SCOTT FORESMAN

SOCIAL STUDIES

GROWTH OF A NATION

Teacher's Edition
Volume One

Editorial Offices: Glenview, Illinois • Parsippany, New Jersey • New York, New York
Sales Offices: Boston, Massachusetts • Duluth, Georgia • Glenview, Illinois
• Coppell, Texas • Sacramento, California • Mesa, Arizona

ISBN: 0-328-23961-5

3 4 5 6 7 8 9 10 V063 15 14 13 12 11 10 09 08 07

TEACHING FREEDOM

Freedom to read and learn
Reading is a #1 priority. Only *Scott Foresman Social Studies* provides explicit, four-step reading instruction.
Page SF4

Freedom to act
Caring, respect, responsibility, fairness, honesty, and courage! Teach the core values of freedom at every grade level.
Page SF6

Freedom to read and learn

Reading is the #1 priority. (We understand.) Can you think of a social studies program as content-area reading? Absolutely. *Scott Foresman Social Studies* is designed to extend your reading curriculum. Explicit reading instruction and proven strategies are built into each unit. At Scott Foresman, reading is at the heart of everything we do.

Teach ····▸
Model ····▸
Practice···▸

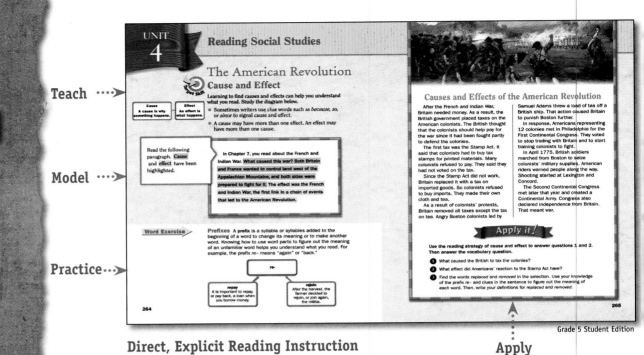

Grade 5 Student Edition

Apply

Direct, Explicit Reading Instruction
Only *Scott Foresman Social Studies* provides explicit, four-step reading instruction in every unit to improve students' comprehension.

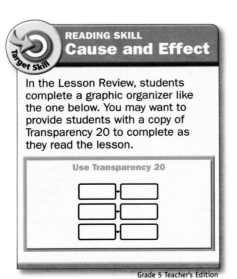

Grade 5 Teacher's Edition

Practice the Skill
Students practice the reading skill throughout each unit, so they can apply it independently.

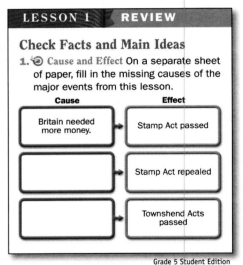

Grade 5 Student Edition

Review the Skill
The target reading skill is monitored continuously in Lesson, Chapter, and Unit Reviews.

Three Content Leveled Readers—the Same Topic, Vocabulary, and Skill!

Leveled readers for each unit of *Scott Foresman Social Studies* help all students access the same grade-level skills and content. Compare this with other social studies programs. (There is no comparison!)

- The same topic at three reading levels
- The same key content vocabulary
- The same reading comprehension skill

Below-Level

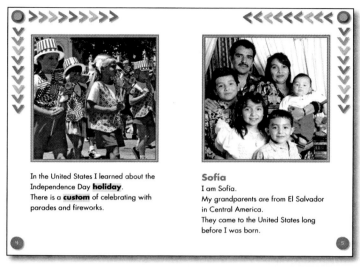

In the United States I learned about the Independence Day **holiday**. There is a **custom** of celebrating with parades and fireworks.

Sofía
I am Sofía.
My grandparents are from El Salvador in Central America.
They came to the United States long before I was born.

On-Level

Leveled Reader Database

ONLINE
sfsuccessnet.com

Find the Books You Need with Lightning Speed!

The Scott Foresman online Leveled Reader Database helps you find and manage the right books for every student in your class.

Select from over 1,000 leveled readers!

- Search by the criteria you need
- Hear fluently read recordings
- Print out and e-mail assignments
- Teach lessons, use practice pages
- Read online at school or home

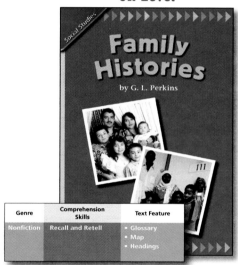

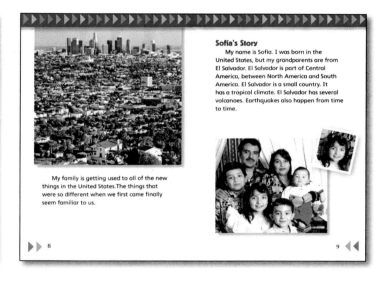

Sofía's Story
My name is Sofía. I was born in the United States, but my grandparents are from El Salvador. El Salvador is part of Central America, between North America and South America. El Salvador is a small country. It has a tropical climate. El Salvador has several volcanoes. Earthquakes also happen from time to time.

My family is getting used to all of the new things in the United States. The things that were so different when we first came finally seem familiar to us.

Advanced

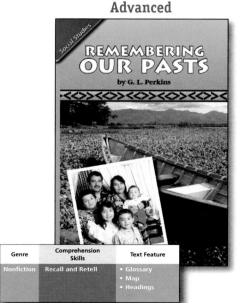

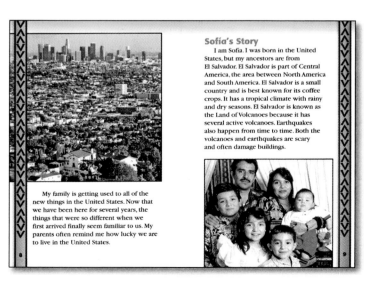

Sofía's Story
I am Sofía. I was born in the United States, but my ancestors are from El Salvador. El Salvador is part of Central America, the area between North America and South America. El Salvador is a small country and is best known for its coffee crops. It has a tropical climate with rainy and dry seasons. El Salvador is known as the Land of Volcanoes because it has several active volcanoes. Earthquakes also happen from time to time. Both the volcanoes and earthquakes are scary and often damage buildings.

My family is getting used to all of the new things in the United States. Now that we have been here for several years, the things that were so different when we first arrived finally seem familiar to us. My parents often remind me how lucky we are to live in the United States.

Freedom to act

You don't have to be a president, a soldier, or a famous celebrity to be a citizen hero. You just need to be responsible and caring. *Scott Foresman Social Studies* fosters the notion that every child can be a citizen hero. Good citizenship is about watching out for each other and lending a hand whenever possible.

CITIZEN HEROES

Racing to the Rescue

On a day of terrifying attacks, the heroic actions of New York City firefighters saved thousands of lives.

New York City's Ladder Company 21 has a long history of fighting fires and saving lives. When the company was first formed in 1890, firefighters rushed to fires on a truck pulled by three horses. Today Ladder Company 21 has computers and modern trucks. But some things have not changed. Firefighting is still a dangerous job that requires great courage. This is why New Yorkers have nicknamed the city's firefighters "New York's Bravest."

On the morning of September 11, 2001, terrorists crashed two planes into New York's World Trade Center. The call for help went out to fire stations all over the city. At Ladder Company 21, Benjamin Suarez was one many firefighters who were just finishing a 24-hour shift. But Suarez did not even think about leaving the job. He called his wife and said,

"I have to help the people."

Then he and his fellow firefighters jumped on their trucks and raced to the scene of the attacks.

As firefighters arrived from around the city, they saw that the twin towers of the World Trade Center were on fire. They rushed into the buildings and up the stairs. "We saw them going up the stairs as we were going down," said a woman who escaped from one of the towers. The firefighters helped people who were injured or lost in the smoke. With the firefighters' help, thousands of people escaped to safety.

Not everyone survived, however. About 4,000 people were trapped in the buildings when they collapsed. More than 300 firefighters, including Benjamin Suarez, died while trying saving the lives of others. Like so many heroes on that terrible day, Suarez put the desire to help other people ahead of his own safety. "That's what Benny was about," said Captain Michael Farrell of Ladder Company 21.

In the days following the terrorist attacks, neighbors visited Ladder Company 21 to show their sympathy for the firefighters who had lost their lives. Many people left flowers and made donations to the firefighters' families. Children wrote letters in which they thanked firefighters for saving lives. Some children drew pictures showing firefighters performing brave actions. The firefighters hung these letters and pictures on the wall of the fire station. Similar scenes took place at fire stations all over the city.

Rudolph Giuliani, the mayor of New York City, thanked firefighters for their incredible courage:

> *"Without courage, nothing else can really happen. And there is no better example, none, than the courage of the Fire Department of the City of New York."*

New York's firefighters not only saved thousands of lives. Their actions inspired the entire nation. In a time of fear and danger, firefighters helped Americans have the courage to face the difficult times ahead.

Courage in Action

Link to Current Events Every day, firefighters, police officers, and other rescue workers perform heroic acts in communities all over the nation. Read a newspaper from your community to find out about the recent actions of your [...] ons did they take?

667

BUILDING CITIZENSHIP
Caring
Respect
Responsibility
Fairness
Honesty
Courage

Grade 5 Student Edition

Citizen Heroes
Special lessons explore how everyday citizens and well-known Americans show good citizenship.

BUILDING CITIZENSHIP

Caring

Respect

Responsibility

Fairness

Honesty

Courage

Teach the Core Values of Freedom!
Students learn the important responsibilities of citizenship at every grade level.

Celebrate Freedom
This special resource helps you inspire patriotism through songs, symbols, and sayings of the United States.

Colonial Williamsburg

The nation's largest living history museum and an exclusive partner of Scott Foresman

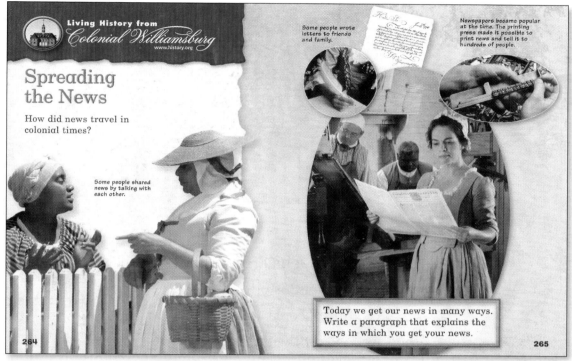

Grade 3 Student Edition

Living History Lessons

Colonial Williamsburg makes history come alive with artifacts, reenactments, and thought-provoking activities.

AWARD WINNING!

Primary Sources CD-ROM

Help students think like historians. Produced in cooperation with Colonial Williamsburg, this award-winning multimedia program introduces primary source documents that spark interest in American history and the ideals of citizenship.

"Awards of Excellence"
Technology And Learning magazine

"Teachers' Choice Award"
Learning magazine

"To be engaged citizens, our children must understand their revolutionary heritage. They must understand that the future of the democracy depends on them."

Bill White, Director of Educational Development, Colonial Williamsburg Foundation

Freedom to explore

Freedom isn't free. People gave their lives for freedom. (And still do every day.) This is why you teach social studies. Students need to see they are the future defenders of America's freedoms. *Scott Foresman Social Studies* presents the story of our nation, the story of families and cultures, the story of our world.

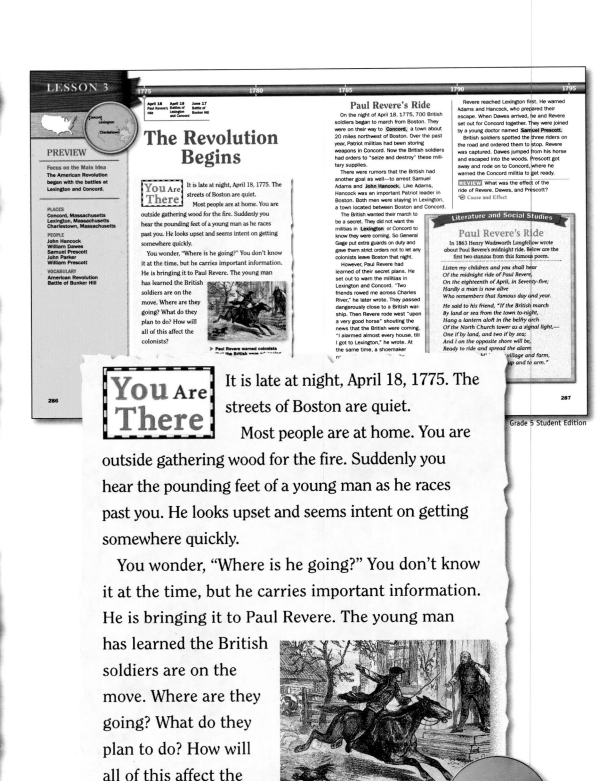

Grade 5 Student Edition

You Are There

It is late at night, April 18, 1775. The streets of Boston are quiet.

Most people are at home. You are outside gathering wood for the fire. Suddenly you hear the pounding feet of a young man as he races past you. He looks upset and seems intent on getting somewhere quickly.

You wonder, "Where is he going?" You don't know it at the time, but he carries important information. He is bringing it to Paul Revere. The young man has learned the British soldiers are on the move. Where are they going? What do they plan to do? How will all of this affect the colonists?

▶ Paul Revere warned colo[nists] that the British were adv[ancing]

AudioText

You Are There
Feel the heart-pounding action! The "You Are There" writing style captivates young readers. Dramatic recordings add power and suspense.

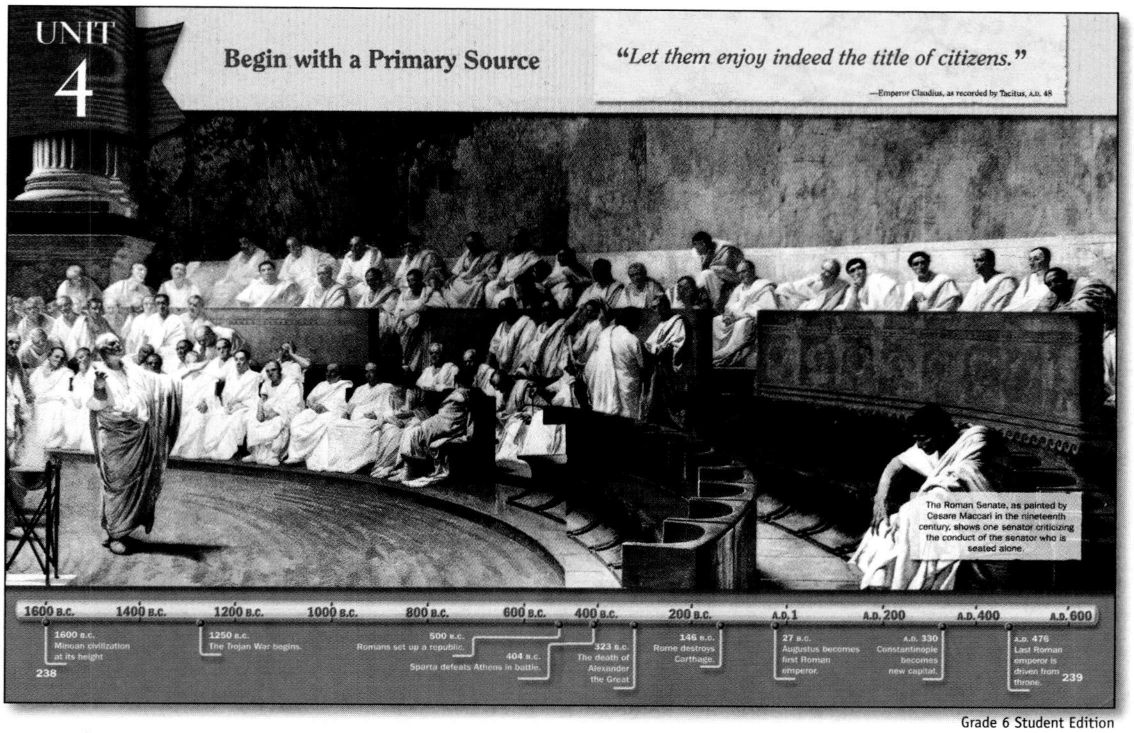
UNIT 4
Begin with a Primary Source
"Let them enjoy indeed the title of citizens."
—Emperor Claudius, as recorded by Tacitus, A.D. 48
The Roman Senate, as painted by Cesare Maccari in the nineteenth century, shows one senator criticizing the conduct of the senator who is seated alone.
1600 B.C.
1400 B.C.
1200 B.C.
1000 B.C.
800 B.C.
600 B.C.
400 B.C.
200 B.C.
A.D. 1
A.D. 200
A.D. 400
A.D. 600
1600 B.C. Minoan civilization at its height
1250 B.C. The Trojan War begins.
500 B.C. Romans set up a republic.
404 B.C. Sparta defeats Athens in battle.
323 B.C. The death of Alexander the Great
146 B.C. Rome destroys Carthage.
27 B.C. Augustus becomes first Roman emperor.
A.D. 330 Constantinople becomes new capital.
A.D. 476 Last Roman emperor is driven from throne.
238
239

Grade 6 Student Edition

Stunning, Powerful, Gripping

Erase the notion that a social studies textbook has to be boring. *Scott Foresman Social Studies* is filled with rich, compelling visuals and content.

- Primary sources
- Museum-quality artwork
- Colorful maps and place locators
- Graphs, diagrams, time lines
- Brilliant photographs
- Full-page biographies

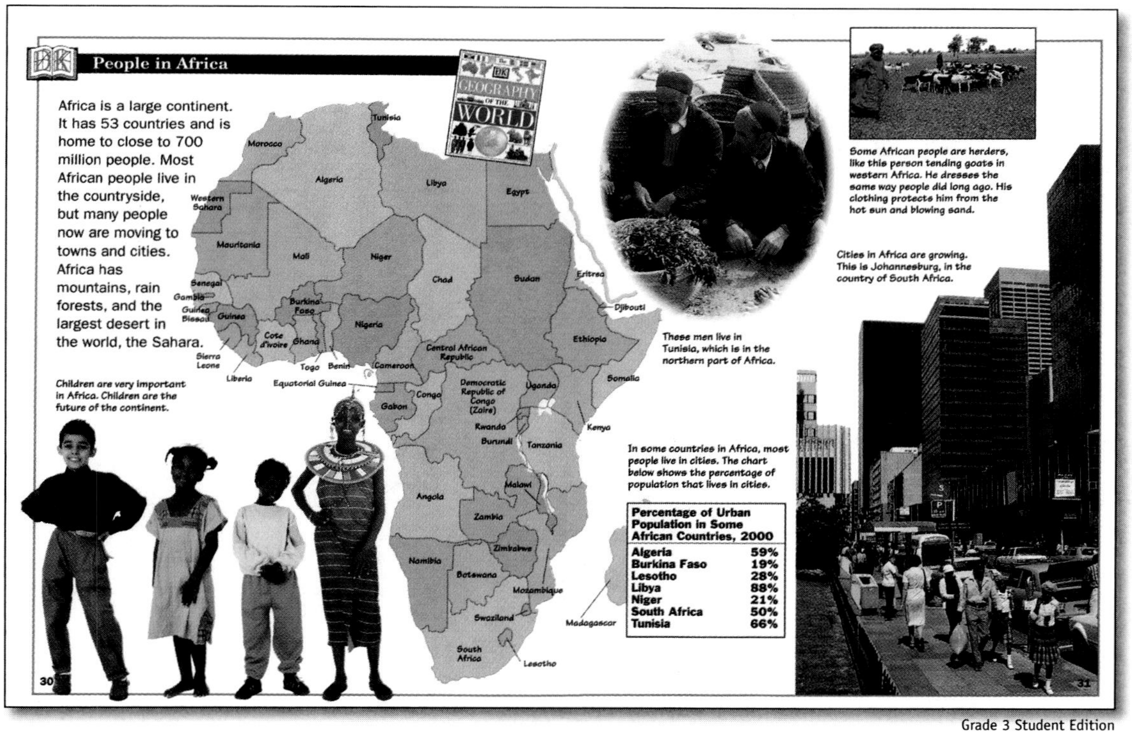
People in Africa
Africa is a large continent. It has 53 countries and is home to close to 700 million people. Most African people live in the countryside, but many people now are moving to towns and cities. Africa has mountains, rain forests, and the largest desert in the world, the Sahara.
Children are very important in Africa. Children are the future of the continent.
Some African people are herders, like this person tending goats in western Africa. He dresses the same way people did long ago. His clothing protects him from the hot sun and blowing sand.
Cities in Africa are growing. This is Johannesburg, in the country of South Africa.
These men live in Tunisia, which is in the northern part of Africa.
In some countries in Africa, most people live in cities. The chart below shows the percentage of population that lives in cities.
Percentage of Urban Population in Some African Countries, 2000
Algeria 59%
Burkina Faso 19%
Lesotho 28%
Libya 88%
Niger 21%
South Africa 50%
Tunisia 66%
30
31

Grade 3 Student Edition

DK Eyewitness Reference Pages

The Eyewitness Book series has sold 50 million copies. Only Scott Foresman embeds richly illustrated, highly accessible DK Eyewitness reference pages into the text.

Freedom to teach

Do you feel you have to be a superhero just to teach reading and math? Who has time for social studies? You have time. Scott Foresman's Quick Teaching Plan and Quick Summary make social studies doable when time is short. Of course, Scott Foresman also provides all the tools you need to really dig into a topic. *Enjoy!*

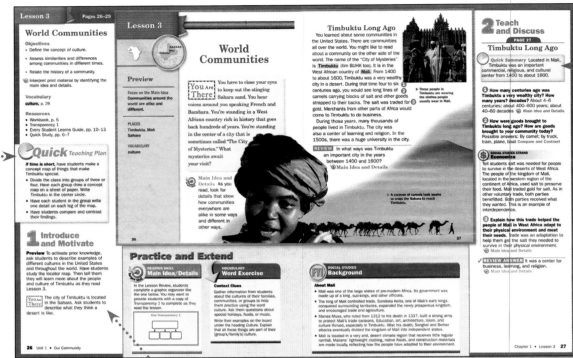

Quick Teaching Plan
Use the Quick Teaching Plan to make lessons a breeze.

Complete Lesson Plan
Dig into a topic with the three-step lesson plan.

Quick Summary
Focus on the key lesson content. It's a snap!

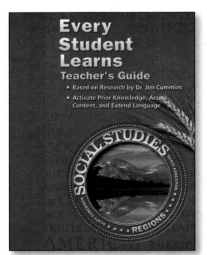

Every Student Learns
Here's quick help for your ESL/ELL students.

Quick Study
Here's quick access to content, vocabulary, and skills.

Components

Practice and Assessment

- Workbook
- Vocabulary Workbook
- Test Talk Practice Book
- Test Talk Transparencies
- Assessment Book

Leveled Readers

- Content Leveled Readers in English and Spanish
- Online Leveled Readers in English and Spanish

Map and Globe Skills

- Primary Atlas
- Student Atlas
- Big Book Atlas
- Outline Maps
- Laminated Desk Maps
- Map Sack
- Floor Map

Social Studies Activities

- Celebrate Freedom
- Social Studies Plus! A Hands-On Approach
- Read Alouds and Primary Sources
- Daily Activity Bank

Supplemental Resources

- Ancient Communities
- World Communities
- Our United States
- Latin America and Canada
- Native Americans
- Learning About Your State and Community

Reading Social Studies/ESL

- Quick Study
- Every Student Learns Teacher's Guide
- Vocabulary Cards
- Colorful Posters
- Transparencies
- Document-Based Questions
- Multi-Leveled Library
- Literature Library
- Literature Big Books

Technology

- Online Teacher's Edition
- Online Student Edition
- Digital Learning CD-ROM Powered by KnowledgeBox®
- Colonial Williamsburg Primary Sources CD-ROM
- MindPoint™ Quiz Show CD-ROM
- Video Field Trips Package

- Hand in Hand Video Package
- Songs and Music Audio CDs
- AudioText CDs
- Map Resources CD-ROM
- Teacher Resources CD-ROM
- ExamView® Test Bank CD-ROM
- sfsocialstudies.com

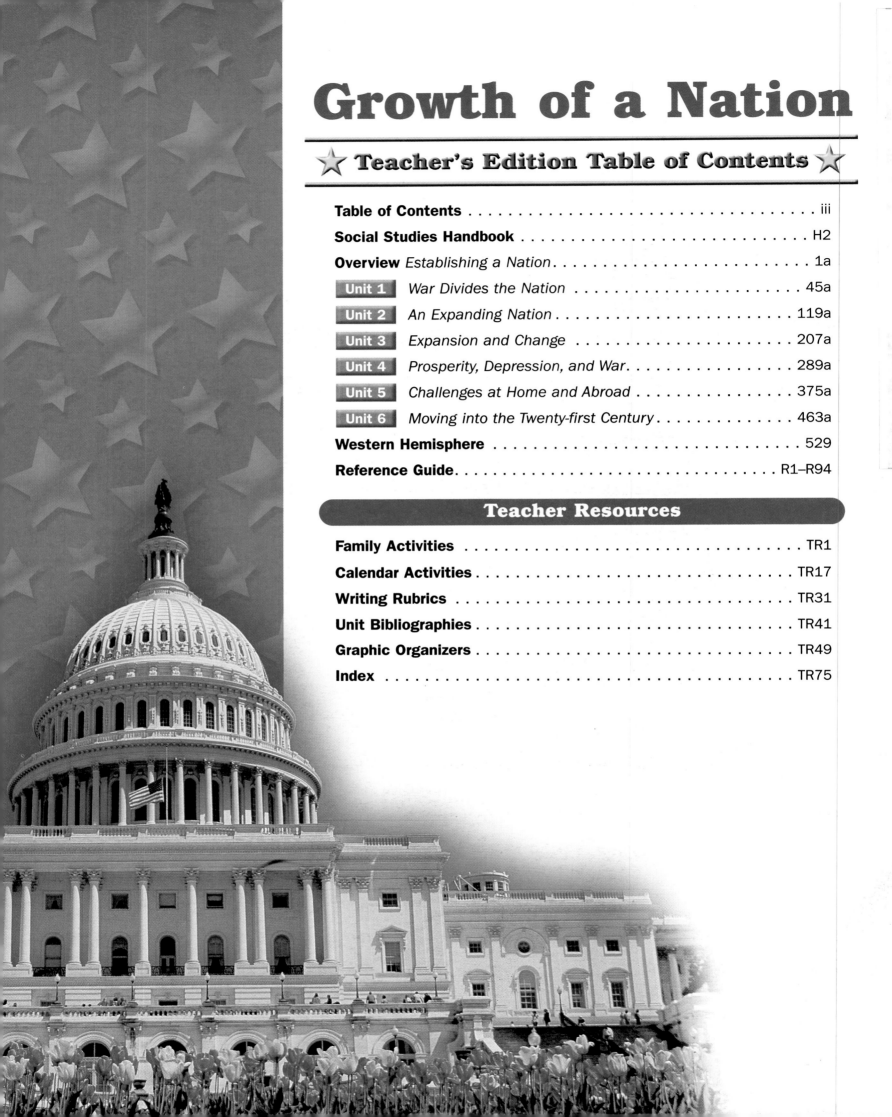

Growth of a Nation

★ Teacher's Edition Table of Contents ★

Teacher Resources

Explore THE UNITED STATES

WALL ST

Objectives

- Explain the purpose of a memorial.
- Describe ways in which monuments honor people, events, or cultures.

Vocabulary

honors shows respect for

century 100 years

1 Introduce and Motivate

Preview To activate prior knowledge, ask students if they have ever seen a monument or a statue dedicated to the memory of a person. Discuss why the person was honored and whether the monument was a fitting memorial or not. Ask students if they have ever seen pictures of or visited Mount Rushmore in South Dakota. Then introduce the travel brochure on pp. E2–E3. Explain that the Crazy Horse Memorial is a monument dedicated to the memory of a famous Oglala Sioux chief. It is located near Mount Rushmore and is also a likeness carved into a mountain. You might want to share information about Crazy Horse from the background material that appears at the bottom of this page.

You Are There Ask students to describe what they think it would be like to visit the Crazy Horse Memorial and climb to the top of the monument. Discuss whether or not they would like to make that trip.

2 Teach and Discuss

Map Study Have students locate the Black Hills on the map on p. E3. Then have students use a map of the Black Hills to locate Mount Rushmore and the Crazy Horse Memorial. Have them use the map scale to determine about how far the two monuments are from one another.

History

History is the study of people and events from the past.

Crazy Horse Memorial

Black Hills, South Dakota

You Are There You're tired. Your muscles ache. You've been climbing for three hours to reach the top of Crazy Horse Monument. You feel honored to be here. People are allowed to walk up to the monument only one weekend a year. Looking out over the Black Hills and beyond, you picture Crazy Horse riding across the Great Plains more than 100 years ago. You turn toward the giant, stone-faced monument. Once it's complete, it will be the largest monument on Earth.

E2

VISIT HISTORY AT

CRAZY HORSE MEMORIAL

The main feature of Crazy Horse Memorial is a monument carved into the rock of the Black Hills of South Dakota. The monument **honors**, or shows respect for, Crazy Horse. It also honors the culture and heritage of all Native Americans of North America. Crazy Horse was an Oglala Sioux chief who fought to preserve Sioux lands and traditions. He died in 1877—more than a **century**, or 100 years, ago. In 1939, Chief Standing Bear and other Native American elders began to plan the Crazy Horse monument. Work on the monument continues to this day.

Native Americans invited sculptor, Koczak Ziolkowski (KOR-chok jewel-CUFF-ski), to carve the giant statue of Crazy Horse. The monument became his life's work, until he died in 1982. Today, his wife and seven of their sons and daughters work to finish his dream.

Practice and Extend

Crazy Horse

- Tashunca-uitco (Crazy Horse) was an Oglala Lakota leader. The Lakota are also known as the Sioux. According to Lakota lore, he was born on the Republican River around 1845, and he led his first war party before he turned twenty.
- Crazy Horse led the Lakota resistance against the U.S. War Department, which had ordered all Lakota onto reservations.
- He is best known for his leadership, along with chiefs Sitting Bull and Gall, in the 1876 victory against General George Custer and the 7th Cavalry in the Battle of Little Bighorn.
- Eventually, Crazy Horse and his band surrendered after the government promised his people their own reservation. The plan fell through, however, and Crazy Horse was killed in captivity at Fort Robinson, Nebraska, in 1877.

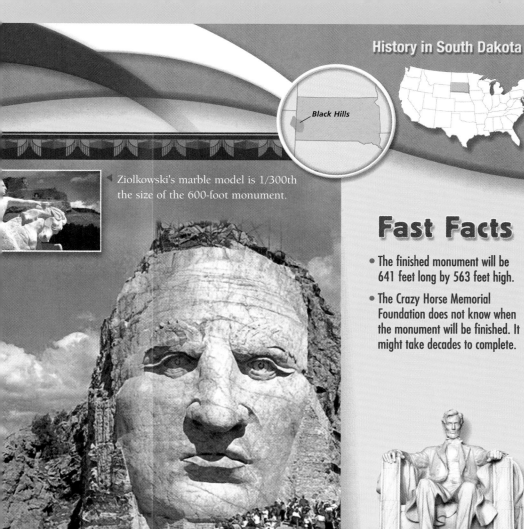

Black Hills

Ziolkowski's marble model is 1/300th the size of the 600-foot monument.

August 1991   July 1994   August 1996

Fast Facts

- The finished monument will be 641 feet long by 563 feet high.
- The Crazy Horse Memorial Foundation does not know when the monument will be finished. It might take decades to complete.

Link to You

Tell about a memorial you have visited or know about that honors a person's role in history. Why do we honor this person?

E3

Read the text on pp. E2–E3 with students. Then discuss the following questions:

Why do you think Chief Standing Bear and other Native American elders wanted to honor Crazy Horse? Possible answer: They wanted to honor the memory of the Oglala Sioux and their leaders.

Work on the memorial began in 1948. How long has work on the memorial proceeded? Answers will depend on the current year. When will the memorial be finished? The Crazy Horse Memorial Foundation does not know when it will be finished. It may take decades more to complete.

What person in history would you honor with a memorial, and what would the memorial be like? Answers will vary, but should reflect an understanding of the purpose of a memorial monument.

3 Close and Assess

Extend student discussion about people they think are worth of a memorial monument. Have the class suggest names and vote on one whom they think most deserves a monument. Have students discuss and, if time allows, design a monument for the winner as a class.

Link to You

Have students use the History graphic organizer to write about a memorial or monument they have visited or know about that honors a person's role in history. Discuss with students why we honor the people they mention. Answers will vary.

CURRICULUM CONNECTION
Writing

Use Graphic Organizers

- Use the Explore History graphic organizer to help students answer the Link to You question.
- Direct students to use pictures and words in their answers.
- Have students share their answers with a partner or in a small group.

Organizer, p. E17

The Memorial

Why do we honor this person?

Economics

Objectives

- Describe how stocks are traded on the New York Stock Exchange.
- Describe how supply and demand affect the stock market.

Vocabulary

stocks pieces, or shares, of companies

trading buying and selling

brokers people who buy and sell stocks for customers

1 Introduce and Motivate

Preview Ask students if they have ever contributed money to buy something as part of a group, such as pooling money to buy a game or a CD. Point out to students that when this happens, each person who contributed owns part of what the group purchased. The part each person owns is called a *share*. Explain that the travel brochure on pp. E4–E5 features the New York Stock Exchange, where people buy and sell shares of ownership in companies.

 Ask students to write about what they think the new broker's first day will be like. Have them explain whether or not they would like to work as a broker.

2 Teach and Discuss

Map Study Have the students use the map on p. E5 to locate New York State and New York City.

Read pp. E4–E5 with students and discuss these questions:

Why do you think it is important to have a broker? Possible answer: It would be impossible for every customer to buy and sell his or her own stocks on the Trading Floor.

E4 Economics

Economics

Economics is the study of the production, distribution, and consumption, or use, of goods and services.

The New York Stock Exchange
New York City, New York

 You can't believe you're standing on the Trading Floor of the New York Stock Exchange (NYSE), the heart of buying and selling shares of ownership in companies. You're a broker who buys and sells shares for others. It's your first day on the job, and you're feeling the pressure. "Calm down," you tell yourself. "Remember, it's simple. Match buyers with sellers and do it fast. How hard can that be?" You take a deep breath and wait for the opening bell to ring.

The New York Stock Exchange (NYSE) is where people can buy and sell pieces or shares of companies called **stocks**. The Trading Floor is where all this buying and selling, or **trading**, takes place. Customers don't make their own trades on the Trading Floor. The people who buy and sell stocks for customers are called **brokers**. Brokers at the NYSE make more than one million trades on an average day. The Trading Floor is one of the fastest-paced, busiest places in the world. Stock prices can change quickly. If many people compete over shares in the same company, the price of the share rises. If no one wants the shares of a company, the share price drops. A good broker works quickly and tries to get the best price.

E4

Practice and Extend

SOCIAL STUDIES
FYI Background

The New York Stock Exchange

- In 1789 government bonds were first sold under a buttonwood tree on Wall Street in New York City, not far from where the NYSE stands today.
- The NYSE was formally founded in 1817 as the New York Stock and Exchange. It has been known by its present name since 1863.
- More than 3,000 people—brokers, specialists, and staff—work on the NYSE Trading Floor.
- The NYSE's opening bell rings at 9:30 A.M. Eastern Time. Many brokers, however, work different hours to accommodate other stock exchanges in cities around the world, such as London and Tokyo.
- Nearly 2,800 companies are listed on the NYSE.
- The New York Stock Exchange provides educational materials on investing and stock trading via its Web site.

Fast Facts

- Every weekday, nearly two billion shares of stock are traded on the NYSE.

- The stock exchange works like an auction. Customers are actually buying and selling stocks to and from one another, with brokers negotiating the price.

STOCK EXCHANGE

With computers to help, trading that once took a day can now be handled in a few minutes. Some day, all stock trading may take place on computers.

The NYSE is on Wall Street in New York City. It is one of the most important financial centers in the world.

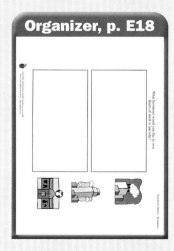

Link to You

What businesses would you like to own shares of stock in? Why?

E 5

What are some ways the stock exchange is like an auction? Possible answers: Customers buy and sell stocks, with brokers and auctioneers negotiating the price; the price of a stock is determined by how many people want that particular stock at that moment.

How does the supply of stocks affect the demand for stocks? Since only a set number of shares in a given company are available, if the demand for the stock is high, the price of a share will rise. If demand is low, many shares will be available, and the price will fall.

Do you think you would you like to own stock? Why or why not? Possible answers: Yes, because I could earn money; no, because prices can drop quickly and I wouldn't want to lose money.

3 Close and Assess

Have the class select three companies to track on the NYSE. Use the stock market report in the newspaper to find the abbreviation for each company's name and the cost per share. Track each stock's progress for one week. Have students decide which stock they think was the best investment.

Link to You

Have students use the Economics graphic organizer to list businesses in which they would like to own shares of stock. Have students share their answers. Answers will vary.

Use Graphic Organizers

- Use the Explore Economics graphic organizer to help students answer the Link to You question.
- Direct students to use pictures and words in their answers.
- Have students share their answers with a partner or in a small group.

Organizer, p. E18

Science and Technology

Objectives

- Explain how technology can be used to study earthquakes.
- Explain why collecting data about earthquakes is important.

Vocabulary

seismologists scientists who study earthquakes

data factual information

1 Introduce and Motivate

Preview To activate prior knowledge, ask students if they have ever watched a weather report on television to see if it was going to be hot, cold, rainy, sunny, or windy outside. Have students share the types of technology meteorologists use as they describe the weather report—technology such as radar, thermometers, and barometers. Introduce the travel brochure about the National Earthquake Information Center on pp. E6–E7. Explain that, like the people who predict and study the weather, the people who work at the NEIC use special technology to record and study earthquakes.

 As a group, make a list of things students "know" about earthquakes. Have the class vote on whether they think each statement is true. Divide students into pairs and help them research to find the answers.

2 Teach and Discuss

Map Study Have students use the map on p. E7 to locate Colorado and Golden.

Science and Technology

Science and technology change people's lives. These changes bring opportunities and challenges.

Technology at Work at the

National Earthquake Information Center

The National Earthquake Information Center
Golden, Colorado

 Your class is touring the National Earthquake Information Center (NEIC). Seismographs that measure and record the strength of earthquakes are humming and scribbling calmly. Suddenly, one of the seismographs starts to scratch out a different pattern, a series of scribbles going back and forth in a wider arc. The scientists spring into action. They call government officials, railroad personnel, and safety organizations in the affected area. "This must be pretty unusual," you say to one of the scientists. "Not really," she says. "We get about 50 of these per day."

Scientists who study earthquakes are called **seismologists**. The seismologists at the NEIC use various instruments to study and record earthquakes around the world as they happen. They can help people understand why earthquakes happen, and how to build homes and cities that will be better able to withstand them. No one, not even seismologists, can prevent or predict earthquakes. They can study **data**, or factual information, to determine places that are more likely to have earthquakes. Based on the information they gather, they are able to understand the Earth's structure in an area that might lead to an earthquake.

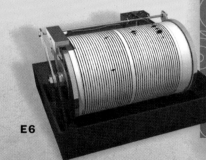

E6

Practice and Extend

FYI SOCIAL STUDIES Background

Earthquakes

- Worldwide, there are about 500,000 detectable earthquakes each year. Of these, only 100,000 will be felt by humans. Only about 100 will cause significant damage.
- The Richter scale measures the energy released by an earthquake. Light tremors register 1.5, while the most destructive earthquakes measure 8.3 and up. Although the Richter scale has no upper limit, a 10.0 earthquake has never been recorded.
- The Modified Mercalli scale measures the intensity of an earthquake. It rates quakes from I (people do not feel movement) to XII (widespread destruction).
- The world's largest recorded earthquake took place in 1960 in Chile. It measured 9.5 on the Richter scale.

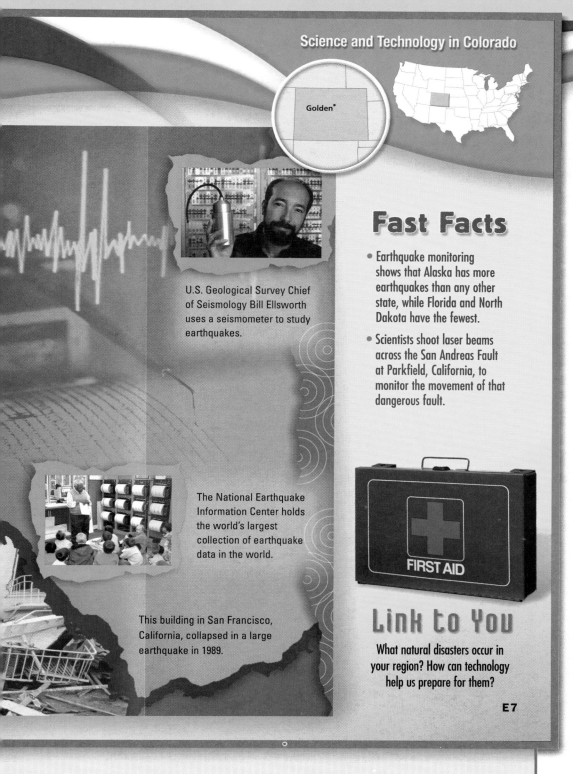

Science and Technology in Colorado

Golden

Fast Facts

- Earthquake monitoring shows that Alaska has more earthquakes than any other state, while Florida and North Dakota have the fewest.

- Scientists shoot laser beams across the San Andreas Fault at Parkfield, California, to monitor the movement of that dangerous fault.

U.S. Geological Survey Chief of Seismology Bill Ellsworth uses a seismometer to study earthquakes.

The National Earthquake Information Center holds the world's largest collection of earthquake data in the world.

This building in San Francisco, California, collapsed in a large earthquake in 1989.

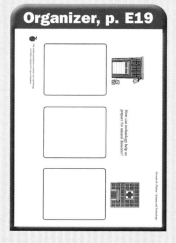

FIRST AID

Link to You

What natural disasters occur in your region? How can technology help us prepare for them?

E7

Read the text on pp. E6–E7 with students. Then discuss the following questions:

How do seismologists use technology to study earthquakes? They use various devices such as seismographs, seismometers, and lasers to study and record data on earthquakes and fault movements.

If seismologists can't prevent earthquakes, why study them? Possible answers: Seismologists can determine places that are more likely to have earthquakes; they can use the data to suggest ways to build homes and cities that are better able to survive an earthquake.

Would you like to be a seismologist? Why or why not? Answers will vary.

3 Close and Assess

Have students use library resources or the Internet to research earthquakes that have occurred in their state. Have them record locations, dates, and magnitudes on a state map. The NEIC maintains a Web site with this information: **neic.usgs.gov**

Link to You

Have students use the Science and Technology graphic organizer to research natural disasters that occur in their region. If natural disasters such as earthquakes, hurricanes, or tornados frequently occur in your region, review with students what to do in case of those natural disasters. Ask them to write about ways science and technology have helped people prepare for natural disasters. Answers will vary.

CURRICULUM CONNECTION
Writing

Use Graphic Organizers

- Use the Explore Science and Technology graphic organizer to help students answer the Link to You question.
- Direct students to use pictures and words in their answers.
- Have students share their answers with a partner or in a small group.

Organizer, p. E19

Geography

Objectives

- Describe a geographic region, such as a desert.
- Identify a habitat, including the plants and animals that live there.

Vocabulary

habitat a place where an animal or plant naturally lives

mesa a small, high plateau with a flat top and steep sides

1 Introduce and Motivate

Preview To activate prior knowledge, ask students to make two lists: one of words they associate with the desert and one of words they associate with caves. Then have students view the photographs on pp. E8–E9 of the travel brochure. Do the pictures reflect any of the words on their lists? If so, how?

 Invite students to write a journal entry as if he or she were the first person ever to see Carlsbad Caverns. Students can refer to the photographs on pp. E8–E9 to help with their descriptions.

2 Teach and Discuss

Map Study Have students locate New Mexico and Carlsbad Caverns National Park on the map on page E9. Ask them to name the state on which the park nearly borders. (Texas) Then have them use a map of the southwest to locate Guadalupe National Park. Tell students that both parks are part of the Chihuahuan Desert.

Geography

Geography is the study of Earth's surface, features, and climates, and the way they impact people in different regions.

Carlsbad Caverns National Park
New Mexico

You Are There It's taken you about an hour to walk the winding path from the natural entrance down to the Big Room of Carlsbad Caverns. Now you stand about 750 feet beneath the desert. Instead of the dry, sunny heat of the surface, the Big Room is dim, cool, and damp. It is also huge—the area of more than six football fields! You set off along the trail to explore the fascinating cave formations that lie within: towering stalagmites; long, slender stalactites; sturdy columns, and walls of flowstone that look as delicate as folded fabric. How different this is from Juniper Ridge, where you hiked yesterday!

E8

Welcome to Carlsbad

Carlsbad Caverns National Park is best known for its series of huge caverns. Nearly half a million people come each year to tour the park's underground wonders and see the famous evening bat flight. However, the park is also known as prime habitat for many desert species. A **habitat** is a place where an animal or plant naturally lives. Carlsbad Caverns National Park lies in the Chihuahuan (chi WAH wahn) Desert. This desert extends from southern New Mexico and western Texas south into Mexico. Desert shrubs and different types of cactus grow in the park's rugged canyons and atop its mesas. A **mesa** is a small, high plateau with a flat top and steep sides. Mule deer, coyote, mountain lions, hawks, and roadrunners are among the wildlife that lives in the park.

▶ This view of Rattlesnake Canyon shows the rugged desert of Carlsbad Caverns National Park.

Practice and Extend

FYI **SOCIAL STUDIES Background**

Carlsbad Caverns National Park

- Carlsbad Caverns National Park has more than 100 caves, including Lechuguilla Cave, one of the world's longest and the nation's deepest cave.
- Although most people visit the park to tour Carlsbad Caverns and see the evening bat flight, the park's extensive backcountry wilderness provides opportunities for primitive hiking and camping. Even short day-hikes offer the opportunity to see desert plants and animals in their natural habitat.
- Although a portion of Carlsbad Caverns was mined for bat guano (used for fertilizer) for years, Jim White explored and later exploited the depths of the cave as a tourist attraction. Carlsbad Caverns became a national monument in 1923, and national park in 1930. It is also a United Nations World Heritage Site.

Caverns National Park!

Each summer evening, hundreds of thousands of Mexican free-tailed bats fly out of Carlsbad Caverns to hunt for insects in the desert night.

▶ Visitors to Carsbad Caverns can tour some of the cave's largest and most spectacular chambers.

▶ Visitors to the park may see a roadrunner. This desert bird is also the state bird of New Mexico.

Carlsbad Caverns National Park

Fast Facts

- Ancient pictographs, or rock paintings, have been found at the entrances to caves in Carlsbad Caverns National Park. Humans found shelter in these caves hundreds or perhaps even thousands of years ago.

- Today, elevators take visitors from the visitor center on the surface to the Big Room 750 feet below in less than a minute.

Link to You

How would you describe the geography of the region where you live? What plant and animal habitats are in your region?

E9

Read the text on pp. E8–E9 with students. Then discuss the following questions:

How would you describe the geographic region in which Carlsbad Caverns National Park lies? Possible answers: It is a desert; the land is dry and has canyons and mesas; it has many plants and animals that live in a desert.

Name two types of plants and three types of animals that live in the Chihuahuan Desert. Plants: cacti, desert shrubs; animals: choose from mule deer, coyote, mountain lions, hawks, roadrunners, bats

Why do you think the caverns and the area around them were declared a national park? Possible answers: To protect them from harm; to preserve them for people to see in the future.

What would you most like to see if you visited Carlsbad Caverns National Park? Why? Answers will vary.

3 Close and Assess

Ask students if they have ever visited a cave, or if they know of other caves in the country. List some on the board. Discuss what types of geographical features one might find in the regions where these caves are found. Compare these geographical features with those of Carlsbad Caverns National Park.

Link to You

Have students use the Geography graphic organizer to describe the geography of the region where they live. Ask them to make a list of plants and animals that live in their region. Answers will vary.

CURRICULUM CONNECTION
Writing

Use Graphic Organizers

- Use the Explore Geography graphic organizer to help students answer the Link to You question.
- Direct students to use pictures and words in their answers.
- Have students share their answers with a partner or in a small group.

Organizer, p. E20

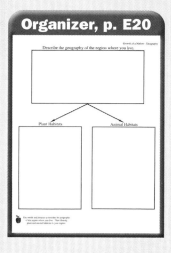

Objectives
- Identify and describe traditions from different cultures.
- Explain the importance of preserving and celebrating cultural traditions.

Vocabulary

ancestor a person who is related to you from the past

customs long-established ways people have of doing things

preserve keep, prevent from change

1 Introduce and Motivate

Preview To activate prior knowledge, ask students if they know where their ancestors came from. Introduce the travel brochure on pp. E10–E11 and explain to students that they are going to read about the Kunta Kinte Festival, a celebration of the African American heritage.

You Are There Ask students why they think storytelling is important to various cultures. Have children share names of stories they know from their own cultures.

2 Teach and Discuss

Map Study Have students use the map on p. E11 to find Maryland and Annapolis. Then help them locate Gambia, Kunta Kinte's home, on the political world map on pp. R4–R5. Then have them find the approximate location of Annapolis on that map (it is not labeled; students will have to use the map on p. E11 as a guide).

Culture

Culture is the customs, traditions, habits and values of a group of people.

The Kunta Kinte Festival
Annapolis, Maryland

You Are There It's a hot day in August and drums are pounding. The aroma of African foods, such as chicken imoyo and plantain fritters, drifts in from every direction. Vendors are selling food, art, clothing, and crafts. It seems as if you are in the middle of an African market. A woman's voice catches your attention. It's the griot (GREE oh). She is telling traditional African stories. Her voice rises and falls as she tells her tales, and you cannot help but listen. She brings people from the past alive.

Roots is a bestselling book. It has been published in thirty languages, and more than six million copies have been sold.

The Kunta Kinte–Alex Haley Memorial

E10

Practice and Extend

FYI SOCIAL STUDIES
Background

The Kunta Kinte Festival
- Kunta Kinte was born in Gambia, West Africa in 1750. He was one of 98 slaves aboard the ship *Lord Ligonier,* which landed in Annapolis in 1767.
- Festival visitors enjoy performances of African music, dance, and storytelling. Vendors sell a variety African arts and artifacts, clothing, and food.
- Alex Haley is the great, great, great, great grandson of Kunta Kinte. His novel, *Roots,* is based on more than 10 years of research. It is a mix of historical facts and fiction.

Culture in Maryland

eserving Culture at the

Kunta Kinte Festival

In 1976 Alex Haley wrote a book called *Roots*. The book told the story of a man named Kunta Kinte, an ancestor of Haley. An **ancestor** is a person who is related to you from the past. Kunta Kinte was kidnapped from his home in Africa when he was 17 years old. He was put on a boat headed for Maryland, where he was sold into slavery. He spent much of his life enslaved but managed to keep the customs of his homeland and family alive. **Customs** are long established ways people have of doing things. The Kunta Kinte Festival honors Kinte's struggle to **preserve**, or keep, his cultural roots.

The Kunta Kinte Heritage Festival is a celebration of the preservation of culture. More than 125,000 people have visited the Kunta Kinte Festival since 1989.

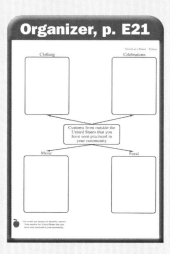

Fast Facts

- Alex Haley began researching Kunta Kinte's life after hearing stories about his ancestors from his grandmother, a griot.

- Before they are allowed to sell at the festival, craftspeople and artists are reviewed for cultural authenticity and historical value.

Link to You

Describe customs from countries outside the United States that you have seen practiced in your community.

E11

Read the text on pp. E10–E11 with students. Then discuss the following questions:

Who is Kunta Kinte? Possible answers: Kunta Kinte was a 17-year-old boy brought to the United States as a slave; he is the main character of a book called *Roots;* he was an ancestor of author Alex Haley.

Why do you think Alex Haley wrote a book about Kunta Kinte? Possible answers: He wanted to know about his family's history; he researched his ancestors and found that Kunta Kinte's story was interesting and important to tell; he wanted to tell others about the culture Kunta Kinte struggled to preserve.

Why do you think people try to preserve and celebrate their cultural traditions? Possible answers: It helps them learn about the past; it makes them proud of their ancestors; they can share their traditions with others, who can also enjoy and learn from them.

3 Close and Assess

Have students think about the cultures of people who live in their community. Compare the Kunta Kinte Festival with festivals they have attended in their community or elsewhere. Ask students to describe ways these festivals are similar and ways they are different.

Link to You

Have students use the Culture graphic organizer to write about some customs from other countries that they have seen practiced or know about. Ask students to share and discuss their answers. Answers will vary.

CURRICULUM CONNECTION
Writing

Use Graphic Organizers

- Use the Explore Culture graphic organizer to help students answer the Link to You question.
- Direct students to use pictures and words in their answers.
- Have students share their answers with a partner or in a small group.

Organizer, p. E21

Objectives

- Recognize struggles citizens have endured to protect their rights.
- Explain the importance of voting.

Vocabulary

civil right a right guaranteed equally to every eligible citizen

republic a form of government under which citizens vote to choose leaders to represent them

1 Introduce and Motivate

Preview To activate prior knowledge, ask students what they might do if they thought a law was unfair, or not being equally applied. Explain that throughout the history of the United States, people have joined together to protest against laws they thought were unjust. Explain that the National Voting Rights Museum featured on the travel brochure on pp. E12–E13 honors citizens who fought for voting rights.

 Invite students to tell about times when they stood up for what they believed was right and fair. They could have remained silent. Why did they speak up? Remind students that one of the responsibilities of citizenship is to uphold and protect the rights of fellow citizens.

2 Teach and Discuss

Map Study Have students locate Alabama and Selma on the map on p. E13. If you can find a road map of Alabama, have students locate both Selma and Montgomery and trace the route the marchers took along Route 80.

Citizenship

Citizenship is all the rights and privileges of being a member of a community, state, or nation.

National Voting Rights Museum, Selma, Alabama

 You are standing on the Edmund Pettus Bridge. Beneath the bridge, the Alabama River flows peacefully by. Your grandparents have told you about this bridge—it is a place where people made a stand to protect their right to vote. Even violence could not stop them. You turn and walk the few steps back to the National Voting Rights Museum, where you will learn about brave American citizens who risked their lives to protect their rights.

E12

Learn about citizenship rights at the

National Votin

The National Voting Rights Museum honors the citizens of Alabama and the nation who risked their own safety to gain civil rights for all. A **civil right** is a right guaranteed equally to every eligible citizen. Voting is a civil right. Throughout the history of our nation people have fought for this right, because it is the basis of our power as citizens of a republic. In a **republic**, citizens vote to choose leaders to represent them in the government. Exhibits at the National Voting Rights Museum honor the struggle African Americans, women, and others have made to win and keep the right to vote. The museum encourages all of us to use our right to vote.

Suffragists, or those who were for women's suffrage, handed out information on their cause. This booth was set up in New York City in 1914.

Practice and Extend

FYI SOCIAL STUDIES Background

The Selma-to-Montgomery March

- The National Voting Rights Museum is very close to the Edmund Pettus Bridge where, on March 7, 1965, hundreds of civil rights marchers met with violence as they attempted to walk from Selma to Montgomery, Alabama. Their attackers were the local police force.
- Two weeks later, the march was attempted again. This time, 3,200 marchers set out on the 54-mile march, led by Dr. Martin Luther King. Four days later, more than 25,000 marchers strode into Montgomery. Their route is now a National Historic Trail.
- The Voting Rights Act of 1965 was passed within five months of this march.
- Today, the march is remembered at the National Voting Rights Museum, along with exhibits such as the "I Was There Wall," "Footsteps to Freedom," and "The Suffrage Room."

Rights Museum

Suffragists protested at the White House.

People from around the country travel to Selma each year to celebrate the anniversary of the march to Montgomery.

WE MARCH FOR FIRST CLASS CITIZENSHIP NOW!

In 1963, thousands of people in Washington, D.C., marched in support of civil rights, including voting rights.

Fast Facts

- Women gained the right to vote in national elections in 1920.
- The Voting Rights Act of 1965 made it illegal to deny voting rights because of race.
- The museum's annual "Bridge Crossing Jubilee," an outdoor festival held on the first weekend in March, attracts as many as 25,000 people.

★ Link to You ★

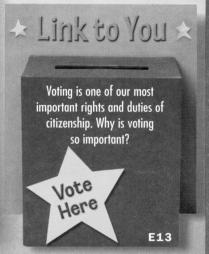

Voting is one of our most important rights and duties of citizenship. Why is voting so important?

Vote Here

E13

Read the text on pp. E12–E13 with students. Then discuss the following questions:

In what ways have citizens worked to win and protect their voting rights? Possible answers: They faced violence; they marched and protested to make their voices heard; they made information available so that others could learn about their cause.

Why is the National Voting Rights Museum a good place to learn about the rights and responsibilities of citizenship? Possible answers: It honors those who have fought to win and protect their voting rights; it has exhibits where you can learn about the struggle for voting rights; it encourages all citizens to use their right to vote.

Why do you think so many people participate in the annual Bridge Crossing Jubilee each year? Possible answers: To honor the original marchers; to call attention to the importance of voting rights for all citizens.

3 Close and Assess

Have students brainstorm a list of issues in their community that they think need to be resolved. Ask students if they think it would be fairer to let citizens vote on these issues or to allow a city leader to decide what to do. Discuss their answers.

Link to You

Have students use the Citizenship graphic organizer to write about why voting is important. Use the Close and Assess discussion as a springboard for this activity. Answers will vary.

CURRICULUM CONNECTION
Writing

Use Graphic Organizers

- Use the Explore Citizenship graphic organizer to help students answer the Link to You question.
- Direct students to use pictures and words in their answers.
- Have students share their answers with a partner or in a small group.

Organizer, p. E22

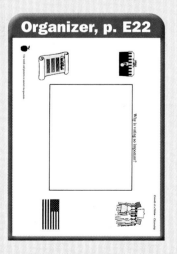

Government

Objectives
- Describe the function of the legislative branch of the U.S. government.
- Explain the importance of the United States Capitol.

Vocabulary
legislative branch branch of government that makes laws

rotunda a round room, usually beneath a dome

1 Introduce and Motivate

Preview To activate prior knowledge, ask students what they know about how laws are made in our nation. Have students explain the process to the best of their ability. Explain to students that the travel brochure on pp. E14–E15 features the United States Capitol where the laws of the United States are made. Point out to students that the Capitol is also a symbol of the American people and our government.

 Ask students to discuss the importance of debates, such as the solar energy research bill discussed in You Are There. Why do students think it's important for the House of Representatives to discuss these issues? Explain that citizens of many countries do not have a representative government such as we do in the United States.

2 Teach and Discuss

Map Study Have students locate Washington, D.C., on the map on p. E15. Explain that *D.C.* stands for "District of Columbia," and that Washington, D.C., is not part of any of the 50 states.

Government

Government is a system for running a community, state, or country.

The United States Capitol
Washington, D.C.

You Are There From your seat in the public gallery, you can watch all the activity below. The Chamber of the House of Representatives is large. It smells of polished wood and leather. You hear the sharp crack of a gavel. The representatives take their seats and begin to discuss a bill to fund solar energy research. You watch as members rise to speak and debate. Even though the speakers hold different points of view, you think they all make sense. You wonder whether this bill will pass.

E14

Watch Government in Action at the

United States Capitol

The U.S. Capitol is one of the most recognizable buildings in the world. Its gleaming white dome has become a symbol of our nation. The Capitol is the central building of the Capitol Complex, which houses the legislative branch of the United States government. The **legislative branch** makes our laws. Both the House of Representatives and the Senate are part of the legislative branch. Visitors to the Capitol can arrange in advance to watch either the House or the Senate in session.

Practice and Extend

FYI SOCIAL STUDIES Background

The United States Capitol
- George Washington laid the cornerstone of the Capitol in 1793. Congress moved to the building in 1800; only the north wing had been completed.
- The *Statue of Freedom* at the top of the Capitol's dome was set in place in 1863.
- The United States Capitol Complex includes the Capitol, the House and Senate Office Buildings, the U.S. Botanic Garden, the Library of Congress buildings, the Supreme Court Building, the Capitol Power Plant, a Capitol Visitor Center, the Capitol Grounds, and various support facilities.
- The Capitol is open to the public for guided tours. Admission to the Public Galleries of the House and Senate chambers is by pass only. Such passes can be obtained through your representative or senator's office.

Government in Washington, D.C.

Washington, D.C.

Visitors can also tour the Capitol to see historical paintings, statues, exhibits, and the **rotunda**, a round ceremonial area that lies beneath the dome.

On top of the U.S. Capitol dome is the *Statue of Freedom*.

Fast Facts

- During the Civil War, a part of the Capitol was used as a Union hospital.

- The first electric lights in the Capitol were installed in the Senate cloakroom, lobby, and stairways in 1885.

Link to You

How does the United States government work for your state or community?

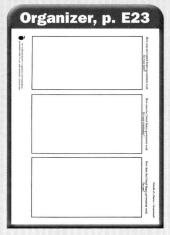

E15

Read the text on pp. E14–E15 with students. Then discuss the following questions:

What are the two houses of Congress, and why is it important that they meet in the same building? House of Representatives and Senate; Possible answer: It is important that the two houses be close by to share ideas and information, and to make it easier to work with each other.

What role does the legislative branch play in the U.S. government? It makes the laws of our nation.

What can visitors see and do at the Capitol? Possible answers: tour the building to see historical paintings, statues, exhibits, and the rotunda; watch the House or the Senate in session.

What question would you ask your representative or senator if you could meet with him or her at the U.S. Capitol? Answers will vary.

3 Close and Assess

Ask students to describe what they think happens in the Capitol on a typical day. Then, if the Internet is available, visit the Web sites of the House of Representatives (**http://www.house.gov/**) or the Senate (**http://www.senate.gov/**) to see what issues are being discussed in Congress that day.

Link to You

Have students use the Government graphic organizer to write about ways the United States government affects their state or community. Answers will vary.

CURRICULUM CONNECTION
Writing

Use Graphic Organizers

- Use the Explore Government graphic organizer to help students answer the Link to You question.
- Direct students to use pictures and words in their answers.
- Have students share their answers with a partner or in a small group.

Organizer, p. E23

Objectives

- Identify symbols of the United States and explain their significance.
- Describe the importance of symbols in creating a national identity.

1 Introduce and Motivate

Preview Ask students to describe some reasons that people come to the United States. Explain that they will discuss some national symbols.

2 Teach and Discuss

Why is Ellis Island considered a national symbol? Possible answer: It celebrates the courage, determination, and hope of immigrants.

How does the Supreme Court uphold the motto "Equal Justice Under Law"? The justices make their rulings based on whether the law upholds the Constitution of the United States, and they try to make sure their rulings are applied equally and fairly to all citizens.

Why do you think the founders chose *E pluribus unum* for our nation's motto? Possible answers: It symbolizes the 13 Colonies unifying as a new nation; it represents the many different people who are citizens of the United States.

3 Close and Assess

Ask students to discuss what they think about when they see these symbols on TV or in newspapers. Discuss what these symbols might suggest to people outside the United States.

National Symbols

U.S. Supreme Court
Washington, D.C.

The Supreme Court is the highest court of the United States, and a symbol of the American justice system. The words "Equal Justice Under Law" are engraved over the doors of the Supreme Court Building. The nine justices of the Supreme Court make their rulings based on whether the law upholds the principles outlined in the U.S. Constitution.

The Great Seal and Motto

On July 4, 1776, the Continental Congress appointed Benjamin Franklin, John Adams, and Thomas Jefferson to create an official seal for the United States of America. The seal is a symbol of the hopes and values of the nation. The Great Seal has two sides. On one side, a bald eagle holds a scroll in its beak, bearing the Latin inscription *E pluribus unum*, our nation's motto. The motto means "out of many, one." The image of the seal is printed on the one dollar bill and on many important government documents.

Ellis Island
New York Harbor, NY

Opened in 1892, Ellis Island became known as the "gateway to America." For more than 50 years, the island was used as a Federal Immigration Station. Millions of immigrants arriving in the United States from Europe were questioned, inspected, and recorded here.

E16

Practice and Extend

CURRICULUM CONNECTION
Writing

Use Graphic Organizers

- Use the Symbols graphic organizer to help students identify important local or school symbols.
- Direct students to use pictures and words in their answers.
- Have students share their answers with a partner or in a small group.

Organizer, p. E24

Why do we honor this person?

The Memorial

 Use words and pictures to describe a memorial you have visited or know about that honors a person's role in history. Then explain why we honor that person.

kidspiration This graphic organizer is also available for use on your school computers. Find this activity and a 30-day Kidspiration trial at www.inspiration.com/sf.

History Organizer **E17**

What businesses would you like to own shares of stock in and why?

Use words and pictures to identify businesses you would like to own shares of stock in. Then explain why.

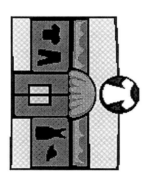

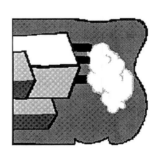

Growth of a Nation - Economics

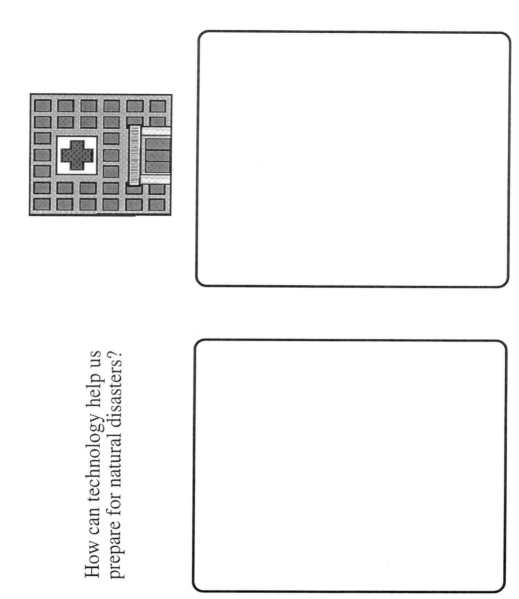

How can technology help us prepare for natural disasters?

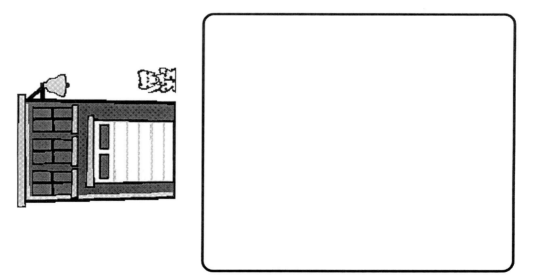

Use words and pictures to explain how technology can help us prepare for natural disasters.

kidspiration This graphic organizer is also available for use on your school computers. Find this activity and a 30-day Kidspiration trial at www.inspiration.com/sf.

Science and Technology Organizer **E19**

Describe the geography of the region where you live.

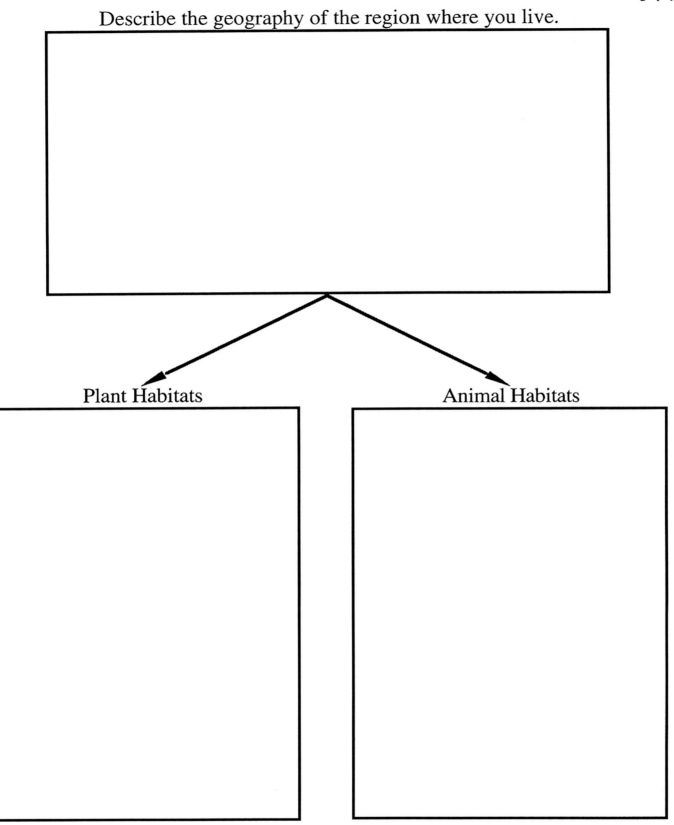

Plant Habitats

Animal Habitats

Use words and pictures to describe the geography of the region where you live. Then identify plant and animal habitats in your region.

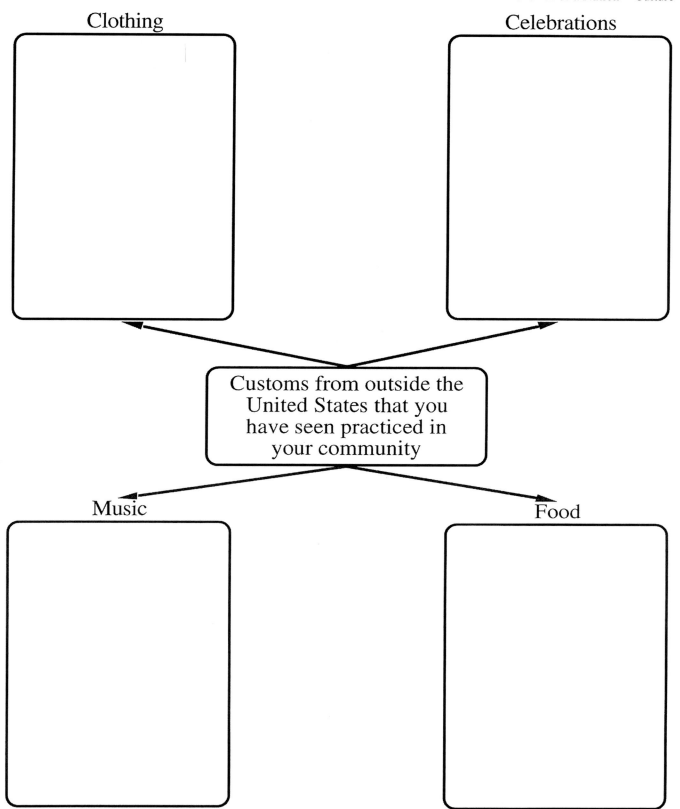

Clothing

Celebrations

Customs from outside the United States that you have seen practiced in your community

Music

Food

Use words and pictures to describe customs from outside the United States that you have seen practiced in your community.

kidspiration This graphic organizer is also available for use on your school computers. Find this activity and a 30-day Kidspiration trial at www.inspiration.com/sf.

Culture Organizer E21

Use words and pictures to answer the question.

Why is voting so important?

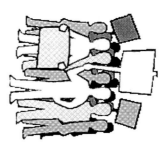

Growth of a Nation - Citizenship

Growth of a Nation - Government

How does the United States government work for you?

How does the United States government work for your community?

How does the United States government work for your state?

Use words and pictures to explain how the United States government works for you, your community, and your state.

kidspiration This graphic organizer is also available for use on your school computers. Find this activity and a 30-day Kidspiration trial at www.inspiration.com/sf.

Government Organizer **E23**

Identify a building in your community that is a symbol and explain your choice.

Design a seal and motto for your school or community. Explain the symbols that you use.

 Use words and pictures to identify and design symbols for your community.

kidspiration This graphic organizer is also available for use on your school computers. Find this activity and a 30-day Kidspiration trial at www.inspiration.com/sf.

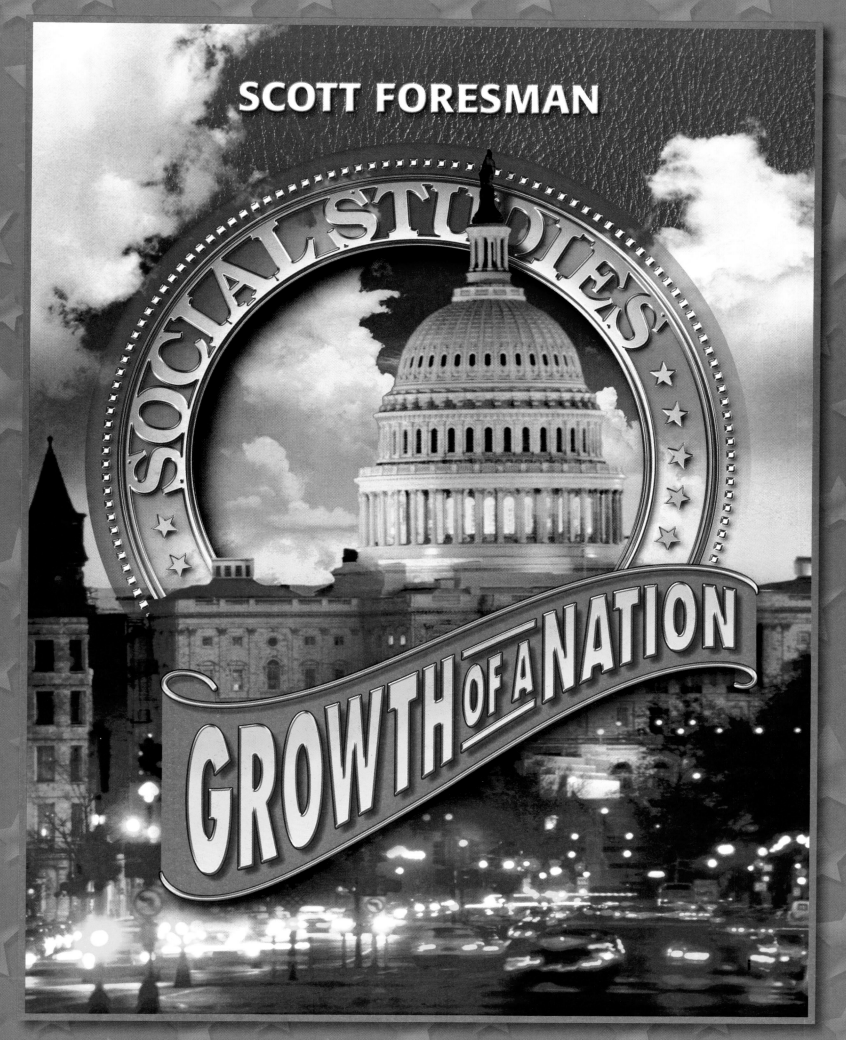

SCOTT FORESMAN

SOCIAL STUDIES

GROWTH OF A NATION

SCOTT FORESMAN

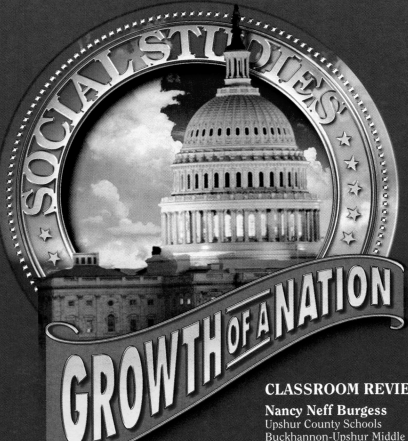

SOCIAL STUDIES

GROWTH OF A NATION

CLASSROOM REVIEWERS

Nancy Neff Burgess
Upshur County Schools
Buckhannon-Upshur Middle School
Upshur County, West Virginia

Stephen Corsini
**Content Specialist in Elementary
Social Studies**
School District 5 of Lexington and
Richland Counties
Ballentine, South Carolina

Deanna Crews
Millbrook Middle School
Elmore County
Millbrook, Alabama

Kevin L. Curry
Social Studies Curriculum Chair
Hickory Flat Elementary School
Henry County, McDonough, Georgia

Sheila A. Czech
Sky Oaks Elementary School
Burnsville, Minnesota

Rebecca Eustace Mills
Supervisor of Social Studies
Spotsylvania County Schools
Spotsylvania, Virginia

Cynthia K. Reneau
Muscogee County School District
Columbus, Georgia

Brandon Dale Rice
Secondary Education Social Science
Mobile County Public School System
Mobile, Alabama

Teresa L. Wilson
NBCT (MCGEN)
Neale Elementary School
Vienna, West Virginia

CONTENT REVIEWERS

**The Colonial Williamsburg
Foundation**
History Education Initiative
Williamsburg, Virginia

Dr. William E. White
**Director, Educational Program
Development**
The Colonial Williamsburg Foundation
Williamsburg, Virginia

Steve Sheinkin
Curriculum Writer
New York, New York

Editorial Offices:
• Glenview, Illinois • Parsippany, New
Jersey • New York, New York

Sales Offices:
• Boston, Massachusetts • Duluth, Georgia
• Glenview, Illinois • Coppell, Texas
• Sacramento, California • Mesa, Arizona

www.sfsocialstudies.com

Contents

Social Studies Handbook

UNIT 1

War Divides the Nation

UNIT 2

An Expanding Nation

UNIT 3

Expansion and Change

UNIT 4

Prosperity, Depression, and War

UNIT 6

Moving into the Twenty-first Century

★ B I O G R A P H Y ★

xii

Charts, Graphs, Tables & Diagrams

Time Lines

xiii

The following aspects of citizenship should be discussed with students. Help students determine ways in which the personal attributes described apply to their lives.

Caring

1 **How is the person in blue in the picture showing that she cares?** She is helping someone find the right classroom. **Analyze Pictures**

Respect

2 **How is the description of respect similar to "the golden rule?"** Both encourage you to "do unto others as you would have them do unto you." **Compare and Contrast**

Responsibility

3 **How do you act responsibly at home? at school?** Possible answer: Both at home and in school, I do what my parents and teachers ask me to do. **Apply Information**

Fairness

4 **Why is it important to take turns and follow the rules?** It is important to allow everyone to participate. Being fair is one way to show both caring and respect. **Generalize**

Honesty

5 **Describe some of the problems that could occur if a person does not tell the truth.** Possible answer: They could cause others not to trust them. **Make Inferences**

Courage

6 **What do you think the girl has done that took courage?** She admitted that she broke the window. **Analyze Pictures**

Citizenship Skills

There are six ways to show good citizenship: caring, respect, responsibility, fairness, honesty, and courage. In your textbook, you will learn about people who used these ways to help their community, state, and country.

Caring
Think about what someone else needs.
1

Respect
Treat others as you would want to be treated, and welcome differences among people.
2

Responsibility
Do what you are supposed to do and think before you act.
3

Fairness
Take turns and follow the rules. Listen to other people and treat them fairly.
4

Honesty
Tell the truth and do what you say you will do.
5

Courage
Do what is right even when the task might be hard.
6

Practice and Extend

SOCIAL STUDIES STRAND
Citizenship

Prejudice Reduction The following activity may help students understand the ramifications of prejudice, racism, and stereotyping.

- Have students write a story in which characters display at least two traits of citizenship.
- Students should write about how good citizenship helps characters solve problems, make decisions or show tolerance.

SOCIAL STUDIES STRAND
Citizenship

Citizen Heroes

In Growth of a Nation, students will read about some of the following Citizen Heroes.

- Ida Tarbell: *Responsibility*
- Ladder Company 21: *Courage*
- Francis Scott Key and Jan Scruggs: *Respect*
- Jacob Lawrence: *Honesty*
- Chief Joseph: *Fairness*
- Jody Williams: *Caring*

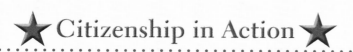

★ Citizenship in Action ★

Good citizens make careful decisions. They solve problems in a logical way. How will the fifth-graders handle each situation as good citizens?

Decision Making

These students are voting in the school election. Before making a decision, each student follows these steps:

1. **Tell what decision you need to make.**
2. **Gather information.**
3. **List your choices.**
4. **Tell what might happen with each choice.**
5. **Make your decision.**
6. **Act according to your decision.**

Problem Solving

These students broke a window near the playground. They follow these steps to solve the problem.

1. **Name the problem.**
2. **Find out more about the problem.**
3. **List ways to solve the problem.**
4. **Talk about the best way to solve the problem.**
5. **Solve the problem.**
6. **Figure out how well the problem was solved.**

Social Studies Handbook **H3**

CURRICULUM CONNECTION
Drama

Make Decisions and Solve Problems

- Have groups of students write short scripts in which they use either the steps of decision making to make a decision or the steps of problem solving to solve a problem.
- Students may write scripts using the decision-making and problem-solving situations shown on this page or they may use situations of their own invention.

- Have students present their decision-making or problem-solving plays to the class.
- After viewing each play, have the class—as a large group or individually—evaluate the different steps of the decision-making process or the problem-solving process that were presented in the play.

As students read about the following situations, have them incorporate their ideas into the models of decision making and problem solving.

Decision Making

Discuss the decision-making scenario. Help students make a careful decision.

1. A decision about whom to vote for in a school election is needed.
2. Students might read campaign literature made by candidates.
3. The choices might include different candidates representing different positions and opinions.
4. Have students discuss different outcomes for different candidates.
5. Have students talk about the type of candidate they might choose.

Problem Solving

Discuss the problem-solving scenario. Help students solve the problem in a logical way.

1. The problem is that students broke a window.
2. Discuss the possible causes and effects of the problem.
3. Possible solutions: replace the window with glass or with clear plastic.
4. Certain solutions might not be permanent—if replaced with glass, the window might break again.
5. Students should choose the solution they feel is best.
6. Have students evaluate the solution that they choose.

Citizenship Throughout History

As students learn more about United States history in this book, have them identify decisions and problems that people have had to make and solve.

Think Like a Historian

Objectives

- Identify the types of primary sources historians use to learn about the past.

- Examine how historians use primary sources, including documents, visual materials, archaeological evidence, and artifacts, to learn about the past.

1 Introduce and Motivate

- Remind students that there are many ways to gather information about people of the past. Historians are thorough researchers and use all available resources to understand what life was like long ago.

- Review with students the different categories of primary sources, including artifacts, journals and diaries, archaeological fragments, oral histories, and printed documents.

- Have students make a list on a sheet of paper of the various kinds of information that primary sources can reveal about people of the past.

2 Teach and Discuss

- **Woman's Gown** This wool gown and petticoat were made and worn in England in the 1760s. These kinds of artifacts can tell historians many things about people, their work, and their daily lives. Ask students to describe how clothing might help historians gain information about people's wealth and fashions of the time.

- **Diary Entry: January 4, 1774** This diary entry was written by Philip Vickers Fithian, tutor to wealthy Virginia planter Robert Carter's seven children. Diaries and journals tell us about the actions and opinions of individuals, as well as what they thought was important. Ask students to discuss what this entry tells us about Mrs. Carter.

Research Skills

Living History from
Colonial Williamsburg
www.history.org

Think Like a Historian

At Colonial Williamsburg, we work to learn what life was like in the 1700s. To do this, we study artifacts from that time period. Artifacts and documents created by the people who lived in a time period and witnessed its events are called primary sources. Primary sources help us learn about people and places from the past. They help us understand events that happened before our time.

▶ Many artifacts survive and allow us to explore the past. We collect artifacts, such as this gown, that tell us how people lived.

Letters and diaries give us information about how people thought and acted. This description of Frances Carter was written by her children's teacher, Philip Vickers Fithian. ▼

Tuesday, January 4, 1774

"Mrs. Carter is prudent, always cheerful, never without something pleasant, a remarkable Economist, perfectly acquainted with the good management of children...."

H4

Practice and Extend

 **SOCIAL STUDIES Background**

Investigating the Past *by Dr. William E. White, Colonial Williamsburg Historian*

- Historians are much like detectives. As soon as an event happens it becomes part of the past. We must depend upon the memories of individual participants and the artifact evidence left by the event to solve the mystery of exactly what happened.

- History teaches how to investigate questions and evaluate evidence. Your students will find that skill valuable every single day of their lives.

- There are many ways for students to become involved in the exciting detective work of history. Encourage them to talk with family and friends about ancestors and family artifacts. The local library can help them investigate the history of their neighborhood and community. Local history museums provide programs and volunteer opportunities for students.

Many family stories are passed down from generation to generation over time. We call these oral histories. ►

Documents such as court records and newspapers tell us the types of things people owned and used. Look at this store advertisement from the *Virginia Gazette*, the local newspaper. ▼

◄ **Archaeologists find many artifacts by excavating the ground where people lived. Pieces of plates, cups, and teapots help us learn what people once used in their homes.**

"Just IMPORTED, and to be sold by the subscriber, in Williamsburg, THE FOLLOWING ARTICLES, VIZ. Irish linens, . . . children's shoes and stays, flannel waistcoats, new rosebags, paste necklaces and earrings . . . dolls and toys, and many other things too numerous to insert. The above GOODS to be sold on reasonable terms for ready money.

C. RATHELL."

By carefully studying many primary sources, we are able to form an idea of what life was like in colonial times. ◄

Find primary sources that describe your family or your school in the past. You might look for yearbooks, newspapers, articles that have been saved, or pictures that were taken. Use those primary sources to write a description of what your family or school was like in the past.

H5

- **Ceramic Teapot** This creamware teapot was made by William Greatbatch in Staffordshire, England, in about 1770. Artifacts often reveal important details about daily life. Have students describe the design of the teapot. Have them share their ideas about what this artifact might tell us about the family who used it.

- **Storytelling** This photograph depicts interpreters portraying slaves, who left few written records. The mother is telling her children a bedtime story. Such stories and oral histories are a type of primary source that provides information about people of the past, their families, and their values. Ask students how oral history and storytelling are used today.

- ***Virginia Gazette* Newspaper Advertisement** This advertisement appeared in the October 20, 1774, issue of the Williamsburg newspaper, the *Virginia Gazette*. The advertisement lists a variety of items for sale in Catherine Rathell's shop. Newspapers distributed local, colonial, and international news, as well as business advertisements, to a large number of people. Ask students what information they get from newspapers today.

- **Family Group** This photograph shows Colonial Williamsburg interpreters portraying an eighteenth-century family. This is an interpretation of what life was like 200 years ago, based on historians' careful research of all available sources. Ask students how historians 200 years in the future will learn about life today.

3 Close and Assess

- Ask students to review the list they created of the kinds of information that can be learned about people of the past by studying primary sources.

- Have students discuss which resources might help them learn about their family or school in the past. Students should visit their school library or ask family members to help them find those sources.

- Once resources have been collected, students should use information to write several paragraphs on their family or school as it was in the past.

CURRICULUM CONNECTION
Writing

- Encourage students to list primary sources that are good indicators of what life is like today.
- Using magazines and newspapers, have students find primary sources that either match or are similar to the items on their lists. Students may also draw the item if they like.
- Instruct students to choose a year in the future. Through the eyes of a "future" historian, have them write a creative story telling how that primary source was discovered and what it tells about life in the early twenty-first century.

Identify Primary and Secondary Sources

Ask students to categorize the following items as either a primary source or a secondary source.

- a diary entry from a general (primary source)
- a history book about the invention of the telephone (secondary source)
- an interview with a politician (primary source)

1 **What are some other examples of secondary sources in the classroom?** Possible answers: Encyclopedias, atlases, and history books.
Main Idea and Details

Print Resources

Use Encyclopedias

- Show students a set of encyclopedias and dictionaries. Based on the guide letters and volume numbers, ask students to find the volume they would use to research such topics as South America or George Washington Carver.
- Ask students to look in a dictionary to find a word they do not know. They should pronounce the word, spell it, and describe its meaning.

Use Atlases and Almanacs

2 **What can you find in an atlas?** Maps that show information, such as elevation, crops, and natural resources
Main Idea and Details

3 **How is an almanac different from an encyclopedia?** An almanac is a yearly publication that provides facts and figures; an encyclopedia is a collection of articles on various topics.
Compare and Contrast

Use Nonfiction Books and Periodicals

4 **Why is it important to check the copyright date of nonfiction books and periodicals when conducting research?** To make sure that the book or periodical is not outdated Make Inferences

---

When gathering information for written reports and research projects, you will need to use resources in addition to your textbook. You can use print technology resources, and community resources. These sources can be of two different kinds.

Primary sources are firsthand documents produced by people who were involved in the event. Primary sources include journals, diaries, letters, speeches, autobiographies, photographs, interviews, and eyewitness accounts.

Secondary sources are descriptions of an event written by people who did not participate in the event. Secondary sources include history books, encyclopedias, and biographies. **1**

Print Resources

Libraries often have books, periodicals, and reference books such as atlases, almanacs, and encyclopedias.

An *encyclopedia* is a collection of articles, listed alphabetically, on various topics. Electronic encyclopedias often have sound and video clips in addition to words.

A *dictionary* is an alphabetical collection of words that includes the meanings of each word. A dictionary is the best source for checking the correct spelling of a word.

An *atlas* is a collection of maps. Some atlases have a variety of maps showing elevation, natural **2** resources, historical events, and so on.

An *almanac* is a book or computer resource that contains facts about a variety of subjects. Almanacs are updated every year, so they usually have the latest statistics on populations, weather, **3** and other number-based facts.

A *nonfiction book* is a factual book about a specific topic. In a library you can search for books by subject, by title, or by author. Once you find a book that you want, the book's catalog number will guide you to the area of the library where you will find the book.

A *periodical,* such as a newspaper or **4** magazine, has information that is usually more up-to-date than that found in an older book. Most libraries have a special periodical section.

Practice and Extend

 CURRICULUM CONNECTION
Writing

Use Print Research to Create Puzzles

- Ask each student to pick a topic word or words—a place such as Williamsburg or a person such as Eleanor Roosevelt.
- Have students use print resources to gather short facts, statistics, or other information about their topic.
- Tell students to write as many clues as there are letters in their topic word. For Williamsburg, a student would write twelve clues. Each clue will relate to the topic, and the answer to each clue will begin with one of the letters in the topic word.
- Have students copy their clues in order on a clean sheet of paper so that when the clues are solved, the topic word will be spelled.
- Ask students to exchange papers and use print resources to solve each other's puzzles.

Technology Resources

The Internet, CD-ROMs, and TV programs are some technology sources that you can use for research.

The Internet is a system of linked computers that store information to be accessed by others. There are online encyclopedias, dictionaries, almanacs, and Web sites for many different companies, individuals, projects, and museums.

Anyone can create a Web site and post information on the Internet. As a researcher, you must determine which information is accurate. It is important to know who put together the information. It is wise to check information by finding several different reliable sources that give the same facts.

Before you turn on your computer, you should plan your research. What do you need to find out? For example, to begin the research project that appears on page H5, list names of communities or schools you want to research. Then use a *search engine* to find more information about these places. If you have not used the Internet before, ask a librarian, teacher, or parent for help.

Searching by Subject To find a search engine, click on SEARCH at the top of your screen. Choose a search engine from the list. Type one of your subject words into the search engine field. Then click SEARCH or GO. Click on the site you are most interested in.

Searching by Address URLs, or Web addresses, are found in many places. Magazines, newspapers, TV programs, and books often give Web addresses. You will see URLs written in this form: *www.sfsocialstudies.com*. Type the URL in the long address field at the top of the screen. Then press ENTER or RETURN.

Technology Resources

To establish guidelines for your students' safe and responsible use of the Internet, use the Scott Foresman Internet Guide.

5 What are some types of technology resources in your school? Possible answer: The Internet and CD-ROMS
Apply Information

6 What are some different places to look for information on the Internet? There are online encyclopedias, dictionaries, almanacs, and Web sites for many different companies, individuals, projects, and museums.
Main Idea and Details

7 When you are researching, how can you determine whether information is accurate? First, you should try to find out who put together the information. Next, it is wise to find several other reliable sources that give the same facts. **Main Idea and Details**

Use Search Engines

- Have students go online to an approved search engine and enter a subject word or words for the research project.

- Have students search for facts about their subject. Students should try to find information from several reliable online sources that give the same fact or facts.

8 How many Web sites are displayed for your subject? Do you need to change the word(s) or term(s) you are using? Answers will vary, but students should change the word(s) or term(s) they are using if too few (or too many) sites are displayed. **Evaluate**

MEETING INDIVIDUAL NEEDS
Leveled Practice

Find Reliable Sources Have students find and evaluate print and technology resources to make a list of reliable sources.

Easy Ask students to find three Internet sources that give the same facts about a historical event or person. **Reteach**

On-Level Have students find several Internet sources and one non-Internet source that all give the same facts about a historical event or person. **Enrich**

Challenge Have students find an Internet and a non-Internet source that offer facts about a historical event or person. Have students evaluate and write a short review of each source, rating its reliability or explaining their evaluation of it. **Extend**

Community Resources

Interviews

- You may wish to ask a local historian to come and speak to the class about United States history or another topic.
- Have students complete the steps under **Plan ahead.** Find background information for students to use to prepare questions.
- As students conduct the interview, remind them to follow the steps under **Ask/Listen/Record.** When students have completed their initial line of questioning, have them review the information they have gathered.
- Remind students to follow the steps under **Wrap-up.** Ask students to prepare a thank-you note to present to their guest.

Surveys

- Have students conduct a survey of their classmates about a topic that they choose.
- Students should use either yes/no questions or short-answer questions as they gather information.
- Have students tally people's answers.
- Students should analyze their data and interpret what they have discovered.
- Have students write about what they found out or make graphs to display their data.

Write for Information

- Have groups of students work together to compose e-mail letters requesting information from a community resource.
- Have students proofread their letters and correct any errors in spelling, punctuation, grammar, and sentence structure.

Community Resources

The people of your community are good sources of information.

Interviews

One way to find out what the people in your community know is to interview them. This means to ask them questions about the topic you are studying. If you want to conduct an interview, follow these steps.

Plan Ahead

- List the people you want to interview.
- Call or write to ask permission. Let the person know who you are and why you need information.
- Agree on a time and place for the interview.
- Find out background information about your topic.
- Write down questions you want to ask.

Ask/Listen/Record

- Ask questions clearly.
- Listen carefully.
- Be polite.
- Take notes to remember important ideas. If possible, use a tape recorder so that you have a recording of what was said.

Wrap-up

- Thank the person for his or her time.
- Send a follow-up thank-you note.

Surveys

Another way to find information in your community is to conduct a survey. A survey is a list of questions that you ask people and a record of their answers. You can use either yes/no questions or short-answer questions. To record the information you find out, make a chart with a column for each question.

The following steps will help you plan a survey:

- Make a list of questions.
- Decide where you want to conduct the survey and how many people you want to ask.
- Use a tally sheet to record people's answers.
- After the survey, look through the responses and write down what you found out.

When did you go to school?	How many kids were in your class?	What is your best memory?	Describe your favorite teacher.
1965-1968	around 15	recess	Mrs. Summers She was smart and fair.
1952-1956	around 20	winning the spelling bee	Mr. Shifflet He was a great storyteller.

Write for Information

Another way to use the people in your community as resources is to e-mail or write a letter asking for information. Use the following steps:

- Plan before you write.
- Tell who you are and why you are writing.
- Be neat and careful about spelling and punctuation.
- Thank the person.

Practice and Extend

ESL ACCESS CONTENT
ESL Support

Practice Interviewing Help students learn and apply approximate language for some of the steps of interviewing.

Beginning Help students choose a historic event and list several types of people they might interview about the event. Have students ask, draw, or act out questions that you write on the board. Play the role of the interviewee and answer students' questions using simple language, pantomime, or pictures.

Intermediate Have students in small groups agree on a historic event and a person to interview. Then, with a volunteer, model making a phone call to set up an interview. Guide pairs of students in practicing similar phone calls.

Advanced Have student pairs choose a social studies topic and use print resources to research it. Then have the pairs write interview questions related to this information and dramatize an interview where the interviewer takes notes.

Writing a Research Report

Prewrite

- Decide on a topic for your report. Your teacher may tell you what kind of report to write and how long it should be.
- Generate questions about your topic to help focus your report.
- Use a variety of sources to find information and answer your questions.
- Evaluate your sources to determine which will be the most helpful.
- Take notes from your sources.
- Review your notes and write down the main ideas related to the topic that you want to present in your report. Two or three main ideas are enough for most reports.
- Organize your notes into an outline, listing each main idea and the details that support it.

Write a First Draft

- Using your outline and your notes, write a draft report of what you have learned. You can correct mistakes at the revising step.
- Write in paragraph form. Each paragraph should be about a new idea.
- When you quote something directly from your sources, write down which source the quote came from.
- Your report should be organized with a strong introduction, a solid summary of information, a conclusion, and the list of sources you used.

Revise

- Read over your first draft. Does it make sense? Does it answer the questions you asked? Does it clearly explain facts and ideas? Do your ideas flow from one to the other in an organized way? Do you need more information about any main idea? Will the report hold a reader's interest?
- Change any sentences or paragraphs that do not make sense. Add anything that will make your ideas clear.
- Check your quotations to make sure you have used people's exact words and that you have noted the source.

Edit

- Proofread your report. Correct any errors in spelling, capitalization, or punctuation.

Publish

- Include illustrations, maps, time lines, or other graphics that will add to the report.
  - Write a table of contents.
  - Write or type a final copy of your report as neatly as possible.

My School

Write a Research Report

Write Reports About Communities or Schools

- Have students write a report about the community or school they chose to research.
- Students should first complete the steps listed under **Prewrite** on p. H9. Remind them to use the resources they learned about on pp. H6–H8.
- Before students work independently, demonstrate how to take notes and how to complete an outline. Point out that notes may be phrases, not sentences. Show how to write down main ideas and details.
- Remind students to keep a record of the specific sources they use. Later, you may wish to ask students to use their list to create a bibliography for their report.
- Students should use their outlines to complete the steps under **Write a First Draft,** then the steps under **Revise.** You may wish to ask students to review their peers' papers as they revise their drafts.
- Finally, ask students to complete the steps under **Edit** and **Publish.** Remind students to use standard grammar, spelling, sentence structure, and punctuation. You may wish to have students use a word processor to publish their reports.

MEETING INDIVIDUAL NEEDS
Learning Styles

Complete Group Reports Have groups of students work together to complete the research report described on this page. Have students use their individual learning styles to enhance their group's research report.

Visual Learning Students with strength in visual learning may determine the maps, time lines, or other graphics that will be added to their groups' report.

Kinesthetic Learning Have students make a model of the community or school that they researched. Other students may make replicas of artifacts that can be displayed.

Five Themes of Geography

From *Guidelines for Geographic Education: Elementary and Secondary Skills,* prepared by the Joint Committee on Geographic Education of the National Council for Geographic Education and the Association of American Geographers

Location

Describing a *location* involves finding the exact or relative position of a place. You may wish to have students use the Student Atlas or the atlas at the end of the Pupil Edition to complete the following activities.

Find Locations

- Have students locate the state of Wyoming and list the states that are located to its north, south, east, and west.
- Point out the lines of latitude and longitude on the map. Have students find the location of Yellowstone National Park using the points of latitude and longitude given in the text.

Place

Tell students they can describe a *place* by identifying its distinguishing features and comparing them to the natural or human-made features of other areas.

1 What makes Yellowstone National Park different from other areas?
Possible answers: Yellowstone is a volcanic region; it has hot springs, mudpots, and geysers; Old Faithful is located there. **Compare and Contrast**

Geography Skills

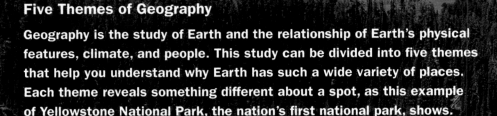

Five Themes of Geography

Geography is the study of Earth and the relationship of Earth's physical features, climate, and people. This study can be divided into five themes that help you understand why Earth has such a wide variety of places. Each theme reveals something different about a spot, as this example of Yellowstone National Park, the nation's first national park, shows.

Location

Where can this park be found?
Yellowstone National Park is located at about 45°N, between 110°W and 111°W.

1 Place

How is this place different from others?
Yellowstone National Park is an area of volcanic activity, with hot springs, mudpots, and geysers such as Old Faithful.

2 Human/Environment Interaction

How have people changed this place?
People have built visitor centers and lodgings in Yellowstone National Park, as well as special walkways so tourists can hike safely among hot springs and geysers.

H10 Social Studies Handbook

Practice and Extend

**SOCIAL STUDIES
Background**

The Essential Elements of Geography
From the National Council for Geographic Education

- **The World in Spatial Terms** Geography studies the relationships among people, places, and environments by showing information about them in spatial context.
- **Places and Regions** The identities of individuals and cultures can be found in particular places and regions.

- **Physical Systems** Physical processes shape Earth's surface and interact with flora and fauna to create, sustain, and change ecosystems.
- **Human Systems** Human activities help shape Earth's surface. Human structures and settlements are part of Earth's surface, and humans control portions of Earth's surface.

- **Environment and Society** The physical environment is modified by human activities, many having to do with the pursuit of Earth's natural resources. Human activities are also influenced by Earth's physical features and processes.
- **The Uses of Geography** Knowledge of geography enables people to develop an understanding of the relationships among people, places, and environments over time.

Movement

Millions of people travel to and through Yellowstone National Park each year to see its beauty and natural wonders.

Region

What is special about the region in which Yellowstone National Park is located? Yellowstone National Park is located in the Rocky Mountains, a system of mountain ranges that stretches from New Mexico north into Canada and Alaska.

Social Studies Handbook **H11**

Human/Environment Interaction

Interaction between *humans* and the *environment* involves people influencing (changing) and being influenced by their surroundings.

2 How have people changed the environment in your community? Possible answers: People have paved the ground with concrete and built buildings. Forests have been cut down to make room for farming. **Draw Conclusions**

Movement

Discuss the theme of *movement*—ways in which people, goods, and information move from one place to another.

3 How are the ways people and goods move around the country similar to and different from the ways ideas move around the country? People and goods are moved by planes, trucks, trains, cars, buses, and bicycles. Ideas can also be moved by any of these means, if, for example, they are printed in books or newspapers. In addition, ideas can be moved by speech, telephone, television, radio, Internet, film, and so on. **Compare and Contrast**

Region

The common features that make an area special help comprise a *region*.

Compare Regions

- Show students pictures of your region and of the regional landscape of Yellowstone National Park. Help students identify the landforms and vegetation of each region. Have students compare and contrast the regions.

Additional Resources

The following resources can be used throughout *Growth of a Nation* to teach and reinforce geography skills.

- Intermediate Big Book Atlas
- Student Atlas
- Outline Maps
- Desk Maps
- Map Resources CD-ROM

FYI SOCIAL STUDIES
Background

Yellowstone National Park

- Yellowstone National Park was the world's first national park, established by Congress in 1872.
- Yellowstone got its name from the Yellowstone River, which winds through the park on its way to its confluence with the Missouri River in eastern Montana. In the park, it passes through Yellowstone Lake and gushes down Upper and Lower Falls into a deep canyon: the Grand Canyon of the Yellowstone.
- Yellowstone contains more than 10,000 hydrothermal features, including its 300 geysers—the largest concentration in the world.
- The park's wildlife includes all species of large mammals known to be present in North America when the first Europeans arrived.
- Yellowstone Lake is the largest lake above 7,000 feet in North America, with 136 square miles of surface area and 110 miles of shoreline.

Use a Globe

- Point to an ocean on a globe. Have students use the globe to locate other oceans. You may also want to have students locate seas, gulfs, lakes, rivers, and other bodies of water.

- Explain to students that some people consider that there is a fifth ocean, the Southern Ocean, which consists of those parts of the Pacific, Indian, and Atlantic Oceans that are south of 60°S latitude.

- Point to a continent on a globe. Have students name the continent to which you are pointing. Then have them use the globe to locate and name other continents. Also have students locate several countries located on the continents they locate.

- Have students use the globe to locate the equator (0° latitude) and the prime meridian (0° longitude).

Geography Skills

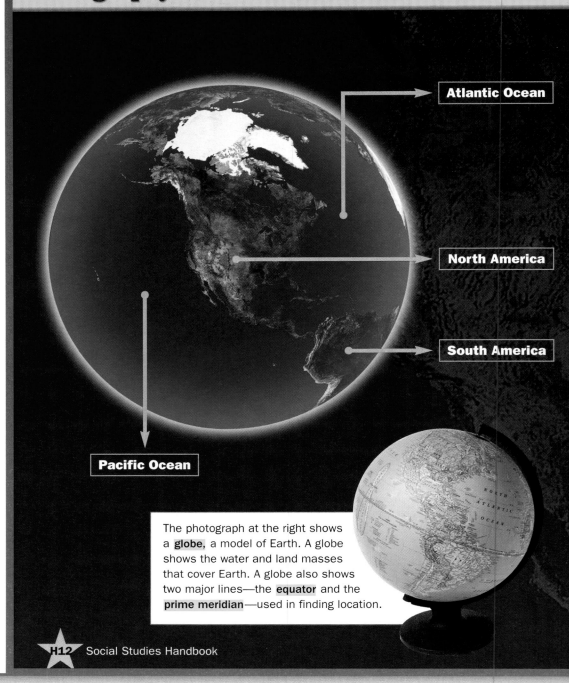

The photograph at the right shows a **globe**, a model of Earth. A globe shows the water and land masses that cover Earth. A globe also shows two major lines—the **equator** and the **prime meridian**—used in finding location.

H12 Social Studies Handbook

Practice and Extend

SOCIAL STUDIES
Background

About Earth and the Sun

- Earth rotates on its axis, making one complete rotation about every 24 hours.

- While rotating, Earth revolves around the sun, making one complete revolution in approximately 365 days.

- Earth is tilted on its axis. Show students a globe on which Earth is tilted.

- The tilt of Earth affects how much sunlight each place on Earth gets at different times of the year.

- When places are tilted toward the sun, they get more direct sunlight and temperatures are warmer. When the Northern Hemisphere is tilted toward the sun, it is summer there. When the Northern Hemisphere is tilted away from the sun, it is winter there.

- Places near the equator, where sunlight is most direct, have a warm, tropical climate. Places near the poles, where sunlight is least direct, have a cold, polar climate.

Hemispheres: Northern and Southern

A globe, like Earth, is shaped like a sphere, or ball, so it can only show one half of Earth at a time. People commonly speak of Earth as being divided into half-spheres called hemispheres. The **Northern Hemisphere** is the half north of the equator, an imaginary line that circles Earth at its widest point between the North and South poles. The **Southern Hemisphere** is the half south of the equator.

Complete views of these hemispheres are not possible when you are looking at a globe only from the side. For a complete view, you have to turn a globe until you are looking down directly at either the North or South Pole. The illustration below shows you these views.

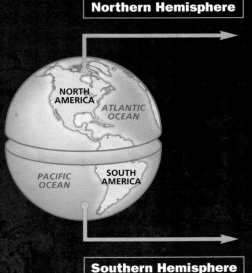

Northern Hemisphere

Southern Hemisphere

Vocabulary

globe
equator
prime meridian
hemisphere

Hemispheres: Northern and Southern

Identify Hemispheres

- Have students use a globe to determine oceans and continents that are in the Northern Hemisphere.

4 In which hemisphere is the entire continent of North America located, the Northern Hemisphere or the Southern Hemisphere? The Northern Hemisphere

Interpret Maps

- Have students locate oceans and continents that are in the Southern Hemisphere.

- Have students locate oceans and continents that are in *both* the Northern and Southern hemispheres.

- You may wish to ask students to find individual countries that are in the Northern Hemisphere, the Southern Hemisphere, or both hemispheres.

Vocabulary

globe: a model of Earth

equator: an imaginary line around Earth, halfway between the North and South Poles

prime meridian: an imaginary line between the North and South Poles that runs through Greenwich, England

hemisphere: one half of Earth

Northern Hemisphere: the half of Earth between the North Pole and the equator

Southern Hemisphere: the half of Earth between the South Pole and the equator

Learn About the Equator Have students extend their knowledge about the equator.

Beginning Have students draw a circle on a piece of paper and then draw a line representing the equator to divide the circle into two equal parts. Have students label the two hemispheres "Northern Hemisphere" and "Southern Hemisphere."

Intermediate Have pairs of students use lengths of yarn to form a circle representing Earth and the equator. Ask students to make and place small labels for hemispheres, the equator, and North America or other continents.

Advanced Have students look in the dictionary to find other words that begin with *equa-* or *equi-,* such as *equivalent, equilateral,* and *equidistant.* Have students determine the meaning of the combining form *equi-* (equal). Ask students how the meaning "equal" applies to the equator. (The equator is an imaginary line that divides Earth into two equal hemispheres.)

Hemispheres: Western and Eastern

Identify Hemispheres

Have students look at the picture of the continents in the Western Hemisphere.

5 **What continents are entirely in the Western Hemisphere?** North America and South America Interpret Maps

Have students look at the picture of the continents and oceans in the Eastern Hemisphere.

6 **What continents are entirely or almost entirely in the Eastern Hemisphere?** Asia, Europe, Africa, and Australia Interpret Maps

7 **Which ocean is entirely in the Eastern Hemisphere?** The Indian Ocean Interpret Maps

Have students use what they know about the Northern, Southern, Eastern and Western Hemispheres.

8 **What continent is in all four hemispheres?** Africa Interpret Maps

Hemispheres: Western and Eastern

Earth has two other hemispheres—the **Eastern Hemisphere** and the **Western Hemisphere.** These are formed by dividing the globe into halves along the prime meridian. The prime meridian is an imaginary line that extends from pole to pole and passes through Greenwich, England. To the east of the prime meridian, halfway around Earth, is the Eastern Hemisphere. To the west of the prime meridian is the Western Hemisphere. The illustration below shows you these views.

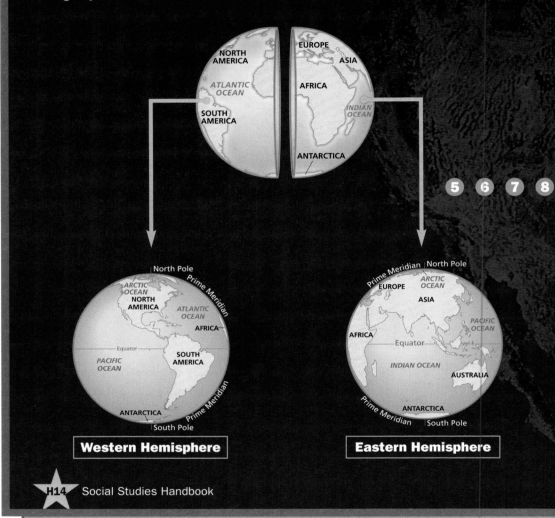

Western Hemisphere

Eastern Hemisphere

H14 Social Studies Handbook

Practice and Extend

MEETING INDIVIDUAL NEEDS
Leveled Practice

Use Latitude and Longitude After students read both pages above, have them complete the following activities using a map of the United States or a globe that indicates both latitude and longitude.

Easy Have students choose one line of latitude or longitude and trace its path across the continental United States. Students should write the names of any states and major cities that the parallel or meridian passes through or near. **Reteach**

On-Level Ask students to work together to determine the latitude and longitude for several different places in the United States. **Extend**

Challenge Ask students to determine the latitude and longitude of various cities and other places of their choosing within the United States. Have students write down the coordinates they determine and exchange them with classmates. Students should identify places using their classmates' coordinates. **Enrich**

Latitude and Longitude on a Globe

Latitude and longitude are imaginary lines that help us find locations on Earth. The lines are found only on globes and maps.

Lines of latitude circle Earth in an east-west direction. They are also called parallels because they are parallel to the equator and to one another. These lines are measured in units called degrees. The equator is the latitude line of 0 degrees (0°) where measurements begin. Latitude lines tell how many degrees north or south of the equator a location is. A change of one degree of latitude in any direction on Earth is equal to about 69 miles.

Lines of longitude circle Earth in a north-south direction. They are also called meridians. The prime meridian is 0 degrees (0°) longitude. Longitude lines tell how many degrees east or west of the prime meridian a location is. Unlike latitude, longitude lines are not parallel. They are farthest apart at the middle of Earth but become closer together as they move toward the poles.

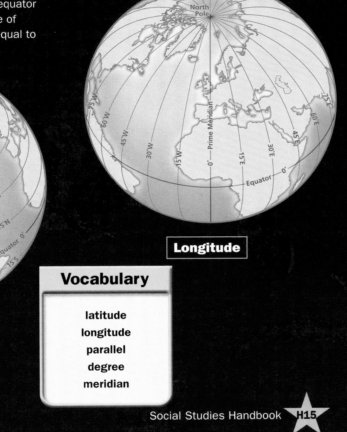

Longitude

Latitude

Vocabulary

latitude
longitude
parallel
degree
meridian

CURRICULUM CONNECTION
Literature

Read About Maps Have students read the following books to learn more about maps, latitude and longitude, and navigation.

How Maps Are Made, by Martyn Bramwell (Lerner Publications Company, ISBN 0-822-52920-3, 1997) **Easy**

Where Am I? The Story of Maps and Navigation, by A. G. Smith (Stoddart Kids, ISBN 0-773-75836-4, 1997) **On-Level**

The Longitude Prize, by Joan Dash (Farror, Straus, & Giroux, ISBN 0-374-34636-4, 2000) **Challenge**

Latitude and Longitude on a Globe

Understand Latitude and Longitude

- Have students find latitude 0°, the equator, on a globe. Then have them examine all the lines of latitude between that point and 90° north latitude. Tell them those are north latitudes. Repeat this process working from the equator south, and tell students those are south latitudes.

- Have students find longitude 0°, the prime meridian, on the globe. Then have them find the next line east of the meridian (15° east), then 30° east, and work their way around the globe to 180°. Tell students these are the east longitudes. Repeat the process working from the prime meridian west, and say these are the west longitudes.

- Point out to students that the prime meridian, unlike the equator, extends only halfway around Earth. The 180° line of longitude extends the rest of the way.

- Explain that latitude and longitude coordinates use the letters *N, S, E,* and *W* to tell which latitude or longitude line a place is located near.

- Model how to find the latitude and longitude of a city on a globe. Then have students find the lines of latitude and longitude nearest to the city or town where they live and write down the latitude and longitude coordinates for their community.

Vocabulary

latitude: a measure of how far north or south of the equator a location is

longitude: a measure of how far east or west of the prime meridian a location is

parallel: one of the lines of latitude, which are imaginary lines that circle Earth in an east-west direction

degree: a unit of measure of latitude or longitude; a full circle around Earth contains 360 degrees

meridian: one of the lines of longitude, which circle Earth in a north-south direction

Political Map

Have students use political maps in this textbook or the Student Atlas to identify examples of their different features. Point out similarities and differences between the various titles, symbols, keys, and locators.

9 **How is this political map different from political maps of the United States today?** Alaska and Hawaii are not shown. Some of the states that are states today are only shown as territories on the map. Compare and Contrast

10 **What is the purpose of a locator?** A locator is a small map within a larger map that locates the subject of the main map in a larger area. Main Idea and Details

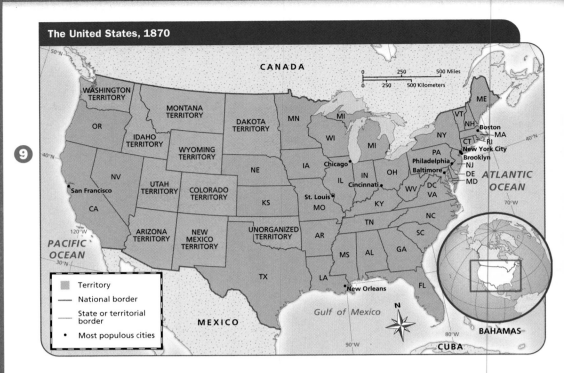

The United States, 1870

Key:
- Territory
- National border
- State or territorial border
- Most populous cities

Political Map

A **political map** shows what humans have created on Earth's surface. This means that a political map can show borders that divide an area into countries, states, and counties. It can also show where cities, roads, buildings, and other human-made elements once were or still are today. Like other kinds of maps, political maps have many of the features below that help us read and use them.

A map's **title** tells what a map is about. What is the title of the historical map on this page?

A map's **symbols** are lines, small drawings, or fields of color that stand for something else. The map's **key,** or legend, is a small box that lists each symbol and tells what it stands for. How can you use the key to identify U.S. territories on this map?

Sometimes a map includes a **locator,** a small map in a box or circle. It locates the subject of the main map in a larger area such as a state, country, continent, or hemisphere. In what larger area is the United States of 1870 shown?

H16 Social Studies Handbook

Practice and Extend

SOCIAL STUDIES
Background

Dakota Territory Why does the map show only one Dakota Territory when today there are two Dakotas, North Dakota and South Dakota?

- The Dakota Territory was established by act of Congress on March 2, 1861. At this time the territory covered the current states of North and South Dakota and most of the land of present-day Montana and Wyoming. In 1863, the territory was reduced to include only the present-day Dakotas.
- By the late 1870s, Dakotans felt it was time their territory became a state. They began to push for statehood.

- As much as Dakotans wanted statehood, they could not agree on a capital city. The northern part of the territory claimed Bismarck as the territorial capital. The southern part of the territory claimed Pierre. In 1889 the territory split into two parts.
- On November 2, 1889, North Dakota and South Dakota became the 39th and 40th states, respectively.

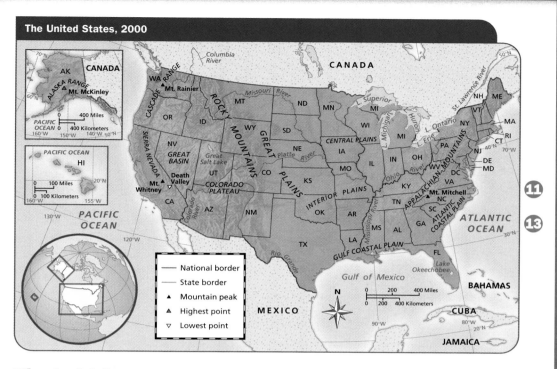

The United States, 2000

National border
State border
▲ Mountain peak
▲ Highest point
▽ Lowest point

Physical Map

A **physical map** shows the major landforms and water features on an area of Earth's surface. What are some examples of mountains, plains, rivers, gulfs, and oceans on the physical map of the United States on this page? Notice that a physical map can have a few elements of a political map.

A **compass rose** is a fancy design with four large pointers that show the cardinal directions. The north pointer, which points toward the North Pole, is marked with an "N." East is to the right, south is opposite north, and west is to the left. The compass rose also shows **intermediate directions,** which are smaller pointers halfway between the cardinal directions. Intermediate directions are northeast, southeast, southwest, and northwest. What direction is the Gulf of Mexico from the Cascade Range?

Four other common features on maps are a scale, inset maps, latitude and longitude, and elevation. These and other features are covered in detail on the next five pages of this handbook.

Vocabulary

political map
title
symbol
key
locator
physical map
compass rose
intermediate
direction

Social Studies Handbook **H17**

Physical Map

⓫ **According to this map, where is the lowest point in the United States?** Death Valley Interpret Maps

⓬ **Where does an intermediate direction get its name?** From the two cardinal directions it is between Draw Conclusions

⓭ **Name the four mountain peaks shown on the map, and the states in which they are located.** Mt. McKinley, Alaska; Mt. Rainier, Washington; Mt. Whitney, California; Mt. Mitchell, North Carolina Interpret Maps

Vocabulary

political map: a map that shows countries, states, and cities

title: a name that tells what a map is about

symbol: a small drawing or field of color that stands for something

key: information that explains what each symbol on a map stands for

locator: a small map that shows where the subject of a main map can be found

physical map: a map that shows landforms and geographic features

compass rose: a pointer on a map that shows directions

intermediate direction: one of four directions that are midway between the cardinal directions

Scale

Use a Map Scale

- Discuss with students that the scale of a map tells the relationship between measurements on the map and actual distances between places in the world.

⑭ About how many miles apart are Little Rock, Arkansas, and Fort Smith, Arkansas? About 125 miles
Interpret Maps

- Supply the class with a map with a clear map scale. Have students practice using the map scale to find distances between locations on the map.

⑮ Why would someone need to know how to read the scale on a map?
Possible answer: To find out how far it really is between cities or other places
Draw Conclusions

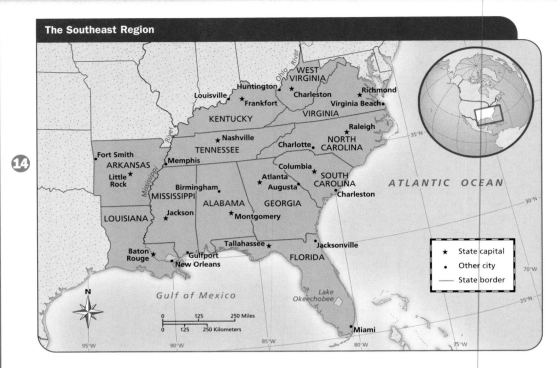

The Southeast Region

⑭

Scale

Usually a map has a **scale**, a set of lines marked off in miles and kilometers. A scale allows you to estimate the actual distances between points on a map. It tells ⑮ you what a small distance on a map equals in actual miles on Earth. For example, one inch on a map may equal one mile,

hundreds of miles, or even thousands of miles. On the scale above, one inch equals 250 miles. If two points on the map are two inches apart, about how many miles apart are they? How many miles apart are Little Rock, Arkansas, and Richmond, Virginia?

H18 Social Studies Handbook

Practice and Extend

SOCIAL STUDIES STRAND
Geography

Scales and Details on a Map

- Using a political map of the United States, discuss with students the appearance of the country's western and eastern coastlines. Note that parts of these coastlines appear somewhat irregular, whereas others appear very smooth.

- Get an enlarged map of a single state that borders either of these oceans. Have students compare the appearance of the portions of coastline appearing on this map with the same portions as they appear on the larger map.

- Discuss the general point that in maps that show relatively large areas, each inch represents a large number of miles (or kilometers), and as a result not as many details can be shown.

Georgia and Its Capital

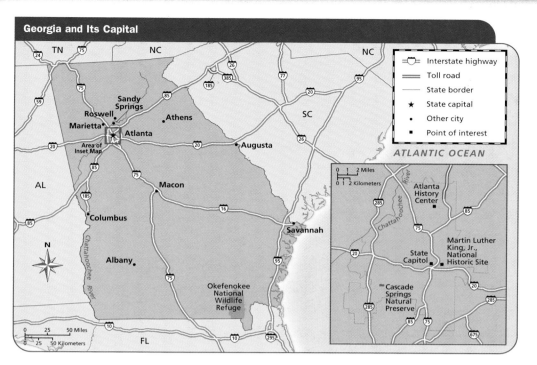

Inset Map

An **inset map** is a small map in a box that is set inside a main map. An inset map is not the same as a locator map. It is not the purpose of an inset map to locate the main map in a larger area. Instead, an inset map shows either more of the main map or details about the main map. The map of the United States on page H17 has two inset maps. They show Alaska and Hawaii, which otherwise would be outside the area shown on the main map. The inset map has its own scale, and this often lets you see something in greater detail. What do you see on the inset map of Atlanta that you cannot see on the main map?

 16

Vocabulary

scale

inset map

Inset Map

Use an Inset Map

- Have students turn to page H17 and point out the inset maps of Alaska and Hawaii. Then locate Alaska and Hawaii on a globe to show students where these states are actually located. Explain to students that because these states are located outside the area shown on the main map, they were included on the main map through the use of inset maps.

- Draw students' attention to the main map of Georgia and the inset map of Atlanta. Discuss the increased level of detail shown in the inset map.

16 Why might a visitor to Georgia use the inset map of Atlanta? Possible answers: To find points of interest to visit; to know which route to take through or around the city **Draw Conclusions**

- Help students find other examples of maps containing insets. These might include historical maps showing, for example, a country and its colonies in other parts of the world.

Vocabulary

scale: a tool for estimating actual distances between points on a map

inset map: a small map that shows details that cannot be shown in a larger map

SOCIAL STUDIES STRAND
Geography

Inset Maps In the News

- Explain to students that newspapers and other publications sometimes use inset maps to help explain current events that are happening throughout the world.

- Find some examples of inset maps in newspapers and magazines and help the class interpret them.

- Ask students to share their experiences in seeing insets in other contexts, such as on news or sports programming on television. Have them discuss what the purposes of these insets are and how they are similar to the purposes of insets on maps (making it possible to directly compare different sets of information that could otherwise not be seen at the same time).

Latitude and Longitude on a Map

Make Maps

- Give students centimeter-square graph paper. Students should turn the paper sideways.

- Have students draw the outline of a continent, country, or landform of their own invention on the paper.

- Students should plot several cities or landmarks on their maps.

- Have students label the horizontal lines with degrees of latitude. Have students label the vertical lines with degrees of longitude. Students should use intervals of 5° or 10°.

- Ask students to exchange maps and determine the latitude and longitude of cities or landmarks on their classmates' maps.

Geography Skills

Mississippi and Alabama

Latitude and Longitude on a Map

Lines of latitude and longitude can appear on maps as well as on globes. They are usually drawn as thin, light blue lines, with numbers at the edge of the map. The point where these horizontal and vertical lines cross shows the exact location of a place. We can find the location of a place by knowing its latitude and longitude.

We refer to degrees (°) east and west (for longitude) and degrees north and south (for latitude). Although this map shows every degree, maps of larger areas do not. That would make them too cluttered and hard to read. So mapmakers usually place the lines at intervals of every 5°, 10°, 15°, 20°, or 30°. On this map, Gadsden, Alabama, is nearly exactly at the point where which lines cross? Which city lies nearest the point at which 35°N and 90°W cross?

 H20 Social Studies Handbook

Practice and Extend

CURRICULUM CONNECTION
Math

Miles per Degree

- Discuss with students why one degree of latitude is approximately equal to the same distance all the way around the world, whether at the equator or the poles.

- Tell students that the approximate circumference of Earth around the poles is 24,800 miles. Ask them to compute the number of miles that are equal to one degree of latitude. (24,800 miles ÷ 360° = 69 miles per degree)

- Discuss why one degree of longitude is not equal to the same distance all around the world. At the equator, a degree of longitude has about the same number of miles as a degree of latitude (69). However, as one moves toward one of the poles, each degree of longitude represents a shorter and shorter distance, eventually becoming zero at the pole.

Time Zones of North America

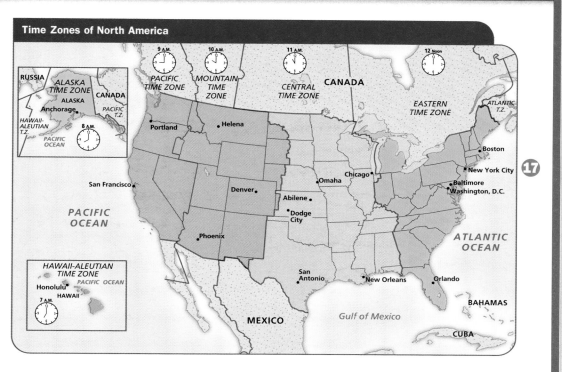

Time Zone Map

The world is divided into 24 time zones, one for each hour of the day. A **time zone map** shows a given region's time zones. A time zone map of the world can show all 24 of the world's time zones. The United States has six times zones. Within a time zone, almost every place has the same time. Look at the map above. What is the name of the time zone in which Anchorage is located? If it is 11 A.M. in Orlando, what time is it in Phoenix?

Vocabulary

time zone map

Time Zone Map

Read a Time Zone Map

• If necessary, review with students that Earth's rotation around the Sun means that the time of day changes depending on where you are on Earth. When it is night in one part of the world, it is day in another part.

• Review the time zone map with students. Point out that the United States lies within six time zones.

• Have students name one city or town in each of the time zones of the United States.

17 **Suppose you flew on a plane from one city shown on the map to another. Would you pass through any time zones? How many hours' difference are there between the times?** Students should identify two cities or towns, their times relative to each other, and any differences between the two. Interpret Maps

Vocabulary

time zone map: a map showing the world's or any country's time zones

SOCIAL STUDIES
Background

Time Zones Around the World

• There are 24 time zones around the world. Each zone represents 15° of longitude—one hour of time.

• From Greenwich, England, going east, each time zone advances in time by one hour. Halfway around Earth at the International Date Line (IDL), the time is 12 hours later than it is at Greenwich. As you continue east and cross the IDL, time goes backward by 24 hours. It then advances as before as you continue east, one hour per time zone, to Greenwich.

• Some countries have chosen different ways of administering their time zones. Russia stretches across 11 time zones and uses all of them. China, although its land falls into six time zones, uses the same time throughout the country.

Elevation Map

Read an Elevation Map

- Make sure that students see the connection between the colors in the key shown for elevation and the colors on the map on p. H22.

- Help students understand that 0 on the elevation map key refers to sea level.

- Discuss with students that although the bands of color for elevations above sea level all have the same width on the elevation key, these bands do not represent equal-sized ranges of elevation. Thus the darker green band represents a range of elevations of 160 feet whereas the orange band represents a range of elevations of 980 feet.

18 **Which part of South Carolina has a higher elevation, the south or the north?** The north Interpret Maps

19 **What landforms labeled on the map help you understand what accounts for the change in elevation in the state?** The Atlantic Coastal Plain is a plain by the coast. It has a low elevation. The Appalachian Mountains in the west of the state is a range of mountains and has a higher elevation. Interpret Maps

Geography Skills

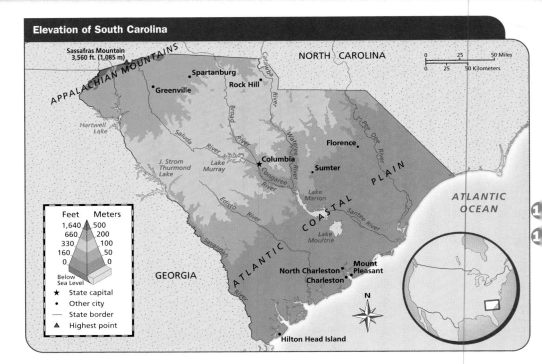

Elevation of South Carolina

Elevation Map

Elevation is the height of land above sea level. The measurement is usually given in both feet and meters.

An **elevation map** like the one on this page uses colors to show different elevations across a landscape. You can see the general heights of mountains, plateaus, and other landforms.

The key on an elevation map often contains a pyramid-shaped graphic to emphasize height. Different colors are used to stand for certain ranges of

elevation in feet and meters. For example, the darker green color stands for land that ranges between sea level and 160 feet above sea level.

On the key, which color shows the highest elevation range? What is the highest elevation range shown on the map? In which elevation range is South Carolina's capital city of Columbia? On average, is the land in South Carolina higher in the east or in the west of the state?

H22 Social Studies Handbook

Practice and Extend

SOCIAL STUDIES STRAND
Geography

Make a Three-Dimensional Relief Map

- Have students use an atlas or the Internet to find elevation maps and physical maps of your state. Have them trace those maps or use outline maps of the state.

- Have students add pieces of clay to the traced or outline map to make a three-dimensional relief map.

- Students should refer to the elevation map and physical maps they gathered as they add clay to the outline map to form mountain ranges, drainage basins, plateaus, and other large landforms.

- Students may wish to create small flags or labels to indicate the names of certain features or landforms.

- Display students' completed maps in the classroom.

Population Density Map

Interpret a Distribution Map

- Tell students that *distribute* means "to spread or scatter." A *distribution map,* therefore, measures how something is spread out over an area.

- Have students look at the population density map of the United States at the top of the page. Review the key with students to make sure they understand that different colors represent different population densities.

- Name a few urban centers on the map and have students use the key to identify the population range of each.

- Then distribute paper squares, pennies, or other small objects to students. Give students sitting in the center of the room several objects, and students sitting at the periphery only one or two objects.

- Sketch a quick map of the class seating chart on the board. Have students make their own copies of this map.

- Have each student tell you how many objects he or she has, and write that number on the board map in the place where the student sits.

- Have the class help you make a key for the map. Perhaps the color red could equal 1–2 objects, the color green could equal 3–4 objects, and so on.

- Have students use the key to make distribution maps showing the distribution of the objects throughout the classroom population.

Population Density of the United States, 2000

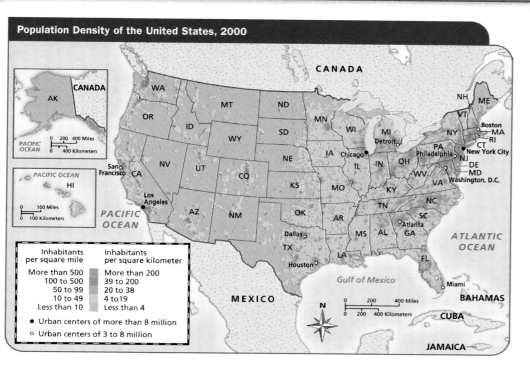

Inhabitants per square mile	Inhabitants per square kilometer
More than 500	More than 200
100 to 500	39 to 200
50 to 99	20 to 38
10 to 49	4 to 19
Less than 10	Less than 4

- Urban centers of more than 8 million
- Urban centers of 3 to 8 million

Population Density Map

A **distribution map** shows the pattern of data, or specific information, spread out over an area. Such a map can show this pattern for a city, a region, a country, a continent, and even the whole world at a time. This distribution map shows **population density,** or the average number of people who live in a given area.

Similar to an elevation key, the key in this population density map has boxes of color and a few other symbols. Do more people live in North Carolina or in Kansas? Which region has the higher population density, the Northwest or the Northeast? Which United States cities have more than 3 million inhabitants? Where would you guess that the mountain and desert regions of the United States are located? What hints at this fact?

Vocabulary

elevation
elevation map
distribution map
population density

Vocabulary

elevation: the height of land above sea level

elevation map: a map that shows the height of land above sea level

distribution map: a map that shows the pattern of something spread out over an area

population density: the number of people living per square mile of land

 **SOCIAL STUDIES Background**

The Growth of World Population As a world power, the United States is concerned with and closely follows trends in world population.

- In 1850, the population of the world reached about 1 billion. It took 80 years for it to double, reaching 2 billion in 1930. It had doubled again, to 4 billion, by 1975, and in 1999 the world population surpassed 6 billion.

- Statisticians estimate that the population of the world will reach about 9 billion by the year 2050.

- Each day, about 230,000 babies are born. The country with the highest birthrate is Niger, with 54 live births per thousand people, and the one with the lowest birthrate is Latvia, with 8 per thousand. The average birthrate in the world is 22 per thousand. The birth rate of the United States was a little more than 14 live births per thousand as estimated in 2003.

Road Map

Read a Road Map

Have students use the map key to determine the different types of roads on the map: interstate highways, U.S. highways, and state highways.

20 **What road would you take to visit Gila Cliff Dwellings National Monument? Is it an interstate highway, a U.S. highway, or a state highway?** Route 15; state highway Interpret Maps

21 **Suppose you planned a trip to three cities or towns in New Mexico. What routes would you take?** Students should identify the numbers and the types of roads they would take. Interpret Maps

Vocabulary

road map: a map that shows routes between towns and cities in a state or a country

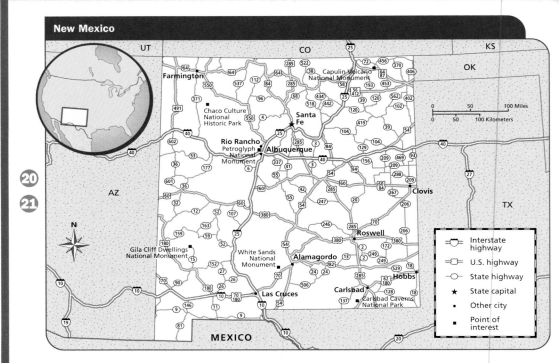

Road Map

A **road map** shows automobile routes between towns and cities for a region, county, state, or country. Major and minor roads or paved and unpaved roads are usually shown with thick or thin lines or with different colors. Most roads are numbered or lettered to make following them easier. Road maps may also show points of interest within a region.

The United States has several types of roads. The largest are Interstate highways that connect states and have the most lanes for traveling. The map key shows you the different types of roads.

The map on this page is a road map of New Mexico. If you lived in Alamagordo and wanted to drive southwest to Las Cruces, which numbered highway would you take? What is the number of the road that is the most direct route from Roswell north to Santa Fe? Which highways would you take from Farmington to Albuquerque?

H24 Social Studies Handbook

Vocabulary

road map

Practice and Extend

 Decision Making

Use a Decision-Making Process

- Write on the board three home addresses in your community and the address of a local movie theater. Have students use a community map with a grid and index of street names to complete this activity: **Suppose you and two friends want to travel together to the movies, taking the most direct route possible. Which route will you follow?**

- Students should use the decision-making process to plan their routes. They should use the grid and the index of street names to locate the homes and the theater. For each step in the process, have them discuss and write about what must be considered. Write the steps on the board or read them aloud.

1. Identify a situation that requires a decision.
2. Gather information.
3. Identify options.
4. Predict consequences.
5. Take action to implement a decision.

★ Overview ★

Vocabulary Routines

The following examples of reading and vocabulary development strategies can be used to instruct students about unit vocabulary.

BEFORE READING

Structural Analysis

Recognizing Word Forms Students can benefit greatly by reviewing how different word endings such as *-ed*, *-ing*, *-s*, or *-er* affect the meaning of a base word. Guiding students to recognize as well as write the different forms of a word will make everyday language more accessible to them.

Think about the word **draft**. *What does it mean? When you draft a story, you are writing out a rough copy or plan of your idea. Adding* **-ed** *to* **draft** *makes the word* **drafted**. *This word means the idea was written at a time before now. How would the meaning of the word* **draft** *change if we added the word endings* **-ing** *or* **-s**? **Drafting** *means "the act or process of writing or the writing is happening now." The drafting of the story took three hours. We are drafting a story. Now think of a sentence that uses the word* **drafts**. *(She drafts three stories a week.) In addition, the word* **draft** *is a noun that means the actual rough copy that you've written down. The result of drafting is a draft!*

DURING READING

Context Clues

Making Choices Reminding students that some words have more than one meaning will reinforce effective reading strategies such as recognizing context clues. Encouraging students to look closely for context clues will help them to determine the meaning of a word that can be used in different ways.

We've all seen the word **shape**. *It can mean the way in which something is formed. It can also refer to the act of forming something, as in an artist shaping clay. The word* **shape** *can be used in other ways as well. Look at this sentence from p. 9:*

On the flat, grass-covered Great Plains, huge herds of buffalo helped shape life for groups such as the Lakota and Pawnee.

Now I'm going to say three more definitions. Which one is the definition for the word **shape** *as it is used on p. 9?*

- *the outline of a house*
- *to have an effect on*
- *to form an idea*

AFTER READING

Word Associations

Graphic Organizers Having students fill in graphic organizers such as word webs to list examples of a vocabulary word will assist them in reviewing and retaining word meanings. These graphic tools can be used before, during, and after reading.

Look at this word web. In the center circle we see the term **natural resources**. *Think about what this word means. Then fill in the outer circles with examples of some natural resources that you know about.*

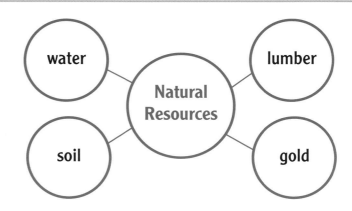

Establishing a Nation

OVERVIEW

Planning Guide

Overview • Establishing a Nation

Begin with a Primary Source pp. 2–3

🎯 *Target Skill* **Reading Social Studies, Summarize** pp. 4–5

Lesson Titles	Pacing	Main Ideas
Lesson 1 **Connections Across Continents** pp. 6–11	2 days	• A wide variety of Native American groups lived in North America when European explorers began arriving in the late 1400s.
Lesson 2 **Life in the Colonies** pp. 12–18 **Biography: John Rolfe** p. 19 **Map and Globe Skills: Compare Maps at Different Scales** pp. 20–21	4 days	• By the early 1600s, many European countries had established colonies in North America. • John Rolfe helped the English colony in Virginia establish peace with the Powhatan and economic stability. • Comparing maps at different scales helps you see areas at different levels of detail.
Lesson 3 **Revolution and Constitution** pp. 22–28 **Biography: Abigail Adams** p. 29	3 days	• The United States won independence from Britain and formed a new government under the Constitution. • Abigail Adams was a trusted advisor and supporter to her husband, John Adams, and other Patriots of the Revolutionary Era.
Lesson 4 **A Growing Nation** pp. 30–36 **Biography: Sequoyah** p. 37 **Chart and Graph Skills: Use Parallel Time Lines** pp. 38–39 ⭐ **Citizen Heroes: Respect** **Respecting the Flag** pp. 40–41	5 days	• During the first half of the 1800s, the United States expanded west to the Pacific Ocean, and the Industrial Revolution changed the way Americans lived and worked. • Sequoyah created a written language for the Cherokee that helped his people preserve their language and culture. • Comparing parallel time lines helps you recognize patterns in the development of different regions. • Francis Scott Key's respect for the flag helped inspire the nation and our national anthem.

✓ **Overview Review** pp. 42–43

✓ **Overview Project** p. 44

✓ = Assessment Options

Corn was an important food for the Pilgrims in Plymouth.

Vocabulary	Resources	Meeting Individual Needs
Ice Age, glacier, migrate, agriculture, culture, colony, Columbian Exchange	• Workbook, p. 4 • Transparency 6 • Every Student Learns Guide, pp. 2–5 • Quick Study, pp. 2–3	• ESL Support, TE p. 7 • Learning Styles, TE p. 8 • Leveled Practice, TE p. 9
cash crop, House of Burgesses, natural resource, economy, plantations, triangular trade routes, French and Indian War, small-scale map, large-scale map	• Workbook, p. 5 • Transparency 7 • Every Student Learns Guide, pp. 6–9 • Quick Study, pp. 4–5 • Workbook, p. 6	• Leveled Practice, TE p. 13 • ESL Support, TE p. 17
Stamp Act, Declaration of Independence, republic, constitution, checks and balances, Bill of Rights	• Workbook, p. 7 • Transparency 6 • Every Student Learns Guide, pp. 10–13 • Quick Study, pp. 6–7	• Leveled Practice, TE p. 23 • ESL Support, TE p. 26
Cabinet, political party, Industrial Revolution, manifest destiny, abolitionist, parallel time lines, decade, century	• Workbook, p. 8 • Transparency 7 • Every Student Learns Guide, pp. 14–17 • Quick Study, pp. 8–9 • Workbook, p. 9	• ESL Support, TE p. 31 • Leveled Practice, TE p. 33

The magnetic compass allowed sailors to determine their direction out at sea.

Providing More Depth
Additional Resources

- Trade Books
- Family Activities
- Vocabulary Workbook and Cards
- Social Studies Plus! pp. 2–19
- Daily Activity Bank
- Read Alouds and Primary Sources
- Big Book Atlas • Student Atlas
- Outline Maps • Desk Maps

 Technology

- AudioText
- Video Field Trips
- Songs and Music
- Digital Learning CD-ROM Powered by KnowledgeBox (Video clips and activities)
- MindPoint® Quiz Show CD-ROM
- ExamView® Test Bank CD-ROM
- Colonial Williamsburg Primary Sources CD-ROM
- Teacher Resources CD-ROM
- Map Resources CD-ROM
- SF SuccessNet: iText (Pupil Edition online), iTE (Teacher's Edition online), Online Planner
- **www.sfsocialstudies.com** (Biographies, news, references, maps, and activities)

To establish guidelines for your students' safe and responsible use of the Internet, use the Scott Foresman Internet Guide.

Additional Internet Links

To find out more about:
- the Bering land bridge, search that term at **www.nps.gov**
- Jamestown, Virginia, visit **www.apva.org**
- the American Revolution, search that term at **www.nps.gov**

Overview Objectives

Beginning of Overview

- Use primary sources to acquire information. (p. 2)
- Analyze information by summarizing to describe a main idea. (p. 4)

Lesson 1 Connections Across Continents pp. 6–11

- Explain how early people were able to migrate from Asia to the Americas.
- Compare the ways different American Indian groups used natural resources.
- Analyze the impact Columbus's voyages had on the Americas.

Lesson 2 Life in the Colonies pp. 12–18

- Identify reasons people moved from Europe to North America.
- Analyze the importance of the Jamestown colony.
- Explain how natural resources influenced the economies of the 13 Colonies.
- Describe the accomplishments of significant colonial leaders such as John Rolfe. (p. 19)
- Compare and use scales to measure distance on maps. (pp. 20–21)

Lesson 3 Revolution and Constitution pp. 22–28

- Explain how British taxes and colonial protests led to the American Revolution.
- Identify major events of the American Revolution.
- Analyze the plan of government described in the United States Constitution.
- Identify the personal qualities that motivated Abigail Adams to become an outspoken and educated woman. (p. 29)

Lesson 4 A Growing Nation pp. 30–36

- Describe how President Washington organized the Executive Branch around the cabinet.
- Describe the Louisiana Purchase, and tell what effect it had on the nation.
- Explain how the Industrial Revolution changed the way goods were made.
- Analyze the development of the abolitionist movement.
- Identify the challenges and contributions of people, including Sequoyah, from selected American Indian groups. (p. 37)
- Use parallel time lines to see how major events in different places occurred during the same period of time. (pp. 38–39)
- Discover the history behind the U.S. national anthem. (pp. 40–41)
- Describe accomplishments of significant colonial figures, such as Francis Scott Key. (pp. 40–41)

The cotton gin was one factor that contributed to the dramatic change in the way Americans lived and worked in the 1800s.

Assessment Options

✓ Formal Assessment

- **Lesson Reviews,** PE/TE pp. 11, 18, 28, 36
- **Overview Review,** PE/TE pp. 42–43
- **Unit Tests,** Assessment Book, pp. 1–4
- **ExamView® Test Bank CD-ROM** (test-generator software)

✓ Informal Assessment

- **Teacher's Edition Questions,** throughout Lessons and Features
- **Section Review,** PE/TE pp. 7, 9, 11, 13–18, 23–26, 28, 31–32, 34–36
- **Close and Assess,** TE pp. 5, 11, 18, 19, 21, 28, 29, 36, 37, 39, 41

Ongoing Assessment

Ongoing Assessment is found throughout the Teacher's Edition lessons using an **If...then** model.

If = students' observable behavior,   **then =** reteaching and enrichment suggestions

✓ Portfolio Assessment

- **Portfolio Assessment,** TE pp. 1, 2, 43
- **Leveled Practice,** TE pp. 9, 13, 23, 33
- **Workbook Pages,** pp. 1–12
- **Overview Review: Write and Share,** PE/TE p. 43
- **Overview Review: Apply Skills,** PE/TE p. 43
- **Curriculum Connection: Writing,** PE/TE p. 36; TE pp. 9, 21, 33

✓ Performance Assessment

- **Hands-on Unit Project** (Overview Performance Assessment), TE pp. 1, 44
- **Internet Activity,** PE p. 44
- **Overview Performance Assessment,** TE p. 42
- **Overview Review: Write and Share,** PE/TE p. 43
- **Scoring Guides,** TE pp. 43–44

Test Talk

Test-Taking Strategies

Understanding the Question
- **Locate Key Words in the Question,** PE/TE p. 42; TE pp. 26, 35
- **Locate Key Words in the Text,** TE pp. 15, 34

Understand the Answer
- **Choose the Right Answer,** Test Talk Practice Book
- **Use Information from the Text,** TE p. 9
- **Use Information from Graphics,** TE pp. 27, 39
- **Write Your Answer to Score High,** TE p. 36

For additional practice, use the Test Talk Practice Book.

Featured Strategy

Locate Key Words in the Question

Students will:
- Find the key words in the question.
- Turn the key words into a statement that begins "I need to find out . . . ."

PE/TE p. 42; **TE** pp. 26, 35

Curriculum Connections

Integrating Your Day

The lessons, skills, and features of the Overview provide many opportunities to make connections between social studies and other areas of the elementary curriculum.

READING

Reading Skill—Summarize, PE/TE pp. 4–5, 6, 12, 22, 30

Lesson Review—Summarize, PE/TE pp. 11, 18, 28, 36

MATH

Link to Mathematics, PE/TE p. 18

Calculate Area, TE p. 9

Calculate Distances, TE p. 20

Calculate Speed, TE p. 34

Use Data, TE p. 39

WRITING

Link to Writing, PE/TE p. 36

Write a Letter, TE p. 9

Plan a Walking Tour, TE p. 21

Write a Persuasive Letter, TE p. 33

LITERATURE

Read About Jamestown, TE p. 14

Read About the Puritans, TE p. 15

Read About Patriots, TE p. 25

Learn More About Lewis and Clark, TE p. 32

SCIENCE

Link to Science, PE/TE p. 11

Exchange of Diseases, TE p. 10

ART

Create a Mural, TE p. 2

Interpret Fine Art, TE p. 3

MUSIC / DRAMA

Interpret Lyrics, TE p. 36

Write an Anthem, TE p. 41

Social Studies

 Look for this symbol throughout the Teacher's Edition to find **Curriculum Connections.**

Professional Development

Preparing Citizens of the 21st Century

by Carole L. Hahn, Ed.D.
Emory University

In the past, the old "expanding environments" view of social studies was that students first became aware of their local, then national, and finally, international communities. Very little, if anything, was said about their growing identity with an ethnic community. We now realize that a child simultaneously comes to identify with his or her ethnic community, a national community, and the global human community.

It is only by teaching social studies and language arts with a multicultural and global perspective that we will prepare students to be effective citizens in our culturally pluralistic democracy in an interdependent world.

Students need to see how decisions made in one part of the world affect citizens in other parts of the world and how decisions made by one generation have consequences for future generations. Students need to study issues that transcend national borders.

If we give students practice in analyzing issues and ask them to take the perspectives of others across time and space, we will help them appreciate their roles as global citizens, as well as citizens in the national, local, and ethnic communities of which they are a part. Below are several ways *Scott Foresman Social Studies* helps students understand how they are connected to people around the world.

- *To complete the Decision Making activity on p. 16, students are asked to think about life as a colonist in New England. The process of thinking through what kind of work they would have liked to do as a colonist is one that students can follow as they make decisions about their roles as members of a community.*

- *Call students' attention to the Citizen Heroes feature on pp. 40–41. Ask students to name ways that Francis Scott Key demonstrated an appreciation for his country.*

ESL Support

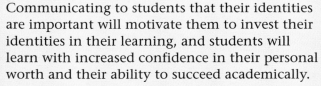

by Jim Cummins, Ph.D.
University of Toronto

In the Overview, you can use the following fundamental strategies to help activate prior knowledge and build background for ESL students.

Activate Prior Knowledge/ Build Background

Teachers can use a variety of strategies to activate prior knowledge and build background. Communicating to students that their identities are important will motivate them to invest their identities in their learning, and students will learn with increased confidence in their personal worth and their ability to succeed academically.

Building context is an effective strategy for helping students understand more complex language and to pursue more cognitively demanding activities. Finding out what students know about a particular topic allows the teacher to supply relevant concepts or vocabulary that some or all students may be lacking but which will be important for understanding the text or lesson.

The following example in the Teacher's Edition will help you activate prior knowledge and build background for ESL students:

- ***Migration Routes** on p. 7 helps ESL students access prior knowledge and build background by using a variety of nonwritten means to trace and describe the migration routes used by early people to travel from Asia to North America.*

Read Aloud

from "America, the Beautiful"
words by Katharine Lee Bates
music by Parke W. Hewins

O beautiful for spacious skies,
For amber waves of grain,
For purple mountain majesties
Above the fruited plain!
America! America!
God shed his grace on thee
And crown thy good with brotherhood
From sea to shining sea!

Build Background
- Katharine Lee Bates's inspiration for writing the poem, to which music was later added, may have been the view from the top of Pikes Peak.
- Bates wrote the first version of the poem in 1893. The final version was published in 1911.

Definitions
- *amber:* golden or dark orange
- *majesties:* splendors
- *thee:* you

Read Alouds and Primary Sources
- *Read Alouds and Primary Sources* contains additional selections to be used with the Overview.

Bibliography

Columbus Day: Celebrating a Famous Explorer, by Elaine Landau (Enslow Publishers, Inc., ISBN 0-766-01573-4, 2001) **Easy** *NCSS Notable Book*

James Towne: Struggle for Survival, by Marcia Sewall (Atheneum, ISBN 0-689-81814-9, 2001) **Easy** *NCSS Notable Book*

Yonder Mountain: A Cherokee Legend, by Kay Thorpe Bannon, et al (Marshall Cavendish Corp., ISBN 0-761-45113-7, 2002) **Easy** *NCSS Notable Book*

American Indian Cooking Before 1500, by Mary Gunderson (Capstone Press, Inc., ISBN 0-736-80605-9, 2000) **On-Level** *NCSS Notable Book*

Journeys in Time: A New Atlas of American History, by Susan Buckley and Elspeth Leacock (Houghton Mifflin Co., ISBN 0-618-31114-9, 2003) **On-Level** *NCSS Notable Book*

John and Abigail Adams: An American Love Story, by Judith St. George (Holiday House, ISBN 0-823-41571-6, 2001) **Challenge** *NCSS Notable Book*

The Signers: The 56 Stories Behind the Declaration of Independence, by Dennis Brindell Fradin and Michael McCurdy (Walker & Co., ISBN 0-802-78849-1, 2002) **Challenge** *NCSS Notable Book*

Slavery: Bondage Throughout History, by Richard Watkins (Houghton Mifflin Co., ISBN 0-395-92289-5, 2001) **Challenge** *NCSS Notable Book*

This Vast Land: A Young Man's Journal of the Lewis and Clark Expedition, by Stephen E. Ambrose (Simon & Schuster, ISBN 0-689-86448-5, 2003) **Challenge**

In the Hands of the Great Spirit: The 20,000-Year History of American Indians, by Jake Page (Free Press, ISBN 0-684-85577-1, 2004) **Teacher reference**

A People's History of the United States: 1492–Present, by Howard Zinn (HarperPerennial Library, ISBN 0-060-52837-0, 2003) **Teacher reference**

The U.S. Constitution: And Fascinating Facts About It, by Terry L. Jordan (Oak Hill Publishers, ISBN 1-891-74300-7, 1999) **Teacher reference**

Discovery Channel School Videos *George Washington: The Unknown Years* Learn about George Washington's colonial life and what prepared him to become one of the country's Founding Fathers. 26 minutes.

The Real Thomas Jefferson Discover the complexities and contradictions of a great American. 26 minutes.

Look for this symbol throughout the Teacher's Edition to find **Award-Winning Selections.** Additional book references are suggested throughout this unit.

OVERVIEW
Establishing a Nation

Why do Americans celebrate the Fourth of July?

1

Establishing a Nation

Unit Overview

After the arrival of the Europeans, life in North America changed in many ways. The American Indian, or Native American, population found their ways of life threatened as England established thirteen colonies along the eastern seaboard. These colonies eventually declared their independence from Great Britain, leading to the establishment of the United States and the reason for our Fourth of July celebration of independence.

Overview Outline

Lesson 1 *Connections Across Continents* pp. 6–11

Lesson 2 *Life in the Colonies* pp. 12–18

Lesson 3 *Revolution and Constitution* pp. 22–28

Lesson 4 *A Growing Nation* pp. 30–36

Unit Question

- Have students read the question under the painting.

- To activate prior knowledge, discuss the meaning of *celebrate*. Ask students to mention some celebrations that they have attended and give the reasons why they were celebrating.

- Create a list of reasons why people celebrate the Fourth of July.

✓**Portfolio Assessment** Keep this list to review with students at the end of the Overview on p. 43.

Practice and Extend

Hands-on Unit Project

✓**Overview Performance Assessment**

- The Hands-on Project, *This Just In,* found on p. 44, is an ongoing performance assessment project to enrich students' learning throughout the unit.

- This project, which has students hold a press conference to report on an event in American history, may be started now or at any time during this unit of study.

- A performance assessment scoring guide is located on p. 44.

Begin with a Primary Source

Objective
- Use primary sources to acquire information.

Resources
- Poster 1
- Workbook, pp. 2–3: Vocabulary Preview
- Vocabulary Cards
- Social Studies Plus!

Interpret a Primary Source

- Tell students that this primary source is the first few words in the second paragraph of the Declaration of Independence.

- The full text of the Declaration of Independence can be found in the back of this book.

- The Declaration of Independence was primarily written by Thomas Jefferson in 1776.

✓ **Portfolio Assessment** Remind students of the list they created of the reasons why people celebrate the Fourth of July. As they read this unit, have students look for and list more reasons why the people of this nation value independence and celebrate their independence each year. Review students' lists at the end of the unit on p. 43.

OVERVIEW

Begin With a Primary Source

 40,000 years ago — 1500 — 1600 — 1700

40,000–10,000 years ago
People migrate from Asia to North America, scientists now believe.

1492
Christopher Columbus reaches the Americas.

1607
English settlers establish Jamestown.

1620
Pilgrims sail from Europe to North America.

2

 1

Practice and Extend

CURRICULUM CONNECTION
Art

Create a Mural
- Provide an assortment of art materials, such as paints, crayons, paper, fabric scraps, and so on.
- Have students create a mural depicting the 4th of July.
- Students may work individually, or in small groups.
- Have students discuss the origin and significance of this holiday.

SOCIAL STUDIES
FYI Background

About the Primary Source
- The Declaration of Independence was written at the request of the Second Continental Congress in 1776.
- The document explained why the colonies were declaring themselves independent of Great Britain.
- The Revolutionary War had been going on for over a year before the Declaration of Independence was written.

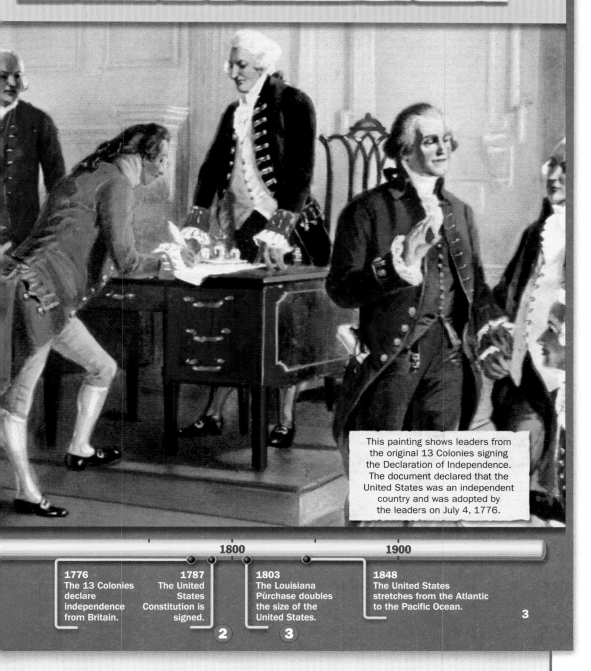

> "We hold these truths to be self-evident;
> that all men are created equal. . . ."
>
> —from the United States Declaration of Independence

This painting shows leaders from the original 13 Colonies signing the Declaration of Independence. The document declared that the United States was an independent country and was adopted by the leaders on July 4, 1776.

1800   **1900**

1776
The 13 Colonies declare independence from Britain.

1787
The United States Constitution is signed.

1803
The Louisiana Purchase doubles the size of the United States.

1848
The United States stretches from the Atlantic to the Pacific Ocean.

3

Interpret Fine Art

- Point out that this painting depicts a very important event in the history of the United States.

- Have students discuss how the people in the painting might feel and how the mood of the painting compares to the mood found at many Fourth of July celebrations today.

Use the Time Line

The time line at the bottom of the page covers the span of time from the initial migration of people from Asia to North America to the expansion of the United States from the Atlantic to the Pacific Ocean.

1 How long after the English settlers established Jamestown did the Pilgrims sail from Europe to North America?
About thirteen years Interpret Time Lines

2 How many years after the colonies declared independence from Britain did the signing of the Constitution happen?
About eleven years Interpret Time Lines

3 What inference might be made from the fact that the United States completed the Louisiana Purchase?
The United States needed more land and was willing to pay for it.
Make Inferences

Vocabulary Preview

- Use Workbook pp. 2–3 to help students preview the vocabulary words in the Overview.
- Use Vocabulary Cards to preview key concept words in the Overview.

Also on Teacher Resources CD-ROM.

Workbook, p. 2

Vocabulary Preview

Directions: Match each vocabulary word to its meaning. Write the number of the word on the blank next to its meaning.

1. Ice Age	_____ Trade networks shaped like a triangles
2. glaciers	_____ Large farms with many workers
3. migrate	_____ The movement of people, animals, plants, and ways of life between Europe and the Americas
4. agriculture	_____ The first law-making assembly in an English colony
5. culture	_____ To move
6. colony	_____ A system for producing and distributing goods and services
7. Columbian Exchange	_____ A settlement far from the country that rules it
8. cash crop	_____ Thick sheets of ice
9. House of Burgesses	_____ Conflict between the British and French and Native American allies
10. natural resource	_____ A crop grown for profit
11. economy	_____ A long period of time during which Earth's climate was colder than it is today
12. plantations	_____ The way of life of a group of people
13. triangular trade routes	_____ A material found in nature that people can use, such as trees or water
14. French and Indian War	_____ The knowledge of how to grow crops and raise farm animals

p. 3

Industrial Revolution
manifest destiny
abolitionist

Overview • Begin with a Primary Source **3**

Reading Social Studies

Summarize

Objective

Analyze information by summarizing to describe a main idea.

Resources

- Workbook, p. 1

About the Unit Target Skill

- The target unit skill for this unit is Summarize.
- Students are introduced to the unit target skill here and are given an opportunity to practice it.
- Further opportunities to use summarizing are found throughout the Overview.

1 Introduce and Motivate

Preview To activate prior knowledge, ask students to give an example of a summary by summarizing what they did last weekend. (Possible answer: Last weekend was very eventful. On Saturday morning I had a soccer game. After the game my friend came to my house to play. On Sunday I slept late and then helped my dad with some yard work. Sunday evening we had dinner with my grandparents.)

2 Teach and Discuss

- Explain that summarizing is telling the main idea of a reading selection (or other information) in only a few words. Most selections can be summarized in one or two sentences. Suggest that students, as they read, look for the most important ideas instead of the specific details.

Establishing a Nation

Summarize

Summarizing means telling the main idea of a paragraph, section, or story. Writers use summarizing sentences to describe a main idea.

- A good summary is short. It tells the most important ideas. It should not include many words or details.

Sometimes a paragraph's **topic sentence** provides a summary. **Details** can be found in other parts of the paragraph.

During the American Revolution, the American colonists and the British fought major battles throughout the colonies. The British won battles at White Plains, New York, and Charleston, South Carolina. The Americans won battles at Saratoga, New York, and Trenton, New Jersey. The American victory at Yorktown, Virginia, was the last major battle of the war.

Word Exercise

Meaning from Context Some words have more than one meaning. You can figure out which meaning is correct by looking at how a word relates to other words in the sentence.

- She **upset** (tipped over) the glass and spilled the water.
- The loss of his wallet **upset** (troubled) him.
- The Colts **upset** (unexpectedly defeated) the Bears and easily won the game.

4

Practice and Extend

ESL ACCESS CONTENT
ESL Support

Create Oral or Written Summaries Have students summarize part or all of the reading selection.

Beginning Help students summarize the first paragraph on p. 5 by asking questions. *What was the last battle? How was the British army trapped by land? How was the British army trapped by sea?*

Intermediate Read the selection on p. 5 with students. Help them identify the most important ideas. After reading, ask students to answer the "Beginning" questions. Using their answers, have students write a one- or two-sentence summary of the first paragraph.

Advanced Have students read the selection on p. 5. Then have pairs of students ask each other questions about each paragraph of the text. Ask students to summarize their answers to form one or two summary sentences about the selection.

The Battle of Yorktown

The American victory at Yorktown, Virginia, was the last major battle of the American Revolution. In September 1781, British General Charles Cornwallis and his army were trapped in Yorktown near the Chesapeake Bay. American and French soldiers, led by General George Washington, surrounded the town by land. The French navy blocked the British from escaping by sea. Washington wrote, "The present moment will decide American independence. . . . The liberties of America . . . are in our hands."

The American and French soldiers fired on the British constantly. The British hoped help would arrive, but it never did. Cornwallis realized that the situation was hopeless. Outnumbered and running out of food, he surrendered on October 19. About 100 American and French soldiers, and 156 British soldiers, were killed in the Battle of Yorktown.

For the official surrender, soldiers on each side put on their best uniforms. American and French soldiers lined up along the road that the British soldiers would walk down. When the British came out of their camp, General Cornwallis was not leading them. He was too upset to attend the surrender ceremony.

One by one, the British soldiers laid down their guns in a large circle. The British band played the song "The World Turned Upside Down." For the British, it seemed as if the world really had been turned upside down.

Use the reading strategy of summarizing to answer the first two questions. Then answer the vocabulary question.

1 Which sentence gives a summary of the ideas in the passage?

2 How did the Americans and French defeat the British at Yorktown?

3 Find this sentence in the selection: *He was too upset to attend the surrender ceremony*. Was he tipped over, troubled, or unexpectedly defeated?

5

Standardized Test Prep

Workbook, p. 1

- Use Workbook p. 1 to give students practice with standardized test format.
- Chapter and Unit Tests in the Assessment Book use standardized test format.
- Test-taking tips are contained in the front portion of the Assessment Book Teacher's Edition.

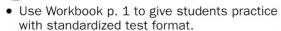
Also on Teacher Resources CD-ROM.

- Have students read the sample paragraph on p. 4. Make sure they can explain why the first highlighted sentence is a topic sentence and a good summary for the paragraph.

- Then have students read the longer practice sample on p. 5 and answer the questions that follow.

- Ask students why it is helpful to summarize when reading about history. (It's not always possible to remember every detail about events in history. By summarizing the main idea, it shows that you understand what you have read.)

Meaning from Context   Word Exercise

Remind students to check the context in which a word is found for clues to the word's meaning. Write the following sentence from the passage on the board: "In September 1781, British General Charles Cornwallis and his army were trapped in Yorktown on the Chesapeake <u>Bay</u>." Help students figure out what the underlined word in this sentence means. Use dictionaries to look up its definitions as necessary. *Bay* can mean several things, including "a part of a sea or lake extending into the land" and "a small evergreen tree." Context clues in the passage include "surrounded the town by land" and "escaping to the sea." These clues tell a reader that in this case, *bay* means "a part of a sea extending into the land."

3 Close and Assess

Apply it!

1. The first sentence: *The American Victory at Yorktown, Virginia, was the last major battle of the American Revolution.*

2. They surrounded the British on land and by sea.

3. Too troubled

Workbook Support

Use the following Workbook pages to support content and skills development as you teach the Overview. You can also view and print Workbook pages from the Teacher Resources CD-ROM.

Workbook, p. 1

Use with Pages 4–5.

Summarize

Directions: Read the passage below. Then fill in the circle next to the correct answer.

In 1607, English colonists established a new settlement at Jamestown. From the start, the colony faced a number of serious problems. The settlement's water supply was of poor quality and caused many to become sick. The nearby swamps were swarming with disease-carrying mosquitoes. Food was in short supply. And conflicts with neighboring Native American groups sometimes turned violent.

In spite of these problems, the Jamestown colonists managed to survive. The introduction of tobacco farming helped put the colony on solid ground economically. The marriage of a colonist to a chief's daughter helped bring peace—for a while. Many new colonists arrived. These factors helped make Jamestown survive—and become the first permanent English colony in North America.

1. Which sentence best summarizes paragraph 1?
   - (A) Jamestown's water supply was almost its undoing.
   - (B) The colonists failed to build a friendship with Native Americans.
   - ● Jamestown faced a series of problems in its early years that threatened its survival.
   - (D) Mosquitoes were not considered to be dangerous.

2. Which of the following is NOT one of the main ideas in paragraph 1?
   - (A) Jamestown was founded in 1607.
   - (B) Jamestown faced a shortage of food.
   - (C) The colony was located near a mosquito-infested swamp.
   - ● Colonists grew tobacco.

3. Which sentence best summarizes paragraph 2?
   - ● Jamestown overcame its problems and survived to become the first permanent English colony in North America.
   - (B) The marriage of a colonist to a Native American helped Jamestown.
   - (C) Native Americans loved the colonists' tobacco.
   - (D) Jamestown was founded in 1607.

4. Which of these is NOT an important detail in paragraph 2?
   - (A) Colonists in Jamestown raised tobacco.
   - ● Jamestown did not have enough food.
   - (C) Marriage between a colonist and a chief's daughter helped stop fighting for a while.
   - (D) New colonists arrived in Jamestown to help strengthen the colony.

Notes for Home: Your child learned to summarize, or tell the main idea, of a passage.
Home Activity: Read a newspaper story with your child. Together, summarize the main idea and look for supporting details.

Use with Pupil Edition, p. 5

Workbook, p. 2

Use with Overview.

Vocabulary Preview

Directions: Match each vocabulary word to its meaning. Write the number of the word on the blank next to its meaning

1. Ice Age
2. glaciers
3. migrate
4. agriculture
5. culture
6. colony
7. Columbian Exchange
8. cash crop
9. House of Burgesses
10. natural resource
11. economy
12. plantations
13. triangular trade route
14. French and Indian War

- **13** Trade network shaped like a triangle
- **12** Large farms with many workers
- **7** The movement of people, animals, plants, and ways of life between Europe and the Americas
- **9** The first law-making assembly in an English colony
- **3** To move
- **11** A system for producing and distributing goods and services
- **6** A settlement far from the country that rules it
- **2** Thick sheets of ice
- **14** Conflict between the British and French and Native American allies
- **8** A crop grown for profit
- **1** A long period of time during which Earth's climate was colder than it is today
- **5** The way of life of a group of people
- **10** A material found in nature that people can use, such as trees or water
- **4** The knowledge of how to grow crops and raise farm animals

Use with Pupil Edition, p. 3

Workbook, p. 3

Use with Overview.

Directions: Choose the word from the box below that best completes each sentence. Write the word on the line provided.

Stamp Act	checks and balances	Industrial Revolution
Declaration of Independence	Bill of Rights	manifest destiny
republic	Cabinet	abolitionist
constitution	political party	

1. The idea of __manifest destiny__ was the belief that the United States should expand west to the Pacific Ocean.
2. A __republic__ is a system in which people elect representatives to make laws and run the government.
3. A system to keep branches of government from gaining too much power is a system of __checks and balances__.
4. A person who called for an end to slavery everywhere was known as an __abolitionist__.
5. The President's advisors were part of the __Cabinet__.
6. The __Bill of Rights__ was added to the Constitution to guarantee certain freedoms.
7. The __Stamp Act__ placed a tax on printed goods used by the colonists.
8. A written plan of government is a __constitution__.
9. The __Industrial Revolution__ was a change in the way goods were produced.
10. The __Declaration of Independence__ explained why the colonies believed they must declare independence from Britain.
11. An organized group of people who share a common view of what government should do is a __political party__.

Notes for Home: Your child has learned the vocabulary words from the Overview.
Home Activity: Have your child create flash cards for each vocabulary word and its definition. Use the cards to quiz your child on meanings and spellings.

Use with Pupil Edition, p. 3

Workbook, p. 4

Use with Pages 6–11.

Lesson 1: Connections Across Continents

Directions: Complete the outline with information from this lesson. You may use your textbook.

Humans in North America up to 1492

I. The First Americans
   A. The first people in North America may have crossed a __land bridge__ from Asia.
   B. The first people got their food by __hunting__.
   C. About 7,000 years ago, people began to practice __agriculture__.

II. Native American Cultures
   A. Groups living in the same region of North America developed similar __cultures__.
   B. Groups relied on available resources.
      1. Eastern Woodland people hunted in forests.
      2. On the Great Plains, people hunted __buffalo__.
      3. In the Southwest, people relied on agriculture.
      4. In the Northwest, coastal waters and __rivers__ supplied plentiful food.

III. Cultures Mix
   A. Inventions promote trade and travel.
   B. Europeans arrived in __North America__ in 1492.
   C. The __Columbian Exchange__ changed life in the Eastern and Western Hemispheres.

Notes for Home: Your child has learned about the early history of human beings in North America.
Home Activity: Help your child develop an illustrated time line of the time period of 20,000 years ago to 1492.

Use with Pupil Edition, p. 11

Workbook, p. 5

Use with Pages 12–18.

Lesson 2: Life in the Colonies

Directions: Answer the following questions on the lines provided. You may use your textbook.

1. What attracted so many people from Europe to come to North America in the 1600s? What was the name and location of the first permanent English colony in North America?
   There was great economic opportunity to be found in North America. Jamestown, located in present-day Virginia

2. What factor led to the foundation of colonies in the New England area?
   Colonists came to New England seeking religious freedom.

3. What were the names and major economic features of the three regions of England's colonies?
   The three regions were the New England Colonies, in which wood products and fishing were important; the Middle Colonies, in which wheat and iron were major products; and the Southern Colonies, where cash-crop plantations were common.

4. Under what circumstances did most Africans come to North America?
   Many Africans came to North America as slaves, traded for goods as part of the triangular trade route.

5. Describe the conflict that lead to the French and Indian War. What was the effect of this war?
   Both the English and the French claimed the Ohio River Valley—a region of fertile land along the Ohio River. It was also home to Native American groups. Britain and France eventually signed a peace treaty that gave Britain control over most of France's land in North America.

Notes for Home: Your child learned about the growth and development of the earliest European colonies in North America.
Home Activity: Ask your child to summarize the causes and effects of European colonization.

Use with Pupil Edition, p. 18

Workbook, p. 6

Use with Pages 20–21.

Compare Maps at Different Scales

Directions: Study the map below and answer the questions.

1. Describe the small scale map pictured above.
   The small scale map shows the state of Virginia and some of its cities.

2. Describe the large scale map pictured above.
   The large scale map shows the Washington, D.C. area.

3. Which map would you use to locate attractions in Washington, D.C.?
   The large scale map would be helpful in locating attractions.

4. Which map would help you to find the distance between cities in Virginia?
   The small scale map

5. Why are both small-scale and large scale maps useful?
   Sometimes it is necessary to have a map that shows a large area, and sometimes it is necessary to have a map that focuses on a small area.

Notes for Home: Your child learned to measure distances on a map using a scale and to tell the difference between large-scale maps and small-scale maps.
Home Activity: Practice finding the scale on maps that you see in newspapers and other materials.

Use with Pupil Edition, p. 21

Workbook Support

Workbook, p. 7

Lesson 3: Revolution and Constitution
Use with Pages 22–28.

Directions: Using information from this lesson, circle the term in parentheses that best completes each sentence.

1. When news of the Stamp Act reached the 13 Colonies, many colonists reacted with (joy, **anger**).

2. Colonists who opposed British rule came to be known as (**Patriots**, Loyalists).

3. In 1775, colonists prepared to (**fight**, elect) their British rulers.

4. During the Revolutionary War, George Washington served as (**general**, president).

5. In the early battles of the war, George Washington led the army to several (**defeats**, victories).

6. A turning point in the Revolutionary War was when the French came to the aid of the (British, **Patriots**).

7. The new government for the independent colonies was to be a (**republic**, monarchy).

8. In 1787, delegates met in Philadelphia to create a (**constitution**, Declaration of Independence).

9. Some people in the United States worried that the Constitution gave the government too (little, **much**) power.

10. Fears about individual liberties were calmed by the addition of a Bill of (**Rights**, Independence).

Notes for Home: Your child learned about the Revolutionary Era in the United States.
Home Activity: Have your child recount the tale of how the United States first grew apart from Great Britain, then fought for its independence, then established a new government.

Use with Pupil Edition, p. 28

Workbook, p. 8

Lesson 4: A Growing Nation
Use with Pages 30–36.

Directions: Suppose you were going to write an article about the first years of the United States. Use the chart below to help you get started. You may use your textbook.

The First Years of the United States	
WHO was the first President?	George Washington
WHAT problem existed in his Cabinet?	He had strong Cabinet members who had different ideas.
HOW did President Jefferson help the United States grow?	He purchased the Louisiana Territory and sent Lewis and Clark to explore it.
WHAT was the Industrial Revolution?	It was a change in the way goods were produced that in turn changed the way people in the United States lived.
WHAT was "manifest destiny"?	It was a popularly held belief that it was the destiny of the United States to spread across the continent, from coast to coast.
WHO were the abolitionists?	They were people who believed that slavery was wrong and should be abolished.

Notes for Home: Your child learned a brief overview of the first half-century of United States history.
Home Activity: Use library or online sources to look up more about the items presented in the Fact File on page 33.

Use with Pupil Edition, p. 36

Workbook, p. 9

Use Parallel Time Lines
Use with Pages 38–39.

Directions: Use the time lines below to answer the following questions.

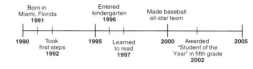

MARTINA

TONY

1. In what ways have Tony and Martina had similar lives?
Both were born in the same year, entered kindergarten the same year, and got "student of the year" in the same year.

2. In what ways have Tony and Martina had different educations?
Tony went to preschool and Martina did not.

3. What can you learn about Tony and Martina based on the events of 2000?
Tony was successful at art and Martina was successful at baseball.

4. What can you learn about Tony and Martina based on the events of 2002?
Both of them are very good students.

Notes for Home: Your child learned to read parallel time lines.
Home Activity: With your child, make parallel time lines of your day. Compare and contrast events.

Use with Pupil Edition, p. 39

Workbook, p. 10

Vocabulary Review
Use with Overview Unit.

Directions: Use the vocabulary words from the Overview to complete each item. Use the numbered letters to answer the clue that follows.

1. A change in the way goods were produced
Industrial Revolution

2. The movement of people, animals, plants, and ways of life between Europe and the Americas
Columbian Exchange

3. An early British tax on printed goods
Stamp Act

4. Thick sheets of ice
glaciers

5. A system in which people elect representatives to make laws and run the government
republic

6. A system to keep branches of government from gaining too much power
checks and balances

7. An organized group of people who share a common view of what government should do
political party

8. A long period of cold temperatures
Ice Age

9. A person who called for the end of slavery everywhere in the United States
abolitionist

10. The belief that the United States should expand west to the Pacific Ocean
manifest destiny

11. To move
migrate

12. A system for producing and distributing goods and services
economy

13. A material found in nature that people can use
natural resource

Use with Pupil Edition, p. 43

Workbook, p. 11

Use with Overview Unit.

14. The way of life of a group of people
culture

15. The knowledge of how to grow crops and raise farm animals
agriculture

16. A written plan of government
constitution

17. Large farms with many workers
plantations

18. A President's advisors
Cabinet

19. Conflict between the British and French and Native American allies
French and Indian War

20. Crop grown for profit
cash crop

21. Added to the Constitution to guarantee certain freedoms
Bill of Rights

22. A settlement located far away from the country that rules it
colony

23. The first law-making assembly in an English colony
House of Burgesses

24. Trade networks shaped like triangles
triangular trade routes

Clue: created by Thomas Jefferson
Declaration of Independence

Notes for Home: Your child learned the vocabulary from the Overview unit.
Home Activity: Talk to your child about how the vocabulary words relate to what they learned in the unit about American history.

Use with Pupil Edition, p. 43

Workbook, p. 12

Overview Project This Just In

Report breaking news in American history. In a group, choose an important event that you have learned about in American history. Then report the event in a press conference.

1. The event that we chose is _____.

2. My role in the press conference is (✔) one
____ news reporter ____ expert
____ government official ____ other: ___

3. Here are some details about the event:
What happened: _____
Where and when the event took place: _____
Who was involved: _____
Effects or importance of the event: _____

4. Here are some questions and answers that we will ask and answer in our news conference:
News Reporter: _____
Expert: _____
News Reporter: _____
Other _____ : _____

Following the press conference, have students discuss why the event is important to America's history.

> **✔ Checklist for Students**
> ____ We chose an event in America's history.
> ____ We found information about the event.
> ____ We answered questions about the event.
> ____ We made a poster about the event to use in our press conference.
> ____ We presented our press conference to the class.

Notes for Home: Your child learned how to report important details of an event in a press conference.
Home Activity: Watch a news program with your child. Discuss what important facts are reported about each event, and why the events might be important to the region where the events occurred.

Use with Pupil Edition, p. 44

Assessment Support

Use these Assessment Book pages and ExamView® Test Bank CD-ROM to assess content and skills in the Overview. You can also view and print Assessment Book pages from the Teacher Resources CD-ROM.

Assessment Book, p. 1

Overview Test

Part 1: Content Test

Directions: Fill in the circle next to the correct answer.

Lesson Objective (1:1)

1. Many scholars think people first migrated to North America by
   Ⓐ boat.
   ● crossing a land bridge between Asia and North America.
   Ⓒ walking north from South America.
   Ⓓ swimming from Caribbean islands.

Lesson Objective (1:2)

2. The first people to arrive in North America survived by
   ● hunting.
   Ⓑ farming.
   Ⓒ trading.
   Ⓓ manufacturing.

Lesson Objective (1:2)

3. Native American cultures differed in part based on
   Ⓐ how long they had been living in North America.
   Ⓑ what part of Asia they came from.
   Ⓒ whether they preferred hunting or farming.
   ● the resources available to them.

Lesson Objective (1:3)

4. Which of the following is NOT a result of the Columbian Exchange?
   Ⓐ Cattle and horses came from Europe to the Americas.
   ● Columbus landed on some islands off the coast of North America.
   Ⓒ Crops such as potatoes and beans came to Europe from the Americas.
   Ⓓ Native Americans were exposed to European diseases.

Lesson Objective (2:1)

5. Which of the following is NOT one of the reasons Europeans came to the American colonies?
   Ⓐ religious freedom
   Ⓑ economic opportunity
   Ⓒ the chance to explore
   ● the absence of a fur trade

Lesson Objective (2:2)

6. The Jamestown colony is remembered mainly because
   ● it was the first permanent English colony in North America.
   Ⓑ it was a major East Coast Spanish colony.
   Ⓒ the first Thanksgiving was held there.
   Ⓓ Squanto helped the Pilgrims there survive.

Lesson Objective (2:3)

7. Plantations were most common in the Southern Colonies because
   Ⓐ most African Americans lived there.
   ● the soil and climate were suitable to plantation agriculture.
   Ⓒ southern farmers did not like growing wheat.
   Ⓓ the South lacked ports for a fishing industry.

Lesson Objective (2:3)

8. Which of the following were NOT factors in the early colonial economy of New England?
   Ⓐ plentiful supply of wood
   Ⓑ rich fishing grounds
   ● warm weather for plantations
   Ⓓ shipping industry

Use with Pupil Edition, p. 42

Assessment Book, p. 2

Lesson Objective (3:1)

9. Why were many colonists angered by the Stamp Act?
   Ⓐ They thought the tax was too high.
   Ⓑ They thought the tax was too low.
   Ⓒ They had already declared independence from Great Britain.
   ● They did not think the British government had the right to tax them.

Lesson Objective (3:2)

10. Which of the following was NOT a key event of the American Revolution?
    Ⓐ Declaration of Independence
    Ⓑ Battle of Saratoga
    Ⓒ Battle of Yorktown
    ● the Constitutional Convention

Lesson Objective (3:3)

11. Which of the following is NOT a key feature of the United States government under the Constitution?
    ● established by the Articles of Confederation
    Ⓑ includes checks and balances
    Ⓒ is a republic
    Ⓓ includes the Bill of Rights

Lesson Objective (4:1)

12. Disagreement between members of George Washington's Cabinet helped lead the development of
    Ⓐ Washington, D.C.
    Ⓑ a strong national government.
    ● political parties.
    Ⓓ the executive branch.

Lesson Objective (4:2)

13. The Louisiana Purchase
    Ⓐ belonged to Sacagawea.
    ● doubled the size of the United States.
    Ⓒ was never explored.
    Ⓓ led to war with France.

Lesson Objective (4:3)

14. The great change in the way goods were manufactured that took place in the early decades of United States history is known as the
    ● Industrial Revolution.
    Ⓑ Monroe Doctrine.
    Ⓒ cotton gin.
    Ⓓ Report on Manufactures.

Lesson Objective (4:4)

15. The abolitionists favored
    Ⓐ manifest destiny.
    Ⓑ war with Mexico.
    ● an end to slavery.
    Ⓓ territorial expansion of the United States.

Use with Pupil Edition, p. 42

Assessment Support

Assessment Book, p. 3

Part 2: Skills Test

Directions: Use complete sentences to answer questions 1–5. Use a separate sheet of paper if you need more space.

1. Describe how scholars think the first humans arrived in North America and developed into different Native American groups. **Summarize**

   Native Americans may have crossed a land bridge between Asia and North America. As they spread across North America, they changed their way of life based on the available resources. This helped different Native American cultures emerge.

2. What was the effect of the creation of the House of Burgesses in Virginia? **Cause and Effect**

   The development of the House of Burgesses helped colonists establish the idea of self-government in the colonies.

3. What can you conclude about the abolitionists and their feelings about slavery? **Draw Conclusions**

   The abolitionists believed slavery was wrong and should be eliminated.

Use with Pupil Edition, p. 42

Assessment Book, p. 4

4. Complete the chart below by summarizing the details about events in the British colonies. **Summarize**

Stamp Act angers colonists.	Patriot leaders meet in Philadelphia.
British soldiers fire on Boston protesters.	Patriots and British fight at Lexington and Concord.

   Relations between Great Britain and the colonies worsened in the 1760s and early 1770s, leading the colonists to declare their independence.

5. Look at the map below. If you wanted to find how to drive from one city in Virginia to another, would you seek a larger-scale map or a smaller-scale map? **Compare Maps at Different Scales**

   You would seek a small-scale map that would provide information about the entire state.

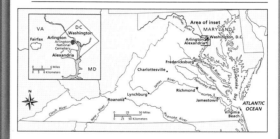

Use with Pupil Edition, p. 42

Connections Across Continents

Objectives

- Explain how early people were able to migrate from Asia to the Americas.
- Compare the ways different American Indian groups used natural resources.
- Analyze the impact Columbus's voyages had on the Americas.

Vocabulary

Ice Age, p. 7; **glacier,** p. 7; **migrate,** p. 7; **agriculture,** p. 7; **culture,** p. 8; **colony,** p. 10; **Columbian Exchange,** p. 10

Resources

- Workbook, p. 4
- Transparency 6
- Every Student Learns Guide, pp. 2–5
- Quick Study, pp. 2–3

Quick Teaching Plan

If time is short, create on the chalkboard a two-column chart, with one column headed *During* and another headed *After*.

- Have students read the lesson independently, and then summarize early Americans' way of life during and after the Ice Age.
- Make sure students include what people ate, how they traveled, what they did for clothing and shelter, and other information from the lesson.

1 Introduce and Motivate

Preview Ask students what they think life would be like without the modern conveniences we have today. Tell students they will learn what life was like for early people as they read Lesson 1.

You Are There Tell students that early people had to rely on hunting for food, clothing, and even shelter. Have students tell what they think an average day was like for a person who lived in this time period.

LESSON 1

ASIA   Bering Strait   NORTH AMERICA

40,000–10,000 years ago
People migrate from Asia to North America, scientists believe.

1400s
Native Americans develop a wide variety of cultures in North America.

1492
Columbus reaches the Americas.

PREVIEW

Focus on the Main Idea
A wide variety of Native American groups lived in North America when European explorers began arriving in the late 1400s.

PLACES
Bering Strait
Asia
North America

PEOPLE
Christopher Columbus

VOCABULARY
Ice Age
glacier
migrate
agriculture
culture
colony
Columbian Exchange

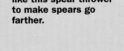

▶ **Woolly mammoth hunters used tools like this spear thrower to make spears go farther.**

Connections Across Continents

You Are There You crouch behind a large rock, shivering in the morning wind. You look at the spear in your hand. It's made of solid wood, with a sharpened stone fastened to the end. You look around at the older members of your small band. They're all watching the snowy field in front of you.

You look out at the field, and there it is—a woolly mammoth. It's a massive elephant-like creature with long, sharp tusks and legs bigger than your whole body. You watch the mammoth walk closer and closer to your hiding place. If you can kill the animal, it will mean weeks of meat for your group.

The leader of your band gives a silent signal. All together, you lift your spears, stand, and throw.

Summarize As you read, look for details that will help you summarize the changing ways of life in North America.

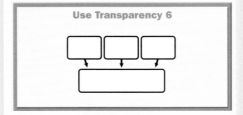

Practice and Extend

READING SKILL — Summarize

In the Lesson Review, students complete a graphic organizer like the one below. You may want to provide students with a copy of Transparency 6 to complete as they read the lesson.

Use Transparency 6

VOCABULARY — Word Exercise

Related Word Study

Students might notice that the words *culture* and *agriculture* appear related. Both words come from the Latin *colere,* which means "to cultivate" or "to cherish." In culture, people cultivate and cherish traditions. In agriculture, they cultivate and cherish plants. The word *cultivate* also comes from *colere.* The word *colony* also comes from *colere.* Discuss how the ideas of planting and settling might be considered related to colonizing.

From Asia to the Americas

The scene you just read about could have occurred about 20,000 years ago, during the **Ice Age.** This was a long period of time during which Earth's climate was colder than it is today. Low temperatures caused much of Earth's water to freeze into **glaciers,** or thick sheets of ice. In fact, so much of Earth's water was frozen in glaciers that the level of the oceans became lower.

Some areas that had been underwater now became dry land. As the map on this page shows, a strip of land called the **Bering Strait** land bridge connected **Asia** and **North America.** This land bridge allowed people to **migrate,** or move, from Asia to the Americas. Many scholars believe that people began to migrate to the Americas between 40,000 and 10,000 years ago.

Over thousands of years, people migrated throughout North America and South America. Getting enough food to eat was often a challenge for these early Americans. People traveled together in small bands, or groups, using stone tools to hunt wandering herds of animals.

About 10,000 years ago, the Ice Age gradually came to an end. The woolly mammoth and some of the other large Ice Age animals became extinct, or died out.

People continued to hunt for smaller animals and to fish. They also gathered wild plants, such as grains, berries, and nuts.

About 7,000 years ago, in present-day Mexico, people began to learn how to grow food themselves. **Agriculture,** or the growing of crops and the raising of farm animals, made it possible for people to settle in one place. Now wandering bands of hunter-gatherers could become members of settled communities.

REVIEW How did the end of the Ice Age change life for early Americans?
➲ Summarize

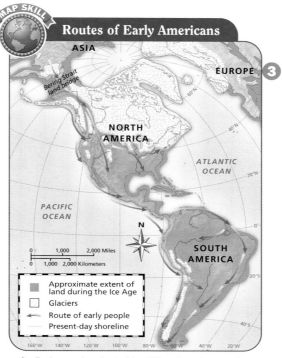

Routes of Early Americans

ASIA

Bering Strait land bridge

EUROPE ❸

NORTH AMERICA

ATLANTIC OCEAN

PACIFIC OCEAN

N

SOUTH AMERICA

0   1,000   2,000 Miles
0 1,000 2,000 Kilometers

160°W 140°W 120°W 100°W 80°W 60°W 40°W 20°W

- Approximate extent of land during the Ice Age
- Glaciers
- Route of early people
- Present-day shoreline

▶ Early people adapted to different environments throughout the Americas.

MAP SKILL Movement *In which main direction were people moving as they traveled through the Americas?*

7

From Asia to the Americas

🕐 *Quick Summary* Scholars believe that during the Ice Age people and animals moved from Asia into North America by crossing a land bridge.

❶ **What caused glaciers to form on Earth's surface during the Ice Age?** A long period of extremely cold temperatures **Cause and Effect**

❷ **Why do you think early people migrated to North America?** Possible answer: To look for food **Express Ideas**

✓ **REVIEW ANSWER** They had to find new ways to get food because the large animals they hunted became extinct.
➲ Summarize

Routes of Early Americans

Point out that a strait is a narrow waterway connecting two large bodies of water. The Bering Strait, which separates Asia and North America, connects the Pacific Ocean and the Arctic Ocean. At the narrowest point of the strait, the two continents are about 53 miles apart.

❸ **What was on either side of people as they crossed the land bridge?** Glaciers **Interpret Maps**

MAP SKILL Answer Most people were moving southeast.

Migration Routes Use the map on this page to help students access prior knowledge and build background about routes that early people may have taken as they migrated from Asia to the Americas.

Beginning Have students locate Asia, the Bering Strait, and the northwest coast of North America. Ask them to trace the route early people may have taken from Asia to North America.

Intermediate Have students describe the routes shown on the map, giving present-day names of locations they know.

Advanced Ask students to describe the possible migration of early people from Asia to the Americas as shown on the map. Ask them to tell the routes people took, including present-day names, and the directions they traveled.

For additional ESL support, use Every Student Learns Guide, pp. 2–5.

Native American Cultures

Quick Summary Over the course of many centuries, Native American groups developed their own cultures and traditions and had access to a variety of natural resources.

4 **How did the Iroquois use their environment to obtain food?** They hunted animals. **Main idea and Details**

Native American Cultural Regions

5 **In which cultural region did the Navajo live?** The Southwest Desert **Interpret Maps**

6 **Which two cultural regions were the largest?** The Great Plains and the Eastern Woodlands **Interpret Maps**

MAP SKILL **Answer** The Northwest Coast

Native American Cultures

Early Americans developed a variety of cultures over the course of many centuries. A **culture** is the way of life of a group of people. Culture can include religion, customs, and language.

By the 1400s, Native Americans, also known as American Indians, had developed into a huge variety of groups that lived all over what is now the United States. While each group had its own culture and traditions, groups that lived in the same region often developed similar cultures. The map on this page shows some of these cultural regions.

In the Eastern Woodlands, Native American groups such as the Iroquois hunted deer, bear, and beaver in the thick forests. They

4

MAP SKILL
Native American Cultural Regions

Legend:
- Eastern Woodlands
- Great Plains
- Northwest Coast
- Southwest Desert
- Present-day boundaries are shown.

▶ The Native Americans of each region had their own culture, including art such as this carved totem pole from the people of the Northwest Coast.

MAP SKILL Location *Which region extended the farthest north?*

8

Practice and Extend

SOCIAL STUDIES STRAND
Economics

Iroquois Economic Patterns
- Tell students that the Iroquois did not use money or own land or property. All resources were shared in the group.
- Point out that the Iroquois practiced *subsistence agriculture*, meaning they raised crops to feed themselves through the winter, but not a surplus for sale or trade.

MEETING INDIVIDUAL NEEDS
Learning Styles

Describe a Means of Transportation
Using their individual learning styles, students explore making birch bark canoes.

Kinesthetic Learning Have students use materials from nature or art materials to make a model of a birch bark canoe.

Linguistic Learning Have students list the supplies and steps required to build a birch bark canoe.

SOCIAL STUDIES
Background

Group Names
- The terms *Native American* and *American Indian* are often used interchangeably.
- Preference as to the use of these terms is mixed even among Native American groups.

used plentiful supplies of wood to build longhouses—long buildings that were shared by as many as 12 families.

On the flat, grass-covered Great Plains, huge herds of buffalo helped shape life for groups such as the Lakota and Pawnee. In summer and fall, Plains Indians traveled to hunt the buffalo. While on the hunt, they lived in tepees made from buffalo hides.

In the hot and dry Southwest, groups including the Hopi and Zuni developed a village way of life based on farming. By digging ditches to carry water from streams, people were able to grow corn, squash, and beans in this dry region.

The forests of the Northwest Coast were rich in animals that could be hunted. Coastal waters and rivers were filled with fish and seals. Groups including the Kwakiutl (kwah kee OO tuhl) and Tlingit (TLIN git) got all they needed from hunting and gathering. They did not have to grow crops for food. **8**

REVIEW What are two ways Native Americans used natural resources?
↻ **Summarize**

An Iroquois Longhouse

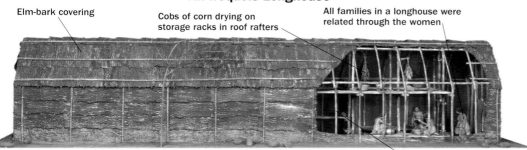

Elm-bark covering

Cobs of corn drying on storage racks in roof rafters

All families in a longhouse were related through the women

Poles for the frame

▶ This model shows an eight-family Iroquois longhouse. There were four shared cooking fires along the central aisle.

DIAGRAM SKILL *Where were the drying cobs of corn kept?*

Connections Among Continents

At the same time that Native American cultures were thriving in North America, connections were growing among Asia, Africa, and Europe. The Chinese developed valuable trade goods, such as silk cloth, tea, and spices. A network of trade routes called the Silk Road connected China to other lands, where demand for Chinese goods was high. Along with trade goods, ideas, skills, and customs moved back and forth along the Silk Road.

▶ This Chinese vase was carried along the Silk Road to Africa.

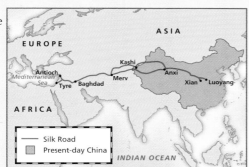

EUROPE
ASIA
Kashi
Antioch
Mediterranean Sea
Merv
Anxi
Tyre
Baghdad
Xian
Luoyang
AFRICA
INDIAN OCEAN

— Silk Road
▨ Present-day China

9

9

East Meets West

 Quick Summary Columbus's expeditions paved the way for other European explorers.

10 How might using a magnetic compass give sailors confidence in their travels? It helps them to determine their direction. **Make Inferences**

C SOCIAL STUDIES STRAND
Culture

Tell students that in honor of Columbus's voyage to the Americas, the United States celebrates Columbus Day.

11 Which animal moved from West to East? Turkey **Which plant moved from East to West?** Sugarcane **Analyze Visuals**

12 How were the goods moving from West to East similar to the goods moving from East to West? Plants and animals traveled in both directions. **Compare and Contrast**

CHART SKILL Answer West

East Meets West

In the 1200s and 1300s, trade was increasing among the peoples of Asia, Africa, and Europe. New inventions were making it easier for people to travel by ship. For example, the magnetic compass, invented in China, made it possible for sailors to determine their **10** direction far out at sea.

In Europe, these new tools were combined with advances in ship design. Explorers could now sail farther from home. This fact, along with the desire to find new trade routes, led to an age of exploration.

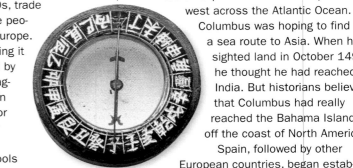
▶ **An early Chinese compass.**

Sailing for Spain, **Christopher Columbus** led an expedition of three ships west across the Atlantic Ocean. Columbus was hoping to find a sea route to Asia. When he sighted land in October 1492, he thought he had reached India. But historians believe that Columbus had really reached the Bahama Islands, off the coast of North America. Spain, followed by other European countries, began establishing colonies in North and South America. A **colony** is a settlement far from the country that rules it. This was the beginning of the **Columbian Exchange**—a movement of people, animals, plants, and

▶ The Columbian Exchange brought changes to both the Eastern and Western Hemispheres.
CHART SKILL *In which direction did horses move?*

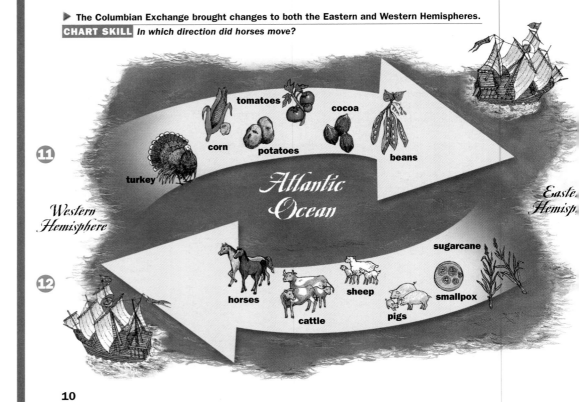

tomatoes · cocoa · corn · potatoes · beans · **11** turkey · *Atlantic Ocean* · *Western Hemisphere* · *Easter. Hemisp.* · sugarcane · **12** · horses · cattle · sheep · pigs · smallpox

10

Practice and Extend

 CURRICULUM CONNECTION
Science

Exchange of Diseases

- Diseases from the Americas also infected Europeans and caused deaths.
- Encourage students to use reference materials to find out more about smallpox and measles.
- Suggest students find answers to these questions: How is the disease spread? What are its symptoms and effects? How were vaccines against it used?

FYI **SOCIAL STUDIES**
Background

Civilization in the Western Hemisphere

- The Inca, who lived in South America when the Spanish explorers arrived, excelled at construction. Some of the stone blocks used to build their cities weighed several tons.
- The Maya had settled in the Yucatan peninsula of Mexico by 1000 B.C. Their farming practices mixed the basic slash-and-burn approach with irrigation and terracing.

ways of life between the Eastern Hemisphere and Western Hemisphere. As the chart shows, European farm animals, such as horses and cattle, were brought to the Americas. Native American foods, such as corn and potatoes, were brought to Europe.

Not all the effects of the Columbian Exchange were positive. Without knowing it, Europeans brought disease germs to the Americas. Many Native Americans died because they had no defense against diseases such as smallpox and measles. As European colonies grew, many Native Americans were enslaved or forced off their land. The Indian way of life was changed forever.

REVIEW What changes did the Columbian Exchange bring to the Eastern and Western Hemispheres? 🌀 **Summarize**

► Columbus made contact with the people of several islands off the coast of North America.

Summarize the Lesson

- **40,000–10,000 years ago** During the Ice Age, people migrated across a land bridge from Asia to North America.

- **1400s** Native Americans had developed a wide variety of cultures in North America.

- **1492** Columbus reached the Americas, beginning a time of exchange between the Eastern and Western Hemispheres.

LESSON 1 REVIEW

Check Facts and Main Ideas

1. 🌀 **Summarize** On a separate sheet of paper, fill in two details that support the summary below.

```
The first Americans hunted mammoths.   |   Some early Native Americans grew crops for food.   |   Europeans introduced farm animals such as horses and pigs to North America.
```
↓
Life in North America changed in many ways from the Ice Age to the arrival of Europeans.

2. How did **Ice Age** glaciers allow people to **migrate** from Asia to the Americas?

3. How did Native Americans of the different geographical regions get their food?

4. How did life for Native Americans change after Columbus's voyage to the Americas?

5. **Critical Thinking:** *Interpret Charts* Based on the chart on page 10, do you think Europe benefited from the **Columbian Exchange**? Explain your answer.

Link to 🔗 Science

Identify Ice Age Animals Using a library or the Internet, find out more about Ice Age animals of North America. Identify three animals that lived here during the Ice Age and later became extinct. According to scientists, what caused these animals to disappear?

11

Workbook, p. 4

Lesson 1: Connections Across Continents
Directions: Complete the outline with information from this lesson. You may use your textbook.

Humans in North America up to 1492

I. The First Americans
A. The first people in North America may have crossed a _____ from Asia.
B. The first people got their food by _____.
C. About 7,000 years ago, people began to practice _____.

II. Native American Cultures
A. Groups living in the same region of North America developed similar _____.
B. Groups relied on available resources.
   1. Eastern Woodland people hunted in forests.
   2. On the Great Plains, people hunted _____.
   3. In the Southwest, people relied on agriculture.
   4. In the Northwest, coastal waters and _____ supplied plentiful food.

III. Cultures Mix
A. Inventions promote trade and travel.
B. Europeans arrived in _____ in 1492.
C. The _____ changed life in the Eastern and Western Hemispheres.

Notes for Home: Your child has learned about the early history of human beings in North America.
Home Activity: Help your child develop an illustrated time line of the time period of 20,000 years ago to 1492.

Also on Teacher Resources CD-ROM.

---

⑬ **Do you think the Columbian Exchange was beneficial to native peoples? Explain.** Possible answer: No; because the way of life of some native groups disappeared. Many died because they had no defense against some diseases. **Draw Conclusions**

⑭ **How might life in the Americas have been different if Columbus had not journeyed here?** Possible answer: Native peoples would not have had certain animals, or been exposed to diseases, or forced to give up their traditional ways, perhaps for many years. **Draw Conclusions**

✓ **REVIEW ANSWER** Europeans were exposed to certain foods; native peoples had access to certain animals but were exposed to diseases. 🌀 Summarize

❸ Close and Assess

Summarize the Lesson

Tell students to examine the vertical time line. Ask them to provide several details for each of the bulleted points.

✓ **LESSON 1 REVIEW**

1. 🌀 **Summarize** For possible answers, see the reduced pupil page.

2. A land bridge connected the two continents at that time.

3. Native Americans of the Northwest Coast, Eastern Woodlands, and Great Plains relied on hunting. In the Southwest Desert, Native American groups relied on farming.

4. Many Native Americans died from disease or were forced off their land.

5. **Critical Thinking:** *Interpret Charts* Possible answer: Europeans benefited from the exposure to new foods and the wealth generated by the colonies.

Link to 🔗 Science

Students should write accurate, descriptive paragraphs about North American Ice Age animals and research scientific theories for their disappearance.

Life in the Colonies

Objective

- Identify reasons people moved from Europe to North America.
- Analyze the importance of the Jamestown colony.
- Explain how natural resources influenced the economies of the 13 Colonies.

Vocabulary

cash crop, p. 14;
House of Burgesses, p. 14;
natural resource, p. 16;
economy, p. 16; **plantations,** p. 16;
triangular trade routes, p. 17;
French and Indian War, p. 18

Resources

- Workbook, p. 5
- Transparency 7
- Every Student Learns Guide, pp. 6–9
- Quick Study Guide, pp. 4–5

Quick Teaching Plan

If time is short, have students make a time line showing the sequence of events in the lesson.

- Ask students to read the lesson independently.
- Have students create journal entries written from the perspective of one of the people at each of the listed events.

1 Introduce and Motivate

Preview To activate prior knowledge, ask students who have moved to a new home or school to share their experiences. Tell them that they will learn more about why people moved from Europe to North America when they read Lesson 2.

You Are There Have students use their senses to describe the sights, sounds, and smells of Manhattan. Then have them imagine what daily life might be like there.

12 Overview • Establishing a Nation

LESSON 2

Quebec
Plymouth
New Amsterdam
Jamestown

1600	1700	1800

1607 English settlers establish Jamestown.

1626 Dutch settlers establish New Amsterdam.

1733 England has 13 colonies along the Atlantic coast.

Life in the Colonies

PREVIEW

Focus on the Main Idea
By the early 1600s, many European countries had established colonies in North America.

PLACES
Quebec
New Amsterdam
Jamestown
Plymouth

PEOPLE
John Smith
John Rolfe
Pocahontas
Squanto

VOCABULARY
cash crop
House of Burgesses
natural resource
economy
plantation
triangular trade route
French and Indian War

You Are There Do you think you would like to settle in New Amsterdam? The year is 1655, and you're here to check out this Dutch colonial town on the island of Manhattan.

As you walk from the busy port, you see a few dirt streets lined with wooden houses and workshops. Some of the buildings have wooden chimneys, which are a serious fire hazard. That's why leather water buckets are kept on the street corners.

You pass by people from many different countries. They're all working, trading goods, and shouting to one another in more languages than you can identify. You also pass lots of pigs, goats, and cows. People let their animals run free. It's cheaper to let the animals feed on garbage in the street than to buy food for them!

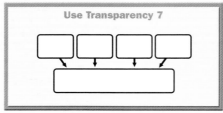

Summarize As you read, keep track of the factors that caused European colonies in North America to grow quickly.

▶ Settlers relied on farm animals such as goats for meat and milk.

12

Practice and Extend

READING SKILL
Summarize

In the Lesson Review, students complete a graphic organizer like the one below. You may want to provide students with a copy of Transparency 7 to complete as they read the lesson.

Use Transparency 7

VOCABULARY
Word Exercise

Individual Word Study

Compound words are words made up of smaller words. Most compound words are combined into one word, as in *football*. However, some compound words remain separate, as in *cash crop*. One way to predict the meaning of a compound word is to break it into the smaller words. Discuss the meanings of *cash* and *crop*. Relate that prior knowledge also helps: students know that cash doesn't grow, so *cash crop* cannot be growing cash.

Founding Colonies

By the early 1600s, Spain, England, France, Sweden, and the Netherlands had all established colonies in North America. Many colonial towns became busy trading centers. The French town of **Quebec,** for example, thrived on the beaver fur trade. Quebec was founded in 1608 on the St. Lawrence River in present-day Canada. This proved to be a good location for a colony, because millions of beavers lived in the forests of this region.

Huron Native Americans trapped the beavers and brought the furs to Quebec for trading. These furs could then be sold for huge profits in Europe. A profit is the money a business has left over after it has paid all its costs.

By 1626 Dutch settlers, from the Netherlands, had established the town of **New Amsterdam** on Manhattan Island. Settlers here also traded with local Native Americans for beaver furs. With an ideal location for trade, New Amsterdam attracted settlers from many countries. By the 1640s, about 18 different languages could be heard on the streets of New Amsterdam. In addition to Dutch, people spoke languages such as French, English, German, Spanish, Portuguese, and Polish.

With thriving industries such as the fur trade, there was money to be made in North America. This attracted new settlers from Europe, causing many colonies to grow quickly. Settlers also had other reasons for moving from Europe to North America. Some came to explore and to spread their religion. Others came in search of land of their own and religious freedom.

Some people came to North America against their will. In the 1500s, European ships began bringing captive Africans to work as slaves in the colonies. However, not all Africans in North America were slaves. In places such as New Amsterdam, some Africans came to the colony as free people and some enslaved people were able to earn their freedom. The son of a former slave, Lucas Santomee, became New Amsterdam's first black doctor.

REVIEW What effect did the beaver fur trade have on the town of Quebec? **Cause and Effect**

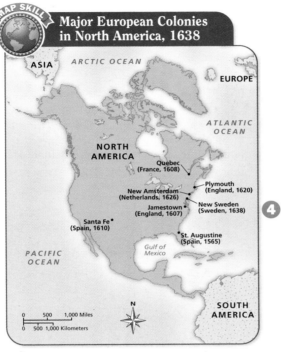

Major European Colonies in North America, 1638

► Look at each colony to see what year it was founded and by which country.

MAP SKILL Use a Historical Map *According to the map, what was the first colony to be founded in North America? Which country established it?*

13

Founding Colonies

Quick Summary The Dutch were the first in a succession of European countries to colonize North America, causing an increase in industry and trade.

1 **What was significant about Quebec's location?** The large beaver population made Quebec a prime location for fur trade. Draw Conclusions

SOCIAL STUDIES STRAND
Geography

Point out that geographic features can affect the decision of where to locate a settlement.

2 **Why did New Amsterdam attract settlers from other countries?** The location was ideal for trade. Draw Conclusions

3 **What were the reasons people wanted to settle in North America?** Strong industry, religious freedom, exploration Main Idea and Details

✓ **REVIEW ANSWER** The town became a center for trade. Cause and Effect

Major European Colonies in North America, 1638

4 **Which colonies on the map were established by England?** Plymouth and Jamestown Interpret Maps

MAP SKILL Answer St. Augustine; Spain

Identifying Key Facts Have students answer questions that ask *Who? When? Where? What? Why?* and *How?* about the founding of French and Dutch colonies.

Easy Prepare a two-column worksheet with questions on the left side and answers on the right. Write the answers in random order. Have students draw a line to connect each question to the correct answer. **Reteach**

On-Level Have students make fact cards and test each other's knowledge about French and Dutch settlements. **Extend**

Challenge Have student groups conduct research to find out about the French explorer, Samuel de Champlain, and the Dutch explorer, Henry Hudson. Have students share what they learn with the class. **Enrich**

For a Lesson Summary, use Quick Study, p. 4.

The First Permanent English Colony

🕐 *Quick Summary* English settlers withstood challenges as they established the first permanent English settlement in North America.

⑤ How did John Smith's leadership help colonists establish Jamestown? He made them work toward survival by building houses, planting crops, and digging wells. Make Inferences

⑥ What caused Jamestown and nearby farms to grow rapidly after 1612? Tobacco, a cash crop, began to be cultivated. Cause and Effect

✓ **Ongoing Assessment**

If... students do not understand the effect of tobacco on the growth of Jamestown and nearby farms,	**then...** briefly explain the concept of supply and demand.

⑦ What was significant about the House of Burgesses? It was the first law-making assembly in an English colony. It began to establish self-government in the English colonies. Main Idea and Details

✓ **REVIEW ANSWER** Settlers might prefer governing themselves as opposed to being governed. Draw Conclusions

The Jamestown Colony

Have students examine the photos of the exhibits at Jamestown Settlement.

⑧ What does the child's toy indicate about the Jamestown Colony? Possible answer: It shows that children lived and played in the Jamestown Colony. Draw Conclusions

The First Permanent English Colony

In 1607 English settlers established the colony of **Jamestown** on the east coast of present-day Virginia. This was the first permanent English settlement in what is now the United States. Lacking food and fresh water, many of the settlers died of starvation and disease during the first year. Then, under the leadership of **John Smith,** the colonists built ⑤ houses, planted crops, and dug wells. Corn from the Powhatan Indians helped keep the settlers alive during this difficult time.

In about 1612, an English settler named **John Rolfe** began raising tobacco in the rich Virginia soil. You will read more about John Rolfe in the biography on page 19. Tobacco soon became Virginia's first **cash crop,** or crop grown for profit. Profits from tobacco exports to England helped the Jamestown colony grow. John Rolfe's marriage to a Powhatan woman named **Pocahontas** helped ⑥ ensure a time of peace between the English and Powhatan people.

Hoping to attract more settlers from England, leaders of the colony decided to give colonists the right to govern themselves. In 1619 the Virginia **House of Burgesses** met for the first time. This was the first lawmaking assembly in an English colony. It was organized much like small-town governments in England. The House of Burgesses began to establish self-government in the English colonies. ⑦

REVIEW Why do you think self-government might have attracted new settlers to Virginia? Draw Conclusions

The Jamestown Colony

Jamestown was built on a heavily wooded peninsula in the James River. When settlers first saw this place, they called it a "paradise." Today you can see Jamestown for yourself. A re-created fort and Powhatan village will give you a better idea of what life was like there 400 years ago.

▶ Actors re-create daily life of the Powhatan (below), as well as the Jamestown settlers (right).

Scientists continue to dig up belongings of the Jamestown settlers, such as this belt buckle and child's toy (above).

14

Practice and Extend

CURRICULUM CONNECTION
Literature

Read About Jamestown Have students read more about the Jamestown colony and then prepare a report about the colony's survival in the early years. Encourage students to be creative in their presentations.

Jamestown: New World Adventure, by James E. Knight (Troll Associates, ISBN 0-816-74554-4, 1998) **Easy**

Pocahontas: The True Story of the Powhatan Princess, by Catherine Iannone (Chelsea House Publishers, ISBN 0-791-02496-2, 1995) **On-Level**

The Paradox of Jamestown: 1585–1700, by Christopher Collier and James Lincoln Collier (Benchmark Books, ISBN 0-761-40437-6, 1998) **Challenge**

After the long journey across the Atlantic Ocean in the *Mayflower* (left), Pilgrim leaders met to establish a government for their new colony (above).

Religious Freedom

In the early 1600s, the search for religious freedom led to the founding of new colonies in what is now Massachusetts. Members of a group called the Pilgrims sailed from Europe to North America in 1620. They had faced persecution, or unjust treatment because of their beliefs, in England. Now they hoped to find a place where they could practice their religion as they pleased.

About 100 Pilgrims crossed the Atlantic Ocean in a small ship called the *Mayflower*. The *Mayflower* landed in a rocky harbor the English called **Plymouth.**

The Pilgrims enjoyed a period of friendly relations with the Wampanoag Indians. A Native American named **Squanto** showed the Pilgrims the best hunting and fishing areas, and he taught them how to grow corn in the rocky New England soil. In the fall of 1621, Pilgrims gathered their first harvest in Plymouth. They invited the Wampanoag to a thanksgiving feast.

In 1630 a group called the Puritans sailed from England to Massachusetts. Like the Pilgrims, they came in search of religious freedom. Puritans founded the Massachusetts Bay Colony. The main settlement was named Boston, which thrived on fishing and trade. It remained the largest city in the English colonies for more than 100 years.

REVIEW Why did the Pilgrims and Puritans come to North America? 🔄 Summarize

The Wampanoag taught the Pilgrims how to grow corn.

15

PAGE 15

Religious Freedom

🕐 *Quick Summary* The Pilgrims and the Puritans left their homeland for North America in search of religious freedom and to escape persecution.

⑨ **What hardship did Pilgrims face in England?** They faced persecution for their religious beliefs.
Main Idea and Details

🧩 **Problem Solving**

⑩ **How did Squanto help solve the Pilgrims' problem about survival?** He showed the Pilgrims where to hunt and fish and how to grow corn.
Solve Problems

⑪ **What was the main settlement of the Massachusetts Bay Colony?** Boston
Main Idea and Details

🦉 **Test Talk**

Locate Key Words in the Text

⑫ **Why did the Massachusetts Bay Colony grow rapidly?** Tell students to skim the section to find key words in the text to answer the question. Fishing and trading were profitable.
Cause and Effect

✓ **REVIEW ANSWER** They came in search of religious freedom and to escape religious persecution.
🔄 Summarize

⊕ **CURRICULUM CONNECTION**
Literature

Read About the Puritans Encourage students to read more about the Puritans and then present one of the selections as a Readers Theater.

The Spinner's Daughter, by Amy Littlesugar (Pippin Press, ISBN 0-945-91222-6, 1994) **Easy**

Increase Mather: Clergyman and Scholar, by Norma Jean Lutz (Chelsea House Publishers, ISBN 0-791-05962-6, 2001) **On-Level**

Pilgrims and Puritans: 1620–1676, by Christopher Collier and James Lincoln Collier (Benchmark Books, ISBN 0-761-40438-4, 1998) **Challenge**

The 13 English Colonies

🕐 *Quick Summary* The three regions of the 13 English Colonies had varying climates and natural resources.

13 What might the barrels produced in New England be used for? Storage of goods Draw Conclusions

14 Why were the Middle Colonies known as the "breadbasket of the colonies"? The Middle Colonies supplied the New England and Southern Colonies with wheat flour.
Main Idea and Details

15 How are the natural resources and climate of the Southern Colonies related to their industry? The rich soil, warm weather, and plentiful rain of the Southern Colonies made it possible to grow crops, such as tobacco and rice.
Analyze Information

MAP SKILL 13 English Colonies

16 How many colonies are in each region? New England—four; Middle—four; Southern—five Interpret Maps

MAP SKILL Answer Maryland, Virginia, North Carolina, South Carolina, and Georgia

✓ **REVIEW ANSWER** New England: fish, ships, and timber; Middle: wheat and iron; Southern: tobacco and rice
Compare and Contrast

The 13 English Colonies

By 1733 the English had established 13 colonies along the east coast of North America. The colonies can be divided into three regions—the New England Colonies, the Middle Colonies, and the Southern Colonies.

Each region was rich in different natural resources. **Natural resources** are materials found in nature that people can use, such as trees or water. The New England, Middle, and Southern Colonies each developed a different type of economy. An **economy** is a system for producing and distributing goods and serv- ices. In New England, for example, trees from the thick forests were used to build houses, **13** ships, and barrels. With ships, colonists could fish in the waters off the New England coast.

Farmers in the Middle Colonies grew so much wheat that the region became known as "the breadbasket of the colonies." Flour from the Middle Colonies was shipped to the New England and Southern Colonies, and **14** sent to other countries. Iron from mines in the Middle Colonies was made into tools.

With rich soil, a warm climate, and plentiful rain, the Southern Colonies developed an economy based on cash crops, such as **15** tobacco and rice. Farms ranged in size from small family farms to large **plantations,** or large farms with many workers who lived on the land they worked. Many of the workers on plantations were enslaved Africans.

REVIEW Compare the important products of the New England, Middle, and Southern Colonies. Compare and Contrast

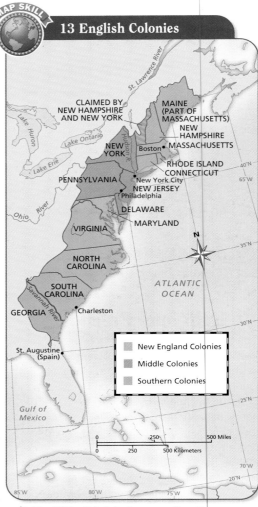

MAP SKILL 13 English Colonies

▶ The 13 English Colonies were all on the Atlantic coast.
MAP SKILL Location *Name the Southern Colonies.*

16

Practice and Extend

🧩 Decision Making

Use a Decision-Making Process

- Have students consider the following decision-making scenario: **Suppose you are a new colonist in New England. You realize that you must work hard to earn your living. You know that most jobs in your colony are based on work related to products from either the forests or the sea.**

- Students should use the following decision-making process to decide which type of work they would prefer to do. For each step in the process, have students work in small groups to discuss and write about what must be considered as they make their decision. Write these steps on the board or read them aloud.

1. Identify a situation that requires a decision.
2. Gather information.
3. Identify options.
4. Predict consequences.
5. Take action to implement a decision.

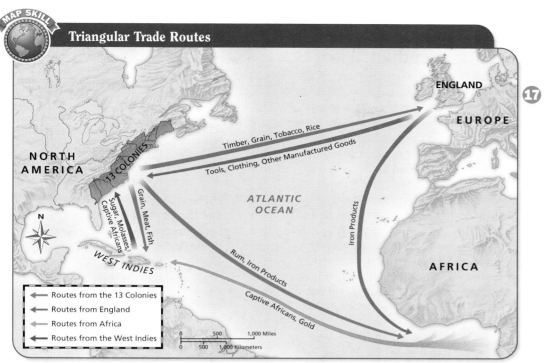

MAP SKILL
Triangular Trade Routes

Timber, Grain, Tobacco, Rice

Tools, Clothing, Other Manufactured Goods

ENGLAND

EUROPE

NORTH AMERICA

13 COLONIES

Sugar, Molasses; Captive Africans

Grain, Meat, Fish

ATLANTIC OCEAN

Iron Products

WEST INDIES

Rum, Iron Products

Captive Africans, Gold

AFRICA

N

← Routes from the 13 Colonies
← Routes from England
← Routes from Africa
← Routes from the West Indies

0   500   1,000 Miles
0   500   1,000 Kilometers

▶ The shipping routes among the colonies, England, and Africa were known as triangular trade routes.

MAP SKILL Use Routes *From where were tools and clothing shipped? To where were these products shipped?*

Slavery and the Slave Trade

As the colonial economies grew, cities such as Boston, New York, Philadelphia, and Charleston became thriving trading centers. An important part of colonial trade was the slave trade. Ships brought captive Africans to the colonies. These enslaved people were sold and then forced to work without wages.

Some trade routes became known as triangular trade routes, because they were shaped like giant triangles. Look at the map on this page and you will see examples of the slave trade and triangular trade routes.

Slavery expanded rapidly in the 13 Colonies during the 1700s. By 1760 about 40,000 enslaved people lived in the New England and Middle Colonies, mostly in towns and cities. They worked in people's homes, as well as in stores and, inns, and as skilled artisans.

The largest number of enslaved people—about 250,000 by 1760—lived in the Southern Colonies. Most slaves in the South worked on plantations. Sometimes hundreds of enslaved people worked on a single large plantation.

REVIEW In which region of the colonies did the largest number of enslaved people live? **Compare and Contrast**

17

Slavery and the Slave Trade

Quick Summary Enslaved people brought by ships from Africa lived and worked in the three colonial regions.

MAP SKILL
Triangular Trade Routes

Help students use the map to identify imports and exports.

17 What goods did the colonies export to England? Timber, grain, tobacco, and rice **Interpret Maps**

✓ Ongoing Assessment

| If... students do not understand the terms *import* and *export*, | then... explain that ex- means *to go out*, as in *exit*, and im- means *to come in*, as in *immigrant*. |

MAP SKILL Answer From England; to the 13 Colonies

18 What conclusions can you draw about the talents and skills of enslaved people in the New England and Middle Colonies based on the kind of work they did? Possible answer: They had many different talents and skills. **Draw Conclusions**

✓ **REVIEW ANSWER** In the South **Compare and Contrast**

Practice and Extend

EXTEND LANGUAGE
ESL Support

Explore Job Words Have students identify and explore the meanings of words that name jobs.

Beginning Write the words *planter, carpenter, blacksmith,* and *tailor* on the board. Have students match each word with words or pictures of items related to each job. For example, show pictures of seeds, wood, axes, and cloth.

Intermediate Write this sentence frame on the board: *A person who is a _____ must _____.* Have students orally or in writing fill in the first blank with a job name and the second with a task the worker does.

Advanced Ask students which job they would choose if they were living in the English colonies in the mid-1600s. Have them write about a typical day and why they enjoy the work.

For additional ESL support, use Every Student Learns Guide, pp. 6–9.

SOCIAL STUDIES
Background

Anthony Benezet
- During the 1750s Anthony Benezet started a movement to raise consciousness against slavery. Later he wrote works against slavery.
- In 1755 he started a school for girls.

Slave Narratives
- The Federal Writers' Project collected life stories of former slaves. Search the American Memory section of the Library of Congress at **memory.loc.gov.**

The French and Indian War

Quick Summary Conflicts over land led settlers and American Indians to war in the west.

19 **What conflict arose when settlers began moving into the Ohio River valley?** British and French both claimed the land. Native Americans also lived there. Make Inferences

20 **Why was the war called the French and Indian War?** The British fought against the French and their American Indian allies. Main Idea and Details

✓ **REVIEW ANSWER** Possible answer: Britain won control over a huge amount of land. Cause and Effect

3 Close and Assess

Summarize the Lesson

Have students add events to the time line and then to summarize the lesson.

✓ | LESSON 2 | REVIEW |

1. 🔄 **Summarize** For possible answers, see the reduced pupil page.

2. Religious freedom, industry, and exploration

3. Tobacco; Jamestown profited from tobacco exports.

4. New England and Middle: slaves worked in cities and towns; Southern: slaves worked on plantations.

5. **Critical Thinking: Apply Information** New England: economy based on fishing and timber; Middle: economy based on mining and farming; Southern: economy based on cash crops.

| Link to 🔗 Mathematics |

Students' graphs should reflect accurate numerical increments.

The French and Indian War

During the 1700s, settlers from the 13 Colonies began moving west in search of land. They entered the Ohio River valley—a region of fertile land and forests along the Ohio River. English settlers felt they could move to the Ohio River valley because England, which was now known as Great Britain, claimed this land. But France also claimed the Ohio River valley. Powerful American Indian groups lived there as well.

19 Conflict over this land led to war in 1754. In the 13 Colonies, the war was called the French and Indian War, because British forces fought against the French and their
20 American Indian allies. Great Britain won the war. In 1763 Britain and France signed a peace treaty that gave Britain control over most of France's land in North America.

REVIEW What was one effect of the French and Indian War? *Cause and Effect*

Summarize the Lesson

- **1607** Settlers founded Jamestown, Virginia, the first permanent English settlement in what is now the United States.

- **1626** Dutch settlers founded New Amsterdam, one of many European colonies in North America.

- **1733** England had 13 colonies on the eastern coast of North America.

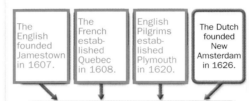

LESSON 2 REVIEW

Check Facts and Main Ideas

1. 🔄 **Summarize** On a separate sheet of paper, fill in three details that support the summary below.

| The English founded Jamestown in 1607. | The French established Quebec in 1608. | English Pilgrims established Plymouth in 1620. | The Dutch founded New Amsterdam in 1626. |

↓

By the 1600s, Europeans had established many colonies in North America.

2. Identify reasons that European settlers moved to North America.

3. What **cash crop** was important to Jamestown, and how did it help the colony grow?

4. How was slavery in the New England and Middle Colonies different from slavery in the Southern Colonies?

5. **Critical Thinking: Apply Information** Explain how **natural resources** helped shape the different **economies** of the New England, Middle, and Southern Colonies.

| Link to 🔗 Mathematics |

Draw a Bar Graph Use the information below to draw a bar graph. Your graph should show the rapid growth of the population of the 13 Colonies.

Year	Population of the 13 Colonies
1730	629,445
1750	1,170,760
1770	2,148,076

18

Practice and Extend

SOCIAL STUDIES Background

Albany Congress

In 1754, at a meeting in Albany, New York, the Iroquois league refused to join the British colonies in the struggle against the British.

- A second purpose of this meeting was to explore a plan for helping the colonies work together.

- Although Benjamin Franklin's Albany Plan of Union was rejected, the U.S. Constitution later included many of his ideas, including representation in a national congress, a separate president with veto power over the decisions of the congress, and congress having power only to make decisions affecting all the states' common interests.

Workbook, p. 5

Lesson 2: Life in the Colonies

Directions: Answer the following questions on the lines provided. You may use your textbook.

1. What attracted so many people from Europe to come to North America in the 1600s? What was the name and location of the first permanent English colony in North America?

2. What factor led to the foundation of colonies in the New England area?

3. What were the names and major economic features of the three regions of England's colonies?

4. Under what circumstances did most Africans come to North America?

5. Describe the conflict that lead to the French and Indian War. What was the effect of this war?

Notes for Home: Your child learned about the growth and development of the earliest European colonies in North America.
Home Activity: Ask your child to summarize the causes and effects of European colonization.

Also on Teacher Resources CD-ROM.

John Rolfe
1585–1622

When John Rolfe arrived in Jamestown from England in 1610, the colony was in trouble. Many people had left the colony. There was also tension between the colonists and the Powhatan. But by the time Rolfe left Jamestown in 1616, the colony was making money and had maintained peace with the Powhatan. How did this happen?

Rolfe wanted to find a product to sell to England that would make a profit. He knew tobacco sold by Spain was popular in England. But the English found the tobacco grown by the Powhatan to be too bitter. In 1612 Rolfe planted tobacco seeds that came from islands in the Caribbean Sea. He also experimented with different ways to dry and prepare tobacco leaves. People in England liked the new tobacco's sweeter taste. **1**

BIOFACT
Rolfe was a member of the Virginia House of Burgesses, which first met in the Jamestown Church. Rolfe and Pocahontas were also married there.

Around the same time, Rolfe fell in love with the Powhatan princess Pocahontas. He asked both the Virginia governor and the Powhatan chief for permission to marry her. Rolfe described Pocahontas as one,

2 *"To whom my heart and best thoughts are, and have a long time been so entangled [involved with]."*

Rolfe and Pocahontas were married in 1614. Two years later they toured England to attract more settlers to Jamestown.

Rolfe's actions had a lasting effect on the colony. He developed the first product sold to England to make a profit. In 1617 colonists sent 20,000 pounds of tobacco to England. In 1630 they shipped 500,000 pounds. Rolfe's marriage to Pocahontas also created a peace between colonists and the Powhatan that lasted eight years. This gave the settlement enough time to become permanent and for its tobacco industry to grow.

For more information, go to *Meet the People* at **www.sfsocialstudies.com.**

Learn from Biographies
How did John Rolfe help the Jamestown colonists?

19

★ B I O G R A P H Y ★

John Rolfe

Objective
- Describe the accomplishments of significant colonial leaders such as John Rolfe.

1 Introduce and Motivate

Preview To activate prior knowledge, ask students what they learned about John Rolfe. Tell them they will learn how he influenced the colony of Jamestown.

2 Teach and Discuss

1 **Why did John Rolfe want to change the way tobacco was grown?** To please the English who found the Powhatan tobacco too bitter **Main Idea and Details**

2 **What may John Rolfe's statement reveal about his feelings toward Pocahontas?** Possible answer: He has had strong feelings about Pocahontas for a long time. **Analyze Primary Sources**

3 Close and Assess

Learn from Biographies Answer
He started growing and selling to England a more popular form of tobacco. His marriage to Pocahontas created peace in the colony.

 ## Problem Solving

Use a Problem-Solving Process
- Have students consider the following scenario: **Suppose you are John Rolfe and want to increase the population of Jamestown. You travel to England to attract more settlers to the colony. How might you set up a plan to convince people to leave their homes and move to a new place?**
- Students should use the following problem-solving process to decide how to persuade people to relocate. For each step, have students work in small groups to discuss and write about what must be considered as they solve the problem. Then have students critique each other's plans.

1. **Identify a decision.**
2. **Gather information.**
3. **List and consider options.**
4. **Consider advantages and disadvantages.**
5. **Choose and implement a solution.**
6. **Evaluate the effectiveness of the solution.**

Compare Maps at Different Scales

Objective
- Compare and use scales to measure distance on maps.

Vocabulary
small-scale map, p. 20;
large-scale map, p. 20

Resource
- Workbook, p. 6

1 Introduce and Motivate

What are small-scale and large-scale maps? Remind students that a map scale is used to measure distance. Ask students why the scale on one map may not be the same as the scale on another map. Then have students read the **What?** section of text on p. 20.

Why use small-scale and large-scale maps? Have students read the **Why?** section of text on p. 21. Ask them what kind of map they would use if they wanted to show someone the location of a historic site in their community. (a large-scale map)

Map and Globe Skills

Compare Maps at Different Scales

What? A map scale uses a unit of measurement, such as one inch, to represent an actual larger distance on Earth, such as one mile. On a **small-scale map,** an inch on the map represents a very large distance on Earth. Therefore, a small-scale map shows a big area of Earth, such as a state or a country. Map A is a small-scale map.

On a **large-scale map,** an inch represents a shorter distance on Earth. Therefore, this kind of map can show more details than a small-scale map. Map B is a large-scale map.

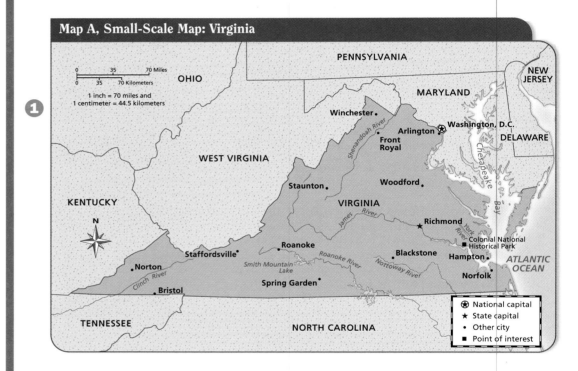

Map A, Small-Scale Map: Virginia

1 inch = 70 miles and
1 centimeter = 44.5 kilometers

20

Practice and Extend

 SOCIAL STUDIES STRAND
Science • Technology

Explore Online Maps
- Introduce students to the Internet map site at **www.mapquest.com.**
- Have students enter a city and state.
- When the map appears, have them use the *zoom in* and *zoom out* functions to change the scale.
- Discuss situations when various scales would be most useful.

 SOCIAL STUDIES STRAND
Geography

The following resources are available:
- Big Book Atlas
- Student Atlas
- Outline Maps
- Desk Maps
- Map Resources CD-ROM

 CURRICULUM CONNECTION
Math

Calculate Distances
- Divide students into groups. Provide groups with a U.S. map and a map of a city outside your state.
- Have each group use the small-scale map to calculate the distance from where they live to the city shown on their large-scale city map.
- Have groups pick three sites they would like to visit on the large-scale map. Have them mark a route and calculate the distance of the trip.

Map B, Large-Scale Map: Colonial National Historical Park

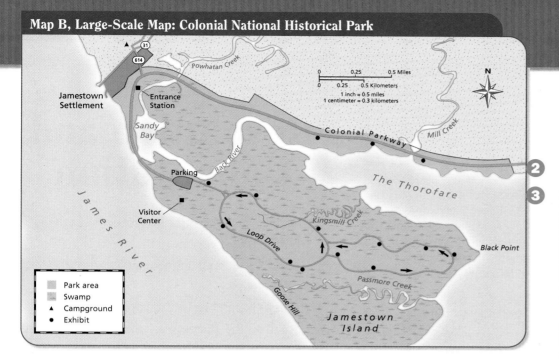

Why? In Lesson 2, you read about the founding of Jamestown. Map B shows Jamestown, which is part of the Colonial National Historical Park. To locate the park in relation to other places in present-day Virginia, you need a small-scale map. To see places in Jamestown and other details of the historical park, you need a large-scale map.

How? You can compare Map A and Map B to see the difference between a large-scale map and a small-scale map. Look at the scale on Map A. How many miles does one inch represent? Measure the distance between the Colonial National Historical Park and Woodford. The park is about 70 miles southeast of Woodford. Now measure the distance between the park and Staunton. How far apart are these places?

Look at the scale on Map B. On this map, one inch represents 1/2 mile. The area

shown is smaller than on Map A, so details of the Colonial National Historical Park can be shown. Find the Visitor Center on this map.

Think and Apply

1. Which map would you use to locate Roanoke?

2. Which map would you use to locate the Colonial Parkway?

3. Turn to the map of the 13 English Colonies on page 16. Is this a large-scale map or a small-scale map?

Internet Activity

For more information, go online to the Atlas at **www.sfsocialstudies.com.**

21

Workbook, p. 6

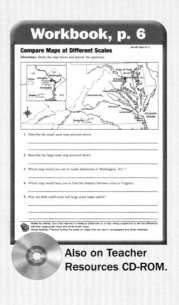

Compare Maps at Different Scales
Directions: Study the map below and answer the questions.

1. Describe the small scale map pictured above.

2. Describe the large scale map pictured above.

3. Which map would you use to locate attractions in Washington, D.C.?

4. Which map would help you to find the distance between cities in Virginia?

5. Why are both small-scale and large scale maps useful?

Also on Teacher Resources CD-ROM.

2 Teach and Discuss

How is this skill used? Examine with students the small-scale map on p. 20 and the large-scale map on p. 21.

- Point out that the small-scale map shows a large area, while the large-scale map shows more details.

- Have students examine both maps closely to detect other similarities and differences.

- Have students read the **How?** section of text on p. 21.

1 **Which map would you use to find the distance between Richmond and Norfolk?** Map A, a small-scale map
Interpret Maps

SOCIAL STUDIES STRAND
Geography

Have students use one of the map resources on p. 21 to help them construct large-scale tourist maps of their community. Remind them to include a compass rose and a legend on their maps.

2 **Which map would you use to help a tourist who is visiting Jamestown? Why?** Map B, because it is a large-scale map which shows places in the city
Interpret Maps

3 **On Map B, what is the distance between the campground and the Visitor Center?** About one and one-fourth miles Interpret Maps

3 Close and Assess

Think and Apply

1. Map A, small-scale map
2. Map B, large-scale map
3. A small-scale map

Revolution and Constitution

Objectives

- Explain how British taxes and colonial protests led to the American Revolution.
- Identify major events of the American Revolution.
- Analyze the plan of government described in the United States Constitution.

Vocabulary

Stamp Act, p. 23;
Declaration of Independence, p. 24;
republic, p. 26; **constitution,** p. 26;
checks and balances, p. 26;
Bill of Rights, p. 28

Resources

- Workbook, p. 7
- Transparency 6
- Every Student Learns Guide, pp. 10–13
- Quick Study Guide, pp. 6–7

Quick Teaching Plan

If time is short, have students write on a chart: *Boston Massacre, Tea Act, Boston Tea Party, Intolerable Acts.*

- Have students write a summary of the roles that the colonists and British played in these events.

1 Introduce and Motivate

Preview To activate prior knowledge, ask students to review the conflicts between the British and the colonists. Tell students they will learn more about conflicts in Lesson 3.

 Explain to students that the British Parliament knows the colonists will not like to be taxed, but the British need to pay off their war debts. Ask students how they would finance war expenses as prime minister of Great Britain.

LESSON 3

1775   1785   1795

1776
13 Colonies declare independence from Britain

1781
Americans defeat British at Yorktown

1787
United States Constitution is signed

PREVIEW

Focus on the Main Idea
The United States won independence from Britain and formed a new government under the Constitution.

PLACES
Boston, Massachusetts
Philadelphia, Pennsylvania
Yorktown, Virginia

PEOPLE
Samuel Adams
George Washington
John Adams
Benjamin Franklin
Thomas Jefferson
Abigail Adams
Peter Salem

VOCABULARY
Stamp Act
Declaration of Independence
republic
constitution
checks and balances
Bill of Rights

▶ The Stamp Act required that stamps like this be placed on all printed materials.

22

Revolution and Constitution

You Are There

This is the biggest news of 1765. Everyone in the streets of Boston is talking about it. Actually, they're shouting about it.

The news is this: The British government has decided to tax the American colonies. A new law called the Stamp Act will place a tax on newspapers, legal documents, even playing cards! You know the British government needs money—it has huge debts from the French and Indian War. But you never thought the British would try to tax the American colonists directly.

How will colonists react to the Stamp Act? Just listen to those angry voices all around you. It is beginning to sound like there might be trouble. What will people do? How will the British react?

Summarize As you read, think of ways to summarize the events that led to the founding of the United States of America.

Practice and Extend

READING SKILL
Summarize

In the Lesson Review, students complete a graphic organizer like the one below. You may want to provide students with a copy of Transparency 6 to complete as they read the lesson.

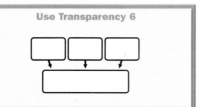

Use Transparency 6

VOCABULARY
Word Exercise

Individual Word Study

Writing definitions in their own words will help students remember the meaning of new terms. Work with students to use their own words to develop definitions of *republic, constitution,* and *checks and balances.* Then ask students to write down each term in their vocabulary journals, along with its definition and a sentence using the term.

Taxes and Protests

When news of the **Stamp Act** reached the 13 Colonies, many colonists reacted with anger. By 1765 the colonies had a long tradition of self-government. Since colonists could not vote for members of the British government, they believed that the British government had no right to tax them. This led to the popular protest cry: "No taxation without representation!"

Samuel Adams became an outspoken opponent of British taxes. In **Boston, Massachusetts,** Adams organized the Sons of Liberty, a group that led protests against the Stamp Act. Soon Sons of Liberty groups were started in towns throughout the colonies.

In response to these protests, the British government repealed, or ended, the Stamp Act. But British leaders insisted that they still had the right to tax the colonies. When the British government passed a new act demanding taxes, the 13 Colonies began to unite against the British. Colonists who opposed British rule became known as Patriots.

In 1774 Patriot leaders from every colony except Georgia met at the Continental Congress in **Philadelphia, Pennsylvania.** Leaders agreed that each colony should begin training militias, or volunteer armies. However, most colonists still hoped their dispute with Britain could be settled peacefully.

REVIEW Explain the meaning of the protest cry: "No taxation without representation."
Summarize

FACT FILE

The Road to Revolution

1765 — **1765 Stamp Act** The British government passes a tax on printed materials sold in the 13 Colonies.

1767 Townshend Acts The British government passes a tax on goods the colonies import from Great Britain.

1770 — **1770 Boston Massacre** British soldiers fire into a crowd of angry protesters in Boston, killing five.

1773 Boston Tea Party Colonists in Boston protest taxes by dumping British tea into Boston Harbor.

1775 — **1774 Intolerable Acts** The British government responds by sending soldiers to Boston and shutting down the city's port.

► Colonists might have served "liberty tea" from this teapot, painted in protest of the Stamp Act.

23

2 Teach and Discuss

PAGE 23

Taxes and Protests

Quick Summary When Britain started taxing colonists, they united against the British and formed protest groups.

$ STUDIES STRAND
Economics

Explain that governments need money to operate and raise it in many ways.

1 **What slogan did the colonists use to protest the Stamp Act?** "No taxation without representation"
Main Idea and Details

2 **Why was this an effective slogan for the anti-tax protesters?** It was short, catchy, and effectively addressed colonists' grievances.
Analyze Primary Sources

3 **What common goal began to create a sense of unity among the colonists?** The repeal of the Stamp Act and the passage of a new act demanding taxes
Draw Conclusions

G SOCIAL STUDIES STRAND
Government

Democratic Values and Institutions Point out to students that a *congress* is an assembly of representatives who meet to vote on a course of action.

4 **How did the Continental Congress show a willingness to fight to end their dispute?** They agreed each colony should begin to train militia.
Draw Conclusions

✓ **REVIEW ANSWER** Colonists felt the members of the British government had no right to tax them since the colonists didn't vote for them. Summarize

FACT FILE

The Road to Revolution

5 **What happened as a result of the Boston Tea Party?** The British punished Boston with the Intolerable Acts.
Cause and Effect

Overview • Lesson 3   **23**

MEETING INDIVIDUAL NEEDS
Leveled Practice

Write a Letter About the Stamp Act Ask each student to write a letter about the effects of the Stamp Act. Have students refer to the You Are There feature on p. 22.

Easy As a colonist, write a letter to a friend listing four things you want or need that the Stamp Act will affect. **Reteach**

On-Level As a colonist, write a short letter to Britain's Prime Minister Grenville. Explain how the Stamp Act affects you and why you oppose it. **Extend**

Challenge As Prime Minister Grenville, explain in a letter to a colonist how the Stamp Act will affect government income, why the government needs additional income, and why the act is fair. **Enrich**

For a Lesson Summary, use Quick Study, p. 6.

Declaring Independence

Quick Summary Americans won their independence from the British in the American Revolution. The Continental Congress approved the Declaration of Independence, which states the reasons for declaring independence.

6 **Why did the British go to Concord?** They went to Concord to seize the Patriot militias' weapons. Summarize

7 **What did the Continental Congress decide to do? Why?** Form the Continental Army; the relationship between the colonists and the British was getting worse. Cause and Effect

8 **Why do you think the Continental Congress wanted to ensure that the 13 Colonies supported the break with Great Britain?** Possible answer: It thought the colonies and the colonists needed to be united. Make Inferences

9 **Why did the committee choose Jefferson to write the first draft of the Declaration of Independence?** He was an excellent writer. Analyze Information

✓ **REVIEW ANSWER** It explained why it was time for American colonies to establish a government of their own. Main Idea and Details

Literature and Social Studies

Have students read one of the most famous sections of the Declaration of Independence.

Primary Source

Cited in the Declaration of Independence.

10 **Reread the section from the Declaration of Independence. What is the tone of Jefferson's words? What makes his statements powerful and effective?** Possible answer: The tone is firm, yet respectful. Jefferson clearly states specific reasons for declaring independence from Britain. He uses persuasive arguments, not angry remarks. Analyze Primary Sources

---

Declaring Independence

On April 19, 1775, tensions around Boston exploded into war. British soldiers marched from Boston to the nearby towns of Lexington and Concord. Their goal was to destroy militia **6** weapons that colonists had been collecting. But militia members in both Lexington and Concord stood up to the British, and the result was a long, bloody day of fighting. This was the beginning of the American Revolution.

Members of the Continental Congress decided it was time to form the Continental Army, an army with soldiers from all 13 **7** Colonies. They selected **George Washington** to lead the new army. General Washington had gained military experience as a Virginia militia officer during the French and Indian War.

Next, the Congress turned to a more difficult decision—was it time for the 13 Colonies to declare independence from Great Britain? By June 1776, members were ready to make this decision. A committee was formed to begin drafting the **Declaration of Independence.** This document explained why the colonies believed they must declare independence **8** from Britain.

The committee included famous Patriot leaders such as **John Adams** of Massachusetts and **Benjamin Franklin** of Pennsylvania. Also on the committee was

24

Thomas Jefferson, a 33-year-old lawyer from Virginia who had a reputation as an excellent writer. Jefferson was given the job of writing **9** the first draft of the Declaration. After making a few changes to Jefferson's draft, the Continental Congress voted to approve the Declaration of Independence on July 4, 1776.

REVIEW What was the purpose of the Declaration of Independence?
Main Idea and Details

Literature and Social Studies

The Declaration of Independence

For more than 200 years, Jefferson's bold words have inspired people all over the world. Below is one of the most famous sections of the Declaration of Independence.

We hold these truths to be self-evident; that all men are created equal, that they are endowed [given] by their Creator with certain unalienable rights, that among these are life, liberty, and the pursuit of happiness.

That to secure these rights, governments are instituted among men, deriving [receiving] their just powers from the consent of the governed; that whenever any form of government becomes destructive of these ends, it is the right of the people to alter or to abolish it, and to institute new government, laying its foundations on such principles, and organizing its powers in such form, as to them shall seem most likely to effect their safety and happiness. **10**

▶ **Thomas Jefferson worked with John Adams and Benjamin Franklin on the Declaration of Independence. A draft of the Declaration is shown here.**

Practice and Extend

FYI **SOCIAL STUDIES**
Background

About the Signers

• The 56 men who signed the Declaration of Independence came from all walks of life. They were physicians, teachers, attorneys, farmers, businessmen, and ministers.

• Despite the differences in their backgrounds, each man promised to give all he had to help America become free.

• In keeping that pledge, some were captured and made prisoners by the British, many lost their homes and possessions, others lost their children, and some even lost their lives.

Grievances Against the King

• Charges against the King in the Declaration of Independence included more than grievances about taxes. Other grievances included:
— misusing the military
— abusing the courts
— ignoring the laws
— restricting travel

► The British surrendered to American and French forces at Yorktown.

Winning the War

The Americans had declared their independence, but they still faced a British government that was determined to hold onto its colonies. In early battles, Washington's army suffered several defeats. The army also faced constant shortages of soldiers and supplies.

An important turning point came in 1777, when Americans defeated a large British army at the Battle of Saratoga in northern New York State. This convinced French leaders that the Continental Army could win the war. France agreed to help the Americans defeat Britain.

Even with this help, victory over Britain still seemed far away. Patriot women helped keep the Revolution alive by collecting food, raising money, and making clothing for the soldiers. **Abigail Adams,** the wife of John Adams, helped the struggle for independence with her pen. She wrote bold letters supporting

American independence. You'll read more about Abigail Adams in the Biography after this lesson.

Peter Salem was one of about 5,000 African Americans who served in the Continental Army. Salem gained fame for his heroism at the Battles of Bunker Hill and Saratoga. Many African American Patriots hoped that victory in the Revolution would mean freedom for all Americans—including those who were enslaved. 12 13

In September 1781, American and French forces trapped a large British army at **Yorktown, Virginia.** The British were forced to surrender to Washington in October. This was the last major battle of the American Revolution. The Americans had finally defeated mighty Great Britain. 14

REVIEW Which two major victories helped the Americans win the Revolution?
🔄 Summarize

25

Winning the War

🕐 **Quick Summary** The American army won several pivotal battles, leading ultimately to British surrender.

11 **What was the effect of winning the Battle of Saratoga?** The victory persuaded the French to join the fight against Britain. Cause and Effect

12 **Why did some African Americans decide to fight with the Patriots?** They believed in freedom for all Americans, including themselves. 🔄 Summarize

⭐ **SOCIAL STUDIES STRAND**
Citizenship

Prejudice Reduction Even though they often faced discrimination, free African Americans often played a positive role in the Revolution.

13 **In what way did African American Patriots set an example for us to follow today?** Possible answer: African Americans who joined the Continental Army fought for freedom for all Americans. Draw Conclusions

14 **Do you think all people living in the United States were equally happy about the outcome of the war? Explain.** Possible answer: No; many African Americans were still enslaved in America, so freedom from Britain did not make them free; Colonists who remained loyal to Britain, or Loyalists, may have feared for their safety after Britain lost the war. Point of View

✓ **REVIEW ANSWER** The Battle of Saratoga and the Battle of Yorktown
🔄 Summarize

CURRICULUM CONNECTION
Literature

Read About Patriots

Sybil Ludington's Midnight Ride, Marsha Amstel (Lerner Publishing Group, ISBN 1-575-05456-6, 2000) **Easy** *Horn Book Award*

The Secret Soldier: The Story of Deborah Sampson, by Ann McGovern (Scholastic, ISBN 0-590-43052-1, 1990) **On-Level**

If You Were There in 1776, by Barbara Brenner (Simon and Schuster, ISBN 0-027-12322-7, 1994) **Challenge**

A New Constitution

🕐 **Quick Summary** After a long process and months of debate, the states agreed on a constitution for the United States.

15 Why did the writers of the Articles of Confederation create a weak national government? They were afraid of giving their new government too much power. Draw Conclusions

16 What do you think might have happened if the United States had kept the Articles of Confederation? Possible answer: The country might have failed; each of the states may have become a separate country with its own government; the country might have fallen to a larger, stronger country in a war. Predict

✓ **Ongoing Assessment**

If... students are unable to make reasonable predictions,	**then...** have them list the problems caused by the Articles of Confederation. Have students make predictions based on the problems they list.

Test Talk

Locate Key Words in the Question

17 What was the goal of the delegates? Have students use the key words *goal* and *delegates* to finish the statement "I need to find out. . . ." To strengthen the government Main Idea and Details

18 What goals for the nation are identified in the Preamble to the Constitution? Justice, peace, defense, welfare, and liberty Main Idea and Details

✓ **REVIEW ANSWER** Americans didn't want their leaders to be too powerful, which reminded them of living under British rule. Draw Conclusions

The Granger Collection

▶ The 55 delegates to the Constitutional Convention included many of the country's most important men. They elected George Washington as leader of the convention.

A New Constitution

After winning independence, Americans had to create new plans for a government of their own. Leaders knew that they wanted their new nation to be a republic. In a **republic,** the people elect representatives to make laws and run the government. Leaders did not want their new government to have too much power, however. They remembered what it was like to live under the very powerful British government.

In 1781 the Continental Congress approved a new plan of government called the Articles of Confederation. The Articles set up a weak national government. As the main governing body, Congress had the power to make laws but not to collect taxes to run the government. This weak government soon faced problems. Paper money printed by Congress became almost worthless. Many leaders decided that it was time to form a stronger national government.

In May 1787, 55 delegates, or representatives, met in Philadelphia. After months of argument, discussion, and compromise, the delegates agreed on a constitution for the United States. A **constitution** is a written plan of government. This meeting became known as the Constitutional Convention.

26

The Preamble, or introduction, to the United States Constitution sets out the major goals of the new government: to establish justice, to ensure peace, to defend the nation, and to protect the people's well-being and liberty.

The Constitution divides the government into three branches, or parts—the Legislative Branch, Executive Branch, and Judicial Branch. To guard against any one branch becoming too powerful, the Constitution provides a system of **checks and balances.** The chart on the next page shows which powers belong to each branch of government. You will also see how the system of checks and balances works.

REVIEW Why do you think Americans were worried about forming a government that had too much power? Draw Conclusions

▶ Congress and the states printed paper money during and after the Revolution.

Practice and Extend

 ESL EXTEND LANGUAGE

ESL Support

Examine Word Meanings Tell students that *compromise* means "to settle a dispute by giving up part of what each side demands."

Beginning Describe a situation in school or your community in which individuals or groups compromised in order to resolve an issue. Have students act out the situation to help them understand what took place.

Intermediate Pose a scenario to illustrate compromising. For example, point to one group of students and say, "They want to eat at 12:00." Point to another group and say, "They want to eat at 1:00. We can compromise and eat at 12:30." Have students describe or pantomime other compromise scenarios.

Advanced Have students work in groups to create skits that show people compromising on an issue. Allow groups to present their work.

For additional ESL support, use Every Student Learns Guide, pp. 10–13.

FACT FILE

The Three Branches of Government

The Constitution of the United States divides our federal, or national, government into three branches. A system of checks and balances limits the power of each branch. The people provide the final check over all three branches.

(19)

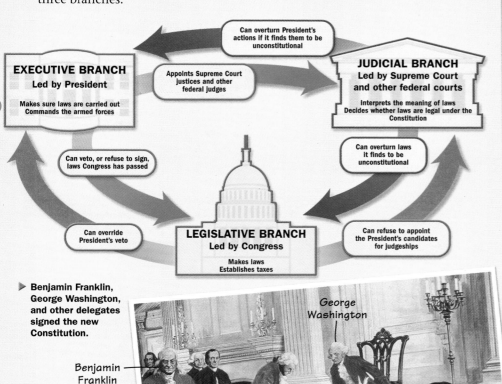

EXECUTIVE BRANCH
Led by President
Makes sure laws are carried out
Commands the armed forces

Can overturn President's actions if it finds them to be unconstitutional

Appoints Supreme Court justices and other federal judges

JUDICIAL BRANCH
Led by Supreme Court and other federal courts
Interprets the meaning of laws
Decides whether laws are legal under the Constitution

Can veto, or refuse to sign, laws Congress has passed

Can overturn laws it finds to be unconstitutional

Can override President's veto

LEGISLATIVE BRANCH
Led by Congress
Makes laws
Establishes taxes

Can refuse to appoint the President's candidates for judgeships

(21)

▶ Benjamin Franklin, George Washington, and other delegates signed the new Constitution.

George Washington

Benjamin Franklin

(22)

27

FACT FILE
The Three Branches of Government

(19) **Why do you think that the writers of the Constitution believed that the government's powers should be limited?** Possible answer: They remembered the abuses of power that led to the American Revolution. Express Ideas

 Test Talk

Use Information from Graphics

(20) **Which branch is in charge of the U.S. armed forces?** Tell students to look at the chart to find the right answer. The Executive Branch Interpret Charts

G STUDIES STRAND
Government

Democratic Values and Institutions The U.S. Congress, established by the new constitution, met for the first time on March 4, 1789, in New York.

(21) **How does the Legislative Branch provide a "check" on the Judicial Branch?** It can refuse to appoint the President's candidates for judgeships. Interpret Charts

(22) **Look at the picture of the delegates signing the Constitution. How do you think they may have felt?** Possible answer: They were happy, concerned, and relieved. Analyze Pictures

 **SOCIAL STUDIES**
Background

Checks and Balances

- One of the first tests of the new system of balanced powers came in 1803 with the court case *Marbury* v. *Madison.*
- Shortly before President John Adams left office in 1801, he appointed several men to judgeships. These men were nicknamed "midnight appointments" because their commissions were written at the last minute.
- When his commission failed to arrive, William Marbury asked the Supreme Court to have Secretary of State James Madison deliver it.
- John Marshall, the Chief Justice of the Supreme Court, ruled that although Marbury's judgeship was legal, the court did not have the right to enforce it. In doing so, he declared part of a previous act of Congress unconstitutional, thus securing for the Court the power to check laws passed by Congress to see if the laws follow the Constitution or not.

The Bill of Rights

Quick Summary The Bill of Rights pledged to guarantee personal freedoms by placing specific limits on government.

23 Why were the first ten amendments to the Constitution called the Bill of Rights? Each amendment guaranteed a certain right that was not specified in the Constitution. *Draw Conclusions*

✓ Ongoing Assessment

If... students are unable to draw conclusions about the Bill of Rights,	**then...** have them read the first ten amendments and ask what rights each amendment addresses.

✓ **REVIEW ANSWER** The Bill of Rights guaranteed freedoms and rights by limiting the power of the government. *Summarize*

Close and Assess

Summarize the Lesson

Create an acrostic using the word *Constitution*. Each letter should form a word, fact, or idea about the Constitution.

✓ LESSON 3 REVIEW

1. **Summarize** For possible answer, see the reduced pupil page.

2. Colonists did not want to be taxed by members of the British government for whom they never voted.

3. The Continental Congress formed the Continental Army and formed a committee to draft the Declaration of Independence.

4. This guards against any one branch being too powerful.

5. **Critical Thinking: *Make Decisions*** Answers will vary.

Link to ⚬—⚬ Art

Posters should use pertinent facts for each branch of government.

28 Overview • Establishing a Nation

The Bill of Rights

Delegates at the Constitutional Convention signed the Constitution on September 17, 1787. Next, it had to be ratified, or officially approved, by at least 9 of the 13 states. Around the country, however, some people worried that the Constitution gave the national government too much power.

To gain more support for the Constitution, leaders agreed to add a list of ten amendments, or additions, to the Constitution. These ten amendments are known as the **Bill of Rights.** The Bill of Rights guarantees freedoms by placing specific limits on government. For example, the First Amendment guarantees freedom of religion, freedom of speech, and freedom of the press.

The Bill of Rights helped convince leaders to ratify the Constitution. Nine states had ratified the Constitution by 1788. The new government of the United States of America took effect on March 4, 1789. The following year, all 13 states had ratified the Constitution.

REVIEW How did the Bill of Rights help convince many people to support the Constitution? *Summarize*

Summarize the Lesson

- **1776** The 13 Colonies declared themselves to be an independent nation.
- **1781** In the last major battle of the Revolution, the American army defeated the British at Yorktown.
- **1787** The United States Constitution was signed, forming a new government for the United States of America.

LESSON 3 REVIEW

Check Facts and Main Ideas

1. **Summarize** On a separate sheet of paper, fill in a sentence that summarizes the details given below.

In 1776 the 13 Colonies declared independence from Great Britain.	In 1781 the United States won the last major battle of the American Revolution.	By 1790 all 13 states approved the United States Constitution.

Americans gained independence from Great Britain and created the United States government.

2. Why did the **Stamp Act** and other British taxes cause conflict in the 13 Colonies?

3. Name two important decisions made by the Continental Congress in 1775 and 1776.

4. What is one benefit of dividing government into three branches?

5. **Critical Thinking: *Make Decisions*** Suppose you were helping to write the **Bill of Rights.** What are three rights you would want to include?

Link to ⚬—⚬ Art

Create a Poster Using the chart on page 27 as a guide, create a poster showing the three branches of government. Give the name and main jobs of each branch. Explain how each branch can check the powers of the others. Include any drawings or photographs you think will improve the poster.

Practice and Extend

FYI SOCIAL STUDIES **Background**

Future Amendments to the Constitution

- Future amendments to the Constitution would guarantee personal and state freedoms by placing specific limits on the central government. Because the Constitution can be changed through a legitimate constitutional amendment process, it is considered a "living document." Share with students some of the following amendments:
- 1865—Thirteenth Amendment: abolished slavery
- 1870—Fifteenth Amendment: guaranteed the right to vote regardless of race
- 1920—Nineteenth Amendment: gave women the right to vote

Workbook, p. 7

Also on Teacher Resources CD-ROM.

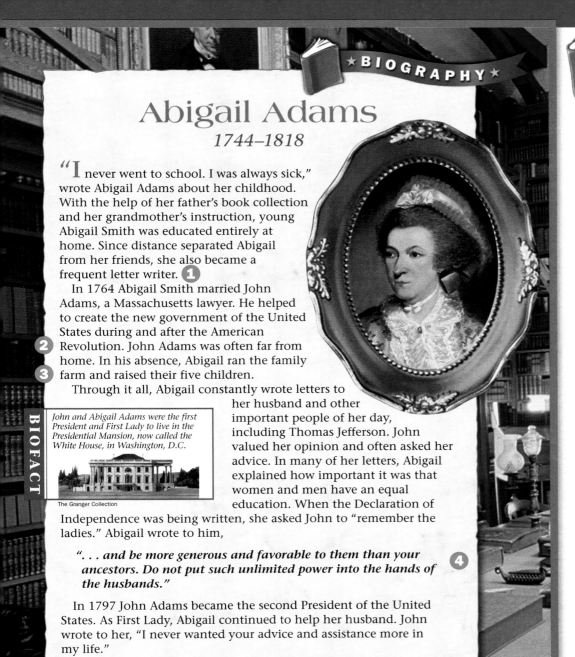

Abigail Adams
1744–1818

"I never went to school. I was always sick," wrote Abigail Adams about her childhood. With the help of her father's book collection and her grandmother's instruction, young Abigail Smith was educated entirely at home. Since distance separated Abigail from her friends, she also became a frequent letter writer. ❶

In 1764 Abigail Smith married John Adams, a Massachusetts lawyer. He helped to create the new government of the United States during and after the American ❷ Revolution. John Adams was often far from home. In his absence, Abigail ran the family ❸ farm and raised their five children.

Through it all, Abigail constantly wrote letters to her husband and other important people of her day, including Thomas Jefferson. John valued her opinion and often asked her advice. In many of her letters, Abigail explained how important it was that women and men have an equal education. When the Declaration of Independence was being written, she asked John to "remember the ladies." Abigail wrote to him,

BIOFACT
John and Abigail Adams were the first President and First Lady to live in the Presidential Mansion, now called the White House, in Washington, D.C.
The Granger Collection

"... and be more generous and favorable to them than your ancestors. Do not put such unlimited power into the hands of the husbands." ❹

In 1797 John Adams became the second President of the United States. As First Lady, Abigail continued to help her husband. John wrote to her, "I never wanted your advice and assistance more in my life."

Learn from Biographies

Why do you think it was so important to Abigail Adams that women have a better chance for education?

For more information, go to *Meet the People* at **www.sfsocialstudies.com.**

29

Abigail Adams

Objective
- Identify the personal qualities that motivated Abigail Adams to become an outspoken and educated woman.

1 Introduce and Motivate

Preview To activate prior knowledge, ask students what they learned about life in Colonial America. Tell them they will learn about how Abigail Adams advocated women's rights.

2 Teach and Discuss

❶ **Why did Abigail Adams become interested in letter writing?** She wanted to stay in touch with her friends who were far away. **Cause and Effect**

❷ **What kept Abigail and John Adams apart?** He was often away helping to build a new government. **Main Idea and Details**

❸ **In what way did Abigail Adams carry more family responsibilities?** When John Adams was away, she took care of the farm and raised their five children. **Draw Conclusions**

❹ **In the quote, what do you think Abigail Adams was telling her husband to do?** Possible answer: To be sure that women and men are given equal consideration when creating the Declaration of Independence **Analyze Primary Sources**

3 Close and Assess

Learn from Biographies Answer

Possible answer: She did not get the opportunity to attend school and wanted women and men to have equal rights.

WEB SITE
Technology

Students can learn more about Abigail Adams by clicking on *Meet the People* at **www.sfsocialstudies.com.**

SOCIAL STUDIES
Background

Abigail Adams
- Her letters have helped historians learn about United States history.
- She was a strong supporter of independence from England.
- She advocated women's rights and the abolition of slavery.

A Growing Nation

Objectives

- Describe how President Washington organized the Executive Branch around the Cabinet.

- Describe the Louisiana Purchase, and tell what effect it had on the nation.

- Explain how the Industrial Revolution changed the way goods were made.

- Analyze the development of the abolitionist movement.

Vocabulary

Cabinet, p. 31; **political party,** p. 31; **Industrial Revolution,** p. 34; **manifest destiny,** p. 35; **abolitionist,** p. 36

Resources

- Workbook, p. 8
- Transparency 7
- Every Student Learns Guide, pp. 14–17
- Quick Study, pp. 8–9

Quick Teaching Plan

If time is short, have students make a time line showing the sequence of events in the lesson.

- Ask students to read the lesson independently.

- Have students create journal entries written from the perspective of one of the people at each of the listed events.

1 Introduce and Motivate

Preview To activate prior knowledge, ask students to share their experiences of significant events in their lives. Tell them that they will learn about important changes that took place in the United States during the early 1800s.

You Are There Tell students that George Washington was sworn in as the first President of the United States on April 30, 1789. Have students describe what they might have seen and heard had they been at Washington's inauguration.

| 1775 | 1800 | 1825 | 1850 |

1789
George Washington becomes the first President of the United States.

1790
The first factory in the United States is built.

1848
The United States stretches from the Atlantic Ocean to the Pacific Ocean.

A Growing Nation

PREVIEW

Focus on the Main Idea
During the first half of the 1800s, the United States expanded west to the Pacific Ocean, and the Industrial Revolution changed the way Americans lived and worked.

PLACES
Washington, D.C.

PEOPLE
Alexander Hamilton
Meriwether Lewis
William Clark
Sacagawea
Sequoyah
James Monroe
Andrew Jackson
Samuel Slater
Frederick Douglass

VOCABULARY
Cabinet
political party
Industrial Revolution
manifest destiny
abolitionist

You Are There What's going on in New York City? The date is April 30, 1789. There are pictures of George Washington everywhere. People are wearing buttons with the initials G. W. on them. The city is so crowded with visitors, many people have been forced to stay in campgrounds.

At about noon, you follow the crowds to Federal Hall. There, up on the balcony, is George Washington. That explains what everyone is doing in New York. They are here to see George Washington sworn in as the first President of the United States.

Washington places one hand on a Bible, raises his other hand, and vows to "preserve, protect and defend the Constitution of the United States." The crowd cheers their new President, shouting "Long live George Washington!"

 Summarize As you read, look for ways to summarize important changes that took place in the United States in the early 1800s.

▶ This button was made in honor of George Washington becoming the first President of the United States. His inauguration was originally scheduled for "March the fourth," as shown on the button.

30

Practice and Extend

READING SKILL
Summarize

In the Lesson Review, students complete a graphic organizer like the one below. You may want to provide students with a copy of Transparency 7 to complete as they read the lesson.

Use Transparency 7

VOCABULARY
Word Exercise

Context Clues

Have students practice new vocabulary terms by completing sentences. Write sentence starters such as the ones below on the board and have students finish them in their own words:

- The President's **Cabinet** had a meeting to…

- She joined the **political party** because…

- He disagreed with **manifest destiny** because…

Alexander Hamilton

George Washington   Henry Knox   Thomas Jefferson

Edmund Randolph

▶ President Washington chose well-known leaders to serve in his Cabinet.

Lithograph by Currier and Ives

President Washington

In 1789 George Washington became the first President of the United States. As President, Washington began dividing the work of the Executive Branch into different departments. Conducting foreign affairs, or relations with other countries, became the job of the Department of State. Washington picked Thomas Jefferson to be secretary of state, the head of the Department of State. The job of handling money matters went to the Department of the Treasury. Washington picked Alexander Hamilton to be secretary of the treasury.

The heads of these and other departments became part of the President's Cabinet. Their job was to advise the President and help him govern.

Members of Washington's Cabinet had very different ideas on how to run the new government. Alexander Hamilton believed in a strong national government. He argued that government should be active in encouraging the growth of cities and trade. Thomas Jefferson, on the other hand, wanted the

nation to remain a land of small farmers and skilled workers. He believed that such a country would not need the strong government that Hamilton supported.

Hamilton and Jefferson each had a large following among Americans. Eventually, the two sides organized themselves into two political parties. A political party is an organized group of people who share a view of what government should do. Political parties work to elect their members to government offices.

The new government met in New York City. This was just a temporary capital for the United States. In 1790, Congress chose a site on the Potomac River for the nation's permanent capital. After Washington's death in 1799, this new city was named Washington, D.C. The letters D.C. stand for District of Columbia. The federal government moved to Washington, D.C., in 1800.

REVIEW How were Hamilton's ideas about government different from Jefferson's? Compare and Contrast

31

🕐 *Quick Summary* President Washington organized the new government by dividing the work of the Executive Branch and choosing a Cabinet to advise him. Cabinet members also organized themselves into political parties.

⭐ SOCIAL STUDIES STRAND
Citizenship

Democratic Values and Institutions
Point out that one of George Washington's major contributions as a national leader was the establishment of a Cabinet consisting of the heads of departments, e.g., the Department of State, or the Department of the Treasury.

❶ **What leadership qualities did Washington demonstrate by creating a Cabinet?** Possible answer: The ability to delegate responsibilities to advisors and recognize essential leadership qualities in others Make Inferences

Decision Making

Washington had to make important decisions when naming the members of his Cabinet. In addition to leaders such as Alexander Hamilton and Thomas Jefferson, Washington chose Henry Knox to be the secretary of war and Edmund Randolf to be the attorney general.

❷ **If you were advising President Washington, what qualities would you look for when recommending possible Cabinet members?** Possible answer: Qualities such as leadership, intelligence, diplomacy, loyalty, and honesty Make Decisions

❸ **What site was chosen as the nation's capital?** The District of Columbia Main Idea and Details

✓ REVIEW ANSWER Hamilton wanted a strong, active federal government; Jefferson wanted a less active federal government, favoring small farmers and skilled workers. Compare and Contrast

The Louisiana Purchase

Quick Summary President Jefferson purchased the Louisiana Territory from France and sent an expeditionary team to explore the West.

4 **Was the Louisiana Purchase a good deal for the United States? Explain your answer.** Possible answer: The Louisiana Purchase was a good deal, since it doubled the size of the country at a moderate cost. Evaluate

5 **Why do you think Jefferson sent a team to explore the West?** He wanted to learn about the newly acquired land. Main Idea and Details

✓ **REVIEW ANSWER** He wanted them to find out about the land and its resources and establish relationships with the Native Americans. Summarize

Map Adventure Answers

1. Missouri River

2. No. They encountered Native Americans along the way.

3. Mountains

The Louisiana Purchase

In 1801 Thomas Jefferson became the third President of the United States. One of Jefferson's most important acts was the Louisiana Purchase in 1803. For a cost of $15 million, the United States bought the vast Louisiana Territory from France. This territory stretched from the Mississippi River west to the Rocky Mountains. The Louisiana Purchase doubled the size of the United States.

Jefferson wanted to find out more about the geography, resources, and Native Americans of this newly acquired land. He chose **Meriwether Lewis,** an army captain, for the job of exploring the West. Lewis chose a fellow army captain, his friend **William Clark,** to share command of the expedition.

Lewis and Clark began their expedition in May 1804. They hired a French Canadian fur trapper and his Shoshone wife, **Sacagawea** (sah KAH gah way ah), to act as interpreters and guides. Sacagawea helped Lewis and Clark establish good relations with Native Americans along the way.

By the time the expedition ended in 1806, Lewis and Clark had explored and mapped a vast area. This helped open the West to new settlers from the United States.

REVIEW What did Jefferson want Lewis and Clark to accomplish? Summarize

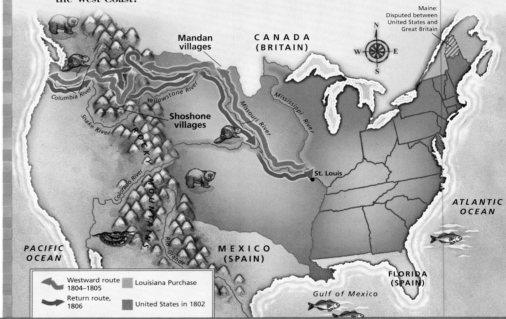

Map Adventure

Lewis and Clark

1. What river did Lewis and Clark follow at the beginning of their trip?
2. Were Lewis and Clark the first people to travel through this area? How can you tell?
3. What natural feature might have made it difficult for Lewis and Clark to reach the West Coast?

Practice and Extend

CURRICULUM CONNECTION
Literature

Learn More About Lewis and Clark

- Have students read a book about Lewis and Clark, such as **The Captain's Dog: My Journey with the Lewis and Clark Tribe,** by Roland Smith (Harcourt Brace, ISBN 0-152-02696-7, 2000).
- Students can present an oral report, video, audio recording, or storyboard that summarizes what they read.

FYI **SOCIAL STUDIES**
Background

Sacagawea

- Sacagawea's Shoshone name was *Boinaiv*. It means "grass maiden."
- The name "Sacagawea" may have been derived from the Hidatsa words for *bird* and *woman*.
- She gave birth to a baby boy, Jean-Baptiste, on February 11, 1805, and carried him on her back when the expedition set out on April 7.
- In addition to translating for the explorers, she identified plants and edible fruits and vegetables for them.
- When a boat tipped over, it was Sacagawea who saved the journals, medicines, and other valuables from being washed away.

Years of Growth and Conflict

1790

1791 New States Vermont became the fourteenth state in 1791. By 1821, the United States had grown to 24 states.

1812 War of 1812 The United States and Great Britain fought in the War of 1812. Neither side won, but the United States showed the world that it could defend itself at sea and on land.

1800

1821 Sequoyah A Cherokee named Sequoyah developed an alphabet for the Cherokee language in 1821.

1823 Monroe Doctrine President James Monroe issued the Monroe Doctrine in 1823. This statement warned European nations against interfering in the Western Hemisphere.

1810

1828 Andrew Jackson After gaining fame as a hero in the War of 1812, Andrew Jackson was elected President in 1828. The son of poor Tennessee settlers, Jackson was the first President who was not from a wealthy Virginia or Massachusetts family.

1820

1830s American Indian Removal In the 1830s, the United States government forced five major American Indian groups in the Southeast to leave their land and move to Indian Territory, in present-day Oklahoma.

1830

Peter Newark's American Pictures

6

7

33

FACT FILE
Years of Growth and Conflict

6 **How did the election of Andrew Jackson as President show that the United States was changing?** He did not come from a wealthy family from the East. Analyze Information

7 **Why do you think the United States forced American Indian groups to leave the southern states and move into Indian Territory?** White settlers wanted the land where these Native Americans lived. Make Inferences

---

![snowflake icon] **MEETING INDIVIDUAL NEEDS**
Leveled Practice

Write a Persuasive Letter Ask students to write about why American Indian groups should be allowed to stay on their lands.

Easy Ask students to describe good reasons for not forcing American Indian groups from their homes. Have different students write two or three sentences for each idea. Have students read their sentences together to form a "persuasive letter." **Reteach**

On-Level Have students write a persuasive letter with at least one paragraph that includes several details to support their argument. **Extend**

Challenge Students should write a persuasive letter to Andrew Jackson that challenges the Indian Removal Act. Ask them to try to influence the President to change his mind and allow American Indian groups to stay in their homes. **Enrich**

For a Lesson Summary, use Quick Study, p. 8.

The Industrial Revolution

Quick Summary The Industrial Revolution changed the way goods were produced and distributed.

Test Talk

Locate Key Words in the Text

⑧ What was an effect caused by the invention of machines? Tell students that the answer to this question can be found in the first paragraph. Goods could be produced faster and more cheaply. **Cause and Effect**

⑨ What led to transportation changes in the early 1800s? People needed better ways to move products and to move themselves. **Cause and Effect**

⑩ Why do you think people decided to develop railroads? They were a fast means of transportation. **Draw Conclusions**

✓ **REVIEW ANSWER** Making goods slowly by hand and with simple tools changed into making goods rapidly with machines. **Main Idea and Details**

⑪ Based on the graph, what can you conclude about cotton production in the early 1800s? It increased greatly each decade. **Analyze Information**

⑫ Between which two dates shown did cotton production increase by almost one million bales? 1840 and 1850 **Interpret Graphs**

GRAPH SKILL Answer About 650,000 bales

The Industrial Revolution

In Great Britain in the middle 1700s, the Industrial Revolution began to change the world. The **Industrial Revolution** was a change in the way goods were produced. Before the Industrial Revolution, goods were made by hand in small workshops or at home. During the Industrial Revolution, people began making goods by machine in factories. Machines helped businesses manufacture clothing and other goods ⑧ much faster and more cheaply than before.

A skilled mechanic named **Samuel Slater** helped bring the Industrial Revolution to the United States. Slater moved from Britain to Rhode Island, bringing with him his knowledge of how to build a factory. In 1790 he built the first cotton-spinning factory in the country. The New England region soon became the center of the country's new clothing industry.

The Industrial Revolution dramatically changed the way Americans lived and worked. Inventors developed new machines that could help produce goods more quickly than ever before. In 1793 Eli Whitney invented the cotton gin, which could clean 50 times as much cotton a day as could be done by hand. With more cotton available, factories could manufacture more goods, often more cheaply than before.

▶ In the 1800s, many children such as this girl worked long hours in factories.

With all of these goods being produced, people needed better ways to get their products to market. This need led to major advances in transportation. In 1807 an engineer named Robert Fulton successfully tested a riverboat powered by a steam engine. In 1830 Peter Cooper built a steam-powered locomotive. Railroads were built, and trains quickly became the easiest and cheapest way to move goods. By 1840 the United States had about 3,000 miles of railroad track.

REVIEW How did the Industrial Revolution change the way goods were produced? **Main Idea and Details**

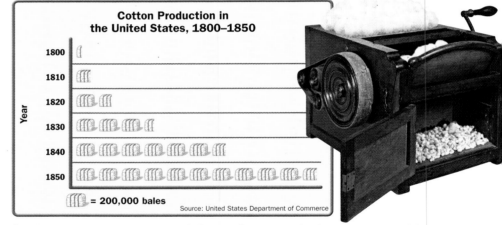

Cotton Production in the United States, 1800–1850

Year	
1800	
1810	
1820	
1830	
1840	
1850	

= 200,000 bales

Source: United States Department of Commerce

▶ Eli Whitney's cotton gin led to a rapid increase in cotton production.

GRAPH SKILL *By about how many bales did cotton production increase from 1830 to 1840?*

34

Practice and Extend

The Erie Canal

- Governor DeWitt Clinton of New York proposed building a canal from the eastern shore of Lake Erie to the upper Hudson River.
- The state legislature allowed a budget of $7 million to build a canal about 363 miles long, 40 feet wide, and 4 feet deep.
- Before the canal was built, freight rates by land from Buffalo to New York City were $100 a ton. Rates on the canal were only $10 a ton.

CURRICULUM CONNECTION **Math**

Calculate Speed

- The steamboat traveled 150 miles in 32 hours. A sailboat made the trip in four days.
- Ask: What was the steamboat's rate in miles per hour? About how many hours quicker was the trip in the steamboat? (About 4.7 miles per hour; about 64 hours quicker)

Expansion of the United States, 1783–1898

ALASKA PURCHASE 1867

CANADA

PACIFIC OCEAN

OREGON TERRITORY TREATY 1846

TREATY WITH BRITAIN 1818

TREATY WITH BRITAIN 1842

L. Superior

L. Michigan

L. Huron

L. Ontario

L. Erie

LOUISIANA PURCHASE 1803

MEXICAN WAR TREATY 1848

PACIFIC OCEAN

N

GADSDEN PURCHASE 1853

TEXAS 1845

UNITED STATES 1783

ATLANTIC OCEAN

FLORIDA 1819

HAWAII 1898

PACIFIC OCEAN

Present-day boundaries are shown.

MEXICO

Gulf of Mexico

▶ As a result of the Mexican War, the territory of the United States extended to the Pacific Ocean.

MAP SKILL Place *What was the last territory or area to become part of the United States?*

An Expanding Nation

In the 1820s settlers from the United States began moving to Texas, which was part of the country of Mexico. At the time, Mexico welcomed settlers to build towns, farms, and cattle ranches in Texas. But settlers soon clashed with the Mexican government over how Texas should be governed. The Texas Revolution began in 1835. By winning this war, Texans won independence from Mexico.

Many Texans wanted the United States to annex, or add, Texas as a new state. In the United States, supporters of annexing Texas talked about the idea of **manifest destiny.** This was the belief that the United States should expand west to the Pacific Ocean.

The United States Congress voted to make Texas a state in 1845. This quickly led to war

with Mexico, which still thought of Texas as part of Mexico's territory. The Mexican War lasted from 1846 to 1848. The United States defeated Mexico. Mexico had to give up most of its northern territory to the United States. In return, the United States paid Mexico $15 million. The map on this page shows the land that became part of the United States after the Mexican War.

The map also shows the Oregon Territory, which became part of the United States as a result of a treaty with Great Britain in 1846. Before this treaty, both the United States and Great Britain had claimed this land. The territory of the United States now stretched across the continent, from the Atlantic to the Pacific.

REVIEW What effect did the Mexican War have on the size of the United States? *Cause and Effect*

35

An Expanding Nation

Quick Summary A revolution in Texas and a war with Mexico expanded the borders of the United States.

⑬ **What caused tension between United States settlers and the Mexican government?** Disagreement about how Texas should be governed **Cause and Effect**

⑭ **Why did some Texans want Texas annexed?** They were in favor of manifest destiny and annexing would support that idea. **Draw Conclusions**

Expansion of the United States, 1783–1898

Test Talk

Locate Key Words in the Question

⑮ **What did an 1867 purchase add to the United States?** Help students recognize that the date 1867 is key information in the question. Tell students to look at the map to find out which territory was gained that year. Alaska **Interpret Maps**

MAP SKILL Answer Hawaii

✓ **REVIEW ANSWER** The United States gained most of Mexico's northern territory, which expanded its borders to the Pacific Ocean. **Cause and Effect**

SOCIAL STUDIES Background

WEB SITE Technology

Agreement with Mexico

• The treaty ending the Mexican War was named after the place where it was signed, Villa de Guadalupe Hidalgo in Mexico City.

• The agreement made the Rio Grande and the Gila River the boundary between the United States and Mexico.

• The United States received 525,000 square miles of land.

You can learn more about United States territories and the years they were acquired by clicking on *Atlas* at **www.sfsocialstudies.com.**

The Abolitionist Movement

Quick Summary Reformers in the 1830s formed a movement to abolish, or eliminate, slavery.

16 Why were some reformers called abolitionists? They believed that slavery should be abolished, meaning erased or eliminated forever. Draw Conclusions

17 What do you think made Frederick Douglass different from white abolitionists? He had been a slave and could speak about slavery from personal experience. Draw Conclusions

✓ **REVIEW ANSWER** To end slavery in the United States 🔁 Summarize

3 Close and Assess

Summarize the Lesson

Have students create Sequence Chains, including a significant event in each box.

✓ **LESSON 4   REVIEW**

1. 🔁 **Summarize** For possible answer, see the reduced pupil page.

2. It is made up of heads of departments who advise the President.

3. They explored and mapped the West.

4. People needed better ways to get their products to market.

5. **Critical Thinking:** *Compare and Contrast* 1803—the United States bought the Louisiana Territory. 1830s—settlers forced Native American groups from their land. 1840s—the United States won territory in the Mexican War.

Test Talk

Write Your Answer to Score High

Link to 🔗 Writing

Biographies should be focused and the ideas should be supported with details.

The Abolitionist Movement

As the United States gained new territory, questions about slavery began causing fierce debate. Should slavery be allowed in the new territories? Should it be abolished, or ended, everywhere in the United States?

Reformers known as abolitionists called for an end to slavery everywhere in the United States. Abolitionists attacked slavery as an evil that must be ended. Frederick Douglass, who escaped from slavery as a young man, was a powerful voice for the abolitionists. Douglass's stories of his own

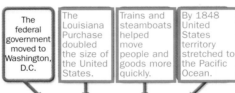

experience as a slave won many supporters for the abolitionist movement.

Questions about slavery would not be easily settled, however. As you will read in Unit 1, this issue would soon tear the country apart.

REVIEW What was the goal of the abolitionist movement? 🔁 Summarize

Summarize the Lesson

— **1789** George Washington became the first President of the United States.

— **1790** Samuel Slater helped bring the Industrial Revolution to the United States by building the nation's first factory.

— **1848** The United States stretched to the Pacific Ocean after its victory in the Mexican War.

▶ Frederick Douglass gave speeches and wrote articles and books that convinced many people to support the abolitionist movement.

LESSON 4 • REVIEW

Check Facts and Main Ideas

1. 🔁 **Summarize** On a separate sheet of paper, fill in three details that support the summary below.

The federal government moved to Washington, D.C.	The Louisiana Purchase doubled the size of the United States.	Trains and steamboats helped move people and goods more quickly.	By 1848 United States territory stretched to the Pacific Ocean.

The United States changed in important ways during the first half of the 1800s.

2. What is the President's **Cabinet**? Describe the role of the Cabinet.

3. What did Lewis and Clark accomplish?

4. How did the **Industrial Revolution** create the need for better transportation?

5. **Critical Thinking:** *Compare and Contrast* Describe the different ways the United States gained territory from 1803 to 1848.

Link to 🔗 Writing

Write a Biography Using a library or the Internet, find out more about one person from this lesson. Write a one-page biography about this person. Explain why he or she is still remembered today.

Practice and Extend

CURRICULUM CONNECTION
Music

Interpret Lyrics

• Have students use the library or online resources to research anti-slavery and abolitionist music that was created in the 1800s.

• If possible, students should locate some lyrics and interpret the meaning.

Workbook, p. 8

Lesson 4: A Growing Nation

Directions: Suppose you were going to write an article about the first years of the United States. Use the chart below to help you get started. You may use your textbook.

The First Years of the United States
WHO was the first President?
WHAT problem existed in his Cabinet?
HOW did President Jefferson help the United States grow?
WHAT was the Industrial Revolution?
WHAT was "manifest destiny"?
WHO were the abolitionists?

Notes for Home: Your child learned a brief overview of the first half-century of United States history.
Home Activity: Use library or online sources to look up more about the items presented in the Fact File on page 33.

Also on Teacher Resources CD-ROM.

Sequoyah
1770?–1843

Sequoyah was born into the Cherokee, a Native American group in which many young men grew up to be fighters. But Sequoyah's leg was injured in a hunting accident, so he became a trader and silversmith. **1** He noticed that white traders had a way to communicate with each other on paper, which many Native Americans called "talking leaves." **2** Sequoyah wanted to create a system of writing for the Cherokee. He believed it would help the Cherokee keep their history and culture.

Sequoyah worked for more than ten years on his writing system. Some people criticized him, believing his work was not worthwhile. But Sequoyah defended himself, saying,

The first Native American newspaper, the Cherokee Phoenix, *was published in 1828 using Sequoyah's writing system.*

"It is not our people that have advised me to [do] this and it is not therefore our people who can be blamed if I am wrong. What I have done I have done from myself." **3**

To create a writing system, Sequoyah created 86 symbols to represent the sounds of the Cherokee language.

After finishing his writing system in 1821, Sequoyah had to convince the major Cherokee chiefs that his writing system was useful. The chiefs asked Sequoyah to teach a group of Cherokees the system. The students were moved far from each other and given messages to write down. When each student could read the other students' notes easily, the chiefs were convinced.

Soon thousands of Cherokee learned how to write their language using Sequoyah's system. Books and newspapers were printed in the Cherokee language. Today Sequoyah is remembered for being the first person known to have created an entire written language alone. **4**

Learn from Biographies
How did not giving up help Sequoyah achieve his goal?

For more information, go to *Meet the People* at **www.sfsocialstudies.com.**

37

Sequoyah

Objective
- Identify the challenges and contributions of people, including Sequoyah, from selected American Indian groups.

1 Introduce and Motivate

Preview Ask students to share what they remember about Native American, or American Indian, groups of the Southeast from the 1820s and 1830s. Tell students they will read about the goals Sequoyah set for himself.

2 Teach and Discuss

1 How was Sequoyah's life different from most other young Cherokee men? He turned to trade and silversmith work instead of becoming a warrior. **Main Idea and Details**

2 What gave Sequoyah the idea to create a writing system? He noticed white traders communicating with each other on paper. **Draw Conclusions**

3 What does Sequoyah's statement reveal about his work? That he is the one responsible for his work because it was his idea **Analyze Primary Sources**

4 What contribution did Sequoyah make to Cherokee culture? He was solely responsible for creating a written language for the Cherokee. **Apply Information**

3 Close and Assess

Learn from Biographies Answer
He did not allow criticism to discourage his efforts.

WEB SITE
Technology

Students can learn more about Sequoyah by clicking on *Meet the People* at **www.sfsocialstudies.com.**

FYI SOCIAL STUDIES
Background

More About Sequoyah
- Sequoyah was not formally educated yet spoke several languages fluently.
- At first, Sequoyah used pictographs instead of words, but soon discovered that the number of symbols in the Cherokee language would be in the thousands.
- The written language, completed in 1821, took Sequoyah 12 years to develop.

Use Parallel Time Lines

Objective

- Use parallel time lines to see how major events in different places occurred during the same period of time.

Vocabulary

parallel time line, p. 38,
decade, p. 38,
century, p. 38

Resource

- Workbook, p. 9

1 Introduce and Motivate

What is a parallel time line? Ask students how parallel time lines help trace events happening in two places at or near the same time. Have students read the **What?** section on p. 38 to set the purpose of the lesson.

Why use parallel time lines? Have students read the **Why?** section of text on p. 38. Ask them what kind of parallel time lines they could develop.

2 Teach and Discuss

How is this skill used? Examine with students parallel time lines on pp. 38–39.

- Point out that the 13 Colonies was the area where colonists first settled. Point out that many historical events occurred in each of the New England, Middle, and Southern colonies.

- Show students that the parallel time lines are aligned for easy use. You can find an increment of 20 years and scan vertically to see what happened in each colonial region during that time.

- Have students read the **How?** section on p. 39.

Use Parallel Time Lines

1 **New England Colonies**

| 1600 | 1620 | 1640 | 1660 | 1680 | 1700 |

1620 Pilgrims arrive in Plymouth.
1630 Puritans establish Boston.
1647 Massachusetts law requires towns to build public schools.

3

Middle Colonies

| 1600 | 1620 | 1640 | 1660 | 1680 | 1700 |

1626 Dutch establish New Amsterdam.
1664 New Amsterdam becomes New York City.
1681 William Penn founds the colony of Pennsylvania.

Southern Colonies

| 1600 | 1620 | 1640 | 1660 | 1680 | 1700 |

1607 English establish settlement in Jamestown.
1619 Virginia House of Burgesses meets for the first time.
1693 The College of William and Mary opens in Virginia.

What? A time line is a diagram that shows the sequence of historical events. **Parallel time lines** are two or more time lines grouped together. They show major events in different places during the same period of time. Time lines are divided into equal spans of time such as a **decade,** 10 years, or a **century,** 100 years. The time lines above are divided into 20-year intervals.

Why? As you know from the map on page 16, the 13 English colonies were divided into three regions—the New England Colonies, the Middle Colonies, and the Southern Colonies. The parallel time lines on these pages show events that took place in each region between 1600 and 1800. By comparing parallel time lines, you can recognize patterns in the development of the different regions.

38

Practice and Extend

 **SOCIAL STUDIES**
Background

Meetings in Philadelphia

- Philadelphia was an important city during colonial times. Established in 1681, the city had a population of at least 30,000 by the 1770s, making it an important business center.

- One of Philadelphia's most famous residents was Benjamin Franklin, who was a member of the Second Continental Congress and served on the committee that assisted Thomas Jefferson in writing the Declaration of Independence. At the age of 81, Franklin was the oldest delegate to the Constitutional Convention.

- The city was chosen for the Continental Congress because of its location at the midpoint of the colonies. Philadelphia served as the capital of the United States from 1790 to 1800.

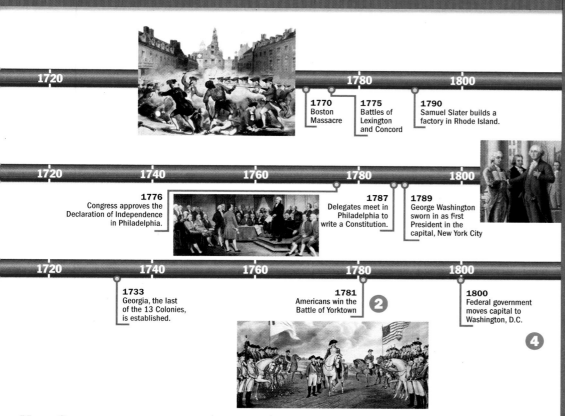

1720   1780   1800

1770
Boston Massacre

1775
Battles of Lexington and Concord

1790
Samuel Slater builds a factory in Rhode Island.

1720   1740   1760   1780   1800

1776
Congress approves the Declaration of Independence in Philadelphia.

1787
Delegates meet in Philadelphia to write a Constitution.

1789
George Washington sworn in as first President in the capital, New York City

1720   1740   1760   1780   1800

1733
Georgia, the last of the 13 Colonies, is established.

1781
Americans win the Battle of Yorktown

❷

1800
Federal government moves capital to Washington, D.C.

❹

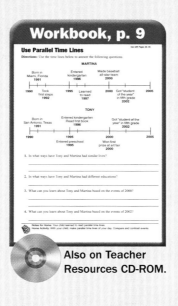

How? Look at the three parallel time lines and compare them. Although the time lines show the same period of time, different events were taking place in each region. Sometimes events that began in one region reached another region.

To use the time lines, first look at each one separately. Then compare what was taking place in two or three different regions during a particular time period. Think about how these events may have been related or may have affected other areas.

Think and Apply

❶ What event was taking place in all three regions in the 1600s?

❷ What occurred in Philadelphia in the same decade that Americans defeated the British at Yorktown?

❸ According to the time lines, which city was one of the capitals of the United States before Washington, D.C.?

39

---

❶ **How are the time lines organized?**
By colonial region **Main Idea and Details**

Test Talk

Use Information from Graphics

❷ **In which region of the colonies did the American Revolution begin? In which region did it end?** Help students recall that the Battles of Lexington and Concord started the American Revolution and the Battle of Yorktown was the final major victory. New England Colonies; Southern Colonies **Categorize**

❸ **What event occurred in Plymouth around the same time that the Virginia House of Burgesses met?** The Pilgrims arrived. **Interpret Time Lines**

❹ **Which event on the time lines is the most recent?** Federal government moves capital to Washington, D.C. **Sequence**

3 Close and Assess

Think and Apply

1. Colonies were being founded in all three regions.

2. Delegates met in Philadelphia to write a constitution.

3. New York City

Workbook, p. 9

Use Parallel Time Lines
Directions: Use the time lines below to answer the following questions.

MARTINA

Born in Miami, Florida
1991

Entered kindergarten
1996

Made baseball all-star team
2000

1990   Took first steps **1992**   1995   Learned to read **1997**   2000   Got "student of the year" in fifth grade **2002**   2005

TONY

Born in San Antonio, Texas
1991

Entered kindergarten Read first book
1996

Got "student of the year" in fifth grade
2002

1990   Entered preschool **1995**   2000   Won first prize at art fair **2000**   2005

1. In what ways have Tony and Martina had similar lives?

2. In what ways have Tony and Martina had different educations?

3. What can you learn about Tony and Martina based on the events of 2000?

4. What can you learn about Tony and Martina based on the events of 2002?

Also on Teacher Resources CD-ROM.

Respecting the Flag

Objectives

- Discover the history behind the U.S. national anthem.

- Describe accomplishments of significant colonial figures, such as Francis Scott Key.

1 Introduce and Motivate

Preview To activate prior knowledge, ask students on what occasion the lyrics to "The Star-Spangled Banner" were written and by whom.

Ask students what a "star-spangled banner" refers to. (The American flag, which seems to shine with stars)

2 Teach and Discuss

1 How did Francis Scott Key become trapped on a British ship? He was sent to rescue his friend William Beanes, who was taken prisoner. **Cause and Effect**

2 What observation confirmed that Fort McHenry did not fall? At dawn the American flag was still flying. **Main Idea and Details**

3 What inspired Francis Scott Key to write "The Star Spangled Banner"? He was overjoyed to see the waving flag. **Make Inferences**

Respecting the Flag

▶ **Francis Scott Key witnessed the British attack on Fort McHenry.**

You know that it is important to show respect for our country's flag. For example, when the flag passes in a parade, you stand and place your right hand over your heart. When people show respect for a flag, it is because they want to show respect for the ideals it represents. For Francis Scott Key, the United States flag represented hope and freedom in a moment of crisis. The flag even inspired him to write what became our country's national anthem— "The Star-Spangled Banner."

In 1812 Great Britain was fighting a war against France. The crews of British ships often stopped American ships, forcing the men on board to fight for Britain against their will. Soon the United States was fighting the British in what was sometimes called a "second war for independence"—the War of 1812. In August 1814, the British invaded Washington, D.C., and set fire to the White House and the Capitol.

At this time, Francis Scott Key was a lawyer working near Washington, D.C. His friend William Beanes was taken prisoner by the British after they left Washington. In September United States military leaders sent Key to try to persuade the British to release Beanes, who was held on a ship in Chesapeake Bay near Baltimore, Maryland. The British agreed to release Key's friend. However, they were about to attack Fort McHenry in Baltimore and did not want Key or Beanes to warn the Americans. Key and Beanes were forced to wait aboard a ship. On September 13, the British began firing on Fort McHenry. When the fighting finally stopped, it was too dark for Key to see what had happened to the fort. He waited anxiously for the sun to rise. In the morning, he saw the American flag flying over Fort McHenry. It was torn but still waving. The fort had not been captured.

▶ **Francis Scott Key**

Practice and Extend

FYI SOCIAL STUDIES
Background

"The Star-Spangled Banner"

- The words were first published in 1814 in a broadside titled "Defence of Fort M'Henry."

- The title was changed to "The Star-Spangled Banner" in 1814 when it appeared as sheet music.

- The song was officially adopted as the U.S. national anthem in 1931 by an act of Congress.

AUDIO CD
Technology

Play the CD *Songs and Music* to listen to "The Star-Spangled Banner."

BUILDING CITIZENSHIP
Caring
Respect
Responsibility
Fairness
Honesty
Courage

Key was overjoyed to see the flag. He was immediately inspired ③ to write a poem about the event. The first part of his poem says,

> Oh, say can you see, by the dawn's early light,
> What so proudly we hailed at the twilight's
>   last gleaming?
> Whose broad stripes and bright stars, ⑤
>   through the perilous fight,
> O'er the ramparts we watched, were so
>   gallantly streaming?
> And the rockets' red glare, the bombs
>   bursting in air,
> Gave proof through the night that our
>   flag was still there.
> Oh say, does that star-spangled banner ⑥
>   yet wave
> O'er the land of the free and the home of
>   the brave?

▶ The original flag that flew over Fort McHenry is located at the National Museum of American History of the Smithsonian Institution in Washington, D.C.

Within a week, the poem, first called "The Defense of Fort McHenry," was published in a Baltimore newspaper. Soon other newspapers all over the country also published the poem. Set to a popular tune of the time, Key's song became known as "The Star-Spangled Banner." Congress officially adopted the song as the national anthem in 1931. Today the very flag that ⑦ inspired Key to write the anthem is on display at the Smithsonian Institution in Washington, D.C.

Respect in Action

When "The Star-Spangled Banner" is sung at a sports game or other event, people stand and men remove their hats. Why do you think this is the custom? In what other ways can you show respect for our country?

41

④ **What words suggest that these events took place in the morning?** "by the dawn's early light" **Draw Conclusions**

⑤ **How did Francis Scott Key describe the American flag in his poem?** Possible answer: The star-spangled banner, with its broad stripes and bright stars, withstood the rockets and bombs going off around it. **Analyze Primary Sources**

⑥ **What do you think Key meant by the words "O say, does that star-spangled banner yet wave o'er the land of the free and the home of the brave?"** Possible answer: He's asking if the flag is still waving over the free country of the United States **Analyze Primary Sources**

⑦ **Why do you think this song was chosen as the U.S. national anthem?** Possible answer: It points out the determination of the United States to fight for and retain its freedom and independence. **Draw Conclusions**

Close and Assess

Respect in Action

- Encourage students to share their opinions.

- Have students identify other ways in which people show respect for the United States.

CURRICULUM CONNECTION
Music

Write an Anthem

Have students work in small groups to write a class, school, or community anthem.

- Students can first choose a familiar tune they will use for their anthem.
- Students should then work together to write the words and perform their anthems for the class.
- Make sure that students show proper respect for their class, school, and community as they compose and perform their anthems.

Resources
- Assessment Book, pp. 1–4
- Workbook, p. 10–11: Vocabulary Review

Main Ideas and Vocabulary — TEST PREP

1. c, **2.** a, **3.** d, **4.** d

Test Talk

Locate Key Words in the Question
Use Main Ideas and Vocabulary, Questions 1 and 4, to model the Test Talk strategy.

Find the key words in the question.
Have students ask themselves, "*Who* or *what* is this question about?" The words that tell who or what the question is about are the key words.

Turn the question into a statement.
Students should use the key words in a sentence that begins, "I need to find out...."

People and Vocabulary
1. e, **2.** d, **3.** f, **4.** a, **5.** c, **6.** b

Apply Skills
- Ensure that students have kept information on the two time lines separate.
- Encourage students to observe any patterns in the events recorded on the two time lines.

Test Talk
Look for key words in the question.

Main Ideas and Vocabulary — TEST PREP

Read the passage below and use it to answer the questions that follow.

During the Ice Age, about 40,000 to 10,000 years ago, people from Asia began moving to North America over a land bridge. After the Ice Age, different cultures developed among Native American groups.

In 1492 Christopher Columbus sailed to an island off the coast of North America. Soon, Spain, England, France, Sweden, and the Netherlands began establishing colonies in North and South America. By 1733 Great Britain had 13 colonies in North America. When the French and Indian War ended in 1763, Britain gained more land from France.

During the American Revolution, from 1775 to 1781, Americans living in the 13 Colonies fought against Great Britain to gain independence. After the Americans won the war, delegates met in Philadelphia to write a constitution for the new United States of America. They formed a government based on three branches of government.

In the early years of the nation, the Industrial Revolution dramatically changed the way Americans lived. New forms of transportation made travel easier and provided cheaper and faster ways to move goods to markets.

The issue of slavery soon divided the country. Abolitionists wanted it ended everywhere in the United States. Slavery became the central issue in the nation.

1 According to this passage, what was the effect of the French and Indian War?
  A Christopher Columbus was allowed to travel to North America.
  B The American colonists gained independence.
  C Britain gained land from France.
  D Spain acquired more colonies.

2 In the passage, the term Ice Age means—
  A a period of colder climate than today
  B a settlement
  C a period of warmer climate than today
  D a period of storms

3 In the passage, the word constitution means—
  A a book
  B a to-do list
  C a declaration of war
  D a written plan of government

4 Which sentence is true?
  A The French and Indian War came after the American Revolution.
  B Columbus landed in North America after the American Revolution.
  C Columbus arrived in North America before the Ice Age.
  D The French and Indian War came before the American Revolution.

42

Practice and Extend

Assessment Options

✓ **Overview Assessment**
- Overview Content test: Use Assessment Book, pp. 1–2.
- Overview Skills Test: Use Assessment Book, pp. 3–4.

Standardized Test Prep
- Overview Tests contain standardized test format.

✓ **Overview Performance Assessment**
- See p. 44 for information about using the Overview Project as a means of Performance Assessment.
- A scoring guide for the Overview Project is provided in the teacher's notes on p. 44.

Test Talk
- Test Talk Practice Book

WEB SITE Technology

For more information, you can select the dictionary or encyclopedia from *Social Studies Library* at **www.sfsocialstudies.com.**

People and Vocabulary

Match each person and term to its definition.

1. **migrate** (p. 7)
2. **Pocahontas** (p. 14)
3. **Thomas Jefferson** (p. 24)
4. **republic** (p. 26)
5. **manifest destiny** (p. 35)
6. **Frederick Douglass** (p. 36)

a. government in which people elect representatives

b. leader in the abolitionist movement

c. belief that the United States should expand west to the Pacific Ocean

d. brought peace between the English and the Powhatan with marriage

e. to move

f. wrote the Declaration of Independence

Apply Skills

Create Parallel Time Lines Make a time line listing major events from your life in the order they occurred. Then ask a friend or family member about major events in his or her life and when they occurred. Make another time line for this person's events. Draw pictures illustrating events in both time lines. Do any events on the time lines match? What are some differences?

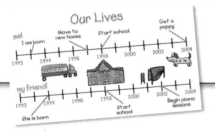

Write and Share

Present an Interview With the help of a classmate, choose one key person from this unit. Write a list of questions you would ask if that person were alive today. Conduct research in the library to answer as many of your questions as you can. Finally, share your findings with the class in the form of an interview. One of you will be the key person and the other will be the interviewer.

Read on Your Own

Look for books like these in the library.

43

Revisit the Unit Question

✓ Portfolio Assessment

- Have students look at the lists they created throughout the Overview about the reasons people celebrate their independence.
- For each idea that students in the class generated, have students write a sentence that explains or describes that idea.
- Have students add these lists and sentences to their Social Studies Portfolio.

Workbook, p. 10

Vocabulary Review

Directions: Use the vocabulary words from the Overview to complete each item. Use the numbered letters to answer the clue that follows.

1. A change in the way goods were produced
2. The movement of people, animals, plants, and ways of life between Europe and the Americas
3. An early British tax on printed goods
4. Thick sheets of ice
5. A system in which people elect representatives to make laws and run the government
6. A system to keep branches of government from gaining too much power
7. An organized group of people who share a common view of what government should do
8. A long period of cold temperatures
9. A person who called for the end of slavery everywhere in the United States
10. The belief that the United States should expand west to the Pacific Ocean
11. To move
12. A system for producing and distributing goods and services
13. A material found in nature that people can use

Also on Teacher Resources CD-ROM.

Write and Share

- Encourage student pairs to select different individuals from others in the class.
- Have students switch roles midway through the interview to give each a chance at asking and answering the questions.
- Use the following scoring guide.

✓ Assessment Scoring Guide

Present an Interview	
6	Major accomplishments and characteristics revealed with complete, accurate, and detailed examples.
5	Major accomplishments and characteristics revealed with mostly complete, accurate, and detailed examples.
4	Interview helps reveal major accomplishments and characteristics. Information is mostly accurate, complete, and somewhat detailed.
3	Interview partially reveals major accomplishments and characteristics. Information is somewhat accurate, complete, and detailed.
2	Interview partially reveals major accomplishments and characteristics. Information is often inaccurate, incomplete, and lacking in detail.
1	Interview fails to reveal major accomplishments and characteristics. Information is inaccurate, incomplete, and lacking in detail.

If you prefer a 4-point rubric, adjust accordingly.

Read on Your Own

Have students prepare oral reports using the following books.

Our Strange New Land: Elizabeth's Diary, Jamestown, Virginia, 1609, by Patricia Hermes (Scholastic Press, ISBN 0-439-11208-7, 2000) **Easy**

How We Crossed the West: The Adventures of Lewis & Clark, by Rosalyn Schanzer (National Geographic Society, ISBN 0-792-26726-5, 2002) **On-Level**

The Declaration of Independence: The Words that Made America, by Sam Fink (text by Thomas Jefferson) (Scholastic Reference, ISBN 0-439-40700-1, 2002) **Challenge**

This Just In

Objective
- Report news in American history.

Resource
- Workbook, p. 12

Materials
paper, pencils, paints, markers, reference materials

Follow This Procedure
- Tell students that they will hold a press conference about an important event in American history. They will describe an event they learned about in this unit. They will need to conduct research about important details of the event.

- Divide students into groups. Students need to choose roles to play in a press conference. Possible roles include government officials or experts, news reporters, and eyewitnesses.

- Instruct students to make a poster that a TV news station might use to announce important news.

- Invite students to present their posters and conduct their press conferences for the class.

- Use the following scoring guide.

✓ Assessment Scoring Guide

This Just In	
6	Clearly describes the event. Includes accurate information about many details.
5	Clearly describes the event. Includes accurate information about several details.
4	Describes the event, including mostly accurate information about one or two details.
3	Describes the event, including some inaccurate information about one or two details.
2	Describes the event using some inaccurate information and no details.
1	Poorly describes the event using inaccurate information and no details.

If you prefer a 4-point rubric, adjust accordingly.

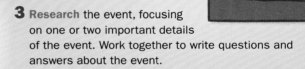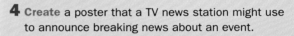

This Just In

Report breaking news in American history.

1 Choose an important event that you have learned about American history.

2 Choose roles to play for a press conference about the event: government officials or experts, news reporters, eyewitnesses, and other participants.

3 Research the event, focusing on one or two important details of the event. Work together to write questions and answers about the event.

4 Create a poster that a TV news station might use to announce breaking news about an event.

5 Hold your press conference as a class activity.

Internet Activity
Find out more about history in North America. Go to **www.sfsocialstudies.com/activities** and select your grade and unit.

44

Practice and Extend

Hands-on Unit Project

✓ Performance Assessment
- The Unit Project can also be used as a performance assessment activity.
- Use the scoring guide to assess each group's work.

WEB SITE
Technology

Students can launch the Internet Activity by clicking on *Grade 5, Overview* at **www.sfsocialstudies.com/activities**.

Workbook, p. 12

Overview Project This Just In
Report breaking news in American history. In a group, choose an important event that you have learned about in American history. Then report the event in a press conference.

1. The event that we chose is _____
2. My role in the press conference is (✔) one:
   ___ news reporter   ___ expert
   ___ government official   ___ other: _____
3. Here are some details about the event.
   What happened: _____
   Where and when the event took place: _____
   Who was involved: _____
   Effects or importance of the event: _____
4. Here are some questions and answers that we will ask and answer in our news conference.
   News Reporter: _____
   Expert: _____
   News Reporter: _____
   Other: _____

✔ Checklist for Students
   ___ We chose an event in America's history.
   ___ We found information about the event.
   ___ We answered questions about the event.
   ___ We made a poster about the event to use in our press conference.
   ___ We presented our press conference to the class.

Notes for Home: Your child learned how to report important details of an event in a press conference.
Home Activity: Watch a news program with your child. Discuss what important facts are reported about each event, and why the events might be important to the region where the events occurred.

Also on Teacher Resources CD-ROM.

★ Unit 1 ★

Vocabulary Routines

The following examples of reading and vocabulary development strategies can be used to instruct students about unit vocabulary.

BEFORE READING

Context Clues

Sentence Completions One way to reinforce word meanings is to provide students with sentences and have them fill in the blanks with words from a word bank. Sentences that are rich in context will assist students in making correct choices when filling in the blanks. Select vocabulary words from a lesson or chapter and write them on the board in a word bank. Next to the bank, write sentences containing blanks that can be filled by the words in the word bank. The following example uses words from Chapter 2, Lesson 4.

Read the words in the word bank. Think about what each one might mean. Then use the words to complete the sentences. Remember to look for context clues to confirm your choices.

assassination	segregation	sharecropping

- *Because he was ___, the farmer had to give some of his potatoes and wheat to the landowner.* (sharecropping)

- *After the ___, the country was without a leader.* (assassination)

- *___ kept some people separate from other people.* (segregation)

DURING READING

Individual Word Study

Have You Ever . . . Having students use newly learned words to describe their own experiences or thoughts will help them understand that there is a place for these new terms in their own vocabulary. The model below draws on content from Chapter 1, Lesson 3.

*Think about the word **compromise**. A compromise is the settlement of a disagreement in which both sides agree to give up part of what is wanted. Have you ever had to make a compromise with a friend or family member when you were having a disagreement? Have you ever read a book or seen a movie where two of the characters had to make a big compromise? Think of a sentence that describes one of these situations. Use the word **compromise** in your sentence.*

AFTER READING

Related Word Study

Word Relationships Recognizing the relationships between different words will help students figure out and retain word meaning as well as organize information. Asking students what other terms come to mind when they are presented with a word will help them make the connections necessary to either determine or recall the meaning. Content-area word mapping can be achieved through the use of graphic organizers such as the one shown below.

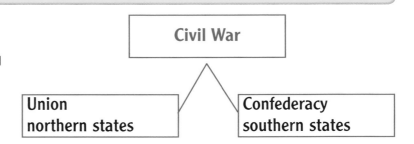

You can use a chart like the one shown to guide students in recognizing word relationships. Fill in one or two of the boxes. Tell students to think about what the word (or words) bring to mind. Students should then be able to complete the chart.

Teaching with Leveled Readers

This series of readers focuses on the brave female heroes of the Civil War.

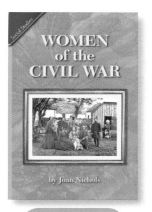

Below Level

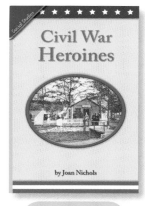

On Level

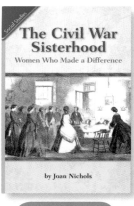

Above Level

LEVELED READER VOCABULARY ACTIVITY

- Before reading, have students preview the vocabulary words.

- After reading, have students create word jumbles for the vocabulary words. Students should write clues for the jumbled words using the definitions.

- Have students share their jumbles with a partner.

r g e i e m n t

regiment

CONNECTIONS TO THE LESSON

Chapter 2, Lesson 2: Life During the War

CONNECTIONS TO TODAY

- Have students read the lesson. Then provide the leveled readers to enhance students' understanding of how the courage of the women of the Civil War era impacted our country.

- **Points for Discussion:**
    1. Have students discuss the difficulties and challenges of women in the 1800s. How have things changed since then?
    2. Students can also discuss ways in which they can overcome challenges in their lives.

War Divides the Nation

UNIT 1

Unit Planning Guide

Unit 1 • War Divides the Nation

Begin with a Primary Source pp. 46–47

Meet the People pp. 48–49

 Reading Social Studies, Main Idea and Details pp. 50–51

Chapter Titles	Pacing	Main Ideas
Chapter 1 **A Divided Nation** pp. 52–77 ✓ **Chapter 1 Review** pp. 78–79	7 days	• Differences between North and South led to growing tensions between the two regions. • Enslaved African Americans resisted slavery in many different ways. • Despite attempts to compromise, the struggle over slavery threatened to tear the United States apart. • Eventually 11 Southern states seceded from the United States, leading to the outbreak of the Civil War.
Chapter 2 **War and Reconstruction** pp. 80–111 ✓ **Chapter 2 Review** pp. 112–113	9 days	• In the early years of the Civil War, the North and South formed strategies in hopes of gaining a quick victory. • As the Civil War continued, people in the North and the South suffered many hardships, including the growing loss of life. • A series of Northern victories led to the end of the Civil War by 1865. • The country faced many difficult challenges after the Civil War ended, including rebuilding the South and protecting the rights of newly freed African Americans.

End with a Song pp. 114–115

✓ **Unit 1 Review** pp. 116–117

✓ **Unit 1 Project** p. 118

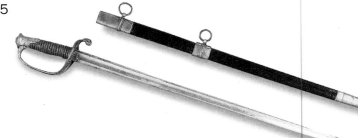

 **✓ = Assessment Options**

This newspaper shares an opinion about the Fugitive Slave Law.

Resources	Meeting Individual Needs
• Workbook, pp. 13–19	• ESL Support, TE pp. 55, 61, 67, 76
• Every Student Learns Guide, pp. 18–33	• Leveled Practice, TE pp. 55, 64, 69, 72
• Transparencies 1, 2, 4, 50, 51, 52, 53	• Learning Styles, TE pp. 63, 70
• Quick Study, pp. 10–17	
• Workbook, p. 20	
✓ Chapter 1 Content Test, Assessment Book, pp. 5–6	✓ Chapter 1 Performance Assessment, TE p. 78
✓ Chapter 1 Skills Test, Assessment Book, pp. 7–8	

• Workbook, pp. 21–26	• Leveled Practice, TE pp. 83, 89, 97, 102, 108
• Every Student Learns Guide, pp. 34–39	• ESL Support, TE pp. 84, 92, 101, 109
• Transparencies 1, 54, 55	• Learning Styles, TE p. 98
• Quick Study, pp. 18–25	
• Workbook, p. 27	
✓ Chapter 2 Content Test, Assessment Book, pp. 9–10	✓ Chapter 2 Performance Assessment, TE p. 112
✓ Chapter 2 Skills Test, Assessment Book, pp. 11–12	

This Confederate sword was used in the Battle of Gettysburg.

Providing More Depth

Additional Resources

- Trade Books
- Family Activities
- Vocabulary Workbook and Cards
- Social Studies Plus! pp. 20–43
- Daily Activity Bank
- Read Alouds and Primary Sources
- Big Book Atlas   • Student Atlas
- Outline Maps   • Desk Maps

Technology

- AudioText
- Video Field Trips
- Songs and Music
- Digital Learning CD-ROM Powered by KnowledgeBox (Video clips and activities)
- MindPoint® Quiz Show CD-ROM
- ExamView® Test Bank CD-ROM
- Colonial Williamsburg Primary Sources CD-ROM
- Teacher Resources CD-ROM
- Map Resources CD-ROM
- SF SuccessNet: iText (Pupil Edition online), iTE (Teacher's Edition online), Online Planner
- **www.sfsocialstudies.com** (Biographies, news, references, maps, and activities)

⚠ *To establish guidelines for your students' safe and responsible use of the Internet, use the Scott Foresman Internet Guide.*

Additional Internet Links

To find out more about:

- the Civil War, visit **www.gliah.uh.edu**
- Clara Barton, visit **www.greatwomen.org**
- abolitionists, visit **www.pbs.org**

Unit 1 Objectives

Beginning of Unit 1

- Use primary sources to acquire information. (p. 46)
- Identify the contributions of significant individuals during the time leading up to and including the U.S. Civil War. (p. 48)
- Analyze information by using supporting details to determine the main idea. (p. 50)

Chapter 1

Lesson 1 North and South Grow Apart pp. 54–57

- Describe the differences between the economies and populations of the North and South.
- Identify the role that slavery played in the South in the mid-1800s.
- Explain how and why views about slavery differed in the North and South.
- Identify facts and opinions in writing. (p. 58)
- Consider the experiences of an individual writer and how those experiences may have shaped the writer's ideas. (p. 58)
- Describe a writer's point of view. (p. 58)

Lesson 2 Resisting Slavery pp. 60–64

- Identify ways African Americans resisted slavery.
- Describe rebellions of African Americans against slavery.
- Explain how the Underground Railroad was used to free enslaved people.
- Describe the lives of free African Americans in the North and South.
- Identify the personal qualities that motivated Harriet Tubman to take risks in helping African Americans escape to freedom. (p. 65)

Lesson 3 The Struggle Over Slavery pp. 66–72

- Describe the causes and effects of the Missouri Compromise and the Compromise of 1850.
- Explain the causes of violence in Kansas in 1854.
- Draw conclusions about how Dred Scott and John Brown affected the split between the North and South.
- Compare the views on slavery of Abraham Lincoln and Stephen Douglas.
- Identify early influences in Abraham Lincoln's life that shaped his character and his deep feelings of patriotism. (p. 73)

Lesson 4 The First Shots Are Fired pp. 74–77

- Describe the reasons why Southern states seceded from the Union.
- Identify the immediate cause of the start of the Civil War.
- Describe the goals the North and South hoped to achieve by fighting the Civil War.

Chapter 2

Lesson 1 The Early Stages of the War pp. 82–86

- Identify the resources of the North and South.
- Compare the strategies of the North and South in the Civil War.
- Describe early battles in the Civil War.
- Explain how new military technology affected the way the war was fought.
- Identify the accomplishments of notable individuals, such as Robert E. Lee. (p. 87)

Lesson 2 Life During the War pp. 88–93

- Compare and contrast life for Northern and Southern soldiers.
- Analyze the effect of the Emancipation Proclamation on African Americans.
- Describe the contributions of African American soldiers to the Union war effort.
- Identify the different ways women contributed to the war effort in the North and South.
- Identify the accomplishments of notable individuals, such as Jody Williams. (p. 94)

Lesson 3 How the North Won pp. 96–101

- Describe the events of the Battle of Gettysburg.
- Analyze President Lincoln's Civil War goals as expressed in the Gettysburg Address.
- Identify the locations and results of the major battles of the Civil War.
- Explain the reasons for the use of total war and its consequences.
- Apply geographic skills to interpret legends and symbols on maps. (p. 102)
- Identify and explain different forms of communication during the Civil War. (p. 104)

Lesson 4 The End of Slavery pp. 106–111

- Explain why Congress disagreed with Johnson's plan for Reconstruction.
- Analyze the effect of the Reconstruction Acts.
- Evaluate the impact of the Thirteenth, Fourteenth, and Fifteenth Amendments.
- Describe life for African Americans after Reconstruction.

End of Unit 1

- Identify significant examples of music from various periods in U.S. history. (p. 114)
- Describe events and people's experiences during the Civil War and Reconstruction. (p. 118)

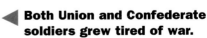

Both Union and Confederate soldiers grew tired of war.

Assessment Options

✓ Formal Assessment

- **Lesson Reviews,** PE/TE pp. 57, 64, 72, 77, 86, 93, 101, 111
- **Chapter Reviews,** PE/TE pp. 78–79, 112–113
- **Chapter Tests,** Assessment Book, pp. 5–12
- **Unit Review,** PE/TE pp. 116–117
- **Unit Tests,** Assessment Book, pp. 13–16
- **ExamView® Test Bank CD-ROM** (test-generator software)

✓ Informal Assessment

- **Teacher's Edition Questions,** throughout Lessons and Features
- **Section Reviews,** PE/TE pp. 55–57, 61–64, 67–72, 75–77, 83–86, 89–92, 97–100, 107, 111
- **Close and Assess,** TE pp. 51, 57, 59–65, 72–73, 77, 86, 87, 93, 95, 101, 103, 105, 111, 115

Ongoing Assessment

Ongoing Assessment is found throughout the Teacher's Edition lessons using an **If...then** model.

If = students' observable behavior, **then** = reteaching and enrichment suggestions

✓ Portfolio Assessment

- **Portfolio Assessment,** TE pp. 45, 46, 117
- **Leveled Practice,** TE pp. 57, 64, 69, 72, 83, 89, 97, 102, 108
- **Workbook Pages,** pp. 13–28
- **Chapter Review: Write About History,** PE/TE pp. 79, 113
- **Unit Review: Apply Skills,** PE/TE p. 117
- **Curriculum Connection: Writing,** PE/TE pp. 72, 93, 111; TE pp. 47, 58, 62, 64, 65, 83, 89, 95, 99, 108

✓ Performance Assessment

- **Hands-on Unit Project** (Unit 7 Performance Assessment), TE pp. 45, 79, 113, 118
- **Internet Activity,** PE p. 118
- **Chapter 1 Performance Assessment,** TE p. 78
- **Chapter 2 Performance Assessment,** TE p. 112
- **Unit Review: Write and Share,** PE/TE p. 117
- **Scoring Guides,** TE pp. 117–118

Test Talk

Test-Taking Strategies

Understand the Question
- **Locate Key Words in the Question,** PE/TE p. 116; TE p. 85
- **Locate Key Words in the Text,** TE p. 90

Understand the Answer
- **Choose the Right Answer,** Test Talk Practice Book
- **Use Information from the Text,** TE p. 70
- **Use Information from Graphics,** TE p. 103
- **Write Your Answer to Score High,** TE p. 79

For additional practice, use the Test Talk Practice Book.

Featured Strategy

Locate Key Words in the Question

Students will:

- Find the key words in the question.
- Turn the key words into a statement that begins "I need to find out. . . ."

PE/TE p. 116, **TE** p. 85

Curriculum Connections

Integrating Your Day

The lessons, skills, and features of Unit 1 provide many opportunities to make connections between social studies and other areas of the elementary curriculum.

Social Studies

READING

Reading Skill—Main Idea and Details, TE pp. 50–51, 54, 60, 66, 82, 88, 96, 106

Lesson Review—Main Idea and Details, TE pp. 57, 64, 72, 86, 93, 101, 111

WRITING

Write a Speech, TE p. 47

Write an Editorial, TE p. 58

Create an Argument, TE p. 62

Write an Article, TE pp. 64, 108

Write Speeches, TE p. 65

Link to Writing, PE/TE pp. 72, 93, 111

Write a Summary, TE p. 83

Write a Letter, TE p. 89

Write an E-mail, TE p. 95

Write a Diary Entry, TE p. 99

Write a Short Story or Poem, TE p. 111

MATH

Disease Statistics, TE p. 86

Link to Mathematics, PE/TE pp. 86, 101

Calculate Totals, TE p. 91

Number Match, TE p. 97

LITERATURE

Read Biographies, TE pp. 48, 73

Read Books About Slavery, TE p. 59

SCIENCE

Link to Science, PE/TE p. 64

MUSIC / DRAMA

"When Johnny Comes Marching Home," PE/TE p. 114

Write a New Verse, TE p. 115

ART

Interpret Fine Art, TE p. 46

Link to Art, PE/TE p. 57

Create an Illustration, TE p. 58

Design Promotional Materials, TE p. 62

 Look for this symbol throughout the Teacher's Edition to find **Curriculum Connections.**

Professional Development

Making Social Studies Exciting

by Fred Risinger, Ph.D.
Indiana University

Elementary social studies is an essential subject. Understanding our society, its history and pluralistic culture, and the skills and processes of participatory citizenship are all taught through the social studies curriculum.

One need not choose between a teaching method that favors systematic information processing instructional strategies and a teaching method that involves a problem-solving, student-centered, project-oriented approach. Effective teaching uses elements of both methodologies.

One thing is certain—the most important person in the instructional process is you, the classroom teacher. When asked to name a best or favorite teacher, more students named a social studies teacher than any other. What does this say? I think it says that social studies—the dramatic, tragic, and uplifting story of men and women on this planet—is the most exciting part of the school curriculum. As a classroom teacher, you have the obligation, and the great opportunity, to bring that story to your students. Below are several ways the Scott Foresman program makes social studies come alive.

- *On p. 56 of the Teacher's Edition, students are told to suppose they are a plantation owner who does not believe in slavery. Students use a problem-solving process to decide how they would harvest their cotton before their crops are ruined.*

- *Students examine pictures on p. 80 of the Pupil's Edition that are springboards for discussion about important historical events.*

- *On p. 87 of the Teacher's Edition, students use a decision-making process to decide whether they should advise Robert E. Lee to accept or to reject the position as commander of the Virginia armed forces.*

ESL Support

by Jim Cummins, Ph.D.
University of Toronto

In Unit 1, you can use the following fundamental strategy to help ESL students access social studies content:

Access Content

Language is central to the teaching of virtually every school subject. When students learn social studies, they are learning a set of concepts related to the ways in which people have organized their communities and societies both historically and currently.

Social studies has its own specialized vocabulary that students must acquire if they are to be successful in learning the content. Examples of such vocabulary include *constitution, preamble, convention,* and many other words rarely heard on the playground.

Similarly, what linguists call *nominalization* is very common in the social studies text. Nominalization refers to the creation of abstract nouns from verbs and adjectives. These nouns, such as *immigrate/immigration* and *represent/representation,* express concepts that can be related to each other.

The following examples in the Teacher's Edition will help ESL students better understand the content of the unit:

- ***Examine Word Meaning*** *on p. 61 helps English Language Learners explore the meaning of the word resist. Advanced learners are led to understand that another form of resist is resistance. Students then discuss the word's meaning.*

- ***Demonstrate Concept Understanding*** *on p. 84 provides opportunities for students to show that they know the meaning of the word retreat.*

Read Aloud

from Abraham Lincoln's first inaugural address:

We are not enemies, but friends. We must not be enemies. Though passion may have strained it must not break our bonds of affection. The mystic chords of memory, stretching from every battlefield and patriot grave to every living heart and hearthstone all over this broad land, will yet swell the chorus of the Union, when again touched, as surely they will be, by the better angels of our nature.

Build Background

- These words are from President Abraham Lincoln's first inaugural address, which he delivered on Monday, March 4, 1861.
- Two weeks before Lincoln's inauguration, many of the states in the Southern part of the United States had left the Union to form a confederacy, or association, of states. Jefferson Davis was its president.
- In his speech, Lincoln addressed the importance of uniting the country. The American Civil War had not yet begun.

Definitions

- *passion:* violent anger or rage
- *affection:* friendship or warmth

Read Alouds and Primary Sources

- *Read Alouds and Primary Sources* contains additional selections to be used with Unit 1.

Bibliography

A Freedom River, by Doreen Rappaport (Hyperion Books for Children, ISBN 0-786-80350-9, 2000) **Easy** **Coretta Scott King Honor Book**

Harriet and the Promised Land, by Jacob Lawrence (Aladdin Paperbacks, ISBN 0-689-80965-4, 1997) **Easy** **New York Times Best Illustrated Book**

Voice of Freedom: A Story About Frederick Douglass, by Maryann N. Weidt (Lerner Publishing Group, ISBN 1-575-05553-8, 2001) **Easy**

Lincoln: A Photobiography, by Russell Freedman (Houghton Mifflin Company, ISBN 0-899-19380-3, 1987) **On-Level** **Newbery Medal**

Steal Away, by Jennifer Armstrong (Scholastic Paperbacks, ISBN 0-590-46921-5, 1993) **On-Level** **ALA Notable Book**

The World in the Time of Abraham Lincoln, by Fiona MacDonald (Chelsea House Publishing, ISBN 0-791-06028-4, 2000) **On-Level**

Anthony Burns: The Defeat and Triumph of a Fugitive Slave, by Virginia Hamilton (Laureleaf, ISBN 0-679-83997-6, 1993) **Challenge** **ALA Notable Book, Boston Globe Horn Book Award, Jane Addams Book Award**

Dear Ellen Bee: A Civil War Scrapbook of Two Union Spies, by Mary E. Lyons and Muriel M. Branch (Atheneum, ISBN 0-689-82379-7, 2000) **Challenge**

House of Dies Drear, by Virginia Hamilton (Aladdin Paperbacks, ISBN 0-020-43520-7, 1984) **Challenge** **Edgar Allan Poe Juvenile Book**

Battle Cry of Freedom: The Civil War Era, by James M. McPherson (Oxford University Press, 0-19-516895-X, 1989) **Teacher reference**

With Malice Toward None: A Life of Abraham Lincoln, by Stephen B. Oates (Harperperennial Library, ISBN 0-060-92471-3, 1994) **Teacher reference**

Discovery Channel School Video Slave Ship Uncover the shocking facts about the transatlantic slave trade as African slaves take over the slave ship *Amistad.* (Item #716787, 52 minutes)

- To order *Discovery Channel School* videos, please call the following toll-free number: 1-888-892-3484
- Free online lesson plans are available at **DiscoverySchool.com.**

Look for this symbol throughout the Teacher's Edition to find **Award-Winning Selections.** Additional book references are suggested throughout this unit.

War Divides the Nation

What might cause a nation to break apart?

45

War Divides the Nation

Unit Overview

Friction between the Northern and Southern states developed as the two regions differed more and more in their viewpoints on crucial issues. Conflicts between the regions resulted in the secession of the Southern states and, eventually, the U.S. Civil War.

Unit Outline

Chapter 1 *A Divided Nation*
pp. 52–79

Chapter 2 *War and Reconstruction*
pp. 80–113

Unit Question

- Have students read the question under the painting.

- To activate prior knowledge, ask students if they know of, or have heard of, nations that have collapsed or divided. What caused those problems? What kinds of differences of opinion or policy could lead to friction between different parts of a nation?

- Create a list of students' ideas about why nations may break apart. Encourage students to include factors they have heard or read about as well as additional factors that they think could contribute.

✓ **Portfolio Assessment** Keep this list to review with students at the end of the unit on p. 117.

Practice and Extend

Hands-on Unit Project

✓ **Unit 1 Performance Assessment**

- The Unit Project, *History Speaks,* found on p. 118, is an ongoing performance assessment project to enrich students' learning throughout the unit.

- This project, which has students prepare a talk about life during the Civil War and Reconstruction, may be started now or at any time during this unit of study.

- A performance assessment scoring guide is located on p. 118.

UNIT 1

Begin with a Primary Source

Objective

- Use primary sources to acquire information.

Resource

- Poster 2

Interpret a Primary Source

- Tell students that this quotation is from the Gettysburg Address, which Lincoln gave at the dedication of the National Cemetery at this Civil War battlefield.

- The main speaker was Edward Everett, and he spoke for two hours. He later acknowledged that Lincoln's short address was brilliant.

- The full text of Lincoln's address is on p. 98.

- ✓**Portfolio Assessment** Remind students of their lists of reasons that a nation might break apart. Have students continue their lists, adding the reasons that the United States began to break apart in the 1850s (see p. 45). As they read the unit, allow time for students to review and add to the list. Review students' lists at the end of the unit on p. 118.

Interpret Fine Art

- This picture shows the fall of Richmond, Virginia, and was printed by Currier and Ives in 1865. It shows Richmond, Virginia, which was the capital of the Confederate States of America.

- Spark discussion on the point of view of this piece. Do students think it was created by someone who was neutral about the outcome of the war?

- Have students discuss what this picture reveals about the costs of the Civil War to "ordinary" citizens.

46 Unit 1 • War Divides the Nation

UNIT 1

Begin with a Primary Source

1820		1850	1860		
1820 Congress passes Missouri Compromise.		**1849** Harriet Tubman escapes slavery on the Underground Railroad.	**1860** Abraham Lincoln is elected President.	**April 1861** Southern forces fire on Fort Sumter, beginning the Civil War.	**January 1863** Emancipation Proclamation takes effect.

46

Practice and Extend

FYI **SOCIAL STUDIES**
Background

About the Primary Source

- Many students will recognize the first words of the Gettysburg Address: *Four score and seven years ago our fathers brought forth on this continent a new nation . . . .* The phrase on p. 47 comes from the last sentence of the speech.

- Although Lincoln's speech was far shorter than that of the main speaker at the National Cemetery dedication and was criticized by many of his opponents, his oration was quoted and praised by many.

- The Battle of Gettysburg, a defeat for Southern forces, took place from July 1 to 3, 1863. The losses in the battle were among the worst of the entire Civil War—more than 43,000 men were killed, wounded, missing, or captured.

- In 1895 the battlefield became a national military park.

> *"...that these dead shall not have died in vain— that this nation, under God, shall have a new birth of freedom..."*
>
> —Said by President Abraham Lincoln in the Gettysburg Address, November 19, 1863

This print by Currier and Ives shows the Fall of Richmond, Virginia, to Union forces in 1865.

1870

July 1863
Battle of Gettysburg is fought.

April 1865
Confederacy surrenders, ending the Civil War. **1**

December 1865
The 13th Amendment ends slavery. **2**

March 1867
Congress passes the first Reconstruction Act. **3**

47

Meet the Artist

- Nathaniel Currier and James Merritt Ives used lithography, a method of printing, to make black-and-white prints, which were then hand colored.

- Known as Currier and Ives from 1857, the company produced more than 7,500 different titles and a total of more than a million copies of these prints.

- Currier and Ives described themselves as "Publishers of Cheap and Popular Pictures."

- The lithographs were very popular. They helped people understand current events.

- Many Currier and Ives works showed daily life in the United States—scenes of family life, or of people at work or play. Today, these lithographs serve as a valuable record of what people's lives were like in an age before photography was widely available.

Use the Time Line

The time line at the bottom of the page covers a time period of nearly fifty years, starting with the Missouri Compromise and ending with the passage of the Reconstruction Act.

1 **How long did the Civil War last?** About four years Interpret Time Lines

2 **About how many years after Harriet Tubman's escape from slavery were all enslaved people legally freed by the 13th Amendment?** 16 years Analyze Information

3 **Which event happened in March of 1867?** Congress passed the Reconstruction Act. Interpret Time Lines

CURRICULUM CONNECTION
Writing

Write a Speech

Have students suppose they have been asked to give speeches at the opening ceremonies for the national park at the site of the Battle of Gettysburg. Provide ideas such as the following to spark students' thinking about speech topics:

- Tell why it is important to remember the sacrifices that were made during the Battle of Gettysburg. Explain why the National Park Service decided to honor those who had fought there.
- Create a short "Hall of Fame" presentation about a person who was important during the time of the U.S. Civil War.
- Read Lincoln's Gettysburg Address. In your speech, explain Lincoln's thoughts in your own words and tell why you agree or disagree with his ideas.

Consider having students write and read their speeches with partners in preparation for presenting their work to the class.

Meet the People

Objective
• Identify the contributions of significant individuals during the time leading up to and including the U.S. Civil War.

Resource
• Poster 4

Research the People

Each of the people pictured on these pages played an important role in the history of the United States between 1820 and 1867. Have students conduct research to find out the answers to the following questions.

• **What was surprising about Ulysses S. Grant's decision to attend the U.S. Military Academy?** Possible answer: He was not interested in the military, and many thought he was too "sloppy" to be a soldier.

• **What office did Henry Clay run for unsuccessfully?** He ran for President twice.

• **Describe some of the jobs that Clara Barton held.** She was a teacher, and she worked in the U.S. Patent Office.

• **What jobs did Harriet Tubman hold after escaping from slavery?** Scout, spy, nurse, laundress, and founder of home for elderly people and orphans

Students may wish to write their own questions about other people on these pages for the rest of the class to answer.

Use the Time Line

Have students use the time line and biographies to answer the following questions.

❶ Which person died before the Civil War began? Henry Clay
Analyze Information

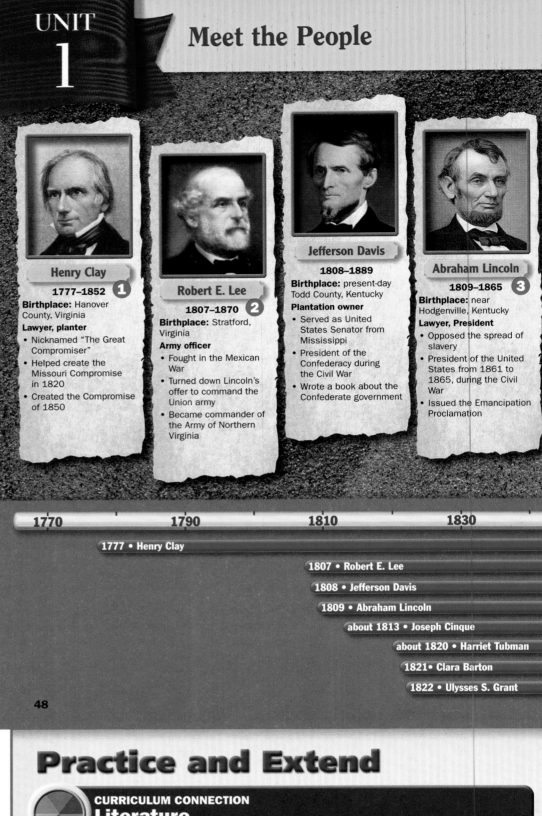

Meet the People

Henry Clay
1777–1852 ❶
Birthplace: Hanover County, Virginia
Lawyer, planter
• Nicknamed "The Great Compromiser"
• Helped create the Missouri Compromise in 1820
• Created the Compromise of 1850

Robert E. Lee
1807–1870 ❷
Birthplace: Stratford, Virginia
Army officer
• Fought in the Mexican War
• Turned down Lincoln's offer to command the Union army
• Became commander of the Army of Northern Virginia

Jefferson Davis
1808–1889
Birthplace: present-day Todd County, Kentucky
Plantation owner
• Served as United States Senator from Mississippi
• President of the Confederacy during the Civil War
• Wrote a book about the Confederate government

Abraham Lincoln
1809–1865 ❸
Birthplace: near Hodgenville, Kentucky
Lawyer, President
• Opposed the spread of slavery
• President of the United States from 1861 to 1865, during the Civil War
• Issued the Emancipation Proclamation

1770   1790   1810   1830

1777 • Henry Clay
1807 • Robert E. Lee
1808 • Jefferson Davis
1809 • Abraham Lincoln
about 1813 • Joseph Cinque
about 1820 • Harriet Tubman
1821• Clara Barton
1822 • Ulysses S. Grant

48

Practice and Extend

CURRICULUM CONNECTION
Literature

Read Biographies
Use the following biography selections to extend the content.

Robert E. Lee, Brave Leader, by Rae Bains (Troll Associates, ISBN 0-816-70546-1, 1989) **Easy**

Harriet Tubman: Conductor on the Underground Railroad, by Ann Petry (Harper Trophy, ISBN 0-064-46181-5, 1996) **On-Level**

Clara Barton: Civil War Nurse, by Nancy Whitelaw (Enslow Publishers, ISBN 0-894-90778-6, 1997) **Challenge**

For more information, go online to *Meet the People* at **www.sfsocialstudies.com**.

Joseph Cinque
about 1813–about 1879 ❹

Birthplace: present-day Sierra Leone, West Africa

Rice farmer, leader of slave ship rebellion

- African name was Sengbe Pieh, which was pronounced by the Spanish as "Cinque"
- Led African captives in a revolt aboard the slave ship *Amistad*
- Served as key witness during the *Amistad* trial

Harriet Tubman
about 1820–1913 ❸ ❺

Birthplace: Dorchester County, Maryland

Conductor on the Underground Railroad, abolitionist

- Escaped from slavery in 1849 and settled in Philadelphia
- Made 19 trips to the South on the Underground Railroad and helped free more than 300 slaves
- Spoke out against slavery and for women's rights

Clara Barton
1821–1912 ❺

Birthplace: Oxford, Massachusetts

Teacher, nurse

- Volunteered as a nurse during the Civil War
- Nicknamed the "Angel of the Battlefield"
- Founded the American Red Cross

Ulysses S. Grant
1822–1885 ❷

Birthplace: Point Pleasant, Ohio

Army officer, President

- Won the first major Union victory of the Civil War at Fort Donelson
- Appointed to command the Union armies by President Lincoln
- Elected President of the United States in 1868

1850 | 1870 | 1890 | 1910

1852
1870
1889
1865
about 1879
1913
1912
1885

49

❷ **How were Robert E. Lee and Ulysses S. Grant similar?** Both were offered the opportunity to command the Union Army by Abraham Lincoln. **Compare and Contrast**

❸ **Which person had the longest life? the shortest life?** Longest: Harriet Tubman; Shortest: Abraham Lincoln **Analyze Information**

❹ **Why do you think that the date of death for Joseph Cinque is "about 1879"?** People are not sure of the exact date of his death; there may not have been records kept of his death. **Analyze Information**

❺ **Which people were alive during the twentieth century?** Harriet Tubman and Clara Barton **Interpret Time Lines**

Biographies

Three of the people shown here are discussed more extensively in the Biography pages in Unit 1.

Read About the People

The people shown here are discussed in the text on the following pages in Unit 1.

WEB SITE
Technology

Students can research the lives of people on this page by clicking on *Meet the People* at **www.sfsocialstudies.com**.

Reading Social Studies

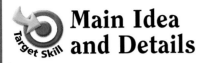
Main Idea and Details

Objective

Analyze information by using supporting details to determine the main idea.

Resource

• Workbook, p. 13

About the Unit Target Skill

• The target reading skill for this unit is Main Idea and Details.
• Students are introduced to the unit target skill here and are given an opportunity to practice it.
• Further opportunities to determine main ideas and details are found throughout Unit 1.

1 Introduce and Motivate

Preview Show students a short article from a newspaper and point out the headline. Ask students what the headline of the article does (tells what the article is about). Link the headline to the concept of main idea. The headline tells what the article is about, or gives the most important idea; and the article gives details that support that idea.

2 Teach and Discuss

• Explain that a main idea is the most important idea of a paragraph. Details are pieces of information related to the main idea. Each detail supports, or tells more about, the main idea.

• Have students read the paragraph on p. 50. Make sure they realize that the highlighting shows the main idea and the details that support the main idea. Each detail tells how the United States was growing and changing.

War Divides the Nation

Main Idea and Details

Look at the diagram to see how details support a main idea. A main idea is the most important idea of a paragraph. Details are information related to the main idea. Each detail helps support the main idea.

Main Idea
Detail	Detail	Detail

Read the following paragraph. The **main idea** and **details** have been highlighted.

In the 1800s the United States was growing and changing. The development of roads, waterways, and railroads allowed people to move west. The nation's land was expanding. The way people lived was also changing. In some places, cities were growing and attracting factory workers. In other parts of the country, people were still living on farms but changing the way they harvested their crops.

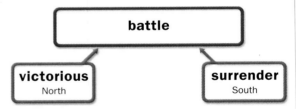

Word Exercise **Word Relationships** One way to understand a word's meaning better and remember what you read is to look for word relationships. Seeing how key words and ideas from the reading are related can help you figure out a word's meaning and organize information.

battle

victorious	**surrender**
North	South

50

Practice and Extend

ACCESS CONTENT
ESL Support

Determine Main Ideas Guide students to understand how to determine the main idea of a paragraph.

Beginning Write a short paragraph on the board that consists of a main idea and several details. Read the first sentence aloud. As you underline this sentence, explain that it is the main idea. Then ask students to circle details.

Intermediate Make copies of a simple paragraph with a main idea sentence and several sentences with details. Cut each paragraph into sentence strips and give groups the strips for one paragraph. Have students put the sentences into an order that makes sense and identify the main idea.

Advanced Cut several paragraphs out of magazine or newspaper articles and distribute them to students. Students can work in pairs to underline the main idea and then use a colored pen to highlight supporting details.

Main Ideas and Details of War Divides a Nation

Differences between the Northern and Southern states led to many problems for the United States. The rural South depended on farming and slavery. The North had more factories and larger cities than the South.

Trouble grew when Abraham Lincoln became President in 1861. South Carolina broke away from the Union. Before long, eleven states in the South had done the same and formed the Confederate States of America. The country was divided and went to war. This war was called the Civil War.

Each side won some battles. In late 1863 Northern victories increased. In 1865 the North was victorious and the South surrendered.

Lincoln hoped to reunite the nation, but he was killed shortly after the Civil War. President Andrew Johnson and

Congress fought over Reconstruction, or the plans for rebuilding the South. Amendments to the Constitution ended slavery and gave the vote to all male citizens, black and white.

Federal troops and Reconstruction laws governed Southern states. The Freedmen's Bureau, a federal agency, provided aid and set up schools for African Americans.

When Reconstruction ended in 1877, some Southerners tried to keep freed slaves from voting. A few people used violence to stop black men who tried to vote. Southern states also passed Jim Crow laws, which said African Americans could not use the same areas as whites in restaurants, trains, buses, hotels, and other public places.

Use the reading strategy of main idea and details to answer these questions.

1 What is the main idea of the first paragraph?

2 What details support that main idea?

3 How are these words from the selection related: *farming, cities, rural, factories?*

51

Workbook, p. 13

Main Idea and Details
Directions: Fill in the circle next to the correct answer.

- Then have students read the longer practice sample on p. 51 and answer the questions that follow.

- Ask students why, when studying history, it is important to know how to figure out the main idea and identify details. (To understand history we need to figure out the most important ideas. Locating supporting details shows us whether or not our main ideas are accurate.)

Words Relationships  Word Exercise

Make sure students relate *farming* with *rural* and *factories* with *cities.* They can organize these four words under a top box with the heading "Ways of Life." Then write the following terms on the board: *Reconstruction, amendments, after Reconstruction,* and *Jim Crow laws.* Ask students how to organize these words and phrases. Help them see that a top box could be headed "Life in the South." Two boxes can come down from the top box for *Reconstruction* and *after Reconstruction.* Then a box for *amendments* can attach to the *Reconstruction* box, and one for *Jim Crow laws* can attach to the *after Reconstruction* box. Finally, have students attach boxes with details to the *amendments* and *Jim Crow laws* boxes, such as "ended slavery" for the first and "said African Americans could not use the same areas as whites" in the second.

3 Close and Assess

Apply it!

1. Differences between the North and South led to many problems for the United States.

2. The South was rural and depended on farming and slavery, while the North had more factories and larger cities than the South.

3. Possible answer: **Farming** is very common in **rural** areas. **Factories** were usually found in **cities.**

Chapter Planning Guide

Chapter 1 • A Divided Nation

Locating Time and Place pp. 52–53

Lesson Titles	Pacing	Main Ideas
Lesson 1 **North and South Grow Apart** pp. 54–57	2 days	• Differences between North and South led to growing tensions between the two regions.
Thinking Skills: **Recognize Point of View** pp. 58–59		• Paying careful attention to descriptions and details can help you determine an author's point of view.
Lesson 2 **Resisting Slavery** pp. 60–64	2 days	• Enslaved African Americans resisted slavery in many different ways.
Biography: Harriet Tubman p. 65		• Harriet Tubman's courage helped her lead African Americans from slavery to freedom.
Lesson 3 **The Struggle Over Slavery** pp. 66–72	2 days	• Despite attempts to compromise, the struggle over slavery threatened to tear the United States apart.
Biography: Abraham Lincoln p. 73		• Reading about George Washington and Benjamin Franklin helped Abraham Lincoln develop his deep regard for the United States.
Lesson 4 **The First Shots Are Fired** pp. 74–77	1 day	• Eventually 11 Southern states seceded from the United States, leading to the outbreak of the Civil War.

Chapter 1 Review
pp. 78–79

◀ **On April 12, 1861, Southern troops fired on Fort Sumter.**

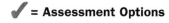

✓ **= Assessment Options**

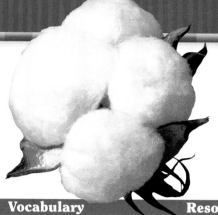

◀ Cotton, an important Southern crop, was usually grown on large plantations.

Vocabulary	Resources	Meeting Individual Needs
sectionalism point of view	• Workbook, p. 15 • Transparency 4 • Every Student Learns Guide, pp. 18–21 • Quick Study, pp. 10–11 • Workbook, p. 16	• ESL Support, TE p. 55 • Leveled Practice, TE p. 57
slave codes Underground Railroad	• Workbook, p. 17 • Transparencies 2, 50 • Every Student Learns Guide, pp. 22–25 • Quick Study, pp. 12–13	• ESL Support, TE p. 61 • Learning Styles, TE p. 63 • Leveled Practice, TE p. 64
free state slave state states' rights Missouri Compromise Fugitive Slave Law Compromise of 1850 Kansas-Nebraska Law	• Workbook, p. 18 • Transparencies 2, 51, 52 • Every Student Learns Guide, pp. 26–29 • Quick Study, pp. 14–15	• ESL Support, TE p. 67 • Leveled Practice, TE pp. 69, 72 • Learning Styles, TE p. 70
secede Confederacy Union border state civil war	• Workbook, p. 19 • Transparencies 1, 53 • Every Student Learns Guide, pp. 30–33 • Quick Study, pp. 16–17	• Leveled Practice, TE p. 76 • ESL Support, TE p. 77
	✓ Chapter 1 Content Test, Assessment Book, pp. 5–6 ✓ Chapter 1 Skills Test, Assessment Book, pp. 7–8	✓ Chapter 1 Performance Assessment, TE p. 78

Providing More Depth

Additional Resources
- Vocabulary Workbook and Cards
- Social Studies Plus! pp. 32–37
- Daily Activity Bank
- Big Book Atlas
- Student Atlas
- Outline Maps
- Desk Maps

 Technology

- AudioText
- MindPoint® Quiz Show CD-ROM
- ExamView® Test Bank CD-ROM
- Teacher Resources CD-ROM
- Map Resources CD-ROM
- SFSuccessNet: iText (Pupil Edition online), iTE (Teacher's Edition online), Online Planner
- **www.sfsocialstudies.com** (Biographies, news, references, maps, and activities)

 To establish guidelines for your students' safe and responsible use of the Internet, use the Scott Foresman Internet Guide.

Additional Internet Links

To find out more about:
- Abraham Lincoln, visit **www.whitehouse.gov**
- Underground Railroad, visit **www.undergroundrailroad. org**
- Frederick Douglass, visit **www.frederickdouglass. org**

Key Internet Search Terms
- Abraham Lincoln
- Civil War
- Underground Railroad
- Harriet Tubman

Workbook Support

Use the following Workbook pages to support content and skills development as you teach Chapter 1. You can also view and print Workbook pages from the Teacher Resources CD-ROM.

Workbook, p. 13

Main Idea and Details
Use with Pages 50–51.

Directions: Fill in the circle next to the correct answer.

Many people believe slavery in the United States ended with the Emancipation Proclamation. This idea is not completely accurate. The Emancipation Proclamation did outlaw slavery, but slavery continued in some areas.

Only certain people were declared free by the Emancipation Proclamation. Those people were slaves who lived in Confederate states that were fighting against the Union. Slaves who lived in border states that were fighting for the Union were not granted freedom by the

proclamation. Also unaffected were those slaves living in Southern areas already under Union control.

Although the Emancipation Proclamation granted legal freedom to slaves living in Confederate states that were fighting against the Union, those states did not recognize Lincoln's laws. Therefore, the slaves saw no change.

All slavery in the United States officially ended in December of 1865 with the passage of the Thirteenth Amendment to the Constitution.

1. How did the Emancipation Proclamation affect slavery?
   - Ⓐ It freed all slaves in all states.
   - Ⓑ It freed slaves in Union territory.
   - ● It freed slaves in some states, but not in others.
   - Ⓓ It did not free slaves.

2. Which slaves were NOT declared free by the Emancipation Proclamation?
   - Ⓐ slaves who wanted to fight for the Union
   - Ⓑ only African American women and children
   - ● those in border states and areas under Union control
   - Ⓓ only male slaves in border states

3. Why did slavery continue in Confederate states fighting against the Union?
   - ● Those states did not recognize Lincoln's laws.
   - Ⓑ The Union allowed it.
   - Ⓒ The Thirteenth Amendment had not been passed.
   - Ⓓ Those slaves did not want to move to the North.

4. What officially ended all slavery in the United States?
   - Ⓐ the Emancipation Proclamation
   - ● the passage of the Thirteenth Amendment to the Constitution
   - Ⓒ the Civil War
   - Ⓓ the Confederate states

 Notes for Home: Your child learned about identifying the main idea and details of a passage.
Home Activity: With your child, choose a magazine or newspaper article of interest and work together to identify the article's main idea and details.

Use with Pupil Edition, p. 51

Workbook, p. 14

Vocabulary Preview
Use with Chapter 1.

Directions: Match each vocabulary word to its meaning. Write the vocabulary word on the line provided. Not all words will be used. You may use your glossary.

sectionalism	states' rights	secede
slave codes	Missouri Compromise	Confederacy
Underground Railroad	Fugitive Slave Law	Union
free state	Compromise of 1850	border state
slave state	Kansas-Nebraska Act	civil war

1. **secede** — to break away from
2. **border state** — state located between the Union and the Confederacy
3. **Compromise of 1850** — plan in which California entered the United States as a free state and the Fugitive Slave Law was passed
4. **Union** — states that remained loyal to the United States government
5. **free state** — state in which slavery was not allowed
6. **Fugitive Slave Law** — law which stated that escaped slaves had to be returned to their owners, even if they had reached Northern states where slavery was not allowed
7. **Kansas-Nebraska Act** — law allowing the people of Kansas and Nebraska to decide whether they would allow slavery in their territory
8. **Underground Railroad** — organized, secret system set up to help enslaved people escape from the South to freedom in the North or Canada
9. **sectionalism** — loyalty to a section or part of the country rather than to the whole country
10. **slave codes** — laws to control the behavior of slaves
11. **Confederacy** — government formed by the seven seceding states, also known as the Confederate States of America
12. **slave state** — state in which slavery was legally allowed

 Notes for Home: Your child learned the vocabulary terms for Chapter 1.
Home Activity: Help your child learn the vocabulary terms by having him or her form comparisons between pairs of terms, such as free state and slave state, Union and Confederacy, and so on.

Use with Pupil Edition, p. 52

Workbook, p. 15

Lesson 1: North and South Grow Apart
Use with Pages 54–57.

Directions: Complete the compare-and-contrast table using information from Lesson 1. You may use your textbook.

Topic	In the North	In the South	Similar or Different?
The way of life in 1850	Most people still lived on farms, but more began working in factories and living in large towns and cities.	People lived a mostly rural way of life. People mostly lived and worked on farms and in small towns.	different
Point of view on tariffs on imported goods	They wanted higher tariffs on imported goods to increase U.S. companies' sales.	They wanted lower tariffs on imported goods to reduce the cost of buying those goods.	different
Point of view on the buying and selling of manufactured goods	They wanted to sell their goods to Americans.	They preferred to buy cheaper goods made in Great Britain.	different
Point of view on slavery	Most states outlawed slavery.	Slavery was profitable, so most states allowed it.	different

 Notes for Home: Your child learned about the different views of the North and the South during the mid-1800s.
Home Activity: With your child, discuss instances when your child's opinion or point of view might differ from that of a friend. Brainstorm positive ways to resolve or live with these differences.

Use with Pupil Edition, p. 57

Workbook, p. 16

Recognize Point of View
Use with Pages 58–59.

Point of view is the way a person looks at or thinks about a topic or situation and describes it. A person's point of view may be affected by his or her experiences and way of life.

Directions: Read the following poem. It was written by a Southern woman during the time when the South had to produce its own goods because it was blockaded by the North. Answer the questions that follow.

> My homespun dress is plain, I know;
>   My hat's palmetto, too.
> But then it shows what Southern girls
>   For Southern rights will do.
> We send the bravest of our land
>   To battle with the foe,
> And we will lend a helping hand
>   We love the South, you know.
> Hurrah! Hurrah!
>   For the sunny South so dear.
> Three cheers for the homespun dress
>   That Southern ladies wear.

1. What is the topic of the poem?
   The ladies of the South will sacrifice to help Southern soldiers.

2. What words does the writer use to show how she feels about Southern soldiers?
   The bravest of our land

3. What words does the writer use to show how she feels about the South?
   We love the South; the sunny South so dear

4. How do you think the writer feels about supporting the South in the war? How do you know?
   Possible answer: The writer is proud to support the South. Her homespun dress, although plain, shows that the South can survive on its own, without luxuries from Europe. This feeling is evident when the writer says "Three cheers for the homespun dress that Southern ladies wear."

Notes for Home: Your child learned to identify the writer's point of view.
Home Activity: With your child, discuss a family situation or a situation at school in which two people had different points of view. Help your child recognize that different points of view can come from different goals or experiences.

Use with Pupil Edition, p. 59

Workbook Support

Workbook, p. 17

Lesson 2: Resisting Slavery
Use with Pages 60–64.

Directions: Categorize each term in the box by writing it in the column of the correct category below. You may use your textbook.

performed acts of cruelty	pretended to be sick
broke the tools they used	separated family members
learned to read	enforced slave codes
required permission to leave plantation	formed the Underground Railroad
used physical punishment	worked slowly

Methods of Controlling Slaves	Ways Slaves Resisted
performed acts of cruelty	**broke the tools they used**
required permission to leave plantation	**learned to read**
used physical punishment	**pretended to be sick**
separated family members	**formed the Underground Railroad**
enforced slave codes	**worked slowly**

Directions: Write the missing cause or effect on the line provided. You may use your textbook.

1. **Cause:** Slaves suffered cruel, harsh treatment.
   Effect: **Slaves resisted.**

2. **Cause:** **Slaves led rebellions.**
   Effect: Slave owners tried to prevent slaves from gathering and meeting with one another.

3. **Cause:** Captive Africans aboard the Spanish vessel *Amistad* seized the ship and ended up in the United States.
   Effect: **The Supreme Court decided their fate and released them. All of the survivors returned to Africa that year.**

 Notes for Home: Your child learned how slaves reacted to the treatment they received.
Home Activity: With your child, discuss how he or she feels when treated unfairly. Relate this feeling to how the slaves reacted when they were treated harshly and unfairly.

Use with Pupil Edition, p. 64

Workbook, p. 18

Lesson 3: The Struggle Over Slavery
Use with Pages 66–72.

Directions: Match each item in the first column to its clue or description in the second column. Write the number of the item on the line before its description.

1. Missouri Compromise
2. Fugitive Slave Law
3. Compromise of 1850
4. Kansas-Nebraska Act
5. *Uncle Tom's Cabin*
6. Dred Scott decision
7. John Brown's plan
8. Abraham Lincoln
9. Stephen Douglas

6 The Supreme Court ruled that slaves were not citizens of the United States and had no rights.

5 This book described the cruelties of slavery and won over many people to the abolitionist cause.

4 The people of each territory were allowed to decide whether it should be free or slave.

8 "If slavery is not wrong, then nothing is wrong. . . . [But I] would not do anything to bring about a war between the free and slave states."

2 Escaped slaves had to be returned to their owners, even if they had reached Northern states where slavery was not allowed.

7 A plan to attack pro-slavery people with weapons from the arsenal at Harpers Ferry further divided the North and the South in 1859.

1 The number of slave states and free states was kept balanced when Missouri was allowed into the Union as a slave state and Maine as a free state.

9 "Each state . . . has a right to do as it pleases on . . . . slavery."

3 California became a free state, and the Fugitive Slave Law was passed.

 Notes for Home: Your child learned about struggles over slavery that threatened to tear the United States apart.
Home Activity: With your child, choose a current controversial issue from the newspaper. Discuss citizens' opposing views and the divisions that can develop.

Use with Pupil Edition, p. 72

Workbook, p. 19

Lesson 4: The First Shots Are Fired
Use with Pages 74–77.

Directions: Sequence the events in the order in which they occurred by numbering them from 1 to 8. You may use your textbook.

7 Lincoln asks Union states for troops to put down the Confederate rebellion.

1 Abraham Lincoln is elected President of the United States.

8 Some states are angered by Lincoln's call for troops. Virginia, Arkansas, Tennessee, and North Carolina secede and join the Confederacy.

3 The Confederate States of America, or the Confederacy, is formed.

6 The Confederates attack Fort Sumter, which is surrendered two days later. The Civil War has started.

5 Jefferson Davis, president of the Confederacy, asks for the surrender of Union-held Fort Sumter in Charleston, South Carolina.

2 The Southern states of South Carolina, Alabama, Florida, Mississippi, Georgia, Louisiana, and Texas secede.

4 By Lincoln's inauguration on March 4, 1861, the Confederacy has control of most of the forts and military property in the South.

Directions: Explain each of the following points of view from the time of the American Civil War. You may use your textbook.

1. Explain the goal Lincoln and his supporters hoped to achieve by fighting the Civil War.
   Possible answer: Lincoln and his supporters wanted to preserve the Union.

2. Explain the goal Southerners hoped to achieve by fighting the Civil War.
   Southerners wanted to preserve states' rights and slavery.

3. Why do you think Northerners called Southerners "rebels"?
   Possible answer: Northerners thought the Southerners were rebelling against the established order of government and trying to get their own way.

 Notes for Home: Your child learned how to determine the sequence of events for the beginning of the Civil War.
Home Activity: With your child, look over a previous lesson. Ask your child to tell the sequence of events in that lesson.

Use with Pupil Edition, p. 77

Workbook, p. 20

Vocabulary Review
Use with Chapter 1.

Directions: Choose the vocabulary word from the box that best completes each sentence. Write the word on the line provided. Not all words will be used.

sectionalism	states' rights	secede
slave codes	Missouri Compromise	Confederacy
Underground Railroad	Fugitive Slave Law	Union
free state	Compromise of 1850	border state
slave state	Kansas-Nebraska Act	civil war

1. The **Union** was made up of states that remained loyal to the United States government.

2. The **Compromise of 1850** allowed California to be admitted to the Union as a free state.

3. **States' rights** is the idea that people of a state can choose the laws that best fit their needs.

4. South Carolina was the first state to **secede** from the Union.

5. The **Missouri Compromise** preserved the balance between free and slave states.

6. The states that seceded from the Union formed the **Confederacy**.

7. The **Kansas-Nebraska Act** allowed people in certain areas to determine whether or not their territory would allow slavery.

8. Although some former slaves had reached the North and found freedom, the **Fugitive Slave Law** said they had to be returned to their owners.

9. **Slave codes** did not allow slaves to own land.

10. Slavery was illegal in California and any other **free state**.

11. Harriet Tubman became famous for helping slaves escape to freedom on the **Underground Railroad**.

 Notes for Home: Your child learned the vocabulary terms for Chapter 1.
Home Activity: Have your child practice using the vocabulary terms in sentences of his or her own.

Use with Pupil Edition, p. 79

Assessment Support

Use these Assessment Book pages and the ExamView® Test Bank CD-ROM to assess content and skills in Chapter 1. You can also view and print Assessment Book pages from the Teacher Resources CD-ROM.

Assessment Book, p. 5

Chapter 1 Test

Part 1: Content Test

Directions: Fill in the circle next to the correct answer.

Lesson Objective (1:1)

1. Where did most Southerners live by the mid-1850s?
   - Ⓐ cities and large towns
   - Ⓑ cities and plantations
   - ● farms and small towns
   - Ⓓ farms and plantations

Lesson Objective (1:1)

2. In what region of the United States were most of the nation's cities located by the 1850s?
   - ● North
   - Ⓑ South
   - Ⓒ East
   - Ⓓ West

Lesson Objective (1:3)

3. What was the North's point of view on slavery by the 1850s?
   - ● Most Northern states had outlawed slavery.
   - Ⓑ Most Northern states supported slavery.
   - Ⓒ Most Northern factories hired slaves for workers.
   - Ⓓ Slaves were found only on farms in the North.

Lesson Objective (1:2)

4. Which of the following describes slavery's role in the Southern economy?
   - Ⓐ Slavery was expensive.
   - Ⓑ Slavery was forbidden.
   - Ⓒ Slavery was a luxury.
   - ● Slavery was profitable.

Lesson Objective (2:1)

5. Which of the following is one way in which slaves resisted slavery?
   - Ⓐ telling family stories
   - Ⓑ meeting with owners
   - Ⓒ singing in the fields
   - ● holding back on work

Lesson Objective (2:2)

6. Which of the following was a slave rebellion that ended in the slaves returning to Africa?
   - Ⓐ New Haven rebellion
   - ● *Amistad* rebellion
   - Ⓒ slave rebellion
   - Ⓓ abolitionists' rebellion

Lesson Objective (2:3)

7. What means did Harriet Tubman and others use to help slaves reach freedom in the North?
   - ● Underground Railroad
   - Ⓑ churches
   - Ⓒ schools
   - Ⓓ *Amistad* rebellion

Lesson Objective (2:4)

8. Which of the following describes the lifestyle of free African Americans?
   - ● They lived in fear of losing their freedom.
   - Ⓑ They lived the same as white citizens.
   - Ⓒ They lived as paid slaves.
   - Ⓓ They received many benefits.

Use with Pupil Edition, p. 78

Assessment Book, p. 6

Lesson Objective (3:1)

9. What problem did the Missouri Compromise solve?
   - Ⓐ Southern states wanted to admit a free state.
   - ● Northerners did not want more slave states than free states.
   - Ⓒ Missouri had to choose to be a free state or a slave state.
   - Ⓓ Missouri wanted to join the United States as a free state.

Lesson Objective (3:2)

10. What led to violence in Kansas in 1854?
    - ● Northerners and Southerners disagreed over the results of the slavery vote.
    - Ⓑ People voted for Kansas to be a slave state.
    - Ⓒ People voted for Kansas to be a free state.
    - Ⓓ Nebraska was split into Kansas and Nebraska.

Lesson Objective (3:3)

11. Why were people outraged at the Supreme Court's decision in the Dred Scott case?
    - Ⓐ They believed it would solve many problems.
    - Ⓑ They agreed with the decision.
    - ● The Court said African Americans had no rights.
    - Ⓓ The Court ruled in favor of Scott.

Lesson Objective (3:4)

12. Which statement represents Lincoln's and Douglas's views on slavery?
    - Ⓐ They agreed on slavery.
    - Ⓑ Neither one cared about slavery.
    - Ⓒ Douglas opposed slavery, but Lincoln believed slavery had its place.
    - ● Lincoln opposed slavery, but Douglas thought slavery had its place.

Lesson Objective (4:1)

13. Which of the following is a reason Southern states seceded from the Union?
    - Ⓐ They wanted to support the Union.
    - Ⓑ They wanted to abolish slavery.
    - Ⓒ They wanted their own flag.
    - ● They wanted to keep slavery.

Lesson Objective (4:2)

14. What officially started the Civil War?
    - ● battle at Fort Sumter
    - Ⓑ disagreements between the North and the South
    - Ⓒ disagreements between Lincoln and Davis
    - Ⓓ disagreements between abolitionists and slave owners

Lesson Objective (4:3)

15. What did the North hope to achieve by fighting the Civil War?
    - Ⓐ preservation of states' rights
    - ● an end to slavery
    - Ⓒ equality for all
    - Ⓓ preservation of the slave system

Use with Pupil Edition, p. 78

Assessment Support

Part 2: Skills Test

Directions: Use complete sentences to answer questions 1–5. Use a separate sheet of paper if you need more space.

1. Why did Southern states fear the outlawing of slavery? **Main Idea and Details**

   Possible answers: Slavery was profitable to the Southern economy. The goods an enslaved person produced brought in at least twice as much money as the cost of owning a slave.

2. In the chart below, give details that explain how the Underground Railroad was able to be so successful in its fight against slavery. **Main Idea and Details**

The Underground Railroad
The Underground Railroad was an organized, secret system. Both whites and African Americans helped slaves escape to the North or to Canada.

3. What was the underlying issue the Missouri Compromise was intended to address? Was it successful or not? **Draw Conclusions**

   Possible answers: The Missouri Compromise was intended to address the issue of balance of power between free and slave states; it was successful for a while because it maintained the balance by allowing one free state and one slave state to join the Union at the same time.

Use with Pupil Edition, p. 78

4. Why do you think Jefferson Davis thought it was important to capture Fort Sumter? **Hypothesize**

   Possible answer: Jefferson Davis knew that the Northern forces would be a "powerful opposition" to the Confederacy. The Confederacy had already taken control of most forts and military property in the South, but Fort Sumter was still under Union control and could be used as a threat.

5. Complete the chart below. List some of the goals people in the United States had as they entered into the Civil War. **Main Idea and Details**

   Possible answer: People fought hoping to achieve different goals. In the Civil War some people were fighting to end slavery, some to preserve slavery, and some to preserve the Union.

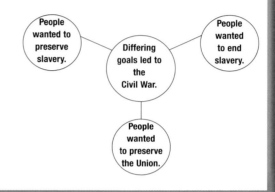

Use with Pupil Edition, p. 78

A Divided Nation

Chapter 1 Outline

Resources

- Workbook, p. 14: Vocabulary Preview
- Vocabulary Cards
- Social Studies Plus!

1820, United States: Lesson 1

Share with students that this picture shows enslaved African Americans working on a plantation in the southern United States. Ask students why some Americans owned slaves at that time.

1849, Philadelphia, Pennsylvania: Lesson 2

This picture shows Harriet Tubman, who escaped from slavery through the Underground Railroad. After her escape, she helped other enslaved people escape to freedom. Ask students to suggest words that describe her.

March 1861, Washington, D.C.: Lesson 3

Remind students that when Abraham Lincoln took office, the United States had "broken" into two groups of states. Ask students what they think Lincoln might have done to restore the Union.

April 1861, Charleston, South Carolina: Lesson 4

This picture shows the battle at Fort Sumter, the first conflict in the Civil War. The bombardment of the fort resulted in victory for the Confederate forces. Ask students to calculate the length of time between Lincoln's taking office and the beginning of the war. (About one month)

CHAPTER

1

A Divided Nation

1820

United States
About 1.5 million enslaved people live in the United States, most in the Southern states.

Lesson 1

1

1849

Philadelphia, Pennsylvania
Harriet Tubman escapes to freedom in Philadelphia on the Underground Railroad.

Lesson 2

2

March 1861

Washington, D.C.
Abraham Lincoln is inaugurated as President.

Lesson 3

3

April 1861

Charleston, South Carolina
Southern troops fire on Fort Sumter.

Lesson 4

4

52

Practice and Extend

Vocabulary Preview

- Use Workbook p. 14 to help students preview the vocabulary words in this chapter.
- Use Vocabulary Cards to preview key concept words in this chapter.

 Also on Teacher Resources CD-ROM.

Workbook, p. 14

Vocabulary Preview

Vocabulary Preview
Directions: Match each vocabulary word to its meaning. Write the vocabulary word on the line provided. Not all words will be used. You may use your glossary.

sectionalism	states' rights	secede
slave codes	Missouri Compromise	Confederacy
Underground Railroad	Fugitive Slave Law	Union
free state	Compromise of 1850	border state
slave state	Kansas-Nebraska Act	civil war

1. _____ to break away from
2. _____ state located between the Union and the Confederacy
3. _____ plan in which California entered the United States as a free state and the Fugitive Slave Law was passed
4. _____ states that remained loyal to the United States government
5. _____ state in which slavery was not allowed
6. _____ law which stated that escaped slaves had to be returned to their owners, even if they had reached Northern states where slavery was not allowed
7. _____ law allowing the people of Kansas and Nebraska to decide whether they would allow slavery in their territory
8. _____ organized, secret system set up to help enslaved people escape from the South to freedom in the North or Canada
9. _____ loyalty to a section or part of the country rather than to the whole country
10. _____ laws to control the behavior of slaves
11. _____ government formed by the seven seceding states, also known as the Confederate States of America
12. _____ state in which slavery was legally allowed

Notes for Home: Your child learned the vocabulary terms for Chapter 1.
Home Activity: Help your child learn the vocabulary terms by having him or her form comparisons between pairs of terms, such as free state and slave state, Union and Confederacy, and so on.

Locating Time and Place

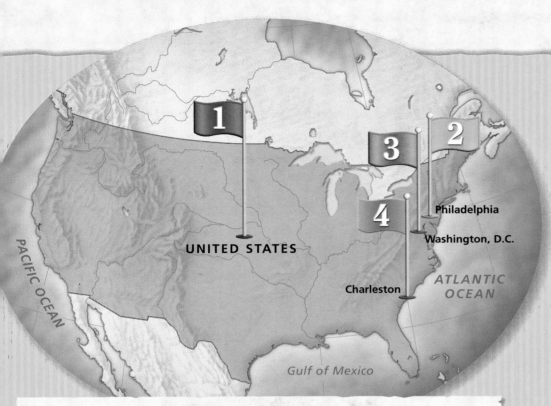

Why We Remember

". . . one nation under God, indivisible, with liberty and justice for all."
These words are part of the Pledge of Allegiance, which Americans have said for many years. But there was a time when the words were not true for all Americans. In the middle 1800s, the United States was one nation divided into two parts, the North and the South. In the South, enslaved people grew crops such as cotton on plantations. In the North, where slavery was illegal in most states, many people worked in factories and lived in cities. Differences between the North and the South sparked serious conflicts, which in 1861 set off a terrible war. By the end of the war, Americans began the long task of rebuilding the country—"with liberty and justice for all."

53

WEB SITE
Technology

You can learn more about Philadelphia, Pennsylvania; Washington, D.C.; and Charleston, South Carolina, by clicking on *Atlas* at **www.sfsocialstudies.com.**

SOCIAL STUDIES
Background

Largest U.S. Cities in 1860

- In 1860 the ten largest cities in the United States were, in order from most to least populous: New York City, NY; Philadelphia, PA; Brooklyn City, NY; Baltimore, MD; Boston, MA; New Orleans, LA; Cincinnati, OH; St. Louis, MO; Chicago, IL; and Buffalo, NY.

- In 1860, New York City had more than 800,000 residents.

- Have students examine the pictures shown on p. 52 for Lessons 1, 2, 3, and 4.

- Remind students that each picture is coded with both a number and a color to link it to a place on the map on p. 53.

Why We Remember

Have students read the "Why We Remember" paragraph on p. 463, and ask them why events in this chapter might be important to them. Ask students to imagine what it would be like to live in this country if it were still divided. What lessons do students think people may have learned from the Civil War? How do these lessons still affect us today?

North and South Grow Apart

Objectives

- Describe the differences between the economies and populations of the North and South.

- Identify the role that slavery played in the South in the mid-1800s.

- Explain how and why views about slavery differed in the North and South.

Vocabulary

sectionalism, p. 55

Resources

- Workbook, p. 15
- Transparency 4
- Every Student Learns Guide, pp. 18–21
- Quick Study, pp. 10–11

 Quick *Teaching Plan*

If time is short, have students create a chart of the characteristics of the North and the South in the mid-1800s.

- Have students make a T-chart with the two headings *Northern United States* and *Southern United States*.

- Students can add details as they read. They should also include viewpoints from each place.

1 Introduce and Motivate

Preview Ask students to list reasons why the two regions might grow apart. Ask students to recall what life in the United States was like in the 1800s. Tell students that in Lesson 1 they will learn more about the differences between these two regions.

You Are There The economy of the Southern United States depended upon cotton, while the Northern United States relied more on industry than on agriculture. Have students predict what effect the differences between the two regions might have on the country as a whole.

54 Unit 1 • War Divides the Nation

LESSON 1

1840		1860
1846 Congress votes to lower tariffs on imports.		**1860** The number of enslaved African Americans in the United States reaches four million.

PREVIEW

Focus on the Main Idea
Differences between the North and South led to growing tensions between the two regions.

PEOPLE
David Walker

VOCABULARY
sectionalism

North and South Grow Apart

You Are There The year is 1850, and you are a sailor on a ship that carries goods to and from ports on the East Coast of the United States. Your ship glides into the port of Charleston, South Carolina, and ties up at a dock. You see hundreds of bundles of cotton waiting to be loaded onto your ship. The cotton has been grown on plantations across the South. You know that most of the work on those plantations is done by people who are enslaved.

You join the other sailors to unload your ship of its cargo of manufactured goods from Boston, Massachusetts. The cargo includes tools, machines, and cloth made by free workers in factories. You know that Charleston and Boston are part of the same country, the United States. Yet they are so different they might well be parts of different countries. Before long their differences will lead to war.

 Main Idea and Details As you read, focus on how the North and South differed and how each of the differences pushed the two regions apart.

54

Practice and Extend

READING SKILL
Main Idea/Details

In the Lesson Review, students complete a graphic organizer like the one below. You may want to provide students with a copy of Transparency 4 to complete as they read the lesson.

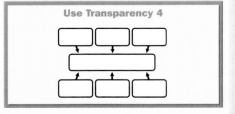
Use Transparency 4

VOCABULARY
Word Exercise

Individual Word Study

Point out to students that the word *section,* meaning "a part separated," is part of *sectionalism.* Tell students that a suffix is a syllable or syllables added to the end of a word to change its meaning or to make a new word. Explain that the suffix *-ism* means "a belief in." Help students understand that *sectionalism* means "a belief in sections" or "a loyalty to a section of the country, rather than to the whole country."

Two Regions

Many changes had taken place in the United States since the country was formed. The North and South were very different geographically, but after the start of the Industrial Revolution, other differences between the two regions increased dramatically. Southerners lived a mostly rural way of life. Most lived and worked on farms and in small towns. By the middle 1800s, few Southern cities had a population of more than 15,000.

In contrast, many Northerners at that time lived an urban way of life. Although most Northerners still lived on farms, more and more people worked in factories and lived in large towns and cities. In 1860 nine of the ten largest cities in the United States were located in the North. The bar graph and circle graphs below show how the populations of the North and South differed in 1850.

The goals of factory owners and factory workers in the North were different from those of plantation owners and farmers in the South. These differences led to a strong disagreement in 1846. A law passed by Congress in that year lowered the tariffs the United States charged for goods imported from other countries. This made Northern factory owners angry.

The Northern states had wanted higher tariffs, or taxes on imported goods. Higher prices on imported goods would encourage Americans to buy manufactured goods from the North.

The Southern states, however, wanted lower tariffs. They preferred to buy the cheaper goods made in Great Britain.

The way of life of one section of the United States was threatening the way of life in the other section of the United States. These differences caused sectionalism in our country. **Sectionalism** is a loyalty to a section or part of the country rather than to the whole country.

REVIEW Explain how differences between the North and South led to conflict between them. Main Idea and Details

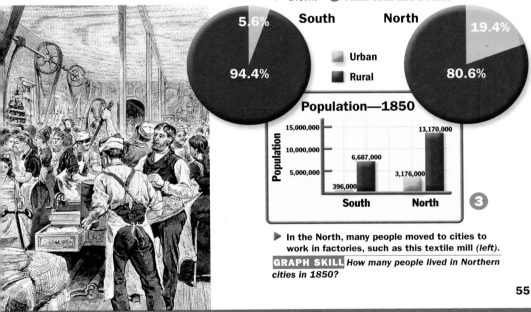

Population—1850

In the North, many people moved to cities to work in factories, such as this textile mill *(left)*.

GRAPH SKILL *How many people lived in Northern cities in 1850?*

55

Two Regions

Quick Summary The rural way of life in the South and the industrial way of life in the North led to sectionalism, or intense loyalty to one part of the country.

1 Why were nine of the ten largest U.S. cities in 1860 in the North rather than in the South? Many Northerners worked in factories and lived in cities. In the South, agriculture was the way of life, so more people lived on farms and in small towns. **Draw Conclusions**

$ SOCIAL STUDIES STRAND Economics

2 How might the lower tariffs on foreign goods affect the wages of workers in the North? Lower tariffs meant that people could buy goods made in foreign countries for less money. With less money coming in to American industry, factory owners might need to lower wages to keep their businesses running. **Cause and Effect**

✓ **REVIEW ANSWER** The way of life in the South was rural, while that of the North was more urban. The North wanted higher tariffs, while the South wanted lower tariffs. Main Idea and Details

3 Which section of the country had the largest total population in 1850? The North **Interpret Graphs**

GRAPH SKILL Answer 3,176,000

ESL EXTEND LANGUAGE ESL Support

Examine Comparatives and Superlatives Have students practice using comparatives and superlatives.

Beginning Write the words *high* and *low* on the board. Illustrate the concepts by drawing a high and a low building or rectangle on the board. Label the rectangles *A* and *C*. Then draw a rectangle that is intermediate in height between *A* and *C*. Label it *B*. Explain that *A* is *higher* than *B* and *C*. Have students use *higher* and *lower* to describe the relationships between the rectangles.

Intermediate Have students scan the chapter to find comparatives and superlatives with *-er* and *-est*. Students should list the words they find and determine their meanings.

Advanced Ask students to write riddles using comparative and superlative forms of words.

For additional ESL support, use Every Student Learns Guide, pp. 18–21.

Slavery in the South

🕐 *Quick Summary* Slavery was profitable to the agricultural South, while the practice was outlawed in most Northern states. African Americans suffered from discrimination in all parts of the United States.

④ Why do you think that most Northern states had outlawed slavery by 1850? Possible answers: Enslaved workers were not as needed there because there were many people living in cities to do the work in factories. Students should recognize that the practice of slavery did exist in the North.
Draw Conclusions

⑤ What kinds of discrimination did free African Americans face in the United States in 1860? They did not always have the same voting rights as whites. In New York, African Americans had to own land before they could vote.
🔎 Main Idea and Details

✓ Ongoing Assessment

| **If...** students are unable to support the main idea that African Americans faced discrimination, | **then...** ask students if they believe people are truly free when they are unable to vote in elections. |

✓ REVIEW ANSWER
The goods an enslaved person produced brought in at least twice as much money as the cost of owning a slave. 🔎 Main Idea and Details

GRAPH SKILL Answer About 400,000

Different Views on Slavery

🕐 *Quick Summary* Abolitionists insisted that slavery should end, but many slave owners disagreed.

Slavery in the South

One very important difference between the North and the South was slavery. Slavery was allowed in the Southern states, where enslaved people grew such crops as cotton, tobacco, and rice. By 1850 most Northern states had outlawed slavery. Northern workers were free and were paid for their work. In many Northern ④ factories, however, workers put in long hours, under difficult conditions, for low pay.

Slavery was profitable to the economy of the South. The goods an enslaved person produced brought in at least twice as much money as the cost of owning the slave. In 1850 about six out of every ten slaves in the South worked in the cotton fields. Cotton was usually grown on large plantations. However, many slaves lived on small farms. On these smaller farms, the owner often worked in the fields alongside a small group of slaves. Still, only about one-third of Southern farmers owned slaves.

By 1860 enslaved African Americans in the United States totaled almost four million people. In some states, they outnumbered the free whites. The line graph on this page shows how the number of enslaved people changed between 1820 and 1860. It also shows changes in the population of free African Americans during the same time. Most of the enslaved African Americans lived in the South, while most of the free African Americans lived in the North.

Even free African Americans did not always have the same voting rights as whites. In some states, only people who owned property could vote, but in some states where this requirement had been dropped for whites, such as in New York, blacks still had to own land before they could vote. ⑤ Throughout the country African Americans suffered from discrimination. They did not have the rights of full citizenship.

REVIEW Identify the main reason why the South wanted to keep slavery.
🔎 Main Idea and Details

Free and Enslaved African Americans 1820–1860

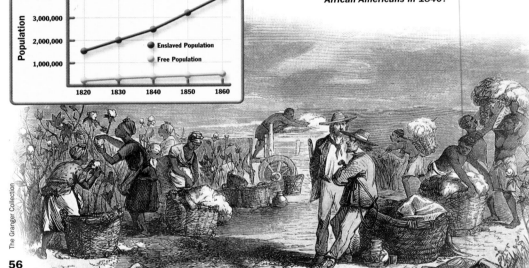

Population
- 4,000,000
- 3,000,000
- 2,000,000
- 1,000,000

Enslaved Population
Free Population

1820 1830 1840 1850 1860

The Granger Collection

56

▶ As Southern cotton plantations *(below)* grew, so did the number of enslaved African Americans.

GRAPH SKILL *About what was the population of free African Americans in 1840?*

Practice and Extend

Problem Solving

Use a Problem-Solving Process

- Have students consider the following problem-solving scenario: **Suppose you are a plantation owner with a large amount of cotton to harvest. You do not believe it is right to own another person, so you do not own slaves. Yet, you need help on your farm and you live far from a city.**
- Students should use the following problem-solving process to decide how they will harvest their cotton before their crops are ruined. For each step in the process, have students work in small groups to discuss and write about what must be considered as they solve the problem. Write the steps above on the board or read them aloud.

1. Identify a problem.
2. Gather information.
3. List and consider options.
4. Consider advantages and disadvantages.
5. Choose and implement a solution.
6. Evaluate the effectiveness of the solution.

Different Views on Slavery

As you have read, abolitionists opposed the practice of slavery and fought to end slavery everywhere in the country. They insisted that slavery should be abolished because it was wrong for one human being to own another. One abolitionist, a free African American named **David Walker,** asked this about the Southern slave owners:

⑥ *"How would they like us to make slaves of . . . them?"*

Southern slave owners continued to defend slavery. They pointed to the evils of factories in the North, where people worked long hours, in bad surroundings, for little pay.

Slave owners argued that slaves were better off than Northern factory workers.

Debate continued throughout the middle 1800s. But, as you will read, words were not the only weapons to be used against slavery.

REVIEW Identify one argument that supported the idea that slavery should be abolished. ⊚ Main Idea and Details

Summarize the Lesson

— **1846** Congress voted to lower the tariff on imports, which angered many Northerners.

— **1860** The number of enslaved African Americans in the United States reached almost four million.

LESSON 1 REVIEW

Check Facts and Main Ideas

1. ⊚ **Main Idea and Details** On a sheet of paper, complete the graphic organizer to show details supporting the main idea.

North

Mostly city life	Wanted higher tariffs	Fewer enslaved people

The North and South differed.

Mostly farming life	Wanted lower tariffs	Many more enslaved people

South

2. Describe how tariffs affected relations between the North and South. Use the word **sectionalism** in your answer.

3. In 1860 were more African Americans enslaved or free? How do you know?

4. **Critical Thinking:** *Make Inferences* What conditions existed in the North that might lead to problems at a later date?

5. Describe the main argument of people opposed to slavery.

Link to ∞ Art

Create a Graph or Illustration Choose one topic from the lesson. Then show with a graph or a picture how the North and the South were growing apart.

57

Primary Source

Cited in *A Documentary History of the Negro People in the United States,* by Herbert Aptheker, ed.

⑥ **What feelings did David Walker express in his question?** Possible answers: Frustration, sadness, defiance
Analyze Primary Sources

✓ **REVIEW ANSWER** It is wrong for one human being to own another.
⊚ **Main Idea and Details**

③ Close and Assess

Summarize the Lesson

Review the time line with students. Then have them use the two main ideas on the time line to create outlines. Remind them that their outlines should include supporting details to explain each main idea. Allow time for students to share their outlines with the class.

✓ **LESSON 1 REVIEW**

1. ⊚ **Main Idea and Details** For possible answers, see the reduced pupil page.

2. Different viewpoints on the tariff helped cause sectionalism, because each side began to show more loyalty to its own part of the country. The North wanted higher tariffs so Americans would buy its goods. This angered the South, which wanted to buy goods cheaply from Great Britain.

3. Enslaved; from the graph on p. 56

4. **Critical Thinking:** *Make Inferences* Possible answers: The North wanted higher tariffs, which threatened Southerners' ability to buy goods from Britain. Factory workers in the North worked long hours for low pay.

5. It is wrong for one human being to own another.

Link to ∞ Art

Students' art should be titled, detailed, clearly labeled, and perhaps focused on daily life, slavery, or tariffs.

Workbook, p. 15

Lesson 1: North and South Grow Apart Use with Pages 54–57
Directions: Complete the compare-and-contrast table using information from Lesson 1. You may use your textbook.

Topic	In the North	In the South	Similar or Different?
The way of life in 1850			
Point of view on tariffs on imported goods			
Point of view on the buying and selling of manufactured goods			
Point of view on slavery			

Notes for Home: Your child learned about the different views of the North and the South during the mid-1800s.
Home Activity: With your child, discuss instances when your child's opinion or point of view might differ from a friend. Brainstorm positive ways to resolve or live with these differences.

⊙ **Also on Teacher Resources CD-ROM.**

Recognize Point of View

Objectives

- Identify facts and opinions in writing.

- Consider the experiences of an individual writer and how those experiences may have shaped the writer's ideas.

- Describe a writer's point of view.

Vocabulary

point of view, p. 58

Resource

- Workbook, p. 16

1 Introduce and Motivate

What is point of view? Read aloud a recent editorial that expresses an opinion. Ask students if they could tell how the writer felt about the topic. After discussion, have students read the **What?** section of text on p. 58 to help set the purpose of the lesson.

Why identify the point of view? Have students read the **Why?** section of text on p. 58. Ask them what details they would use to support an editorial with the point of view that recess should be longer (e.g., need for exercise; a break helps people work better).

2 Teach and Discuss

How is this skill used? Examine with students the selections on p. 59.

- Point out that the two selections have very different points of view.

- Ask students to summarize the point of view of each of the selections. Help students identify words that indicate point of view.

- Have students read the **How?** section of text on p. 58.

Recognize Point of View

What? Point of view is the way a person looks at or thinks about a topic or situation. A person's point of view may be affected by his or her experiences and way of life. As you have read in Lesson 1, people had very different points of view about slavery.

In the selections on these pages, two writers expressed their points of view about slavery. The writers tried to support their points of view with descriptions and details.

Selection A was written by George Fitzhugh, a lawyer who was a supporter of slavery. His family had lived in the South for many years and had owned a 500-acre plantation.

Selection B was written by Frances Anne (Fanny) Kemble, a famous British actress married to Pierce Butler, an American. In 1836 Butler inherited two Southern plantations and became one of the largest slaveholders in the country. His wife became an opponent of slavery and moved back to Britain. Years later she wrote of her experiences in *Journal of a Residence on a Georgian Plantation.*

George Fitzhugh

Fanny Kemble

Why? As a reader, you need to be able to identify a writer's point of view so that you can understand the writer's choice of details. Writers may use their own feelings and beliefs when they decide what to include and how to tell their story.

How? To recognize a writer's point of view, you may follow these steps:

1 Identify the topic.

2 Determine which statements are fact and which are opinions.

3 Look for words or phrases that tell how a writer feels about the topic.

4 Consider the writer's experiences and way of life. How might these affect the writer's point of view?

5 Describe the writer's point of view.

58

Practice and Extend

 CURRICULUM CONNECTION
Writing

Write an Editorial

- Ask students to write editorials for the school newspaper. They could focus on a school or community topic.

- Suggest that students begin with an opinion. They should include persuasive facts and opinions that would influence readers to have the same point of view about the topic.

 CURRICULUM CONNECTION
Art

Create an Illustration

- Remind students that an illustration can reveal an artist's point of view.

- Ask students to make illustrations for the two selections on p. 469. Point out that the subject will be the same, but the details will reflect different points of view.

- Allow time for students to display their artwork. Classmates can try to determine which illustrations should accompany each piece.

Selection A

1 "The negro slaves of the South are the happiest, and in some sense, the freest people in the world. The children and the aged and infirm [sick or weak] work not at all, and yet have all the comforts and necessaries [needs] of life provided for them. They enjoy liberty, **2** because they are oppressed [weighed down] neither by care nor labor. The women do little hard work, and are protected from . . . their husbands by their masters [slave owners]. The negro men and . . . boys work, on the average, in good weather, not more than nine hours a day. The balance of their time is spent in [relaxation]. Besides, they have their Sabbaths and holidays. . . . They can sleep at any hour. . . . We do not know whether free laborers [in the North] ever sleep."

—George Fitzhugh

Selection B

"I have sometimes been haunted [worried] with the idea that it was . . . [a] duty, knowing what I know, and having seen what I have seen, to do all that lies in my power to show the dangers and the evils of this frightful institution [slavery]. . . . The handcuff, the lash—the tearing away of children from parents, of husbands from wives— the weary trudging [walking] . . . along the common highways, the labor of body, the despair of mind [hopelessness], the sickness of heart—these are the realities which belong to the system, and form the rule, rather than the exception, in the slave's experience." **3**

—Fanny Kemble

Think and Apply

1 What is the subject of both of these writers?

2 What details does each writer use to support his or her point of view?

3 What are the points of view each writer reveals?

4 How might the experiences and way of life of each writer affect his or her point of view?

59

1 **Which words in the first sentence of Selection A reveal the writer's point of view?** "happiest," "freest people" Point of View

2 **Fitzhugh states in his article the point of view that slaves are "free." What does he think makes enslaved people free?** Possible answer: Some of the slaves, such as the children and the aged, do not work, yet they are given necessities of life, such as food and shelter. Draw Conclusions

3 **Why do you think Kemble believed it was her "duty" to show the dangers of slavery?** Possible answer: She wanted other people to know about the suffering of enslaved people so that more people would pressure the government to end slavery. Hypothesize

3 Close and Assess

Think and Apply

1. The condition of the life of a slave

2. Fitzhugh says slaves work only nine hours a day and that children and old and sick people are taken care of; Kemble says slaves suffer from handcuffs, lashes, separation of families, hard labor, and despair.

3. Fitzhugh's point of view is that a slave's life is an easy life, and a slave is better off than a free worker. Kemble's point of view is that slaves are treated harshly and cruelly.

4. Fitzhugh was from an old Southern family that had probably owned slaves; after seeing the mistreatment of enslaved people, Kemble became an opponent of slavery.

CURRICULUM CONNECTION
Literature

Read Books About Slavery Have students identify points of view and supporting details in literature.

Sweet Clara and the Freedom Quilt, by Deborah Hopkinson (Random House, ISBN 0-679-87472-0, 1995) **Easy**

The Africans (We Came to North America), by Jen Green (Crabtree Publishing, ISBN 0-778-70198-0, 2000) **On-Level**

Nightjohn, by Gary Paulsen (Delacorte Press, ISBN 0-385-30838-8, 1993) **Challenge**

Workbook, p. 16

Recognize Point of View

Point of view is the way a person looks at or thinks about a topic or situation and describes it. A person's point of view may be affected by his or her experiences and way of life.

Directions: Read the following poem. It was written by a Southern woman during the time when the South had to produce its own goods because it was blockaded by the North. Answer the questions that follow.

My homespun dress is plain, I know;
My hat's palmetto, too.
But then it shows what Southern girls
For Southern rights will do.
We send the bravest of our land
To battle with the foe,
And we will lend a helping hand
We love the South, you know.
Hurrah! Hurrah!
For the sunny South so dear;
Three cheers for the homespun dress
That Southern ladies wear!

1. What is the topic of the poem?

2. What words does the writer use to show how she feels about Southern soldiers?

3. What words does the writer use to show how she feels about the South?

4. How do you think the writer feels about supporting the South in the war? How do you know?

Notes for Home: Your child learned to identify the writer's point of view.
Home Activity: With your child, discuss a family situation or a situation at school in which two people had different points of view. Help your child recognize that different points of view can come from different experiences.

Also on Teacher Resources CD-ROM.

Resisting Slavery

Objectives

- Identify ways African Americans resisted slavery.

- Describe rebellions of African Americans against slavery.

- Explain how the Underground Railroad was used to free enslaved people.

- Describe the lives of free African Americans in the North and South.

Vocabulary

slave codes, p. 61;
Underground Railroad, p. 63

Resources

- Workbook, p. 17
- Transparency 2
- Every Student Learns Guide, pp. 22–25
- Quick Study, pp. 12–13

Quick Teaching Plan

If time is short, have students create a word web about resisting slavery.

- Ask students to write the title of the lesson in the middle of a piece of paper and draw a circle around it.

- As students read, they can create detail webs by drawing spokes from the central circle and writing methods that were used to resist slavery.

1 Introduce and Motivate

Preview To activate prior knowledge, ask students what it means to *resist* (refuse to give in or go along). Tell students that in Lesson 2 they will learn more about how enslaved African Americans resisted slavery.

You Are There Students may recognize Patrick Henry's words "liberty or...death." Ask students what meaning those words might have had for enslaved people and how those people may have tried to gain liberty.

LESSON 2

PREVIEW

Focus on the Main Idea
Enslaved African Americans resisted slavery in many different ways.

PLACES
Southampton County, Virginia
New Haven, Connecticut

PEOPLE
Nat Turner
Joseph Cinque
Harriet Tubman
Levi Coffin
Catherine Coffin

VOCABULARY
slave codes
Underground Railroad

1830

1831
Nat Turner leads a slave rebellion in Virginia.

1841
The Supreme Court frees the prisoners from the slave ship *Amistad*.

1850

1849
Harriet Tubman escapes from slavery on the Underground Railroad.

60

Resisting Slavery

You Are There
September 11, 1853, in Richmond, Virginia. In a house in the city, J.H. Hill, an escaped slave, waits for a message.

Later Hill wrote, "Nine months I was trying to get away. I was secreted [hidden] a long time in a kitchen of a merchant." And then the long awaited message arrives. He is to meet a guide who will try to lead him to freedom in the North. Early next morning, Hill leaves his hiding place and carefully makes his way to the guide. "I felt composed [calm]," Hill reports, "for I had started . . . that morning for liberty or for death." Hill reached the North where, at last, he found liberty.

Main Idea and Details As you read, note the details that support the main idea that African Americans resisted slavery.

Practice and Extend

READING SKILL
Main Idea/Details

In the Lesson Review, students complete a graphic organizer like the one below. You may want to provide students with a copy of Transparency 2 to complete as they read the lesson.

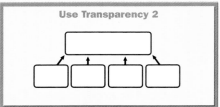

Use Transparency 2

VOCABULARY
Word Exercise

Context Clues

Remind students to be aware of the context in which a word or phrase is used. Point out that *Underground Railroad* literally would mean a train that runs under the ground, like a subway. Explain that when these words are used in the context of discussing slavery, *underground* means "secret" and *railroad* means "system of routes to travel by, including places where escaping slaves could hide, called *stations*."

African Americans Resist Slavery

Some enslaved people, like J.H. Hill, resisted slavery by risking their lives in daring escapes. Other slaves found different ways to resist.

When enslaved people resisted slavery, they were fighting for freedom. They were also fighting against a cruel system. They had no choices. They would be moved when they were sold, and they could not control who bought them. Many owners treated slaves well, but some beat or abused their slaves.

Another form of cruelty was the breaking up of families. Abream Scriven, a slave sold by his owner in 1858, was forced to leave his wife, father, and mother. He wrote these words to his wife:

"Give my love to my father and mother and tell them good bye for me, and if we shall not meet in this world I hope to meet in heaven."

Slave owners had almost complete control over slaves' lives. The owners told them when to start work and when to end work.

Slaves could not leave the plantation without permission. Slave owners also decided whether slaves could marry and the age at which their children had to begin working.

Slave codes, or laws to control the behavior of slaves, also made life difficult for them. For example, most slave codes did not allow a slave to hit a white person, even in self-defense. Slaves were not allowed to own property, and few were allowed to buy and sell goods.

Resistance took many forms. Some slaves simply refused to obey the owner. Other slaves resisted by holding back the main thing they could control, their work. They worked more slowly or pretended to be sick. Others broke the tools that were needed to do work.

Many enslaved people resisted by breaking rules that were meant to keep them ignorant. For example, slaves often were not allowed to learn to read or write. Some slaves learned in secret, risking punishment if they were found out.

REVIEW Describe some ways enslaved African Americans resisted slavery.
 Main Idea and Details

▶ Family members were often separated when slaves were sold.

61

African Americans Resist Slavery

🕐 *Quick Summary* In order to gain their freedom, slaves resisted by refusing to obey, holding back in their work, or secretly breaking laws.

Primary Source
Cited in *A People's History of the United States,* by Howard Zinn

1 Why do you think that some slaveholders broke up enslaved people's families? Possible answers: To demonstrate power over enslaved people; they could only afford one slave; they needed workers for specific jobs **Draw Conclusions**

2 How were some slaveholders cruel to enslaved people? Possible answers: Broke up families, controlled people's lives, sometimes beat or abused them **Main Idea and Details**

🧩 Problem Solving

3 Enslaved people resisted in several ways. Which solution to the problem do you think was the best? Explain. Possible answer: Refusing to work because it would cause economic hardships for slaveholders **Solve Problems**

4 Why do you think slave codes prohibited enslaved people from learning to read and write? Possible answer: To prevent them from communicating effectively and planning a revolt **Draw Conclusions**

✓ **REVIEW ANSWER** Refused to obey owners, worked more slowly, pretended to be sick, broke tools, and learned to read and write **Main Idea and Details**

Examine Word Meaning Work with students to explore the meaning of *resist*.

Beginning Have students in pairs use a dictionary to look up *resist*. Talk through the meaning of the term with them. Then invite them to pantomime the meaning (e.g., fists raised in a fighting posture).

Intermediate Consider giving a sentence frame for students to complete: African Americans resisted slavery by _____. Students can work with partners to find examples in the text, insert the examples in the sentence, and share their sentences with the class.

Advanced Discuss other forms of *resist* with students: *resisted, resisting, resister, resistance.* Then have students identify the suffixes and discuss how the different suffixes change the form of the word (e.g., One form of *resistance* to slavery was _____.).

For additional ESL support, use Every Student Learns Guide, pp. 22–25.

Slave Rebellions

 Quick Summary Slave owners tried to prevent rebellions, but rebellions, such as the one led by Nat Turner, did occur.

5 **Why did slave owners try to keep slaves from meeting with each other?**
To prevent them from planning rebellions
Cause and Effect

6 **Retell, in chronological order, the events surrounding the *Amistad*.** A group of captive Africans seized control of the *Amistad*; they were tricked into sailing to the United States; the U.S. Navy captured and imprisoned the Africans; they were freed by the U.S. Supreme Court and returned to Africa. Sequence

Ongoing Assessment

If... students are unable to retell the events in order,	**then...** write the words *first*, *second*, *third*, *then*, and *finally* on the board. Ask volunteers to record the major events next to the words.

 SOCIAL STUDIES STRAND
Citizenship

Democratic Values and Institutions
Remind students that because the Africans from the *Amistad* were not U.S. citizens, they had no right to an attorney or a trial by jury. Ask students what they know about due process rights.

✓ **REVIEW ANSWER** The Nat Turner rebellion was stopped and the rebels were executed. The *Amistad* rebellion was successful and led to the freeing of the captives. Compare and Contrast

 The *Amistad*

7 **Why do you think that people might want to visit the *Amistad*?** Possible answer: Visitors may want to celebrate the bravery of the people involved.
Express Ideas

62 Unit 1 • War Divides the Nation

Slave Rebellions

5 To prevent enslaved people from planning rebellions, slave owners tried to keep slaves from gathering and meeting with one another. Still, rebellions did occur. One was planned and led by **Nat Turner** in Virginia.

In August 1831, Turner and his followers killed about 60 whites in **Southampton County, Virginia.** United States and Virginia troops were called in to stop them. The soldiers killed more than 100 African Americans before the rebellion was ended. Turner escaped but was later captured. He was hanged on November 11, 1831.

A later rebellion had a different ending. In 1839, a group of 53 captive Africans seized control of the *Amistad*, a Spanish slave ship carrying them from one port to another in Cuba. The Africans were led by a farmer from West Africa who became known as **Joseph Cinque** (SEEN kay). He told the Africans: "We may as well die in trying to be free."

After taking control of the ship, the Africans told a Spanish sailor to sail them back to Africa. But the Spaniard tricked them and instead sailed the *Amistad* north along the coast of the United States. The United States Navy captured the *Amistad* near Long Island, New York. The Africans were taken as prisoners to **New Haven, Connecticut.**

At first, the United States planned to return the ship and the Africans to the Spanish. Abolitionists and Northern newspapers printed articles against this plan and in support of the Africans. With their help, the Africans' fight for freedom eventually came before the Supreme Court. There, former President John Quincy Adams presented the Africans' case. He argued that the Africans were not property but human beings and should not be returned to Spain.

On March 9, 1841, the Supreme Court reached its decision. It agreed with Adams and freed the Africans. All 35 of the Africans who survived the rebellion sailed back to Africa later that year.

REVIEW Contrast the Nat Turner and *Amistad* rebellions. Compare and Contrast

 The *Amistad*
In 2000, a full-size reproduction of the *Amistad* was launched at Mystic Seaport, a museum in Connecticut. People can visit the ship there, or at ports to which it sails, to hear the story of the *Amistad* rebellion.

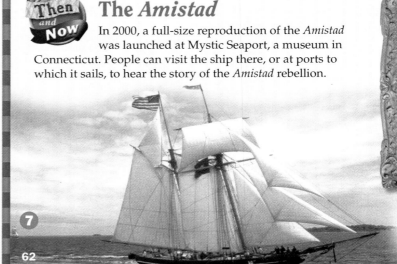

▶ Joseph Cinque (*above*) led the rebellion that took control of the Spanish slave ship, *Amistad*. The picture at left shows the reproduction of the *Amistad*.

Practice and Extend

CURRICULUM CONNECTION
Art

Design Promotional Materials
- Have students suppose that they are promoting the launch of the *Amistad* reproduction.
- Invite them to design a poster or brochure to celebrate the launch. Their work should express the importance of the exhibit.
- Readers should have a good idea of what they will learn from visiting the ship and museum.

CURRICULUM CONNECTION
Writing

Create an Argument
- Ask students to consider the actions of John Quincy Adams and create arguments to present to the Supreme Court on behalf of the Africans on the *Amistad*.
- Their arguments should persuade the justices to free the Africans.
- Tell students to use a formal tone and support their argument with facts.

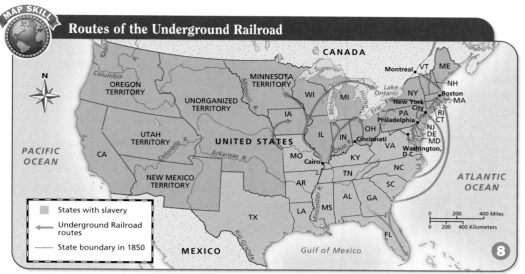

Routes of the Underground Railroad

This map shows some of the routes traveled by people escaping from slavery on the Underground Railroad.

MAP SKILL Use Routes *To what other country did many slaves escape?*

Underground Railroad

Thousands of enslaved African Americans resisted slavery by trying to escape. The **Underground Railroad** was an organized, secret system set up to help enslaved people escape from the South to freedom in the North or Canada. The map on this page shows its routes.

The Underground Railroad probably got its name when railroads became popular. The guides, or people who helped those escaping, were called "conductors." The houses, barns, and other places where runaways hid along their journey were known as "stations."

To find their way north, escaping slaves were guided by the North Star. On cloudy nights they felt for moss on tree trunks, because moss tends to grow on the north side of a tree. All along the journey, they faced the risk of capture, a severe beating, or death.

Between 40,000 and 100,000 slaves escaped using the Underground Railroad. **Harriet Tubman** was the most famous

"conductor." In about 1849, Tubman escaped from slavery herself and settled in Philadelphia. Before the Civil War she returned south 19 times to lead more than 300 people, including her mother and father, to freedom. Tubman later said, "On my underground railroad, I never ran my train off the track and I never lost a passenger." You can read more about Tubman in the Biography on page 65.

Not all "conductors" on the Underground Railroad were African Americans. **Levi Coffin** was a white teacher who had opened a school for slaves in North Carolina. After slave owners closed his school, Coffin moved to Indiana. There he became one of the leading "conductors" of the Underground Railroad. He and his wife, **Catherine Coffin,** helped more than 2,000 slaves escape to freedom.

REVIEW Write a brief summary of the way the Underground Railroad helped people escape slavery. **Summarize**

63

Underground Railroad

 Quick Summary An organized, secret system, the Underground Railroad, helped enslaved people from the South escape to freedom in the North or Canada.

Routes of the Underground Railroad

8 **Which city is the origin of a route that led some enslaved people to the Minnesota Territory?** Cairo
Interpret Maps

MAP SKILL **Answer** Canada

9 **Compare and contrast the Underground Railroad with a "real" railroad.** Both railroads had set routes, moved people from one place to another, and had "conductors" and "stations." The Underground Railroad was not an actual rail system with tracks.
Compare and Contrast

10 **What risks did enslaved people face when using the Underground Railroad?** Possible answer: Capture, punishment, or even death Main Idea and Details

11 **What personal characteristics does Harriet Tubman reveal in her quotation?** Courage, self-confidence, pride, and a sense of humor Draw Conclusions

✓ **REVIEW ANSWER** Guides, called "conductors," led escaped slaves from one hiding place, or "station," to another, until the enslaved people reached freedom in the North or in Canada. Summarize

---

MEETING INDIVIDUAL NEEDS
Learning Styles

The Underground Railroad Using their individual learning styles, students explore the Underground Railroad.

Musical Learning Have students work in small groups to compose songs that would help enslaved people remember a route on the railroad. Remind students to refer to the map as they write.

Individual Learning Ask students to write at least three journal entries that an enslaved person may have written while using the Underground Railroad to escape to freedom. Journal entries could include information about the route as well as the hopes and fears of the escaping slave.

Logical Learning Encourage students to use the map on this page as well as a map with a mileage scale to compute the distances of the routes of the Underground Railroad. Ask students to calculate how long it might take to follow several of the routes if escaping slaves could travel 25 miles in a day.

Free African Americans

> ⏱ **Quick Summary** By 1860 only one out of nine African Americans in the United States was free.

⑫ In 1860 where did most free African Americans in the United States live?
In cities ↺ Main Idea and Details

✓ **REVIEW ANSWER** Without a certificate of freedom, they could be sent back into slavery. Escaped slaves in the North could be kidnapped and returned to slavery in the South.
↺ **Main Idea and Details**

Close and Assess

Summarize the Lesson

Have groups of students list details about or illustrate one of the main ideas. Students can combine their work to create a large class outline.

✓ | **LESSON 2** | **REVIEW** |

1. ↺ **Main Idea and Details** For possible answers, see the reduced pupil page.

2. The purpose of the slave codes was to control the behavior of slaves.

3. **Critical Thinking: Cause and Effect** To prevent enslaved people from planning rebellions.

4. Guides led escaped enslaved people from one hiding place to another.

5. Laws prevented them from holding some jobs; threats and violence from white workers made it difficult to find work; they feared being sent back into slavery.

Link to ⛓ **Science**
Encourage students to draw pictures showing the North Star and the surrounding stars. Ask students which other groups of people may have used the North Star to find their way (e.g., sailors).

64 Unit 1 • War Divides the Nation

Free African Americans

⑫ By 1860 about 4.5 million African Americans lived in the United States. About 4.1 million lived in the South. Only one out of every nine African Americans in the country was free. Most free African Americans lived in cities. Although they were free, they feared losing their freedom. Any white person could accuse a free black person of being a slave. Without a certificate of freedom, African Americans in the South could be sent back into slavery. Escaped slaves in the North could be kidnapped by slave catchers and returned to slavery in the South.

Many Southern states passed laws preventing free African Americans from holding certain jobs. In the North and the South, finding work was made more difficult by threats and violence from white workers. Still,

thousands of free blacks found jobs and bought property. In New Orleans, 650 African Americans owned land by 1850. This was by far the largest number of black landowners of any city in the United States.

REVIEW Why did free African Americans have much to fear about keeping their freedom? ↺ Main Idea and Details

Summarize the Lesson

- **1831** Nat Turner led a slave rebellion in Virginia.

- **1841** Africans who had seized control of the slave ship *Amistad* gained their freedom in the Supreme Court.

- **1849** Harriet Tubman escaped slavery and began leading people to freedom on the Underground Railroad.

| **LESSON 2** | **REVIEW** |

Check Facts and Main Ideas

1. ↺ **Main Idea and Details** On a separate sheet of paper, complete the graphic organizer to show the details that support the main idea that enslaved African Americans resisted slavery.

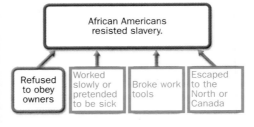

2. What was the purpose of the **slave codes**?

3. **Critical Thinking: *Cause and Effect*** Why would slave owners want to keep slaves from gathering or meeting one another?

4. Describe how enslaved African Americans escaped to freedom on the **Underground Railroad.**

5. What challenges were faced by free African Americans in the North and South?

Link to ⛓ **Science**
Locate the North Star Escaping African Americans used the North Star to help them find the direction north. Do research to locate the North Star. Then one evening, when it is dark enough, look for the star and determine north.

64

Practice and Extend

 MEETING INDIVIDUAL NEEDS
Leveled Practice

Write an Article Have students write an article as if they were a reporter in the 1860s. Students may need to do additional research.

Easy Have students write three or four sentences about the Nat Turner rebellion. They should answer *Who? What? Where? When? Why?* and *How?* **Reteach**

On-Level Have students write a newsletter article for Underground Railroad conductors to read. **Extend**

Challenge Students can write an article about the *Amistad* incident and speculate how it might affect the future slave trade. **Enrich**

For a Lesson Summary, use Quick Study p. 12.

Workbook, p. 17

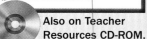

Also on Teacher Resources CD-ROM.

Harriet Tubman
1820(?)–1913

As a teenager in Maryland, Harriet Tubman had only known a life of slavery, yet she grew tougher by resisting, or fighting back. She even survived a serious head injury that she suffered while helping another slave escape. As a result of the injury, for the rest of her life Harriet could not control falling asleep at odd times, suffered from bad headaches, and had a deep scar. Yet nothing could prevent her from seeking freedom.

When she was about 28 years old, Harriet Tubman escaped and made her way 90 miles on the Underground Railroad to Philadelphia. Although she was afraid, she later explained,

1 *"I had reasoned this out in my mind. . . . I had a right to liberty or death; if I could not have one, I would have the other, for no man should take me alive."*

2 Despite the dangers, before the Civil War Tubman returned again and again to the South to help lead other African Americans from slavery to freedom. No one in her care was ever caught.

BIOFACT
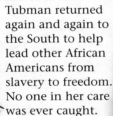
During the Civil War, Tubman served the United States Army as a nurse and a scout, helping to free almost 800 slaves in one attempt.

Learn from Biographies
How do you think Harriet Tubman's scar and trouble with sleeping could have made her escape more dangerous? Why do you think that she returned to the South so many times despite all of the dangers?

 For more information, go online to *Meet the People* at **www.sfsocialstudies.com.**

65

Harriet Tubman

Objective
- Identify the personal qualities that motivated Harriet Tubman to take risks in helping African Americans escape to freedom.

1 Introduce and Motivate

Preview To activate prior knowledge, ask students to recall what they learned about Harriet Tubman in Lesson 2. Tell students they will read more about her courage.

2 Teach and Discuss

1 **What two choices did Harriet Tubman say she had the right to choose between?** Liberty or death
Analyze Primary Sources

2 **What did Tubman do during the Civil War?** Served the U.S. Army as a nurse and a scout; helped free almost 800 slaves at once **Main Idea and Details**

3 Close and Assess

Learn from Biographies Answer
Possible answer: Her scar made her easy to recognize, and she might fall asleep at any time. She knew the value of freedom and wanted to help others achieve their goal of liberty.

 WEB SITE
Technology

Students can find out more about Harriet Tubman by clicking on *Meet the People* at **www.sfsocialstudies.com.**

 **CURRICULUM CONNECTION**
Writing

Write Speeches
- Tell students to suppose that Harriet Tubman is going to be honored with a museum display at a Heroes Hall of Fame.
- Invite students to write speeches that could be given at the opening of the display.
- Students' speeches should describe Tubman's life, explain why she is remembered today, and tell why she deserves the status of "hero."

The Struggle Over Slavery

Objectives

- Describe the causes and effects of the Missouri Compromise and the Compromise of 1850.

- Explain the causes of violence in Kansas in 1854.

- Draw conclusions about how Dred Scott and John Brown affected the split between the North and South.

- Compare the views on slavery of Abraham Lincoln and Stephen Douglas.

Vocabulary

free state, p. 67; **slave state,** p. 67; **states' rights,** p. 67; **Missouri Compromise,** p. 67; **Fugitive Slave Law,** p. 68; **Compromise of 1850,** p. 68; **Kansas-Nebraska Act,** p. 69

Resources

- Workbook, p. 18
- Transparency 2
- Every Student Learns Guide, pp. 26–29
- Quick Study, pp. 14–15

Quick Teaching Plan

If time is short, ask students to create a time line as they read.

- Students can begin by recording main ideas about the Missouri Compromise.
- Remind students to add other dates and details from the lesson.

1 Introduce and Motivate

Preview To activate prior knowledge, have students summarize the conflicts over slavery. Tell students that they will find out more about the issue of slavery in Lesson 3.

You Are There Remind students that, in 1850, the United States was still acquiring territory and admitting new states. Ask them to predict how adding new states might cause problems.

LESSON 3

1820 Missouri Compromise

1850 Fugitive Slave Law

1857 Dred Scott case

1860 Abraham Lincoln is elected President.

PREVIEW

Focus on the Main Idea
Despite attempts to compromise, the struggle over slavery threatened to tear the United States apart.

PLACES
Nebraska Territory
Kansas Territory
Harpers Ferry, Virginia

PEOPLE
John C. Calhoun
Henry Clay
Daniel Webster
Stephen Douglas
Harriet Beecher Stowe
Dred Scott
John Brown
Abraham Lincoln

VOCABULARY
free state
slave state
states' rights
Missouri Compromise
Fugitive Slave Law
Compromise of 1850
Kansas-Nebraska Act

The Struggle over Slavery

You Are There Your old home in Ohio lies hundreds of miles behind you as you ride into the Kansas Territory. On this spring day in 1854, you meet a group of 650 settlers from New England. They tell you they have all pledged to keep Kansas free of slavery.

You have also met other people coming to Kansas who have different views. One group is from neighboring Missouri, a slave state. Their aim is to make the Kansas Territory a place where people can own slaves.

Wherever you go, you hear arguments about whether or not Kansas should allow slavery. You also hear stories of violence between people on both sides of this argument. The issue of slavery is splitting Kansas apart. Soon it will threaten to split apart the entire country.

 Main Idea and Details As you read, look for details that support the main idea that slavery was threatening to split apart the country in the middle 1800s.

Practice and Extend

READING SKILL
Main Idea/Details

In the Lesson Review, students complete a graphic organizer like the one below. You may want to provide students with a copy of Transparency 2 to complete as they read.

Use Transparency 2

VOCABULARY
Word Exercise

Related Word Study

Using graphic organizers can help students categorize and learn new vocabulary terms. Model a Venn diagram with the labels *free state* and *slave state.* Have students write similarities in the overlapping portion and differences in the non-overlapping parts. Similarities could include that they both had two United States senators. Differences could include that free states did not allow slavery, and slave states did.

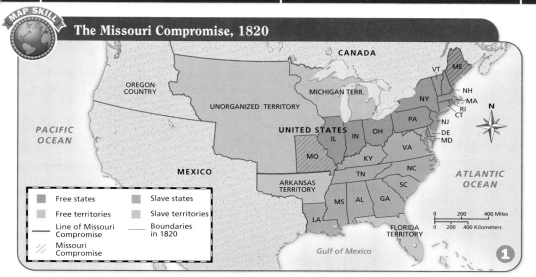

The Missouri Compromise, 1820

▶ The Missouri Compromise kept the balance between free states and slave states.

MAP SKILL Use a Map Key *Which two states were admitted as part of the Missouri Compromise?*

Missouri Compromise

In 1819 the United States was made up of 11 free states and 11 slave states. A **free state** was one in which slavery was not allowed. A **slave state** was one in which slavery was allowed. Since each state had two United States senators, the Senate was balanced evenly between senators that favored slavery and senators that opposed slavery.

In 1819 the people of Missouri asked for statehood as a slave state. Northern states did not want Missouri to be admitted as a slave state. Southern states took the opposite position.

John C. Calhoun from South Carolina was a leader of the Southerners in the Senate. Calhoun was a believer in **states' rights**— the idea that states have the right to make decisions about issues that concern them. According to Calhoun, slavery should be legal if a state's citizens wanted it to be.

Senator **Henry Clay** of Kentucky, who would become known as "The Great Compromiser," urged a solution called the **Missouri Compromise.** In 1820 Missouri was admitted as a slave state, and Maine was admitted as a free state. There were now 24 states, evenly balanced between free states and slave states.

What would happen when more new states were formed from land gained in the Louisiana Purchase? The Missouri Compromise tried to settle this question. Look at the map above and find the Missouri Compromise line. According to the Missouri Compromise, new states north of this line would be free states. New states south of this line could allow slavery.

REVIEW How did the Missouri Compromise affect the way in which future states would be admitted to the United States?
Main Idea and Details

67

2 Teach and Discuss

PAGE 67

Missouri Compromise

Quick Summary Henry Clay's Missouri Compromise kept the balance between free and slave states.

The Missouri Compromise, 1820

❶ Did the Missouri Compromise allow more free states or slave states?
Neither, the states were equally balanced **Interpret Maps**

MAP SKILL Answer Maine and Missouri

❷ How would the balance of the Senate be affected by new states that were admitted to the United States?
Two senators were elected from every state. If more slave states than free states were admitted to the United States, there would be more senators who represented the interests of slave states. Many wanted the Senate to be equal. **Cause and Effect**

SOCIAL STUDIES STRAND
Geography

The Mason-Dixon line is commonly used to describe the boundary between the slave states of the South and the free states of the North after the Missouri Compromise, although it was originally drawn in the 1760s to determine precise borders between Delaware, Maryland, and Pennsylvania.

✓ **REVIEW ANSWER** The Missouri Compromise established a line of latitude north of which (with the exception of Missouri) slavery would not be allowed and south of which slavery would be allowed.
Main Idea and Details

ACCESS CONTENT
ESL Support

Discuss Compromise Help students understand *compromise*.

Beginning Demonstrate the meaning of *compromise* with this scenario: "John wants to go to a ball game; his sister wants to go to a movie. They *compromise* by going to a movie about a ball game." Have students role-play the scenario.

Intermediate Using the map above, point to the states that were part of the U.S. before Missouri and Maine were admitted. Have students count the number of slave states and free states. Ask what would happen if one new state was a slave state or a free state. Discuss how the compromise maintained a balance.

Advanced Have students work in groups of four to role-play a discussion that might have occurred between Henry Clay and John C. Calhoun. Two students can role-play Clay and Calhoun, and two students can listen and discuss. Then have students switch roles.

For additional ESL support, use Every Student Learns Guide, pp. 26–29.

The Compromise of 1850

Quick Summary The Compromise of 1850 admitted California as a free state while enacting the Fugitive Slave Law.

SOCIAL STUDIES STRAND
Geography

Point out on a map California, Missouri, and the latitude line for the Missouri Compromise (36° 30'N). Show students that the line traverses California.

③ Why was the Missouri Compromise unable to settle the question of California being admitted as a free state? The latitude line dividing slave states and free states cuts through the middle of California; the balance between free and slave states was threatened.
Apply Information

Primary Source

Cited in *The Oxford History of the American People,* by Samuel Eliot Morison

④ What does John Calhoun's letter reveal about his attitude toward the North? He is angry and frustrated with it.
Analyze Primary Sources

⑤ What did the Fugitive Slave Law say? Slaves who escaped, even if they had reached the North, would be returned to their owners if caught.
⊛ **Main Idea and Details**

⑥ How did the Compromise of 1850 fit into the idea of states' rights? People living in the territories gained from Mexico could vote for whether or not they wanted to allow the practice of slavery.
Apply Information

⑦ At first Calhoun opposed admitting California as a free state, yet he supported the Compromise of 1850. What do you think may have changed his mind? The Compromise of 1850 led to passage of the Fugitive Slave Law. **Draw Conclusions**

✓ **REVIEW ANSWER** California would be admitted as a free state if a Fugitive Slave Law was passed. Slavery would be allowed in the territories acquired from Mexico if people in those territories voted for slavery. ⊛ **Main Ideas and Details**

The Compromise of 1850

For a time, the Missouri Compromise settled the question about the balance of free and slave states. But in 1849, California—which was part of the lands the United States had gained from the Mexican War—applied for statehood as a free state. At that time the United States was made up of 15 free states and 15 slave states. Once again, the balance between free and slave states was threatened.

John Calhoun wrote to his daughter about the South's reaction to California's request:

> "*I trust we shall persist in our resistance [to California]. . . . We have borne the wrongs and insults of the North long enough.*"

Calhoun hoped that the Southern members of Congress would force the North to turn down California's request to enter as a free state.

Henry Clay again suggested a compromise. Clay proposed that the South accept California as a free state. In return, the North should agree to pass the **Fugitive Slave Law.** This law said that escaped slaves had to be returned to their owners, even if they had reached Northern states where slavery was not allowed. Clay's compromise also suggested a way to accept other new states from the territories gained from Mexico. He proposed that slavery be allowed in these territories if the people living there voted for it.

Daniel Webster, a senator from Massachusetts, spoke in favor of the compromise. Webster was an opponent of slavery. Yet like Clay, he wanted to keep the country together. Webster said, "We must view things as they are. Slavery does exist in the United States."

68

With the support of Calhoun and Webster, Congress passed Clay's plan. It was called the **Compromise of 1850.** California became a free state, and the Fugitive Slave Law was passed. But the battle over slavery was far from over.

The Compromise of 1850 was made to keep the North and the South from splitting apart over slavery. But as Senator Salmon P. Chase of Ohio said later, "The question of slavery in the territories has been avoided. It has not been settled." The truth of his words became clear in 1854, as huge numbers of settlers were entering the Nebraska Territory west of the Missouri River.

REVIEW What were the main proposals of the Compromise of 1850?
⊛ **Main Idea and Details**

▶ Many newspapers printed opinions about the new Fugitive Slave Law.

Practice and Extend

SOCIAL STUDIES
Background
FYI

About Daniel Webster

- At the age of 15, Daniel Webster entered Dartmouth College, where he excelled at public speaking. When he graduated, he taught school and studied law. He soon became a prominent lawyer.
- After becoming a member of the House of Representatives, Webster became an influential and well-paid lawyer.
- Webster directly opposed John C. Calhoun's declarations of states' rights. As Webster defended the powers of the federal government, he said, "Liberty *and* Union, now and forever, one and inseparable!"
- Webster supported the Compromise of 1850 not because he defended the rights of states, but because he thought that the terrain in the West would not support plantations or farms, making slavery unnecessary.

The Kansas-Nebraska Act, 1854

Free states
Free territories
Slave states
Decision on slavery left to territories
Boundaries in 1854

▶ This map shows how the Kansas-Nebraska Act affected the United States.

MAP SKILL Region *What was the only state in the West region in 1854?*

"Bleeding Kansas"

In 1854 Senator **Stephen Douglas** of Illinois proposed that Nebraska be split into two territories: the **Nebraska Territory** in the north and the **Kansas Territory** in the south. Because both territories were north of the Missouri Compromise line, both would be free territories. However, many Southerners insisted that slavery be allowed in both the Nebraska and the Kansas territories.

Congress again looked for a solution. Senator Douglas suggested a compromise: let the people of each territory decide whether it should be free or slave. Congress passed this law, which came to be known as the **Kansas-Nebraska Act.** Instead of solving the problem, the law created a new one in Kansas.

Because a majority vote would decide whether Kansas would be free or slave, people who favored one side or the other rushed to settle in Kansas. People against slavery

came from the North. People for slavery came from the South, especially from neighboring Missouri, a slave state.

The people of Kansas voted for slavery. But many who voted were not Kansans at all. They had crossed the border from Missouri just to vote for slavery. Northerners claimed the vote was illegal. Southerners disagreed. Although most people in Kansas just wanted to establish homes and live in peace, there were leaders on both sides of the slavery issue who were trying to cause a fight. Violence broke out in many parts of the Kansas Territory. Because of the many acts of violence, Kansas became known as "bleeding Kansas." These would not be the last drops of blood spilled between those who favored and opposed slavery.

REVIEW In what way did the Kansas-Nebraska Act change a part of the Missouri Compromise? **Compare and Contrast**

69

"Bleeding Kansas"

🕐 *Quick Summary* Although the Kansas-Nebraska Act was created to solve the problem of whether slavery would be allowed in the two territories, it prompted violent disputes.

The Kansas-Nebraska Act, 1854

8 **According to the terms of the Missouri Compromise, would Kansas have been a free state or a slave state?** Free state **Apply Information**

MAP SKILL Answer California

9 **Why did people from neighboring states rush to Kansas to vote on the question of slavery?** A majority vote would decide the outcome, so people against slavery came from the North and those for slavery came from the South to vote. **Cause and Effect**

10 **Why do you think that the issue of slavery caused so much violence?** Possible answer: People had strong feelings about the way of life in their region of the country, and they did not want their way of life threatened by another region. **Express Ideas**

✓ **REVIEW ANSWER** The Missouri Compromise declared that states and territories north of a certain line of latitude should be free. The Kansas-Nebraska Act left the decision to the people of the two territories, even though they were north of this latitude. **Compare and Contrast**

MEETING INDIVIDUAL NEEDS
Leveled Practice

Review Acts Have students review acts regarding new states (The Missouri Compromise, the Compromise of 1850, and the Kansas-Nebraska Act).

Easy Write *Missouri Compromise* on the board and say, "This act made Maine a free state." Students should show thumbs up because the statement is true. Continue with the other acts. Students show thumbs down for false. **Reteach**

On-Level Write the names of the acts on the board and have groups of students choose one. They should list the main features of the act. Allow time for students to share their lists. **Extend**

Challenge Students participate in panel discussions, acting as one of the people from the lesson. In character, students explain their viewpoints. Audience members can question the characters. **Enrich**

For a Lesson Summary, use Quick Study, p. 14.

A Divided Country

 Quick Summary Events such as the publication of *Uncle Tom's Cabin* and the Dred Scott decision heightened emotions about the issue of slavery and further divided the United States.

Test Talk

Use Information from the Text

11 **How did the publication of *Uncle Tom's Cabin* affect people's feelings about slavery? Why did the book have that effect?** Students should skim the first paragraph to find out what the effect was. The book, which sold many copies, won some people over to the abolitionist cause because it described the cruelties of slavery. **Cause and Effect**

12 **Why did John Brown lead a raid on the arsenal at Harper's Ferry?** To steal weapons for attacking slave owners in Virginia **Main Idea and Details**

✓ Ongoing Assessment

If... students do not understand Brown's importance to the abolitionist cause,

then... read them variants of the song "John Brown's Body" to illustrate how people later drew inspiration from his actions.

✓ REVIEW ANSWER Dred Scott sought to gain his freedom from slavery peacefully. John Brown sought to abolish slavery violently. **Compare and Contrast**

Literature and Social Studies

Read the passage aloud for students, asking them to listen for vivid words that provoke strong emotions.

13 **What does this passage reveal about slavery?** Possible answer: It shows the cruelty of the slave traders and the harsh and frightening conditions under which enslaved people lived. It shows how mothers and their children suffered. **Apply Information**

A Divided Country

In addition to the violence in "bleeding Kansas," other events deepened the split between the North and the South. One was the publication of *Uncle Tom's Cabin*, a novel by **Harriet Beecher Stowe,** in 1852. Stowe's novel described the cruelties of slavery. It sold about 300,000 copies in the first year after it was published, winning over many people to the abolitionist cause.

Another important event was the case of **Dred Scott,** an enslaved African American from Missouri. Scott's owner had taken him to Illinois, a free state, and to Wisconsin, a free territory, and then back to Missouri, a slave state. Then Scott's owner died. Scott went to court claiming he was a free man because he had lived in a free state.

Scott's case reached the United States Supreme Court. The 1857 decision written by Chief Justice Roger Taney said that Scott "had no rights" because African Americans were not citizens of the United States. Many Americans were outraged by the Supreme Court's decision. Frederick Douglass said that the decision would bring about events that would "overthrow . . . the whole slave system."

Another event that further divided the North and the South occurred in 1859. Abolitionist **John Brown,** who had led attacks on pro-slavery people in Kansas, made plans to attack slave owners in Virginia. To carry out his plan, Brown needed weapons. He planned to steal them from the army's arsenal at **Harpers Ferry, Virginia** (now West Virginia). An arsenal is a place where weapons are stored.

On October 16 Brown and 21 other men, black and white, started on their raid. But federal and state soldiers stopped them, killing some of the raiders. Brown was taken prisoner and, after being found guilty, was sentenced to death and hanged. However, his actions showed that the struggle over slavery was growing. Compromise was becoming harder to find.

REVIEW Contrast the goals of Dred Scott and John Brown. **Compare and Contrast**

Literature and Social Studies

In this excerpt from *Uncle Tom's Cabin,* Harriet Beecher Stowe describes the struggle of an enslaved mother named Eliza to keep her child from slave traders who wanted to take her child away from her.

"[Eliza's] room opened by a side door to the river. She caught her child, and sprang down the steps toward it. The [slave] trader caught a full glimpse of her, just as she was disappearing down the bank, and throwing himself from his horse . . . he was after her like a hound after a deer. In that dizzy moment her feet . . . [hardly] seemed to touch the ground, and a moment brought her to the water's edge. . . . and, nerved with strength such as God gives only to the desperate, with one wild cry and flying leap, she vaulted sheer [jumped clear] over the . . . current by the shore, on to the raft of ice beyond. It was a desperate leap,—impossible to anything but madness and despair."

70

Practice and Extend

Learning Styles
MEETING INDIVIDUAL NEEDS

Review Events in the Struggle Over Slavery Using their individual learning styles, students review the different actions taken in response to conflicts about slavery.

Visual Learning Students can make illustrated time lines to show lesson events. Make certain they include specific dates, complete descriptions, and appropriate illustrations.

Linguistic Learning Ask students to suppose they are developing a documentary film about lesson events. Work with students to brainstorm a list of important events to include. Have them work independently or in small groups to write a script for a portion of the documentary, describing one of the events. If time allows, students can perform their scripts for the class.

The Granger Collection

▶ Abraham Lincoln spoke out against the spread of slavery while running for the Senate against Stephen Douglas.

A New Political Party

The issue of slavery led to the end of one political party and the beginning of another. The Whigs, split between a group against slavery and a group for it, ceased to exist. In 1854 some of its members who opposed slavery joined with other slavery opponents to form the Republican party. Now two major political parties, Republican and Democrat, battled over the issues of slavery and states' rights.

No election showed this conflict more clearly than the 1858 campaign for the United States Senate in Illinois. The Republicans chose **Abraham Lincoln** as their candidate. Lincoln was a lawyer from Springfield, Illinois.

15 Many people called him "The Rail Splitter" because when he was young, he split logs with an axe to make the rails of fences. Lincoln was opposed to the spread of slavery and spoke of the "ultimate extinction," or final end, of slavery.

Lincoln's opponent was Democratic Senator Stephen Douglas. Douglas was known as the "Little Giant" because, although he was short, he was a giant when it came to making speeches that changed people's ideas. Douglas believed in states' rights. He said, "Each state . . . has a right to do as it pleases on . . . slavery."

The candidates made speeches and debated throughout Illinois about the spread of slavery. The Lincoln-Douglas debates became well known because both candidates were such good speakers. Lincoln said:

> *"If slavery is not wrong, then nothing is wrong. . . . [But I] would not do anything to bring about a war between the free and slave states."*

Douglas stated:

> *"If each state will only agree to mind its own business . . . this republic can exist forever divided into free and slave states."*

Douglas won the election, but the debates made Lincoln the new leader of the Republican party. Within two years, he would be the Republican candidate for President. You can read more about Lincoln in the Biography on page 73.

REVIEW Summarize the views on slavery held by Lincoln and Douglas. **Summarize**

71

A New Political Party

🕐 ***Quick Summary*** The Whig Party disbanded and the Republican Party was born. The Lincoln-Douglas debates set the stage for Abraham Lincoln's presidential candidacy.

14 **Explain what caused the end of the Whig Party.** Within the party, one group was against slavery, and another group was for it. **Cause and Effect**

15 **What do the details in the picture tell you about the Lincoln-Douglas debates?** Possible answer: The flag and the people's formal clothing show that the debates were important. **Analyze Pictures**

H SOCIAL STUDIES STRAND
History

Prejudice Reduction Remind students that Illinois was a Northern state and that slavery had been outlawed in Illinois.

16 **What do you think Douglas thought about slavery? What did Douglas think was important?** Possible answer: It is not clear from the information here; states' right to choose **Evaluate**

Primary Source

Cited in *The Impending Crisis*, by David M. Potter

17 **Based on Lincoln's quotation, what do you think he considered the most important issue in the election?** Preserving the Union; keeping slave states and free states from fighting **Analyze Primary Sources**

✓ **REVIEW ANSWER** Lincoln believed that slavery was wrong. Douglas believed that each state should decide whether or not to allow slavery. **Summarize**

FYI SOCIAL STUDIES
Background

About the Whig Party

- The Whig Party was organized in 1834 by people who opposed President Andrew Jackson.
- The Whig Party took its name from the British political party that opposed royal privileges.

About the Lincoln-Douglas Debates

- Democratic Senator Stephen Douglas and Republican challenger Abraham Lincoln had seven debates.
- Lincoln stressed the importance of unity: "A house divided against itself cannot stand."

Lincoln Is Elected President

🕐 *Quick Summary* Southerners feared that President Lincoln would try to end slavery and refuse to let the South have a voice in the government.

18 **Do you think Southerners were justified in their fears about Lincoln? Why or why not?** Possible answer: No, Lincoln had spoken out against slavery, but he also favored unity. **Evaluate**

✓ **REVIEW ANSWER** Lincoln feared that the United States might split up if the North and South became enemies. If possible, read the Read Aloud passage on p. 45h to students again. **Draw Conclusions**

3 Close and Assess

Summarize the Lesson

Have students create a graphic organizer using one of the events on the time line and supporting it with details.

✓ | **LESSON 3** | **REVIEW** |

1. 🔁 **Main Idea and Details** For possible answers, see the reduced pupil page.

2. Missouri became a slave state; Maine became a free state.

3. California was a free state. Territories were allowed to vote on whether or not they wanted to allow slavery.

4. Dred Scott was a slave who sought freedom through the courts; John Brown was an abolitionist who tried to overthrow slavery violently; caused a further split.

5. **Critical Thinking:** *Make Inferences* Preserving the nation; he thought slavery was wrong, but he did not want a war between the states.

Link to ⚭ Writing

Remind students to use quotation marks for speakers' exact words.

Lincoln Is Elected President

In the election of 1860, the Democratic party split. Northern Democrats chose Stephen Douglas to run for President. Southern Democrats chose John Breckinridge of Kentucky. The Republicans chose Abraham Lincoln.

Lincoln won the election, but without winning any Southern electoral votes. Southerners feared that Lincoln would attempt to end slavery not only in the western territories but in the Southern states as well. Southerners also worried that they would have no voice in the new government. Lincoln said to the South, "We must not **18** be enemies." However, many on both sides viewed the other side as their enemy. In the North and South, the time of compromise had passed.

REVIEW Why do you think Lincoln said, "We must not be enemies" after he became President? **Draw Conclusions**

Summarize the Lesson

- **1820** Congress passed the Missouri Compromise.

- **1850** The Fugitive Slave Law was passed as part of the Compromise of 1850.

- **1857** In the Dred Scott case, the Supreme Court ruled that slaves were not citizens and had no rights, even in free states.

- **1860** Abraham Lincoln was elected President without any Southern support.

LESSON 3 **REVIEW**

Check Facts and Main Ideas

1. 🔁 **Main Idea and Details** On a separate sheet of paper, complete the graphic organizer with details that support the main idea.

There were many attempts to compromise, but the struggle over slavery threatened to tear the United States apart.

| The Missouri Compromise | The Fugitive Slave Law and the Compromise of 1850 | The Kansas-Nebraska Act | Dred Scott and John Brown |

2. How did the **Missouri Compromise** keep the balance of **free and slave states**?

3. How did the **Compromise of 1850** affect slavery in California and the territories gained from Mexico?

4. Who were Dred Scott and John Brown? How did their actions affect the split between the North and South?

5. **Critical Thinking:** *Make Inferences* What was more important to Abraham Lincoln, abolishing slavery or preserving the nation? Explain.

Link to ⚭ Writing

Write a Conversation Write a conversation about the spread of slavery that might have occurred among Americans in the 1850s. You can base your conversation on the words of American leaders in this lesson, such as John C. Calhoun, Daniel Webster, Frederick Douglass, Harriet Beecher Stowe, Abraham Lincoln, and Stephen Douglas. Use the term **states' rights** in your conversation.

72

Practice and Extend

 MEETING INDIVIDUAL NEEDS **Leveled Practice**

Give an Oral Presentation Have students draw from the lesson to present information orally.

Easy Ask students to discuss a person from the lesson whom they admire. They should give reasons. **Reteach**

On-Level Students should prepare and deliver a speech about states' rights and how they affected slavery and the conflict between the North and South. **Extend**

Challenge Students prepare and deliver persuasive speeches explaining which act they think had the greatest impact on the slavery issue. **Enrich**

For a Lesson Summary, use Quick Study, p. 14.

Workbook, p. 18

Lesson 3: The Struggle Over Slavery

Directions: Match each item in the first column to its clue or description in the second column. Write the number of the item on the line before its description.

1. Missouri Compromise
2. Fugitive Slave Law
3. Compromise of 1850
4. Kansas-Nebraska Act
5. Uncle Tom's Cabin
6. Dred Scott decision
7. John Brown's plan
8. Abraham Lincoln
9. Stephen Douglas

_____ The Supreme Court ruled that slaves were not citizens of the United States and had no rights.

_____ This book described the cruelties of slavery and won over many people to the abolitionist cause.

_____ The people of each territory were allowed to decide whether it should be free or slave.

_____ "If slavery is not wrong, then nothing is wrong ... [but I] would not do anything to bring about a war between the free and slave states."

_____ Escaped slaves had to be returned to their owners, even if they had reached Northern states where slavery was not allowed.

_____ A plan to attack pro-slavery people with weapons from the arsenal at Harpers Ferry further divided the North and the South in 1859.

_____ The number of slave states and free states was kept balanced when Missouri was allowed into the Union as a slave state and Maine as a free state.

_____ "Each state ... has a right to do as it pleases on ... slavery."

_____ California became a free state, and the Fugitive Slave Law was passed.

Notes for Home: Your child learned about struggle over slavery that threatened to tear the United States apart.
Home Activity: With your child, choose a current controversial issue from the newspaper. Discuss positions and the divisions that can develop.

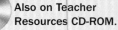 **Also on Teacher Resources CD-ROM.**

Abraham Lincoln 1809–1865

Young Abraham Lincoln had to help his father on the family farm and only attended school for a total of about one year during his life. Yet Abe read anything he could get his hands on. He once said, "My best friend is the man who'll get me a book." So when a neighboring farmer, Josiah Crawford, offered to lend him a biography of George Washington, Abe was thrilled. Unfortunately, one rainy night, the book was left near the leaky cabin walls and got soaked. Abe told the truth, and Crawford was not angry. Abe paid him back by working in his fields.

The book on Washington became one of Abe's favorites, along with the autobiography of Benjamin Franklin. ❶ From these, Abe learned about the men who founded the United States and why the dream of a free country was so important to them.

BIOFACT
Lincoln grew his beard in response to a suggestion from 11-year-old Grace Bedell, who wrote him a letter.

Throughout his life, Lincoln educated himself through reading. When he decided to become a lawyer, he taught himself by studying law books. Even when he was the President, Lincoln read books to learn how to lead the war effort. After the election of 1860, President Lincoln made a speech sharing his deep belief in the future of the United States that he had read about since his childhood. With tension rising between the North and South, he said:

❷ *"If we do not make common cause to save the good old ship of the Union on this voyage, nobody will have a chance to pilot her on another voyage."*

Learn from Biographies
How do you think Lincoln's reading of how Washington met the challenges of the American Revolution helped Lincoln meet the challenges of the Civil War?

For more information, go online to *Meet the People* at **www.sfsocialstudies.com.**

73

CURRICULUM CONNECTION
Literature

Read Biographies Encourage students to read about Abraham Lincoln. Have students create an annotated bibliography for future reference.

Abe Lincoln Remembers, by Ann Warren Turner (HarperCollins Juvenile Books, ISBN 0-060-27577-4, 2003) **Easy**

Abraham Lincoln the Writer: A Treasury of His Greatest Speeches and Letters, edited by Harold Holzer (Boyds Mills Press, ISBN 1-563-97772-9, 2000) **On-Level**

Lincoln: In His Own Words, by Milton Melzer, ed. (Harcourt, ISBN 0-152-45437-3, 1993) **Challenge**

★BIOGRAPHY★

Abraham Lincoln

Objective
• Identify early influences in Abraham Lincoln's life that shaped his character and his deep feelings of patriotism.

1 Introduce and Motivate

Preview To activate prior knowledge, ask students to list what they learned about Abraham Lincoln in Lesson 3. Tell students they will read more about Lincoln's early influences.

2 Teach and Discuss

❶ **Who were Lincoln's heroes? Why do you think he admired these people?** George Washington and Benjamin Franklin; they helped found the United States and believed that the dream of a free country was very important.
➲ **Main Idea and Details**

❷ **What did Lincoln mean by the "ship of the Union"? To what voyage was Lincoln referring?** The ship was the United States, and the voyage was the attempt to preserve the Union.
Make Inferences

3 Close and Assess

Learn from Biographies Answer
Possible answer: He may have been inspired by Washington's courage, dedication, and dream of a free country.

The First Shots Are Fired

Objectives

- Describe the reasons why Southern states seceded from the Union.

- Identify the immediate cause of the start of the Civil War.

- Describe the goals the North and South hoped to achieve by fighting the Civil War.

Vocabulary

secede, p. 75; **Confederacy,** p. 75; **Union,** p. 75; **border state,** p. 76; **civil war,** p. 77

Resources

- Workbook, p. 19
- Transparency 1
- Every Student Learns Guide, pp. 30–33
- Quick Study, pp. 16–17

Quick Teaching Plan

If time is short, ask students to create a three-column chart with the headings *Causes, Events,* and *Effects.*

- Have students list important events as they read through the lesson independently.

- For each event, students should list a cause for that event and/or an effect that the event had on people and other events of the time.

1 Introduce and Motivate

Preview To activate prior knowledge, review the tensions that had arisen between the North and South. Tell students that in Lesson 4 they will learn about what happened when attempts to reach a peaceful solution failed.

You Are There The bombing of Fort Sumter by Confederate forces rallied the North. Ask students what they think will happen now that the first shots have been fired.

LESSON 4

1860   1862

December 1860
South Carolina is the first state to break away from the United States.

February 1861
Seven Southern states form the Confederate States of America.

April 1861
Confederate forces fire on United States troops at Fort Sumter.

PREVIEW

Focus on the Main Idea
Eventually 11 Southern states seceded from the United States, leading to the outbreak of the Civil War.

PLACES
Fort Sumter, South Carolina

PEOPLE
Jefferson Davis

VOCABULARY
secede
Confederacy
Union
border state
civil war

The First Shots Are Fired

You Are There Dawn is about to break in Charleston, South Carolina. The date is April 12, 1861. Mary Boykin Chesnut, the wife of a Southern officer, is staying as a guest in a house near Charleston Harbor. Troops of the Southern states begin firing on Fort Sumter, a United States fort on an island in the harbor.

Chesnut describes the event in her diary:

"I do not pretend to go to sleep. . . . How can I?" She is kept awake by the "heavy booming of a cannon." She springs out of bed and falls to her knees. "I prayed as I never prayed before." Chesnut then puts on her shawl and climbs to the top floor of the house to get a better view. "The shells were bursting." The roar of the cannons fills the air. "We watched up there, and everybody wondered that Fort Sumter did not fire a shot."

Sequence As you read, identify the events that led to the start of the Civil War.

74

Practice and Extend

READING SKILL
Sequence

In the Lesson Review, students complete a graphic organizer like the one below. You may want to provide students with a copy of Transparency 10 to complete as they read the lesson.

Use Transparency 10

VOCABULARY
Word Exercise

Individual Word Study

Tell students that sometimes the same word can have multiple meanings. For example, in *civil war, civil* means "occurring among citizens of one community, state, or nation." Another meaning of *civil* is "polite and courteous." Tell students that both meanings of this word evolved from the Latin word *civis,* meaning "citizen."

Southern States Secede

Many Southerners believed that the South should **secede,** or break away, from the United States. In December 1860, almost two months after Abraham Lincoln was elected President, South Carolina decided to secede.

By February 1, 1861, six more states—Alabama, Florida, Mississippi, Georgia, Louisiana, and Texas—had seceded. Representatives from the seven seceding states met in Montgomery, Alabama. On February 8, they formed their own government. It was called the Confederate States of America, or the **Confederacy.**

The Confederacy adopted a constitution that supported states' rights and slavery. The Confederate constitution said that its congress could not pass laws that denied "the right of property in . . . slaves."

The Confederacy also elected **Jefferson Davis,** a former United States senator from Mississippi, as its president. Like Abraham Lincoln, Jefferson Davis was born in

Kentucky, in a log cabin. But Davis grew up in Mississippi on a plantation owned by his family. Later he developed his own plantation on land given to him by his oldest brother.

After becoming president of the Confederacy, Davis said the Southern states should "look forward to success, to peace, and to prosperity." But in a letter to his wife, Varina, he wrote that the Southern states were "threatened by a powerful opposition." That opposition came from the United States and its newly elected President, Abraham Lincoln. ❷

Lincoln was inaugurated on March 4, 1861. By then the Confederacy had taken control of most of the forts and military property of the United States in the South. The states that remained loyal to the United States government were called the **Union.** One of the forts still under Union control was **Fort Sumter,** in the harbor of Charleston, South Carolina.

REVIEW Summarize the events that occurred as the Confederacy was formed. Summarize

▶ **Jefferson Davis** *(below)* **was president of the Confederacy. The Confederate attack on Fort Sumter** *(left)* **was the start of the Civil War.**

75

🕐 *Quick Summary* Shortly after Abraham Lincoln's election, seven Southern states seceded from the Union to form the Confederacy. Jefferson Davis became the president of the Confederate States of America.

❶ **Contrast the Confederate Constitution with the U.S. Constitution.** U.S. Constitution: gave many powers to the federal government; Confederate Constitution: more power to the states; slavery was lawful **Compare and Contrast**

✓ Ongoing Assessment

If... students have difficulty contrasting the two constitutions,

then... have students reread the paragraph about the Confederate Constitution. Discuss how it might differ from the U.S. Constitution.

❷ **How did President Jefferson Davis feel about the Confederacy?** The Southern states could be peaceful and prosperous, but they were also threatened by opposition from the United States. **Main Idea and Details**

✓ REVIEW ANSWER Abraham Lincoln was elected President. South Carolina seceded from the United States, followed by six other states. The Confederate States of America was formed. The Confederate Constitution was adopted and Jefferson Davis was elected president of the Confederacy. Summarize

SOCIAL STUDIES Background

About the Confederate States of America

- The Confederate States adopted symbols to show that they were an independent country. They designed their own postage stamps and created a flag known as the "Stars and Bars."

- The Confederates felt that their cotton industry would gain them formal recognition from the governments of foreign countries, but the Confederacy was unable to successfully establish relations with Great Britain, France, or any other power in Europe.

- Students may think that all the slave states were part of the Confederacy, but four of the slave states stayed in the Union. (Delaware, Maryland, Missouri, and Kentucky)

The War Begins

 Quick Summary Confederate forces fired the first shots of the Civil War when they fired on Fort Sumter in the harbor of Charleston, South Carolina. Abraham Lincoln responded by asking Union states to supply soldiers to put down the rebellion.

MAP SKILL The Union and the Confederacy, 1861–1865

Guide students as they use the key to determine which states and territories were controlled by the Union or by the Confederacy.

3 Which states were border states?
Missouri, Kentucky, West Virginia, Maryland, and Delaware **Interpret Maps**

MAP SKILL Answer Texas

4 Why did Confederate forces begin firing on Fort Sumter? A Union officer agreed to surrender the fort but asked for three days' wait. The Confederate commander gave orders to fire on the fort if it was not surrendered in one hour after the demand was made. When Union officers did not give up the fort within the demanded amount of time, Confederate forces began shelling it.
Cause and Effect

5 Why do you think the call for troops caused more states to secede?
Possible answer: These states may have been worried about the issue of states' rights. They may have felt that their right to own slaves was being threatened by the upcoming war.
Draw Conclusions

6 Why do you think that the border states stayed in the Union but would not provide soldiers to fight in the war?
Possible answer: These states may have believed it was important to remain part of the United States, but they did not want to fight against people who held some of the same beliefs that they did.
Evaluate

MAP SKILL The Union and the Confederacy, 1861–1865

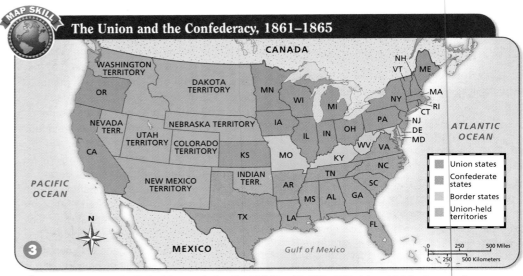

▶ This map shows the United States during the Civil War. Find West Virginia, which broke away from Virginia and voted to stay in the Union. West Virginia became a state in 1863.

MAP SKILL Place *Name the Confederate state that was farthest west.*

The War Begins

On April 9, 1861, Jefferson Davis met with his advisers to discuss Fort Sumter. One adviser said that making the first strike would put the Confederacy "in the wrong." Davis disagreed and decided to send officers to ask for the surrender of the fort.

A Union officer, Robert Anderson, commanded Fort Sumter. He agreed to surrender if the Confederacy would wait three more days. But the Confederate commander, Pierre G. T. Beauregard (BOH ruh gard), had given orders to fire on Fort Sumter if Anderson did not surrender in one hour.

The Confederates began firing on Fort Sumter on Friday, April 12, at 4:30 A.M. The bombing continued into Saturday. With little food and water, Major Anderson was forced to surrender. He and his troops left the fort on Sunday.

Lincoln responded to the attack on Fort Sumter and its surrender by asking Union states to supply 75,000 soldiers to put down

76

the Confederate rebellion. Lincoln believed that this could be done quickly and said the soldiers would be needed for only 90 days.

Lincoln's call for troops so angered the states of Virginia, Arkansas, Tennessee, and North Carolina that they seceded and joined the Confederacy. There were now 11 states in the Confederacy and 23 in the Union. Four of the Union states—Delaware, Maryland, Missouri, and Kentucky—were slave states that seemed unsure whether to stay in the Union or join the Confederacy. These were called the **border states** because they were located between the Union and Confederacy. Three of these states—Delaware, Missouri, and Kentucky—said they would not provide soldiers. Maryland said it would, but only to defend Washington, D.C.

Lincoln believed it was important to keep these border states in the Union, even though they were slave states. That is why in 1861 he continued to say that his aim was to hold the United States together, not to abolish slavery.

Practice and Extend

 **MEETING INDIVIDUAL NEEDS**
Leveled Practice

Act as Reporters Have students act as on-the-scene reporters giving firsthand accounts of the shelling of Fort Sumter.

Easy Students can reread the account of the bombing, using tone and word emphasis to underscore important events. Each time a student reads, a volunteer can provide a "recap," summarizing what was said. **Reteach**

On-Level Have students paraphrase or summarize the lesson. They can add ideas about what these events may mean for the future of the Union and the Confederacy. Remind them to use vivid, colorful language that will help their listeners feel as if they are witnessing the events themselves. **Extend**

Challenge Building on the "On-Level" idea, groups of students can interview "bystanders" and important figures from history, such as the commander of Fort Sumter, Jefferson Davis, and Abraham Lincoln. **Enrich**

For a Lesson Summary, use Quick Study, p. 16.

The conflict between the states arose for a number of reasons. For Lincoln and his supporters, the main reason for fighting the war was to preserve, or keep together, the Union. However, other supporters of the North believed they were fighting to end slavery. Southerners fought the war to preserve states' rights and slavery. They also believed they were defending their homeland and their way of life.

The battle at Fort Sumter began the American Civil War. A **civil war** is a war between people of the same country. Some Northerners described the war as a rebellion and the Confederacy as a group of rebels. Many Southerners accepted the name *rebel* with pride. To them the conflict was known as the War for Southern Independence. They also called it the War of Northern Aggression. The title War Between the States is also com-monly used. But no matter what it was called, the war would be longer and bloodier than anyone guessed in the spring of 1861.

REVIEW What were the main differences between the reasons the North and South fought the Civil War? **Compare and Contrast**

Summarize the Lesson

- **December 1860** South Carolina became the first state to secede from the United States.
- **February 1861** Seven Southern states formed the Confederate States of America.
- **April 1861** Confederate forces fired on United States troops at Fort Sumter, a battle that began the Civil War.

LESSON 4   REVIEW

Check Facts and Main Ideas

1. **Sequence** On a separate sheet of paper, complete the graphic organizer to show the events that led up to the start of the Civil War.

   Seven Southern states seceded from the United States and formed the Confederate States of America.

   ↓

   The Confederacy elected Jefferson Davis as its president.

   ↓

   Jefferson Davis sent Confederate soldiers to make Fort Sumter surrender.

   ↓

   The Civil War began on April 12, 1861

2. Why did the Southern states **secede?**

3. **Critical Thinking:** *Draw Conclusions* What might have been Jefferson Davis's reason for attacking Fort Sumter?

4. Describe Abraham Lincoln's main reason for fighting the Civil War.

5. Why at the beginning of the Civil War did Lincoln not say that he was fighting the war to end slavery?

Link to Writing

Write an Article Suppose you are part of the **Union** or **Confederacy** at the start of the war in 1861. Research the man who is your president and write a brief article explaining why he is qualified for his position.

77

---

7 **Compare and contrast Abraham Lincoln's reasons for involvement in the Civil War with reasons of other Northerners.** Although he thought that slavery was wrong, Lincoln's main reason for fighting was to preserve the Union. Other Northerners believed they were going to war to end slavery. **Compare and Contrast**

✓ **REVIEW ANSWER** Northerners fought the war to keep the Union together and to end slavery. Southerners fought the war to preserve states' rights and slavery and to defend their homeland and way of life. **Compare and Contrast**

3 Close and Assess

Summarize the Lesson

Have students create a cause and effect chart using two of the points on the time line.

✓ **LESSON 4   REVIEW**

1. **Sequence** For possible answers, see the reduced pupil page.

2. To preserve the rights of states and to uphold the practice of slavery

3. **Critical Thinking:** *Draw Conclusions* Possible answer: To show that the fort now belonged to the Confederacy.

4. To preserve the Union

5. The border states were still part of the Union, yet they allowed slavery. If Lincoln had said he was fighting the war to end slavery, the border states may have joined the Confederacy.

Link to Writing

Review the information about the two men found in the lesson before students begin their research.

Workbook, p. 19

Lesson 4: The First Shots Are Fired
Directions: Sequence the events in the order in which they occurred by numbering them from 1 to 8. You may use your textbook.

____ Lincoln asks Union states for troops to put down the Confederate rebellion.

____ Abraham Lincoln is elected President of the United States.

____ Some states are angered by Lincoln's call for troops. Virginia, Arkansas, Tennessee, and North Carolina secede and join the Confederacy.

____ The Confederate States of America, or the Confederacy, is formed.

____ The Confederates attack Fort Sumter, which is surrendered two days later. The Civil War has started.

____ Jefferson Davis, president of the Confederacy, asks for the surrender of Union-held Fort Sumter in Charleston, South Carolina.

____ The Southern states of South Carolina, Alabama, Florida, Mississippi, Georgia, Louisiana, and Texas secede.

____ By Lincoln's inauguration on March 4, 1861, the Confederacy has control of most of the forts and military property in the South.

Directions: Explain each of the following points of view from the time of the American Civil War. You may use your textbook.

1. Explain the goal Lincoln and his supporters hoped to achieve by fighting the Civil War.

2. Explain the goal Southerners hoped to achieve by fighting the Civil War.

3. Why do you think Northerners called Southerners "rebels"?

Notes for Home: Your child learned to identify the main idea and supporting details of an assigned reading selection.
Home Activity: With your child, talk over a previous lesson. Ask your child to point out the main ideas and identify the supporting facts and details.

Also on Teacher Resources CD-ROM.

Resources
- Assessment Book, pp. 5–8
- Workbook, p. 20: Vocabulary Review

Chapter Summary

For possible answers, see the reduced pupil page.

Vocabulary

1. b, **2.** d, **3.** a, **4.** e, **5.** c

People and Terms

1. David Walker was a free African American who spoke against slavery.
2. Nat Turner led an armed uprising of slaves in Virginia.
3. Southern states seceded from the Union and formed the Confederacy.
4. Harriet Tubman led many slaves from the South to freedom in the North.
5. John C. Calhoun was a U.S. senator from South Carolina who believed in a state's right to decide which laws best served its own needs.
6. The Fugitive Slave Law said that escaped slaves had to be returned.
7. Harriet Beecher Stowe wrote *Uncle Tom's Cabin*, which convinced many people to support abolition.
8. In the Dred Scott case, the Supreme Court ruled that slaves had no rights because they were not citizens.
9. Jefferson Davis became the president of the Confederate States.
10. The states loyal to the U.S. government were called the Union.

Facts and Main Ideas

1. When slaves worked, where they went, and whether they could marry
2. Anti-slavery members of the Whig Party formed the Republican Party.
3. About 26 years
4. Attitudes toward states' rights, tariffs, and slavery
5. Slave escapes, refusals to obey orders, and slave rebellions
6. It was difficult for people with differing opinions about slavery to get along.
7. The South worried that Lincoln would prohibit slavery. This belief led Southern states to secede and form their own government.
8. So that an equal number of senators represented each group in Congress

---

CHAPTER 1
REVIEW

1820	1830	1840

1820
Missouri Compromise

1831
Nat Turner leads a slave rebellion in Virginia

1846
Congress votes to lower tariffs on imports

Chapter Summary

Target Skill

Main Idea and Details

On a separate sheet of paper, fill in the main compromises made in Congress before the Civil War.

Congress made several compromises to keep the North and South from splitting apart.

- Missouri Compromise
- Compromise of 1850
- Kansas-Nebraska Act

▶ Tattered flag from the battle at Fort Sumter

Vocabulary

Match each word with the correct definition or description.

1. **sectionalism** (p. 55)
2. **slave codes** (p. 61)
3. **free state** (p. 67)
4. **secede** (p. 75)
5. **Underground Railroad** (p. 63)

a. state that does not permit slavery

b. loyalty to a part of a country, not to the whole country

c. secret system to help slaves escape to freedom

d. laws controlling behavior of slaves

e. break away

People and Terms

Write a sentence explaining why each of the following people or terms was important in the events that led to the start of the Civil War. You may use two or more in a single sentence.

1. **David Walker** (p. 57)
2. **Nat Turner** (p. 62)
3. **Confederacy** (p. 75)
4. **Harriet Tubman** (p. 63)
5. **John C. Calhoun** (p. 67)
6. **Fugitive Slave Law** (p. 68)
7. **Harriet Beecher Stowe** (p. 70)
8. **Dred Scott** (p. 70)
9. **Jefferson Davis** (p. 75)
10. **Union** (p. 75)

78

Practice and Extend

Assessment Options

✓ Chapter 1 Assessment
- Chapter 1 Content Test: Use Assessment Book, pp. 5–6.
- Chapter 1 Skills Test: Use Assessment Book, pp. 7–8.

Standardized Test Prep
- Chapter 1 Tests contain standardized test format.

✓ Chapter 1 Performance Assessment
- Have students work in small groups to create displays (or plan displays) for a museum that showcases U.S. history in the years leading up to the Civil War.
- Students might include drawings of important figures with short biographies, maps, excerpts from speeches, and descriptions of the compromises. Students should explain why these resources are important to understanding this period.
- As students present their work, assess their knowledge of key concepts in the chapter.

1849
Harriet Tubman escapes slavery on the Underground Railroad

1857
Dred Scott case

1860
Abraham Lincoln is elected President

February 1861
Confederate States of America formed

April 1861
Southern forces fire on U.S. troops at Fort Sumter

Facts and Main Ideas

1 What kinds of control did slave owners have over the lives of slaves?

2 How did the issue of slavery lead to a new political party?

3 **Time Line** How many years were there between the Nat Turner revolt and the Dred Scott case?

4 **Main Idea** What were some differences between the North and South that increased tensions between the two regions?

5 **Main Idea** How did many slaves resist slavery?

6 **Main Idea** How did the differences over slavery threaten the existence of the United States?

7 **Main Idea** What effect did Lincoln's election have on the South?

8 **Critical Thinking:** *Draw Conclusions* Why did people work to keep a balance between the number of slave states and free states?

Write About History

1 **Write a journal entry** as a person who observed the battle at Fort Sumter.

2 **Write a poem** about a person mentioned in this chapter whom you admire.

3 **Write a short speech** you might have given as a senator for or against the Missouri Compromise.

Apply Skills

Recognize Point of View
Read the two sections below from the Lincoln-Douglas debates. Then answer the questions.

"If slavery is not wrong, then nothing is wrong. . . . [But I] would not do anything to bring about a war between the free and slave states."

—Abraham Lincoln

"If each state will only agree to mind its own business . . . this republic can exist forever divided into free and slave states."

—Stephen Douglas

1 What is the subject of each section?

2 What is Lincoln's viewpoint about slavery?

3 What is Douglas's viewpoint about slavery?

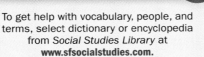

Internet Activity

To get help with vocabulary, people, and terms, select dictionary or encyclopedia from *Social Studies Library* at **www.sfsocialstudies.com.**

79

Write About History

Test Talk

Write Your Answer to Score High

1. Remind students that a journal entry should be written from the first-person point of view. Tell students to use details from the chapter to make their journal entry realistic.

2. Remind students that poems do not have to rhyme. Students should use words and images to "paint a picture" of the subject they choose.

3. Encourage students to list their opinions and persuasive facts supporting those opinions. Remind them that their speeches should have a formal and respectful tone.

Apply Skills

1. The subject is slavery and its effect on the relationship of free states and slave states.

2. Lincoln believes that slavery is wrong, but does not believe there should be a war between free states and slave states.

3. Douglas believes that the question of slavery should be left up to each state.

Hands-on Unit Project

✓ Unit 1 Performance Assessment

- See p. 118 for information about using the Unit Project as a means of performance assessment.
- A scoring guide is provided on p. 118.

WEB SITE
Technology

For more information, students can select the dictionary or encyclopedia from *Social Studies Library* at **www.sfsocialstudies.com.**

Workbook, p. 20

Vocabulary Review

Directions: Choose the vocabulary word from the box that best completes each sentence. Write the word on the line provided. Not all words will be used.

sectionalism	states' rights	secede
slave codes	Missouri Compromise	Confederacy
Underground Railroad	Fugitive Slave Law	Union
free state	Compromise of 1850	border state
slave state	Kansas-Nebraska Act	civil war

1. The _____ was made up of states that remained loyal to the United States government.

2. The _____ allowed California to be admitted to the Union as a free state.

3. _____ is the idea that people of a state can choose the laws that best fit their needs.

4. South Carolina was the first state to _____ from the Union.

5. The _____ preserved the balance between free and slave states.

6. The states that seceded from the Union formed the _____.

7. The _____ allowed people in certain areas to determine whether or not their territory would allow slavery.

8. Although some former slaves had reached the North and found freedom, the _____ said they had to be returned to their owners.

9. _____ did not allow slaves to own land.

10. Slavery was illegal in California and any other _____.

11. Harriet Tubman became famous for helping slaves escape to freedom on the _____.

Notes for Home: Your child learned the vocabulary terms for Chapter 1.
Home Activity: Have your child practice the vocabulary terms in sentences of his or her own.

Also on Teacher Resources CD-ROM.

Chapter Planning Guide

Chapter 2 • War and Reconstruction

Locating Time and Place pp. 80–81

Lesson Titles	Pacing	Main Ideas
Lesson 1 **The Early Stages of the War** pp. 82–86	2 days	• In the early years of the Civil War, the North and South formed strategies in hopes of gaining a quick victory.
Biography: Robert E. Lee p. 87		• Robert E. Lee made the difficult decision to command the Virginia forces.
Lesson 2 **Life During the War** pp. 88–93	2 days	• As the Civil War continued, people in the North and the South suffered many hardships, including the growing loss of life.
Citizen Heroes: Caring **Working for Lasting Peace** pp. 94–95		• Jody Williams continues her efforts to rid the world of land mines.
Lesson 3 **How the North Won** pp. 96–101	3 days	• A series of Northern victories led to the end of the Civil War by 1865.
Map and Globe Skills: **Read a Road Map** pp. 102–103		• Road maps allow you to figure out how to get from one place to another.
Communications During the **Civil War** pp. 104–105		• Both Union and Confederate armies used Morse code and secret military codes to communicate.
Lesson 4 **The End of Slavery** pp. 106–111	2 days	• The country faced many difficult challenges after the Civil War ended, including rebuilding the South and protecting the rights of newly freed African Americans.

✔ **Chapter 2 Review**
pp. 112–113

African American men were granted the right to vote by the Fifteenth Amendment.

✔ = Assessment Options

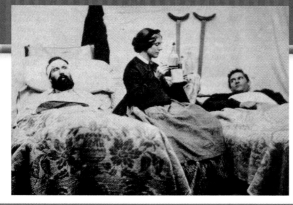

◀ **During the war some women cared for soldiers.**

Vocabulary	Resources	Meeting Individual Needs
blockade Anaconda Plan First Battle of Bull Run Battle of Antietam	• Workbook, p. 22 • Transparency 1 • Every Student Learns Guide, pp. 34–37 • Quick Study, pp. 18–19	• Leveled Practice, TE p. 83 • ESL Support, TE p. 84
draft Emancipation Proclamation	• Workbook, p. 23 • Transparency 1 • Every Student Learns Guide, pp. 38–41 • Quick Study, pp. 20–21	• Leveled Practice, TE p. 89 • ESL Support, TE p. 92
Battle of Gettysburg Gettysburg Address Battle of Vicksburg total war road map interstate highway	• Workbook, p. 24 • Transparencies 1, 54, 55 • Every Student Learns Guide, pp. 42–45 • Quick Study, pp. 22–23 • Workbook, p. 25	• Leveled Practice, TE p. 97 • Learning Styles, TE p. 98 • ESL Support, TE p. 101 • Leveled Practice, TE p. 102
assassination, Reconstruction, Thirteenth Amendment, black codes, Freedmen's Bureau, Fourteenth Amendment, Fifteenth Amendment, impeachment, Jim Crow laws, segregation, sharecropping	• Workbook, p. 26 • Transparency 1 • Every Student Learns Guide, pp. 46–49 • Quick Study, pp. 24–25	• Leveled Practice, TE p. 108 • ESL Support, TE p. 109
	✓ Chapter 2 Content Test, Assessment Book pp. 9–10 ✓ Chapter 2 Skills Test, Assessment Book, pp. 11–12	✓ Chapter 2 Performance Assessment, TE p. 112

Providing More Depth

Additional Resources

- Vocabulary Workbook and Cards
- Social Studies Plus! pp. 38–43
- Daily Activity Bank
- Big Book Atlas
- Student Atlas
- Outline Maps
- Desk Maps

 Technology

- AudioText
- MindPoint® Quiz Show CD-ROM
- ExamView® Test Bank CD-ROM
- Teacher Resources CD-ROM
- Map Resources CD-ROM
- SFSuccessNet: iText (Pupil Edition online), iTE (Teacher's Edition online), Online Planner
- **www.sfsocialstudies.com** (Biographies, news, references, maps, and activities)

 To establish guidelines for your students' safe and responsible use of the Internet, use the Scott Foresman Internet Guide.

Additional Internet Links

To find out more about:

- Women in the Civil War, visit **www.nara.gov**
- International Campaign to Ban Landmines, visit **www.icbl.org**
- Gettysburg National Military Park, visit **www.nps.gov**

Key Internet Search Terms

- Civil War
- Abraham Lincoln
- Robert E. Lee
- Reconstruction

Workbook Support

Use the following Workbook pages to support content and skills development as you teach Chapter 2. You can also view and print Workbook pages from the Teacher Resources CD-ROM.

Workbook, p. 21

Vocabulary Preview

Use with Chapter 2.

Directions: Circle the vocabulary term that best completes each sentence.

1. The (Anaconda Plan, Reconstruction) was a three-part war strategy to crush the South during the Civil War.

2. Slavery was abolished by the (Thirteenth Amendment, Fourteenth Amendment) to the Constitution.

3. The (First Battle of Bull Run, Battle of Gettysburg) lasted three days and was one of the most important battles of the Civil War.

4. African Americans became U.S. citizens under the (Fourteenth Amendment, Thirteenth Amendment) to the Constitution.

5. At the (Battle of Antietam, Battle of Vicksburg) Union forces blockaded the city and bombarded it for 48 days.

6. (Segregation, Sharecropping) is the separation of blacks and whites.

7. Both the North and the South instituted the (blockade, draft) to get men to fight in the war.

8. The (Gettysburg Address, Emancipation Proclamation) granted freedom to slaves in any Confederate states that were still battling the Union.

9. The time after the war when the country was rebuilding and healing is known as (Reconstruction, segregation).

10. The (black codes, blockade) kept supplies from reaching Southern soldiers.

11. One of the early battles of the war was the (Battle of Gettysburg, First Battle of Bull Run).

12. People in many U.S. cities paid their respects to President Lincoln after his (assassination, impeachment).

13. The (Freedmen's Bureau, Emancipation Proclamation) was established to help former slaves after the war.

14. All male citizens received the right to vote with the ratification of the (Thirteenth Amendment, Fifteenth Amendment) to the Constitution.

15. The (Emancipation Proclamation, Jim Crow laws) enforced separation of blacks and whites.

16. Republicans in Congress called for the (total war, impeachment) of President Andrew Johnson.

Notes for Home: Your child learned the vocabulary terms for Chapter 2.
Home Activity: With your child, review each vocabulary term and its definition to make sure the term fits in the sentence. Then make your own sentences using the vocabulary terms.

Use with Pupil Edition, p. 80

Workbook, p. 22

Lesson 1: The Early Stages of the War

Use with Pages 82–86.

Directions: Complete each compare-and-contrast table with information about the Union and the Confederacy. You may use your textbook.

	Supporters of the North	Supporters of the South
Reason for fighting	to preserve the Union	to preserve their way of life

	Northerners	Southerners
Believed advantage over the opposition	Armies needed supplies, and the North produced more than 90 percent of the country's weapons, cloth, shoes, and iron.	The South's more rural way of life would better prepare soldiers for war. The South had a history of producing military leaders.

	Union	Confederacy
War strategies	Three-part plan of action: (1) set up a blockade of the Confederacy's Atlantic and Gulf coasts, (2) capture territory along the Mississippi to weaken the Confederacy by cutting the Southern states in two, (3) attack the Confederacy from both the east and the west.	Defend the Confederacy until the North grows tired and gives up. Northerners, who have nothing to gain, will not fight as fiercely as Southerners. Britain will assist in the war because English clothing mills depend on Southern cotton.

Notes for Home: Your child learned about different attitudes toward war and different strategies used by the North and South during the Civil War.
Home Activity: With your child, discuss possible problems the Union and the Confederacy might have had to consider when forming their war strategies. Ask your child what could have gone wrong in each case.

Use with Pupil Edition, p. 86

Workbook, p. 23

Lesson 2: Life During the War

Use with Pages 88–93.

Directions: For each main idea, write a supporting detail on the line provided. You may use your textbook.

1. **Main Idea:** News of the war spread in many ways.
   Detail: The news spread through letters, newspaper articles, and photographs.

2. **Main Idea:** As the war continued, both sides had trouble getting more soldiers.
   Detail: Possible answers: The number of volunteers decreased, so both sides passed draft laws; in the Union, men paid $300 to avoid fighting; in the Confederacy, some men paid substitutes to fight in their place.

3. **Main Idea:** Most of the soldiers who died in the Civil War did not die in battle.
   Detail: Possible answer: Disease was the most common cause of death in the Civil War.

4. **Main Idea:** The Civil War did not begin as a war against slavery.
   Detail: Lincoln's goal was to keep the nation united.

5. **Main Idea:** African Americans who wished to serve in the war were not treated the same as white soldiers.
   Detail: Possible answers: At first, African Americans were not allowed to join the Union army; African American soldiers were paid less than white soldiers at first.

6. **Main Idea:** Women contributed to the war effort in many ways.
   Detail: Possible answers: Women ran businesses and farms and became teachers and office workers; some women became spies; some women became nurses; some women gathered supplies for soldiers.

Notes for Home: Your child learned to identify the main idea and supporting details of a reading selection.
Home Activity: With your child, look over a previous lesson. Ask your child to point out the main ideas and then identify supporting facts and details.

Use with Pupil Edition, p. 93

Workbook, p. 24

Lesson 3: How the North Won

Use with Pages 96–101.

Directions: Match each term in the box with its clue. Write the term on the line provided.

Battle of Gettysburg	Ulysses S. Grant	total war
Gettysburg Address	Battle of Vicksburg	Robert E. Lee
Anaconda Plan	William Tecumseh Sherman	Appomattox Court House

1. Place where Generals Lee and Grant met to discuss the terms of the Confederates' surrender of the Civil War **Appomattox Court House**

2. "I would rather die a thousand deaths." **Robert E. Lee**

3. President Lincoln made a short speech at a ceremony to dedicate a national cemetery. In his speech, Lincoln inspired the Union to keep fighting for a united nation and the end of slavery. **Gettysburg Address**

4. A method of warfare designed to destroy the opposing army and the people's will to fight **total war**

5. This three-day battle began on July 1, 1863. It was one of the most important battles of the Civil War. It was an important victory for the North and a costly battle for both sides. **Battle of Gettysburg**

6. Head of the Union forces in the Battle of Vicksburg **Ulysses S. Grant**

7. The surrender of this battle by the Southerners cut the Confederacy in two. **Battle of Vicksburg**

8. The Union blockade at the Battle of Vicksburg was part of this strategy to gain control of the Mississippi River and weaken the Confederacy. **Anaconda Plan**

9. Led soldiers in a destructive "March to the Sea" **William Tecumseh Sherman**

Notes for Home: Your child learned how the North used strategies to win the Civil War.
Home Activity: With your child, brainstorm strategies for winning a game such as checkers, chess, or cards. Discuss the advantages of using a strategy to defeat an opponent.

Use with Pupil Edition, p. 101

Workbook Support

Workbook, p. 25

Read a Road Map

Use with Pages 102–103.

A road map shows roads, cities, and places of interest. Drivers use road maps to figure out how to get from one place to another.

Directions: Use the road map to answer the following questions.

1. General Sherman's army probably walked and rode horses from Atlanta to Savannah, Georgia. What major roads might you take today to drive between these two cities?

   Interstate 75 and Interstate 16

2. What major city would you pass through when traveling along this route from Atlanta to Savannah? **Macon**

3. According to this map, what other roads might you take to travel from Atlanta to Savannah? **Possible answers: Hwy 23 and Hwy 80**

4. Examine the map. Why do you think General Sherman's march was known as the "March to the Sea"? **Possible answer: Savannah is located on the ocean, and the march from Atlanta to Savannah would go toward the sea.**

5. General Sherman's army left Savannah and went to South Carolina. If you were to drive from Savannah to South Carolina today, what major road might you take?

   Interstate 95

 Notes for Home: Your child learned how to read a road map.
Home Activity: With your child, look at a road map of your state. Together, determine the most direct route from your city to one of your state's borders. Next, find the most scenic route.

Use with Pupil Edition, p. 103

Workbook, p. 26

Lesson 4: The End of Slavery

Use with Pages 106–111.

Directions: Define each term or phrase. Use a separate sheet of paper if you need more room. You may use your textbook.

1. Reconstruction **The rebuilding and healing of the country after the Civil War**

2. Thirteenth Amendment **The amendment that abolished slavery in the United States**

3. black codes **Laws that denied African Americans many things, including the right to vote, to take part in jury trials, to own land or guns, or to take certain jobs; allowed unemployed African Americans to be fined or arrested**

4. Freedmen's Bureau **Bureau established to help the 4 million former slaves after the war**

5. Ku Klux Klan **Group formed to restore white control over African Americans after the war**

6. Fourteenth Amendment **Gave African Americans citizenship and equal protection of the law**

7. Jim Crow laws **Laws that enforced segregation**

8. sharecropping **The practice of renting land from landowners and then paying the rent with a portion of the crop produced on that land**

 Notes for Home: Your child learned about how the United States changed after the Civil War.
Home Activity: With your child, review the series of changes that took place during Reconstruction and discuss who benefited from each change.

Use with Pupil Edition, p. 111

Workbook, p. 27

Vocabulary Review

Use with Chapter 2.

Directions: Use the vocabulary words from Chapter 15 to complete the following sentences. Write the correct word in the space provided. You may use your textbook.

1. **Segregation** is the separation of blacks and whites.

2. The shutting off of an area by troops or ships to keep people and supplies from moving in or out is known as a **blockade**.

3. At the Battle of **Vicksburg**, Union forces blockaded the city and bombarded it with cannon fire by land and sea for 48 days.

4. **Sharecropping** is the practice of renting land from a landowner and paying rent with a portion of the crop produced on that land.

5. The murdering of a government or political leader is known as an **assassination**.

6. Laws that denied blacks the right to vote or take part in jury trials were known as **black codes**.

7. A method of warfare that destroys not only the opposing army but also the people's will to fight is known as **total war**.

8. In the Battle of **Antietam**, Union and Confederate forces clashed near the town of Sharpsburg in Maryland.

9. The First Battle of **Bull Run**, one of the early battles of the Civil War, was won by the Confederates.

10. The **Freedmen's Bureau** was established to help the more than 4 million former slaves after the war.

11. **Reconstruction** refers to the rebuilding of the country after the Civil War.

12. The Battle of **Gettysburg** lasted three days and was one of the most important battles of the Civil War.

13. **Jim Crow** laws enforced the separation of blacks and whites.

14. The **Anaconda** Plan was a war strategy designed to "squeeze" the Confederacy.

 Notes for Home: Your child learned the vocabulary terms for Chapter 2.
Home Activity: With your child, analyze the relationships among the vocabulary terms for this unit. Begin by having your child place each term on a time line for the Civil War era.

Use with Pupil Edition, p. 113

Workbook, p. 28

UNIT 1 Project   We Interrupt This Program

Directions: In a group, present a special report about an event described in this unit. Group members should choose a role and complete the assignment for that role.

1. The event that we chose is

2. My role in the news program is (✔)

   ____ news anchor   ____ reporter   ____ government official   ____ citizen

3. News Anchor: Write a summary of the event.

4. Reporter: Write questions to ask the government official and the citizen.

5. Government Official: Describe the event from your point of view.

6. Citizen: If you are an eyewitness, write a description of what you saw. If you were involved in the event, tell what happened from your point of view.

Following the presentation, have students discuss why the event was important.

✔ Checklist for Students

____ We chose an event.
____ We chose a role to play in the news program.
____ We wrote about the event from the point of view of our assigned role.
____ Our group made a banner and background for our news program.

 Notes for Home: Your child learned how to report important details of an event in a news program.
Home Activity: Watch a news program with your child. Discuss what important facts are reported about each event, and why each event might be important.

Use with Pupil Edition, p. 118

Assessment Support

Use these Assessment Book pages and the ExamView® Test Bank CD-ROM to assess content and skills in Chapter 2 and Unit 1. You can also view and print Assessment Book pages from the Teacher Resources CD-ROM.

Assessment Book, p. 9

Chapter 2 Test

Part 1: Content Test

Directions: Fill in the circle next to the correct answer.

Lesson Objective (1:1)

1. Which of the following did the South see as its advantage in the war?
   - Ⓐ The South had plenty of cotton for cloth.
   - Ⓑ The South produced more than half of the country's wheat.
   - Ⓒ The army needed supplies.
   - ● Southerners' rural lifestyles better prepared soldiers for war.

Lesson Objective (1:2)

2. Which of the following was a war strategy used by the Union?
   - Ⓐ stampede
   - ● blockade
   - Ⓒ bombing
   - Ⓓ air raid

Lesson Objective (1:2)

3. Which of the following did Confederates believe?
   - Ⓐ Northerners would fight a long time.
   - Ⓑ Britain would help the Union.
   - ● Northerners would grow tired of fighting and give up.
   - Ⓓ The Union would use the Anaconda Plan.

Lesson Objective (1:3)

4. Which of the following describes the early battles of the Civil War?
   - ● They were confusing because most of the troops were new to war.
   - Ⓑ They were well organized and efficient.
   - Ⓒ The Union always won because the North had better soldiers.
   - Ⓓ The Confederacy always won because the South had better soldiers.

Lesson Objective (1:4)

5. Which of the following describes the effect of new military technology on the Civil War?
   - Ⓐ More accurate weapons resulted in fewer casualties.
   - ● More accurate weapons resulted in many casualties.
   - Ⓒ Stronger ships resulted in fewer sea battles.
   - Ⓓ New weapons reduced the need for blockades.

Lesson Objective (2:1)

6. Which of the following was NOT experienced by both Northern and Southern soldiers?
   - Ⓐ Soldiers were unhappy with the food.
   - Ⓑ Soldiers saw friends die.
   - ● Soldiers often had to fight in bare feet.
   - Ⓓ Soldiers were drafted.

Lesson Objective (2:2)

7. What was the Emancipation Proclamation?
   - Ⓐ a statement giving freedom to all women
   - Ⓑ a statement giving freedom to all people in the United States
   - Ⓒ a statement giving freedom to all Confederate states still at war with the Union
   - ● a statement giving freedom to slaves in all Confederate states still at war with the Union

Use with Pupil Edition, p. 112

Assessment Book, p. 10

Lesson Objective (2:3)

8. What is one way African Americans served the Union's war effort?
   - ● They engaged in combat.
   - Ⓑ They protested against slavery.
   - Ⓒ They supported freedom and went to Canada.
   - Ⓓ They staged demonstrations to end the war.

Lesson Objective (2:4)

9. Which is NOT one way women contributed to the war effort?
   - Ⓐ They cared for the soldiers.
   - ● They ran the government.
   - Ⓒ They ran businesses.
   - Ⓓ They were spies.

Lesson Objective (3:1)

10. Which of the following describes the Battle of Gettysburg?
    - Ⓐ Lee and Pickett battled against each other, and the North won.
    - Ⓑ Lee's retreat to Virginia won the battle for the South.
    - Ⓒ The Pennsylvania battle was won by the South.
    - ● The three-day struggle was won by the North.

Lesson Objective (3:3)

11. Which cut the Confederacy in two?
    - ● Battle of Vicksburg
    - Ⓑ Battle of Gettysburg
    - Ⓒ Battle of Savannah
    - Ⓓ Battle of Bull Run

Lesson Objective (3:4)

12. Which is a result of total war?
    - Ⓐ Everybody helps out any way they can.
    - Ⓑ An area is squeezed the way a snake would squeeze its prey.
    - Ⓒ Supplies are cut off.
    - ● The people's will to fight is destroyed.

Lesson Objective (4:1)

13. Why did Congress disagree with President Andrew Johnson's Reconstruction plan?
    - ● They thought it was too easy on the South.
    - Ⓑ They did not want to include all of the Southern states.
    - Ⓒ They did not want to allow all African Americans to be free.
    - Ⓓ They thought the plan was cruel to Southerners.

Lesson Objective (4:2)

14. Which of the following was an effect of the Reconstruction Acts?
    - Ⓐ All African Americans had the right to vote.
    - ● African American men had the right to vote.
    - Ⓒ African Americans could lobby Congress for the right to vote.
    - Ⓓ African Americans were not allowed to vote.

Lesson Objective (4:3)

15. What did the passage of the Thirteenth, Fourteenth, and Fifteenth Amendments mean for African Americans?
    - ● African Americans were free citizens, and the men could vote.
    - Ⓑ African Americans became citizens.
    - Ⓒ Slavery was abolished.
    - Ⓓ Equal protection could not be denied any citizen.

Use with Pupil Edition, p. 112

Assessment Book, p. 11

Part 2: Skills Test

Directions: Use complete sentences to answer questions 1–5. Use a separate sheet of paper if you need more space.

1. How did the South plan to win the war? **Summarize**

   > Southerners planned to wear down the North because they believed that Northerners would quickly grow tired of fighting and give up. They also were hoping to get aid from Britain.

2. Support the statement in the box below with details. **Main Idea and Details**

   > Life was difficult for soldiers during the Civil War.

   Detail 1
   > Supplies were short, and soldiers had to make do with food they disliked.

   Detail 2
   > They had to walk long distances and often wore out their shoes.

   Detail 3
   > They were exposed to harsh weather conditions with no protection.

   Detail 4
   > They suffered and died from disease and infection.

Use with Pupil Edition, p. 112

Assessment Book, p. 12

3. Why do you think General Grant allowed total war to be used to defeat Lee but then offered to feed Lee's men after their surrender? **Draw Conclusions**

   > **Possible answer:** Grant did what was necessary to win the war. However, he realized that the Confederate soldiers were again his countrymen and that everyone would have to forgive each other for the nation to heal.

4. Why did Reconstruction include the Thirteenth, Fourteenth, and Fifteenth Amendments? **Make Inferences**

   > **Possible answer:** The goal of Reconstruction was to rebuild and heal the nation. Abolishing slavery was the first step in recognizing African Americans as valuable people. Granting citizenship and the right to vote helped make all men equal.

Road Map of Georgia

5. Use the map to answer the questions. **Read a Road Map**

   a. What route would you take to travel from Vidalia to Albany?

   > You would follow U.S. highway 280 west to U.S. highway 19 south to Albany.

   b. What distance in miles would you travel if you went from Atlanta to Macon?

   > You would travel about 80 miles.

Use with Pupil Edition, p. 112

Assessment Support

Assessment Book, p. 13

Unit 1 Test

Part 1: Content Test

Directions: Fill in the circle next to the correct answer.

Lesson Objective (1–1:1)

1. Which of the following was becoming more popular among people in the North during the 1850s?
   Ⓐ working on small farms
   ● working in factories
   Ⓒ living on small farms
   Ⓓ living in small towns

Lesson Objective (1–1:3)

2. Why did Southerners want to preserve slavery?
   Ⓐ Slaves were their friends.
   Ⓑ Slaves obeyed them.
   ● Slavery was profitable for them.
   Ⓓ Slavery made them feel important.

Lesson Objective (1–2:1)

3. Which of the following is a way slaves resisted slavery?
   ● They pretended to be sick.
   Ⓑ They held prayer meetings.
   Ⓒ They told family stories.
   Ⓓ They sang while they worked.

Lesson Objective (1–2:3)

4. What was the purpose of the Underground Railroad?
   Ⓐ It was a secret railroad that ran only at night.
   Ⓑ It was a secret organization to turn in slaves.
   Ⓒ It carried people to other cities at night.
   ● It helped slaves escape to freedom.

Lesson Objective (1–3:1)

5. What was the result of the Missouri Compromise?
   Ⓐ Missouri would be divided into two territories.
   Ⓑ Mississippi could be a slave state.
   Ⓒ Missouri could choose to be a free or a slave state.
   ● The balance was kept between free and slave states.

Lesson Objective (1–3:3)

6. What was an effect of the Dred Scott decision?
   Ⓐ The North and South agreed on the decision.
   Ⓑ Many Northerners agreed with the decision.
   ● The split between the North and the South worsened.
   Ⓓ Most Southerners disagreed with the decision.

Lesson Objective (1–3:4)

7. How did many Southerners feel about Lincoln's election to the presidency?
   Ⓐ Many were happy because Lincoln was a fair man.
   ● Many were unhappy because Lincoln was against slavery.
   Ⓒ Many did not care because Lincoln promised to make no changes.
   Ⓓ Many were happy because they wanted to end slavery.

Use with Pupil Edition, p. 116

Assessment Book, p. 14

Lesson Objective (1–4:1)

8. Why did Southern states secede from the Union?
   Ⓐ Lincoln came from the North.
   ● They wanted to keep slavery.
   Ⓒ They had not voted for Lincoln.
   Ⓓ They wanted to change slavery laws.

Lesson Objective (1–4:3)

9. What did the South hope to achieve by fighting the Civil War?
   ● preservation of slavery
   Ⓑ an end to slavery
   Ⓒ equality for all
   Ⓓ preservation of the Union

Lesson Objective (2–1:1)

10. Which of the following was NOT an advantage held by the North during the Civil War?
    Ⓐ It produced most of the country's shoes and wheat.
    Ⓑ It had more railroads than the Confederacy.
    Ⓒ It produced more than 90 percent of the country's weapons.
    ● It had a history of producing military leaders.

Lesson Objective (2–1:4)

11. How did new technology affect the war?
    Ⓐ Women could join the forces.
    Ⓑ Battles were less deadly.
    Ⓒ Soldiers healed more quickly.
    ● Soldiers could use weapons more accurately.

Lesson Objective (2–2:2)

12. How did African Americans respond to the Emancipation Proclamation?
    Ⓐ Many fled to Canada.
    Ⓑ Many chose to remain slaves.
    ● Many joined the Union army.
    Ⓓ Many protested.

Lesson Objective (2–3:3)

13. Where did Sherman use a strategy of total war to defeat the South?
    ● Georgia
    Ⓑ Pennsylvania
    Ⓒ Maryland
    Ⓓ Virginia

Lesson Objective (2–3:4)

14. Which of the following best describes total war?
    Ⓐ Destroy all buildings and farms that might help the enemy win.
    Ⓑ Destroy all weapons.
    ● Destroy anything that might help the enemy win, including the people's will to fight.
    Ⓓ Destroy all military establishments in enemy territory.

Lesson Objective (2–4:1)

15. Why did Congress object to Johnson's Reconstruction plan?
    Ⓐ Congress wanted stricter laws for African Americans.
    ● Congress objected to Johnson's efforts to limit African Americans' rights.
    Ⓒ Congress wanted to allow the South to do as it pleased.
    Ⓓ Congress wanted laws that were less harsh for the South.

Use with Pupil Edition, p. 116

Assessment Book, p. 15

Part 2: Skills Test

Directions: Use complete sentences to answer questions 1–5. Use a separate sheet of paper if you need more space.

1. How did lifestyles in the North and the South differ during the mid-1800s?
   Compare and Contrast
   > Possible answer: In the South, most people had a rural lifestyle. They lived on farms and in small towns. Although most Northerners still lived on farms, more and more of them worked in factories and lived in large towns and cities. They had an urban lifestyle.

2. What do you think were two long-term effects of the Dred Scott decision? **Draw Conclusions**
   > Accept all reasonable answers. Possible answers: It firmly divided the nation into antislavery and pro-slavery groups; it established that African Americans did not have legal rights that were equal to those of whites.

3. What steps led to the outbreak of the Civil War? **Sequence**
   > Possible answer: North and South split over slavery; Lincoln is elected President; Southern states secede and form Confederacy; Jefferson Davis's forces capture Fort Sumter; Lincoln uses Union forces to put down Confederate rebellion.

4. Complete the chart below. Support the main idea in the box with details.
   Main Idea and Details

Main Idea	Details
African Americans' lives were different at the end of Reconstruction.	→ New laws were passed that placed African Americans under many restrictions. Life became very difficult for most. Work was scarce, and many became sharecroppers.

Use with Pupil Edition, p. 116

Assessment Book, p. 16

Road Map of Maryland and Eastern Virginia

5. Use the map to answer the questions. **Read a Road Map**
   a. What interstate highway would you use to travel from Charlottesville to Richmond?
   > You would use interstate highway 64.

   b. How many miles along interstate highway 95 would you travel going from Richmond to Petersburg?
   > You would travel about 25 miles.

   c. How could you use this map to plan a trip to visit Civil War sites?
   > Possible answer: The map shows me the location of some sites and helps me figure out how far apart they are.

Use with Pupil Edition, p. 116

CHAPTER 2
War and Reconstruction

Chapter 2 Outline

- **Lesson 1,** *The Early Stages of the War,* pp. 82–86
- **Biography:** *Robert E. Lee,* p. 87
- **Lesson 2,** *Life During the War,* pp. 88–93
- **Citizen Heroes:** *Working for Lasting Peace,* pp. 94–95
- **Lesson 3,** *How the North Won,* pp. 96–101
- **Map and Globe Skills:** *Read a Road Map,* pp. 102–103
- 𝔻𝕂 *Communications During the Civil War,* pp. 104–105
- **Lesson 4,** *The End of Slavery,* pp. 106–111

Resources
- Workbook, p. 21: Vocabulary Preview
- Vocabulary Cards
- Social Studies Plus!

1861, Manassas Junction, Virginia: Lesson 1

This picture shows hand-to-hand combat in the Civil War. Ask students what dangers troops faced. (Possible answers: Being shot; being trampled)

1863, Charleston, South Carolina: Lesson 2

Tell students that this picture shows African American Union troops.

1865, Appomattox Court House, Virginia: Lesson 3

This picture shows General Robert E. Lee surrendering to Ulysses S. Grant at Appomattox Court House. Ask students about how long the Civil War lasted. (About 4 years, from 1861 to 1865)

1865, Washington, D.C.: Lesson 4

This picture shows John Wilkes Booth assassinating President Lincoln. Ask students what the President was doing when he was shot. (Watching a play)

80 Unit 1 • War Divides the Nation

CHAPTER 2
War and Reconstruction

1861
Manassas Junction, Virginia
Confederate troops win the first major battle of the Civil War.
Lesson 1

1

1863
Charleston, South Carolina
African American troops of the Union army attack Fort Wagner.
Lesson 2

2

1865
Appomattox Court House, Virginia
The South surrenders.
Lesson 3

3

1865
Washington, D.C.
President Lincoln is assassinated.
Lesson 4

4

80

Practice and Extend

Vocabulary Preview

- Use Workbook p. 21 to help students preview the vocabulary words in this chapter.
- Use Vocabulary Cards to preview key concept words in this chapter.

 Also on Teacher Resources CD-ROM.

Workbook, p. 21

Vocabulary Preview
Directions: Circle the vocabulary term that best completes each sentence.

1. The (Anaconda Plan, Reconstruction) was a three-part war strategy to crush the South during the Civil War.
2. Slavery was abolished by the (Thirteenth Amendment, Fourteenth Amendment) to the Constitution.
3. The (First Battle of Bull Run, Battle of Gettysburg) lasted three days and was one of the most important battles of the Civil War.
4. African Americans became U.S. citizens under the (Fourteenth Amendment, Thirteenth Amendment) to the Constitution.
5. At the (Battle of Antietam, Battle of Vicksburg), Union forces blockaded the city and bombarded it for 48 days.
6. (Segregation, Sharecropping) is the separation of blacks and whites.
7. Both the North and the South instituted the (blockade, draft) to get men to fight in the war.
8. The (Gettysburg Address, Emancipation Proclamation) granted freedom to slaves in any Confederate states that were still battling the Union.
9. The time after the war when the country was rebuilding and healing is known as (Reconstruction, segregation).
10. The (black codes, blockade) kept supplies from reaching Southern soldiers.
11. One of the early battles of the war was the (Battle of Gettysburg, First Battle of Bull Run).
12. People in many U.S. cities paid their respects to President Lincoln after his (assassination, impeachment).
13. The (Freedmen's Bureau, Emancipation Proclamation) was established to help former slaves after the war.
14. All male citizens received the right to vote with the ratification of the (Thirteenth Amendment, Fifteenth Amendment) to the Constitution.
15. The (Emancipation Proclamation, Jim Crow laws) enforced separation of blacks and whites.
16. Republicans in Congress called for the (total war, impeachment) of President Andrew Johnson.

Notes for Home: Your child learned the vocabulary terms for Chapter 2.
Home Activity: With your child, review each vocabulary term and its definition to make sure the term fits in the sentence. Then make up your own sentences using the vocabulary terms.

Locating Time and Place

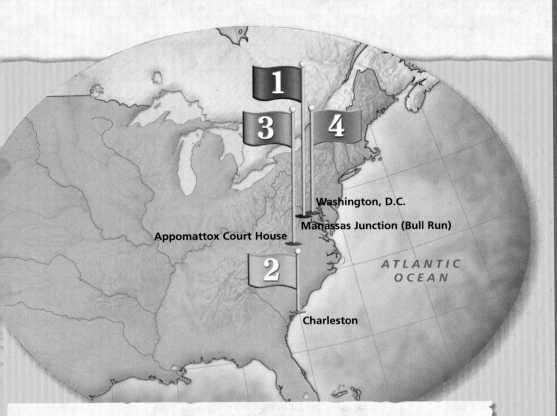

Washington, D.C.

Manassas Junction (Bull Run)

Appomattox Court House

ATLANTIC OCEAN

Charleston

Why We Remember

". . . that government of the people, by the people, for the people, shall not perish from the earth."

In 1863, in the middle of the Civil War, these words rang out over a scarred battlefield where many Union and Confederate soldiers had died a few months before. The battlefield was at Gettysburg, Pennsylvania. The speaker was President Abraham Lincoln. At the time, no one was sure who would win the war. But Lincoln was sure of his goal—to preserve the nation that had been born only 87 years earlier.

81

Locating Time and Place

- Have students examine the pictures shown on p. 80 for Lessons 1, 2, 3, and 4.

- Remind students that each picture is coded with both a number and a color to link it to a place on the map on p. 81.

Why We Remember

Have students read the "Why We Remember" paragraph on p. 81, and ask them why events in this chapter might be important to them. Ask students what "government of the people, by the people, and for the people" means and why it is so important to Americans.

WEB SITE
Technology

You can learn more about Manassas Junction, Virginia; Charleston, South Carolina; Appomattox Court House, Virginia; and Washington, D.C., by clicking on *Atlas* at **www.sfsocialstudies.com.**

SOCIAL STUDIES STRAND
Geography

Mental Mapping On an outline map of the United States, have students draw and label the city of New Orleans, the Mississippi River, and the states of Virginia and Tennessee. These four locations were Union objectives during the Civil War. Have students decide which of these locations was most important to winning the war. Have them rank locations in order of importance. Discuss answers.

The Early Stages of the War

Objectives

- Identify the resources of the North and South.
- Compare the strategies of the North and South in the Civil War.
- Describe early battles in the Civil War.
- Explain how new military technology affected the way the war was fought.

Vocabulary

blockade, p. 84; **Anaconda Plan,** p. 84; **First Battle of Bull Run,** p. 85; **Battle of Antietam,** p. 85

Resources

- Workbook, p. 23
- Transparency 1
- Every Student Learns Guide, pp. 34–37
- Quick Study, pp. 18–19

Quick Teaching Plan

If time is short, have students read the lesson independently and copy and complete the following chart.

	NORTH	SOUTH
Advantages		
Strategies		
First Battle of Bull Run		
Battle of Antietam		
Ships		

1 Introduce and Motivate

Preview To activate prior knowledge, ask students what they remember about the causes of the Civil War. Tell students that they will learn about early battles in the Civil War in Lesson 1.

You Are There Soldiers in the Civil War often found themselves fighting against family members. Have students discuss their opinions about members of the same family joining armies on different sides.

LESSON 1

April 1861
Union begins blockade of Southern ports.

July 1861
First Battle of Bull Run

September 1862
Battle of Antietam

Washington, D.C.
Manassas Junction
Richmond

PREVIEW

Focus on the Main Idea
In the early years of the Civil War, the North and South formed strategies in hopes of gaining a quick victory.

PLACES
Richmond, Virginia
Manassas Junction, Virginia

PEOPLE
Winfield Scott
Thomas "Stonewall" Jackson
Robert E. Lee

VOCABULARY
blockade
Anaconda Plan
First Battle of Bull Run
Battle of Antietam

▶ This canteen was carried by a Confederate soldier in the Civil War.

The Early Stages of the War

You Are There It is the summer of 1861. Dawn breaks over your Kentucky farm. You hear a rooster crowing. Below your attic bedroom, your mother lets out a cry. You peer down from your room and see her holding a sheet of paper. It is a letter from your oldest brother, Joshua. He left last night to join the Union army.

Joshua and your second-oldest brother, William, had been arguing about the war since spring. "The Union forever!" Joshua would say. "Down with Northern tyranny!" William would shout. You just hope the war ends soon.

You read in the newspaper that the Confederates have just won a victory in Virginia. Expecting a short war, many Southern men are rushing to join the army before the war ends. You wonder if William will leave to join the Confederate forces. If he does, could he and Joshua end up fighting against each other, brother against brother?

Main Idea and Details As you read, note how the North and South prepared for war.

82

Practice and Extend

READING SKILL
Main Idea/Details

In the Lesson Review, students complete a graphic organizer like the one below. You may want to provide students with a copy of Transparency 1 to complete as they read the lesson.

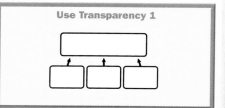

Use Transparency 1

VOCABULARY
Word Exercise

Context Clues

Help students build context knowledge by having them plan a blockade. Provide students with simple map of a coastline with several cities. Have students form groups and make up plans for how they would blockade the cities. Ask students to write a one or two paragraph summary of how they would form their blockade and what effect the blockade would have on the cities.

Advantages and Disadvantages

Many supporters of the North believed they were fighting to preserve the Union. However, most Southern supporters thought that they were fighting to preserve their way of life. Sometimes these different opinions divided families. Some of President Lincoln's own family sided with the South. Four brothers of his wife, Mary, fought for the Confederacy.

Besides strong feelings, each side thought that it had an advantage over the other. Southerners believed that their more rural way of life would better prepare soldiers for war. Many Southerners hunted and were familiar with weapons. The South also had a history of producing military leaders. A larger share of the Mexican War veterans came from the South.

But an army needed supplies. In 1860 the Northern states produced more than 90 percent of the country's weapons, cloth, shoes, and iron. They also produced more than half of the country's corn and 80 percent of the wheat.

Moving supplies was also important to an army. The Union had far more railroads, canals, and roads than the Confederacy. In addition, the Union was able to raise far more money. By the end of the war, the Union had spent more than $2.6 billion. The Confederacy had spent only $1 billion.

REVIEW Why did each side believe that it would win the war? **Summarize**

FACT FILE

Union and Confederacy, 1861

Look at the graphs below to compare the resources each side had.

■ Union
□ Confederacy

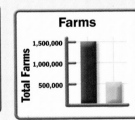
Union Flag

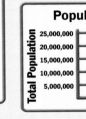

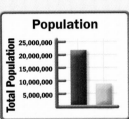
States
Total States

Population
Total Population

Soldiers
Total Soldiers

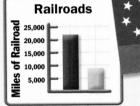
Factories
Total Factories

Farms
Total Farms

Railroads
Miles of Railroad

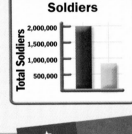
Confederate Flag

83

2 Teach and Discuss

PAGE 83

Advantages and Disadvantages

Quick Summary The North had better access to supplies and transportation. The South felt its soldiers were better prepared to fight.

1 How did the North's reason for fighting the war differ from the South's? The North wanted to preserve the Union, whereas the South was fighting to preserve its way of life. **Compare and Contrast**

2 What advantages did the various transportation systems give the North during the Civil War? Possible answer: The North was better able to move supplies. **Make Inferences**

✓ **REVIEW ANSWER** South: More rural way of life would prepare them for war; had more Mexican War veterans; they were fighting for their homeland; North: More resources, including railroads, canals, roads, and money **Summarize**

FACT FILE
Union and Confederacy, 1861

3 What was the difference in the number of factories between the North and South? What effect might this have had? The North had over 90,000 more factories than the South and could produce more supplies. **Interpret Graphs**

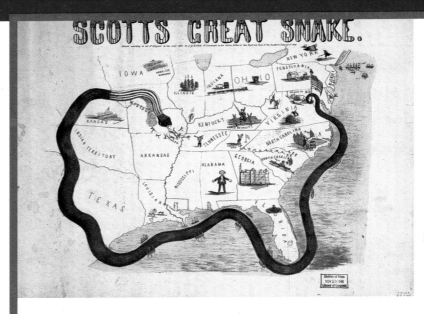

SCOTTS GREAT SNAKE.

▶ This cartoon illustrated the Anaconda Plan by showing an anaconda snake surrounding the Confederacy.

Strategies

🕐 **Quick Summary** The North and South planned different strategies in hopes of quickly ending the war.

④ What strategies did the Confederacy believe would bring them victory? Defend territory until the North gave up; Southern soldiers would fight more fiercely for their land; Britain would help the South 🔄 **Main Idea and Details**

If... students do not understand the South's strategies,

then... guide them to copy and complete this Main Idea and Details chart.

Confederate strategy for victory

| Defend territory until Northerners give up | Fight fiercely | Receive help from Britain |

🧩 **Problem Solving**

⑤ What problem did Britain's cotton surplus cause for the South? Britain no longer needed as much of the South's cotton, so there was little reason to assist the South in the war. **Solve Problems**

✓ **REVIEW ANSWER** First there would be a blockade of Southern ports to prevent supplies from reaching the Confederate states. Then the Union would gain control of the Mississippi River, cutting the Confederacy in half. Then the Union would invade the Confederacy from the east and west. 🔄 **Main Idea and Details**

Strategies

President Abraham Lincoln sought advice on how to win the war from General **Winfield Scott,** who had fought in the Mexican War. Scott planned a strategy with three parts. The first part was a blockade of the Atlantic and Gulf coasts of the Confederacy. A **blockade** is the shutting off of an area by troops or ships to keep people and supplies from moving in or out. With a blockade the South would not be able to ship its cotton for sale in Europe. Cotton sales were the South's main way of getting money to pay for the war.

The second stage of Scott's plan was to capture territory along the Mississippi River, the heart of the Confederacy. Gaining control of the Mississippi River would weaken the Confederacy by cutting the Southern states in two.

Third, the Union would attack the Confederacy from the east and west. Scott's strategy was called the **Anaconda Plan,** because he said that it would squeeze the Confederacy like an anaconda. An anaconda

is a huge snake that kills prey by wrapping itself around an animal and suffocating it. Lincoln liked the plan. He ordered the blockade on April 19, one week after the fall of Fort Sumter.

The Confederate government had its own strategy for victory. First, it believed that the Confederacy only had to defend its territory until the Northerners got tired and gave up. Many Southerners believed that Northerners had nothing to gain from victory and would not be willing to fight for long. Southerners assumed that their soldiers would fight more fiercely for their land and their way of life.

The Confederacy also believed that Britain would assist it in the war because British clothing mills depended on Southern cotton. But Britain already had a surplus of cotton and was looking to India and Egypt for new sources of cotton. Britain allowed the South to build several warships in its shipyards, but it did not send any soldiers.

REVIEW How did Winfield Scott's Anaconda Plan attempt to weaken the Southern states? 🔄 **Main Idea and Details**

Practice and Extend

ESL **ACCESS CONTENT**
ESL Support

Demonstrate Concept Understanding After they read p. 85, have students demonstrate their understanding of the concept of "retreat" in a war.

Beginning Divide the class into two groups. Have one group carry a sign labeled "North" and the other group "South." At your prompting, have students act out the sequence of advances and retreats during the First Battle of Bull Run.

Intermediate Have students write journal entries as if they were retreating soldiers in the First Battle of Bull Run.

Advanced Have students write a speech for Robert E. Lee to raise the morale of Confederate troops after their defeat at Antietam.

For additional ESL support, use Every Student Learns Guide, pp. 34–37.

Early Battles

Early successes gave the Confederacy confidence. President Lincoln sent 35,000 troops to invade Richmond, Virginia, the capital of the Confederacy. On the way, on July 21, 1861, they met Confederate troops at a small stream called Bull Run near the town of Manassas Junction, Virginia.

The First Battle of Bull Run was a confusing event. Early on, the fighting went in the Union's favor. Some Confederate soldiers began to turn back, but one general from Virginia told his men to hold their place. Because the general and his men stood "like a stone wall," he became known as Thomas "Stonewall" Jackson.

As more Confederates arrived, the tide turned in their favor. The Union soldiers retreated. The casualties at Bull Run were about 3,000 for the Union and 2,000 for the Confederacy. Casualties include soldiers killed, wounded, captured, or missing.

Many battles took place across the South.

Union forces won some, but the Confederates seemed to be winning the war. In May 1862, "Stonewall" Jackson defeated the Union army in Virginia, and some feared that he could take over Washington, D.C.

On September 17, 1862, Union and Confederate forces met near the town of Sharpsburg, Maryland, in the **Battle of Antietam** (an TEET um). The battle involved one of the Confederacy's most capable generals, **Robert E. Lee.** He had been asked to fight for the Union but refused. Lee decided to serve the Confederacy after Virginia, the state of his birth, joined the other Southern states. You will read more about Robert E. Lee in the Biography on page 87.

The battle was an important victory for the Union. After Antietam, Great Britain ended its support for the Southern states. The Confederacy would have to fight alone.

REVIEW What effect did winning the Battle of Antietam have on the Union?
Cause and Effect

Lithograph by Kurz & Allison

▶ **With more than 23,000 casualties, the Battle of Antietam was the single bloodiest day of the Civil War.**

85

Early Battles

Quick Summary The Confederacy won the First Battle of Bull Run but lost the Battle of Antietam.

Test Talk

Locate Key Words in the Question

6 **About how much time passed between the First Battle of Bull Run and the Battle of Antietam?** Have students tell who or what in the questions are key words. About one year and two months **Sequence**

7 **Why do you think Robert E. Lee decided to fight for the Confederacy?** Possible answer: He was loyal to Virginia, the state of his birth. **Point of View**

✓ **REVIEW ANSWER** After the Battle of Antietam, the Union did not have to worry about Britain supporting the Confederacy. **Cause and Effect**

SOCIAL STUDIES
Background

About the Early Battles

- The First Battle of Bull Run is known in the South by a different name: "The First Battle of Manassas," or simply "First Manassas."
- During the beginning of the First Battle of Bull Run, people came out from Washington, D.C., in carriages to watch the battle as if it were a spectator sport. They made a hasty retreat when the tide turned against the Union.
- Antietam spurred Lincoln to issue the Emancipation Proclamation.
- The Battle of Antietam got its name from a creek near the site of the battle. In the South it is called the Battle of Sharpsburg, for the nearby town.
- Antietam was the bloodiest battle of the Civil War up to that point.

Technology and War

🕐 **Quick Summary** The soldiers of the Civil War used new technologies to fight.

SOCIAL STUDIES STRAND
Science • Technology

8 **What new technology did the *Virginia* and the *Monitor* have?** An iron covering **Draw Conclusions**

✓ **REVIEW ANSWER** Advantages: Soldiers could shoot farther and more accurately; Disadvantages: More casualties **Compare and Contrast**

Close and Assess

Summarize the Lesson

Tell students to write and answer one question about each event in the summary. Students can share their questions.

✓ **LESSON 1** | **REVIEW**

1. 🔄 **Main Idea and Details** For possible answers, see the reduced pupil page.

2. Union: Produced wheat, corn, weapons, clothes, and iron; had more railroads, canals, roads, and money; Confederacy: More Mexican War generals, familiarity with weapons

3. North: Blockade ports, control of the Mississippi; South: Defend land until North gives up and hope Britain will help

4. Union was winning; Jackson refused to retreat; more Confederate troops arrived; Union troops retreated

5. **Critical Thinking:** *Analyze Information* Allowed them to kill or wound more enemies; caused more death from disease and infection

---

Link to ∞ Mathematics

About 13 million more people; about 13,000 more miles; more people could serve in the army or produce supplies. More miles of railroad would improve transportation.

86 Unit 1 • War Divides the Nation

Technology and War

Recent technologies were used and new technologies were developed during the Civil War. Soldiers used rifles that could shoot farther and more accurately than guns used in previous wars. Railroads quickly moved troops and supplies to battlefronts. The Confederacy built several submarines—ships that could travel under the water's surface—to overcome the Union's blockade. Both sides used an early version of the hand grenade.

Another new weapon was the ironclad, or iron covered ship. The Confederates built an ironclad by taking an abandoned Union ship called the *Merrimack* and covering it with iron. They renamed it the *Virginia*. In March 1862, the *Virginia* easily sank several wooden Union ships. Union cannonballs simply bounced off the *Virginia's* iron sides. Then, on March 9, a Union ironclad named the *Monitor* arrived to

8 battle the *Virginia*. The two ships fired at each other for hours. But neither ship was able to seriously damage the other.

These new technologies made the war more deadly, resulting in huge numbers of casualties. Unfortunately, medical knowledge had not advanced as much as other technologies. Many soldiers died from disease and infection.

REVIEW What were the advantages and disadvantages of new technology in the Civil War? **Compare and Contrast**

Summarize the Lesson

- **April 19, 1861** The Union began a blockade of Southern ports.
- **July 21, 1861** Confederate forces defeated Union troops in the First Battle of Bull Run in Manassas.
- **September 17, 1862** Union and Confederate troops fought a bloody battle at Antietam, an important Union victory.

LESSON 1 **REVIEW**

Check Facts and Main Ideas

1. 🔄 **Main Idea and Details** On a separate sheet of paper, fill in the details of the **Anaconda Plan.**

General Winfield Scott's Anaconda Plan attempted to weaken the Confederate states.

A Union blockade of Southern ports would cut off supplies to the South.	The Union would gain control of the Mississippi River and cut the Confederacy in half.	Union armies would attack the Confederacy from east and west.

2. Compare advantages the Union had at the beginning of the war to those of the Confederacy.

3. How did the strategies of the North and South differ?

4. Summarize the events of the **First Battle of Bull Run.**

5. Critical Thinking: *Analyze Information* What effect did military technology have on Civil War soldiers?

Link to ∞ Mathematics

Analyze Graphs Look again at the graphs on page 83. How many more people lived in the Northern states than in the Southern states? How many more miles of railroad did the North have compared to the South? Why would a larger population and more miles of railroad be an advantage?

86

Practice and Extend

CURRICULUM CONNECTION
Math

Disease Statistics

Display the following chart and have students draw conclusions about which diseases caused the most deaths for the Northern army during the Civil War. (Diarrhea/Dysentery and Typhoid)

Disease	Deaths
Diarrhea/Dysentery	44,558
Malaria	10,063
Typhoid	34,833
Typhus	958
Yellow Fever	436

Workbook, p. 22

Lesson 1: The Early Stages of the War
Directions: Complete each compare-and-contrast table with information about the Union and the Confederacy. You may use your textbook.

	Supporters of the North	Supporters of the South
Reason for fighting		

	Northerners	Southerners
Believed advantage over the opposition		

	Union	Confederacy
War strategies		

💿 **Also on Teacher Resources CD-ROM.**

Robert E. Lee *1807–1870*

Robert E. Lee did not know his father for long. When Robert was six, his father, Harry Lee, visited a friend who published a newspaper that criticized the United States for going to war with Great Britain in 1812. Like his friend, Harry Lee opposed this war. A group of angry people attacked the newspaper offices while Harry Lee was inside, and he was badly beaten. Robert had to say goodbye as his father boarded a ship to Barbados, where he went to heal from his wounds. Harry Lee died before he could return home.

Many years later, at the beginning of the Civil War, Robert E. Lee was asked to make the most difficult decision of his life. Lee was a rising star in the United States Army. But Lee had been born and raised in Virginia, and, although he personally disapproved of slavery, he loved his home and his state. Perhaps he thought of his father, who had defended the things he loved at great cost to himself. Lee resigned from the United States Army and wrote:

> *"I have not been able to make up my mind to raise my hand against my relatives, my children, my home."*

Lee hoped that Virginia would not take sides in the conflict, and he would not have to fight at all. But when Virginia seceded and joined the Confederacy, his path became clear to him. Lee accepted a position commanding Virginia's forces. Later, Lee's wife, Mary, remembered the night of his decision. She said that he "wept tears of blood." **2**

Learn from Biographies

Why was Lee's decision so difficult to make? What do you think his wife meant when she said that he "wept tears of blood"?

For more information, go online to *Meet the People* at **www.sfsocialstudies.com**.

87

Robert E. Lee

Objective
- Identify the accomplishments of notable individuals, such as Robert E. Lee.

1 Introduce and Motivate

Preview To activate prior knowledge, ask students to share what they remember about Robert E. Lee from p. 85.

2 Teach and Discuss

1 What might have affected Lee's decision to resign from the U.S. Army? He might have thought of his father, who had lost his life defending the things he loved. **Cause and Effect**

2 What personal traits do you think Lee possessed? Possible answer: He was compassionate, brave, loyal, and conscientious. **Draw Conclusions**

3 Close and Assess

Learn from Biographies Answer

He was doing well in the army but he was loyal to Virginia. She meant that he was very torn about his decision.

Decision Making

Use a Decision-Making Process

- Have students consider the following decision-making scenario: **Suppose you are an advisor to Robert E. Lee. You have just heard that he must decide whether or not to command the forces in Virginia. You understand he is against slavery, yet loyal to his state.**

- Students should use the following decision-making process to decide whether to advise Lee to accept or reject the position as commander of the Virginia armed forces. For each step in the process, have students discuss and write about what must be considered as they make their decision. Write these steps on the board or read them aloud.

1. Identify a situation that requires a decision.
2. Gather information.
3. Identify opinions.
4. Predict consequences.
5. Take action to implement a decision.

Life During the War

Objectives

- Compare and contrast life for Northern and Southern soldiers.
- Analyze the effect of the Emancipation Proclamation on African Americans.
- Describe the contributions of African American soldiers to the Union war effort.
- Identify the different ways women contributed to the war effort in the North and South.

Vocabulary

draft, p. 89;
Emancipation Proclamation, p. 90

Resources

- Workbook, p. 23
- Transparency 1
- Every Student Learns Guide, pp. 38–41
- Quick Study, pp. 20–21

Quick Teaching Plan

If time is short, have students create word webs for the lesson.

- Have students write *Soldiers,* *African Americans,* and *Women* in separate webs.
- As they read, students should add details to each web.

1 Introduce and Motivate

Preview Ask students to share any personal knowledge they may have about life in the armed forces. Tell students that in Lesson 2 they will learn about life in the armed forces during the Civil War.

 You Are There Both soldiers and civilians are affected by war, no matter which side they are on. Have students discuss whether or not they believe being victorious in battle makes the war experience any easier.

LESSON 2

1863		1864
January 1863 Emancipation Proclamation takes effect.	**July 1863** African American troops attack Fort Wagner.	**June 1864** Congress gives black and white troops equal pay.

PREVIEW

Focus on the Main Idea
As the Civil War continued, people in the North and the South suffered many hardships, including the growing loss of life.

PLACES
Fort Wagner, South Carolina

PEOPLE
Mathew Brady
William Carney
Belle Boyd
Clara Barton

VOCABULARY
draft
Emancipation Proclamation

Life During the War

You Are There These letters are from soldiers who fought in the Battle of Fredericksburg in Virginia on December 13, 1862. They were on opposing sides, but whether fighting for the Union or the Confederacy, soldiers were horrified by the loss of life.

December 16, 1862

Gone are the proud hopes, the high aspirations [goals] that swelled our bosoms [chests] a few days ago. Once more unsuccessful, and only a bloody record to show our men were brave.

Captain William T. Lusk, Union soldier

January 11, 1863

I can inform you that I have seen the Monkey Show [battle] at last, and I don't want to see it anymore. Martha I can't tell you how many dead I did see. . . . one thing is sure, I don't want to see that sight anymore.

Private Thomas Warrick, Confederate soldier

 Main Idea and Details As you read, note the difficulties during the Civil War for both soldiers and civilians.

88

Practice and Extend

READING SKILL
Main Idea/Details

In the Lesson Review, students complete a graphic organizer like the one below. You may want to provide students with a copy of Transparency 1 to complete as they read the lesson.

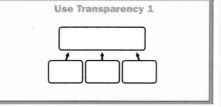

Use Transparency 1

VOCABULARY
Word Exercise

Related Word Study

Tell students that *emancipate* comes from Latin words meaning "to take away the hand." The Latin word *manus* means "hand." Often people use the idea of "hands" to talk about owning something, as in the phrases *to change hands* and *to get your hands on.* The Latin word *manus* also helped form the word *manual.* To do something manually means to do it by hand, instead of using a machine to do it.

Life for Soldiers

Families of soldiers like Captain Lusk and Private Warrick learned about the war from soldiers' letters and newspaper articles. They could also see the horrors of war thanks to a new technology—photography. Civil War photographers like Mathew Brady took pictures in camps and on the war's many battlefields. Photographs showed the dead and wounded, but also showed soldiers warming themselves by campfires, or resting after a long day's march.

The average age of a Civil War soldier was about 25. However, drummer boys as young as twelve years old went to the battlefield. A soldier's life was a hard one, even when he was not in battle. Soldiers might march as many as 25 miles a day while carrying about 50 pounds of supplies in knapsacks, or backpacks. They grew thirsty marching in summer's heat and shivered through winter's cold.

Marching was especially tough for Confederate soldiers. The Union blockade prevented many supplies from reaching Southern armies. Soldiers wore out their shoes and often fought in bare feet until they could get another pair.

On both sides, soldiers were usually unhappy with the food. They were given beans, bacon, pickled beef, salt pork, and a tough flour-and-water biscuit called "hardtack." When they could, troops hunted for food in nearby forests, or even raided local farms.

As the war continued, volunteers for the war decreased. A volunteer is a person who chooses freely to join or do something. Both sides passed draft laws. A **draft** requires men of a certain age to serve in the military if they are called. However, Confederates who owned 20 or more slaves could pay substitutes to take their place. In the Union, men could pay $300 to avoid fighting in the war. The draft was unpopular, because it favored the wealthy. In July 1863, riots broke out in New York City to protest the draft. Many called the conflict "a rich man's war and a poor man's fight." ❶

Losses on each side were terrible. A total of about 1 million Union and Confederate soldiers were killed or wounded. In comparison, only about 10,600 Patriots were killed in the Revolutionary War. Disease was the most common cause of death in the Civil War. Of the more than 360,000 soldiers that died in the Union army, only about 110,000 died in battle. In the Confederate army, 258,000 soldiers died, but only about 94,000 died in battle. As you read in Lesson 1, disease and infections killed many soldiers. This is because no one knew about germs yet, so doctors did not know how to keep wounds from getting infected. ❷

REVIEW What were some of the challenges faced by Civil War soldiers?
⤷ Main Idea and Details

▶ Life was difficult and dangerous for both Union soldiers (*left*) and Confederate soldiers (*right*).

89

2 Teach and Discuss

PAGE 89

Life for Soldiers

🕐 **Quick Summary** Both the Union and Confederate soldiers suffered on and off the field.

❶ **What was meant by the expression identifying the Civil War as "a rich man's war and a poor man's fight"?** Rich people could pay money or substitute others to avoid fighting in the war, leaving poor people to fight the battles. **Draw Conclusions**

✓ Ongoing Assessment

If… students do not understand the expression, "a rich man's war and a poor man's fight,"

then… have them list the draft requirements for both the North and South.

⭐ **SOCIAL STUDIES STRAND**
Citizenship

Democratic Values and Institutions
Joining the armed forces of a country is just one way individuals can participate in civic affairs at the national level.

❷ **What contribution did soldiers in the Civil War make to their country?** Possible answer: They fought against the enemy and many gave their lives.
⤷ Main Idea and Details

✓ **REVIEW ANSWER** Soldiers had to deal with the threat of death, disease, or injury, difficult marches, lack of water and poor food, little protection from the elements, and shortages in supplies.
⤷ Main Idea and Details

❋ **MEETING INDIVIDUAL NEEDS**
Leveled Practice

Write a Letter Have students write a letter as if they were soldiers in the Northern or Southern armies.

Easy Have students write a letter to their family telling about one aspect of their experiences, such as the food, the marches, or the living conditions. **Reteach**

On-Level Have students write a letter home describing a sequence of experiences over one week. **Extend**

Advanced After students read the text, have them write a letter to the editor of a newspaper describing their experiences as a soldier and giving their opinion of the war and the draft rules. **Enrich**

For a Lesson Summary, use Quick Study, p. 20.

The Emancipation Proclamation

Quick Summary The Emancipation Proclamation freed slaves in the Confederate states at war with the Union.

3 **What was Lincoln's attitude toward slavery? How can you tell?** He believed it should be abolished. He issued the Emancipation Proclamation. **Point of View**

Primary Source

Cited in *From Slavery to Freedom: A History of African Americans,* by John Hope Franklin and Alfred A. Moss, Jr.

Explain that the Emancipation Proclamation made it clear that one of Lincoln's goals was to end slavery.

Test Talk

Locate Key Words in the Text

4 **Why did some slaves not gain their freedom after this proclamation?** Have students locate key words in the text that match key words in the question, such as *proclamation.* Because it proclaimed freedom only for enslaved people who were in states that were at war with the Union **Analyze Primary Sources**

✓ **REVIEW ANSWER** The Emancipation Proclamation said that slaves in Confederate states not controlled by the Union were free, and many African Americans were encouraged to fight for the Union cause. **Cause and Effect**

Slaves and Serfs

5 **What conclusion can you draw about enslavement during the 1800s?** Possible answer: Enslavement was a worldwide condition that began coming to an end during the late nineteenth century. **Draw Conclusions**

The Emancipation Proclamation

At first, the Civil War was not a war against slavery. Lincoln's goal was to preserve the Union, or keep the country together. By 1862, though, Lincoln began to believe that he could save the Union only by making the abolition of slavery a goal of the war.

Lincoln's advisers feared that ending slavery would hurt the war effort. Some said that it would unite the South and divide the North. But Lincoln explained, "Slavery must die that the nation might live."

On January 1, 1863, President Lincoln issued the **Emancipation Proclamation.** Emancipate means "to set free." A proclamation is a statement. The Emancipation Proclamation was a statement that freed all slaves in the Confederate states at war with the Union. Moments before signing the proclamation Lincoln said, "I never in my life felt more certain that I was doing right." The **3** Proclamation said:

> "*Slaves within any State . . . in rebellion against the United States, shall be then . . . and forever free.*"

The Emancipation Proclamation did not end slavery in the border states or in Confederate land that Union forces already controlled. It did declare an end to slavery in the rest of the Confederacy. But since Union forces did not control these areas, most African Americans remained enslaved.

Free African Americans like Frederick Douglass supported Lincoln's efforts. Douglass encouraged African Americans to assist the Union in the war. "Fly to arms," he wrote. Large numbers of African Americans responded by joining the Union army.

REVIEW What was a result of the Emancipation Proclamation? **Cause and Effect** **4**

Slaves and Serfs

At About the Same Time that President Lincoln was issuing the Emancipation Proclamation, people in other areas of the world were gaining liberty. In 1861 leaders in Russia began freeing people called serfs. Serfs worked on an owner's land in exchange for protection and housing. Like slaves, serfs could not marry, change their occupation, or leave the land without the owner's permission.

EUROPE RUSSIA ASIA

5

90

Practice and Extend

SOCIAL STUDIES
Background

Serfdom

- Serfdom was a condition of tenant farmers in medieval Europe and Asia in which serfs were obligated to farm a plot of land belonging to their landlord.
- Serfs had to provide their own food and clothing, and also give a portion of their crops to the landlord.
- A serf could become free only through liberation by the landlord, being rescued, or escaping.
- In 1861 serfs in Russia were granted freedom and their own pieces of land under Alexander II's Edict of Emancipation.

The African American soldiers of the 54th Regiment gained fame for their brave attack on Fort Wagner.

The Granger Collection

Library of Congress

African Americans in the War

In the beginning of the war, African Americans were not allowed to join the army. But they did serve as cooks, servants, and other workers. They were first allowed to join the Union army in 1862.

African American soldiers were not treated the same as whites. They received less pay than white soldiers. They had to buy their own uniforms, while white soldiers did not.

The situation improved for African Americans before the end of the war. One reason for this change was the role played by the Massachusetts 54th Colored Regiment. A regiment is a group of 600 to 1,000 soldiers. The 54th was one of the first groups of black troops to be organized for combat in the Union army.

On July 18, 1863, the 54th Regiment led an attack on **Fort Wagner** in South Carolina.

Confederate fire was heavy, but the men of the 54th charged the fort before being forced back. The group lost more than four out of every ten men.

William Carney, a sergeant in the battle, was seriously wounded. Yet he never dropped the regiment's flag. Carney later said that he had fought "to serve my country and my oppressed brothers." He was one of 16 African Americans to win the Congressional Medal of Honor during the war.

The Union did not win the battle at Fort Wagner. But the bravery of the 54th Regiment changed the minds of many Northerners who had doubted the abilities of black soldiers to fight. Nearly 200,000 black soldiers fought for the Union in the Civil War, and 37,000 lost their lives. In June 1864, Congress voted to give black and white troops equal pay. **6**

REVIEW What conclusion can you draw about why African American troops fought in the Civil War? Draw Conclusions

African Americans in the War

Quick Summary The role of African Americans in the Civil War changed as they proved their ability and willingness to fight for their country and their freedom.

6 **Because of the 54th Regiment, how did the situation improve for African American soldiers?** They were recognized as heroes. Many Northerners no longer doubted the abilities of black soldiers to fight, and Congress voted to give black and white troops equal pay. Cause and Effect

✓ **REVIEW ANSWER** Many African Americans felt loyalty to the Union and wanted to fight for its cause. Some may have wanted to prove their abilities on the battlefield. Draw Conclusions

91

CURRICULUM CONNECTION
Math

Calculate Totals

- Have students calculate the approximate number of African American soldiers who survived the Civil War. (About 163,000)
- Have advanced students find the percentage of African American soldiers who died in the Civil War by completing the following calculation:

$37,000 \div 200,000 = 37 \div 200 = 0.185 = 18.5\%$

Women and the War

🕐 **Quick Summary** Women contributed to the war effort by working on farms, in offices, schools, and hospitals, by spying, and by caring for soldiers on the battlefield.

💲 **SOCIAL STUDIES STRAND**
Economics

Explain that prices typically rise when the supply of a good is limited and/or demand increases.

7 **How did supply and demand affect consumers in the South during the Civil War?** Because there was a shortage of much-needed supplies for the war effort in the South, consumers had to pay higher prices for whatever supplies they could get. **Cause and Effect**

8 **Compare and contrast the contributions made by women in the North and South.** Both helped by working, caring for the wounded, and sending food for armies; women in the South protested the rise in cost of supplies, which were in short supply in the South. **Compare and Contrast**

✓ **REVIEW ANSWER** Possible answers: Women ran farms and businesses and became teachers, office workers, spies, soldiers, and nurses. They also sewed clothing for the soldiers and sent them any food they could spare.
🕐 **Main Idea and Details**

The War Goes On

🕐 **Quick Summary** Both the North and South were tired of the ravages of war and wanted it to end.

9 **What do you think was the most difficult thing soldiers had to endure?** Possible answer: Watching family and friends die **Express Ideas**

✓ **REVIEW ANSWER** In both places, they were tired of it.
Compare and Contrast

▶ Belle Boyd (below) worked as a spy. Other women cared for soldiers in hospitals (right).

Women and the War

Women contributed to the war effort in many ways. They ran farms and businesses while their husbands were fighting. They became teachers and office workers. Some even became involved in the war more directly. Frances Clalin, for example, disguised herself as a man so that she could fight in the Union army.

Some women became spies. Women were less likely to be suspected as spies and were punished less severely if they were caught. They often hid weapons and documents under their large hoop skirts to avoid being caught. **Belle Boyd,** nicknamed "La Belle Rebelle," was one of the most famous Confederate spies. She continued spying even after six arrests. She once communicated to a Confederate by hiding messages inside rubber balls and throwing them out of her cell window.

Women in the North and the South worked in hospitals as nurses and other caregivers. Sojourner Truth gathered supplies for black regiments. One Northern woman, **Clara Barton,** explained why she cared for soldiers, "While our soldiers stand and fight, I can stand and feed and nurse them." Barton earned the nickname "Angel of the Battlefield" as she cared for wounded soldiers during the First Battle of Bull Run. In 1881 Barton organized the American Association of the Red Cross to help victims of wars and natural disasters.

Women in the South also had to deal with shortages of supplies. Because demand was greater than supply, prices rose dramatically. The average Southern family's monthly food bill rose from $6.65 just before the war to $68 in 1863. In April of that year, hundreds of women rioted in Richmond to protest the rise in prices. Similar bread riots occurred in other Southern cities as well. **7**

Despite their own difficulties, women in the North and South did all they could for the soldiers. They sewed clothing, rolled bandages, sold personal possessions, and sent any food they could spare to the armies. **8**

REVIEW How did women help the war effort? 🕐 **Main Idea and Details**

92

Practice and Extend

ESL **EXTEND LANGUAGE**
ESL Support

Examine Word Meanings A *bandage* is a strip of fabric, usually gauze, which is used to wrap wounds. Women rolled bandages to make them easy to use when needed.

Beginning Show students examples of different kinds of bandages, which you can most likely obtain from the school nurse. Have students take turns "bandaging" by following your verbal directions.

Intermediate Have students write a paragraph from the point of view of a Civil War nurse. Students should use the word *bandage* in their paragraph.

Advanced Have students work in pairs to create a dialogue between a Civil War doctor or nurse and a patient. Students should use the word *bandage* as both a noun and a verb.

For additional ESL support, use Every Student Learns Guide, pp. 38–41.

The War Goes On

In 1863 the Vice President of the Confederacy, Alexander Stephens, said, "A large majority on both sides are tired of the war." And it was true. Union and Confederate soldiers alike were singing a song called "When This Cruel War Is Over." The lack of supplies, delays in pay, sleeping uncovered in the rain, and the terrible death of friends and family members were taking their toll.

By 1863 some soldiers were refusing to go to war. Thousands of Union and Confederate men deserted, or left their military duty without permission.

Explained one Union soldier, "I'm tired of the war anyhow, and my time's up soon."

▶ Soldiers on both sides were tired of war.

But, as you will read, Union victories would soon lead to the war's end.

REVIEW Compare how people in the North and the South felt about the war after the first two years. **Compare and Contrast**

Summarize the Lesson

— **January 1863** President Abraham Lincoln formally issued the Emancipation Proclamation, freeing slaves in territories still fighting Union forces.

— **July 1863** The Massachusetts 54th, one of the first African American regiments to fight for the Union, attacked Fort Wagner in South Carolina.

— **June 1864** Congress gave black soldiers the same pay as white soldiers.

LESSON 2 REVIEW

Check Facts and Main Ideas

1. **Main Idea and Details** On a separate sheet of paper, fill in the details that support the main idea.

> Soldiers and civilians faced many difficulties during the Civil War.

> Soldiers faced lack of supplies, poor shelter, difficult marches, and threats of death and injury.

> African American soldiers faced unequal pay and the doubts of citizens in their abilities to fight.

> Women in the South faced shortages and inflation; all families faced the possibility of losing a loved one.

2. Why was the Civil War called a "rich man's war and a poor man's fight"?

3. Critical Thinking: *Problem-Solving* Suppose you had to help President Lincoln decide when to issue the **Emancipation Proclamation.** How would you solve this problem?

4. How did the Massachusetts 54th help change people's minds?

5. What role did women play in the Civil War?

Link to ⸺ **Writing**

Write Letters Letters written by soldiers and their families often described conditions on the battlefield or at home. Write a letter detailing life as a Civil War soldier. Write another letter in response that relates the situation at home in the city or on a farm. Use the word **draft** in your answer.

93

Close and Assess

Summarize the Lesson

Tell students to examine the vertical time line. Ask them to summarize the lesson by reviewing how the events are related.

✓ **LESSON 2 REVIEW**

1. **Main Idea and Details** For possible answers, see the reduced pupil page.

2. South: A man could pay for a substitute if he owned 20 or more slaves; North: A man could pay $300 to avoid fighting.

3. **Critical Thinking: *Problem Solving*** Possible answer: First I would analyze how the war was going for both sides. Then I would advise President Lincoln of his options, weighing the advantages and disadvantages.

4. Many Northerners no longer doubted the ability and bravery of black soldiers.

5. Possible answers: Took over the jobs their husbands held before the Civil War; became soldiers, spies, nurses, or made clothing and sent food

Link to ⸺ **Writing**

Consider having students deliver their letters as soldiers to another classmate who then responds as a family member at home.

FYI SOCIAL STUDIES **Background**

Civil War Anesthesia

- Explain how scientific discoveries and technological innovations have benefited individuals in the United States.

- William Thomas Morton, an American, was among the first to use a general anesthetic on surgical patients. He used an inhaler that he had devised to administer ether to a patient before surgery on October 16, 1846. This made surgery painless.

- Doctors began using this technique on wounded Civil War soldiers before performing surgery—when ether was available.

Workbook, p. 23

Lesson 2: Life During the War

Directions: For each main idea, write a supporting detail on the line provided. You may use your textbook.

1. **Main Idea:** News of the war spread in many ways.
   Detail: _____

2. **Main Idea:** As the war continued, both sides had trouble getting more soldiers.
   Detail: _____

3. **Main Idea:** Most of the soldiers who died in the Civil War did not die in battle.
   Detail: _____

4. **Main Idea:** The Civil War did not begin as a war against slavery.
   Detail: _____

5. **Main Idea:** African Americans who wished to serve in the war were not treated the same as white soldiers.
   Detail: _____

6. **Main Idea:** Women contributed to the war effort in many ways.
   Detail: _____

Also on Teacher Resources CD-ROM.

Working for Lasting Peace

Objective
- Identify the accomplishments of notable individuals, such as Jody Williams.

1 Introduce and Motivate

Preview To activate prior knowledge, have students describe a time when they or another person was treated unfairly. Ask them if they took any action to stop this mistreatment, and if so, have them describe it.

2 Teach and Discuss

Primary Source
Cited in a CNN report on 1997 Nobel Prize winners: "Jody Williams: The Woman Who Waged War on Land Mines"

1 What point was Jody Williams trying to make in this quote? Land mines continue to kill innocent people even after a war has ended. Analyze Primary Sources

Working for Lasting Peace

Many years after the terrible bloodshed of the Civil War, new kinds of weapons, such as landmines, pose a threat to the lives of innocent people.

When Jody Williams heard schoolchildren pick on her brother, Stephen, she got angry. "I couldn't understand why people would be mean to him because he was deaf," says Williams. From that early experience of cruelty in Poultney, Vermont, came Williams's fierce desire to "stop bullies [from] being mean to . . . people, just because they are weak."

Today defending innocent people against landmines is Jody Williams's life work. Landmines have been used since the late 1800s. They are hidden in the ground and are intended to harm enemy soldiers during war by exploding when people walk over them. When the wars end, however, many landmines remain. Today millions and millions of landmines are in the ground in about 70 countries—mainly poor ones like Angola, Afghanistan, and Cambodia. Williams says:

"The landmine cannot tell the difference between a soldier or a civilian [a person who is not soldier]. . . . Once peace is declared, the landmine does not recognize that peace.

"The landmine is eternally [always] prepared to take victims." 1

▶ Jody Williams shared the 1997 Nobel Peace Prize with Tun Channareth, a victim of a landmine in Cambodia.

Practice and Extend

FYI SOCIAL STUDIES
Background

More About Jody Williams
- Williams was born on October 9, 1950.
- Williams was awarded degrees at the University of Vermont and Johns Hopkins School of Advanced International Studies.
- Williams has held jobs as Deputy Director of Medical Aid for El Salvador and has taught in Mexico, the United Kingdom, and Washington, D.C.

BUILDING CITIZENSHIP

★ **Caring**

Respect
Responsibility
Fairness
Honesty
Courage

In the 1980s Jody Williams learned of the dangers of landmines while working for human rights in war-torn Central America. There she saw children who had lost legs or arms after stepping on buried landmines. She met families who could not farm land because there were so many landmines buried there.

In 1991 Jody Williams and others started the International Campaign to Ban Landmines (ICBL). Their goal is a landmine-free planet. Williams works tirelessly for a ban on landmines, visiting affected countries and sending e-mails and faxes to tell people around the world about the dangers of these buried killers.

In recognition of their efforts, Jody Williams and ICBL were awarded the Nobel Peace Prize in December 1997. At the end of 1997, leaders from 121 countries signed a treaty to outlaw landmine production and destroy existing landmines. ③

Caring in Action

Link to Current Events "When we began we were just three people sitting in a room," says Williams about ICBL's beginnings. "It's breathtaking what you can do when you set a goal and put all your energy into it." Get together with two other classmates. What caring action can you plan for your school or community? What are some steps your group could take to carry it out?

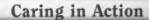

2 **Why did land mines prevent farmers from farming their land in Central America?** If they tried to plant crops, they might dig up or step on a land mine and be injured or killed. **Cause and Effect**

Problem Solving

3 **How does the ICBL propose to solve the problem of land mines around the world?** They hope all countries will agree to ban land mines, outlaw land mine production in the future, and destroy existing land mines. **Solve Problems**

3 Close and Assess

Caring in Action

Link to Current Events

- Have students research the problem they want to solve in their community and present information to others.

- Point out that solving problems in the community involves citizenship skills, such as mobilizing information, people, and other resources.

CURRICULUM CONNECTION
Writing

Write an E-mail

- Have students suppose they are working with Williams in the ICBL.

- Have them write an e-mail they would send to leaders of countries around the world to make them aware of the dangers of the buried land mines.

- Students should include ideas about how the leaders could help eliminate land mines now and in the future.

How the North Won

Objectives

- Describe the events of the Battle of Gettysburg.
- Analyze President Lincoln's Civil War goals as expressed in the Gettysburg Address.
- Identify the locations and results of the major battles of the Civil War.
- Explain the reasons for the use of total war and its consequences.

Vocabulary

Battle of Gettysburg, p. 97;
Gettysburg Address, p. 98;
Battle of Vicksburg, p. 99;
total war, p. 100

Resources

- Workbook, p. 24
- Transparency 1
- Every Student Learns Guide, pp. 42–45
- Quick Study, pp. 22–23

Quick Teaching Plan

If time is short, have students copy and complete the following diagram as they read the lesson independently. Have students add more boxes using the *Places* from Lesson 3.

Where: Gettysburg	→	Where:
When: 1863		When:
What Happened:		What Happened:

1 Introduce and Motivate

Preview Ask students to recall how the North and South were affected by the Civil War. Tell students they will learn about how the Civil War finally ended in Lesson 3.

 The Gettysburg Address was one of Lincoln's most famous speeches. It honored soldiers who died in the Battle of Gettysburg. Ask students what they think Lincoln might have said in the speech.

LESSON 3

1863			1865
July 1863 The Union gains control of the Mississippi River.	**November 1863** President Lincoln delivers the Gettysburg Address.		**April 1865** The Confederacy surrenders to the Union.

Gettysburg
Appomattox
Court House
Atlanta
Vicksburg
Savannah

PREVIEW

Focus on the Main Idea
A series of Northern victories led to the end of the Civil War by 1865.

PLACES
Gettysburg, Pennsylvania
Vicksburg, Mississippi
Atlanta, Georgia
Savannah, Georgia
Appomattox Court House, Virginia

PEOPLE
Ulysses S. Grant
William Tecumseh Sherman

VOCABULARY
Battle of Gettysburg
Gettysburg Address
Battle of Vicksburg
total war

96

How the North Won

You Are There The date is November 19, 1863. About 15,000 people have gathered at Gettysburg, Pennsylvania. They are here for a ceremony to honor the soldiers who died in the Battle of Gettysburg just four months earlier. President Lincoln has been asked to speak.

The main speaker at the event is former Massachusetts governor Edward Everett. He delivers a speech that lasts almost two hours. Finally, President Lincoln rises and addresses the crowd for about three minutes. The speech is so short that no one realizes that Lincoln is finished. The crowd is silent for a moment. Then a few people begin to clap. Lincoln sits down before the photographer can take his picture.

One newspaper calls his speech "silly." Lincoln calls it "a flat failure." But his speech, the Gettysburg Address, will become known as one of the greatest speeches in United States history.

 Main Idea and Details As you read, keep in mind the goals of the North as the war reached an end.

Practice and Extend

READING SKILL
Main Idea/Details

In the Lesson Review, students complete a graphic organizer like the one below. You may want to provide students with a copy of Transparency 1 to complete as they read the lesson.

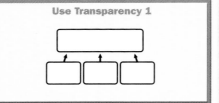

Use Transparency 1

VOCABULARY
Word Exercise

Individual Word Study

Point out to students that the word *address* can mean "the place to which mail is directed," "speaking or writing to," and "a speech." Ask students which meaning *address* has in *Gettysburg Address.* (a speech) Tell students that the word *address* comes from a Latin word that means "to direct." Discuss how each meaning of the word *address* relates to the idea of directing something.

The Battle of Gettysburg

One of the most important battles of the Civil War was a three-day struggle fought in Gettysburg, Pennsylvania. This was the farthest north that Confederate forces had advanced into Union territory.

The Battle of Gettysburg began on July 1, 1863. The Confederates, led by Robert E. Lee, pushed the Union soldiers back, but missed an opportunity to pursue the Northerners and follow up their attack.

By the second day of fighting, more Union soldiers had arrived. The Confederates attacked again, but the Union troops held their ground. One Confederate from Texas remembered "the balls [bullets] were whizzing so thick that it looked like a man could hold out a hat and catch it full."

On July 3, more than 150 Confederate cannons fired at Union troops. Northern cannons responded. The noise was so loud it was heard 140 miles away in Pittsburgh. Southern General George Pickett then led an attack on Union troops known as "Pickett's Charge." Thousands of Confederates marched in the open and uphill toward the well-protected Union troops. The attack was a disaster. Of the nearly 10,500 Confederates in Pickett's Charge, more than 5,000 were killed or wounded, and hundreds were captured.

The Battle of Gettysburg was an important victory for the North. Lee's advance into the North was stopped, and he retreated back into Virginia. It was also a costly battle for both sides. There were more than 23,000 Union casualties. The South suffered more than 28,000 casualties.

REVIEW Describe the events of each day in the Battle of Gettysburg. **Sequence**

Map Adventure

Battle of Gettysburg, 1863
Suppose you are visiting the battle site where the fighting at Gettysburg took place. Today it is a national military park. Answer the questions about the battle site.

1. Describe the location of the Union and Confederate headquarters.
2. In which direction was Pickett's Charge made?
3. What advantage did the location of Little Round Top give the Union forces?

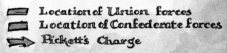
Location of Union forces
Location of Confederate forces

Pickett's Charge

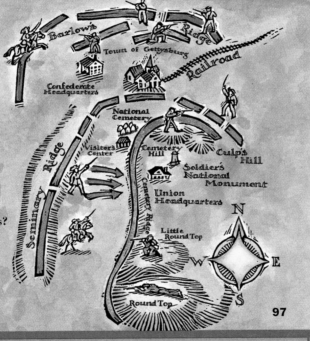

97

Number Match Have students match estimates with facts.

Easy Reorder the facts in Column B. Have students match the numbers in Column A with a fact in Column B. (Correct facts are shown.) **Reteach**

On-Level List the numbers in Column A. Have students find and write the fact in Column B. **Extend**

Challenge Have students choose one fact to research and write about for a class presentation. **Enrich**

Battle of Gettysburg	
Column A	Column B
About 140	Number of miles to Pittsburgh
About 4,000	Number of captured Confederates in "Pickett's Charge"
More than 23,000	Number of Union casualties
More than 28,000	Number of Confederate casualties

For a Lesson Summary, use Quick Study, p. 22.

---

2 Teach and Discuss

PAGE 97

The Battle of Gettysburg

Quick Summary The well-protected Union troops won the Battle of Gettysburg, causing the Confederates to retreat to Virginia.

1 What mistake did the Confederate soldiers make that caused them to lose the battle? They did not follow up on their first attack quickly enough. By the next day more Union soldiers had arrived. **Cause and Effect**

Ongoing Assessment

If... students cannot identify the mistake that caused the Confederate loss,	then... ask what might have happened if the Confederates had pursued the Northerners and followed up their attack at the end of the first day of fighting.

✓ **REVIEW ANSWER** During the first day Confederate soldiers pushed Union soldiers back but failed to follow up their attack. By the second day, more Union soldiers had arrived. The Confederates attacked again, but Union soldiers held their ground. "Pickett's Charge" occurred during the third day. Thousands of Confederates were captured. **Sequence**

Map Adventure Answers

1. The Union headquarters was located just east of Cemetery Ridge. The Confederate headquarters was located just north of Seminary Ridge.

2. East

3. It helped protect them because the Confederates had to march uphill.

The Gettysburg Address

 Quick Summary President Lincoln gave the Gettysburg Address at the dedication of the Gettysburg cemetery in November, 1863.

⭐ **SOCIAL STUDIES STRAND**
Citizenship

Democratic Values and Institutions
Point out that Lincoln's leadership qualities were evident in his Gettysburg Address.

❷ In what ways was the message of the Gettysburg Address consistent with Lincoln's wish to preserve the Union before the Civil War began? In the Gettysburg Address, Lincoln urged people to remain together to support the cause of preserving the Union.
🔄 Main Idea and Details

✓ **REVIEW ANSWER** Lincoln said that the soldiers had given their lives so that the nation might live. He believed their bravery would be long remembered.
🔄 Main Idea and Details

Primary Source
Cited in *The Annals of America*, Volume 9, published by Encyclopædia Britannica, Inc.

Explain that the Gettysburg Address honored the soldiers who died at Gettysburg and inspired the Union.

❸ In the Gettysburg Address, how did Lincoln suggest that people honor the soldiers who died at the Battle of Gettysburg? By increasing their devotion to support the cause of saving the Union
Analyze Primary Sources

The Gettysburg Address

In November 1863, the Gettysburg battlefield was made into a national cemetery to honor the men who died there. As you have read, President Lincoln was one of the people asked to speak at the ceremony. Read his speech, known as the **Gettysburg Address.**

The Gettysburg Address inspired the Union to keep fighting. The speech made it clear that a united nation and the end of slavery were worth fighting for. ❷

REVIEW How did President Lincoln express his admiration for the soldiers who had died at Gettysburg? 🔄 Main Idea and Details

The Gettysburg Address

Four score [80] and seven years ago our fathers brought forth on this continent a new nation, conceived [formed] in Liberty, and dedicated [devoted] to the proposition [idea] that all men are created equal.

Now we are engaged in a great civil war, testing whether that nation, or any nation so conceived and so dedicated, can long endure. We are met on a great battlefield of that war. We have come to dedicate a portion of that field, as a final resting place for those who here gave their lives that that nation might live. It is altogether fitting and proper that we should do this.

But, in a larger sense, we cannot dedicate—we cannot consecrate [make worthy of respect]—we cannot hallow [make holy]—this ground. The brave men, living and dead, who struggled here, have consecrated it, far above our poor power to add or detract [take away]. The world will little note, nor long remember what we say here, but it can never forget what they did here. It is for us the living, rather, to be dedicated here to the unfinished work which they who fought here have thus far so nobly advanced. It is rather for us to be here dedicated to the great task remaining before us—that from these honored dead we take increased devotion to that cause for which they gave the last full measure of devotion—that we here highly resolve [are determined] that these dead shall not have died in vain—that this nation, under God, shall have a new birth of freedom—and that government of the people, by the people, for the people, shall not perish [die out] from the earth. ❸

Painting by J. L. G. Ferris

Practice and Extend

❄ **MEETING INDIVIDUAL NEEDS**
Learning Styles

Review the Gettysburg Address Using their individual learning styles, students review the contents of the Gettysburg Address.

Verbal Learning Have a group of students present a choral reading of the Gettysburg Address with proper tone and expression.

Auditory Learning Have students listen to the choral reading to find the main idea of the speech. (To honor the soldiers who died at the Battle of Gettysburg by continuing to support the Union)

The Tide Turns

The Battle of Gettysburg was one of a series of battles that turned the tide of the war in favor of the Union. As you read in Lesson 1, one part of the Anaconda Plan called for Union troops to gain control of the Mississippi River to weaken the Confederacy. Capturing **Vicksburg, Mississippi,** which lay on the east bank of the river, would achieve this goal.

General **Ulysses S. Grant,** who had served with General Robert E. Lee in the Mexican War, headed the Union forces in the **Battle of Vicksburg.** In May 1863, Union forces began a blockade of the city. They bombarded Vicksburg with cannon fire by land and sea

for 48 days. Many people in the town dug caves in the hillside for protection.

Confederate civilians and soldiers in Vicksburg faced starvation under the Union blockade. Butcher shops sold rats, and soldiers received one biscuit and one piece of bacon a day. **4**

Finally, on July 4, 1863, one day after the Battle of Gettysburg ended, the Southerners surrendered Vicksburg. The Confederacy was cut in two. Study the map below to see where Vicksburg and other major battles of the Civil War took place.

REVIEW Why do you think it took so long for the Confederates to surrender at Vicksburg? **Draw Conclusions**

5

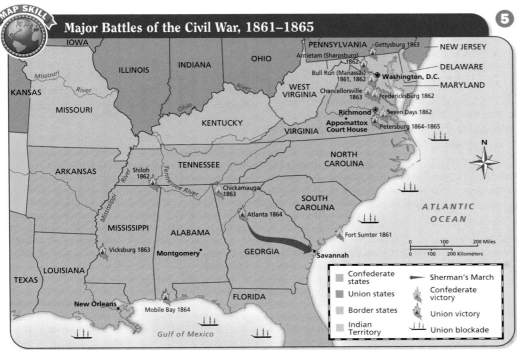

Major Battles of the Civil War, 1861–1865

MAP SKILL

▶ In July 1863, Union victories at Gettysburg and Vicksburg turned the tide of the war.

MAP SKILL Use a Map Scale *How many miles apart were the battles of Gettysburg and Vicksburg?*

The Tide Turns

Quick Summary The Union victory at the Battle of Vicksburg resulted in cutting the Confederacy in half.

4 **How did blockading the city of Vicksburg cause the Confederates to surrender?** They could not get supplies through and people faced starvation, so they surrendered. **Cause and Effect**

✔ **REVIEW ANSWER** Possible answer: The Confederates held out because they believed in their cause and thought more Confederate soldiers would arrive to help them. **Draw Conclusions**

Major Battles of the Civil War, 1861–1865

Point out that the Civil War was fought in both Confederate and Union states.

5 **In which state was the Battle of Gettysburg? Was it a Union or a Confederate state?** Pennsylvania; Union **Interpret Maps**

MAP SKILL **Answer** About 1,000 miles

CURRICULUM CONNECTION
Writing

Write a Diary Entry

- Have one group of students write a diary entry as a Confederate living in Vicksburg during the time of the siege.
- Have another group write a diary entry as a Union soldier taking part in the siege.
- Students can share and compare entries.

The War Ends

🕐 *Quick Summary* Sherman's march through Georgia ended with his army linking with Grant's army and the fall of Richmond. Lee then surrendered and ended the war.

6 **Why did the Confederate army not fight when Sherman marched on Savannah?** Possible answer: They realized it was of no use since Sherman had just destroyed Atlanta and had so many Union soldiers. **Make Inferences**

Primary Source

Cited in *The Civil War: A Narrative–Red River to Appomattox,* by Shelby Foote

7 **What do Lee's words suggest about him?** Possible answer: He was a proud man, but sensible. He realized his soldiers could not achieve victory and more would die if he did not surrender.
Analyze Primary Sources

8 **What can you conclude about Grant's characteristics, based on his actions in Appomattox Court House? Explain.** Possible answer: He was a fair and considerate person who did not take advantage of those whom he had defeated. He gave food to the Confederate soldiers and allowed them to keep their horses and weapons.
Draw Conclusions

Primary Source

Cited in *The Oxford History of the American People,* by Samuel Eliot Morison

9 **To whom was Grant referring with the term "rebels"?** Confederate soldiers
Analyze Primary Sources

✓ **REVIEW ANSWER** Possible answer: In addition to winning battles and capturing territory, Sherman wanted to break the Confederacy's will to fight.
Cause and Effect

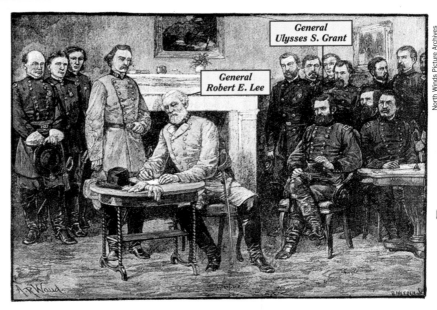

General Ulysses S. Grant

General Robert E. Lee

North Winds Picture Archives

▶ After four years of fighting, General Lee agreed to surrender his army to General Grant.

The War Ends

General Grant was given control of all Union forces in March 1864. Grant continued to wear down the Confederate army with the help of Union General **William Tecumseh Sherman.**

Sherman moved his army toward **Atlanta, Georgia,** a vital industrial and railway center. The opposing Confederate army could not defend the city and retreated. Atlanta fell to the Union on September 2, 1864.

General Sherman used a method of warfare called **total war.** The aim of total war is to destroy not just the opposing army, but the people's will to fight. Sherman's men ordered everyone to leave Atlanta and burned almost the entire city.

Starting in November, his army moved southeast toward **Savannah, Georgia.** The Union soldiers marched 300 miles in a 60 mile-wide path. As they went, they destroyed anything that might help the South keep fighting, including houses, railroads, barns, and fields. Soldiers caused $100 million dollars worth of damage in Sherman's "March to the Sea."

Savannah fell without a fight on December 21, 1864. Sherman wrote to Lincoln, "I . . . present you as a Christmas gift the city of Savannah." Sherman's men then moved to South Carolina, causing even more destruction in the state where the war began.

Sherman's army moved north to link with Grant's army. The Northerners were closing in on Lee's army in Virginia. In April 1865 Confederate soldiers left Richmond, and Union troops entered on April 3. President Lincoln arrived to tour the captured Confederate capital. The city's former slaves cheered him.

Lee's army of 55,000 was tired and starving. The men tried to escape west, but Grant's force of about 113,000 outnumbered and trapped them. Lee admitted to his men,

"There is nothing left for me to do but go and see General Grant, and I would rather die a thousand deaths."

100

Practice and Extend

FYI **SOCIAL STUDIES**
Background

The Beginning and End of the War

- In 1861, Wilmer McLean was making a stew for Confederate General P.G.T. Beauregard in his home on the Bull Run in northern Virginia. During the action at the First Battle of Bull Run, an artillery shell fell down the chimney and into the stew.
- McLean decided to find a safer place to live and bought a farmhouse in Appomattox County.
- It was in this farmhouse that Lee and Grant would meet for the surrender.
- It could be said that the Civil War began in the kitchen of McLean's first home and ended in the parlor of his second home.

Generals Lee and Grant met in a farmhouse in **Appomattox Court House, Virginia,** on April 9, 1865, to discuss the terms of surrender. Grant allowed Lee's men to go free. The Southerners were allowed to keep their personal weapons and any horses they had. Grant also offered to give Lee's men food from Union supplies. Lee accepted. As Lee returned to his men, the Union soldiers began to cheer. Grant silenced them, explaining,

> *"The war is over; the rebels are our countrymen again."*

The Civil War was the most destructive war in United States history. About 620,000 soldiers died. Towns, farms, and industries—mostly in the South—were ruined. Families had been torn apart by the struggle.

Even so, Lincoln expressed sympathy for the South. After news of the Confederate surrender reached Washington, D.C., he appeared before a crowd and asked a band to play the song "Dixie," one of the battle songs of the Confederacy. "I have always thought 'Dixie' one of the best tunes I ever heard," he told the people.

Lincoln wanted the country to be rebuilt. He had a plan to heal the nation's deep divisions. But he would never see his plans carried out.

REVIEW What were the results of General Sherman's strategy of total war?
Cause and Effect

Summarize the Lesson

- **July 4, 1863** Union soldiers led by General Grant cut the Confederacy in two by capturing Vicksburg, Mississippi.

- **November 19, 1863** President Abraham Lincoln gave the Gettysburg Address honoring the men who died in battle there.

- **April 9, 1865** General Robert E. Lee surrendered to General Ulysses S. Grant at Appomattox Court House, Virginia, ending the Civil War.

LESSON 3 REVIEW

Check Facts and Main Ideas

1. **Main Idea and Details** On a separate sheet of paper, fill in the missing details that support the main idea.

> The Union used several strategies to achieve decisive victories in the last years of the Civil War.

> The Union held a high position during the Battle of Gettysburg, protecting them from the attacking Confederates.

> The Union blockaded Vicksburg, forcing them to surrender when they faced starvation.

> General Sherman used total war, destroying any resources that the South might use to keep fighting.

2. What circumstances led the Union to victory on the third day in the **Battle of Gettysburg**?

3. What were Lincoln's goals as expressed in the **Gettysburg Address**?

4. **Critical Thinking:** *Interpret Maps* Look at the map on page 99. In what state did most of the major battles occur in the Civil War? Give a reason you think this would be so.

5. What was the purpose of **total war** and Sherman's "March to the Sea"?

Link to Mathematics

Analyze a Speech Reread President Lincoln's Gettysburg Address on page 98. What year was he referring to in the speech when he said "Four score and seven years ago"? Why would he have referred to that year?

101

Summarize the Lesson

Have pairs of students share details about each event.

✓ **LESSON 3 REVIEW**

1. **Main Idea and Details** For possible answers, see the reduced pupil page.

2. Possible answer: The Union army was well protected on hills while the Confederates marched toward them in the open.

3. Lincoln wanted to honor the soldiers who had died and to rally the people to preserve the Union.

4. **Critical Thinking:** *Interpret Maps* Virginia; The Union army might have concentrated its forces in this area in an attempt to capture the Confederate capital, Richmond, and to defend Washington, D.C.

5. To capture Savannah; the Union destroyed almost everything in its path because Sherman wanted to weaken the Confederacy.

Link to Mathematics

Explain that a *score* means 20 years and that students first have to calculate how many years four score and seven are. Lincoln believed the Civil War soldiers were fighting to preserve the nation the Patriots had fought to create in 1776.

EXTEND LANGUAGE
ESL ESL Support

Explore Words About the South Help students identify and explore words about people and places.

Beginning Have students look at the map on p. 76. Name states and have students say *yes* or *no* to indicate whether they were in the Confederacy.

Intermediate Have students use words such as *Confederacy, rebels,* and *Dixie* in a paragraph. Then have students read their paragraphs to partners.

Advanced Have students create and share a dialogue between Lincoln and Grant or Lee discussing how the country might be rebuilt.

For additional ESL support, use Every Student Learns Guide, pp. 42–45.

Workbook, p. 24

Lesson 3: How the North Won
Directions: Match each term in the box with its clue. Write the term on the line provided.

Battle of Gettysburg	Ulysses S. Grant	total war
Gettysburg Address	Battle of Vicksburg	Robert E. Lee
Anaconda Plan	William Tecumseh Sherman	Appomattox Court House

1. Place where Generals Lee and Grant met to discuss the terms of the Confederates' surrender of the Civil War. _____

2. "I would rather die a thousand deaths." _____

3. President Lincoln made a short speech at a ceremony to dedicate a national cemetery. In his speech, Lincoln inspired the Union to keep fighting for a united nation and the end of slavery. _____

4. A method of warfare designed to destroy the opposing army and the people's will to fight. _____

5. This three-day battle began on July 1, 1863. It was one of the most important battles of the Civil War. It was an important victory for the North and a costly battle for both sides. _____

6. Head of the Union forces in the Battle of Vicksburg. _____

7. The surrender of this battle by the Southerners cut the Confederacy in two. _____

8. The Union blockade at the Battle of Vicksburg was part of this strategy to gain control of the Mississippi River and weaken the Confederacy. _____

9. Led soldiers in a destructive "March to the Sea" _____

Notes for Home: Your child learned how the North used strategies to win the Civil War.
Home Activity: With your child, brainstorm strategies for winning a game such as checkers, chess, or cards. Discuss the advantages of using a strategy to defeat an opponent.

Also on Teacher Resources CD-ROM.

Read a Road Map

Objective
- Apply geographic skills to interpret legends and symbols on maps.

Vocabulary
road map, p. 102;
interstate highway, p. 102

Resource
- Workbook, p. 25

1 Introduce and Motivate

What is a road map? Ask students how people might use a road map. What information can be found on a road map? Then have students read the **What?** section of text on p. 102 to help set the purpose of the lesson.

Why use a road map? Have students read the **Why?** section of text on p. 102. Ask them how using a road map might make it easier to locate and visit places of interest.

2 Teach and Discuss

How is this skill used? Examine the map on p. 103 with students.

- Point out that interstate highways are identified by a shield with a black top and the number of the highway. These are usually three- or four-lane highways.

- Explain that cities are marked with small circles, and points of interest, such as battlefields, are marked with small squares.

- Have students read the **How?** section of text on p. 103.

Map and Globe Skills

Read a Road Map

What? A road map is a map that shows roads, cities, and places of interest. Different types of lines show large and small highways and even smaller roads. Symbols show if a road is a major interstate highway, a large road that connects cities in different states. Other symbols show state roads, and still others show smaller roads.

Different sizes of color areas and dots are used to show cities and towns of various sizes. Many road maps use special symbols to show places of interest. Some road maps also show distances from one place to another.

Why? People often have to drive to places they do not know. They may be traveling for business, vacation, or other reasons. Drivers use road maps to figure out how to get from one place to another.

Many people are interested in the history of the Civil War. Some visit Civil War sites. Our nation keeps many Civil War sites as parks or monuments. Tourists may go from one site to another during a vacation. Often they visit places they have never been before, and they find their way with road maps.

▶ **Today the Gettysburg battlefield is a national military park.**

102

Practice and Extend

MEETING INDIVIDUAL NEEDS
Leveled Practice

Give Directions Ask students to use the road map on p. 103 to give directions from one city to another.

Easy Have students complete sentence frames similar to the following by telling the direction and road to travel: To go from Richmond to Washington, D.C., travel north on highway 95. **Reteach**

On-Level Have students choose two cities shown on the map and write directions telling the road, direction, and distance to travel to go from one city to the other. **Extend**

Challenge Have students choose three cities on the map and write sets of directions to go from the first city to the second and from the second city to the third. **Enrich**

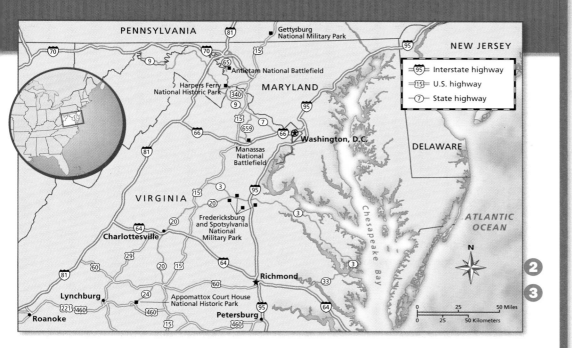

PENNSYLVANIA

Gettysburg National Military Park

NEW JERSEY

Antietam National Battlefield

MARYLAND

Harpers Ferry National Historic Park

Washington, D.C.

DELAWARE

Manassas National Battlefield

Legend:
- Interstate highway
- U.S. highway
- State highway

VIRGINIA

Fredericksburg and Spotsylvania National Military Park

Charlottesville

Chesapeake Bay

ATLANTIC OCEAN

N

Richmond

Lynchburg

Appomattox Court House National Historic Park

Petersburg

Roanoke

0   25   50 Miles
0   25   50 Kilometers

How?

To use a road map, you need to know where you are and where you want to go. Then you find these places on the map. You also have to understand what kinds of roads are shown and how they are marked on the map.

Say that you are starting at Richmond, Virginia, and want to get to Gettysburg, Pennsylvania. Look at the road map on this page, which shows many Civil War sites in Pennsylvania, Maryland, and Virginia. You notice that Gettysburg is about 180 miles north of Richmond. You see that Route 64 goes northwest from Richmond to Route 15. From there, Route 15 goes north all the way to Gettysburg.

Think and Apply

1. How would you travel from Gettysburg National Military Park to Manassas National Battlefield?

2. What interstate highway is part of the shortest route from Manassas National Battlefield Park to Washington, D.C.?

3. How would you travel from Washington, D.C., to the Fredericksburg and Spotsylvania National Military Park?

Internet Activity

For more information, go online to the *Atlas* at **www.sfsocialstudies.com.**

103

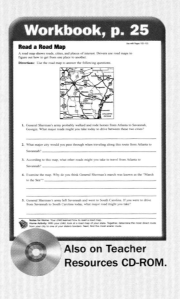

Communications During the Civil War

Objective

• Identify and explain different forms of communication during the Civil War.

1 Introduce and Motivate

• Tell students that the quality of communication during a war can lead to victory or defeat.

• Before students read this page, ask them to brainstorm a list of facts they know about telegraphs. Have them include parts of a telegraph, items needed to operate telegraphs, and types of codes. Tell students they will learn more about telegraphs as they read these pages.

• Students will add to their lists later as part of the assessment for this page.

2 Teach and Discuss

1 **What limitation did signal drums have that telegraphs did not?** They could only be heard short distances. Telegraph signals could be sent across many miles. **Compare and Contrast**

2 **What important capability did the army field telegrapher's wagon have?** It could move from place to place, so telegraphs could be sent and received wherever the troops might have to move to during battle. **Draw Conclusions**

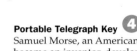 DORLING KINDERSLEY VISUAL DICTIONARY

Communications During the Civil War

The Civil War was one of the first large conflicts in which armies could communicate instantly using the telegraph, which sent messages along wires. By 1861 every state east of the Mississippi River was linked by telegraph wires. That April, when the Confederacy attacked Fort Sumter in South Carolina, word went out immediately: "Fort Sumter is fired upon." Both Union and Confederate armies used Morse code and secret military codes to communicate.

Signal Drum
Drums and bugles were played on the field, signaling instructions for firing and troop movements. This drum was found on the Gettysburg battlefield.

Animal hide drum head

Handpainted eagle and crest

Strapping to keep drum head taut

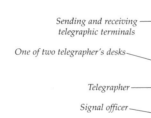

Polished wood key tip

Key arm

Electrical contact

Wire terminals

Spring rod

Key contact

Wooden base

Portable Telegraph Key 4
Samuel Morse, an American artist who became an inventor, developed a way to send telegraph messages using a code called Morse code.

Rolled canvas window blind

Sending and receiving telegraphic terminals

One of two telegrapher's desks

Telegrapher

Signal officer

2 **Army Field Telegrapher's Wagon**
This portable telegrapher's office had sending and receiving sets.

104

Practice and Extend

FYI SOCIAL STUDIES **Background**

Morse Code

• Students may enjoy writing out messages using Morse Code.
• Display the following symbols or have students find them in a reference source in the library or on the Internet.

Morse Code Alphabet

A · —	I · ·	Q — — · —	X — · · —
B — · · ·	J · — — —	R · — ·	Y — · — —
C — · — ·	K — · —	S · · ·	Z — — · ·
D — · ·	L · — · ·	T —	comma — — · · — —
E ·	M — —	U · · —	period · — · — · —
F · · — ·	N — ·	V · · · —	question mark · · — — · ·
G — — ·	O — — —	W · — —	
H · · · ·	P · — — ·		

Hanging Military Telegraph Wires

As armies moved, telegraph wires had to be strung to areas that might not have been wired yet. Army telegraph poles were often trees from which bark and limbs had been removed.

Insulated wire hook

Bamboo field poles for temporary hook-ups to existing heavy lines

Wire spool

Field telegrapher's wagon

❸

Sending and receiving key and letter indicator

Brass wheel with stamped letters

Sending terminals

Receiving terminals

❹

Beardslee Telegraph

Most soldiers could not read Morse code, so the Union army adopted the Beardslee telegraph. Electric signals sent or received over the Beardslee system moved a metal arrow around a large brass wheel with the letters of the alphabet stamped on it. These letters spelled out messages in English or secret code. The Beardslee's range was limited to five miles.

Letter wheel gear mechanism

Wire wrapping

Service door

Carrying strap

Brass fittings

105

---

❸ Why were telegraph wires necessary? So electrical signals could travel from one place to another **Draw Conclusions**

❹ How were Beardslee's telegraph and Samuel Morse's telegraph alike? How were they different? Alike: Both transmitted electrical signals; Different: Beardslee's telegraph spelled out messages using letters while Morse's used a code. **Compare and Contrast**

❸ Close and Assess

- Encourage students to learn more about other means of communication in encyclopedias or history books.

- Ask students to add to the lists they began earlier. Have students discuss what new information they learned from the pictures on these pages.

SOCIAL STUDIES
Background

Communicating by Flag

- Albert J. Myer developed a way to communicate on the battlefield by using flags.

- The system, which used only one flag, was called *wigwag*. It was effective for communications between troops miles apart.

The End of Slavery

Objectives

- Explain why Congress disagreed with Johnson's plan for Reconstruction.
- Analyze the effect of the Reconstruction Acts.
- Evaluate the impact of the Thirteenth, Fourteenth, and Fifteenth Amendments.
- Describe life for African Americans after Reconstruction.

Vocabulary

assassination, p. 107; **Reconstruction,** p. 107; **Thirteenth Amendment,** p. 107; **black codes**, p. 107; **Freedmen's Bureau,** p. 108; **Fourteenth Amendment,** p. 109; **Fifteenth Amendment,** p. 109; **impeachment,** p. 109; **Jim Crow laws,** p. 110; **segregation,** p. 110; **sharecropping,** p. 110

Resources

- Workbook, p. 26
- Transparency 1
- Every Student Learns Guide, pp. 46–49
- Quick Study, pp. 24–25

Quick Teaching Plan

If time is short, have students work in pairs to copy and complete this chart:

Effects of Reconstruction on African Americans	
Reconstruction under Congress	End of Reconstruction

1 Introduce and Motivate

Preview To activate prior knowledge, ask students to recall Lincoln's goals in fighting the Civil War. Tell students that in Lesson 4 they will learn whether or not Lincoln's goals were realized.

You Are There — Not everyone was happy with the way the Civil War ended. Ask students to predict how Lincoln's assassination might affect relations between the North and South.

LESSON 4

1865			1867
April 1865 President Lincoln is killed.	December 1865 The Thirteenth Amendment ends slavery.		March 1867 Congress passes the first Reconstruction Act.

Washington, D.C.

PREVIEW

Focus on the Main Idea
The country faced many difficult challenges after the Civil War ended, including rebuilding the South and protecting the rights of newly freed African Americans.

PLACES
Washington, D.C.

PEOPLE
Andrew Johnson
Hiram R. Revels
Blanche K. Bruce

VOCABULARY
assassination
Reconstruction
Thirteenth Amendment
black codes
Freedmen's Bureau
Fourteenth Amendment
Fifteenth Amendment
impeachment
Jim Crow laws
segregation
sharecropping

106

The End of Slavery

You Are There — It is Friday, a little after 10:00 P.M. President Abraham Lincoln and his wife, Mary, are enjoying a play. The President and his guests are seated in a box above the stage of Ford's Theater.

Suddenly, the audience hears something like an explosion. Blue-colored smoke comes from the box where the President is seated. Mary Lincoln screams. President Lincoln has been shot. The bullet has entered the back of his head near his left ear. Lincoln is still breathing but is unconscious.

A young doctor comes forward to aid the President. After checking his wound, he says, "It is impossible for him to recover."

Main Idea and Details As you read, look for details about rebuilding the nation after the Civil War.

▶ Poster for the play President Lincoln was seeing when he was shot.

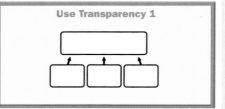

Practice and Extend

READING SKILL
Main Idea/Details

In the Lesson Review, students complete a graphic organizer like the one below. You may want to provide students with a copy of Transparency 1 to complete as they read the lesson.

Use Transparency 1

VOCABULARY
Word Exercise

Context Clues

Use these questions or create your own in order to help students learn new vocabulary. Have students draw upon their own knowledge in answering questions.

- Which does **segregation** do, separate people or give people the right to vote? (separate)
- Which would someone who is **sharecropping** do, pay rent with crops or give crops away to neighbors? (pay rent)

A New President

After being shot, President Abraham Lincoln died in the early morning of April 15, 1865, in Washington, D.C. Until that time, no United States President had ever been assassinated. Assassination is the murder of a political or government leader.

Lincoln's killer was John Wilkes Booth, a 26-year-old actor who supported the Confederacy. Federal troops found Booth in a Virginia barn where he was shot and killed after he refused to surrender. Others who took part in the assassination plan were also caught and later hanged.

A funeral train carried President Lincoln's body to his hometown of Springfield, Illinois, where he was buried. People in New York City, Philadelphia, Cleveland, Chicago, and other cities paid their respects as the train passed through their communities.

▶ People lined the streets when Lincoln's funeral train passed through New York City.

THE NATION MOURNS.

Collection of the New York Historical Society

Vice President Andrew Johnson became the new President. The former senator from Tennessee intended to carry out Lincoln's plan for Reconstruction—the rebuilding and healing of the country after the war.

One of the first steps toward reconstruction was ending slavery throughout the nation. The Thirteenth Amendment, which abolished slavery in the United States, took effect on December 18, 1865.

Johnson also had a plan to readmit the former Confederate states into the Union. Each state had to form a new state government. It had to pledge to obey all federal laws and deal fairly with newly freed African Americans. By the end of 1865, President Johnson believed that Reconstruction was complete.

Under Johnson's plan, though, Southern states were free to pass laws called black codes. These laws denied African American men the right to vote or act as jurors in a trial. Black people also could not own guns, take certain jobs, or own land. African Americans who were out of work might be fined or arrested. The laws had the effect of making an African American's life much the same as it had been under slavery. **①**

Many in Congress were angered by the black codes. They thought Johnson's Reconstruction plan was too easy on the South. The Republicans, who had won a majority in both houses of Congress, did not trust Johnson, who was a Southerner and had been a Democrat before becoming Lincoln's Vice President. Members of Congress began developing a new plan of Reconstruction. **②**

REVIEW What effect did black codes have on African Americans? *Cause and Effect*

107

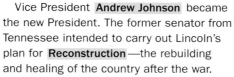

PAGE 107

A New President

⏱ *Quick Summary* Although the Thirteenth Amendment prohibited slavery, Southern states passed black codes that made conditions for African Americans similar to those under slavery.

① Why do you think the Southern states passed black codes? Possible answer: To prevent African Americans from gaining freedom even though slavery had been abolished **Make Inferences**

✓ **Ongoing Assessment**

| **If...** students cannot make an inference about the purpose of black codes, | **then...** ask the following questions and discuss students' responses. What did the Thirteenth Amendment do? (End slavery) How did the Southern states feel about slavery? (They were in favor of slavery.) What did the black codes do? (Allowed the Southern states to treat African Americans in a way similar to when they were enslaved) |

② How did Lincoln and Johnson differ in their policies? Possible answer: Lincoln was less sympathetic toward the South. **Compare and Contrast**

✓ **REVIEW ANSWER** Black codes tried to place limitations on African Americans similar to those they faced under slavery. Under black codes, African Americans could not vote, participate in jury trials, own guns or land, or hold certain jobs. **Cause and Effect**

Reconstruction Under Congress

Quick Summary The Reconstruction Acts gave many freedoms to African Americans. White Southerners resisted these changes.

Problem Solving

3 **What problems did people in the war-torn South face? How did Congress attempt to solve them?** Possible answer: People needed greater access to hospitals and schools. The Freedmen's Bureau built hospitals and schools for blacks in the South. Solve Problems

C SOCIAL STUDIES STRAND
Culture

Prejudice Reduction Tell students that the Freedmen's Bureau maintained extensive records of the births, marriages, and deaths of many former slaves. These documents have been preserved by many local organizations and have helped African Americans in researching their family histories. The book *Roots,* by Alex Haley, introduced new possibilities in researching African American genealogy and focused new interest on family reunions. At these reunions, extended families of African Americans meet to exchange traditions and family lore.

4 **Who were carpetbaggers?** Northerners who moved south to start businesses; they often carried suitcases made of carpet. Main Idea and Details

5 **What was the main method the Ku Klux Klan used to restore white control in the South?** Terror and violence Main Idea and Details

✓ **REVIEW ANSWER** Under Congress's Reconstruction plan, Southern states had to draft new constitutions giving African American men the right to vote. African Americans were allowed to hold public office, but former Confederate leaders could not vote or hold office. Buildings, roads, and bridges were repaired. New railroads were built, and a system of free education was established. Main Idea and Details

Reconstruction Under Congress

Congress passed the first Reconstruction Act in 1867. The former Confederate states were divided into five military districts, and about 20,000 federal troops were sent to the South. The troops, led by military governors, were responsible for maintaining order, supervising elections, and preventing discrimination against African Americans.

The Reconstruction Acts required Southern states to write new state constitutions giving African American men the right to vote. The Acts also prevented former Confederate leaders and military officers from voting or holding elected office.

The Freedmen's Bureau was established to help the 4 million freedmen, or former slaves, after the war. The Freedmen's Bureau built hospitals and schools for blacks in the South. **3** The Bureau hired black and white teachers from the North and the South.

For the first time in United States history, African Americans became elected officials. In Mississippi, two African Americans were elected United States senators. In 1870 Republican **Hiram R. Revels,** a minister and teacher, was elected to the Senate seat that Jefferson Davis held before the Civil War. In 1874 **Blanche K. Bruce,** a former slave, was elected to the Senate. Twenty other African Americans from the South were also elected to the House of Representatives.

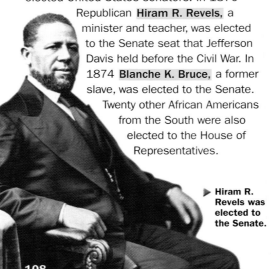
▶ Hiram R. Revels was elected to the Senate.

108

▶ During Reconstruction, African American children studied at new schools in the South.

Many white Southerners did not like the changes brought by Reconstruction. Some resented the new state governments, which they felt were forced on them by outsiders. Some were angered by Northerners who moved south to start businesses. These new arrivals were called carpetbaggers, because they often arrived carrying their belongings in suitcases made of carpet. Southerners who supported Reconstruction were called scalawags. Carpetbaggers and scalawags were accused of trying to profit from the hardships of the South. **4**

New leaders raised taxes to help rebuild roads, construct railroads, and establish a free education system. Many Southerners had a hard time paying these taxes. They were trying to rebuild their own farms and businesses.

Some white Southerners also objected to the rights gained by African Americans. After the new state governments repealed black codes, a small group of white Southerners formed the Ku Klux Klan. The Klan's goal was to restore white control over the lives of African Americans. Members of the Klan burned African American schools and homes, and attacked blacks for trying to vote. **5**

REVIEW What changes did Congress bring about in the South during Reconstruction? Main Idea and Details

Practice and Extend

MEETING INDIVIDUAL NEEDS
Leveled Practice

Write an Article Ask students to write a newspaper article about Reconstruction.

Easy Have students write headlines for an article announcing the passage of the Reconstruction Acts. **Reteach**

On-Level Have students write a newspaper article describing the new rights and resources African Americans will have as part of the Reconstruction Acts. **Extend**

Challenge Have students write a newspaper article that contains an interview with an African American who experienced life in the South before and after the Civil War. **Enrich**

For a Lesson Summary, use Quick Study, p. 24.

New Amendments

Before being readmitted into the Union, former Confederate states had to accept two new amendments. The **Fourteenth Amendment,** ratified in July 1868, gave African Americans citizenship and said that no state could deny the equal protection of the law to all citizens.

The **Fifteenth Amendment,** ratified in February 1870, gave all male citizens the right to vote. It stated,

> "... the right of citizens of the United States to vote shall not be denied ... on account of race, color, or previous condition of servitude [slavery]."

Sojourner Truth pointed out that a woman had "a right to have just as much as a man." But the Fifteenth Amendment did not give voting rights to women. This angered many women who had fought for abolition and thought women as well as African Americans should have the right to vote.

President Johnson opposed the Fourteenth Amendment and other Reconstruction laws. He believed that the Reconstruction Acts were unlawful because they were passed without the representation of Southern states in Congress. He tried to block the passage of several laws that granted further rights to African Americans.

Angry about Johnson's actions, the Republicans in Congress tried to remove him from office by **impeachment.** Impeachment is the bringing of charges of wrongdoing against an elected official by the House of Representatives. If found guilty in a Senate trial, an impeached President is removed from office. Johnson avoided being removed from office by one vote in May 1868, but his ability to lead the nation was weakened.

REVIEW Why did Congress want to impeach President Johnson? *Summarize*

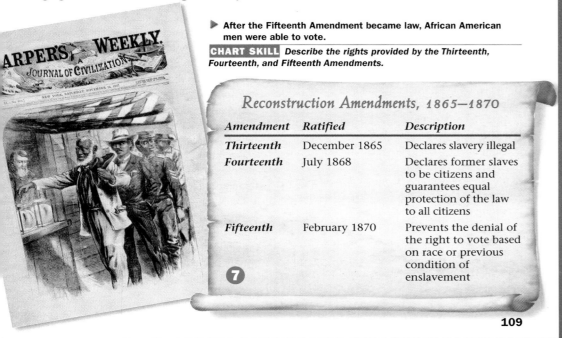

▶ After the Fifteenth Amendment became law, African American men were able to vote.

CHART SKILL *Describe the rights provided by the Thirteenth, Fourteenth, and Fifteenth Amendments.*

Reconstruction Amendments, 1865–1870

Amendment	Ratified	Description
Thirteenth	December 1865	Declares slavery illegal
Fourteenth	July 1868	Declares former slaves to be citizens and guarantees equal protection of the law to all citizens
Fifteenth	February 1870	Prevents the denial of the right to vote based on race or previous condition of enslavement

7

109

Quick Summary The Fourteenth and Fifteenth Amendments were passed during Reconstruction. President Johnson tried to block the passage of laws that granted rights to African Americans.

Primary Source

Cited in *The World Almanac 2001*

6 **How did the Fifteenth Amendment both expand and continue to limit which citizens had the right to vote?** It stated that citizens could not be denied the right to vote based on race, color, or previous condition of servitude; it did not give voting rights to women.
Analyze Primary Sources

✓ **REVIEW ANSWER** Because Johnson tried to block the passage of several laws that granted further rights to African Americans **Summarize**

7 **What was the main purpose of the Thirteenth, Fourteenth, and Fifteenth Amendments?** To provide more rights for people who were formerly enslaved
Main Idea and Details

CHART SKILL **Answer** Thirteenth Amendment: right to freedom; Fourteenth Amendment: rights of citizenship and equal protection; Fifteenth Amendment: right to vote

Reconstruction Ends

 Quick Summary By 1877 white Southern Democrats had regained their power in state governments and restricted most of the rights African Americans won during Reconstruction.

H SOCIAL STUDIES STRAND
History

Many states in the South passed "grandfather clauses" to increase the number of white voters. Southerners who could not pay the poll tax or pass a literacy test were allowed to vote if their grandfathers had the right to vote.

8 **Why were African Americans in the South unable to vote even though the Constitution gave them the right to vote?** Possible answer: Southern Democrats passed new laws and state constitutions that prevented them from voting. Cause and Effect

9 **What were the Jim Crow laws?** Jim Crow laws enforced segregation of blacks and whites. Main Idea and Details

Library of Congress

▶ **Federal troops left the South in 1877, marking the end of Reconstruction.**

Reconstruction Ends

By 1870 all of the former Confederate states had met the requirements of Reconstruction. They had written new state constitutions that accepted the Thirteenth, Fourteenth, and Fifteenth Amendments to the U.S. Constitution and extended freedom and citizenship rights to African Americans. The Southern states were then readmitted to the Union. Also, many Northerners were tired of having their taxes used to help rebuild the South. In 1877 the remaining federal troops were withdrawn from the South.

Reconstruction had some successes in the South. A public school system was established and many industries were expanded. However, many of Reconstruction's goals failed to have a lasting impact.

After Reconstruction, white Southern Democrats regained their power in state governments. Almost immediately, new laws were passed that again restricted the rights of African Americans. Whites tried to prevent blacks from voting in several ways. They set up voting booths far from African American communities, or changed the location of the booths without informing blacks. Some states required a poll tax, or a payment, in order to vote. Many African Americans could not afford the poll tax.

In some places blacks were forced to take a reading test before voting. Under slavery, many people had not been allowed to learn to read or write, and so they failed the test. A "grandfather clause" was added to some state constitutions. It said that men could only vote if their father or grandfather had voted before 1867. The "grandfather clause" kept most African Americans from voting because they had not gained the right to vote until 1870.

Jim Crow laws were also passed. These laws enforced **segregation,** or separation of blacks and whites. Under Jim Crow laws, blacks could not sit with whites on trains or stay in certain hotels. They also could not eat in certain restaurants or attend certain theaters, schools, or parks.

During Reconstruction, Congressman Thaddeus Stevens said that every African American adult should be given "40 acres and a mule." His hope was to help former slaves begin new lives. However, there was no land to be distributed.

Many African Americans had no choice but to return to the plantations where they had worked as slaves, because they could not find jobs elsewhere. Many blacks as well as whites became trapped in a system called **sharecropping.** Sharecroppers rented land

8

9

110

Practice and Extend

 SOCIAL STUDIES
Background

More About the End of Reconstruction

- Only African Americans were required to pass reading tests before voting. Many whites were illiterate as well, but they were not often compelled to take literacy tests and therefore did not lose their right to vote.

- Some whites were also entrapped in the sharecropping system, although it was more widespread among blacks.

 SOCIAL STUDIES STRAND
Government

Participation in Government

- Remind students that one way people in a republic participate in government is through voting.

- For example, in a national election, registered voters vote for the President. Votes are counted state by state. In most states the candidate with the most votes gets all of that state's electoral votes.

- Explain that preventing African Americans from voting meant that they could not participate in the government.

from landowners. They paid for their rent with a portion of their crop. Sharecroppers sold the rest of their crop to pay for food, clothing, and farming equipment.

Usually, the costs of sharecropping were higher than the income received. Sharecropper John Mosley related, "When our crop was gathered, we would still be in debt."

The end of Reconstruction set the stage for a new phase in American history. The era of slavery was over. The federal government had established its power over individual states. The Fourteenth and Fifteenth Amendments provided a constitutional basis for equal rights, although it would take a long time for these rights to be fully recognized.

As you will read in the following units, after Reconstruction the nation continued expanding westward and building a strong economy. The South, however, continued to rely on an agricultural economy. It remained the poorest section of the country.

REVIEW What conclusions can you draw about how life changed in the South after Reconstruction ended?
Draw Conclusions

Summarize the Lesson

- **April 1865** President Abraham Lincoln was assassinated.

- **December 1865** The Thirteenth Amendment was adopted, abolishing slavery in the United States.

- **March 1867** Congress passed the first Reconstruction Act, sending military forces to the former Confederate states.

LESSON 4   REVIEW

Check Facts and Main Ideas

1. **Main Idea and Details** On a separate sheet of paper, fill in the details to the main idea.

```
        The nation faced many
        challenges after the Civil War.

The assassi-   | Carrying out   | Need to protect
nation of      | the plan of    | rights of African
Lincoln        | Reconstruction | Americans, including
               | to rebuild after| amendents ending
               | the war        | slavery and giving
                                | them the vote.
```

2. Why did Republicans in Congress dislike Johnson's **Reconstruction** plan?

3. **Critical Thinking:** *Cause and Effect* How did the Reconstruction Acts affect the South?

4. Why were three amendments added to the Constitution during Reconstruction?

5. How were the lives of African Americans made more difficult after the end of Reconstruction? Use the word **segregation** in your answer.

Link to ⚭ **Writing**

Research Biographies Many African Americans became government leaders for the first time during Reconstruction. Research Hiram R. Revels, Blanche K. Bruce, or another African American member of Congress elected during Reconstruction. Were they enslaved or free before the Civil War? How did they become involved in politics? How did the end of Reconstruction affect them? Write a summary of what you learn.

111

CURRICULUM CONNECTION
Writing

Write a Short Story or Poem

- Have students work in pairs to write a short story or poem on one of the following topics: Life as a Sharecropper, The African American Experience During Reconstruction, The African American Experience After Reconstruction.

- Encourage students to use literary devices, such as dialogue and figurative language.

- Students may wish to do further research to learn more about the topic they choose.

Workbook, p. 26

Lesson 4: The End of Slavery
Directions: Define each term or phrase. Use a separate sheet of paper if you need more room. You may use your textbook.

1. Reconstruction _____
2. Thirteenth Amendment _____
3. black codes _____
   _____
   _____
4. Freedmen's Bureau _____
5. Ku Klux Klan _____
6. Fourteenth Amendment _____
7. Jim Crow laws _____
8. sharecropping _____

Notes for Home: Your child learned about how the United States changed after the Civil War.
Home Activity: With your child discuss some of the changes that took place during Reconstruction and discuss who benefited from each change.

Also on Teacher Resources CD-ROM.

✓ **REVIEW ANSWER** After Reconstruction ended, the way of life for African Americans in the South became much like it had been during slavery. Southern lawmakers set up policies, including poll taxes, reading tests, and "grandfather clauses," to prevent African Americans from voting. Jim Crow laws segregated blacks and whites. Many African Americans also became indebted under the system of sharecropping.
Draw Conclusions

3 Close and Assess

Summarize the Lesson

Tell students to read the lesson summary. Then have them write about the dates 1868, 1870, and 1877, describing events for each.

✓ **LESSON 4   REVIEW**

1. **Main Idea and Details** For possible answers, see the reduced pupil page.

2. Southern states were still free to pass black codes, limiting the rights of African Americans.

3. **Critical Thinking:** *Cause and Effect* They expanded the rights of African Americans, but white Southerners resented this intrusion, and many of these policies did not last.

4. Possible answer: To ensure the basic rights of all African Americans

5. Jim Crow laws restricted where they could go, resulting in segregation; poll taxes and reading tests limited their right to vote; sharecropping trapped them in debt.

Link to ⚭ **Writing**
Give students the option of presenting their findings as an oral report, visual presentation, audio report, or written report.

CHAPTER 2
REVIEW

Resources

- Assessment Book, pp. 9–12
- Workbook, p. 27: Vocabulary Review

Chapter Summary

For possible answers, see the reduced pupil page.

Vocabulary

1. a, **2.** e, **3.** d, **4.** b, **5.** c

People and Terms

Possible answers:

1. The Anaconda Plan called for blockading Confederate ports, capturing land along the Mississippi River, and attacking from the east and west.
2. Thomas "Stonewall" Jackson helped the Confederates win the First Battle of Bull Run by refusing to retreat.
3. Mathew Brady's photographs showed civilians the realities of war.
4. The Emancipation Proclamation, issued by Lincoln on Jan. 1, 1863, freed slaves in all areas of the Confederacy not under Union control.
5. Clara Barton cared for wounded Union soldiers during the Civil War.
6. The Battle of Gettysburg turned the tide of the Civil War for the North.
7. William Tecumseh Sherman's men used the strategy of "total war" to destroy the South's will to fight.
8. The Freedmen's Bureau helped freed slaves after the Civil War by building hospitals and schools for them.
9. Hiram R. Revels became one of the first African Americans elected to Congress during Reconstruction.
10. Jim Crow laws enforced racial segregation.

Facts and Main Ideas

1. Rifles that shot farther and more accurately, railroads, submarines, ironclad ships, and hand grenades
2. It proved to many that black soldiers were capable of fighting just as effectively as white soldiers.

CHAPTER 2
REVIEW

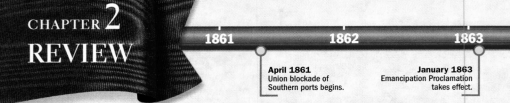

1861   1862   1863

April 1861
Union blockade of Southern ports begins.

January 1863
Emancipation Proclamation takes effect.

Chapter Summary

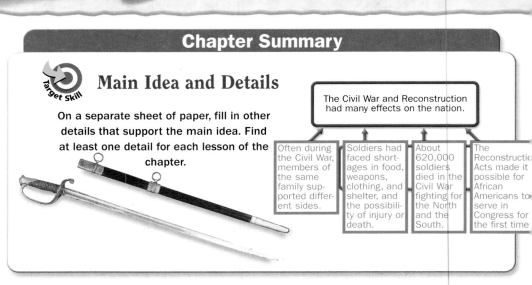

Main Idea and Details

On a separate sheet of paper, fill in other details that support the main idea. Find at least one detail for each lesson of the chapter.

The Civil War and Reconstruction had many effects on the nation.

- Often during the Civil War, members of the same family supported different sides.
- Soldiers had faced shortages in food, weapons, clothing, and shelter, and the possibility of injury or death.
- About 620,000 soldiers died in the Civil War fighting for the North and the South.
- The Reconstruction Acts made it possible for African Americans to serve in Congress for the first time

Vocabulary

Match each word with the correct definition or description.

1 blockade (p. 84)

2 draft (p. 89)

3 total war (p. 100)

4 black codes (p. 107)

5 impeachment (p. 109)

a. preventing supplies from moving in or out

b. laws denying rights to African Americans

c. charging an official with unlawful action

d. destroying an enemy's will to fight

e. law requiring people to serve in the military

People and Terms

Write a sentence explaining why each of the following people or terms was important. You may use two or more in a single sentence.

1 Anaconda Plan (p. 84)

2 Thomas "Stonewall" Jackson (p. 85)

3 Mathew Brady (p. 89)

4 Emancipation Proclamation (p. 90)

5 Clara Barton (p. 92)

6 Battle of Gettysburg (p. 97)

7 William Tecumseh Sherman (p. 100)

8 Freedmen's Bureau (p. 108)

9 Hiram R. Revels (p. 108)

10 Jim Crow laws (p. 110)

112

Practice and Extend

Assessment Options

✓ Chapter 2 Assessment

- Chapter 2 Content Test: Use Assessment Book, pp. 9–10.
- Chapter 2 Skills Test: Use Assessment Book, pp. 11–12.

Standardized Test Prep

- Chapter 2 Tests contain standardized test format.

✓ Chapter 2 Performance Assessment

- Have students think about what it was like to be a Northern or Southern soldier during the Civil War. Have them draw a picture and write a one- or two-sentence summary about soldiers' living conditions.
- Have partners role-play a conversation between a Northerner and Southerner discussing their opinions about Reconstruction in the South.
- Assess students' understanding of the Civil War and Reconstruction experiences in their drawings and conversations.

July 1863
Battle of Gettysburg is a victory for Union forces.

November 1863
President Lincoln delivers the Gettysburg Address.

April 1865
The Confederacy surrenders. President Lincoln is killed.

December 1865
The Thirteenth Amendment abolishes slavery.

Facts and Main Ideas

1. What kinds of new technology were used during the Civil War?

2. Describe the significance of the attack on Fort Wagner.

3. **Time Line** How long did the Civil War last?

4. **Main Idea** What early strategies did each side plan for quick victories?

5. **Main Idea** What hardships did people on each side suffer during the Civil War?

6. **Main Idea** How did the Union army gain key victories in the final years of the war?

7. **Main Idea** What were the goals of Reconstruction?

8. **Critical Thinking:** *Compare and Contrast* Compare the lives of African Americans living in the South before the Civil War and after Reconstruction.

Write About History

1. **Write a newspaper story** about one of the battles discussed in your text.

2. **Write a journal entry** as a soldier describing General Robert E. Lee's surrender to General Grant.

3. **Write a letter** telling a friend about the *Monitor* or the *Virginia,* how these ironclads worked, and what they were like.

Apply Skills

Use Road Maps
Study the road map below. Then answer the questions.

1. Which three interstate highways lead into and out of Atlanta?

2. How would you travel from Atlanta to Savannah?

3. Andersonville National Historic Site is the location of a Civil War prisoner of war camp. How would you travel to Andersonville from Kennesaw Mountain National Battlefield?

Internet Activity

To get help with vocabulary, people, and terms, select dictionary or encyclopedia from *Social Studies Library* at **www.sfsocialstudies.com.**

113

Hands-on Unit Project

✓ **Unit 1 Performance Assessment**

- See p. 118 for information about using the Unit Project as a means of performance assessment.
- A scoring guide is provided on p. 118.

WEB SITE
Technology

For more information, students can select the dictionary or encyclopedia from *Social Studies Library* at **www.sfsocialstudies.com.**

Workbook, p. 27

Vocabulary Review

Directions: Use the vocabulary words from Chapter 15 to complete the following sentences. Write the correct word in the space provided. You may use your textbook.

1. _____ is the separation of blacks and whites.
2. The shutting off of an area by troops or ships to keep people and supplies from moving in or out is known as a _____.
3. At the Battle of _____, Union forces blockaded the city and bombarded it with cannon fire by land and sea for 48 days.
4. _____ is the practice of renting land from a landowner and paying rent with a portion of the crop produced on that land.
5. The murdering of a government or political leader is known as an _____.
6. Laws that denied blacks the right to vote or take part in jury trials were known as _____.
7. A method of warfare that destroys not only the opposing army but also the people's will to fight is known as _____.
8. In the Battle of _____, Union and Confederate forces clashed near the town of Sharpsburg in Maryland.
9. The First Battle of _____, one of the early battles of the Civil War, was won by the Confederates.
10. The _____ was established to help the more than 4 million former slaves after the war.
11. _____ refers to the rebuilding of the country after the Civil War.
12. The Battle of _____ lasted three days and was one of the most important battles of the Civil War.
13. _____ laws enforced the separation of blacks and whites.
14. The _____ Plan was a war strategy designed to "squeeze" the Confederacy.

Notes for Home: Your child learned the vocabulary terms for Chapter 2.
Home Activity: With your child, analyze the relationships among the vocabulary terms for this unit. Begin by having your child place each term on a time line for the Civil War era.

Also on Teacher Resources CD-ROM.

3. About four years, from April 1861 to April 1865

4. North: Blockade Southern ports, gain control of the Mississippi River, and attack from the east and west; South: Defend land until North gave up and hope Britain would help

5. Soldiers: death, disease, injury; Civilians: not enough food or clothing; loss of family and friends

6. Gettysburg: On high land, well protected; Vicksburg: Surrounded city to cut off supplies; Atlanta to Savannah: destroyed nearly everything

7. To guarantee the rights of African Americans, reunite the country, rebuild the war-torn South, and, for some, punish the South for seceding from the Union

8. Before the Civil War, most African Americans in the South were enslaved and had very few rights; Jim Crow laws, poll taxes, reading tests, grandfather clauses, and sharecropping denied rights and equal opportunities to African Americans.

Write About History

1. Suggest that students include *Who, What, When, Where,* and *Why* in their stories.

2. Students can suppose they are an eyewitness to the surrender.

3. You might also suggest that students write from the point of view of someone who saw the ships fight, or even as someone who was on one of the ships.

Apply Skills

1. Interstate highways 75, 85, and 20

2. One route is to go southeast on Highway 75 and then take Highway 16 to Savannah.

3. One route is to take Highway 75 to Route 19 and then take local road 49 to the site.

When Johnny Comes Marching Home

Objective

- Identify significant examples of music from various periods in U.S. history.

1 Introduce and Motivate

Preview To activate prior knowledge, ask students about the conditions both Northern and Southern soldiers endured during the Civil War. Discuss how they probably felt about the end of the war. Ask how students think the families of the soldiers felt.

2 Teach and Discuss

1 **For about how long did the war go on after this song was written?** About two more years **Analyze Information**

2 **How did this song attempt to raise the morale of soldiers?** It suggested that those back home supported them and were anxious for their return. **Draw Conclusions**

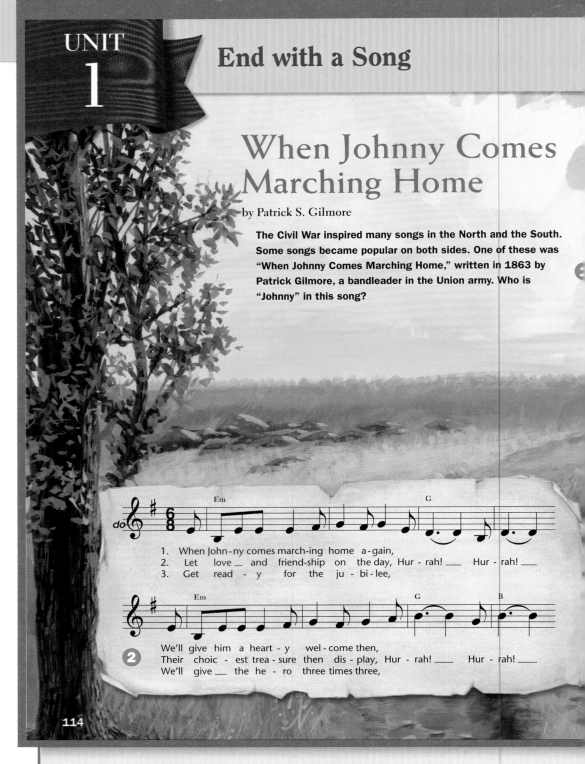

When Johnny Comes Marching Home

by Patrick S. Gilmore

The Civil War inspired many songs in the North and the South. Some songs became popular on both sides. One of these was "When Johnny Comes Marching Home," written in 1863 by Patrick Gilmore, a bandleader in the Union army. Who is "Johnny" in this song?

1. When John-ny comes march-ing home a-gain,
2. Let love _ and friend-ship on the day, Hur - rah! ___ Hur - rah! ___
3. Get read - y for the ju - bi - lee,

We'll give him a heart - y wel - come then,
Their choic - est trea - sure then dis - play, Hur - rah! ___ Hur - rah! ___
We'll give _ the he - ro three times three,

114

Practice and Extend

 **SOCIAL STUDIES Background**

"When Johnny Comes Marching Home"

- Patrick S. Gilmore was a bandmaster of the Union army.
- Soldiers in both armies sang this song and identified with "Johnny."
- People waiting at home sang with hope and joy about the day "When Johnny Comes Marching Home."

 **AUDIO CD Technology**

Play the CD, *Songs and Music*, to listen to "When Johnny Comes Marching Home."

The_men will cheer,_the boys will shout, The la-dies they_will all turn out,
And_let each one_per-form some part, To fill with joy_the war-rior's heart,
The_laur-el wreath_is read-y now To place up-on_his roy-al brow,

And we'll shout "Hur - rah" when John-ny comes march-ing home! _

115

③ What does the song suggest will happen when the war ends? People at home will cheer and all come out to honor and welcome home the soldiers.
Interpret Primary Sources

3 Close and Assess

- Have one group of students practice singing the first verse, another practice the second, and another practice the third. Have each group perform its verse.

- Ask students why they think this song was popular in both the North and the South. (Possible answer: Both sides were tired of the war and wanted their families reunited.)

CURRICULUM CONNECTION
Music

Write a New Verse
- Have students work in pairs or groups to write another verse to the song.
- Students can use the first verse as a model.
- Students may wish to write a new verse from the perspective of a soldier arriving home.

Resource
- Assessment Book, pp. 13–16

Main Ideas and Vocabulary TEST PREP

1. b, **2.** d, **3.** b, **4.** c

Test Talk

Locate Key Words in the Question
Use Main Ideas and Vocabulary, Question 3, to model the Test Talk strategy.

Make sure that you understand the question.
Have students ask themselves, "Who or what is this question about?" The words that tell *who* or *what* the question is about are key words.

Find key words in the question.
Students should use the key word *seceded* in a sentence that begins "I need to find out. . . ."

People and Terms

1. e, **2.** a, **3.** f, **4.** c, **5.** d, **6.** b

Test Talk
Look for the key words in the question.

Main Ideas and Vocabulary TEST PREP

Read the passage below and use it to answer the questions that follow.

The growing nation faced problems of sectionalism. Northerners and Southerners disagreed about whether slavery should be allowed in new states. Northern and Southern states also had different ways of life. Many Northerners and Southerners were loyal to their region of the country.

Abraham Lincoln joined the Republican party, which opposed the spread of slavery. After he was elected President in 1860, South Carolina seceded from the Union. Other Southern states followed and formed the Confederacy. Confederate troops attacked Union-held Fort Sumter in April 1861, beginning the Civil War.

The Civil War dragged on for four years. New weapons of war left many soldiers dead or wounded. A lack of knowledge about disease killed many more. In the spring of 1865, the Confederacy surrendered. President Lincoln was killed shortly afterwards by a Confederate supporter.

Congress passed the Reconstruction Acts to rebuild the country and readmit the Southern states to the Union. Federal troops were sent to the South to maintain order and regulate elections. During this period, much of the damage from the war was repaired. African American men were granted the right to vote and some became members of Congress. The Freedmen's Bureau built hospitals and schools to help freed slaves.

When Reconstruction ended in 1877, many laws were passed to restrict the rights of African Americans again. Jim Crow laws segregated blacks and whites.

1 According to the passage, what was one difference between the North and South?
- **A** Northerners and Southerners had similar ways of life.
- **B** Northerners and Southerners disagreed about slavery in new states.
- **C** The South had more resources.
- **D** The North had fewer resources.

2 In the passage, the word sectionalism means—
- **A** wanting to divide the country in half
- **B** ending slavery in part of the country
- **C** loyalty to one's country
- **D** loyalty to one's region

3 In the passage, the word seceded means—
- **A** joined with others
- **B** broke away from a group
- **C** objected to something
- **D** formed a new government

4 What is the main idea of the first paragraph in passage?
- **A** The North won the Civil War.
- **B** The Civil War ended slavery.
- **C** Differences between North and South led to the Civil War.
- **D** War destroys people and places.

116

Practice and Extend

Assessment Options

✓ Unit 1 Assessment
- Unit 1 Content Test:
  Use Assessment Book, pp. 13–14.
- Unit 1 Skills Test:
  Use Assessment Book, pp. 15–16.

Standardized Test Prep
- Unit 1 Tests contain standardized test format.

✓ Unit 1 Performance Assessment
- See p. 118 for information about using the Unit Project as a means of Performance Assessment.
- A scoring guide for the Unit 1 Project is provided in the teacher's notes on p. 118.

Test Talk
- Test Talk Practice Book

WEB SITE Technology

For more information, students can select the dictionary or encyclopedia from *Social Studies Library* at **www.sfsocialstudies.com**.

People and Terms

Match each person and term to its definition.

1. **Joseph Cinque** (p. 62)
2. **John Brown** (p. 70)
3. **border state** (p. 76)
4. **Catherine Coffin** (p. 63)
5. **Ulysses S. Grant** (p. 99)
6. **segregation** (p. 110)

a. abolitionist who attacked an arsenal at Harpers Ferry

b. separating people

c. helped slaves escape to freedom

d. leader of Union forces at the Battle of Vicksburg

e. leader of *Amistad* rebellion

f. allowed slavery but did not secede

Apply Skills

Prepare a scrapbook about different points of view on a current subject. First, choose the topic. Then clip articles that present opposing points of view about the topic. Paste the articles into a scrapbook. Under each article, write a sentence that summarizes the writer's point of view.

Write and Share

Create a Quiz Show Work with a group of students to create a quiz show about some of the main events and people in the period just before, during, and after the Civil War. Select a quiz show host and assistants to write the questions and answers. Then select contestants and develop a scoring system. Decide on a prize for the winner, and present the show to your class.

Read on Your Own

Look for these books in the library.

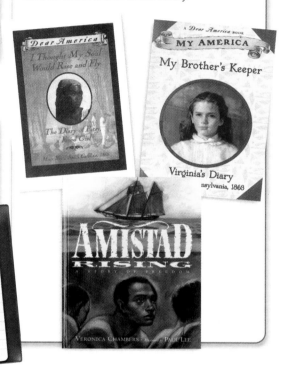

117

Revisit the Unit Question

✓ Portfolio Assessment

- Have students look at the lists they compiled throughout Unit 1 of ideas about why nations may break apart.
- Have students compare and contrast their lists.

- Direct students to write a one-paragraph summary of these ideas from the lists. After each idea, suggest that students write a way to prevent the action from causing a nation to break apart.
- Have students add these lists and summaries to their Social Studies Portfolio.

Apply Skills

- Students can use newspapers and magazines to find articles and copy them for their scrapbooks.
- Encourage students to use a variety of sources for each point of view.

Write and Share

- Have students use the People, Places, and Vocabulary of each lesson as the subjects for some of their questions.
- Students can also change section headings into questions.
- Use the following scoring guide.

✓ Assessment Scoring Guide

	Create a Quiz Show
6	Many questions covering all main topics in unit. Answers and scoring system are complete and accurate.
5	Many questions covering most main topics in unit. Answers and scoring system are complete and accurate.
4	A number of questions covering many main topics in unit. Answers are accurate. Scoring system is sensible.
3	A number of questions covering some main topics in unit. Answers are mostly accurate. Scoring system is sensible.
2	Few questions covering some of the main topics in unit. Answers are mostly accurate but may be incomplete. Scoring system may not be accurate.
1	Few or no questions covering few main topics in unit. Answers are incorrect or incomplete. Scoring system is inaccurate.

If you prefer a 4-point rubric, adjust accordingly.

Read on Your Own

Have students prepare oral reports using the following books.

I Thought My Soul Would Rise and Fly: The Diary of Patsy, a Freed Girl, by Joyce Hansen (Scholastic, Inc., ISBN 0-590-84913-1, 1997) **Easy**

My Brother's Keeper: Virginia's Diary—Gettysburg, Pennsylvania, by Mary Pope Osborne (Scholastic, ISBN 0-439-15307-7, 2000) **On-Level**

Amistad Rising: A Story of Freedom, by Veronica Chambers (Harcourt Brace, ISBN 0-152-01803-4, 1998) **Challenge**

We Interrupt This Program

Objective
- Describe events and people's experiences during the Civil War and Reconstruction.

Resource
- Workbook, p. 28

Materials
paper, pens, pencils, reference materials

Follow This Procedure
- Tell students they will present a "news update" about an event from this unit. Discuss with students what they know about news reports. List on the board such key elements as commentary from news anchors, background from experts, and interviews with people who witnessed the event.

- Help students brainstorm people who could provide eyewitness accounts: soldiers, slaves, people freed from slavery, children, plantation owners, and so on.

- Divide students into groups. Have students write questions and answers and choose who will play reporters, witnesses, and so on.

- Invite each group to present their news update to the class.

- Use the following scoring guide.

✓ Assessment Scoring Guide

History Speaks	
6	Elaborate details, accurate content, variety of topics
5	Good details, accurate content, variety of topics
4	Good details, mostly accurate content, some variety of topics
3	Several details, mostly accurate content, some variety of topics
2	Few details, some inaccurate content, little variety of topics
1	Few or no details, inaccurate content, no variety of topics

If you prefer a 4-point rubric, adjust accordingly.

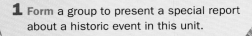
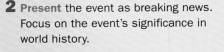
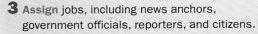
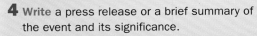

UNIT 1 Project

We Interrupt This Program

Participate in a "live, at the scene" news update from the past.

1 Form a group to present a special report about a historic event in this unit.

2 Present the event as breaking news. Focus on the event's significance in world history.

3 Assign jobs, including news anchors, government officials, reporters, and citizens.

4 Write a press release or a brief summary of the event and its significance.

5 Create a banner and bring in materials that help describe the event. You may choose to create a scenic background.

Internet Activity

Explore the Civil War. Go to **www.sfsocialstudies.com/activities** and select your grade and unit.

118

Practice and Extend

Hands-on Unit Project

✓ Performance Assessment
- The Unit Project can also be used as a performance assessment activity.
- Use the scoring guide to assess each group's work.

WEB SITE Technology

Students can launch the Internet Activity by clicking on *Grade 5, Unit 1* at **www.sfsocialstudies.com/activities**.

Workbook, p. 28

[Workbook page 28 reproduction: "1 Project We Interrupt This Program" with directions and checklist for students]

Also on Teacher Resources CD-ROM.

★ Unit 2 ★

Vocabulary Routines

The following examples of reading and vocabulary development strategies can be used to instruct students about unit vocabulary.

BEFORE READING

Related Word Study

Words With Suffixes The structural analysis of words that contain a suffix can be accomplished by calling attention to the relationship between a base word and a suffix that has been added to the base word. By understanding how a suffix changes a base word, students will be better equipped to determine the meanings of words with suffixes.

We all know what the word willing *means. It means "wanting or being ready to do something." Listen to this sentence:*

Some Native Americans were <u>willing</u> to sell their land.

When we add -ness *to the word* willing *we create a new word:* willingness. *The meaning of this new word is related to* willing. Willingness *means "the state of wanting or being ready to do something." Now listen to this sentence:*

Some Native Americans displayed a <u>willingness</u> to sell their land.

How are these sentences alike? How are they different?

Now think about the word settle. *What happens when we add the suffix* -ment *to* settle? *That's right. The new word is settlement. Now use both* settle *and* settlement *in sentences.*

willing	+	ness	=	willingness
settle	+	ment	=	settlement

DURING READING

Individual Word Study

Providing Meaning Sometimes as they are reading, students will encounter words they don't know. There may or may not be enough context within the sentence or the surrounding sentences to enable students to determine the meaning of the word. To ensure student comprehension, you may want to provide meaning as words are encountered during reading.

Look at the word treaty *(p. 155). Do you know what a* treaty *is? It is a formal agreement between groups or nations. What are some reasons that groups of people sign treaties? Some reasons nations sign treaties are to agree to trade, to promise help, to stop or avoid wars, or to settle boundary disagreements. What did the treaty between the Lakota and the United States do? Why was a treaty needed? Why do you think both groups were willing to sign the treaty?*

AFTER READING

Context Clues

Using Words in Reading and Writing Situations In a large body of text, students will likely encounter many new content-related words. Having students use new content-area vocabulary in their writing will help them recall both the definitions of these words and how they are used in context.

In Unit 2, you came across many important vocabulary words. Some of these words may have been unfamiliar to you. Others you may have seen before. Think about these words from the unit:

nation	communication	telegraph
stagecoach	transcontinental	homesteaders

Write a paragraph that uses all of these words. Try to show how some of the words are related. Feel free to use any other related vocabulary words you learned in the unit.

★ Unit 2 ★

Teaching with Leveled Readers

This series of readers focuses on the experiences of pioneers traveling west to new territories of the United States.

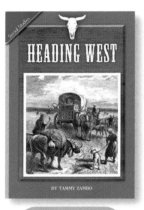

Below Level

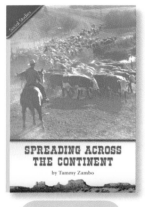

On Level

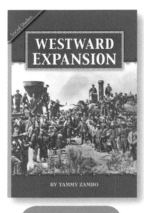

Above Level

LEVELED READER VOCABULARY ACTIVITY

- Before students read, have them preview the list of vocabulary words.

- Explain to students that *-ology* is a common word ending, and it means "any science or branch of knowledge."

- Have students find the vocabulary word with the *-ology* ending. Then have students brainstorm a list of other *–ology* words.

techn | ology

ec | ology

ge | ology

CONNECTIONS TO THE LESSON

Chapter 3, Lesson 3: Cowboys and Miners

CONNECTIONS TO TODAY

- Have students read the lesson. Then provide the leveled readers to enhance their understanding of the migration of Americans to the land west of the Mississippi.

- **Points for Discussion:**
   1. Have students discuss what it might have felt like to travel west in search of gold. What sorts of challenges would they have faced?

   2. Students can also discuss what factors need to be considered when making a decision to move.

An Expanding Nation

PUBLIC SCHOOL

THROUGH LINE

NEW YORK

Unit Planning Guide

Unit 2 • An Expanding Nation

Begin with a Primary Source pp. 120–121

Meet the People pp. 122–123

 Reading Social Studies, Sequence pp. 124–125

Chapter Titles	Pacing	Main Ideas
Chapter 3 **Crossing the Continent** pp. 126–161	13 days	• In the 1860s new railroad lines made it possible to travel and move goods across the United States much more quickly than ever before. • Farmers began settling in the Great Plains in the 1860s, and they soon turned the plains into a productive farming region. • Cattle drives and the search for gold offered new opportunities and led to lasting changes in the western United States. • As more and more settlers came to the western United States, Native American groups fought to maintain control of their lands.
✔ **Chapter 3 Review** pp. 162–163		
Chapter 4 **Industry and Immigration** pp. 164–199	12 days	• In the late 1800s and early 1900s, new inventions changed the way people lived and led to the rise of new industries. • In the late 1800s and early 1900s, big businesses helped the United States economy grow quickly. • During the late 1800s and early 1900s, millions of immigrants arrived in the United States in search of freedom and opportunity. • Workers formed labor unions to fight for better wages and working conditions.
✔ **Chapter 4 Review** pp. 200–201		

End with a Song pp. 202–203

✔ **Unit 2 Review** pp. 204–205

✔ **Unit 2 Project** p. 206

✔ = Assessment Options

 A stagecoach

Resources	Meeting Individual Needs
• Workbook, pp. 29–37	• ESL Support, TE pp. 130, 139, 150, 152, 157
• Every Student Learns Guide, pp. 50–65	• Leveled Practice, TE pp. 129, 140, 151, 158
• Transparencies 10, 11	• Learning Styles, TE p. 142
• Quick Study, pp. 26–33	
• Workbook, p. 38	
✓ Chapter 3 Content Test, Assessment Book, pp. 17–18	✓ Chapter 3 Performance Assessment, TE p. 162
✓ Chapter 3 Skills Test, Assessment Book, pp. 19–20	

• Workbook, pp. 39–44	• ESL Support, TE pp. 167, 178, 185, 195
• Every Student Learns Guide, pp. 66–81	• Leveled Practice, TE pp. 171, 174, 177, 188, 197
• Transparencies 1, 6, 10, 23	
• Quick Study, pp. 34–41	
• Workbook, pp. 45–46	
✓ Chapter 4 Content Test, Assessment Book, pp. 21–22	✓ Chapter 4 Performance Assessment, TE p. 200
✓ Chapter 4 Skills Test, Assessment Book, pp. 23–24	

Providing More Depth
Additional Resources

- Trade Books
- Family Activities
- Vocabulary Workbook and Cards
- Social Studies Plus! pp. 44–67
- Daily Activity Bank
- Read Alouds and Primary Sources
- Big Book Atlas   • Student Atlas
- Outline Maps   • Desk Maps

Technology

- AudioText
- Video Field Trips
- Songs and Music
- Digital Learning CD-ROM Powered by KnowledgeBox (Video clips and activities)
- MindPoint® Quiz Show CD-ROM
- ExamView® Test Bank CD-ROM
- Colonial Williamsburg Primary Sources CD-ROM
- Teacher Resources CD-ROM
- Map Resources CD-ROM
- SF SuccessNet: iText (Pupil Edition online), iTE (Teacher's Edition online), Online Planner
- **www.sfsocialstudies.com** (Biographies, news, references, maps, and activities)

 To establish guidelines for your students' safe and responsible use of the Internet, use the Scott Foresman Internet Guide.

Additional Internet Links
To find out more about:

- the California gold rush, search for *gold rush* at **www.pbs.org**
- cowboys and cattle drives, visit **www.old-cowtown.org**
- labor unions, search that term at **www.carnegielibrary.org**

Unit 2 Objectives

Beginning of Unit 2

- Use primary sources to acquire information (p. 120)
- Identify the contributions of significant individuals in the United States in the late 1800s and early 1900s. (p. 122)
- Analyze information by identifying the sequence of events. (p. 124)

Chapter 3

Lesson 1 Rails Across the Nation
pp. 128–133

- Identify innovations that allowed people and news to cross the country more quickly.
- Describe the challenges faced by the Union Pacific railroad.
- Evaluate the importance of Chinese workers to the Central Pacific railroad.
- Explain how the transcontinental railroad changed travel in the United States.
- Interpret information in maps. (p. 134)
- Identify key events involved in and reasons for Americans' movement westward. (p. 136)
- Identify the physical constraints and technological advances that challenged and aided Americans' movement westward, including natural terrain and advances in modes of transportation. (p. 136)

Lesson 2 Pioneers on the Plains
pp. 138–144

- Describe the purpose of the Homestead Act.
- Evaluate the challenges that homesteaders faced.
- Analyze the reasons why exodusters came to the Great Plains.
- Explain how technology helped pioneers turn the Great Plains into productive farmland.
- Identify the contributions of people from selected immigrant groups. (p. 145)
- Interpret information in climographs. (p. 146)

Lesson 3 Cowboys and Miners
pp. 148–153

- Explain the factors that made cattle drives profitable.
- Identify the reasons why cattle drives came to an end.
- Evaluate the lasting effect of the search for gold in the West.

Lesson 4 War in the West
pp. 154–159

- Identify changes that threatened the traditional way of life for Native Americans of the Great Plains.
- Summarize the outcome of wars between United States soldiers and Native Americans.
- Describe ways in which Native Americans are keeping their traditions alive today.
- Describe the accomplishments of significant leaders in United States history, such as Chief Joseph. (p. 160)
- Analyze the diverse cultures that have contributed to the heritage of the United States. (p. 160)

Chapter 4

Lesson 1 Inventors Change the World pp. 166–173

- Identify important inventions by Alexander Graham Bell and Thomas Edison.
- Describe some of the inventions that changed transportation.
- Explain how inventions led to the rise of new industries.
- Organize information in an outline. (p. 174)

Lesson 2 The Rise of Big Business
pp. 176–182

- Identify key industrial leaders and the businesses they started.
- Explain how railroads helped the United States economy grow.
- Compare the role of business owners and consumers in a free enterprise system.
- Describe important effects of the rise of big business in the United States.
- Describe the accomplishments of significant leaders in United States history, such as Andrew Carnegie. (p. 183)

Lesson 3 New Americans
pp. 184–190

- Identify reasons why immigrants came to the United States in the late 1800s and early 1900s.
- Compare and contrast the immigration stations at Ellis Island and Angel Island.
- Evaluate the challenges that faced new immigrants.
- Analyze the experience of immigrants, such as Mary Antin. (p. 191)

Lesson 4 The Labor Movement
pp. 192–197

- Describe conditions that led to the rise of labor unions.
- Explain the main goals of labor unions such as the AFL.
- Identify ways in which conditions began to improve for workers in the early 1900s.
- Explain how the Industrial Revolution caused changes in society that led to clashes between certain groups of Americans. (p. 198)
- Explain how industry changed many Americans' way of life. (p. 198)
- Explain how an individual is able to take part in civic affairs at the national level. (p. 198)

End of Unit 2

- Identify pieces of music from different periods in United States history. (p. 202)
- Explain how pieces of music reflect the times in which they were written. (p. 202)
- Research an invention from the late 1800s or early 1900s and create an advertisement. (p. 206)

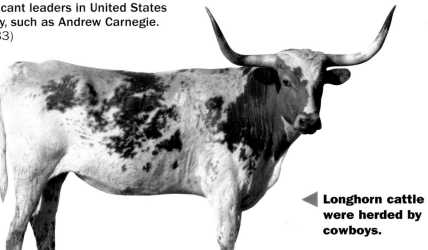

◀ **Longhorn cattle were herded by cowboys.**

Assessment Options

✓ Formal Assessment

- **Lesson Reviews,** PE/TE pp. 133, 144, 153, 159, 173, 182, 190, 197
- **Chapter Reviews,** PE/TE pp. 162–163, 200–201
- **Chapter Tests,** Assessment Book, pp. 17–24
- **Unit Review,** PE/TE pp. 204–205
- **Unit Tests,** Assessment Book, pp. 25–28
- **ExamView® Test Bank CD-ROM** (test-generator software)

✓ Informal Assessment

- **Teacher's Edition Questions,** throughout Lessons and Features
- **Section Reviews,** PE/TE pp. 129–133, 139–142, 144, 149–151, 153, 155–157, 159, 167–170, 172–173, 177–182, 185–187, 189–190, 193–197
- **Close and Assess,** TE pp. 125, 133, 135, 137, 144, 145, 147, 153, 159, 161, 173, 175, 182, 183, 190, 191, 197, 199, 203

Ongoing Assessment

Ongoing Assessment is found throughout the Teacher's Edition lessons using an **If…then** model.

If = students' observable behavior,   **then** = reteaching and enriching suggestions

✓ Portfolio Assessment

- **Portfolio Assessments,** TE pp. 119, 120, 205
- **Leveled Practice,** TE pp. 129, 140, 151, 158, 171, 174, 177, 188, 197
- **Workbook Pages,** pp. 29–46
- **Unit Review: Apply Skills,** PE/TE p. 205
- **Curriculum Connection: Writing,** PE/TE pp. 144, 190; TE pp. 133, 169, 199

✓ Performance Assessment

- **Hands-on Unit Project** (Unit 2 Performance Assessment), TE pp. 119, 163, 201, 206
- **Internet Activity,** PE p. 206
- **Chapter 3 Performance Assessment,** TE p. 162
- **Chapter 4 Performance Assessment,** TE p. 200
- **Unit Review: Write and Share,** PE/TE p. 205
- **Scoring Guides,** TE pp. 205–206

 Test Talk

Test-Taking Strategies

Understand the Question
- **Locate Key Words in the Question,** TE pp. 141, 180, 185
- **Locate Key Words in the Text,** PE/TE p. 204; TE pp. 151, 196

Understand the Answer
- **Choose the Right Answer,** Test Talk Practice Book
- **Use Information from the Text,** TE p. 129
- **Use Information from Graphics,** TE p. 169
- **Write Your Answer to Score High,** TE p. 157

For additional practice, use the Test Talk Practice Book.

Featured Strategy

Locate Key Words in the Text

Students will:
- Make sure that they understand the key words in the question.
- Find key words in the text that match key words in the question.

PE/TE p. 204; **TE** pp. 151, 196

Curriculum Connections

Integrating Your Day

The lessons, skills, and features of Unit 2 provide many opportunities to make connections between social studies and other areas of the elementary school curriculum.

MATH

Link to Mathemathics, PE/TE pp. 133, 182

Calculate Travel Time, TE p. 137

Calculate Crop Yields, TE p. 141

Calculate Hourly Wages, TE p. 149

Calculate Investment Earnings, TE p. 181

Calculate Hours and Pay Rates, TE p. 193

READING

Reading Skill—Sequence, PE/TE pp. 124–125, 128, 138, 148, 154, 166

Lesson Review—Sequence, PE/TE pp. 133, 144, 153, 159, 173

WRITING

Link to Writing, PE/TE pp. 144, 190

Write a Speech, TE p. 133

Write a Letter, TE pp. 169, 199

LITERATURE

Read Biographies, TE p. 122

Read About Chief Joseph, TE p. 161

Read About Inventors, TE p. 173

Read About Andrew Carnegie, TE p. 183

Read About Immigration, TE p. 189

Mary Antin's Book, TE p. 191

Social Studies

SCIENCE

Make a Climograph, TE p. 147

Link to Science, PE/TE p. 173

ART

Link to Art, PE/TE p. 153

Recreate Native American Art, TE p. 159

Paint a Setting, TE p. 203

MUSIC / DRAMA

Link to Language Arts, PE/TE p. 159

 Look for this symbol throughout the Teacher's Edition to find **Curriculum Connections.**

Professional Development

Economics in a Crowded Curriculum

by Bonnie Meszaros, Ph.D.
University of Delaware

Elementary teachers are faced with the daunting task of figuring out how to fit social studies, particularly economics, into a crowded curriculum. After teaching reading, language arts, and math each day, just how much time is left? There just never seems to be enough time to teach all that needs to be taught.

Teachers often question why it is necessary to introduce economics in the elementary grades, arguing that the discipline is more relevant to older students. But research shows that even young students can learn economics. Studies also show that ethnic and income backgrounds and gender of students matter very little. The most important variable explaining students' learning is the extent to which economic concepts are taught.

Students live in an economic world and bring economic knowledge and experience into the classroom. At an early age, they make consumer choices involving spending, saving, and even borrowing. They are exposed through the media to an array of economic problems facing their community and the world. But even with articulated national and state standards, economics continues to be underrepresented in the elementary grades. Below are several ways *Scott Foresman Social Studies* incorporates the study of economics into its program.

- *Chapter 4 explores how big businesses in the late 1800s and early 1900s helped the United States economy grow quickly. It also discusses how workers formed labor unions to obtain better wages and working conditions.*

- *Calculate Hours and Pay Rates on p. 193 helps students calculate and understand the typical wages earned by workers at the Homestead factory.*

ESL Support

by Jim Cummins, Ph.D.
University of Toronto

In Unit 2, you can use the following fundamental strategy to activate students' prior knowledge and build background.

Activate Prior Knowledge/ Build Background

Allowing students to relate what they already know to the abstract content of a unit is important for all students, but especially for English Language Learners. Gaps in students' prior knowledge will either be filled by contributions from other students, as in group brainstorming, or become evident to the teacher who can then build the necessary background knowledge.

Discussion and dramatization are both effective strategies that help build background and activate prior knowledge. When teachers activate students' prior knowledge, it communicates a sense of respect for what students already know and an interest in their cultural background.

The following examples in the Teacher's Edition will help you activate prior knowledge and build background for ESL students:

- *Describe the Distribution of Cattle on p. 150 assists students in building background about the issues and challenges of the cattle industry.*

- *Compare Points of View on p. 157 activates students' prior knowledge of American Indians' and American settlers' views about land.*

Read Aloud

from a letter from Hiram Dwight Pierce to his wife, Sara Jane Pierce, written from San Francisco during the gold rush

I am sitting in the tent a box covered with a cloth is our eating table on which I write. . . . Clothing of all descriptions strews the ground all over. Left by those that have camped here and gone to the mines. Shirts never worn but once or twice are thrown away rather than pay for washing. Fifty cents is the charge for washing a piece or six dollars per dozen and no less—so [items] are thrown away indiscriminately. . . .

Build Background

- This letter was written in 1849, in the midst of the California gold rush.
- San Francisco was the point at which miners who traveled by boat arrived in California. From there, they would travel eastward to the gold fields.
- Prior to the gold rush, San Francisco had been a town of just a few hundred people. Within months of the discovery of gold, thousands upon thousands of miners were camping in its streets.

Definitions

- *strews:* spreads about
- *indiscriminately:* without thought or purpose

Read Alouds and Primary Sources

- *Read Alouds and Primary Sources* contains additional selections to be used with Unit 2.

Bibliography

Eyewitness: Cowboy, by David Hamilton Murdoch (DK Publishing, ISBN 0-789-45854-3, 2000) **Easy**

The New Land: A First Year on the Prairie, by Marilynn Reynolds (Orca Books, ISBN 1-551-43071-1, 1999) **Easy**

Pony Express!, by Steven Kroll (Scholastic, ISBN 0-590-20239-1, 2000) **Easy**

Ellis Island, by Patricia Ryon Quiri (Children's Press, ISBN 0-516-26374-9, 1998) **On-Level**

Immigrant Kids, by Russell Freedman (Penguin Putnam Books for Young Readers, ISBN 0-140-37594-5, 1995) **On-Level**

Industry and Business (Life in America 100 Years Ago), by Linda Leuzzi (Chelsea House, ISBN 0-791-02846-1, 1997) **On-Level**

Hurry Freedom: African Americans in Gold Rush California, by Jerry Stanley (Crown Publishers, ISBN 0-517-80094-2, 2000) **Challenge**

Legendary Labor Leaders, by Thomas Streissguth (Oliver Press, ISBN 1-881-50844-7, 1998) **Challenge**

(AWARD) *Sitting Bull and His World,* by Albert Marrin (Dutton Books, ISBN 0-525-45944-8, 2000) **Challenge** **NCSS Notable Book**

Encyclopedia of Indian Wars: Western Battles and Skirmishes 1850–1890, by Gregory F. Michno (Mountain Press Publishing Co., ISBN 0-878-42468-7, 2003) **Teacher reference**

History of the Labor Movement in the United States, by Philip Sheldon Foner (International Publishers Co., ISBN 0-717-80376-7, 1979) **Teacher reference**

Nothing Like It in the World: The Men Who Built the Transcontinental Railroad 1863–1869, by Stephen E. Ambrose (Touchstone Books, ISBN 0-743-20317-8, 2001) **Teacher reference**

Discovery Channel School **Video** *The Real American Cowboy* Learn about the real life of the American cowboy: It was tough and lonely. (Item #716688, 26 minutes)

- To order *Discovery Channel School* videos, please call the following toll-free number: 1-888-892-3484.
- Free online lesson plans are available at **DiscoverySchool.com**.

(AWARD) Look for this symbol throughout the Teacher's Edition to find **Award-Winning Selections.** Additional book references are suggested throughout this unit.

An Expanding Nation

How do new transportation methods affect where people live?

An Expanding Nation

Unit Overview

In the late 1800s, expanding transportation networks and the lure of land and wealth brought settlers to the American West—and into conflict with Native Americans. Meanwhile, technological changes and the rise of big business transformed life for consumers and workers, millions of whom were immigrants.

Unit Outline

Chapter 3 Crossing the Continent, pp. 126–163

Chapter 4 Industry and Immigration, pp. 164–201

Unit Question

- Have students read the question under the picture.

- To activate prior knowledge, ask students what forms of transportation they use. Discuss how far students travel for various events.

- Create a list of different methods of transportation used in the United States.

- ✓**Portfolio Assessment** Keep this list to review with students at the end of the unit on p. 205.

Practice and Extend

Hands-on Unit Project

✓**Unit 2 Performance Assessment**

- The Unit Project, *Inventions Change the Country,* found on p. 206, is an ongoing performance assessment project to enrich students' learning throughout the unit.

- This project, which has students researching and "promoting" an invention from the late 1800s, may be started now or at any time during this unit of study.

- A performance assessment scoring guide is located on p. 206.

The First Typewriter

Begin with a Primary Source

Objective
- Use primary sources to acquire information.

Resource
- Poster 3

Interpret a Primary Source

- Tell students that this quotation was delivered by one of the key figures in the construction of the nation's first transcontinental railroad, which crossed tall mountains.

- Ask the following question: Why do you think people laughed at the idea of building a railroad across tall mountains? Encourage students to understand why the enormous technical challenge of such a project seemed daunting for people.

- Crocker's railroad company succeeded in crossing the mountains—often by blasting enormous tunnels right through them.

- ✓**Portfolio Assessment** Remind students of the list they created of transportation methods based on the content of p. 119. Have students add information to the list about types of transportation used in the 1800s and 1900s as they read the unit. Review students' lists at the end of the unit on p. 205.

Interpret Fine Art

- The picture shows a small town near a railroad.

- It was created by Currier and Ives in 1868.

- Have students discuss what the presence of the railroad might mean to the inhabitants of the town. How would the railroad change the distances they traveled?

1845		1855		1865		1875	

120

1849
The California gold rush begins.

1861
The first telegraph line crosses the country.

1876
The Lakota defeat Custer at Little Bighorn.

1877
African American pioneers establish Nicodemus, Kansas.

1879
Thomas Edison invents a working light bulb.

Practice and Extend

SOCIAL STUDIES
Background

About the First Transcontinental Railroad
- Work began on the first transcontinental railroad in 1862 after Congress passed the Pacific Railroad Act, which authorized its construction.
- It was built by two companies, the Central Pacific, which started in California and built eastward, and the Union Pacific, which worked toward the West starting from Omaha, Nebraska.
- The two railroads met at Promontory Point, near Ogden, Utah Territory, in May, 1869.

> *"People laughed at the time [at the idea] of building a railroad across those mountains."*
>
> —Charles Crocker, an owner of the Central Pacific Railroad

This 1868 picture by Currier and Ives shows a small town in the West that was built near a railroad.

1885	1895	1905	1915	1925

1882
The first Labor Day celebration is held in New York City.

1900
The United States is the world's leading producer of manufactured goods. ②

1924
The United States government passes a law limiting immigration. ③

121

Meet the Artist

- Nathaniel Currier was born in Massachusetts in 1813. He was an apprentice in a Boston lithography shop. He worked in various shops before starting his own firm in 1834.

- James Merritt Ives joined the firm as a bookkeeper in the 1850s. He rapidly became indispensable.

- Lithography is a printing method that allows many prints to be made from a single image. A mirror-image picture is drawn with a grease pencil on a smooth block of limestone. Water is then put on the stone. The stone accepts the water except in the areas protected by the grease pencil. Then ink, which adheres to the areas with the grease pencil, is applied. The image can then be printed on a sheet of paper. Lithographs are usually one color, but there were several methods used to add color. At one point, Currier and Ives had employees who tinted their prints.

Use the Time Line

The time line at the bottom of the page shows the dates for some major national and global events in which the United States was involved during the mid 1800s and early 1900s.

① **How many years passed between the first telegraph line crossing the country and the invention of a working light bulb?** About 18 years
Interpret Time Lines

② **Which event suggests that American industry expanded rapidly during this era?** The United States became the world's leading manufacturer in 1900.
Draw Conclusions

③ **What can you infer from the event that took place in 1924?** The United States had experienced a huge wave of immigration and wanted to control it.
Make Inferences

CURRICULUM CONNECTION
Science

Research an Invention

- Have students use library and Internet resources to research one of the following inventions: the mechanical windshield wiper, the telegraph, the light bulb, the telephone, the radio.

- Have students compile a fact sheet on the invention they choose, listing the inventor, the year of invention, and the major characteristics of the invention.

- Tell students to write a brief essay explaining how their invention worked and how it altered life in the country.

- Encourage students to create a bibliography for their essay.

Meet the People

Objective

- Identify the contributions of significant individuals in the United States in the late 1800s and early 1900s.

Resource

- Poster 5

Research the People

Each of the people pictured on these pages influenced or was affected by the rapid growth and development of the late 1800s and early 1900s. Have students do research to find answers to the following questions.

- **Which of these people made his or her fortune in post-gold-rush California?** Levi Strauss

- **What were some of the charitable causes that Andrew Carnegie supported with his wealth?** Possible answers: Building of libraries and theaters, improvement of universities

- **What were the first words Alexander Graham Bell spoke into his invention, the telephone?** "Mr. Watson, come here, I want to see you."

- **What was the title of Lewis Latimer's book on Edison's great invention?** *Incandescent Electric Lighting*

Students may wish to write their own questions about other people on these pages for the rest of the class to answer.

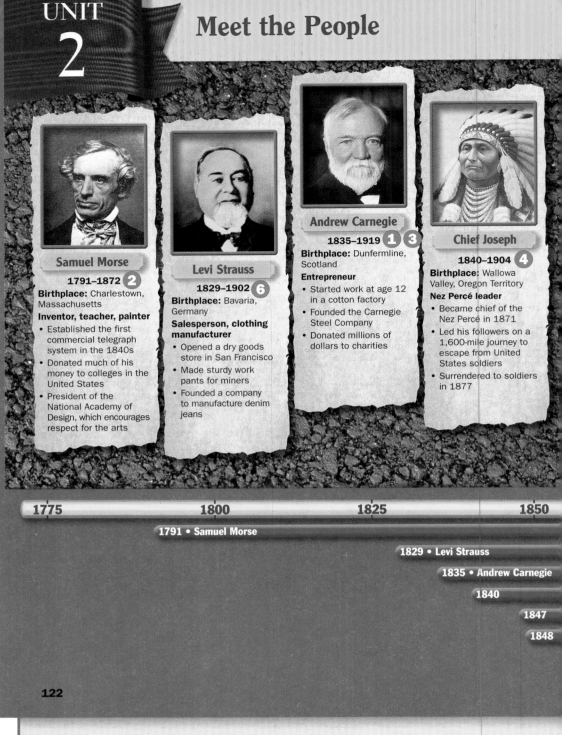

Samuel Morse
1791–1872 2
Birthplace: Charlestown, Massachusetts
Inventor, teacher, painter
- Established the first commercial telegraph system in the 1840s
- Donated much of his money to colleges in the United States
- President of the National Academy of Design, which encourages respect for the arts

Levi Strauss
1829–1902 6
Birthplace: Bavaria, Germany
Salesperson, clothing manufacturer
- Opened a dry goods store in San Francisco
- Made sturdy work pants for miners
- Founded a company to manufacture denim jeans

Andrew Carnegie
1835–1919 1 3
Birthplace: Dunfermline, Scotland
Entrepreneur
- Started work at age 12 in a cotton factory
- Founded the Carnegie Steel Company
- Donated millions of dollars to charities

Chief Joseph
1840–1904 4
Birthplace: Wallowa Valley, Oregon Territory
Nez Percé leader
- Became chief of the Nez Percé in 1871
- Led his followers on a 1,600-mile journey to escape from United States soldiers
- Surrendered to soldiers in 1877

1775	1800	1825	1850

1791 • Samuel Morse

1829 • Levi Strauss

1835 • Andrew Carnegie

1840

1847

1848

122

Practice and Extend

CURRICULUM CONNECTION
Literature

Read Biographies

Use the following biography selections to extend the content.

Streets of Gold, by Rosemary Wells (Dial Books for Young Readers, ISBN 0-803-72149-8, 1999) **Easy**

The Story of Alexander Graham Bell: Inventor of the Telephone, by Margaret Davidson (Gareth Stevens Publishing, ISBN 0-836-81483-5, 1997) **On-Level**

Lewis Latimer, by Winifred Latimer Norman (Chelsea House, ISBN 0-791-01977-2, 1993) **Challenge**

For more information, go online to *Meet the People* at **www.sfsocialstudies.com.**

Alexander Graham Bell

1847–1922 1

Birthplace: Edinburgh, Scotland

Inventor

• Developed techniques to teach speech to the deaf
• Invented the telephone in 1876
• Became president of the National Geographic Society to teach people about distant lands

Lewis Latimer

1848–1928 2

Birthplace: Chelsea, Massachusetts

Inventor

• Served in the United States Navy during the Civil War
• Made improvements on Thomas Edison's electric light bulb
• Taught English and drawing to immigrants

George Shima

1863(?)–1926 3

Birthplace: Japan

Farmer

• Overcame poverty to become the "Potato King"
• Developed a system to pump water out of the soil
• Donated food and money to help those in need

Mary Antin

1881–1949 5

Birthplace: Polotsk, Russia

Writer

• Immigrated to the United States in 1894
• Wrote several books about the experiences of immigrants
• Fought against anti-immigration laws

1875   1900   1925   1950

1872

1902

1919

• Chief Joseph   1904

• Alexander Graham Bell   1922

• Lewis Latimer   1928

1863(?) • George Shima   1926

1881 • Mary Antin   1949

123

WEB SITE
Technology

Students can research the lives of the people on this page by clicking on *Meet the People* at **www.sfsocialstudies.com.**

Use the Time Line

Have students use the time line and biographies to answer these questions.

1 **Which two people were both born in Scotland?** Alexander Graham Bell and Andrew Carnegie Analyze Information

2 **Which people shown were born in states within the United States?** Samuel Morse and Lewis Latimer Compare and Contrast

3 **Which two people were noted for making donations to help other people?** Andrew Carnegie and George Shima Compare and Contrast

4 **Which person was born in an area that later became part of the United States?** Chief Joseph Make Inferences

5 **Which person used writing to inform people about the immigrant experience?** Mary Antin Make Inferences

6 **Which person opened a dry goods store in San Francisco?** Levi Strauss Main Idea and Details

Biographies

Three of the people shown here are discussed more extensively in the Biography pages in Unit 2.

• George Shima, p. 145
• Andrew Carnegie, p. 183
• Mary Antin, p. 191

Read About the People

The people shown here are discussed in the text on the following pages in Unit 2.

• Samuel Morse, p. 129
• Levi Strauss, p. 152
• Andrew Carnegie, pp. 177, 180, 183, 193
• Chief Joseph, pp. 157, 160–161
• Alexander Graham Bell, pp. 166, 167
• Lewis Latimer, p. 168
• George Shima, pp. 144, 145
• Mary Antin, pp. 185, 191

Reading Social Studies

Sequence

Objective

Analyze information by identifying the sequence of events.

Resource

- Workbook, p. 29

About the Unit Target Skill

- The target reading skill for this unit is Sequence.
- Students are introduced to the unit target skill here and are given an opportunity to practice it.
- Further opportunities to use sequence are found throughout Unit 2.

1 Introduce and Motivate

Preview To activate prior knowledge, have students recall a sequence of events from the last unit in the book. (For example, Abraham Lincoln is elected President. Southern states begin to secede. Conflict arises at Fort Sumter. The first shots of the Civil War are fired, and the Civil War begins.)

2 Teach and Discuss

- Explain that a sequence is a logical and meaningful order of events. In history, events take place in a particular order. As students read, suggest that they look for clues such as dates and words that indicate order (e.g., *first, then, after*).

- Have students read the sample paragraph on p. 124. Make sure they recognize that the highlighted phrases are clues that help them recognize the sequence, and that the dates can also be used to place events in order.

An Expanding Nation

Sequence

Word clue	Date	Event
First	1844	Telegraph message sent.
Then	1861	Transcontinental telegraph built.
Finally	1876	Invention of telephone.

Learning to find the sequence of events—the order in which things happen—will help you understand many kinds of writing. Study the chart at left.

Dates help establish sequence. Clue words such as *first, once, before, later, after, then,* and *finally* also help signal the order in which events took place.

Read the paragraph. **Words** that help signal sequence have been highlighted in blue. **Dates** are highlighted in yellow.

> Many communication improvements were made in the 1800s. The Pony Express began delivering mail in 1860. After one year, though, the transcontinental telegraph line replaced it. Earlier, in 1844, Samuel Morse sent the first telegraph message. With the invention of the telephone in 1876, voices could be carried over wires.

Word Exercise

Words with Suffixes [communication, construction, invention, transportation, improvement, advancement]

Suffixes are word endings such as *-ion, -ment, -ness,* and *-tion*. When a suffix is added to a word, the new word is related in meaning to the original, or base, word.

construction = | construct (put together) | + | -ion (act of) |

The act of putting together the National Road began in 1811.
Construction on the National Road began in 1811.

improvement = | improve (make better) | + | -ment (the result of) |

The result of making equipment better made farming less difficult.
Improvements in equipment made farming less difficult.

124

Practice and Extend

ESL ACCESS CONTENT
ESL Support

Create a Sequence Have students put items in a sequence that describes how to do or make something.

Beginning Have students act out the steps of the sequence of some familiar activity, such as making a sandwich or brushing one's teeth. Ask students to emphasize the correct order for the steps by indicating "first," "next," "last," and so on.

Intermediate Have students create a written, properly sequenced list of instructions for the activity described above.

Advanced Have students write a paragraph that describes the sequence of events of some or all of their day. Tell them to make sure the paragraph follows a logical sequence and uses clue words to describe the sequence.

Connecting the Country: A Sequence of Events

Throughout the 1800s, improvements in communication and transportation helped to bring people in the United States closer together. Stagecoaches drawn by horses took passengers from city to city on roads. Construction on the National Road began in 1811. The invention of the steamboat in 1807 made navigation of inland waterways easier.

The country's first railroad was built in 1830. Almost 40 years later, in 1869, the transcontinental railroad was completed. Passengers could go across the continent by train. Automobiles—or "horseless carriages"—began appearing on roads in the United States in the 1890s.

At the same time that transportation was improving, advancements in communications also were being made. In 1860 horses and riders of the Pony

Express started delivering mail in only ten days from Missouri to California. Even the Pony Express seemed slow when, in the following year, a transcontinental telegraph line was completed. In moments, a message could be sent from one end of the country to the other. Samuel Morse had helped develop a way, in the 1830s, to send messages over the telegraph.

Alexander Graham Bell later improved instant communication when he invented the telephone in 1876. The telephone also used wires but allowed two people far apart to speak to each other. Then, with the invention of radio communication in 1895, it was possible for many people with radios to listen to the same message at the same time.

Use the reading strategy of sequence to answer the first two questions. Then answer the vocabulary question.

1 Was the transcontinental railroad completed before or after the telephone was invented?

2 In what sequence did the following events take place: radio communication is invented, Pony Express begins, a way of sending telegraph messages is developed, steamboat is invented, construction begins on the National Road? How many years passed between the first event and the last?

3 Find a word in the above passage that has a suffix. Use a graphic organizer like the one shown at the bottom of page 124 to explain the meanings of the base word, the suffix, and the new word. Then use each form of the word in a sentence.

125

Standardized Test Prep

- Use Workbook p. 29 to give students practice with standardized test format.
- Chapter and Unit Tests in the Assessment Book use standardized test format.
- Test-taking tips appear in the front portion of the Assessment Book Teacher's Edition.

Also on Teacher Resources CD-ROM.

Workbook, p. 29

- Now have students read the longer practice sample on p. 125 and answer the questions that follow.

- Ask students why it is important to understand the sequence of events when reading about history. (Understanding the order in which events took place can help you understand how certain events affect one another.)

Words with Suffixes  Word Exercise

Ask students to find two words from the selection that have suffixes and have not yet been discussed, such as *transportation* and *advancement*. Model for students how to find the base word and look up its definition in a dictionary if it is unfamiliar. Draw on the board two graphic organizers like the ones on p. 124. Fill them in with the definitions of *transport* (carry from one place to another), *-ion* (act of), *advance* (to move forward), and *-ment* (the result of). Guide students in defining *transportation* as "the act of carrying something from one place to another" and *advancement* as "the result of something having moved forward." Then ask students to write a sentence for each form of the word.

3 Close and Assess

Apply it!

1. The transcontinental railroad was completed in 1869, before the invention of the telephone in 1876.

2. The steamboat is invented in 1807. Construction begins on the National Road in 1811. A way of sending telegraph messages is developed in the 1830s. The Pony Express begins in 1860, and radio communication arrives in 1895. About 88 years passed between the first and last event.

3. Possible answer: *immigration* = *immigrate* (to come or move to) + *-ion* (act of). *The act of moving* to the United States contributed to the growth and development of the country. *Immigration* to the United States contributed to the growth and development of the country.

Chapter Planning Guide

Chapter 3 • Crossing the Continent

Locating Time and Place pp. 126–127

Lesson Titles	Pacing	Main Ideas
Lesson 1 **Rails Across the Nation** pp. 128–133		• In the 1860s new railroad lines made it possible to travel and move goods across the United States much more quickly than ever before.
Map and Globe Skills: Read a Time Zone Map pp. 134–135	4 days	• A time zone map shows the different times in the time zones on Earth.
Colonial Williamsburg: Westward Growth of America, 1607–1862 pp. 136–137		• The development of railroads in the 1800s helped the U.S. expand and created new business opportunities.
Lesson 2 **Pioneers on the Plains** pp. 138–144		• Farmers began settling in the Great Plains in the 1860s, and they soon turned the plains into a productive farming region.
Biography: George Shima p. 145	4 days	• George Shima created a successful potato-farming empire and became a community leader.
Chart and Graph Skills: Read Climographs pp. 146–147		• Learning to read climographs can help you understand vital climate information about a place.
Lesson 3 **Cowboys and Miners** pp. 148–153	2 days	• Cattle drives and the search for gold offered new opportunities and led to lasting changes in the western United States.
Lesson 4 **War in the West** pp. 154–159	3 days	• As more and more settlers came to the western United States, Native American groups fought to maintain control of their lands.
⭐ **Citizen Heroes:** Fairness **Fighting for a Homeland** pp. 160–161		• Chief Joseph fought a long battle to win fair treatment for his people, the Nez Perce.

✓ **Chapter 3 Review** pp. 162–163

✓ = Assessment Options

◀ **Posters such as this one advertised free land in the West.**

Vocabulary	Resources	Meeting Individual Needs
Pony Express telegraph transcontinental railroad time zone standard time	• Workbook, p. 31 • Transparency 11 • Every Student Learns Guide, pp. 50–53 • Quick Study, pp. 26–27 • Workbook, p. 32 • Workbook, p. 33	• Leveled Practice, TE p. 129 • ESL Support, TE p. 130
pioneer Homestead Act homesteader sodbuster exoduster technology climograph	• Workbook, p. 34 • Transparency 10 • Every Student Learns Guide, pp. 54–57 • Quick Study, pp. 28–29 • Workbook, p. 35	• ESL Support, TE p. 139 • Leveled Practice, TE p. 140 • Learning Styles, TE p. 142
cattle drive gold rush entrepreneur	• Workbook, p. 36 • Transparency 10 • Every Student Learns Guide, pp. 58–61 • Quick Study, pp. 30–31	• ESL Support, TE pp. 150, 152 • Leveled Practice, TE p. 151
reservation Battle of Little Bighorn	• Workbook, p. 37 • Transparency 10 • Every Student Learns Guide, pp. 62–65 • Quick Study, pp. 32–33	• ESL Support, TE p. 157 • Leveled Practice, TE p. 158
	✓ Chapter 3 Content Test, Assessment Book, pp. 17–18 ✓ Chapter 3 Skills Test, Assessment Book, pp. 19–20	✓ Chapter 3 Performance Assessment, TE p. 162

Providing More Depth

Additional Resources

- Vocabulary Workbook and Cards
- Social Studies Plus! pp. 56–61
- Daily Activity Bank
- Big Book Atlas
- Student Atlas
- Outline Maps
- Desk Maps

 Technology

- AudioText
- MindPoint® Quiz Show CD-ROM
- ExamView® Test Bank CD-ROM
- Teacher Resources CD-ROM
- Map Resources CD-ROM
- SFSuccessNet: iText (Pupil Edition online), iTE (Teacher's Edition online), Online Planner
- **www.sfsocialstudies.com** (Biographies, news, references, maps, and activities)

 To establish guidelines for your students' safe and responsible use of the Internet, use the Scott Foresman Internet Guide.

Additional Internet Links

To find out more about:

- the transcontinental railroad, search for this term at **www.pbs.org**
- the Homestead Act, search for this term at **www.nps.gov**
- the Indian Wars, search for this term at the Center for Military History at **www.army.mil**

Key Internet Search Terms

- cowboys
- gold rush
- Chief Joseph
- Little Bighorn

Workbook Support

Use the following Workbook pages to support content and skills development as you teach Chapter 3. You can also view and print Workbook pages from the Teachers Resources CD-ROM.

Workbook, p. 29

Sequence

Use with Pages 124–125.

Directions: Sequence means the order in which events take place. Dates, times of day, and clue words such as *first, next, then, after, finally, during,* and *meanwhile* help signal the order of events. Use page 125 of your textbook to answer the following questions. Fill in the circle next to the correct answer.

1. Which of the following occurred before construction began on the National Road?
   - ● The steamboat was invented.
   - Ⓑ People began using automobiles.
   - Ⓒ The country's first railroad was built.
   - Ⓓ The telegraph was invented.

2. According to the essay, what happened at the same time that the nation's transportation systems were advancing?
   - Ⓐ People were relying on stagecoaches.
   - ● Communications were also improving.
   - Ⓒ The National Road was nearing completion.
   - Ⓓ Radio was invented.

3. Which of the following occurred first?
   - Ⓐ The Pony Express started delivering mail.
   - Ⓑ "Horseless carriages" began appearing on roads.
   - ● The country's first railroad was built.
   - Ⓓ The transcontinental railroad was completed.

4. Which words tell you that the telegraph was developed after the start of the Pony Express?
   - Ⓐ "started delivering mail"
   - ● "in the following year"
   - Ⓒ "at the same time"
   - Ⓓ "even the Pony Express seemed slow"

5. Based on the essay, which happened last?
   - Ⓐ Samuel Morse developed a way of sending telegraph messages.
   - Ⓑ The telephone was invented.
   - Ⓒ A transcontinental telegraph was completed.
   - ● Radio communication was invented.

 Notes for Home: Your child learned to sequence events and to understand the relationship between events in a sequence.
Home Activity: Provide your child with a list of events from his or her life in random order. Have your child list them in the proper sequence.

Use with Pupil Edition, p. 125

Workbook, p. 30

Vocabulary Preview

Use with Chapter 3.

Directions: Write each vocabulary word from Chapter 3 beside its example or description. You may use your textbook.

1. __reservation__ — area of land set aside for Native Americans
2. __exoduster__ — African American pioneer
3. __Pony Express__ — business that delivered mail from Missouri to California in just ten days
4. __Homestead Act__ — law that offered free land to American citizens and immigrants who were willing to start new farms on the Great Plains
5. __gold rush__ — period when thousands of people went to search for gold
6. __technology__ — use of new ideas to make tools that improve people's lives
7. __sodbuster__ — Great Plains farmer
8. __telegraph__ — invention that sent messages along wires using electricity
9. __entrepreneur__ — person who starts a new business hoping to make a profit
10. __Battle of Little Bighorn__ — battle in which Crazy Horse helped lead the Lakota to victory against United States forces
11. __cattle drive__ — when cowboys guided huge herds of cattle north to new railroad lines extending across the Great Plains
12. __homesteader__ — settler who claimed land through the Homestead Act
13. __pioneer__ — new settler
14. __transcontinental railroad__ — railroad across the continent

Notes for Home: Your child learned the vocabulary terms for Chapter 3.
Home Activity: Encourage your child to tell or write a story using at least five of these words.

Use with Pupil Edition, p. 126

Workbook, p. 31

Lesson 1: Rails Across the Nation

Use with Pages 128–133.

Directions: Write the number of each item in Column A on the blank next to its description in Column B.

Column A	Column B
1. stagecoach	**7** told Union Pacific workers that they were scaring away the buffalo
2. Pony Express	**9** place where the Union Pacific and the Central Pacific met
3. telegraph	**1** horse-drawn wagons that traveled in regular stages
4. Samuel Morse	**3** invention that sent messages along wires using electricity
5. Union Pacific	**4** developed a way to send telegraph messages
6. Central Pacific	**6** part of transcontinental railroad that ran east from Sacramento, California
7. Red Cloud	**5** part of transcontinental railroad that ran west from Omaha, Nebraska
8. General William Tecumseh Sherman	**10** major natural obstacle to the Central Pacific
9. Promontory Point, Utah Territory	**2** business that delivered mail from Missouri to California in just ten days
10. Sierra Nevada	**8** warned Native American leaders that they could not stop the locomotive

 Notes for Home: Your child learned about the building of the first transcontinental railroad.
Home Activity: Talk to your child about travel between the East and West today. How do people usually make this journey, and how long does it take?

Use with Pupil Edition, p. 133

Workbook, p. 32

Read a Time Zone Map

Use with Pages 134–135.

Directions: A time zone is a region in which all places have the same time. Time zone maps show different time zones. Study the map below and answer the questions that follow.

1. How many times zones exist in the United States?
   There are six time zones in the United States.

2. Does the time become earlier or later as you move from east to west across the United States?
   The time becomes earlier as you move from east to west.

3. In what time zone is Miami located?
   Miami is located in the Eastern time zone.

4. If it is 11 A.M. in Seattle, what time is it in Dallas?
   It is 1:00 P.M. in Dallas.

5. Suppose you want to call a friend when he gets out of class at 1 P.M. in Hawaii. At what time should you make your call from Washington, D. C.?
   The call should be made at 6:00 P.M.

 Notes for Home: Your child learned to read a time zone map.
Home Activity: Help your child use the Internet or library resources to locate a world time zone map. Together, use the map to calculate differences between your time zone and time zones in other parts of the world.

Use with Pupil Edition, p. 135

Workbook, p. 33

Use with Pages 136–137.

Directions: Suppose that you are an American moving west on the Oregon Trail during the mid-1800s. Write a diary entry about your travels. Describe the people you meet and the challenges and opportunities you face along the way.

Students' diary entries should accurately reflect information from the time period.

 Notes for Home: Your child learned about the westward expansion of the United States.
Home Activity: Study the map and time line on pages 136–137 with your child. Discuss what it might have been like to live in the changing United States during each period.

Use with Pupil Edition, p. 137

Workbook Support

Workbook, p. 34

Lesson 2: Pioneers on the Plains
Use with Pages 138–144.

Directions: Using information from the lesson, circle the term in parentheses that best completes each sentence.

1. The government hoped that the (Homestead Act, sodbusters) would encourage pioneers to move to the Great Plains.

2. The famous novel *O Pioneers!*, by (Benjamin Singleton, Willa Cather) describes homesteaders' changing feelings about the Great Plains.

3. Europeans' desire to move to the Great Plains was so strong it became known as ("America Fever,") the "Great American Desert").

4. African American pioneers called themselves (homesteaders, exodusters) after a book in the Bible that tells the story of Moses leading the Israelites out of slavery.

5. (Grasshoppers, Technology) helped make life easier for Great Plains farmers.

Directions: In the space below, write a letter to a friend as a pioneer on the Great Plains in the 1860s. Describe the hardships and the opportunities you face.

> Dear _____,
> **Students' letters should identify both the hardships of life on the Great Plains, such as the tough sod, weather, lack of wood, and other natural hazards; and the opportunities, such as inexpensive land, freedom, and fertile soil.**
>
> Your Friend,
> _____

 Notes for Home: Your child learned about the settlement of the Great Plains during the late 1800s and how new technologies helped these settlers.
Home Activity: Review the Fact File on page 143 with your child. Then talk with your child about technologies that have helped improve your daily lives.

Use with Pupil Edition, p. 144

Workbook, p. 35

Read Climographs
Use with Pages 146–147.

Directions: A climograph shows the temperature and the average precipitation of a place. Look at the climograph below. Then answer the questions that follow.

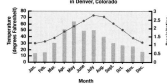

Average Temperature and Precipitation in Denver, Colorado

KEY
Line graph shows temperature.
Bar graph shows precipitation.

1. Which month received the greatest precipitation in Denver?
   May receives the greatest amount of precipitation.

2. What generalization can you make about the relationship between precipitation and temperature in Denver?
   In general, precipitation is higher when the temperatures are higher.

3. What is the warmest season in Denver?
   Summer (June, July, and August) is the warmest season in Denver.

4. What is the driest season in Denver?
   In general, winter (December, January, and February) is the driest season in Denver.

5. How would you summarize the climate of Denver overall?
   Denver has warm, wet summers and cool, dry winters.

 Notes for Home: Your child learned to read a climograph.
Home Activity: Work with your child to compare and contrast the climate where you live with the climate in Denver, Colorado.

Use with Pupil Edition, p. 147

Workbook, p. 36

Lesson 3: Cowboys and Miners
Use with Pages 148–153.

Directions: Complete the outline with information from this lesson. You may use your textbook.

Life in the West

I. **Cattle Drives**
   A. Cattle drives were a way for ranchers to get their cattle to **market** in the East.
      1. The drives began in **Texas** and ended in Great Plains railroad towns such as Dodge City, Kansas.
         a. The Goodnight-Loving Trail, established by **Charles Goodnight** in 1866, ran from Texas to Colorado.
   B. By the late 1880s, cattle drives came to an end.
      1. **Homesteaders** began fencing in their lands with barbed wire to keep cattle off their farmland.
      2. Once **railroads** reached Texas, it was no longer necessary for ranchers to drive their cattle north.

II. **Dreams of Gold**
   A. During the California **gold rush**, thousands of people moved west in search of gold.
      1. By 1850, California had enough people to become a **state**.
   B. When **George Jackson** discovered gold in the Rocky Mountains, miners began searching for gold all over the West.
      1. The flood of newcomers created opportunities for **entrepreneurs** like Luzena Stanley Wilson and Levi Strauss.
   C. The mining boom had lasting effects in the West.
      1. San Francisco, California, and **Denver, Colorado** are two examples of important cities that emerged from supply stations for miners.

Notes for Home: Your child learned about the events that changed the American West.
Home Activity: Discuss with your child what it might have been like for you and your family to move west in search of gold during the mid-1800s.

Use with Pupil Edition, p. 153

Workbook, p. 37

Lesson 4: War in the West
Use with Pages 154–159.

Directions: Answer the following questions on the lines provided. You may use your textbook.

1. What changes took place in the West during the late 1800s that threatened the Native American way of life?
   Thousands of settlers and the changing landscape of the Great Plains threatened the traditional ways of Native Americans. Herds of buffalo, on which many groups depended, began to disappear.

2. Why did the United States government try to move Native Americans to reservations?
   The government wanted the region to be open for expanding railroad lines, growing farms and ranches, and new towns.

3. Why was the Battle of Little Bighorn both a victory and a defeat for Native Americans?
   The battle was a victory in that the Native Americans badly defeated the United States soldiers. It was a defeat in that it convinced the United States to take stronger action against them.

4. Why did Chief Joseph agree to surrender?
   He was told that the Nez Percé would be allowed to return to Oregon.

5. What happened at Wounded Knee in 1890 and what was its significance?
   United States soldiers killed hundreds of Native Americans. It was the last major battle between Native Americans and United States soldiers.

Notes for Home: Your child learned how western expansion of the United States affected Native American groups.
Home Activity: Help your child use Internet or library sources to find information about Native American groups that once lived in your region.

Use with Pupil Edition, p. 159

Workbook, p. 38

Vocabulary Review
Use with Chapter 3.

Directions: Use each of the vocabulary terms from Chapter 3 in a sentence. Write the sentences on the lines provided. You may use more than one term in a sentence. You may use your glossary.

Pony Express	homesteader	gold rush
telegraph	sodbuster	entrepreneur
transcontinental railroad	exoduster	reservation
pioneer	technology	Battle of Little Bighorn
Homestead Act	cattle drive	

Students should use each vocabulary term correctly.

Notes for Home: Your child learned the vocabulary terms for Chapter 3.
Home Activity: Create flashcards of these terms and their meanings to quiz your child.

Use with Pupil Edition, p. 163

Assessment Support

Use these Assessment Book pages and the ExamView® Test Bank CD-ROM to assess content and skills in Chapter 3. You can also view and print Assessment Book pages from the Teacher Resources CD-ROM.

Assessment Book, p. 17

Chapter 3 Test

Part 1: Content Test

Directions: Fill in the circle next to the correct answer.

Lesson Objective (1:1)

1. Which innovation used electricity to send news across the country?
   - (A) the transcontinental railroad
   - (B) the Pony Express
   - ● the telegraph
   - (D) the stagecoach

Lesson Objective (1:2)

2. Which of the following best describes a major challenge faced by the Union Pacific railroad?
   - ● conflict with Native Americans
   - (B) conflict with Chinese immigrants
   - (C) competition among other railroad companies
   - (D) the steep slopes of the Sierra Nevada

Lesson Objective (1:3)

3. Which group made up the largest part of the Central Pacific's workforce?
   - (A) Irish immigrants
   - ● Chinese immigrants
   - (C) African Americans
   - (D) former Union Army soldiers

Lesson Objective (1:4)

4. Which innovation allowed people and goods to travel across the country in just a week?
   - (A) the stagecoach
   - (B) the Pony Express
   - ● the transcontinental railroad
   - (D) the Morse Code

Lesson Objective (2:1)

5. What was the main purpose of the Homestead Act?
   - (A) to bring an end to cattle drives
   - ● to encourage settlement on the Great Plains
   - (C) to defeat the Native Americans
   - (D) to provide a market for steel plows

Lesson Objective (2:2)

6. Which of the following was NOT one of the challenges typically faced by homesteaders?
   - ● high cost of land
   - (B) harsh weather
   - (C) large amount of grasshoppers
   - (D) thick sod

Lesson Objective (2:3)

7. Why did many exodusters come to the Great Plains?
   - (A) European immigrants forced them from their homes in the East.
   - (B) They wanted to hunt buffalo.
   - ● They faced discrimination and lack of opportunity in the East.
   - (D) They were seeking religious freedom.

Lesson Objective (2:4)

8. Which of the following was NOT a way that technology helped pioneers turn the Great Plains into productive farmland?
   - (A) Stronger steel plows were used on the thick grasslands.
   - (B) Windmills were used to pump water to the land's surface.
   - (C) Barbed wire was used to keep animals away from crops.
   - ● Sod was used as a building material to keep out bugs.

Use with Pupil Edition, p. 162

Assessment Book, p. 18

Lesson Objective (3:1)

9. Why were cattle drives profitable for Texas ranchers?
   - (A) Cattle grew fatter as they traveled the trails.
   - (B) People paid to watch the cattle drives.
   - ● Cattle could be sold for more money in the East.
   - (D) Railroads paid ranchers to use their services.

Lesson Objective (3:2)

10. Which of the following best describes a reason why cattle drives came to an end?
    - (A) Thousands of cattle ranchers moved west in search of gold.
    - (B) Consumers became more interested in gold than cattle.
    - (C) Farmers on the Great Plains began raising cattle.
    - ● They were no longer necessary once railroads reached Texas.

Lesson Objective (3:3)

11. Which of the following describes a lasting effect of the search for gold?
    - ● The quest for gold lured many settlers to the West.
    - (B) Gold rushes left the West deserted with ghost towns.
    - (C) Dreams of finding gold continue to attract many settlers each year.
    - (D) Few miners actually found gold nuggets.

Lesson Objective (4:1)

12. Which of the following was NOT a change that threatened the way of life for Native Americans of the Great Plains?
    - (A) decline in buffalo herds
    - ● widespread European diseases
    - (C) spreading telegraph and railroad lines
    - (D) arrival of miners, farmers, and ranchers

Lesson Objective (4:2)

13. Why is the Battle of Little Bighorn also known as "Custer's Last Stand"?
    - (A) Custer resigned after witnessing the brutal Lakota defeat.
    - (B) Custer was seriously injured as he led his forces to victory.
    - ● Custer was killed along with his entire forces.
    - (D) Custer surrendered after his forces were surrounded by the Lakota.

Lesson Objective (4:2)

14. Which of the following describes the significance of the Battle of Wounded Knee?
    - (A) It was the biggest victory Native Americans ever won over United States forces.
    - ● It was the last major battle between the United States and Native Americans.
    - (C) It convinced the United States government to take stronger action against the Lakota and other Native American groups.
    - (D) It allowed Native Americans to return to their traditional homelands.

Lesson Objective (4:3)

15. Which of the following is NOT an example of how Native American groups are keeping traditions alive today?
    - (A) gaining control of more land
    - (B) maintaining tribal languages
    - (C) sharing tribal stories
    - ● launching raids on United States military sites

Use with Pupil Edition, p. 162

Assessment Support

Assessment Book, p. 19

Part 2: Skills Test

Directions: Use complete sentences to answer questions 1–5. Use a separate sheet of paper if you need more space.

1. Write the following events about transportation and communication in the order in which they happened. **Sequence**

   The first telegraph line across the country was completed.

   A new business called the Pony Express began delivering mail from Missouri to California in just 10 days.

   The tracks of the Union Pacific and Central Pacific met at Promontory Point, Utah.

   Samuel Morse developed a method of sending messages along wires.

   > A new business called the Pony Express began delivering mail from Missouri to California in just 10 days.
   >
   > ↓
   >
   > Samuel Morse developed a method of sending messages along wires.
   >
   > ↓
   >
   > The first telegraph line across the country was completed.
   >
   > ↓
   >
   > The tracks of the Union Pacific and Central Pacific met at Promontory Point, Utah.

Use with Pupil Edition, p. 162

Assessment Book, p. 20

2. Use details from the chapter to support the following statement. **Main Idea and Details**

   Gold rushes of the mid-1800s had lasting effects in the West.

   Possible answer: The hope of finding gold drew thousands of settlers to the West. Supply stations for miners grew into important cities. Growing towns offered opportunities for entrepreneurs.

3. What can you infer from the fact that the United States government forced many Native Americans of the Great Plains to move to reservations in the late 1800s? **Make Inferences**

   Possible answer: The United States government wanted the region to be open for expanding railroad lines, growing farms and ranches, and new towns.

4. What effect did the Battle of Little Bighorn have on Native Americans? **Cause and Effect**

   It convinced the United States government to take stronger action against Native Americans and led to the end of freedom for Native Americans of the Great Plains.

5. Study the climograph below. What generalization can you make about precipitation in Burlington, Vermont? **Read Climographs**

   Precipitation is consistent throughout the year, although it is heaviest in the summer months.

Average Temperature and Precipitation in Burlington, Vermont

KEY
Line graph shows temperature.
Bar graph shows precipitation.

Use with Pupil Edition, p. 162

CHAPTER 3

Crossing the Continent

Chapter 3 Outline

Resources

- Workbook, p. 30: Vocabulary Preview
- Vocabulary Cards
- Social Studies Plus!

1869, Promontory Point, Utah Territory: Lesson 1

Ask students why the joining of the nation's first transcontinental railroad might have been important. (Possible answer: The East was joined to the West.)

1877, Nicodemus, Kansas: Lesson 2

Have students explain why the growth of the nation might have been important to African American pioneers after the Civil War. (Possible answer: They needed better economic opportunities.)

1880s, Virginia City, Nevada: Lesson 3

What effect has the lack of gold and silver to mine had on this town? (Possible answer: Citizens have left, turning it into a ghost town.)

1890, Wounded Knee, South Dakota: Lesson 1

Ask students why the site might be memorialized today. (Possible answer: The site marks an important battle.)

CHAPTER 3

Crossing the Continent

1869

Promontory Point, Utah Territory
The first transcontinental railroad is completed.

Lesson 1

1877

Nicodemus, Kansas
African American pioneers called exodusters found a town on the Great Plains.

Lesson 2

1880s

Virginia City, Nevada
The boom town of Virginia City becomes a ghost town when the gold and silver run out.

Lesson 3

1890

Wounded Knee, South Dakota
A memorial now stands where a battle occurred between Native Americans and United States soldiers.

Lesson 4

126

Practice and Extend

Vocabulary Preview

- Use Workbook p. 30 to help students preview the vocabulary words in this chapter.
- Use Vocabulary Cards to preview key concept words in this chapter.

 Also on Teacher Resources CD-ROM.

Workbook, p. 30

Vocabulary Preview

Directions: Write each vocabulary word from Chapter 3 beside its example or description. You may use your textbook.

1. _____ area of land set aside for Native Americans
2. _____ African American pioneer
3. _____ business that delivered mail from Missouri to California in just ten days
4. _____ law that offered free land to American citizens and immigrants who were willing to start new farms on the Great Plains
5. _____ period when thousands of people went to search for gold
6. _____ use of new ideas to make tools that improve people's lives
7. _____ Great Plains farmer
8. _____ invention that sent messages along wires using electricity
9. _____ person who starts a new business hoping to make a profit
10. _____ battle in which Crazy Horse helped lead the Lakota to victory against United States forces
11. _____ when cowboys guided huge herds of cattle north to new railroad lines extending across the Great Plains
12. _____ settler who claimed land through the Homestead Act
13. _____ new settler
14. _____ railroad across the continent

Notes for Home: Your child learned the vocabulary terms for Chapter 3.
Home Activity: Encourage your child to tell or write a story using at least five of these words.

Locating Time and Place

Why We Remember

By the late 1800s, the map of the United States would have looked familiar to you. The nation's territory stretched to the Pacific Ocean, and new states were being admitted to the Union. Telegraph wires and railroad tracks were built across the plains and mountains, linking the East and West Coasts. Soon pioneers began to settle on this land. At the same time, Native Americans, also known as American Indians, were being forced from their homes. The way of life of all Americans was being changed in ways no one could have predicted.

127

- Have students examine the pictures shown on page 126 for Lessons 1, 2, 3, and 4.

- Remind students that each picture is coded with both a number and a color to link it to a place on the map on page 127.

Why We Remember

Have students read the "Why We Remember" paragraph on p. 127, and ask them to identify ways in which the map above differs from a map of the United States today. Ask students to consider how today's map might look if Native American groups in the West had been allowed to retain their land.

WEB SITE
Technology

You can learn more about Promontory Point, Utah Territory; Nicodemus, Kansas; Virginia City, Nevada; and Wounded Knee, South Dakota by clicking on *Atlas* at **www.sfsocialstudies.com.**

SOCIAL STUDIES STRAND
Geography

Mental Mapping Have students draw an outline map of the contiguous United States. Then have students see if they can fill in the present-day states from memory. Ask students to consider how little the United States has actually changed since the late 1800s.

Rails Across the Nation

Objectives
- Identify innovations that allowed people and news to cross the country more quickly.
- Describe the challenges faced by the Union Pacific railroad.
- Evaluate the importance of Chinese workers to the Central Pacific railroad.
- Explain how the transcontinental railroad changed travel in the United States.

Vocabulary
Pony Express, p. 129; **telegraph,** p. 129; **transcontinental railroad,** p. 130

Resources
- Workbook, p. 31
- Transparency 11
- Every Student Learns Guide, pp. 50–53
- Quick Study, pp. 26–27

Quick Teaching Plan

If time is short, have students write the headings *Before* and *After* at the top of a sheet of paper.
- Have students write down details about travel and communication in the United States before the building of the transcontinental railroad.

1 Introduce and Motivate

Preview To activate prior knowledge, ask students to think about a long trip they have taken in a car or a bus. Tell students that they will learn about transportation in the United States and how it changed in the 1800s.

You Are There Coach travel over poor roads in the West was slow, uncomfortable, and often quite dangerous. Have students suggest the benefits a railroad would bring and predict its effects on the West.

128 Unit 2 • An Expanding Nation

LESSON 1

1860   1870

1861
The first telegraph line crosses the country.

1862
Construction of the transcontinental railroad begins.

1869
The transcontinental railroad is completed.

PREVIEW

Focus on the Main Idea
In the 1860s new railroad lines made it possible to travel and move goods across the United States much more quickly than ever before.

PLACES
Omaha, Nebraska
Sacramento, California
Promontory Point, Utah Territory

PEOPLE
Samuel Morse
Red Cloud

VOCABULARY
Pony Express
telegraph
transcontinental railroad

128   ▶ **Stagecoach**

Rails Across the Nation

You Are There It is a scorching hot day in July 1859. You are sitting in the back of a horse-drawn wagon, bouncing across an endless plain. You feel a little sick from the constant bumping and swaying of the seat. You are covered with dust and itching all over from some kind of bug bites. The man next to you sees you scratching. "It's the sand flies," he says.

This journey began three days ago in Missouri. Now you are in either Kansas or Nebraska, but you are not exactly sure. You do know you are traveling west toward California, and you know the trip will take at least three weeks.

Do you regret your decision to cross the country by stagecoach? Not really. This is your first chance to see huge herds of buffalo and snow-covered mountains. It is going to be an adventure.

Sequence As you read, pay attention to the order of the events that linked the eastern and western parts of the United States.

Practice and Extend

READING SKILL
Sequence

In the Lesson Review, students complete a graphic organizer like the one below. You may want to provide students with a copy of Transparency 11 to complete as they read the lesson.

Use Transparency 11

VOCABULARY
Word Exercise

Individual Word Study

Knowing the meaning of parts of a word can help students understand other words. Explain that the prefix *tele-* means "far." Add that *-graph* means "writing." Therefore, *telegraph* means "a machine that can send a written message from far away." Have students think of words beginning with *tele-* that mean the following: a machine that can carry voices from far away *(telephone);* a machine that can send moving images from far away *(television).*

Linking East and West

There was no easy way to get across the United States in the 1850s. Nearly all of the country's railroads were east of the Mississippi River. To travel from the East Coast to the West Coast, you had two choices. You could take a train west to Missouri, where the railroad tracks ended. From there you could continue traveling west by stagecoach. Stagecoaches were horse-drawn wagons that traveled in regular stages, or sections of a route.

Your second choice was to sail south to Central America, travel west across Panama by train, and then get on another boat and sail north to California. You also might sail all the way around South America. Just like traveling by stagecoach, the ocean voyage was long, expensive, and often dangerous. People began looking for faster ways to move people, mail, and goods across the United States.

In 1860 a new business called the **Pony Express** began delivering mail from Missouri to California in just 10 days. The Pony Express was like a 2,000-mile relay race.

Each express rider rode about 75 miles, then handed his bags of mail to the next rider. By changing horses every 10 or 15 miles, Pony Express riders were able to keep moving at about 10 miles per hour all day long. Most of the riders were teenagers, some as young as thirteen years old.

The Pony Express was soon put out of business by an invention called the telegraph. The **telegraph** sent messages along wires using electricity. An American inventor named **Samuel Morse** helped develop a way to send telegraph messages using a code called Morse code. He also built the first working telegraph system and sent the first telegraph message. With this technology, people could share news and information much more quickly than ever before. The first telegraph line across the country was completed in October 1861. Morse code messages could now be sent from coast to coast in just a few minutes!

REVIEW What event in 1861 brought the Pony Express to an end? ⟳ Sequence

▶ It was expensive to send letters by Pony Express, but people were willing to pay to have their mail delivered quickly.

129

Make an Illustrated Map Have students recreate the routes for traveling across the United States in the mid-1800s.

Easy Have students draw (or provide them with) an outline map of North America. Then encourage them to draw in the routes by which people traveled from East to West. **Reteach**

On-Level Have students draw (or provide them with) an outline map of North America. Then have students illustrate with appropriate icons the methods and routes of travel across the continent. **Extend**

Challenge Have students draw a map of North America (or provide them with an outline map), illustrate the methods and routes of travel in the mid-1800s, and calculate the mileage of a journey from New York to San Francisco. **Enrich**

For a Lesson Summary, use Quick Study, p. 26.

2 Teach and Discuss

PAGE 129

Linking East and West

🕐 *Quick Summary* The vast distances between the East and West in the United States were partially closed by improvements in communication in the mid-1800s.

❶ What were the steps involved in traveling across the continent from the eastern United States to the West? A person would have to take a train to Missouri. Then the person would have to travel by stagecoach across the rest of the continent. ⟳ Sequence

❷ What can you infer about the Pony Express from the fact that its riders were usually young people? Possible answer: The work was hard and physically demanding for both riders and horses. **Make Inferences**

Test Talk

Use Information from the Text

❸ What does the text suggest about why the Pony Express went out of business soon after the introduction of the telegraph? Students should ask themselves, "Do I have enough information to answer the question?" Possible answer: People no longer wanted to use the Pony Express to send information because the telegraph was faster. **Make Inferences**

✓ **REVIEW ANSWER** The first telegraph line across the country was completed. ⟳ Sequence

The Transcontinental Railroad

Quick Summary The distances between the East and West in the United States were also partially closed by transportation improvements in the mid-1800s.

④ What problem did the telegraph *not* help solve? Possible answer: The telegraph did not make possible the transportation of people or goods.
Main Idea and Details

✓ Ongoing Assessment

If... students do not understand the significance of the difficulty in moving people and goods across the country,

then... have students explain what they would do if they wanted to send a birthday card to a relative across the country in 1860.

Primary Source

Cited in *A Practical Plan for Building the Pacific Railroad*—a report by Theodore Judah.

❺ What did Judah mean when he said, "The answer is as short as the question"? Possible answer: The trip from East to West would be very short.
Analyze Primary Sources

SOCIAL STUDIES STRAND
History

Explain that in 1861, President Lincoln wanted to ensure that California would remain loyal to the Union. This was one reason he favored building the railroad—and building it through northern states.

❻ How do you think the building of the transcontinental railroad could help strengthen the Union? Possible answer: It would provide better economic links between the states. **Make Inferences**

✓ **REVIEW ANSWER** The Civil War began first. **Sequence**

MAP SKILL
Transcontinental Railroads, 1869–1893

❼ Which railroads connected Omaha and San Francisco? Central Pacific and Union Pacific **Interpret Maps**

MAP SKILL Answer Southern Pacific

The Transcontinental Railroad

The telegraph allowed news to travel quickly, but it did not help people or goods cross the country; that still took weeks, and ❹ even months. Many people believed that the best way to link East and West would be to build a **transcontinental railroad,** a railroad across the continent. A railroad engineer named Theodore Judah made a bold prediction about how the transcontinental railroad would change travel in the United States:

> *"How long will it take to go from St. Louis [Missouri] to San Francisco [California]? The answer is as short as the question. It can be run in three days, or seventy-two hours."*
❺

▶ Most of the thousands of workers on the transcontinental railroad were immigrants from Europe and China.

130

President Abraham Lincoln was a strong supporter of the transcontinental railroad. As you read in Unit 1, the Civil War began soon after Lincoln took office in 1861. Lincoln looked forward to a time when new railroads would help bind the country together. ❻

In 1862 the United States government gave two companies the job of building the transcontinental railroad. The Union Pacific began building track west from **Omaha, Nebraska.** The Central Pacific began building east from **Sacramento, California.**

REVIEW Which began first, the Civil War or construction of the transcontinental railroad?
Sequence

MAP SKILL
Transcontinental Railroads, 1869–1893

❼

▶ By 1893 several transcontinental railroad lines had been completed.
MAP SKILL Use Routes *Which railroad line served the city of New Orleans?*

Practice and Extend

ESL
EXTEND LANGUAGE
ESL Support

Examine the Prefix *Trans-* Help students expand their understanding of language by exploring the use of this prefix.

Beginning Have students look up *trans-* in an English-language dictionary. Then have students act out its meaning. (For example, by walking across a room)

Intermediate Have students look up the prefix *trans-* and the word *continental* in an English-language dictionary. Then have students write sentences to explain how these two pieces go together to describe the transcontinental railroad.

Advanced Ask students to think of two other words that have the prefix *trans-*, and then have them use those words in sentences. (Examples include *transportation, transform,* and *transplant.*)

For additional ESL support, use Every Student Learns Guide, pp. 50–53.

Union Pacific workers laid about one to three miles of track a day across the plains.

Across the Plains

The United States government paid the Central Pacific and Union Pacific for every mile of track completed. The companies were paid in land and money. As a result, the two companies raced against each other. Each company tried to build track more quickly than the other.

Geography gave the Union Pacific an advantage in this race. The Union Pacific began building on the broad, flat plains of Nebraska. The Central Pacific had the difficult job of building in the rugged Sierra Nevada mountain range in California.

The Union Pacific did face challenges, however. One problem was finding enough workers in a region that was far from big towns and cities. This problem was solved when the Civil War ended in 1865. Thousands of Irish immigrants who had served in the Union Army moved west to work on the railroad. The Union Pacific's workers also included former Confederate Army soldiers and formerly enslaved African Americans.

A more serious challenge was conflict with Native Americans. As the railroad moved west, tracks began cutting across the traditional hunting grounds of such groups as the Lakota and Cheyenne. A Lakota chief named **Red Cloud** told Union Pacific workers, "We do not want you here, you are scaring away the buffalo."

The Union Pacific was determined to continue building, and the United States government fully supported the railroad. General William Tecumseh Sherman warned Native American leaders: "We will build iron roads, and you cannot stop the locomotive." Soldiers began guarding Union Pacific workers, and the tracks continued moving west.

REVIEW How did the Union Pacific benefit from the end of the Civil War in 1865? 🔄 Sequence

► Red Cloud

Across the Plains

🕐 *Quick Summary* Two companies built the transcontinental railroad: the Central Pacific and the Union Pacific. The Union Pacific, which built from the eastern portion through the Great Plains, faced conflict with Native Americans living there.

8 **Why do you think the two companies raced to build track more quickly?** Possible answer: Because they were paid for each mile built, it was in their interest to build as many miles as possible. **Main Idea and Details**

Problem Solving

9 **How did the Union Pacific railroad solve its labor shortage?** Possible answer: It hired African Americans, Irish immigrants, and former soldiers who needed jobs after the Civil War. **Solve Problems**

10 **What effects do you think the building of the railroad had on the Native Americans of The Great Plains?** Possible answer: The railroad increased settlement and led to more conflict with the Native Americans there. **Predict**

REVIEW ANSWER The end of the war ✓ helped make many workers available. 🔄 Sequence

Decision Making

Use a Decision-Making Process

• Have students consider the following decision-making scenario: **Suppose you are a former Civil War soldier. You hear there is work on the Union Pacific railroad. You could use a job, but you are also concerned about the dangers facing the workers.**

• Students should use the following decision-making process to decide whether or not to go to work on the Union Pacific railroad. For each step in the process, have students work in small groups to discuss and write about what must be considered as they make their decision. Write the steps above on the board or read them aloud.

1. Identify a situation that requires a decision.
2. Gather information.
3. Identify options.
4. Predict consequences.
5. Take action to implement a decision.

Over the Mountains

🕐 *Quick Summary* The Central Pacific and its largely Chinese workforce struggled to build eastward through the rugged Sierra Nevada.

⑪ **Why do you think "people laughed" at the idea of building through the Sierra Nevada?** Possible answer: They thought it would be impossible to build in such an environment.
Analyze Primary Sources

⑫ **What can you infer about the effects of unfair treatment of Chinese immigrants in California mining camps?** Possible answer: It made it difficult for Chinese Americans to earn money mining for gold. **Make Inferences**

⑬ **Why did newspapers around the country carry stories about the building of the transcontinental railroad?** Possible answer: The project was a source of pride and interest to the American people. **Main Idea and Details**

✓ **REVIEW ANSWER** By then, the slow work of construction in the mountains was finished; construction on flatter land went more quickly. 🔄 Sequence

Over the Mountains

While the Union Pacific built track across the Great Plains, the Central Pacific was stuck in the steep slopes of the Sierra Nevada. "People laughed at the time [at the idea] of building a railroad across those ⑪ mountains," recalled Charles Crocker, one of the owners of the Central Pacific.

Like the Union Pacific, the Central Pacific had a hard time finding enough workers. Many of the people in California had come there to search for gold. They were not interested in railroad jobs that paid $35 a month. But thousands of young Chinese immigrants were interested in these jobs. Like so many other people, they had come to California with dreams of finding gold. Most, however, were treated unfairly at gold mining camps, ⑫ so they began looking for other opportunities.

Chinese immigrants made up about 80 percent of the Central Pacific workforce. Most of them were teenagers. These young men did the difficult work of blasting tunnels through the solid rock of the mountains. In a typical week, they used more explosives than were used during the biggest Civil War battles. Many workers were killed in accidents, but the work never stopped.

▶ Tunneling through mountains to lay railroad tracks was difficult and often dangerous work.

The Central Pacific finally finished building track through the mountains in 1867. Work then sped up, as tracks were built east across the Nevada desert. Almost every day, newspapers around the country printed stories about the race to build the transcontinental railroad. This project was a source of excitement and pride for many Americans. One Chicago newspaper wrote that people would soon "have an opportunity of bathing in the Atlantic one week and in the Pacific the next." This may not seem so amazing to us today, but it was a very new idea to Americans in the 1860s. ⑬

REVIEW Why was the Central Pacific able to build track more quickly after 1867? 🔄 Sequence

Practice and Extend

FYI SOCIAL STUDIES
Background

Building the Central Pacific

- Ground was broken in January 1863, in Sacramento, California.
- In addition to the Sierra Nevada, early construction was hampered by the fact that nearly all the materials had to be shipped around the tip of South America—a journey of 18,000 miles.
- The railroad included tunnels of 800 and 1,600 feet, along with numerous shorter tunnels, all blasted through the rock of the Sierra Nevada.
- After leaving the mountains, the Central Pacific crew set a record by laying more than 10 miles of track in a single day.

The Golden Spike

On May 10, 1869, the tracks of the Union Pacific and Central Pacific met at **Promontory Point, Utah Territory.** A special golden railroad spike was made to symbolize the success of the project. Leland Stanford, president of the Central Pacific, was given the honor of hammering the golden spike into the tracks. Stanford lifted a hammer, swung at the spike—and missed. People began celebrating anyway—the railroad was finished! The message "Done" was telegraphed from Utah to cities around the country.

The transcontinental railroad changed travel in the United States. Before this railroad, traveling across the continent took months and cost about $1,000. Now the trip could be made in a week for less than $100. As you will read, these new railroads brought change and conflict to the United States.

REVIEW How many years did it take to complete the transcontinental railroad?
> Sequence

Summarize the Lesson

- **1861** The first telegraph line across the United States was completed.

- **1862** The Union Pacific and Central Pacific began building the transcontinental railroad.

- **1869** The transcontinental railroad was completed at Promontory Point, Utah Territory.

LESSON 1 REVIEW

Check Facts and Main Ideas

1. > **Sequence** On a separate sheet of paper, fill in key events from this lesson in the order they happened.

> 1860: The Pony Express begins delivering mail across the West.

> 1861: The first telegraph line across the United States is completed.

> 1862: Building begins on the transcontinental railroad.

> 1867: The Central Pacific finishes building track through the mountains.

> 1869: The Transcontinental railroad is completed.

2. Why did new **telegraph** lines put the **Pony Express** out of business?

3. Describe two problems faced by the Union Pacific railroad.

4. What role did Chinese workers play in building the Central Pacific railroad?

5. **Critical Thinking: *Predict*** Suppose you lived in the United States in 1869. What kinds of changes would you expect the new **transcontinental railroad** to bring?

Link to Mathematics

Planning the Pony Express Suppose you were planning the Pony Express. You know the route is 2,000 miles. And you know each rider will ride 75 miles. What is the minimum number of riders you will need to hire?

133

CURRICULUM CONNECTION
Writing

Write a Speech

Have students write a speech to celebrate the completion of the transcontinental railroad. Students should focus on its significance to the business and the culture of the United States.

Workbook, p. 31

Lesson 1: Rails Across the Nation

Directions: Write the number of each item in Column A on the blank next to its description in Column B.

Column A	Column B
1. stagecoach	___ told Union Pacific workers that they were scaring away the buffalo
2. Pony Express	___ place where the Union Pacific and the Central Pacific met
3. telegraph	___ horse-drawn wagons that traveled in regular stages
4. Samuel Morse	
5. Union Pacific	___ invention that sent messages along wires using electricity
6. Central Pacific	
7. Red Cloud	___ developed a way to send telegraph messages
8. General William Tecumseh Sherman	___ part of transcontinental railroad that ran east from Sacramento, California
9. Promontory Point, Utah Territory	___ part of transcontinental railroad that ran west from Omaha, Nebraska
10. Sierra Nevada	___ major natural obstacle to the Central Pacific
	___ business that delivered mail from Missouri to California in just ten days
	___ warned Native American leaders that they could not stop the locomotive

Notes for Home: Your child learned about the building of the first transcontinental railroad.
Home Activity: Talk to your child about travel between the East and West today. How do people usually make this journey, and how long does it take?

Also on Teacher Resources CD-ROM.

The Golden Spike

⏱ **Quick Summary** The Union Pacific and Central Pacific railroads finally linked up at Promontory Point, Utah Territory, opening a new era of transportation in the United States.

14 What was the significance of the golden spike? Possible answers: It represented the successful completion of the project, as well as the financial success the railroad would bring.
Interpret Symbols

✓ **REVIEW ANSWER** Completing the railroad took about seven years.
> Sequence

3 Close and Assess

Summarize the Lesson

Tell students to read the lesson summary aloud. For each event, have them write another sentence that explains its significance.

✓ **LESSON 1 REVIEW**

1. > **Sequence** For possible answers, see the reduced pupil page.

2. The telegraph lines could carry messages in moments, much faster than the Pony Express.

3. The Union Pacific faced a shortage of labor and conflict with Native American groups along the route.

4. Chinese workers provided the labor necessary to accomplish the difficult, dangerous work of building the Central Pacific railroad.

5. **Critical Thinking: *Predict*** Possible answer: The railroad would bring more contact with people from different parts of the country. It would allow people to travel more frequently. It would lead to greater settlement in California and along the route.

Link to Mathematics

Make sure students set up the proper equation: 2000 divided by 75. Answer: 27 riders

Read a Time Zone Map

Objective
• Interpret information in maps.

Vocabulary
time zone, p. 134; **standard time,** p. 134

Resource
• Workbook, p. 32

1 Introduce and Motivate

What is a time zone map? Ask students how people might use time zone maps to plan different events. Then have students read the **What?** section of text on p. 134 to help set the purpose of the lesson.

Why use time zone maps? Have students read the **Why?** section of text on p. 134. Ask them to describe problems that might occur today if there was no standard time.

2 Teach and Discuss

How is this skill used? Examine with students the time zone map on p. 134.

Read a Time Zone Map

What? A **time zone** is an area on Earth that runs north and south in which all places have the same time. Earth is divided into 24 different time zones. **Standard time** is the time set by law for all the places in a time zone.

Why? At one time, each community decided its own time. Because of this, two communities that were close to each other might have different times. This could be confusing and was not practical. Problems increased when trains started to cross the country in the 1870s. Think of how confusing train schedules would have been if ① each town on a railroad line decided its own time. People needed a time system they could depend on.

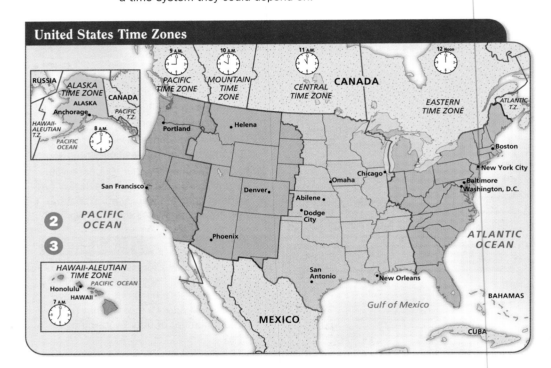

United States Time Zones

134

Practice and Extend

SOCIAL STUDIES STRAND
Geography

The following map resources are available:
• Big Book Atlas
• Student Atlas
• Outline Maps
• Desk Maps
• Map Resources CD-ROM

Decision Making

Use a Decision-Making Process

• Have students consider the following scenario: **You live in Massachusetts. You want to call your cousin who lives in Alaska. Your cousin goes to sleep at 9:00 P.M. and wakes up at 7:00 A.M. When should you call so that you do not wake her up?**

• Students should use the following process to decide what time to call. For each step, have students discuss and write about what must be considered as they make their decision. Write the steps above on the board or read them aloud.

1. **Identify a situation that requires a decision.**
2. **Gather information.**
3. **Identify options.**
4. **Predict consequences.**
5. **Take action to implement a decision.**

| Alaska Time | Pacific Time | Mountain Time | Central Time | Eastern Time |

To solve this problem, in the late 1870s, Canadian railway engineer Sandford Fleming worked out a plan for the 24 worldwide time zones that are used today.

If you drive from New York to California, you go through four of these time zones. It is important for you to know when the time changes and what time it is in the new zone. You would also need to have this information if you have promised to telephone someone at a particular time in a part of the country that is in a different time zone.

How? The map shows the six time zones of the United States. Standard time in each is one hour different from the time in the zone on either side. To help you understand how this works, look at the clocks shown with each time zone. Notice that each time zone has a name. Standard time is the same throughout each time zone.

To use a time zone map, you need to know whether you are east or west of another time zone. The time in a zone that is east of you is later than the time in your zone. The time in a zone that is west of you is earlier than the time in your zone.

If you were to travel east, you would move your watch ahead one hour for each time zone you entered. If you were to travel west, you would move your watch back one hour for each time zone you entered.

For example, say you live in San Antonio, and your watch shows that the time is 3:00 P.M. What is the time in New York City and in San Francisco? Find all three cities on the map and note the time zone of each. San Antonio is in the Central time zone. In which time zone is New York City? San Francisco? New York City is one time zone to the east of San Antonio. So the time there is one hour later than your time, or 4:00 P.M. San Francisco is two time zones to the west, so the time there is two hours earlier than your time, or 1:00 P.M.

Think and Apply

1. What time zone do you live in?

2. In what time zones are Denver and Boston? What time is it in Denver when it is 12 noon in Boston?

3. If you are in Baltimore and want to watch a ballgame that starts at 2:00 P.M. in Chicago, what time should you turn on your television set?

Internet Activity

For more information, go online to the *Atlas* at www.sfsocialstudies.com.

135

- Point out that the map shows the boundaries between each of the six time zones in the United States.

- Tell students that the times on the clocks show the times that correspond to each time zone at one particular time. Ask them to name a few places in each time zone.

- Students may be interested to learn that China, a large country that is slightly smaller than the United States, has only one time zone.

- Have students read the **How?** section of text on p. 135.

1 **Why were time zones developed?** Possible answer: A dependable time system made train travel practical and less confusing. Main Idea and Details

2 **What happens to time as you go from east to west in the United States?** The time gets earlier. Analyze Information

Test Talk

Use Information from Graphics

3 **What is the time difference between Washington, D.C., and New Orleans?** Tell students to use details from the map to support their answer. 1 hour Interpret Maps

3 Close and Assess

Think and Apply

1. Answers will vary; help students use the map to find their time zone.

2. Denver is in the Mountain Time Zone, and Boston is in the Eastern Time Zone. It is 10:00 A.M. in Denver when it is 12 noon in Boston.

3. 3:00 P.M.

CURRICULUM CONNECTION
Math

Solve Time Word Problems

- Suppose you are in Georgia. At 6:32 P.M. you phone a friend in San Antonio, Texas. If the conversation lasts for 42 minutes, what time is it in Texas when the call ends? (6:14 P.M. Central Time)

- You are in Portland, Oregon, and must make a 15-minute call to a company in Baltimore. If the company closes at 5:00 P.M. Eastern Time, what is the latest time that you could place the call? (1:45 P.M. Pacific Time)

Also on Teacher Resources CD-ROM.

Westward Growth of America, 1607–1862

Objectives

- Identify key events involved in and reasons for Americans' movement westward.

- Identify the physical constraints and technological advances that challenged and aided Americans' movement westward, including natural terrain and advances in modes of transportation.

1 Introduce and Motivate

- Review with students the location of the original 13 colonies. Explain that before the year 1800, most Americans lived east of the Mississippi River.

- Have students point out on the map the natural physical barriers that may have made travel west difficult. Include major landforms, such as the Appalachian Mountains, Mississippi River, and Rocky Mountains, as well as terrain obstacles (dense forests, vegetation, etc.).

- Have students list the reasons they think many Americans wanted to move west. Reasons should include land ownership, farmland, economic opportunity, and religious freedom.

2 Teach and Discuss

SOCIAL STUDIES STRAND
History

"A Map of the British and French Dominions in North America."
This map was created by John Mitchell, a mapmaker in London, England, in 1755. Mitchell never traveled to North America. He constructed this map using drawings, maps, and surveys created by others. The boundary lines stretching westward show that Americans were looking toward the west from the very beginning.

Westward Growth of America, 1607-1862

John Mitchell published this map of North America in 1775. You can see from the map that Americans were looking west very early in our history. Over time, people moved west and the nation expanded. Here are some key events in the westward growth of our nation.

136

Practice and Extend

FYI **SOCIAL STUDIES**
Background

Looking to the West *by Dr. William E. White, Colonial Williamsburg Historian*

- During the eighteenth and nineteenth centuries, Americans moved westward. Some people sought the freedom and adventure of living on the frontier. Some people wanted to find land of their own to farm. Some people set up new businesses. Some people harvested the natural resources of the wilderness.

- According to James Madison, by 1803 America had "fixed its destiny westward and secured room to grow in freedom for generations to come."

- Over time, technology made travel west much faster. Canals created smooth travel, without challenges in terrain. Wagon trains made cross-country travel possible for pioneer families. Steamboats turned rivers into major travel routes.

- As people moved west, travel became faster and more efficient. Pioneers took months to reach the Pacific from the Midwest. When the Union Pacific opened in 1870, a person could go from Omaha to San Francisco in just four days.

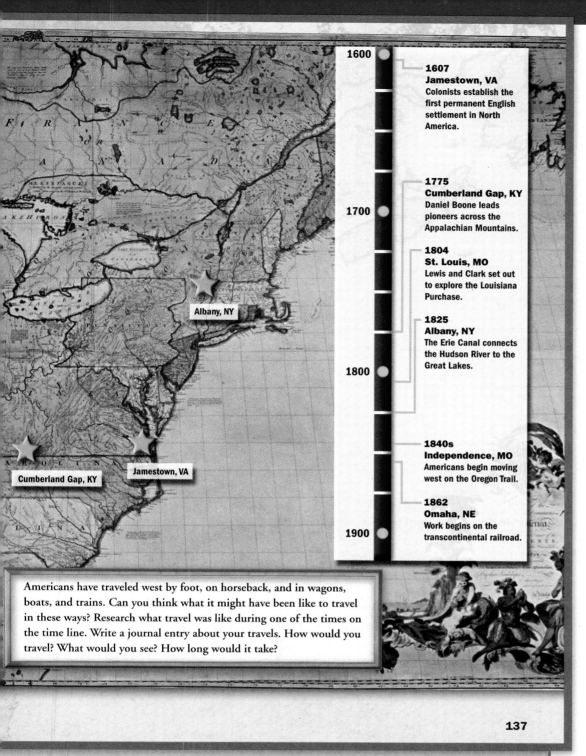

1600

1607
Jamestown, VA
Colonists establish the first permanent English settlement in North America.

1700

1775
Cumberland Gap, KY
Daniel Boone leads pioneers across the Appalachian Mountains.

1804
St. Louis, MO
Lewis and Clark set out to explore the Louisiana Purchase.

1825
Albany, NY
The Erie Canal connects the Hudson River to the Great Lakes.

1800

1840s
Independence, MO
Americans begin moving west on the Oregon Trail.

1862
Omaha, NE
Work begins on the transcontinental railroad.

1900

Albany, NY

Cumberland Gap, KY   Jamestown, VA

Americans have traveled west by foot, on horseback, and in wagons, boats, and trains. Can you think what it might have been like to travel in these ways? Research what travel was like during one of the times on the time line. Write a journal entry about your travels. How would you travel? What would you see? How long would it take?

137

- Jamestown, 1607—Settlers from England arrived aboard three ships—the *Discovery,* the *Godspeed,* and the *Susan Constance.* The journey from Europe took about 144 days. Ask students what difficulties they might encounter traveling on a boat for such a long period of time.

- Cumberland Gap, 1775—Pioneers traveled on foot and horseback along the Wilderness Road. The gap was widened in the 1790s to allow for Conestoga wagons to pass through. Ask students why pioneers would have wanted this trail widened.

- Lewis and Clark Expedition, 1804–1806—The Lewis and Clark expedition traveled by boat, on foot, and on horseback. They moved west against river currents and over the Rocky Mountains. Ask students what supplies they think would be helpful for Lewis and Clark to have brought on their expedition.

- Erie Canal, 1825—The Erie Canal connected Albany, New York, on the Hudson River, to Lake Erie. Once completed, goods could be shipped by boat throughout New York. Ask students how they think life changed along the canal once it was built.

- Oregon Trail, 1840s—Pioneers traveled by covered wagons, horseback, and on foot. The trip, which covered rugged terrain and Indian territory, took about four to six months.

- Transcontinental Railroad, 1862—This railroad allowed for travel across the entire continent by steam locomotive in ten days. Have students discuss why this technology might encourage more Americans to move west.

Calculate Travel Time

- Mention that St. Louis, Missouri, is about 562 miles from Pittsburgh, Pennsylvania.

- Ask students to calculate how long it would take a person to travel from Pittsburgh to St. Louis in each of the following ways (for each, divide 562 by the number of miles per hour):

    1. On foot, at 3 miles per hour. *187.3 hours, or almost 8 days*

    2. On horseback, at 5 miles per hour. *112.4 hours, or about 4-1/2 days*

    3. By steam locomotive, at 30 miles per hour. *18.7 hours*

Workbook, p. 33

Directions: Suppose that you are an American moving west on the Oregon Trail during the mid-1800s. Write a diary entry about your travels. Describe the people you meet and the challenges and opportunities you face along the way.

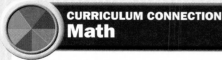

Also on Teacher Resources CD-ROM.

3 Close and Assess

- Have each student choose one method of travel from the time line. Brainstorm with students what details they might include in a travel journal.

- Have students research their mode of travel. Encourage students to look for things such as how travelers prepared and what obstacles they encountered. Have students write, from a pioneer traveler's perspective, a journal entry describing what it was like to travel in that manner.

Pioneers on the Plains

Objectives

- Describe the purpose of the Homestead Act.

- Evaluate the challenges that homesteaders faced.

- Analyze the reasons why exodusters came to the Great Plains.

- Explain how technology helped pioneers turn the Great Plains into productive farmland.

Vocabulary

pioneer, p. 139; **Homestead Act,** p. 139; **homesteader,** p. 139; **sodbuster,** p. 140; **exoduster,** p. 141; **technology,** p. 142

Resources

- Workbook, p. 34
- Transparency 10
- Every Student Learns Guide, pp. 54–57
- Quick Study, pp. 28–29

Quick Teaching Plan

If time is short, have students go through the lesson and write each of the section headings on a piece of paper.

- Have students convert each heading into a question, and then find answers to these questions as they read the lesson independently.

1 Introduce and Motivate

Preview To activate prior knowledge, ask students to think about a time when they have faced a difficult or exciting challenge. (Examples include moving to a new town or going on a camping trip.) Tell them that they will learn about the challenges and difficulties settlers faced to settle and cultivate the Great Plains.

 Have students think about the many things that might be going through Howard Ruede's mind as he wrote the letter. Tell them that they will be learning more about the highs and lows of life on the plains.

138 Unit 2 • An Expanding Nation

LESSON 2

GREAT PLAINS
•Nicodemus

1860			1880
1862 Lincoln signs the Homestead Act.	**1874** Joseph Glidden invents barbed wire.	**1877** African American pioneers establish Nicodemus, Kansas.	

PREVIEW

Focus on the Main Idea
Farmers began settling in the Great Plains in the 1860s, and they soon turned the plains into a productive farming region.

PLACES
Great Plains
Nicodemus, Kansas

PEOPLE
Willa Cather
Benjamin Singleton
George Shima

VOCABULARY
pioneer
Homestead Act
homesteader
sodbuster
exoduster
technology

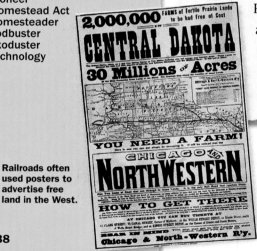

► Railroads often used posters to advertise free land in the West.

138

Pioneers on the Plains

You Are There Howard Ruede (ROO day) has just finished building his new home—if you can call it a home. Actually, it is a hole in the ground, with a roof of wood. At least it will keep out the wind and some of the rain.

It is the summer of 1877, and this 23-year-old from Pennsylvania has just moved west to Kansas. He brought his entire life savings of about $50. Luckily, his underground house only cost $10 to build.

Sitting on a homemade chair in his dark, damp home, Ruede writes a letter to his family in Pennsylvania. He describes his new land and the farm he dreams of building. "The sweat runs off of me," he writes, "and some of the drops wet the paper; so if you can't read it you'll know the reason."

Sequence As you read, list the sequence of events that brought change to the Great Plains.

Practice and Extend

READING SKILL Sequence

In the Lesson Review, students complete a graphic organizer like the one below. You may want to provide students with a copy of Transparency 10 to complete as they read the lesson.

Use Transparency 10

```
┌─────────────┐
│             │
└─────────────┘
      ↓
┌─────────────┐
│             │
└─────────────┘
      ↓
┌─────────────┐
│             │
└─────────────┘
      ↓
┌─────────────┐
│             │
└─────────────┘
```

VOCABULARY Word Exercise

Related Word Study

Write *pioneer, homesteader, sodbuster,* and *exoduster* on the board. Ask students to figure out how to create a word map illustrating the relationship between these words. For example, the center oval could be labeled *pioneers,* since all of these settlers were pioneers. An oval off of this oval could be labeled *homesteader,* and then two ovals off of that could be labeled *sodbuster* and *exoduster.*

The Great Plains

How would you like to move to a place nick-named the "Great American Desert"? This is what many Americans called the **Great Plains** in the mid-1800s. They looked at the plains and saw a vast region of dry grassland in the middle of the country. They saw few trees, harsh weather, and low rainfall. People did not think the Great Plains would ever make good farmland.

The United States government wanted to encourage **pioneers,** or new settlers, to move to the Great Plains. Leaders hoped that with hard work, pioneers could turn the plains into productive farmland. New railroad lines could then carry farm goods from the Great Plains to growing cities in the East.

But how do you encourage people to move to the "Great American Desert"? The govern-ment's solution was to give the land away. In 1862 President Abraham Lincoln signed the **Homestead Act.** This law offered free land to American citizens and immigrants who were willing to start new farms on the Great Plains.

If you were a man over the age of twenty-one, or a woman who was the head of a family, you could claim 160 acres of land. You had to pay a small fee—usually about $10. You had to farm your land and live on it for five years. Then the land was yours.

Now you know why Howard Ruede left his home and family in Pennsylvania to move to the Great Plains in Kansas. Ruede dreamed of owning land of his own. With a life savings of just $50, he could afford land on the Great Plains because of the Homestead Act.

Settlers who claimed land through the Homestead Act were called **homesteaders.** Like many homesteaders, Howard Ruede traveled by train to his new home. Getting there was the easy part. Building a success-ful farm on the Great Plains would take many years of hard work.

REVIEW What steps did a homesteader have to take to become a landowner?
⟳ Sequence

▶ Much of the Great Plains may look flat, but the land actually rises slowly from east to west. The land reaches elevations of more than 5,000 feet at the base of the Rocky Mountains.

139

2 Teach and Discuss

PAGE 139

The Great Plains

🕐 *Quick Summary* The Great Plains was known as the Great American Desert, but the Homestead Act led thousands of pioneers to move there.

❶ What factors made many people believe that the Great Plains would not make good farmland? Possible answer: Lack of wood, rainfall, and transportation, as well as harsh weather
Main Idea and Details

✓ **Ongoing Assessment**

If... students do not understand the significant obstacles that faced farmers on the Great Plains,

then... have them write a list of conditions and resources that farmers need to be successful, and have them compare this list to the conditions and resources facing farmers on the Great Plains.

❷ Why do you think the United States government wanted people to settle on the Great Plains? Possible answer: It would help the nation grow and expand.
Draw Conclusions

G **STUDIES STRAND**
Government

Democratic Values and Institutions Explain that governments use laws and policies to encourage behavior and to promote specific goals.

❸ Why did the United States government institute the Homestead Act? Possible answer: The government wanted to encourage people to settle on the Great Plains, and the Homestead Act made settlement there attractive.
Summarize

✓ **REVIEW ANSWER** The would-be homesteader had to reach age 21, claim land, pay a fee, and then remain on the land for 5 years. **⟳ Sequence**

Settling on the Plains

🕐 **Quick Summary** The sod of the Great Plains was difficult to break through—and tough enough to use as a building material. It also covered rich soil.

4 **Why were the early pioneers on the Great Plains known as "sodbusters"?** Possible answer: The task of breaking up the sod for planting was very difficult and took up much of their time. Summarize

5 **What did the pioneers discover when they were able to plant their crops?** Possible answer: To their surprise, the soil was rich and supported crops very well. **Main Idea and Details**

Primary Source

Cited in *O Pioneers!,* by Willa Cather

6 **What does Cather mean when she says the soil "had its little joke"?** Possible answer: It appeared to be poor, when in fact it was very rich. **Analyze Primary Sources**

✓ **REVIEW ANSWER** The Great Plains had few trees for building houses. **Main Idea and Details**

Settling on the Plains

Before they could plant crops on their properties, homesteaders had to rip up the grass on their land. This was not as easy as it sounds. The grasses on the Great Plains had thick, tangled roots that reached several inches down into the soil. Because they had to bust through this "sod" before planting crops, Great Plains farmers were called **4** sodbusters.

After ripping up the sod from their land, most sodbusters used the sod to build houses. In a region with few trees, sod was a very useful building material. Houses built from blocks of sod stayed cool in summer and warm in winter, and they were fireproof. Unfortunately for homesteaders, the sod walls were often home to bugs, mice, and snakes.

Once homesteaders were able to plant crops, they found that the soil was very **5** fertile. This was not the "Great American Desert" after all! Author **Willa Cather,** who grew up on the plains of Nebraska, described changing feelings about the Great Plains in her famous novel *O Pioneers!* In one scene a pioneer named Alexandra tells her friend Carl about her struggle to build a farm:

"We hadn't any of us much to do with it, Carl. The land did it. It had its little joke. It pretended to be poor because nobody knew how to work it right; and then, all at once, it worked itself. It woke up out of its sleep and stretched itself, and it was so big, so rich, that we suddenly found we were rich, just from sitting still." **6**

REVIEW Why was sod a useful building material for homesteaders? **Main Idea and Details**

▶ This pioneer family built a sod house in Nebraska.

140

Practice and Extend

MEETING INDIVIDUAL NEEDS
Leveled Practice

Research the Great Plains Have students use library and Internet resources to explore the environment that pioneers on the Great Plains encountered.

Easy Have students write a one-paragraph explanation of the vegetation, climate, and soil conditions of the Great Plains. **Reteach**

On-Level Have students write one paragraph each on the vegetation, climate, soil, and other resources of the Great Plains. **Extend**

Challenge Have students create an illustrated notebook, with one page each on the major geographic characteristics of the Great Plains. **Enrich**

For a Lesson Summary, use Quick Study, p. 28.

America Fever

Stories about the fertile soil of the Great Plains spread quickly to Europe. The desire to move to this region was so strong that it became known as "America Fever." Thousands of families from Germany, Sweden, Norway, Russia, and other European countries crossed the Atlantic Ocean to begin new lives on the Great Plains.

Many of these immigrants brought valuable farming skills to the United States. Farmers from Russia, for example, brought seeds for a hardy type of wheat they had grown at home. American farmers were having a hard time finding a type of wheat that could survive the weather on the Great Plains. The wheat brought from Russia grew well on the plains. The Great Plains soon became one of the world's most productive wheat-growing regions—and it still is today.

The Homestead Act also provided opportunities for African American homesteaders. As you have read, African Americans continued to face unfair treatment after the end of slavery. In the 1870s, a carpenter named **Benjamin Singleton** began urging his fellow African Americans to leave the South and move to the Great Plains. "We needed land for our children," he later explained.

Calling themselves **exodusters**, thousands of African American pioneers started new lives in communities on the Great Plains, such as **Nicodemus, Kansas**. The name "exodusters" came from a book of the Bible called Exodus. This book tells the story of Moses leading the Israelites out of slavery. Many southern African Americans felt that their story was similar—they too were making a journey to freedom. An exoduster named John Solomon Lewis never forgot the first thing he said when he arrived in Kansas: "This is free ground." **8**

REVIEW How did European farmers contribute to the success of farming on the Great Plains? Draw Conclusions

Nicodemus, Kansas

The town of Nicodemus (nik uh DEE muhs), Kansas, was founded by African American pioneers in 1877. By the end of the 1880s, Nicodemus had grown **9** into a bustling town, with stores, churches, newspapers, a school, and a baseball team. Today Nicodemus lives on as a symbol of freedom and opportunity. Visitors come from all over the country to see the town's historic buildings and celebrate the important contributions of African American pioneers.

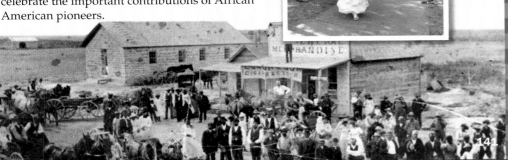

CURRICULUM CONNECTION
Math

Calculate Crop Yields

- Suppose a homesteader had planted 150 of his or her 160 acres.
- With old, conventional seeds, the farmer could harvest 75 bushels of wheat per acre. How much wheat could he or she raise? (75 × 150 = 11,250 bushels)
- New seeds from Europe could yield 100 bushels per acre. How much wheat could the farmer grow using the new seeds? (100 × 150 = 15,000 bushels)

America Fever

Quick Summary The Great Plains soon attracted opportunity-seekers from around the world and across the United States. Immigrants from Europe and African Americans seeking freedom led the way.

Test Talk

Locate Key Words in the Question

7 **Why do you think people in Europe developed "America Fever"?** Have students turn the question into a statement. Students should use the key words in a sentence that begins, "I need to find out why. . . ." Possible answer: The United States and the Great Plains offered opportunities that were unavailable in Europe. Draw Conclusions

8 **What can you infer about life on the Great Plains from the fact that African Americans sought opportunity there?** Possible answer: People were likely to be treated more fairly there than in the South. Make Inferences

✓ **REVIEW ANSWER** They introduced new farming techniques and new crop varieties. Draw Conclusions

Nicodemus, Kansas

9 **What details support the idea that Nicodemus was a successful community?** Possible answer: It had stores, churches, newspapers, a school, and a baseball team. Main Idea and Details

Life on the Plains

⏱ *Quick Summary* The Great Plains had great soil—but the area also had many hazards and obstacles for those who chose to farm there.

⑩ How did the weather on the Great Plains threaten pioneers? Possible answers: Extreme temperatures and storms threatened their crops and their lives. Summarize

Primary Source
Cited in *Story of the Great American West*, by the editors of *Reader's Digest*

⑪ What does this quotation suggest about the destructiveness of prairie fires? Possible answer: The fires could destroy a huge area and everything it contained. Analyze Primary Sources

⑫ How did grasshoppers threaten the farmers of the Great Plains? They ate their crops—and even their fencing and tools. Main Idea and Details

✓ **REVIEW ANSWER** Harsh weather, natural disasters, and grasshoppers made life difficult for homesteaders. Summarize

---

Life on the Plains

The Great Plains may have had fertile soil, but that does not mean it was easy to build a successful farm. As the Fact File on the next page shows, new technology helped make life on the Great Plains a little bit easier. **Technology** is the use of new ideas to make tools that improve people's lives. Even with technology, though, homesteaders had to work hard to survive. A pioneer from England named Percy Ebbutt put it simply: "You must make up your mind to rough it."

Roughing it included facing the harsh weather and natural disasters of the Great Plains. Bitter cold and deadly blizzards swept along the plains in winter. Spring often brought tornadoes, hailstorms, and flooding. Summer could mean blazing heat and little rain. In fall the grasses dried and settlers ⑩ had to watch out for fires. A pioneer from Norway named Gro Svendsen described these fires in a letter to his family:

⑪ *"It is a strange and terrible sight to see all the fields a sea of fire. Quite often the scorching flames sweep everything along in their path—people, cattle, hay, fences."*

▶ A farmer hopes for rain on the Great Plains.

If the weather was not enough to worry about, farmers also faced the dreaded grasshopper. In the mid-1870s, millions of grasshoppers swarmed across the Great Plains. Green bugs darkened the sky and covered the ground in layers up to six inches thick. Grasshoppers ate everything in their path—crops, grass, and even fences and axe handles. After seeing her crops destroyed by one of these invasions, homesteader Mattie Oblinger wrote, "Nebraska would have had a splendid crop if the grasshoppers had stayed away a while." ⑫

REVIEW What challenges made life difficult for homesteaders? Summarize

▶ This painting by Winslow Homer from 1871, called *The Country School,* gives an idea what school was like for children of pioneers in the West.

142

Practice and Extend

MEETING INDIVIDUAL NEEDS
Learning Styles

Describe the Dangers of the Great Plains Using their individual learning styles, students will describe the dangers facing homesteaders on the Great Plains.

Linguistic Learning Have students write creative descriptions of hazards facing pioneers living on the Great Plains.

Musical Learning Have students compose and/or perform a song that conveys the extremes of weather and the other hazards that pioneers faced on the Great Plains.

Social Learning Have students work in groups to discuss the dangers of life on the Great Plains. Students should write and present a short skit about one hazard pioneers faced.

FACT FILE

Technology on the Plains

Farming the Great Plains presented many new challenges. Here are some of the technologies that helped pioneers turn the "Great American Desert" into one of the world's richest farming regions.

Steel Plows Iron plows used in the East did not work well on the tough sod and thick soil of the Great Plains. An inventor named John Deere began building stronger steel plows in 1837. In the 1860s farmers could buy steel plows that were specially made for farming on the Great Plains.

Windmills Most of the water in the Great Plains is deep underground. New types of windmills were designed to pump this water up to the surface. Steady winds on the Great Plains made windmills a useful power source for farmers. **13**

Barbed Wire Farmers always need fences to keep animals away from their crops. In a region with little wood, however, Great Plains farmers had a hard time finding material to build fences. Joseph Glidden solved this problem by inventing barbed wire in 1874. Barbed wire fences were cheap and easy to build.

Dry Farming The dry Great Plains climate forced farmers to find new ways to grow their crops. Farmers adapted to the lack of rain by developing a method called "dry farming." This method uses moisture stored in the soil, rather than rainfall. Dry farming allowed Great Plains farmers to grow wheat and other crops.

143

FACT FILE

Technology on the Plains

13 **Which of the items allowed farmers to take advantage of a feature of the Great Plains climate?** The windmill used the steady winds of the Great Plains as a way to provide water.
Analyze Information

Problem Solving

14 **How did barbed wire help solve the problem of a lack of wood on the Great Plains?** Possible answer: It made it possible for farmers to build long fences without using a lot of wood.
Solve Problems

15 **Summarize the idea behind dry farming.** Possible answer: Dry farming was a method of growing crops without using as much water on the surface as regular farming. It made maximum use of the available water. Summarize

---

SOCIAL STUDIES
Background

The Great Plains

- The grasses of the Great Plains often grew over three feet tall. The roots of these grasses stretched even deeper down into the soil in an effort to reach water deep in the ground.

- Hailstorms are common on the Great Plains. Large hailstones—some several inches in diameter—can destroy crops.

- Parts of the Great Plains experience frequent tornadoes because of their location north of the warm, moist Gulf of Mexico and the absence of mountain barriers. Much of the region is part of what people call "tornado alley."

- Another unusual weather phenomenon on the Great Plains is the Chinook—a warm winter wind that can drive temperatures up 50°F and cause considerable melting of snow.

Growth in the West

Quick Summary The growth of the Great Plains took place at a time when many people were settling other parts of the western United States.

SOCIAL STUDIES STRAND
Geography

Help students recognize that the West Coast of the United States is to Asia as the East Coast is to Europe.

16 **Why do you think the West attracted immigrants from Asia?** Possible answer: People seeking economic opportunities in the United States would arrive in California, which is located directly across the Pacific Ocean from Asia. **Draw Conclusions**

✓ **REVIEW ANSWER** Railroads helped transport people and supplies to the West, and they linked the West to the markets of the East. **Cause and Effect**

Close and Assess

Summarize the Lesson

Tell students to examine the time line. Ask them to summarize the lesson by reviewing how the events are related.

✓ **LESSON 2** **REVIEW**

1. **Sequence** For possible answers, see the reduced pupil page.

2. That it would lead to the settlement of the Great Plains

3. Exodusters were people recently freed from slavery who sought opportunities and an escape from discrimination.

4. Possible answers: The steel plow, the windmill, barbed wire, dry farming

5. **Critical Thinking:** *Decision Making* Possible answers: Yes, the benefits of going outweighed the risks; No, the risks were too great.

Link to ——— Writing
Make sure students' letters accurately reflect pioneer life.

144 Unit 2 • An Expanding Nation

Growth in the West

While pioneers were settling on the Great Plains, people were also moving farther west. New railroad lines brought thousands of people to Washington, Oregon, and California. Towns at the western end of railroad lines, such as Seattle, in Washington, and Los Angeles, in California, quickly grew into important cities.

The West also attracted farmers from other countries. In the late 1800s, thousands of Japanese immigrants began arriving in California. Many Japanese families built successful farms in the West. You will read about one successful Japanese farmer, **George Shima** (SHEE mah), in the Biography on the next page.

16

REVIEW How did railroads help the West to grow? **Cause and Effect**

Summarize the Lesson

- **1862** The Homestead Act gave Americans and immigrants free land on the Great Plains.

- **1874** Joseph Glidden invented barbed wire, one of many technologies that made life easier for Great Plains farmers.

- **1877** Nicodemus, Kansas, was founded, one of many towns built by African American pioneers.

LESSON 2 **REVIEW**

Check Facts and Main Ideas

1. **Sequence** Redraw this diagram on a separate sheet of paper, putting the events in their correct order. Include the year of each event.

> 1837 John Deere built stronger steel plow
>
> ↓
>
> 1862 Homestead Act passed
>
> ↓
>
> 1874 Barbed wire invented
>
> ↓
>
> 1877 Nicodemus, Kansas, founded

2. What did the government hope that the **Homestead Act** would accomplish?

3. Who were the **exodusters**? What caused them to move to the Great Plains?

4. Describe two inventions that helped pioneers on the Great Plains.

5. **Critical Thinking:** *Decision Making* You know about the difficulties of living and farming on the Great Plains. Would you have wanted to be a **homesteader**? Use the Decision Making steps on page H3.

Link to ——— Writing

Write a Letter Suppose you are a young homesteader in Kansas. Write a letter to your family in the East describing your new life. What have you accomplished? What challenges do you face? Do you expect to stay in Kansas for a long time? Why or why not?

144

Practice and Extend

FAST FACTS

- Los Angeles was linked to the East when a rail line was established in 1876, connecting the still small city to San Francisco. Later, the Southern Pacific railroad created a southern route that linked Los Angeles to New Orleans.

- The Great Northern railroad linked Seattle to the East in 1893. Later in that decade, Seattle became a boomtown and jumping off point for the Yukon Gold Rush.

Workbook p. 34

Lesson 2: Pioneers on the Plains

Directions: Using information from the lesson, circle the term in parentheses that best completes each sentence.

1. The government hoped that the (Homestead Act, sodbusters) would encourage pioneers to move to the Great Plains.

2. The famous novel *O Pioneers!*, by (Benjamin Singleton, Willa Cather), describes homesteaders' changing feelings about the Great Plains.

3. Europeans' desire to move to the Great Plains was so strong it became known as ("America Fever," the "Great American Desert").

4. African American pioneers called themselves (homesteaders, exodusters), after a book in the Bible that tells the story of Moses leading the Israelites out of slavery.

5. (Grasshoppers, Technology) helped make life easier for Great Plains farmers.

Directions: In the space below, write a letter to a friend as a pioneer on the Great Plains in the 1800s. Describe the hardships and the opportunities you face.

Dear _____

_____

_____

_____

_____

Your Friend,

_____

Notes for Home: Your child learned about the settlement of the Great Plains during the late 1800s and how new technologies helped these settlers.
Home Activity: Review the Fast Facts on page 143 with your child. Then talk with your child about how they hoped improve your daily lives.

Also on Teacher's Ancillary Library CD-ROM.

George Shima
1863(?)–1926

George Shima, who was born in Japan, arrived in California in 1888. He was so poor that he had nothing to eat. He soon got a job harvesting potatoes and pulling up tree stumps on a farm in the San Joaquin (wah KEEN) Valley. Shima did whatever he could to learn about farming. He later remembered:

Shima was the first grower to wash and classify potatoes before selling them, so that the best of his crop could be sold for more money.

BIOFACT

"I began to study books, talk to farmers, and learn about growing things."

Soon, Shima had made enough money to rent ten acres of land, where he experimented with growing potatoes. He made farmland on the many small, marshy islands in the San Joaquin River by pumping water out of the soil, creating ideal conditions for growing potatoes. Over time, he bought and drained more land, planting potatoes everywhere. Soon, he had a quickly expanding business that made him wealthy. Shima became known as the "Potato King."

But things were not always easy. Despite his success, Shima sometimes met discrimination. When he bought a new home near a university, some white people protested. But Shima would not move. The United States was his home, he said, and his family would stay.

Shima became an important leader in his community. He was president of the Japanese Association of California for many years. Shima also donated food to those in need and paid for college educations for poor students.

Learn from Biographies

Like many immigrants, George Shima made contributions to the United States. What were some of his contributions?

For more information, go to *Meet the People* at **www.sfsocialstudies.com.**

145

SOCIAL STUDIES STRAND
Economics

Staple Crops Tell students that some countries' economies depend heavily on the success of a particular crop.

- In the early 1800s, potatoes were the principal food eaten by about half of the population of Ireland.
- In 1845, and for four years following, diseased potato crops rotted in the fields in Ireland.
- More than one million Irish people died of starvation or other diseases. Many others immigrated to North America and to Britain.

WEB SITE
Technology

Students can find out more about George Shima by clicking on *Meet the People* at **www.sfsocialstudies.com.**

George Shima

Objective
- Identify the contributions of people from selected immigrant groups.

1 Introduce and Motivate

Preview To activate prior knowledge, ask students what they know about growing plants. Tell students they will read about a Japanese immigrant who faced challenges and developed a successful method for growing potatoes.

2 Teach and Discuss

1 How do you think George Shima got the idea of pumping water out of the land? He learned about the conditions needed for growing potatoes by working on farms, reading, and talking to farmers. **Draw Conclusions**

2 What is one detail that supports the idea that Shima experienced discrimination? Some white people did not want him to live in their neighborhood. **Main Idea and Details**

3 Close and Assess

Learn from Biographies **Answer**

Shima was an important leader in his community. He donated food to those in need and paid for college educations for some poor students.

Read Climographs

Objective
- Interpret information in climographs.

Vocabulary
climograph, p. 146

Resources
- Workbook, p. 35

1 Introduce and Motivate

What is a climograph? Ask students to list reasons why they might need information about the climate of a place (For example, if they were traveling to or thinking of starting a business in a place). Then have students read the **What?** section of text on p. 146 to help set the purpose of the lesson.

Why use climographs? Have students read the **Why?** section of text on p. 146. Ask them to think about how climate may have been a special concern of people living in the past, and how it remains a concern today. Guide students to infer the advantages that climographs give people today.

2 Teach and Discuss

How is this skill used? Examine with students the climograph on p. 146.

- Point out that the climograph gives two key pieces of information about Omaha, Nebraska: information on precipitation and on average temperature.

- Point out that the climograph presents information by the month. This helps students see how the climate changes with each month and with each season.

- Have students read the **How?** section of text on p. 147.

Chart and Graph Skills

Read Climographs

What? A climograph is a graph that shows two kinds of information about the climate of a place. It shows both the average temperature and the average precipitation—rain or snow—for a particular place over a period of time. You can see examples of climographs on this page and the next page.

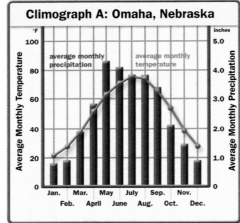

Climograph A: Omaha, Nebraska

Why? Climographs help you understand the typical climate of a place. You have been reading about farmers of the Great Plains during the late 1800s. Some people called this region the "Great American Desert." You learned that despite harsh weather and little rain, farmers were able to successfully grow crops. To study the climate of the Great Plains today, you can use a climograph.

▶ **Omaha, Nebraska**

146

Practice and Extend

 Decision Making

Use a Decision-Making Process

- Have students consider the following scenario: **You live near Omaha, Nebraska. You have some seeds you would like to plant. The package says that the seeds grow best when the average temperature stays above 60 degrees for the 3 months it takes the plants to mature. When should you plant your seeds?**

- Students should use the following process to decide when to plant. For each step, have students discuss and write about what must be considered as they make their decision. Write the steps above on the board or read them aloud.

1. **Identify a situation that requires a decision.**
2. **Gather information.**
3. **Identify options.**
4. **Predict consequences.**
5. **Take action to implement a decision.**

How? Climograph A shows the average monthly temperature and precipitation today in Omaha, Nebraska, a city in the Great Plains. Read each of the labels at the sides. The left side labels the average monthly temperatures in degrees Fahrenheit (°F).

1 Temperature is shown on the line graph. You can see that the average January temperature for Omaha is about 21° Fahrenheit. You can see that the average temperature in July for Omaha is about 77°F.

The right side of the graph shows average monthly precipitation. Precipitation is shown

2 on the bar graph. The average precipitation in January for Omaha is about 0.8 inches. What is the average monthly precipitation in July for Omaha?

Climograph B shows the average monthly temperatures and precipitation for Winchester, Virginia. Author Willa Cather was born near Winchester and moved with her family at age nine to Nebraska. Compare the average January temperatures for Omaha, Nebraska, and Winchester, Virginia. Which is colder? How do you know? Which receives more precipitation in November? How do you know?

▶ **Winchester, Virginia**

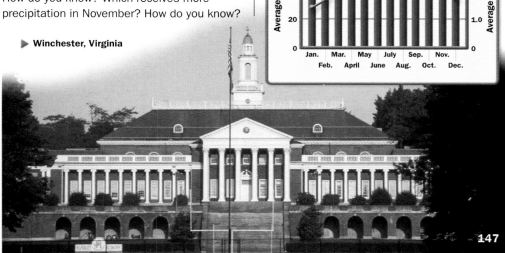

Think and Apply

1 During which months in Omaha is the average daily temperature below freezing (32°F)? Are there months when the average daily temperature is at or below freezing in Winchester?

2 Which month gets the most precipitation in Omaha?

3 In Winchester, what is the warmest month? What are the two wettest months?

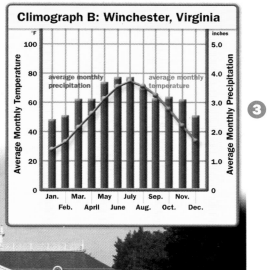

Climograph B: Winchester, Virginia

1 **What part of the climograph shows the average temperature?** The line graph Analyze Pictures

2 **What part of the climograph provides information about precipitation?** The bar graph Analyze Pictures

3 **During what months is the average temperature in Winchester, Virginia, below 50°F?** January, February, March, November, December Analyze Pictures

3 Close and Assess

Think and Apply

1. In Omaha, it is below freezing in January, February, and December. Yes, it is at or below freezing in Winchester in January and February.

2. In Omaha, May has the most precipitation.

3. July is the warmest month in Winchester. The two wettest months are June and July.

CURRICULUM CONNECTION
Science

Make a Climograph

- Have students use a thermometer and a cylindrical can to collect information about rainfall and temperatures at their homes for a single month.

- Have them write down the temperature every day and measure the amount of water collected in any rainstorms. (Have them record the temperature at the same time every day.)

- Have students construct a climograph from their data. They should present average weekly rainfall and temperatures.

Workbook, p. 35

Also on Teacher Resources CD-ROM.

Cowboys and Miners

Objectives
- Explain the factors that made cattle drives profitable.
- Identify the reasons why cattle drives came to an end.
- Evaluate the lasting effect of the search for gold in the West.

Vocabulary
cattle drive, p. 149; **gold rush,** p. 151; **entrepreneur,** p. 152

Resources
- Workbook, p. 36
- Transparency 10
- Every Student Learns Guide, pp. 58–61
- Quick Study, pp. 30–31

Quick Teaching Plan

If time is short, have students write the words *cattle* and *gold* at the head of a two-column chart.
- Ask students to look for examples of how cattle and gold helped shape the settlement of the West as they read the lesson independently.
- Have students list these supporting details on their charts.

1 Introduce and Motivate

Preview To activate prior knowledge, ask students to recall some of the economic factors that brought Europeans to the New World. Tell them that they will learn how economic factors changed the face of the American West.

You Are There Ask students to think of a time when they had to prove themselves in front of a crowd (for example, batting in a baseball game or performing in a play or a concert). Ask them to consider how much hinged on Nat Love's ability to ride a horse and to predict how life will change for Love in the West.

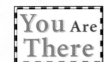

1840			1860

1849 The California gold rush begins.

1859 Gold is found in the Rocky Mountains.

1860s Cattle drives begin.

Virginia City · Chicago · Denver · Dodge City

PREVIEW

Focus on the Main Idea
Cattle drives and the search for gold offered new opportunities and led to lasting changes in the western United States.

PLACES
Dodge City, Kansas
Chicago, Illinois
Denver, Colorado
Virginia City, Nevada

PEOPLE
Charles Goodnight
Nat Love
Luzena Stanley Wilson
Levi Strauss
Mark Twain

VOCABULARY
cattle drive
gold rush
entrepreneur

▶ Cowboys herded longhorn cattle.

Cowboys and Miners

You Are There Nat Love wants to be a cowboy. Born into slavery in Tennessee in 1854, Love gained his freedom at the end of the Civil War. Now it is 1869 and Love is 15 years old. He has come west to Dodge City, Kansas, in search of opportunity and adventure.

Love finds a group of Texas cowboys, walks right up to the boss, and asks for a job. "He asked me if I could ride a wild horse," Love later wrote. "I said, 'Yes sir.' He said, 'If you can I will give you a job.'"

The cowboys bring Love a wild horse named Good Eye. Love jumps on, and Good Eye starts bucking and kicking. Love holds on until the horse gets tired. The cowboys are impressed. "The boss said he would give me a job and pay me $30.00 per month," Love wrote. His new life as a cowboy had begun.

 Sequence As you read, follow the sequence of events that brought lasting change to the western United States.

148

Practice and Extend

READING SKILL
Sequence

In the Lesson Review, students complete a graphic organizer like the one below. You may want to provide students with a copy of Transparency 10 to complete as they read the lesson.

Use Transparency 10

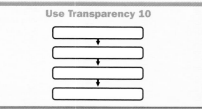

VOCABULARY
Word Exercise

Context Clues

Review the idea that an *entrepreneur* is someone who starts a new business hoping to make a profit. Then describe some people; students should tell you if the person described is an entrepreneur or not.

- Someone who knits sweaters and sells them (yes)
- Someone who does chores to earn an allowance from his or her parents (no)
- Someone who opens a store (yes)

▶ Working long days on horseback, cowboys earned about $30 a month. A group of about ten cowboys could handle a herd of more than 2,000 head of cattle.

Cowboy Life

By the end of the Civil War, there were five million head of cattle in Texas. They were a tough breed known as Texas longhorns. These longhorns sold for just $4 each in Texas, but they were worth about $40 each in the growing cities of the East, where beef was scarce. Ranchers realized that they could make huge profits if they could figure out a way to get their cattle across the country.

The solution was the **cattle drive.** On cattle drives, cowboys guided huge herds of cattle north to the new railroad lines extending across the Great Plains. The cattle drives began in Texas and ended in towns along the railroad, such as **Dodge City, Kansas.** From these towns, the cattle were taken by train to eastern cities

One of the main cattle drive trails was the Goodnight-Loving Trail, which ran from Texas to Colorado. **Charles Goodnight,** a rancher who established this trail in 1866, remembered cowboy life as the happiest time of his life:

"Most of the time we were solitary [lone] adventurers in a great land as fresh and new as a spring morning."

Cowboy life may have been an adventure, but it was also exhausting and dangerous. Cowboys worked sixteen-hour days on horseback. They worked seven days a week for the two or three months it took to drive the cattle north. At night cowboys took turns watching the herd, guarding against the constant danger of stampedes. In a stampede, entire herds of longhorns took off running wildly. They could trample horses and people, or charge into rivers and drown. Almost anything could set off a stampede—a burst of lightning, a coyote's howl, even the sound of cooking pots banging together. To try to keep the animals calm, cowboys would sing to them.

Cowboys were a varied group. About one-third of all cowboys were Mexican American or African American. Many were very young. As you read, **Nat Love** began working as a cowboy when he was just fifteen years old.

REVIEW By how much did the price of one longhorn in Texas and in eastern cities differ? Why?
Compare and Contrast

▶ Nat Love was a famous cowboy.

149

Quick Summary The desire to transport cattle from Texas to the markets of the East led to the cattle drive and the distinctive culture of the cowboy.

$ SOCIAL STUDIES STRAND
Economics

Remind students of the relationship between prices and supply and demand.

 Why would the scarcity of beef in the East drive up prices? Possible answer: Because little beef was available, people were willing to pay more for it. Cause and Effect

Problem Solving

 What problem was the cattle drive created to solve? Possible answer: Transporting longhorns from where they were raised to where they were worth the most money Solve Problems

Primary Source

Cited in *The West, an Illustrated History,* by Geoffrey C. Ward

3 What words indicate that the author has positive memories of his time as a cowboy? Possible answers: *adventurers, great land,* and *fresh and new as a spring morning* Analyze Primary Sources

✓ **REVIEW ANSWER** One longhorn cost ten times more in eastern cities than it did in Texas. Beef was scarce in the East, but plentiful in Texas. Compare and Contrast

---

 CURRICULUM CONNECTION
Math

Calculate Hourly Wages

Some cowboys worked 16 hours a day, seven days a week, in order to earn $30 a month. Assuming 30 days in a month, how much would a cowboy be earning per hour? (Students should multiply 16 hours by 30 days to get 480 hours worked per month. Then they should divide $30 by 480 to discover that the cowboy earned six and one-quarter cents ($0.0625) per hour.

C SOCIAL STUDIES STRAND
Culture

Cowboy Contributions

Cowboys and the cattle drive contributed much to American culture. This includes

- Cowboy songs, such as "Git Along, Little Dogies"
- Vocabulary, such as *lariat* and *bronco,* much of which came from the Spanish language used by Mexican cowboys, who introduced ranching in Texas

The End of the Drives

🕐 **Quick Summary** Conflict between cattle ranchers and the growth of railroads combined to make cattle drives less efficient and, in time, unnecessary.

4 Why do you think the fencing of farmland hurt cattle drives? Possible answer: The cattle could no longer travel across open land. Fences blocked the cattle trails. **Cause and Effect**

5 Name two effects that the railroads had on the ranching industry. Possible answer: Railroads helped end the cattle drives. They also helped ranchers get their products to a growing number of markets. **Cause and Effect**

🌐 **SOCIAL STUDIES STRAND**
Geography

Remind students of Chicago's central location in the country. Explain that it was a place where many railroad lines to and from the East and West met.

6 Describe Chicago's role in the meat industry. Possible answer: It was a central place to which cattle could be shipped and from which meat could then be sent to all parts of the country. **Summarize**

✓ **REVIEW ANSWER** Possible answer: It continued to raise cattle and other animals, but it relied on railroads to transport them. 🔄 **Sequence**

Map Adventure Answers

1. Chisholm Trail

2. About 60 days

3. Cattle trails led to railroad lines. These lines came together in Chicago, making it a logical center for the beef industry.

The End of the Drives

Cattle drives came to an end by the late 1880s. One cause was the growing conflict between cattle ranchers and farmers on the Great Plains. To keep cattle off their farmland, homesteaders began fencing in their land with barbed wire. Expanding railroad **4** lines also helped end the cattle drives. As new railroad lines reached into Texas, it was no longer necessary for ranchers to drive their cattle north.

The cattle drives had ended, but cattle ranching continued to be an important industry. People all over the country still wanted fresh meat at prices they could afford. To meet this demand, ranchers raised millions of cows, as well as hogs and sheep. Expanding railroad lines made it easier and cheaper to transport animals from ranches to cities such as **Chicago, Illinois.** As a major **5** railroad center near the middle of the country, Chicago was perfectly located to become the nation's leading supplier of fresh meat. From Chicago, train cars quickly transported meat to cities around the country. **6**

REVIEW What happened to the cattle ranching industry after the end of cattle drives? 🔄 Sequence

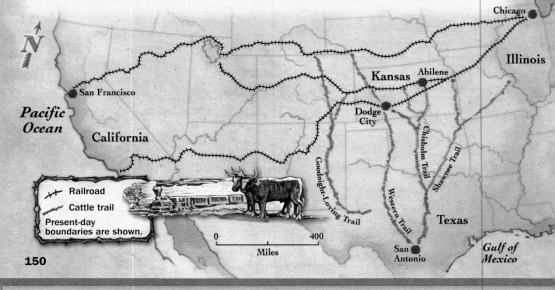

Map Adventure

The Long Cattle Drives

Starting from Texas, there are several routes you can take to drive your cattle to the railroad.

1. Which trail would you follow if you wanted to drive your cattle to Abilene, Kansas?

2. Traveling 10 miles a day, how long would it take to drive your cattle from San Antonio to Dodge City?

3. By the 1880s, the city of Chicago had become the nation's leading supplier of fresh beef. How does the map help explain this?

Railroad
Cattle trail
Present-day boundaries are shown.

Pacific Ocean — San Francisco — California — Kansas — Abilene — Dodge City — Chicago — Illinois — Goodnight-Loving Trail — Western Trail — Chisholm Trail — Shawnee Trail — Texas — San Antonio — Gulf of Mexico

0 — 400 Miles

150

Practice and Extend

ESL BUILD BACKGROUND
ESL Support

Describe the Distribution of Cattle Students will use various means to describe the issues and challenges of the cattle industry.

Beginning Have students draw pictures illustrating the following concepts: cattle drives and transporting cattle by railroad.

Intermediate Have students write one or two sentences that explain how the ranching industry changed in the late 1800s.

Advanced Have students write a one-paragraph essay entitled *Changes in the Ranching Industry in the 1800s.* The essay should include details about the cattle drive and the spread of railroads.

For additional ESL support, use Every Student Learns Guide, pp. 58–61.

▶ It was rare for gold miners to find large gold nuggets like this one *(right)*. More often they just found gold dust, which they searched for in the ground near or in rivers.

Dreams of Gold

You have read that Great Plains farmers and cattle ranchers changed the United States. People who moved to the West for gold also helped change the country.

Luzena Stanley Wilson was living with her family in Missouri when she heard the news that gold had been found in California. "The gold excitement spread like wildfire," she remembered. "And as we had almost nothing to lose, and we might gain a fortune, we early caught the fever." The year was 1849. Just like thousands of other families from all over the country, the Wilsons rushed west. They settled in Nevada City, California.

The California gold rush changed the West. During the gold rush thousands of people went to California to search for gold. By 1850 California had enough people to become a state. Another effect of the gold rush was that people began to wonder where else in the West gold might be found.

This explains why a hopeful miner named George Jackson was exploring the freezing Rocky Mountains in January 1859. In a creek near the small town of Denver, Colorado,

Jackson found a few gold flakes. "I went to bed and dreamed of riches galore," he wrote in his diary.

When Jackson and his partners took some of the gold they had found to Denver, people in town cheered. "The stuff is here after all!" one man shouted. News of gold in the Rockies quickly spread across the country, and a new gold rush was on. Thousands of miners starting searching all over the mountains and deserts of the West.

While everyone dreamed of finding big nuggets of shining gold, such discoveries were actually very rare. Gold mining required long, hard days of work and patience. Using a metal pan, miners scooped sand from the bottom of streams. Then they carefully washed out the sand, hoping to see tiny pieces of gold, known as "gold dust." If miners were lucky, they slowly filled bags with gold dust. The bags were then taken to the nearest town, where the gold could be traded for supplies or deposited in a bank.

REVIEW What was the effect of George Jackson's discovery of gold in the Rockies? *Cause and Effect*

151

Dreams of Gold

 Quick Summary The discovery of gold in the West lured people from around the world to California and Colorado.

Test Talk

Locate Key Words in the Text

7 **Why do you think the fact that Wilson "had almost nothing to lose" made the quest for gold seem more attractive?** Ask students if the answer is right there or if they have to think and search for it. Possible answer: Seeking gold was risky, and having "nothing to lose" meant that the gold-seeker had very little to place at risk.
Analyze Primary Sources

8 **In what ways did the California gold rush change the West?** Possible answer: It brought thousands of people to the area and it inspired people to seek gold in other Western locations.
Summarize

✓ Ongoing Assessment

| If... students do not grasp the significance of the California gold rush, | then... have them make a list titled *Changes in the West.* Encourage students to skim the text and write changes that took place in California between 1848 and 1850. |

9 **Why would the discovery of gold in the Rocky Mountains make the people of Denver happy?** Possible answers: They wanted to find gold themselves. They knew that Denver would become a boomtown when news of the gold strike reached the rest of the world.
Cause and Effect

✓ REVIEW ANSWER Possible answer: It helped bring thousands of people to the area. **Cause and Effect**

MEETING INDIVIDUAL NEEDS
Leveled Practice

Write a Journal Have each student adopt the point of view of a miner during the California gold rush and record their thoughts in a journal.

Easy Have students suppose they are on their way to a gold rush boomtown and record a brief journal entry expressing their hopes and fears. **Reteach**

On-Level Have students write a series of three journal entries—one before their arrival at the mining sites, one during their time seeking gold, and one afterwards. **Extend**

Challenge Have students write five journal entries, beginning with them receiving news of the gold strike and concluding with their return from the gold rush. **Enrich**

For a Lesson Summary, use Quick Study, p. 30.

Boomtowns and Blue Jeans

⏱ *Quick Summary* The rush for gold swelled mining camps into boomtowns. It also created economic opportunities for enterprising people.

💲 **SOCIAL STUDIES STRAND**
Economics

Tell students that fast-growing towns often experienced shortages of essential goods. These shortages created a great demand—which could drive prices sky high.

🔟 **Why do you think "boomtowns" created exciting opportunities for entrepreneurs?** Possible answer: Thousands of miners required the goods and services that entrepreneurs could provide. Cause and Effect

⓫ **What opportunity did Luzena Stanley Wilson see in the gold rush?** Possible answer: She saw the opportunity to make money by feeding hungry miners. Summarize

⓬ **How did the rivets that Levi Straus used to hold his blue denim pants together help make the pants popular?** The rivets helped make the pants strong. They did not fall apart as easily under tough working conditions. Draw Conclusions

Literature and Social Studies

Have students read the excerpt from Mark Twain's *Roughing It.*

⓭ **Based on the excerpt, why are the people of Virginia City happy?** Possible answer: They all considered themselves to be wealthy. Analyze Primary Sources

Boomtowns and Blue Jeans

Miners were always quick to rush to any spot where gold was found. They set up camps of canvas tents, then went right to work. As more and more miners rushed in, mining camps often grew into booming towns with diverse populations.

These "boomtowns" offered exciting opportunities for entrepreneurs such as Luzena Stanley Wilson. An **entrepreneur** is a person who starts a new business, hoping to make ⑩ a profit. After moving with her family to the mining town of Nevada City, California, Wilson saw a way to make money. "The miners were glad to get something to eat, and were always willing to pay for it," she wrote. She built a long table and opened a restaurant in her home. The first night, 20 hungry miners sat at her table. "Each man as he rose put a dollar in my hand and said I might count him ⑪ as a permanent customer," she wrote.

An immigrant from Germany named **Levi Strauss** found opportunity in San Francisco, California. Strauss learned that miners wanted sturdy pants that would not fall apart under tough working conditions. He began making pants out of blue denim, a strong cotton material. He used rivets, or metal pins, to hold the pants together. These were the world's first blue jeans. The jeans were very popular with miners, and Strauss's business grew. ⑫

▶ Levi Strauss

One of the West's biggest boomtowns was **Virginia City, Nevada.** When gold and silver were discovered there, Virginia City grew from a small mining camp to a town of nearly 30,000 people in just a few years. A young writer named **Mark Twain** arrived in 1862. Years before he wrote his classic tales about

Literature and Social Studies

Roughing It

Mark Twain wrote for a Virginia City newspaper during the boom years of the early 1860s. In his book *Roughing It,* Twain described the excitement of living in a town where people dug for gold and silver right under the city streets.

"*Virginia had grown to be the 'livest' town, for its age and population, that America had ever produced. The sidewalks swarmed with people. . . . So great was the pack [crowd], that buggies [wagons] frequently had to wait half an hour for an opportunity to cross the principal street. Joy sat on every countenance [face], and there was a glad, almost fierce, intensity in every eye, that told of the money-getting schemes [plans] that were seething in every brain. . . . Money was as plenty as dust; every individual considered himself wealthy.*" ⑬

Practice and Extend

🔵 **ESL** **ACCESS CONTENT**
ESL Support

Explore the Quotation

- Have students work in small groups to read the selection, explore its meaning, and answer questions about language and usage.
- Students should use an English-language dictionary to look up the meanings of unfamiliar words.
- To check on student understanding, work as a complete group to write a summary of the meaning of the passage.

For additional ESL support, use Every Student Learns Guide, pp. 58–61.

Huckleberry Finn and Tom Sawyer, Twain wrote news reports for Virginia City's newspaper, the *Territorial Enterprise*. In Virginia City, Twain found crowded streets lined with hotels, restaurants, banks, and theaters. "Large fire-proof brick buildings were going up in the principal streets," Twain wrote, "and the wooden suburbs were spreading out in all directions."

The boom times did not last forever. When the gold and silver ran out in Virginia City in the 1880s, people left town. Like many mining towns, Virginia City became a "ghost town," or a town of empty buildings.

All over the West, however, the mining boom had a lasting effect. The hope of finding gold had drawn thousands of new settlers to the region. Towns that had once been supply stations for miners soon grew into

important cities. Denver, Colorado, and San Francisco, California, are two examples. Miners had changed the West forever. **⑭**

REVIEW How did Virginia City change after the gold and silver ran out? 🔄 Sequence

Summarize the Lesson

— **1849** The California gold rush lured thousands of settlers to California.

— **1859** Gold was found in the Rocky Mountains, causing miners to begin searching for gold all over the West.

— **1860s** The ranching industry grew when cowboys began driving cattle from Texas to towns along the railroad.

LESSON 3 REVIEW

Check Facts and Main Ideas

1. 🔄 **Sequence** On a separate sheet of paper, fill in the missing dates in this chart.

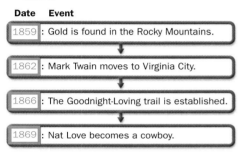

Date	Event
1859	: Gold is found in the Rocky Mountains.
1862	: Mark Twain moves to Virginia City.
1866	: The Goodnight-Loving trail is established.
1869	: Nat Love becomes a cowboy.

2. Why did ranchers decide to drive their cattle from Texas to towns along the railroad?

3. What changes brought **cattle drives** to an end?

4. Summarize the lasting effects of the search for gold in the West.

5. **Critical Thinking:** *Analyze Primary Sources* You read Mark Twain's description of life in Virginia City. List three details that Twain uses to give the reader an idea of what life was like there.

Link to 🔗 Art

Advertise Your Business Suppose you have just moved to a booming mining town in the 1860s. You decide to be an **entrepreneur** and start a business of your own. What kind of business would you want to open? What would you name it? Draw a poster advertising your new business.

153

---

3 Close and Assess

Summarize the Lesson

Tell students to examine the vertical time line. Have students identify three additional events from the section to include on the time line.

✓ **LESSON 3 REVIEW**

1. 🔄 **Sequence** For possible answers, see the reduced pupil page.

2. They wanted to bring their cattle to eastern markets, where they were worth many times what they were worth in Texas.

3. The spread of fencing on the farms and the arrival of railroads in Texas helped reduce the benefits of and need for the cattle drives.

4. The search for gold brought thousands of people to the West and produced boomtowns, some of which survived and grew into major cities.

5. **Critical Thinking:** *Analyze Primary Sources* Possible answers: Swarming sidewalks; buggies waiting half an hour to cross the street; happy, intense looks on people's faces

Link to 🔗 Art

Make sure student artwork clearly includes the business name and identifies the product or service that the business provides.

 SOCIAL STUDIES Background

Supply, Demand, and Inflation in the California Gold Rush

- In 1847 few people called San Francisco home. Two years later, land that had cost less than $20 sold for $45,000.

- In the East, flour sold for four dollars a barrel; in California that price rose to one dollar per pint.

- The demand for goods was so great in response to the gold rush that some have claimed it helped stop a significant economic downturn in the United States.

Workbook, p. 36

Lesson 3: Cowboys and Miners
Directions: Complete the outline with information from this lesson. You may use your textbook.

Life in the West

I. Cattle Drives
  A. Cattle drives were a way for ranchers to get their cattle to _____ in the East.
    1. The drives began in _____ and ended in Great Plains railroad towns such as Dodge City, Kansas.
    a. The Goodnight-Loving Trail, established by _____ in 1866, ran from Texas to Colorado.
  B. By the late 1800s, cattle drives came to an end.
    1. _____ began fencing in their lands with barbed wire to keep cattle off their farmland.
    2. Once _____ reached Texas, it was no longer necessary for ranchers to drive their cattle north.
II. Dreams of Gold
  A. During the California _____, thousands of people moved west in search of gold.
    1. By 1850, California had enough people to become a _____.
  B. When _____ discovered gold in the Rocky Mountains, miners began searching for gold all over the West.
    1. The flood of newcomers created opportunities for _____ like Luzena Stanley Wilson and Levi Strauss.
  C. The mining boom had lasting effects in the West.
    1. San Francisco, California, and _____ are two examples of important cities that emerged from supply stations for miners.

Notes for Home: Your child learned about the events that changed the American West.
Home Activity: Discuss with your child what it might have been like for you and your family to move west in search of gold during the mid-1800s.

💿 **Also on Teacher Resources CD-ROM.**

War in the West

Objectives

- Identify changes that threatened the traditional way of life for Native Americans of the Great Plains.

- Summarize the outcome of wars between United States soldiers and Native Americans.

- Describe ways in which Native Americans are keeping their traditions alive today.

Vocabulary

reservation, p. 155;
Battle of Little Bighorn, p. 156

Resources

- Workbook, p. 37
- Transparency 10
- Every Student Learns Guide, pp. 62–65
- Quick Study, pp. 32–33

Quick Teaching Plan

If time is short, have students create a web diagram, with the words *Indian Wars in the West* in the middle.

- Have students write down details of the wars in the West as they read the lesson independently.

1 Introduce and Motivate

Preview To activate prior knowledge, ask students to think about what they have read about changes in the West—the new cities, the new railroads, and other changes on the land.

Have students think about how these changes might affect the native people living in the West. Ask students to think about how Native Americans might respond.

 You Are There Sitting Bull believed that development damaged, rather than improved, the environment and people's living conditions. Ask students to predict how his belief might bring him into conflict with settlers.

154 Unit 2 • An Expanding Nation

LESSON 4

1875		1890
1876 Lakota forces defeat Custer at Little Bighorn.	**1877** The Nez Percé surrender in Montana.	**1890** Wars in the West come to an end.

PREVIEW

Focus on the Main Idea
As more and more settlers came to the western United States, Native American groups fought to maintain control of their lands.

PLACES
Black Hills

PEOPLE
Sitting Bull
George Custer
Crazy Horse
Chief Joseph
Geronimo

VOCABULARY
reservation
Battle of Little Bighorn

War in the West

 You Are There The Lakota chief Sitting Bull sees that the Great Plains are changing. Telegraph lines and railroads are slicing across the plains. Farmers, ranchers, and miners are arriving in growing numbers.

The vast herds of buffalo are beginning to disappear. Newcomers are killing buffalo by the thousands—for their hides, to feed railroad workers, and for sport.

For centuries the Lakota have followed buffalo herds over the open plains, relying on these animals for food, clothing, and shelter. Sitting Bull believes that most Lakota want to continue this traditional way of life. "The life my people want is a life of freedom," he says. "I have seen nothing that a white man has, houses or railways or clothing or food, that is as good as the right to move in the open country and live in our fashion."

Sequence As you read, pay attention to the order of events that led to the defeat of Native Americans in the western United States.

▶ Lakota leader Sitting Bull

Practice and Extend

READING SKILL
Sequence

In the Lesson Review, students complete a graphic organizer like the one below. You may want to provide students with a copy of Transparency 10 to complete as they read the lesson.

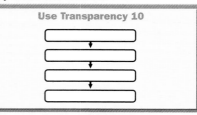

Use Transparency 10

VOCABULARY
Word Exercise

Related Word Study

Explain that sometimes students can determine the meaning of a word without looking at a dictionary or glossary. Write *reservation* on the board. Point out the base word *reserve,* which means "to set apart." Help students use this information to understand that *reservation* means "a place that is kept, held, or set aside." Then help students determine the meanings of *reservist, reservoir,* and *reserved.*

Conflict on the Plains

As you have read, thousands of settlers began moving to the Great Plains in the 1860s. This led to conflict between new settlers and Native Americans of the Great Plains. Such American Indian groups as the Lakota, Cheyenne, and Crow could see that their traditional way of life was threatened. Battles between these groups and settlers became more and more common on the Great Plains.

The United States government was determined to support the settlers. The government wanted the region to be open for expanding railroad lines, growing farms and ranches, and new towns. At first, the government offered money and goods to Native Americans. However, as you read, Sitting Bull did not value the white man's goods. So government leaders decided that Native Americans should move onto reservations. A **reservation** is an area of land set aside for Native Americans. The government was ready to use military force to move Native Americans onto reservations.

Realizing that they could not defeat the United States army, many Native Americans agreed to move to reservations. In 1868 Lakota leaders signed a treaty with the United States creating the Great Lakota Reservation. This large reservation included the **Black Hills,** a region of rugged cliffs and dark green valleys in what is now South Dakota and Wyoming. According to the treaty, this land was to belong to the Lakota people forever.

Then gold was found in the Black Hills in 1874. As always, the news spread quickly. About 15,000 gold miners illegally rushed onto the Lakota reservation.

The United States government now hoped that the Lakota would be willing to sell the Black Hills. A government representative told Lakota leaders, "Gold is useless to you, and there will be fighting unless you give it up." But Lakota leaders refused to move again. "I do not want to sell any land to the government," **Sitting Bull** declared. He picked up a tiny bit of dirt between two fingers. "Not even as much as this."

REVIEW What key events took place after gold was found in the Black Hills?
◉ Sequence

▶ Trains often slowed down to allow railroad workers and passengers to shoot buffalo. There were once about 30 million buffalo on the Great Plains. By the late 1880s, there were fewer than 1,000.

155

ISSUES AND VIEWPOINTS
Critical Thinking

Write the lists below on the board or read them aloud. Ask students to describe why people in these groups may have felt as they did.

United States government

- wanted the nation to grow
- felt that American Indians should be moved onto reservations
- believed that nothing should keep it from valuable resources

Lakota

- felt that their way of life was threatened
- had agreed to move to the Black Hills reservation to avoid a fight
- refused to sell their Black Hills reservation

Conflict on the Plains

🕐 *Quick Summary* Settlers moving into the West came into conflict with American Indians already living there. The United States government backed the settlers—with force.

1 **What can you infer from the fact that the United States government wanted to remove Native Americans to make possible the development of the West?** Possible answer: The government did not think Native Americans could or should take part in its vision of development. They thought the Native Americans would try to stop that development. Make Inferences

2 **Why did many Native Americans eventually choose to move to reservations?** Possible answer: They knew that the United States army was too powerful for them to defeat. Cause and Effect

3 **What choice did the United States government present to the Lakota people?** Possible answer: The Lakota had to choose between selling their land or fighting the United States army. Summarize

Ongoing Assessment ✓

If... students do not understand the difficult decision facing the Lakota after the discovery of gold in the Black Hills,

then... have them summarize all of the Lakota's options and speculate on what could have happened in each instance.

✓ **REVIEW ANSWER** Miners rushed into the area. The Lakota were asked to either sell their Black Hills land or face war.
◉ Sequence

The Battle of Little Bighorn

🕐 *Quick Summary* The growing conflict between the United States government and the Lakota erupted in violence. At the Battle of Little Bighorn, American Indians won a costly victory.

4 **Why do you think Cheyenne fighters were willing to help the Lakota?**
Possible answers: The two groups were friends. The Cheyenne felt that the Lakota were just in their cause.
Draw Conclusions

5 **Why do you think Custer chose to attack in spite of being outnumbered?**
Possible answers: He may have underestimated the size and strength of his enemy. He may have felt that the element of surprise would help make up for his small numbers. Make Inferences

6 **From what point of view can the Battle of Little Bighorn be seen as a defeat for the Native Americans?**
Possible answer: It was a defeat in the sense that it convinced the United States government to apply stronger force against the Native Americans—force they could not resist. Point of View

✓ **REVIEW ANSWER** The United States government sent more troops to the region and successfully forced the Lakota onto a new reservation.
Cause and Effect

The Battle of Little Bighorn

In March 1876 an American soldier named Thomas Eagan wrote a letter to his sister. "I think we will have some hard times this summer," Eagan wrote. "The old chief Sitting Bull says that he will not make peace with the whites as long as he has a man to fight." Eagan was part of the Seventh Cavalry. Led by Colonel **George Custer**, the Seventh Cavalry's mission was to defeat the Lakota and force them onto a new reservation.

Sitting Bull and the Lakota were camped on the banks of the Little Bighorn River in Montana. **Crazy Horse**, one of the Lakota's most successful young war leaders, was in camp along with many Cheyenne fighters. The Cheyenne were ready to battle alongside **4** the Lakota.

Custer found the Lakota camp on June 25. The American soldiers were badly outnum- **5** bered, but Custer decided to attack anyway. "The soldiers charged so quickly we could not talk," said a Lakota chief named Red Horse. Lakota fighters grabbed their guns and the battle began.

Crazy Horse helped lead the Lakota to victory at the **Battle of Little Bighorn**. This battle is also known as "Custer's Last Stand," because George Custer was killed along with his entire force of more than 200 soldiers.

Little Bighorn is remembered as an important battle for two reasons. First, it was the biggest victory Native Americans ever won over United States forces. Second, it soon led to the end of freedom for Native Americans

▶ **Colonel George Custer**

of the Great Plains. Custer's defeat convinced the United States government to take stronger action against the Lakota and other Native American groups. **6**

More soldiers were sent to the Great Plains. By the end of 1877, Crazy Horse and most Lakota had been forced onto reservations. Sitting Bull had escaped to Canada. The Black Hills were now open to gold miners and settlers from the United States.

REVIEW How did the United States government react to the Battle of Little Bighorn? Cause and Effect

▶ **This is part of the land in the Black Hills that the Lakota fought for.**

156

Practice and Extend

FYI **SOCIAL STUDIES Background**

About George Armstrong Custer
- A poor student, Custer graduated at the very bottom of his class at West Point.
- Custer won fame and a promotion during the Civil War for his aggressive and fearless style.
- After the war, Custer was court-martialed and suspended for one year.

About Crazy Horse
- His American Indian name was Tashunca-uitco.
- He won fame as a warrior and a defender of Lakota traditions.
- He refused to allow himself to be photographed.
- He was killed in 1877 while in the custody of U.S soldiers.

Chief Joseph

West of the Great Plains, other Native American groups were also struggling to hold on to their land. The Nez Percé (nez per SAY) lived in the Wallowa Valley of Oregon. In 1877 the United States government decided to move the Nez Percé to a reservation in Idaho Territory. The government wanted the Wallowa Valley to be open to settlers. Many Nez Percé, however, did not want to leave their traditional land. "It has always belonged to our people," said Nez Percé leader Chief Joseph.

In June 1877 United States soldiers were sent to capture the Nez Percé and take them to a reservation. The Nez Percé refused to be taken. For the next three months, the army chased Chief Joseph and about 700 Nez Percé across Oregon, Idaho, and Montana. Several fierce battles were fought along this 1,600-mile chase.

Running short of food and supplies, the Nez Percé tried to escape across the Canadian border. They hoped to get help at Sitting Bull's camp in Canada. They were just 40 miles from the border when they were surrounded by American soldiers.

General Nelson Miles promised Chief Joseph that if the Nez Percé surrendered they would be allowed to return to Oregon. This convinced Chief Joseph to stop fighting. He told the American soldiers,

> *"I am tired of fighting. Our chiefs are killed. . . . The little children are freezing to death. . . . I am tired; my heart is sick and sad. From where the sun now stands I will fight no more forever."*

General Miles's promise was not kept, however. The Nez Percé soon learned they were to be taken to a reservation in Oklahoma. This came as a shock to Chief Joseph. "I believed General Miles, or I never would have surrendered," he said. You will read more about Chief Joseph in the Citizen Heroes following this lesson.

REVIEW What reasons did Chief Joseph give when he agreed to stop fighting? **Summarize**

▶ Chief Joseph surrendering

▶ Chief Joseph

157

Quick Summary Rather than submit to life on a reservation, Chief Joseph and the Nez Percé attempted a daring but failed escape.

7 **Why do you think the United States government did not leave the Nez Percé alone and simply give settlers the reservation land in Idaho?** Possible answer: The reservation land might not have been as attractive to settlers—for example, because of its distance from other settlements or transportation links. **Make Inferences**

SOCIAL STUDIES STRAND
G **Government**

Tell students that United States soldiers cannot cross into the territory of a foreign country without approval from that country.

Test Talk

Write Your Answer to Score High

8 **Why do you think the Nez Percé tried to cross the Canadian border?** Remind students that their written answers should be correct, complete, and focused. Possible answer: In addition to getting help at Sitting Bull's camp, they believed that United States soldiers could not follow them there. **Draw Conclusions**

Primary Source
Cited in *Bury My Heart at Wounded Knee,* by Dee Brown

9 **What can you conclude about the experience of Chief Joseph and the Nez Percé during their flight?** Possible answers: The people endured harsh conditions and suffered greatly. **Analyze Primary Sources**

✓**REVIEW ANSWER** His people had suffered, he became tired and discouraged, and he believed the promise that his people could live in Oregon. **Summarize**

ESL Support

ACTIVATE PRIOR KNOWLEDGE

Compare Points of View Based on what they have read in previous lessons, students will compare the views of American settlers to those of Native Americans.

Beginning Have students identify two English words to describe how settlers viewed the land and how American Indians viewed the land.

Intermediate Have students write a sentence each on how settlers viewed the land and how American Indians viewed the land.

Advanced Tell students to write a one-paragraph essay comparing and contrasting how settlers viewed the land and how the American Indians viewed the land.

For additional ESL support, use Every Student Learns Guide, pp. 62–65.

After the Wars

Quick Summary In the late 1800s, the United States government completed the conquest of American Indian groups in the West. Confined to reservations, these groups began a new era in their history.

⑩ Why do you think the Lakota families decided to leave the reservation? Possible answers: They found it difficult to survive there. They may have thought life on the reservation was not worth living. They may have felt they had the right to leave. **Point of View**

Major Native American Reservations, 1890

Point out that some groups lived on more than one reservation.

⑪ Which two groups lived closest to the border between Canada and the United States? Blackfoot, Spokane **Interpret Maps**

MAP SKILL **Answer** Ute, Hopi

⑫ What can you infer about Wolf Chief's beliefs about learning English and opening a business? Possible answer: He saw them as a way to build a good life. **Analyze Primary Sources**

⑬ What can you conclude from the fact that the Native American population of the United States in 1900 was lower than it was when Columbus arrived? Possible answer: Native Americans had suffered as settlers from Europe arrived and prospered in North America. **Draw Conclusions**

After the Wars

The Lakota and Nez Percé were just two of many American Indian groups that fought for their land. In the southwestern United States, the Apache continued fighting well into the 1880s. An Apache leader named **Geronimo** (je RON ih moh) resisted capture by leading a small group into the mountains of northern Mexico. When Geronimo was finally forced to surrender in 1886, he told American soldiers, "Once I moved about like the wind. Now I surrender to you and that is all."

The last major conflict between United States soldiers and Native Americans took place in 1890. A group of Lakota families ⑩ decided to leave their reservation. They were soon surrounded by United States soldiers at Wounded Knee, South Dakota. While the Lakota were giving up their weapons, someone fired a shot. United States soldiers began firing their guns, and about 300 Lakota were killed.

The fighting at Wounded Knee marked the end of the wars between United States forces and Native Americans. Native Americans all over the western half of the United States had been moved onto reservations. The map on this page shows the locations of the major reservations in 1890.

Native Americans now had to adjust to life on reservations. A Hidatsa woman named Buffalo Bird Woman said, "Our Indian life, I know, is gone forever." Even on the reservation, however, Buffalo Bird Woman continued speaking the Hidatsa language and farming in the traditional way of her people. Buffalo Bird Woman's brother, Wolf Chief, chose a different way of adjusting to life on a reservation. Wolf Chief learned English and started his own store. "I want to be strong and go forward," he said. ⑫

In 1900 there were about 230,000 Native Americans living in the United States. This was fewer than at any time since the arrival of Columbus more than 400 years before. ⑬

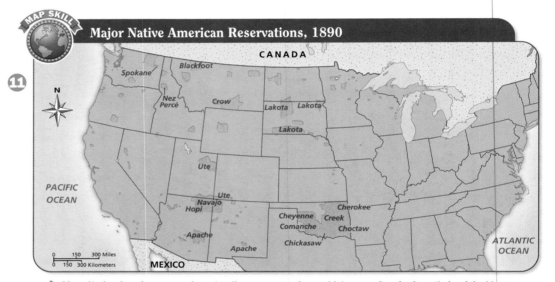

Major Native American Reservations, 1890

⑪

CANADA

Spokane · Blackfoot · Nez Percé · Crow · Lakota · Lakota · Lakota · Ute · Ute · Navajo · Hopi · Cheyenne · Comanche · Creek · Cherokee · Choctaw · Apache · Apache · Chickasaw

PACIFIC OCEAN

ATLANTIC OCEAN

MEXICO

0 150 300 Miles
0 150 300 Kilometers

▶ Many Native Americans were forced to live on reservations, which were often far from their original homes.

 **MAP SKILL** Location *Which two groups lived near the Navajo reservation?*

Practice and Extend

MEETING INDIVIDUAL NEEDS
Leveled Practice

Make a Time Line Students use the text and library and online resources to create a time line of U.S.-Native American relations.

Easy Have students create a time line of key events in this lesson involving the United States government and Native Americans. **Reteach**

On-Level Have students create a time line of events discussed in this chapter that affected development of the West and the Native Americans living there. **Extend**

Challenge Using their texts and additional resources, have students create a time line of major events in the history of the United States involving the United States government and Native Americans. **Enrich**

For a Lesson Summary, use Quick Study, p. 32.

Today the Native American population has grown to more than 2.5 million. About half of the Native Americans in the United States live on or near reservations. By winning court cases and helping to pass new laws, Native Americans have gained more control over reservation land.

► After his surrender, Apache leader Geronimo became a farmer in Oklahoma.

Both on and off reservations, a wide variety of American Indian groups are keeping their traditional cultures alive. Young people are learning the languages of their ancestors. About 200 tribal languages are still spoken in the United States today. Native American writers and filmmakers continue to tell stories about their people's history and way of life.

REVIEW How did life change for Native Americans after 1890? **Compare and Contrast**

Summarize the Lesson

1876 The Lakota won a major victory over United States forces at the Battle of Little Bighorn.

1877 Chief Joseph and the Nez Percé surrendered after a long chase across the West.

1890 The wars between United States forces and Native Americans ended.

LESSON 4 REVIEW

Check Facts and Main Ideas

1. 🔄 **Sequence** On a separate sheet of paper, create a chart of the struggle of Native Americans for their land. Fill in one key event for each year shown.

1868:	Lakota leaders and the United States government sign a treaty creating the Great Lakota reservation.
1874:	Lakota leaders refuse to move from the Black Hills after gold is found there.
1876:	The Lakota win a major victory over United States soldiers at the Battle of Little Bighorn.
1877:	United States soldiers capture the Nez Percé 40 miles from the Canadian border.

2. What changes threatened the way of life for Native Americans of the Great Plains in the 1860s?

3. Why was the **Battle of Little Bighorn** important?

4. What are some ways in which Native Americans are keeping their traditions alive today?

5. **Critical Thinking: *Summarize*** Summarize the outcome of the wars between United States forces and Native Americans.

Link to 🔗 Language Arts

Tell a Story One of the ways in which Native Americans keep their traditions alive is by telling stories. Find a book of Native American stories in the library. Choose one story you like and tell the story to your class.

159

Workbook, p. 37

Lesson 4: War in the West

Directions: Answer the following questions on the lines provided. You may use your textbook.

1. What changes took place in the West during the late 1800s that threatened the Native American way of life?

2. Why did the United States government try to move Native Americans to reservations?

3. Why was the Battle of Little Bighorn both a victory and a defeat for Native Americans?

4. Why did Chief Joseph agree to surrender?

5. What happened at Wounded Knee in 1890 and what was its significance?

Notes for Home: Your child learned how western expansion of the United States affected Native American groups.
Home Activity: Help your child use Internet or library sources to find information about Native American groups once lived in your region.

Also on Teacher Resources CD-ROM.

---

14 **What can you conclude from the fact that the Native American population has grown from 230,000 in 1900 to more than 2.5 million today?** Possible answer: Native American groups have managed to survive and grow on the reservations and beyond. **Draw Conclusions**

✓ **REVIEW ANSWER** Most Native Americans lived on or near reservations. Groups have gained greater control over reservation land and have worked hard to keep their customs alive. **Compare and Contrast**

3 Close and Assess

Summarize the Lesson

Have students read the events described on the vertical time line. Ask them to list at least one effect of each event.

✓ **LESSON 4 REVIEW**

1. 🔄 **Sequence** For possible answers, see the reduced pupil page.

2. The arrival of railroads and settlers spurred development that threatened their way of life.

3. It was a military victory for the Native Americans, but it also convinced the United States to apply decisive force against the Native Americans.

4. They are preserving native languages. They are recording stories of Native American history and ways of life. They are seeking greater control of reservation lands.

5. **Critical Thinking: *Summarize*** Although they had some battlefield successes, Native Americans were eventually defeated by United States troops and forced onto reservations.

Link to 🔗 Language Arts

Encourage students to retell their stories with expression and enthusiasm.

Fighting for a Homeland

Objectives

- Describe the accomplishments of significant leaders in United States history, such as Chief Joseph.

- Analyze the diverse cultures that have contributed to the heritage of the United States.

1 Introduce and Motivate

Preview To activate prior knowledge, have students recall what they have read about past conflicts between settlers and Native American groups. Tell students they will be reading about another conflict that took place in the American Northwest.

2 Teach and Discuss

1 Why had Chief Joseph's father refused to move his people to Idaho? Possible answer: He had previously reached an agreement with the United States government that allowed his people to stay on their land, and the United States was changing the terms after the fact. **Summarize**

2 What events caused Chief Joseph to fear an attack from the United States forces? After Chief Joseph agreed to move his people, a group of Nez Percé fighters attacked some settlers. Chief Joseph feared that this would provoke an attack by the soldiers.
Sequence

Fighting for a Homeland

The Nez Percé lived in the Wallowa Valley of Oregon. As more and more new settlers arrived, the Nez Percé lost their land and were forced to move onto reservations. Chief Joseph spent his life fighting for the right of his people to be treated fairly.

▶ The Nez Percé National Forest is in Idaho.

The Nez Percé had always had friendly relations with settlers, ever since Lewis and Clark passed through their land in the early 1800s. Chief Joseph's father, Joseph the Elder, was a Nez Percé chief who had worked with the United States government on an agreement that gave lands in Oregon and Idaho to his people. In 1863, gold was found on Nez Percé land, however, and more settlers arrived in the region. The United States government took back six million acres of land promised to the Nez Percé and told them they would have to move to a reservation in Idaho. Joseph the Elder refused to move his people there.

When Joseph the Elder died in 1871, his son became chief and soon had to deal with the same problems his father had. In 1877 General Oliver Otis Howard threatened to attack the Nez Percé if they would not move to the Idaho reservation. Chief Joseph was a peaceful man who did not want to see his people killed so he agreed to move. A group of Nez Percé fighters did not agree and attacked nearby settlers. Fearing punishment for the attack, Chief Joseph decided to take his people to Canada.

For three months, United States soldiers chased 700 Nez Percé 1,600 miles across Oregon, Idaho, and Montana. Finally, the army surrounded the Nez Percé in the Bear Paw

160

▶ Chief Joseph

Practice and Extend

FYI SOCIAL STUDIES Background

About the Nez Percé

- The Nez Percé refer to themselves as the Nee-Me-Poo.

- In the mid-1800s, many Nez Percé adopted Christianity after contact with Christian missionaries from the United States. The rest retained their traditional religion.

- After the discovery of gold on Nez Percé land, many Christian Nez Percé accepted the new demands by the United States for their land. The non-Christian Nez Percé refused.

- After their relocation to Oklahoma, the Nez Percé who converted to Christianity were allowed to return to Idaho. Those who did not, including Chief Joseph, were taken to a reservation in Washington state.

Mountains, just 40 miles from the Canadian border. With escape cut off, Chief Joseph surrendered on October 5, 1877. The Nez Percé were taken to a reservation in Oklahoma, where many became sick and died. In 1885 the Nez Percé were allowed to return to reservations in the Northwest. Some were sent to Idaho, others to Washington. However, no reservations were set aside in their original homelands.

Chief Joseph spent the rest of his life working and speaking for the fair and equal treatment of Native Americans. He traveled to Washington, D.C., to speak with President Rutherford B. Hayes and, later, President Theodore Roosevelt. During his visit to see President Hayes in 1879, Chief Joseph said,

"Treat all men alike. Give them the same laws. Give them all an even chance to live and grow. . . . You might as well expect all rivers to run backward as that any man who was born a free man should be contented [satisfied] penned up and denied liberty to go where he pleases. . . . Let me be a free man, free to travel, free to stop, free to work, free to trade where I choose, free to choose my own teachers, free to follow the religion of my fathers, free to talk, think and act for myself— and I will obey every law."

► A group of Nez Percé from the early 1900s

Fairness in Action

Do Chief Joseph's words describe your understanding of the term *fairness*? Write a paragraph called "What Fairness Means to Me." Give examples from the story of the Nez Percé, other examples from history, or even present-day examples.

161

Read About Chief Joseph

Use these selections to extend the content.

***Chief Joseph: Chief of the Nez Percé,* by Cynthia Fitterer Klingel and Robert B. Noyed (Child's World, ISBN 1-567-66165-3, 2002) Easy**

***Chief Joseph: Nez Percé Leader,* by Marian Taylor (Chelsea House, ISBN 0-791-01972-1, 1993) On-Level**

***Chief Joseph and the Nez Percés,* by Robert A. Scott (Facts on File, Inc., ISBN 0-816-02475-8, 1993) Challenge**

---

③ **How many years after their defeat in the Bear Paw Mountains were the Nez Percé allowed to return to the Northwest?** About 8 years ⏺ Sequence

Primary Source

Cited in *Chief Joseph: The Biography of a Great Indian,* by Chester Anders Fee

④ **What does Chief Joseph suggest is the likely result when a person is penned up, denied liberty, and told what he or she should think?** Possible answer: That person will be unhappy and will not be a good, law-abiding citizen.
Analyze Primary Sources

SOCIAL STUDIES STRAND
Citizenship

Democratic Values and Institutions Explain that the United States Constitution guarantees citizens freedom of speech, freedom to associate with whomever one wishes, and freedom of religion.

⑤ **Summarize Chief Joseph's demands in this quotation.** Possible answer: People should be free to live, think, and believe what they want, and live where they want under laws that are applied equally to all people.
Analyze Primary Sources

③ Close and Assess

Fairness in Action

• Encourage students to share their writing.

• Ask students to explain how their examples illustrate the idea of fairness (or the absence of fairness).

Resources

- Assessment Book, pp. 17–20
- Workbook, p. 38: Vocabulary Review

Chapter Summary

For possible answers, see the reduced pupil page.

Vocabulary

1. b, **2.** d, **3.** a, **4.** e, **5.** c

People and Places

Possible answers:

1. Samuel Morse developed a system that allowed people to communicate quickly over long distances using a telegraph.

2. The Central Pacific railroad began building its part of the transcontinental railroad in Sacramento, California.

3. Benjamin Singleton urged African Americans to move to the Great Plains in the 1870s.

4. Japanese immigrant George Shima ran his own successful potato farm.

5. Many ranchers in the West sent their cattle by railroad to Chicago, Illinois.

6. A gold rush occurred near Denver, Colorado, after miner George Jackson found gold in a creek there.

7. German immigrant Levi Strauss sold denim pants to miners in San Francisco, California.

8. After gold was found in the Black Hills in 1874, the United States government wanted the Lakota living there to move.

9. George Custer was killed by the Lakota in the Battle of Little Bighorn, the biggest Native American victory over United States forces.

10. Nez Percé leader Chief Joseph tried to escape with his people to Canada.

1840	1850	1860
	1849 The California gold rush begins.	**1861** The first telegraph line crosses the country.

Chapter Summary

Sequence

On a separate sheet of paper, copy the chart and place the following events in the sequence in which they happened. Include the date for each one.

▶ Ad for barbed wire

1890	The last major Native American conflict ends in Wounded Knee, South Dakota.
1866	The Goodnight-Loving Trail is established.
1874	Barbed wire is invented.
1860	The Pony Express begins.
1859	Gold is discovered near Denver.

Vocabulary

Match each word with the correct definition or description.

1. **telegraph** (p. 129)
2. **exoduster** (p. 141)
3. **technology** (p. 142)
4. **cattle drive** (p. 149)
5. **Battle of Little Bighorn** (p. 156)

a. use of new ideas to make tools that improve people's lives

b. sends messages along wires

c. Lakota defeat of George Custer

d. African American pioneer

e. cowboys guiding cattle to railroad lines

People and Places

Write a sentence explaining why each of the following people or places was important in the United States in the middle and late 1800s.

1. **Samuel Morse** (p. 129)
2. **Sacramento, California** (p. 130)
3. **Benjamin Singleton** (p. 141)
4. **George Shima** (p. 144)
5. **Chicago, Illinois** (p. 150)
6. **Denver, Colorado** (p. 151)
7. **Levi Strauss** (p. 152)
8. **Black Hills** (p. 155)
9. **George Custer** (p. 156)
10. **Chief Joseph** (p. 157)

Practice and Extend

Assessment Options

✓ Chapter 3 Assessment

- Chapter 3 Content Test: Use Assessment Book, pp. 17–18.
- Chapter 3 Skills Test: Use Assessment Book, pp. 19–20.

Standardized Test Prep

- Chapter 3 Tests contain standardized test format.

✓ Chapter 3 Performance Assessment

- Assign individuals one of the following roles: gold miner, homesteader, cowboy (or cowgirl), railroad worker, or Native American. Have each student draw a picture and write a short summary of his or her life in that role.
- Ask pairs of students to role play a conversation in which they compare how they came to live in the West.
- Assess students' understanding of life in the West in the late 1800s.

1862
President Lincoln signs the Homestead Act.

1869
The transcontinental railroad is completed.

1876
Lakota defeat Custer at Little Bighorn.

1877
African American pioneers establish Nicodemus, Kansas.

1877
Nez Percé surrender in Montana.

Late 1880s
Cattle drives come to an end.

Facts and Main Ideas

1. Why did the telegraph replace the Pony Express?

2. How did the gold rush help California become a state?

3. **Time Line** How many years after the first telegraph line crossed the country was the transcontinental railroad completed?

4. **Main Idea** What challenges did companies building the transcontinental railroad face?

5. **Main Idea** Why did many African Americans move to the Great Plains?

6. **Main Idea** Why did cattle drives come to an end by the late 1800s?

7. **Main Idea** How and why were Native American lands threatened by newcomers?

8. **Critical Thinking:** *Compare and Contrast* Contrast the ways in which Buffalo Bird Woman and Wolf Chief adjusted to life on a reservation. Explain why both made good choices.

Write About History

1. **Write a brief news message** describing events at Promontory Point, Utah Territory, on May 10, 1869.

2. **Write a letter** home about your experience as a homesteader.

3. **Write a help-wanted ad** for a cowboy. Describe the responsibilities and benefits of the job.

Apply Skills

Study the climograph of Houston, Texas, below. Then use the climograph to answer the questions that follow.

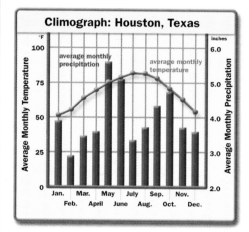

Climograph: Houston, Texas

1. In which month is the average precipitation highest?

2. Which month is usually coldest?

3. Describe the climate during an average day in July in Houston.

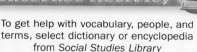
Internet Activity

To get help with vocabulary, people, and terms, select dictionary or encyclopedia from *Social Studies Library* at **www.sfsocialstudies.com**.

163

Hands-on Unit Project

✓ Unit 3 Performance Assessment

- See p. 206 for information about using the Unit Project as a means of performance assessment.
- A scoring guide is provided on p. 206.

WEB SITE
Technology

For more information, students can select the dictionary or encyclopedia from *Social Studies Library* at **www.sfsocialstudies.com**.

Workbook, p. 38

Vocabulary Review

Also on Teacher Resources CD-ROM.

Facts and Main Ideas

Possible answers:

1. The telegraph replaced the Pony Express because the telegraph could send messages more quickly—in minutes instead of days.

2. Thousands of people came to California during the 1849 gold rush, giving the territory enough people to become a state the following year.

3. About eight years

4. Companies building the transcontinental railroad dealt with conflicts with Native Americans, building track through mountains, and accidents from explosives.

5. They hoped to escape discrimination, obtain land, and provide a better life for their children.

6. Cattle drives ended when new railroad lines provided a faster way to send cattle north.

7. United States soldiers forced Native Americans to move to reservations to make land available for newcomers.

8. Possible answer: Buffalo Bird Woman chose to continue speaking the Hidatsa language and farming in the traditional way. Her brother, Wolf Chief, chose to learn English and open a store. Both choices were good because each of them worked to support their families and community.

Write About History

1. Explain to students that their message should describe the event and the feelings it produced.

2. Tell students that their letter should cite some of the hopes and hardships that homesteaders experienced.

3. Each ad should include details about the responsibilities and benefits that come with the job.

Apply Skills

1. May

2. January

3. In July, it would be warm with a low chance of rain.

Chapter Planning Guide

Chapter 4 • Industry and Immigration

Locating Time and Place pp. 164–165

Lesson Titles	Pacing	Main Ideas
Lesson 1 **Inventors Change the World** pp. 166–173	3 days	• In the late 1800s and early 1900s, new inventions changed the way people lived and led to the rise of new industries.
Research and Writing Skills: Write an Outline pp. 174–175		• An outline can serve as a study guide or a summary of a reading selection.
Lesson 2 **The Rise of Big Business** pp. 176–182	3 days	• In the late 1800s and early 1900s, big businesses helped the United States economy grow quickly.
Biography: Andrew Carnegie p. 183		• Immigrant Andrew Carnegie used education and hard work to build a business empire and to support charitable causes.
Lesson 3 **New Americans** pp. 184–190	3 days	• During the late 1800s and early 1900s, millions of immigrants arrived in the United States in search of freedom and opportunity.
Biography: Mary Antin p. 191		• Mary Antin's ability to write allowed her to share the experience of her immigrant family's journey to the U.S.
Lesson 4 **The Labor Movement** pp. 192–197	3 days	• Workers formed labor unions to fight for better wages and working conditions.
Issues and Viewpoints: Working Against Child Labor pp. 198–199		• From the 1800s through today, people have worked to end child labor.

✔ **Chapter 4 Review**
pp. 200–201

✔ = Assessment Options

Vocabulary	Resources	Meeting Individual Needs
investor outline	• Workbook, p. 40 • Transparency 10 • Every Student Learns Guide, pp. 66–69 • Quick Study, pp. 34–35 • Workbook, p. 41	• ESL Support, TE p. 167 • Leveled Practice, TE pp. 171, 174
corporation stock monopoly free enterprise consumer human resource capital resource	• Workbook, p. 42 • Transparency 1 • Every Student Learns Guide, pp. 70–73 • Quick Study, pp. 36–37	• Leveled Practice, TE p. 177 • ESL Support, TE p. 178
prejudice diversity	• Workbook, p. 43 • Transparency 6 • Every Student Learns Guide, pp. 74–77 • Quick Study, pp. 38–39	• ESL Support, TE p. 185 • Leveled Practice, TE p. 188
sweatshop labor union strike	• Workbook, p. 44 • Transparency 23 • Every Student Learns Guide, pp. 78–81 • Quick Study, pp. 40–41	• ESL Support, TE p. 195 • Leveled Practice, TE p. 197
	✓ Chapter 4 Content Test, Assessment Book, pp. 21–22 ✓ Chapter 4 Skills Test, Assessment Book, pp. 23–24	✓ Chapter 4 Performance Assessment, TE p. 200

Providing More Depth

Additional Resources

- Vocabulary Workbook and Cards
- Social Studies Plus! pp. 62–67
- Daily Activity Bank
- Big Book Atlas
- Student Atlas
- Outline Maps
- Desk Maps

 Technology

- AudioText
- MindPoint® Quiz Show CD-ROM
- ExamView® Test Bank CD-ROM
- Teacher Resources CD-ROM
- Map Resources CD-ROM
- SFSuccessNet: iText (Pupil Edition online), iTE (Teacher's Edition online), Online Planner
- **www.sfsocialstudies.com** (Biographies, news, references, maps, and activities)

 To establish guidelines for your students' safe and responsible use of the Internet, use the Scott Foresman Internet Guide.

Additional Internet Links

To find out more about:
- immigration in the United States, visit **www.ellisisland.org**
- Andrew Carnegie and big business, search under *Carnegie* at **www.pbs.org**
- child labor, visit the Learning Page and search for the term *child labor* at **http://memory.loc.gov**

Key Internet Search Terms
- immigrants
- inventors
- labor unions

Workbook Support

 Use the following Workbook pages to support content and skills development as you teach Chapter 4. You can also view and print Workbook pages from the Teacher Resources CD-ROM.

Workbook, p. 39

Vocabulary Preview
Use with Chapter 4.

Directions: Match each vocabulary word to its meaning. Write the number of the word on the blank next to its meaning.

1. investor
2. corporation
3. stock
4. monopoly
5. free enterprise
6. consumer
7. human resource
8. capital resource
9. prejudice
10. diversity
11. sweat shop
12. labor union
13. strike

8 tool or machine that a company can use to produce goods and services

3 share of a company

10 variety

13 when workers refuse to work to try to force business owners to meet their demands

7 people who work to produce goods and services

2 business that is owned by investors

6 person who buys or uses goods and services

5 system in which people are free to start their own businesses and own their own property

12 group of workers who join together to fight for improved working conditions and better wages

9 unfair negative opinion about a group of people

11 hot, cramped workshop

1 person who gives money to a business or project hoping to gain a profit

4 company that has control of an entire industry

Notes for Home: Your child learned the vocabulary terms for Chapter 4.
Home Activity: Help your child use media sources to find current examples of the use of these terms.

Use with Pupil Edition, p. 164

Workbook, p. 40

Lesson 1: Inventors Change the World
Use with Pages 166–173.

Directions: Complete the chart with details from this lesson. You may use your textbook.

Inventor	Invention	Significance
Alexander Graham Bell	Telephone	Changed the way people communicated
Thomas Edison	Phonograph	Musicians could record music and sell records
Lewis Latimer	Method for making carbon filaments	Made electric light practical for everyday use
Frank Sprague	Electric Streetcar	Improved urban transportation
Orville and Wilbur Wright	Airplane	Changed the way people traveled

Notes for Home: Your child learned about inventions that changed the United States at the turn of the twentieth century.
Home Activity: Ask your child whether and how these inventions affect your daily lives today.

Use with Pupil Edition, p. 173

Workbook, p. 41

Write an Outline
Use with Pages 174–175.

Directions: An outline is a written plan for organizing information about a subject. Look at the outline below. Then answer the questions that follow.

Andrew Carnegie

I. Childhood
  A. Born in Scotland
  B. Moved to the United States as a boy
II. Young adulthood
  A. Worked to help support his family rather than attending school
  B. Read on his own and attended night classes
III. Adulthood
  A. Business career
    1. Worked his way up in jobs at telegraph and railroad companies
    2. Made large amounts of money by making shrewd investments
    3. Became rich by building a huge steel empire
  B. Supporter of charitable causes
    1. Gave away millions of his fortune
    2. Is especially well known for supporting libraries

1. What is the main topic of this outline?
Andrew Carnegie

2. How is the biographical information in this outline organized?
The information is organized chronologically.

3. What evidence supports the idea that education was important to Carnegie?
He read on his own and took night classes.

4. According to the outline, how did Carnegie become wealthy?
He made investments and built a steel company.

5. According to the outline, what were two main aspects of Carnegie's adult life?
He had a successful business career and was a supporter of charitable causes.

Notes for Home: Your child learned to organize and read information in an outline.
Home Activity: Help your child outline the main ideas of a magazine or newspaper article.

Use with Pupil Edition, p. 175

Workbook, p. 42

Lesson 2: The Rise of Big Business
Use with Pages 176–182.

Directions: Using information from this lesson, circle the term in parentheses that best completes each sentence.

1. A new process for making (steel, iron) helped spark a boom in industry in the late 1800s.

2. Carnegie built his fortune by (buying, selling) a number of businesses involved in the steel-making process.

3. (Railroad, Oil) companies became the nation's first large corporations.

4. Corporations are owned by (investors, employees).

5. By selling (stock, capital resources), corporations can raise money to help their businesses grow.

6. Standard Oil became a (free enterprise, monopoly) by gaining control of the nation's oil industry.

7. The oil industry boomed in the early 1900s along with the rise of the (automobile, electric) industry.

8. In a free enterprise system, (business owners, consumers) decide what to produce and what to charge for products and services.

9. A company's employees are its (human resources, capital resources).

10. The rise of big business in the late 1800s helped the United States become the world's leading producer of (manufactured goods, natural resources).

Notes for Home: Your child learned about the rise of big business in the late 1800s and early 1900s.
Home Activity: Use a newspaper to read with your child about some of the issues facing big businesses today.

Use with Pupil Edition, p. 182

Workbook Support

Workbook, p. 43

Lesson 3: New Americans
Use with Pages 184–190.

Directions: Fill in the blanks with information from this lesson. You may use your textbook.

Between 1880 and 1920, more than ___**23 million**___ immigrants arrived in the United States. Before 1890, most came from countries in ___**northern Europe**___. After that time, most came from ___**southern and eastern Europe**___. Many came to escape poverty, hunger and a lack of jobs. Some, such as Russian Jews, came in search of ___**religious freedom**___.

Millions of immigrants arriving on the East Coast passed through ___**Ellis Island**___. Here they were checked for illnesses and asked questions about their plans. Chinese immigrants stopped at ___**Angel Island**___. The purpose of this stop was to ensure that they had ___**relatives**___ already living here. Many were forced to remain there for weeks or even longer. Once allowed into the United States, most immigrants had to find a ___**job**___ and a place to live. Many had to learn a new ___**language**___, and some faced the hardship of ___**prejudice**___.

Directions: Suppose you are an immigrant arriving on Ellis Island in the late 1800s. Write a diary entry describing your experience. You may use a separate sheet of paper if you need more space.

_____
_____
_____
_____
_____
_____
_____
_____
_____

Notes for Home: Your child learned about the era of immigration between 1880 and 1920.
Home Activity: Help your child use library or Internet resources to learn more about the immigrant experience in America at the turn of the century.

Use with Pupil Edition, p. 190

Workbook, p. 44

Lesson 4: The Labor Movement
Use with Pages 192–197.

Directions: Complete the chart with information from this lesson. You may use your textbook.

Cause	Effect
Factory workers were sometimes paid for the amount of goods they produced.	They worked faster and sometimes hurt themselves.
Triangle Shirtwaist Company owners did not provide fire exits or fire escapes.	146 workers died when a fire broke out in the factory.
Pay was so low in many factories that parents could not support their families.	Many children worked instead of going to school.
Samuel Gompers led an unsuccessful strike of cigar makers.	He decided unions should be larger to get more bargaining power, leading to the formation of the AFL.
Labor unions gained more members in the late 1800s and early 1900s.	Working conditions improved somewhat.

Notes for Home: Your child learned about the early days of the labor movement.
Home Activity: Discuss with your child how the labor movement of the late 1800s and early 1900s still affects workers today. Talk about current labor laws, labor unions, and strikes. Refer to events in the news and/or the jobs of people your child knows.

Use with Pupil Edition, p. 197

Workbook, p. 45

Vocabulary Review
Use with Chapter 4.

Directions: Use the vocabulary terms from Chapter 4 to complete the crossword puzzle.

Crossword answers:
- PREJUDICE
- DIVERSITY
- CAPITAL
- SWEATSHOP
- INVEST
- HUMAN RESOURCE
- FREE ENTERPRISE
- MONOPOLY
- CONSUMER
- LABOR UNION
- STOCK
- SOURCE
- CORPORATION
- STRIKE

Across
1. unfair negative opinion about a group of people
8. people who work to produce goods and services
10. person who buys or uses goods and services
11. share of a company
12. business that is owned by investors
13. when workers refuse to work to try to force business owners to meet their demands

Down
2. tool or machine that a company can use to produce goods and services
3. variety
4. hot, cramped workshop
5. system in which people are free to start their own businesses and own their own property
6. person who gives to a business or project hoping to gain a profit
7. company that has control of an entire industry
9. group of workers who join together to fight for improved working conditions and better wages

Notes for Home: Your child learned the vocabulary terms for Chapter 4.
Home Activity: Have your child use these words to write a brief summary of what he or she learned in Chapter 4.

Use with Pupil Edition, p. 201

Workbook, p. 46

2 Project Inventions Change the Country
DISCOVERY SCHOOL

Directions: Make a poster or advertisement for an invention from the late 1800s or early 1900s.

1. The invention we chose is _____
2. The name of the inventor is _____
3. The purpose of the invention is _____
4. Special features of this invention include _____
5. The (✔) shows how this invention helped people:
   _____ saved money _____ saved time _____ other: _____
6. Reasons people should use this invention are _____
7. This invention changed the world because _____
8. This is what the invention looked like:

> Gather relevant resources from your school library. Assist students, as needed, to locate answers to the questions listed above.

✔ Checklist for Students
_____ We chose an invention from the late 1800s.
_____ We identified the inventor, and we described the invention's purpose, features, and benefits.
_____ We made a poster or advertisement for the invention.
_____ We included a picture of the invention on the poster.
_____ We presented our poster or advertisement to the class.

Notes for Home: Your child researched an invention from the late 1800s and advertised its features to the class.
Home Activity: With your child, identify a modern invention you both agree has changed the world. Discuss how it has impacted your life.

Use with Pupil Edition, p. 206

Assessment Support

 Use these Assessment Book pages and the ExamView® Test Bank CD-ROM to assess content and skills in Chapter 4 and Unit 2. You can also view and print Assessment Book pages from the Teacher Resources CD–ROM.

Assessment Book, p. 21

Chapter 4 Test

Part 1: Content Test

Directions: Fill in the circle next to the correct answer.

Lesson Objective (1:1)

1. Who invented the telephone?
   - ● Alexander Graham Bell
   - Ⓑ Lewis Latimer
   - Ⓒ Frank Sprague
   - Ⓓ Frank Duryea

Lesson Objective (1:1)

2. Which of the following did Thomas Edison invent?
   - Ⓐ the airplane
   - Ⓑ the electric streetcar
   - ● the phonograph
   - Ⓓ the gasoline engine

Lesson Objective (1:2)

3. Which of the following represents an invention that changed transportation at the turn of the twentieth century?
   - Ⓐ the wagon
   - Ⓑ the Pony Express
   - ● the electric streetcar
   - Ⓓ the stagecoach

Lesson Objective (1:3)

4. Which of the following is NOT an example of how inventions of the late 1800s and early 1900s led to the rise of new industries?
   - Ⓐ Companies all over the country began selling and designing cars.
   - Ⓑ People started businesses to offer telephone service.
   - ● Airplane manufacturing became the country's leading industry.
   - Ⓓ Entrepreneurs built power stations to bring electricity to cities.

Lesson Objective (2:1)

5. Andrew Carnegie is known for which of the following?
   - Ⓐ inventing a new method for making steel
   - ● building a huge steel empire
   - Ⓒ building oil refineries
   - Ⓓ forming the Westinghouse Electric Company

Lesson Objective (2:1)

6. Which business leader founded Standard Oil Company?
   - Ⓐ Edwin Drake
   - ● John D. Rockefeller
   - Ⓒ William Randolph Hearst
   - Ⓓ Madame C. J. Walker

Lesson Objective (2:2)

7. Which of the following best describes how railroads helped the United States economy grow?
   - Ⓐ They charged high rates to farmers.
   - Ⓑ They used many tons of steel.
   - Ⓒ They helped end the shipping industry.
   - ● They helped businesses reach distant markets.

Use with Pupil Edition, p. 200

Assessment Book, p. 22

Lesson Objective (2:3)

8. Which of the following describes a free enterprise system?
   - Ⓐ Consumers have few choices about where they can buy goods and services.
   - Ⓑ Competition rarely exists among business owners.
   - Ⓒ The government regulates what business owners can produce and how much they can charge for products and services.
   - ● Business owners can decide what to produce and how much to charge for products or services.

Lesson Objective (2:4)

9. The growth of big business led to all EXCEPT which of the following?
   - Ⓐ By 1900, more Americans worked in factories than on farms.
   - ● People moved by the millions to rural areas.
   - Ⓒ Big business created millions of jobs.
   - Ⓓ The United States became the world's leading producer of manufactured goods.

Lesson Objective (3:1)

10. Which of the following is one of the main reasons immigrants came to the United States in the late 1800s and early 1900s?
    - Ⓐ They did not want religious freedom.
    - ● They hoped for economic opportunity.
    - Ⓒ They faced a lack of prejudice.
    - Ⓓ They wanted to live more simply.

Lesson Objective (3:2)

11. Angel Island differed from Ellis Island in that
    - Ⓐ it was the main immigrant station for European immigrants.
    - ● it was the main immigrant station for Chinese immigrants.
    - Ⓒ Angel Island was located on the East Coast.
    - Ⓓ most people stopped there for only a few hours.

Lesson Objective (3:3)

12. Immigrants often lived in communities with others from their home country because
    - Ⓐ it was illegal for them to live elsewhere.
    - Ⓑ they had no interest in building new lives in the United States.
    - ● it was a way to help make the adjustment to the United States easier.
    - Ⓓ housing was not available in other areas.

Lesson Objective (4:1)

13. Which of the following was NOT a contributing factor that led to the rise of labor unions?
    - Ⓐ Many workers earned low wages and worked long hours.
    - ● Many business owners were going on strike.
    - Ⓒ Working conditions were often unhealthy and dangerous.
    - Ⓓ Many workers labored in hot, cramped workshops.

Use with Pupil Edition, p. 200

Assessment Book, p. 23

Lesson Objective (4:2)

14. Which of the following was NOT a main goal of the American Federation of Labor?
    - Ⓐ safer working conditions
    - Ⓑ end child labor
    - Ⓒ better wages
    - ● a 12-hour workday

Lesson Objective (4:3)

15. Which of the following events shows how conditions improved for workers in the early 1900s?
    - Ⓐ the Homestead strike
    - Ⓑ the Triangle Shirtwaist fire
    - Ⓒ the completion of the transcontinental railroad
    - ● the establishment of Labor Day

Part 2: Skills Test

Directions: Use complete sentences to answer questions 1–5. Use a separate sheet of paper if you need more space.

1. Write the following events in the order in which they happened. **Sequence**

   Lewis Latimer developed a method that made electric light practical for every day use.

   Thomas Edison built an electric power station in New York City.

   Frank Sprague designed the world's first system of electric streetcars.

   Thomas Edison built a light bulb that glowed for two days.

   > **Thomas Edison built a light bulb that glowed for two days.**
   >
   > ↓
   >
   > **Lewis Latimer developed a method that made electric light practical for every day use.**
   >
   > ↓
   >
   > **Thomas Edison built an electric power station in New York City.**
   >
   > ↓
   >
   > **Frank Sprague designed the world's first system of electric streetcars.**

Use with Pupil Edition, p. 200

Assessment Book, p. 24

2. Why do monopolies threaten the free enterprise system? **Draw Conclusions**

   If companies do not compete with each other, consumers will not have the freedom to decide what goods and services they purchase. Companies can keep prices high.

3. How did the growth of the automobile industry effect the oil industry? **Cause and Effect**

   The growth of the automobile industry created a huge demand for oil products such as gasoline and motor oil.

4. What challenges did many immigrants face once they gained entry into the United States? **Main Idea and Details**

   They had to find a job and a place to live. Many had to learn a new language and adjust to new traditions and ways of living. Others faced the hardship of prejudice.

5. Complete the outline by filling in the missing topics and details about the labor movement. **Write an Outline**

   ### The Labor Movement

   I. Poor working Conditions
      A. **Many workers earned low wages and worked long hours.**
         1. Steelworkers at Carnegie's Homestead Steel Works labored for 12 hours a day, seven days a week.
         2. Many children worked for just 10 to 20 cents a day.
      B. **Working environments were often unhealthy and dangerous.**
         1. Workers were trapped inside when a fire started at the Triangle Shirtwaist Company.

   II. The Rise of Labor Unions
      A. Workers joined together to fight for improved conditions.
         1. **Samuel Gompers formed the American Federation of Labor.**
         2. **Many workers went on strike until business owners met their demands.**

   III. **Conditions Improve for Workers**
      A. New laws shorten working hours and improve safety in the workplace.
      B. Congress declares Labor Day a national holiday.

Use with Pupil Edition, p. 200

Assessment Support

Assessment Book, p. 25

Unit 2 Test

Part 1: Content Test

Directions: Fill in the circle next to the correct answer.

Lesson Objective (3–1:1)

1. Which of the following could deliver mail from Missouri to California in just 10 days?
   - Ⓐ the telegraph
   - Ⓑ the "horseless carriage"
   - ● the Pony Express
   - Ⓓ the stagecoach

Lesson Objective (3–1:2)

2. Which of the following describes a challenge faced by the Union Pacific railroad?
   - Ⓐ It had to build through the Sierra Nevada.
   - ● It faced conflict with Native Americans.
   - Ⓒ It faced conflict with Chinese immigrants.
   - Ⓓ The government did not support a transcontinental railroad.

Lesson Objective (3–2:2)

3. Which best describes a challenge facing homesteaders on the Great Plains?
   - Ⓐ They had to pay about $10 for 160 acres of land.
   - Ⓑ Land on the Great Plains was dry but very fertile.
   - Ⓒ They had to pass through miles of barbed wire.
   - ● They had to bust through sod before planting crops.

Lesson Objective (3–2:4)

4. Steel plows were especially important to Great Plains farmers because
   - Ⓐ there was a shortage of iron.
   - Ⓑ there was a shortage of farm animals to pull plows.
   - ● the sod was extremely thick on the Great Plains.
   - Ⓓ steel plows were less costly than iron ones.

Lesson Objective (3–3:2)

5. The arrival of railroads in Texas helped end the cattle drives because
   - ● they made it unnecessary to drive cattle to distant railroad centers.
   - Ⓑ the railroads blocked key cattle trails.
   - Ⓒ easterners could come to Texas to buy meat.
   - Ⓓ buffalo replaced cattle as a major meat source.

Lesson Objective (3–3:3)

6. Which of the following was NOT an effect of the search for gold in the West?
   - Ⓐ Supply stations for miners grew into important cities.
   - ● Gold rushes left the East deserted with ghost towns.
   - Ⓒ Dreams of finding gold attracted thousands of settlers.
   - Ⓓ Growing towns offered opportunities for entrepreneurs.

Use with Pupil Edition, p. 204

Assessment Book, p. 26

Lesson Objective (3–4:2)

7. The Battle of Little Bighorn convinced the United States that
   - Ⓐ it would not be able to defeat certain Native American groups.
   - Ⓑ the conflict would not be resolved until Native Americans could return to their traditional homelands.
   - Ⓒ moving Native American groups to reservations was not a good idea.
   - ● it should take stronger action against Native Americans.

Lesson Objective (4–1:1)

8. Which of the following did Thomas Edison invent?
   - ● a light bulb with a carbon filament
   - Ⓑ the typewriter
   - Ⓒ the radio
   - Ⓓ the automobile

Lesson Objective (4–1:2)

9. What do the electric street car and the "horseless carriage" have in common?
   - Ⓐ They were invented by Thomas Edison.
   - Ⓑ They were both outlawed at one time.
   - ● They changed transportation at the turn of the twentieth century.
   - Ⓓ They were outdated by the early 1900s.

Lesson Objective (4–2:1)

10. George Westinghouse is known for
    - Ⓐ his monopoly of the oil industry.
    - ● developing a new technology for delivering electricity.
    - Ⓒ controlling the banking industry.
    - Ⓓ building a steel empire.

Lesson Objective (4–2:4)

11. Which of the following is a result of the rise of big business in the late 1800s and early 1900s?
    - Ⓐ More people left the United States to live in other countries.
    - Ⓑ Many people moved from cities to rural areas.
    - ● The United States became the world's biggest producer of manufactured goods.
    - Ⓓ Many United States cities became ghost towns.

Lesson Objective (4–3:1)

12. Which of the following is NOT a reason why many immigrants came to the United States in the late 1800s and early 1900s?
    - Ⓐ to escape poverty
    - Ⓑ to escape hunger
    - ● they had many rights at home
    - Ⓓ they faced a lack of religious freedom at home

Lesson Objective (4–3:2)

13. What did Ellis Island and Angel Island share in common?
    - Ⓐ Both were located on the West Coast.
    - Ⓑ Both were located on the East Coast.
    - Ⓒ Both held immigrants until they could prove they had relatives living in the country.
    - ● Both were main immigration stations for immigrants arriving in the country.

Use with Pupil Edition, p. 204

Assessment Book, p. 27

Lesson Objective (4–4:1)

14. Which of the following describes the typical week of a steelworker at Carnegie's Homestead Steel Works?
    - Ⓐ five days a week, eight hours a day
    - Ⓑ five days a week, ten hours a day
    - Ⓒ seven days a week, four hours a day
    - ● seven days a week, twelve hours a day

Lesson Objective (4–4:2)

15. Which of the following best describes the main goals of labor unions such as the American Federation of Labor?
    - ● to get higher pay, shorter working hours, and safer working conditions
    - Ⓑ to hire new workers and start new holidays
    - Ⓒ to organize strikes and find new jobs
    - Ⓓ to pass child labor laws

Part 2: Skills Test

Directions: Use complete sentences to answer questions 1–5. Use a separate sheet of paper if you need more space.

1. Describe the changes that took place in transportation in the late 1800s.
   Main Idea and Details

   The growth of railroads allowed people to travel and transport goods more quickly. The transcontinental railroad allowed people to travel across the United States in just a week. Electric streetcars greatly improved urban transportation. The first cars were built in the 1890s.

2. What was the purpose of the Homestead Act? **Summarize**

   The purpose of the Homestead Act was to encourage settlers to move to the Great Plains.

3. What conditions led to the rise of labor unions in the late 1800s and early 1900s?
   Cause and Effect

   Many workers had to work for long hours and received low wages. Many had to work in hot, cramped workshops, and conditions were often unhealthy and dangerous. Many young children worked in unsafe conditions.

Use with Pupil Edition, p. 204

Assessment Book, p. 28

4. Write the following events in the order in which they happened. **Sequence**

   Crazy Horse led the Lakota to victory at the Battle of Little Bighorn.

   Gold was discovered in the Black Hills.

   The Lakota signed a treaty with the United States that created the Great Lakota Reservation.

   > The Lakota signed a treaty with the United States that created the Great Lakota Reservation.
   >
   > ↓
   >
   > Gold was discovered in the Black Hills.
   >
   > ↓
   >
   > Crazy Horse led the Lakota to victory at the Battle of Little Bighorn.

5. Look at the map below. What time is it in Boston when it is 4:00 P.M. in Los Angeles?
   Read a Time Zone Map
   It is 7:00 p.m. in Boston.

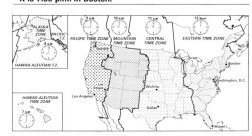

Use with Pupil Edition, p. 204

Industry and Immigration

Chapter 4 Outline

Resources

- Workbook, p. 39: Vocabulary Preview
- Vocabulary Cards
- Social Studies Plus!

1879, Menlo Park, New Jersey: Lesson 1

Ask students to describe what impact the light bulb had. (Possible answer: People could be productive for longer hours.)

1870s, Pittsburgh, Pennsylvania: Lesson 2

Have students consider how steel might help change the nation. (Possible answer: Steel would make larger buildings and longer bridges possible.)

1894, Boston, Massachusetts: Lesson 3

This picture shows Mary Antin, an immigrant who settled in the United States. Ask students what challenges she might have found. (Possible answer: new language, new culture, discrimination)

1899, New York, New York: Lesson 4

Strike means to stop working to demand better pay or conditions. Ask students to predict how the public responded to strikes. (Possible answer: Some people supported the actions, others did not.)

Industry and Immigration

1879

Menlo Park, New Jersey
Thomas Edison invents a useful light bulb.

Lesson 1

1

1870s

Pittsburgh, Pennsylvania
Andrew Carnegie begins making steel at affordable prices.

Lesson 2

2

1894

Boston, Massachusetts
Mary Antin, one of millions of new immigrants, settles in Boston with her family.

Lesson 3

3

1899

New York, New York
New York "newsies" go on strike to protest the rise in the price of newspapers.

Lesson 4

4

164

Practice and Extend

Vocabulary Preview

- Use Workbook p. 39 to help students preview the vocabulary words in this chapter.
- Use Vocabulary Cards to preview key concept words in this chapter.

 Also on Teacher Resources CD-ROM.

Workbook, p. 39

Vocabulary Preview

Directions: Match each vocabulary word to its meaning. Write the number of the word on the blank next to its meaning.

1. inventor
2. corporation
3. stock
4. monopoly
5. free enterprise
6. consumer
7. human resource
8. capital resource
9. prejudice
10. diversity
11. sweat shop
12. labor union
13. strike

___ tool or machine that a company can use to produce goods and services
___ share of a company
___ variety
___ when workers refuse to work to try to force business owners to meet their demands
___ a person
___ business that is owned by investors
___ person who buys or uses goods and services
___ system in which people are free to start their own businesses and own their own property
___ group of workers who join together to fight for improved working conditions and better wages
___ unfair negative opinion about a group of people
___ hot, cramped workshop
___ person who gives money to a business or perhaps hoping to gain a profit
___ company that has control of an entire industry

Notes for Home: Your child learned the vocabulary terms for Chapter 4.
Home Activity: Help your child use media sources to find current examples of the use of these terms.

Locating Time and Place

CANADA

UNITED STATES

Pittsburgh

Boston

New York City
Menlo Park

ATLANTIC OCEAN

Why We Remember

"Give me your tired, your poor,
Your huddled masses yearning to breathe free..."

These words are part of a poem by Emma Lazarus that was written for the Statue of Liberty in New York Harbor. "Lady Liberty" has been a symbol of hope and freedom for the millions of immigrants who have come to the United States from all over the world. In this unit you will see how Americans—both newcomers and those born here—contributed to the remarkable growth and change that altered our nation forever.

165

Locating Time and Place

- Have students examine the pictures shown on p. 164 for Lessons 1, 2, 3, and 4.

- Remind students that each picture is coded with both a number and a color to link it to a place on the map on p. 165.

Why We Remember

Have students read the "Why We Remember" paragraph on p. 165, and ask them to suggest why the poem specifically invites the tired, poor, and the huddled masses to come to the United States. What effect do students think this message had on immigrants?

WEB SITE
Technology

You can learn more about Menlo Park, New Jersey; Pittsburgh, Pennsylvania; Boston, Massachusetts; and New York, New York, by clicking on *Atlas* at **www.sfsocialstudies.com.**

FYI **SOCIAL STUDIES**
Background

The Statue of Liberty

Ask students to share experiences or personal knowledge about the Statue of Liberty.

- France gave the statue to the United States as a sign of friendship.
- One of the statue's engineers, Gustave Eiffel, also designed the Eiffel Tower.
- The seven spikes in the statue's crown stand for the seven seas and seven continents of the world.
- The tablet in the statue's left hand reads "July 4, 1776."

Inventors Change the World

Objectives

- Identify important inventions by Alexander Graham Bell and Thomas Edison.

- Describe some of the inventions that changed transportation.

- Explain how inventions led to the rise of new industries.

Vocabulary

investor, p. 168

Resources

- Workbook, p. 40
- Transparency 10
- Every Student Learns Guide, pp. 66–69
- Quick Study, pp. 34–35

Quick Teaching Plan

If time is short, have students write the headings *Key Inventors* and *Key Inventions* at the top of a sheet of paper.

- Have students write down details about the important inventors and inventions in the late 1800s and early 1900s as they read independently.

1 Introduce and Motivate

Preview To activate prior knowledge, ask students to think about the improvements in communication discussed in Chapter 3. Tell students that they will learn about other communication developments in Lesson 1.

You Are There Tell students that the "talking-machine" experiment would lead to an invention that would change communications forever. Ask them to predict what that invention might be.

LESSON 1

|1875| | |1900|

1876
Alexander Graham Bell invents the telephone.

1879
Thomas Edison develops a working light bulb.

1903
The Wright Brothers make the world's first airplane flight.

PREVIEW

Focus on the Main Idea
In the late 1800s and early 1900s, new inventions changed the way people lived and led to the rise of new industries.

PLACES
Menlo Park, New Jersey
Richmond, Virginia
Kitty Hawk, North Carolina

PEOPLE
Alexander Graham Bell
Thomas Edison
Lewis Latimer
Frank Sprague
Frank Duryea
Charles Duryea
Wilbur Wright
Orville Wright
Blanche Stuart Scott

VOCABULARY
investor

▶ The world's first telephone

Inventors Change the World

You Are There The year is 1863. The place is Edinburgh, Scotland. A 16-year-old boy named Alexander has just finished building a very strange machine out of tin, rubber, and wood. He calls it a "talking-machine," because it is designed to imitate the human voice. He built it with the help of his brother Melville, who is 18.

The brothers have set up their machine to say the word *Mamma*. But will anyone think it sounds like a real person? They decide to find out. They bring the machine out into the street. The brothers hide while the machine calls out, "Mamma, mamma."

And sure enough, people come outside to see who is calling. "Good gracious," cries one neighbor, "what can be the matter with that baby?"

The brothers congratulate each other on a successful experiment.

Sequence As you read, keep track of the sequence of important events that changed the way Americans lived.

Practice and Extend

READING SKILL Sequence

In the Lesson Review, students complete a graphic organizer like the one below. You may want to provide students with a copy of Transparency 10 to complete as they read the lesson.

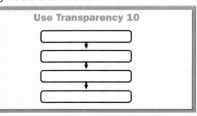

Use Transparency 10

VOCABULARY Word Exercise

Individual Word Study

Tell students that the suffix *-or* means "one who does something." Point out that the word *invest* means "to put money in a business or project hoping for a profit." Ask students to use this information to figure out what *investor* means. (someone who puts money in a business or project hoping for a profit) Ask students what we would call someone who invents things and someone who investigates things. (*inventor, investigator*)

The First Telephone

Alexander Graham Bell was always interested in sound and speech. As a very young boy in Scotland, he tried to teach his dog, Mr. Perd, how to speak. It did not work. But he learned a valuable lesson about being an inventor—you have to learn from your failures, and you have to keep trying.

As you just read, Bell built a talking-machine when he was 16. By the time he was in his twenties, he had a new idea. He believed it was possible to make a machine that would allow people to talk to each other across wires. He called this idea the "talking telegraph."

In 1871 Bell moved to Boston, Massachusetts. He worked at the Boston School for the Deaf, teaching deaf students to speak. Developing better ways to teach deaf children was another of Bell's main interests.

At night Bell continued working on his talking telegraph, or telephone. He hired Thomas Watson to help him design and build models of his invention. Bell and Watson knew they had to work quickly if they wanted to invent the first working telephone. Other inventors were also trying to develop a telephone.

On March 10, 1876, Bell and Watson were ready to test their invention. They stood in separate rooms, with the doors closed. Into one end of the telephone, Bell shouted,

> *"Mr. Watson, come here, I want to see you."*

Watson raced into Bell's room and announced that he had heard the sentence clearly.

Bell predicted that the telephone would soon change the way people communicated with each other. He was right. By the time Bell died in 1922, there were millions of telephones in use in the United States.

REVIEW What events in Alexander Graham Bell's life led up to his invention of the telephone? **Sequence**

▶ Bell's invention helped change the way Americans communicate (*above*).

▶ Alexander Graham Bell is seen here (*left*) placing the first long-distance telephone call, between New York and Chicago.

167

Quick Summary In 1876, Alexander Graham Bell capped a lifetime of work with the invention of the telephone. In the process, he forever changed the way people communicate.

① **Why was the lesson Bell learned from his experiments with Mr. Perd so valuable?** Possible answer: It taught him to stay focused on his ideas, even when he had no success. **Express Ideas**

G **SOCIAL STUDIES STRAND**
Government

Tell students that in order to encourage invention, the government grants a patent to the person who invents something. This gives the inventor the sole right to profit from an invention for a certain period of time.

② **Why was it important for Bell and Watson to be the first to invent the telephone?** Possible answer: The first inventor to develop the telephone would gain economic benefits. **Apply Information**

Primary Source

Cited in *The Importance of Alexander Graham Bell,* by Robyn Weaver

③ **Why was it important that Watson heard Bell's request?** It meant that they had succeeded in developing a working telephone. **Analyze Primary Sources**

④ **What fact from the text supports Bell's prediction that the telephone would change the way people communicated?** By 1922, there were millions of phones in use in the United States. **Main Idea and Details**

✓ **REVIEW ANSWER** Possible answer: Sound and speech interested Bell as a child. By the age of 16, he invented a talking machine. He worked to help deaf people learn to speak. **Sequence**

ESL **ACTIVATE PRIOR KNOWLEDGE**
ESL Support

Chart Changes in Communications Technology Students will place the development of the telephone on a time line of other changes in communications technology.

Beginning Have students create an illustrated time line showing the changes in communications technology discussed here and in Chapter 3.

Intermediate Have students create a time line that identifies the changes in communications technology discussed here and in Chapter 3.

Advanced Have students create a time line that names and briefly describes the changes in communications technology discussed here and in Chapter 3.

For additional ESL support, use Every Student Learns Guide, pp. 66–69.

Edison's Light Bulb

🕐 **Quick Summary** Thomas Edison invented the phonograph, but his greatest invention may have been the electric light bulb.

5 **In addition to recording music, in what other ways could a machine that records voices be used?** Possible answer: Speeches and other important events could be recorded and shared. People could record and send spoken messages. **Categorize**

6 **What advantages might an electric light bulb have over a lamp fueled by gas or candles?** Possible answer: An electric light bulb would be safer than one with an open flame. It might be cleaner, too. **Compare and Contrast**

7 **What did Edison mean when he said "I've just found 10,000 ways that won't work"?** Possible answer: He knew there was a solution to the problem, but he had not found it yet.
Analyze Primary Sources

✓ **REVIEW ANSWER** Edison tested filaments to find a way to make the light bulb glow for more than a few seconds. Latimer found a way to make the light bulb practical for everyday use.
Summarize

Edison's Light Bulb

Another inventor who helped change the world was **Thomas Edison.** A year after Bell built the first telephone, Edison used some of the same scientific ideas to invent the phonograph. Edison's phonograph was the first machine that could record a voice and then play it back. This technology would soon allow musicians to record music and **5** sell records.

After the phonograph, Edison turned to a different idea. He wanted to build a safe and dependable electric light bulb. At that time, people used gas lamps or candles for indoor **6** lighting. Scientists already knew how to build light bulbs, but they could not build one that lasted long enough to be used in homes. Edison began working on this problem with a team of young scientists in his laboratory in **Menlo Park, New Jersey.** Many inventors like Edison did not have enough money of their own to pay for experiments. They relied on investors. **Investors** are people who give money to a business or project, hoping to gain a profit.

▶ Thomas Edison, with his light bulb above, made more than 1,000 inventions.

The hardest part about building the light bulb was finding the right material to use for the filament. The filament is the thin wire inside a light bulb that glows when electricity passes through it. Every filament that Edison tried either burned out quickly or exploded. "I've tried everything," Edison wrote. "I have not failed. I've just found 10,000 ways that won't work." In 1879 Edison and his team **7** solved the problem. They built a bulb with a carbon filament that glowed for two days.

This was a great start, but would you want to replace your light bulbs every two days? An inventor named **Lewis Latimer** helped improve the light bulb. Latimer developed a method of making carbon filaments that lasted much longer. This invention helped make electric light practical for everyday use.

REVIEW How did Thomas Edison and Lewis Latimer each contribute to the effort to make a working light bulb? **Summarize**

▶ Lewis Latimer was also an artist. Alexander Graham Bell hired him to draw up plans for his new invention, the telephone.

Practice and Extend

FYI **SOCIAL STUDIES**
Background

About Lewis Latimer

- Latimer was born in Boston in 1848 to parents who had escaped from slavery.
- He taught himself mechanical drawing while working in a patent attorney's office.
- In addition to being a skilled engineer and inventor with many patents to his credit, Latimer also played a key role in helping Thomas Edison win patents for his inventions.
- Latimer wrote *Incandescent Electric Lighting,* a landmark book about electric lights.

Electricity Brings Change

Thomas Edison knew that electric light could change life in the United States. First, however, there would have to be some way to get electricity into people's homes and businesses. Edison decided to build an electrical power station in New York City. From this station, wires could carry electricity to buildings in the city.

Edison knew that it would be risky to build his first power station in the country's biggest city. If he failed, everyone would know about it. However, like many inventors, Edison was also an entrepreneur. He wanted to show the world that his power station really worked. Then people would pay his company to bring **8** them electricity.

Edison began testing his power station in the summer of 1882. "It was a terrifying experience as I didn't know what was going to happen," he said. After a few failures, Edison got the system working. When he turned the power station on, lights in 40 different buildings began glowing. Soon other cities began building power stations of their own. Stores, offices, newspapers, factories, and theaters began installing electric lights. **9**

Change came more slowly to people's homes. At first only wealthy families could afford to have electric lighting at home. As the graph on this page shows, only eight percent of all U.S. homes had electric service in 1907. The number of homes with electricity began rising quickly after that. **10**

REVIEW Why did Edison decide to build a power station in New York City?
Main Idea and Details

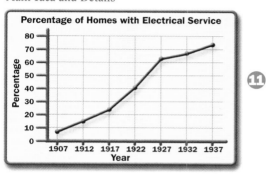

Percentage of Homes with Electrical Service

11

▶ Home use of electricity increased quickly.

GRAPH SKILL By what year did 40 percent of homes have electricity?

▶ Electricity lit up this Coney Island amusement park in New York City.

169

Electricity Brings Change

🕐 **Quick Summary** Edison took the risky step of building a power station to distribute electricity to individual homes. His efforts helped make electricity available to millions of Americans.

8 **Why did Edison want to build the first power station?** Possible answer: He wanted to prove that his electrical system worked so that people would pay to get electricity. Summarize

9 **Why do you think businesses were among the first to make wide use of electricity?** Possible answer: They had the money to invest in electricity. Electricity could help them earn more money for themselves. Analyze Information

10 **Why do you think the number of homes with electricity rose in the 1900s?** Possible answer: As more plants were built, more people could have electricity in their homes. Make Inferences

✔ **REVIEW ANSWER** Edison chose New York City because it was the country's largest city. If he succeeded there, everyone would know about it. Main Idea and Details

 Test Talk

Use Information from Graphics

11 **Based on the graph, during which five-year period did electricity grow the most?** Tell students to study the graph to find the right answer. Between 1922 and 1927 Interpret Graphs

GRAPH SKILL **Answer** 1922

CURRICULUM CONNECTION
Writing

Write a Letter

- Have students adopt the point of view of a person in the early 1900s who has just installed electricity in his or her house.
- Ask them to write a letter to a friend in the country explaining how electricity works and how it has changed life for him or her.
- Encourage students to locate details for their letters from elsewhere in the chapter, as well as from outside resources.

Streetcars and Horseless Carriages

🕐 *Quick Summary* New inventions began to transform the nation's streets in the late 1800s. Electric streetcars replaced horse-drawn streetcars, and automobiles made their first appearance.

12 **What can you infer about the power of electricity compared to the power of horses?** Possible answer: Electricity could provide more power than horses. Make Inferences

13 **What does the text suggest was the main source of transportation in cities and towns before the arrival of cars?** Horses Make Inferences

14 **What other industries might be affected by the growth of cars?** Possible answer: The growth of cars would affect industries that produce materials used to manufacture cars, such as metal, glass, and rubber, and those that sell fuel, such as oil and gasoline. Cause and Effect

✓ **REVIEW ANSWER** Electric streetcars were faster and could carry more passengers than horse-drawn streetcars. Compare and Contrast

▶ The traffic in New York City in the 1890s included both horse-drawn carriages and electric streetcars.

Streetcars and Horseless Carriages

American cities began building streetcar systems in the 1830s. Horses pulled these early streetcars along steel tracks laid in the street. Just like buses today, streetcars would pick up and drop off passengers at different stops around the city. With the rise of electricity and power stations in the 1880s, people started thinking of ways to improve the streetcar.

An electrical engineer named Frank Sprague was the first to succeed. He designed the world's first system of electric streetcars in Richmond, Virginia, in 1888. Electric streetcars traveled more quickly and held more people than horse-drawn streetcars. Within a few years, electric streetcar **12** systems were built in cities all over the world.

At the same time, other inventors were working on the world's first cars. People called this invention the "horseless carriage," because it was like a carriage that did not need horses to pull it. The first cars with gasoline-powered engines were built in **13** Germany in the late 1880s.

Two brothers named Frank Duryea and Charles Duryea were the first to build a working automobile in the United States. In their workshop in Springfield, Massachusetts, the Duryea brothers built the first American car in 1893. A newspaper announced the news with the headline, "No Use for Horses: Springfield Mechanics Devise a New Mode of Travel."

This was the beginning of a new American industry. Companies all over the country began designing and selling cars. Still, it would be many years before companies built cars that most people could afford. **14**

REVIEW What advantages did electric streetcars have over horse-drawn streetcars? Compare and Contrast

▶ These men are riding in one of the earliest automobiles.

170

Practice and Extend

 ## Problem Solving

Use a Problem-Solving Process

- Have students consider the following: **Suppose you are a car-maker in the late 1800s. The cars you make are so expensive that few people can afford them. It is hard for you to make a living on the few cars you can sell.**

- Students should use the following problem-solving process to decide how the car-maker could either sell more cars or produce them at a lower price. For each step in the process, have students work in small groups to discuss and write about what must be considered as they solve the problem. Then have students compare their solution with others in the class. Write the steps of the process on the board or read them aloud.

1. **Identify a problem.**
2. **Gather information.**
3. **List options.**
4. **Consider advantages and disadvantages.**
5. **Choose and implement a solution.**
6. **Evaluate the effectiveness of the solution.**

FACT FILE

Invention Time Line

Here are some inventions that changed life in the United States and around the world. Can you picture what life would be like today without some of these inventions?

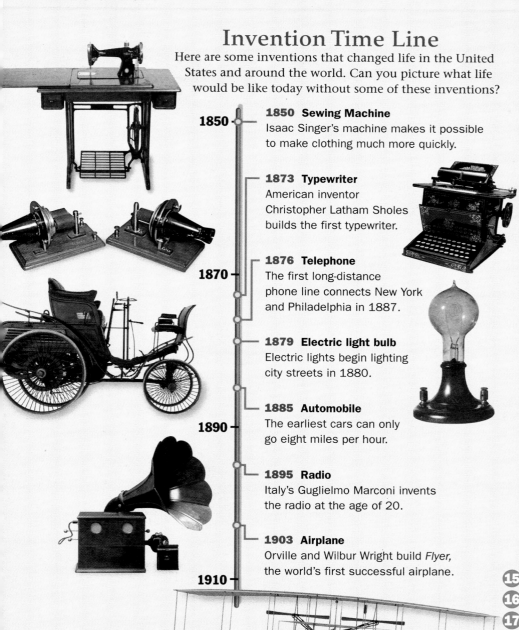

1850 Sewing Machine
Isaac Singer's machine makes it possible to make clothing much more quickly.

1873 Typewriter
American inventor Christopher Latham Sholes builds the first typewriter.

1876 Telephone
The first long-distance phone line connects New York and Philadelphia in 1887.

1879 Electric light bulb
Electric lights begin lighting city streets in 1880.

1885 Automobile
The earliest cars can only go eight miles per hour.

1895 Radio
Italy's Guglielmo Marconi invents the radio at the age of 20.

1903 Airplane
Orville and Wilbur Wright build *Flyer,* the world's first successful airplane.

15
16
17

171

FACT FILE
Invention Time Line

15 Which inventions shown changed the way people communicated? The typewriter, telephone, and radio **Categorize**

16 Which of the inventions brought improvements in transportation? The automobile and the airplane **Categorize**

17 Which of the inventions were most likely to affect the home life of the average person? Possible answers: the sewing machine, the telephone, the electric light, and the radio **Categorize**

✓ **Ongoing Assessment**

If... students do not appreciate the potential of these inventions to change the lives of ordinary people,

then... have them keep a list of how many times each week they use these inventions or other products made possible by them.

MEETING INDIVIDUAL NEEDS
Leveled Practice

Create an Advertisement Students will create an advertisement for one of the new products invented in the late 1800s or early 1900s.

Easy Have students choose one invention discussed in the lesson and create a slogan that promotes that product and its advantages. **Reteach**

On-Level Have students choose one product discussed in this lesson and create an advertisement that uses text and illustrations to promote the product. **Extend**

Challenge Have students choose one product discussed in this lesson and create an advertisement that uses text and pictures to promote the product and to explain how the product is better than an existing product. **Enrich**

For a Lesson Summary, use Quick Study, p. 34.

The Wright Brothers

Quick Summary The Wright brothers knew little about flight. However, with experimentation and hard work, they became the first to build a working airplane.

18 **Why do you think the Wright brothers wanted to work in secret?** Possible answer: They realized that a successful flying machine could be valuable, and they didn't want anyone taking their ideas. Draw Conclusions

19 **What might explain why the plane took off with Orville aboard, but not when Wilbur was aboard?** Possible answers: Perhaps Wilbur weighed more than Orville, or perhaps the weather conditions were better on December 17. Make Inferences

20 **If the plane traveled 120 feet in 12 seconds, what was its rate of speed?** Ten feet per second Analyze Information

✓ **REVIEW ANSWER** They learned about flying, built experimental planes, and took planes to Kitty Hawk, North Carolina, to try them out. Sequence

The Wright Brothers

In Dayton, Ohio, **Wilbur Wright** and **Orville Wright** were working on another invention that would change the world. The Wright brothers built and repaired bicycles for a living. In their free time, they thought about building a flying machine.

The first challenge they faced was that they knew almost nothing about flying. They would have to begin experimenting. In 1899 the Wright brothers built a glider, or a plane with no engine that can glide on the wind. They traveled to the small fishing village of **Kitty Hawk, North Carolina,** to test their glider. The beach at Kitty Hawk was a good location because it had strong winds and soft sand for landing. Because it was far from any big towns, the brothers could do their experiments in secret. **18**

After two years of failures, the Wright brothers were discouraged. Wilbur Wright remembered, "At this time I made the prediction that man would sometime fly, but that it would not be in our lifetime."

But they kept trying. They built a new plane, called *Flyer.* They designed a special lightweight motor for *Flyer,* with a propeller to pull the plane forward. They took *Flyer* to Kitty

Hawk to test it. When the plane was ready, the brothers tossed a coin to see who would get to fly first. Wilbur won. He tried to fly, but *Flyer* would not take off. **19**

Three days later, on December 17, 1903, the brothers tried again. This time it was Orville's turn—and *Flyer* actually took off! The plane flew just 120 feet before landing, but the Wright brothers knew they had made history. "This flight lasted only 12 seconds," Orville wrote, "but it was nevertheless the first in the history of the world in which a machine carrying a man had raised itself by its own power into the air in full flight." **20**

REVIEW After deciding to build a plane, what steps did the Wright brothers take to achieve their goal? Sequence

▶ **The first airplane flight lasted only 12 seconds. This historic flight is pictured below. Today the Wright brothers' airplane, *Flyer* (above), is in the National Air and Space Museum in Washington, D.C.**

172

Practice and Extend

FAST FACTS

- The Wright brothers developed a sophisticated wind tunnel to test parts of their airplane.
- Because there was no commercially available engine that was both strong enough and light enough for their plane, the Wright brothers had to build their own.
- Shortly after Orville's successful flight, Wilbur also succeeded in flying the plane.
- The *Flyer* was badly damaged on the day of its first flight when a gust of wind blew it over and broke several key parts.

FYI SOCIAL STUDIES Background

The *Hindenburg* Disaster

- Dirigibles, or airships, preceded airplanes as a way for people to cross the Atlantic Ocean. In the early 1900s, airplanes were not yet capable of carrying the weight of many passengers.
- Airships were lifted by large bags filled with hydrogen, a very flammable gas.
- In 1936 the *Hindenburg,* the largest airship ever built, was constructed.
- On May 6, 1937, the *Hindenburg* was docking in New Jersey when a fire started. The ship burst into flames and within seconds it crashed.
- This disaster signaled the end of airship travel. Airplane technology accelerated during World War II and soon passengers were traveling across the Atlantic Ocean in airplanes.

Inventions and Industry

The inventions you have read about in this lesson all led to new industries. People started businesses to offer telephone service and electrical service. They started companies to make streetcars, automobiles, and airplanes. Many of these new companies began competing with each other for business.

This kind of competition was good news for a young woman named **Blanche Stuart Scott.** Scott helped advertise a new car company by driving one of its cars across the country in 1910. This trip made her famous, but she soon got an even more exciting opportunity. She joined a team of pilots who worked for the Curtiss Airplane and Motor Company. Her job was to fly Curtiss airplanes at fairs and air shows. Scott was the first American woman to fly an airplane. "I soared to the dizzying height of 25 feet," she said of her first flight. "It seemed like a hundred!"

21

REVIEW What was one effect of the inventions you read about in this lesson? **Cause and Effect**

Summarize the Lesson

1876 Alexander Graham Bell invented the telephone.

1879 Thomas Edison developed the first working light bulb.

1903 The Wright brothers made the world's first airplane flight.

LESSON 1 REVIEW

Check Facts and Main Ideas

1. **Sequence** Redraw this chart on a separate sheet of paper, putting the events in their correct order. Include the year of each event.

1882 Thomas Edison opens a power plant in New York City.

↓

1888 The first electric streetcar system opens in Richmond, Virginia.

↓

1893 The Duryea brothers build the first car in the United States.

↓

1903 The Wright brothers make the world's first airplane flight.

2. How did Alexander Graham Bell's invention affect communication in the United States?

3. What are two important inventions for which Thomas Edison is remembered?

4. Describe three inventions that changed the way people traveled.

5. **Critical Thinking:** *Cause and Effect* How did inventions such as the telephone, electric light, and car lead to the rise of new industries?

Link to — Science

Study Inventors Many inventors have changed the way people live. Choose one inventor and find out more about him or her, including whether the inventor relied on **investors** for help. Write a one-page report about the inventor. Explain how the inventor's work changed the way people lived.

173

Inventions and Industry

🕐 *Quick Summary* The inventions of the late 1800s and early 1900s created new industries and business opportunities.

21 **How did Blanche Stuart Scott become the first American woman to fly an airplane?** After driving a car across the country to advertise a new car company, she joined a team of pilots. Her job was to fly airplanes at fairs and air shows. Summarize

✓ **REVIEW ANSWER** Possible answer: These inventions all led to the creation of new industries and new business opportunities. Cause and Effect

3 Close and Assess

Summarize the Lesson

Have students read the events described in the vertical time line. Then ask them to explain the significance and influence of each invention.

✓ **LESSON 1 REVIEW**

1. **Sequence** For possible answers, see the reduced pupil page.

2. Bell's telephone made it possible for people to speak directly with each other over long distances.

3. The phonograph and the light bulb

4. Possible answer: The electric streetcar, the automobile, the airplane

5. **Critical Thinking:** *Cause and Effect* The inventions created the need for companies to manufacture new products, to produce materials and parts needed for manufacturing, and to provide new services.

Link to — Science

Make sure student reports accurately describe the inventor and clearly explain how his or her work changed the way people lived. Remind students to find out if the inventor had any investors.

CURRICULUM CONNECTION
Literature

Read About Inventors Use these selections about inventors to extend the content.

The Real McCoy: The Life of an African-American Inventor, by Wendy Towle (Scholastic, ISBN 0-590-48102-9, 1995) **Easy**

Always Inventing: A Photobiography of Alexander Graham Bell, by Tom L. Matthews (National Geographic Society, ISBN 0-792-27391-5, 1999) **On-Level**

Thomas A. Edison: Young Inventor, by Sue Guthridge (Simon & Schuster Children's Publishing , ISBN 0-020-41850-7, 1986) **Challenge**

Workbook, p. 40

Lesson 1: Inventors Change the World

Directions: Complete the chart with details from this lesson. You may use your textbook.

Inventor	Invention	Significance
		Changed the way people communicated
Thomas Edison		
	Method for making carbon filaments	
	Electric Streetcar	
Orville and Wilbur Wright		

Notes for Home: Your child learned about inventors that changed the United States at the turn of the twentieth century.
Home Activity: Ask your child whether and how these inventions affect your daily lives today.

💿 **Also on Teacher Resources CD-ROM.**

Write an Outline

Objective
- Organize information in an outline.

Vocabulary
outline, p. 174

Resources
- Workbook, p. 41

Introduce and Motivate

What is an outline? Ask students why they might want to have a short, well-organized summary of a longer written work, such as a chapter or unit of a textbook. Then have students read the **What?** section of text on p. 174 to help set the purpose of the lesson.

Why use outlines? Have students read the **Why?** section of text on p. 175. Ask them to think about how knowing how to make outlines could help them in their studies.

Teach and Discuss

How is this skill used? Examine with students the sample story on p. 174 and the sample outline on p. 175.

- Point out that the sample outline has much fewer words than the sample story about the invention of the windshield wiper.

- Help students see that the outline clearly identifies the main topics and provides easy-to-see supporting details.

- Have students read the **How?** section of text on p. 175.

 Research and Writing Skills

Write an Outline

What? An outline is a written plan for organizing information about a subject. An outline can be used as a study guide or as a summary of a reading selection. It is made up of main ideas and details that support the main ideas.

Outlines are often made up of three parts. First are the main ideas. These statements usually have Roman numerals (I, II, III, IV . . .) in front of them. Next are the subtopics, which support the main ideas. They are often labeled with capital letters. Third are the details of the topic. The details may have Arabic numerals (1, 2, 3, 4 . . .) in front of them. Below is a selection about an inventor in the early 1900s. An outline of this selection is shown on the following page.

Inventor of the Windshield Wiper

Mary Anderson was inspired to invent the windshield wiper when she took a trip from her home in Alabama to New York City in the winter of 1903. While she was riding on a streetcar, a snowstorm started. Anderson noticed that the shivering streetcar operator had to keep leaning out of the window to wipe off the snow from his windshield so he could see. This was inconvenient and dangerous!

Anderson had an idea to improve visibility for drivers during stormy weather. She quickly drew a picture of the idea in her sketchbook. Her invention was a sort of swinging arm with a rubber blade that swept off ice and snow. The driver could move the arm with a handle inside the car. During warmer weather, the arm could easily be removed.

Anderson believed the public could use her invention. A few months after her trip, she applied for and received a patent for the mechanical windshield wiper. A patent is a grant given by the government to an inventor. It gives the inventor the sole right to make and sell the invention for a set period of time. Anderson's invention was very popular. By 1913 the windshield wiper was standard equipment in most American cars. Her invention helped save lives by allowing drivers to see clearly in snow, rain, and sleet.

174

# Practice and Extend

MEETING INDIVIDUAL NEEDS
Leveled Practice

Make an Outline Have students discuss why outlines are helpful before working on their own outlines.

Easy Have students create a blank outline that correctly illustrates the basic outline structure (that is, with Roman numerals for main ideas, capital letters for major subtopics, and so on). **Reteach**

On-Level Have students create an outline of this skill lesson. **Extend**

Challenge Have students create an outline of Chapter 4, Lesson 1. Suggest that students use the section headings as major subtopics. **Enrich**

Why? Writing an outline will help you better organize your thoughts and remember what you read. When you study for an exam, you will be able to see the main ideas at a glance. Outlines also help you write a clear report or speech. They allow you to organize the information you find before you start writing. This can make your writing better and help you remember all the points you want to cover.

I. **Mary Anderson's trip, 1903**
  A. **Inspiration**
    1. **Streetcar operator had to lean out of window to wipe away snow**
    2. **Inconvenient and dangerous**
  B. **Invention to improve visibility for drivers**
    1. **Swinging arm with rubber blade to sweep away snow, ice, or rain**
    2. _____
    3. **Arm can be removed in warm weather**

II. **Ready for the public**
  A. _____
    1. **A grant given by the government**
    2. **She had the right to make and sell her invention**
  B. **Standard equipment in cars by 1913**
    1. **Allowed drivers to see clearly in snow, rain, and sleet**
    2. **Saved lives**

How? Follow these steps to write an outline:

- As you read, think about what the main ideas are. Write the headings next to Roman numerals. Read the passage on the previous page. If you were to write an outline based on this selection, one heading might be *Mary Anderson's trip, 1903*.
- Next, divide the text you read into subtopics under the headings. Write these subtopics next to capital letters. A possible subtopic for this passage could be *Inspiration*.
- Using your own words, write important details below the subtopics. List the details next to numbers. One detail you might include in your outline for the passage is *Streetcar operator had to lean out of window to wipe away snow*.

Think and Apply

1. In the outline on this page, what detail can go next to *2*, under Roman numeral *I*, letter *B*?

2. What subtopic can go next to *A* under Roman numeral *II*?

3. How can writing outlines help you study or write a report?

175

1 **What are the three main parts of an outline?** The main ideas, the subtopics, and the details that support the main ideas **Main Idea and Details**

2 **What are the subtopics shown in the outline for Mary Anderson's 1903 trip?** "Inspiration" and "Invention to improve visibility for drivers" **Apply Information**

3 **What are two details under the subtopic "Standard equipment in cars by 1913"?** "Allowed drivers to see clearly in snow, rain, and sleet" and "Saved lives" **Apply Information**

3 Close and Assess

Think and Apply

1. Driver can move arm with a handle inside car.

2. Anderson receives a patent.

3. Writing an outline helps you write reports by organizing facts, and allows you to see main ideas at a glance.

CURRICULUM CONNECTION
Literature

Read About Study Skills

Use these selections to extend the content.

School Success: The Inside Story, by Peter Kline (Great Ocean Publishing, ISBN 0-915-55625-1, 1994) **Easy**

How to Study, by David H. Griswold (Wayside Publishing, ISBN 1-877-65351-9, 1994) **On-Level**

Student Success Secrets, by Eric Jensen (Barron's Educational Series, ISBN 0-764-12007-7, 2003) **Challenge**

Workbook, p. 41

Write an Outline

Also on Teacher Resources CD-ROM.

The Rise of Big Business

Objectives

- Identify key industrial leaders and the businesses they started.
- Explain how railroads helped the United States economy grow.
- Compare the role of business owners and consumers in a free enterprise system.
- Describe important effects of the rise of big business in the United States.

Vocabulary

corporation, p. 178; **stock,** p. 178; **monopoly,** p. 179; **free enterprise,** p. 180; **consumer,** p. 180; **human resource,** p. 181; **capital resource,** p. 181

Resources

- Workbook, p. 42
- Transparency 1
- Every Student Learns Guide, pp. 70–73
- Quick Study, pp. 36–37

Quick Teaching Plan

If time is short, have students take all the section headings in the lesson and write them down in the form of a question.

- Have students write down answers to their questions as they read the lesson independently.

1 Introduce and Motivate

Preview To activate prior knowledge, ask students to describe what they envision when they think of factories and big business today. Tell students they will learn about the era in the United States when big business was born.

You Are There Explain that the steel mill Garland visited was part of one of the earliest "big businesses." Ask students to predict what other industries might have expanded rapidly during the 1800s and early 1900s.

LESSON 2

1850   1900

1859
Oil is found in Pennsylvania.

1893
The United States has more than 160,000 miles of railroad track.

1900
The U.S. is the leading producer of manufactured goods.

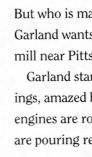
• Cleveland
• Pittsburgh

PREVIEW

Focus on the Main Idea
In the late 1800s and early 1900s, big businesses helped the United States economy grow quickly.

PLACES
Pittsburgh, Pennsylvania
Cleveland, Ohio

PEOPLE
Andrew Carnegie
John D. Rockefeller
George Westinghouse
William Randolph Hearst
Madame C. J. Walker
J. P. Morgan

VOCABULARY
corporation
stock
monopoly
free enterprise
consumer
human resource
capital resource

The Rise of Big Business

You Are There

The year is 1894. All over the nation, steel is being used to build new bridges, railroads, and buildings. But who is making the steel? A writer named Hamlin Garland wants to find out. He is visiting a huge steel mill near Pittsburgh, Pennsylvania.

Garland stands in one of the mill's massive buildings, amazed by all the action and noise. Everywhere engines are roaring, cranes are swinging, and workers are pouring red-hot liquid steel out of giant pots. A young man walks past Garland, panting and sweating.

"That looks like hard work," Garland says.

"Hard! I guess it's hard," the man says. "I often drink two buckets of water during twelve hours; the sweat drips through my sleeves, and runs down my legs and fills my shoes."

Main Idea and Details As you read, pay attention to the important industrial leaders and the businesses they started.

▶ Steel was used to build the Empire State Building, once the tallest building in the world at 1,250 feet.

176

Practice and Extend

In the Lesson Review, students complete a graphic organizer like the one below. You may want to provide students with a copy of Transparency 1 to complete as they read the lesson.

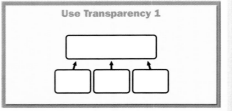
Use Transparency 1

Related Word Study

Point out to students that *resource* means "something that will meet a need." Invite volunteers to look up *natural, human,* and *capital* in the dictionary and to select the definitions for each that apply to the terms *natural resource, human resource,* and *capital resource.* Discuss how each of these three words describes a different type of resource.

Building with Steel

Human beings have been making steel for more than 2,000 years. Steel is made by heating iron until it melts and then adding carbon. The advantage of steel is that it is a stronger material than iron. Steel can hold more weight than iron, and it can bend without cracking.

Until the middle 1800s, however, steel was very expensive to produce. An English inventor named Henry Bessemer helped change this. In 1856 Bessemer developed the Bessemer process, a new way of making steel. Bessemer's furnaces produced strong steel at affordable prices. Now it was possible to produce steel in massive quantities.

An entrepreneur named **Andrew Carnegie** saw that there could be a huge market for steel in the rapidly growing United States. In the 1870s, Carnegie began using the Bessemer process to make steel in **Pittsburgh, Pennsylvania.**

Carnegie's goal was to produce steel at the lowest possible cost. He accomplished this by controlling all the steps of the steel-making process. He bought iron and coal mines to provide his steel mills with these necessary resources. He bought ships and railroads to bring the resources to his mills, and to deliver the finished steel all over the country. Carnegie helped steel become a "big business," or a major industry, in the United States. By 1900 the United States was producing more steel than any other country in the world. Carnegie's mills alone were producing more steel than the entire nation of Great Britain.

Steel was strong and now it was widely available. People used it to build buildings, bridges, automobiles, trains, and railroads. With so much steel being used, Carnegie became one of the richest men in the world. You will read more about how he spent his money in the Biography on page 183.

REVIEW How did the steel industry change after 1856? ⊙ Sequence

► Andrew Carnegie produced steel for bridges, buildings, automobiles, and railroads.

177

② Teach and Discuss

PAGE 177

Building with Steel

🕐 *Quick Summary* Improvements in technology made large-scale steel production possible. It also created an opportunity for entrepreneurs, who helped supply a growing demand for steel.

① **How did Bessemer's invention help enable the production of steel in massive quantities?** Possible answer: His process produced strong steel at affordable prices. **Cause and Effect**

$ **SOCIAL STUDIES STRAND**
Economics

Explain that Carnegie's control of all steps in the manufacturing process is called *integration*. In an unintegrated industry, the process involves several "middlemen." Each "middleman" controls and profits from one part in the production process—and this drives up costs.

② **How did Carnegie's control of the production process allow him to produce steel at a lower cost?** Possible answer: He didn't have to pay high prices to others for raw materials and shipping. **Solve Problems**

③ **What was risky about Carnegie's plan?** Possible answer: He had to invest a lot of money to gain control of each step in the production process. **Analyze Information**

✓ **REVIEW ANSWER** As steel became more affordable, it became much more popular as a building material. Large companies emerged to provide the growing need for steel. ⊙ Sequence

PAGE 178

Railroads Link Markets

 Quick Summary Railroads expanded quickly in the late 1800s and were among the first of the nation's large corporations. They also helped markets and cities expand.

 Decision Making

4 **Why would people decide to buy a corporation's stocks?** Possible answer: They believe that the corporation will become more successful, and that they will earn a share of its future profits. **Make Decisions**

5 **Explain how a railroad might help a factory produce more tools.** Possible answer: The railroad would help the factory deliver tools over a larger area to reach more customers. This would encourage the production of more tools. **Cause and Effect**

✓ **REVIEW ANSWER** Because railroads were expensive to build and operate, many companies became corporations to sell stocks to raise money. **Main Idea and Details**

MAP SKILL **Major Railroad Lines, 1880**

6 **Which large cities in the West could be reached using the railroad?** San Francisco and Los Angeles **Interpret Maps**

MAP SKILL **Answer** Most people lived in the East and the Midwest. There were many more rail lines in the East and the Midwest indicating that there were more people to use the railroads.

Railroads Link Markets

Railroad companies needed steel to build tracks and trains. You read that the first transcontinental railroad was completed in 1869. By 1893 four more railroad lines crossed the country. The United States now had more than 160,000 miles of railroad track!

Railroad companies became one of the nation's first large corporations. A **corporation** is a business that is owned by investors. Corporations sell shares of the company, called **stocks,** to investors. A corporation can use the money from selling stocks to buy equipment for the company. By becoming corporations, railroad companies were able to raise enough money to buy the equipment they needed.

Railroads were the fastest and cheapest way to transport goods. Railroads linked cities, farms, factories, and mines all over the United States. A farmer on the Great Plains could grow more wheat and corn, because trains transported crops to cities where the food could be sold. A factory owner in the East could produce more tools because trains could take the tools to stores all over the country.

By providing these links, railroads helped the United States economy grow. Cities that were major railroad centers also grew. Railroad centers such as Chicago were soon among the biggest cities in the country.

REVIEW Why did many railroad companies form corporations? **Main Idea and Details**

MAP SKILL **Major Railroad Lines, 1880**

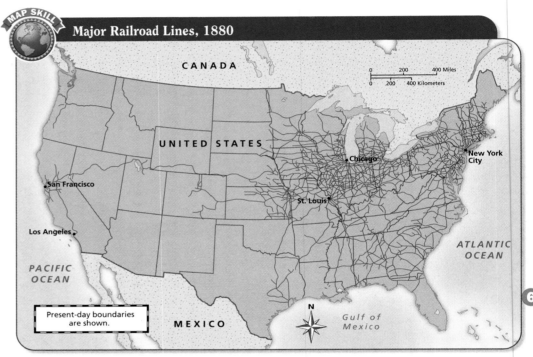

▶ The populations of cities such as Chicago and St. Louis grew as the cities became railroad centers.

MAP SKILL Use a Transportation Map *In which parts of the United States do you think most people lived in 1880? How did you reach this conclusion?*

178

Practice and Extend

 ACCESS CONTENT
ESL Support

Explore the Language of Big Business Students will examine terms used to discuss large businesses.

Beginning In small groups, have students look up the word *share* in an English language dictionary. Have them work together to identify which definition relates to corporations.

Intermediate Encourage students to write a sentence that uses the nouns *share, stock,* and *corporation* correctly.

Advanced Have students write a paragraph that describes the basic idea behind a corporation and that uses the terms *share, stock,* and *corporation.*

For additional ESL support, use Every Student Learns Guide, pp. 70–73.

The Oil Industry

On August 27, 1859, a former railroad conductor named Edwin Drake drilled a hole in the ground in western Pennsylvania. When he reached a depth of 69 feet, a thick, black liquid came up from the ground. This was oil—exactly what Drake had been hoping to find. People rushed to the region to drill for oil, or "black gold," as it was sometimes called. The young oil industry was suddenly big business.

This discovery was big news to a teenager named John D. Rockefeller. Rockefeller saw a great opportunity to start a business of his own. "I want to make a hundred thousand dollars," he told his friends. He realized that he could earn money in the oil business by refining oil, or turning it into useful products such as kerosene. At that time, kerosene lamps were the main source of lighting in the United States.

Rockefeller built his first oil refinery in Cleveland, Ohio, in 1863. Using the profits from this business, he bought other refineries. Rockefeller's company, Standard Oil, slowly gained control of the nation's oil industry.

By the early 1880s, Standard Oil controlled about 90 percent of the oil business in the United States. Standard Oil had become a monopoly (muh NOP uh lee). A monopoly is a company that has control of an entire industry. Monopolies have little or no competition, so they can charge any price they want for their products. As you will read in the next unit, some people began arguing that monopolies were bad for the country.

By the early 1900s, electric lights were replacing kerosene lamps as the most important source of lighting. But this did not mean the end of the oil industry. Americans were beginning to buy cars in large numbers. This created a huge demand for other products made from oil, such as gasoline and motor oil. People started searching for oil all over the country. Major oil discoveries were made in Texas, Oklahoma, and California. The oil industry continued to grow, and it remains one of the biggest industries in the country today.

REVIEW What effect did the rise of the car industry have on the oil industry?
Cause and Effect

▶ The 1901 Spindletop gusher in Texas (*left*) was the biggest oil strike so far in the country. John D. Rockefeller (*right*) built refineries to make oil into useful products.

179

PAGE 179

The Oil Industry

Quick Summary The young oil industry became a big business when oil was discovered in Pennsylvania in 1859. This "black gold" proved valuable in fueling a growing nation, and the oil industry became a big business.

7 **What does the term "black gold" suggest about oil?** Possible answer: It suggests that oil was valuable. **Make Inferences**

8 **How did John D. Rockefeller intend to make a fortune?** Possible answer: He intended to refine oil, or turn it into useful products such as kerosene. **Main Idea and Details**

Problem Solving

9 **What problem are monopolies trying to solve? What problem do they create?** Possible answer: Monopolies solve the problem of competition, which can make it harder for a business to make money. They create a problem for consumers because they can charge any price they want for their products. **Solve Problems**

✓ **REVIEW ANSWER** Possible answer: Cars required oil and gasoline, an oil product, which increased demand. **Cause and Effect**

SOCIAL STUDIES
Background

About Financing the Railroads

- Not all railroads were entirely financed by stockholders.
- Many early railroads, such as the Union Pacific and Central Pacific, obtained large grants of land by the United States government. The companies sold this land to help pay for railroad construction.

SOCIAL STUDIES
Background

Oil in the United States

- Prior to the discovery of petroleum in Pennsylvania, many Americans relied on oil made from the fat of whales.
- Drake had difficulty finding investors to support his plan. In fact, his project was very nearly stopped before he made his strike.
- Though Pennsylvania was the site of the nation's first oil boom, the amount of petroleum found there was relatively small.
- The discovery of oil at the Spindletop Oilfield in Texas marked the first great strike in the Gulf of Mexico region, which immediately became the nation's most important oil producing region.

Free Enterprise

 Quick Summary The free enterprise system helped make possible the growth of big business. Consumers benefited from competition, and successful entrepreneurs made fortunes.

⑩ How might companies compete for consumers? Possible answer: They could offer the lowest prices or try to make a better product. **Solve Problems**

✓ Ongoing Assessment

| If... students do not understand the importance of competition in the American economic system, | then... have students predict what would happen if all people in the United States had the choice of only one type of car or one type of video game system. |

 Test Talk

Locate Key Words in the Question

⑪ What does the text imply about the fate of Edison's electric company? Ask students to look for key words in the question. Possible answer: It lost customers. **Make Inferences**

⑫ Explain how big headlines, illustrations, and color sections helped William Randolph Hearst compete in the newspaper business. Possible answer: Hearst offered things that people wanted but that weren't offered by other newspapers. He sold more newspapers. **Make Inferences**

✓ REVIEW ANSWER
Possible answer: Westinghouse developed a better product. **Summarize**

Free Enterprise

Andrew Carnegie, John D. Rockefeller, and others were able to start their own businesses because the United States economy is based on the system of free enterprise. In a **free enterprise** system, people are free to start their own businesses and own their own property. Business owners are free to decide what to produce, and how much to charge for their products or services. Consumers are free to make choices about how to spend their money. A **consumer** is a person who buys or uses goods and services.

Since consumers are free to decide what to buy, companies must compete with each other to sell their products. Competition between companies is an important part of ⑩ the free enterprise system. For example, a major competition took place in the electricity industry in the late 1800s. An inventor and entrepreneur named **George Westinghouse** formed the Westinghouse Electric Company in 1886. Westinghouse used a new technology called alternating current, or AC, to deliver electricity to homes and businesses. Thomas Edison's electric company used a system called direct current, or DC. Both Westinghouse and Edison argued that they had the better system.

This competition grew so fierce, it became known as the "War of the Currents." Westinghouse won the war for one simple reason. He had the better product. When consumers had a chance to see both systems in action, they saw that Westinghouse's AC worked better than Edison's DC. The Westinghouse Electric Company quickly grew into a large corpora- ⑪ tion with thousands of employees.

A newspaper owner named **William Randolph Hearst** thought of new ways to compete in the newspaper business. Hearst used big, eye-catching headlines in his newspapers. He added illustrations and color sections. These changes helped Hearst sell more newspapers than anyone else in the early 1900s.

Madame C. J. Walker took a different road to success. In 1906 Walker began bottling shampoo and other products in her attic. She could not afford employees or a store, so she sold her products door-to-door. "I got my start by giving myself a start," she often said. Ten years later, she had thousands of employees. Walker was the first African American woman to become a millionaire.

REVIEW Why did Westinghouse win the "War of the Currents"? **Summarize**

▶ William Randolph Hearst's newspaper the *New York Journal* reported the death of President William McKinley in 1901.

180

Practice and Extend

ISSUES AND VIEWPOINTS
Critical Thinking

The entrepreneurs who built big businesses were admired by some as "captains of industry." But others criticized them as "robber barons." Write the lists below on the board or read them aloud. Ask students to describe why people might have held one of these views:

"Robber Baron" view claimed that big business leaders:
• got rich at the expense of workers and consumers
• destroyed competition to enrich themselves
• used their great wealth and power for selfish purposes

"Captains of Industry" view claimed that big business leaders:
• took risks in order to create wealth
• provided and made affordable essential goods and services
• provided jobs for many people

Resources and Big Business

You have read about many of the reasons for the rise of big business. Inventions led to new industries. Railroads linked markets around the country. Entrepreneurs and their new ideas helped businesses grow. Another reason business grew was that the United States is rich in important resources.

Economists, people who study the economy, divide resources into three categories: natural resources, human resources, and capital resources. Each type of resource was, and still is, important to American industries.

▶ J. P. Morgan

Natural resources are things found in nature that people can use. You read that Carnegie used railroads to bring natural resources such as iron and coal to his steel mills. Rockefeller used oil pumped from the ground to make valuable products.

Human resources are people who work to produce goods and services. The United States had a rapidly growing population in the late 1800s and early 1900s. Millions of people had valuable knowledge and skills. This meant that there were plenty of human resources to run the country's businesses.

Capital resources are the tools and machines that companies use to produce goods and services. The money used to buy this equipment is also a capital resource. Think about a steel company, for example. A furnace that is used to make steel is a capital resource. So is the money that is used to buy the furnace.

During the rise of big business, banks helped companies get the capital resources they needed. **J. P. Morgan** was the country's richest and most powerful banker. Morgan's banks invested hundreds of millions of dollars in railroads, steel mills, and other companies. This helped American industries keep growing.

REVIEW Define the three types of resources discussed on this page. **Main Idea and Details**

▶ These women made detachable shirt collars in a factory in Troy, New York, in 1890.

181

Resources and Big Business

Quick Summary Businesses require natural resources, human resources, and capital resources.

13 What are economists? Economists are people who study the economy. Main Idea and Details

14 In what ways can people contribute to a business or industry? Possible answer: They can contribute their ideas, they can perform labor, and they apply their knowledge and skills. Summarize

15 What key role do banks play in American business? Possible answer: They help businesses obtain the capital resources they need. Main Idea and Details

16 Why do you think banks make capital available to businesses? Possible answer: They earn a return on the money they invest. Make Inferences

✓ **REVIEW ANSWER** Natural resources are things found in nature that people can use. Human resources are people. Capital resources are the money, tools, and machines used to produce goods and services. Main Idea and Details

---

CURRICULUM CONNECTION
Math

Calculate Investment Earnings

Have students solve the following math problem.

- A person pays $5,000 to buy 1 share in a corporation.
- The corporation has 100 shares.
- How much money can the corporation raise by selling shares? (100 multiplied by $5,000, or $500,000)
- In the year after the share is purchased, the corporation earns a profit of $5,000. This is returned to the shareholders.
- How much does each shareholder make per share from his or her investment? ($5,000 divided by 100, or $50)

Help Wanted

 *Quick Summary* The rise in big business required many Americans to work in industries and factories.

17 Who filled many of the new jobs created by the growing businesses and industries? Possible answer: People from rural areas in the United States and immigrants from all over the world. **Summarize**

✓ **REVIEW ANSWER** Growing businesses created thousands of jobs, and as people came to fill these jobs, the population in cities grew. **Draw Conclusions**

3 Close and Assess

Summarize the Lesson

Have students read the events in the vertical time line. Ask students to suggest an effect for each event.

✓ **LESSON 2**   **REVIEW**

1. **Main Idea and Details** For possible answers, see the reduced pupil page.

2. He controlled each step in the production of steel, so he could keep costs lower.

3. Railroads transported goods across the country, creating larger markets for producers of goods.

4. Business owners are free to produce what they want, to charge what they want, and to profit from their effort. Consumers are free to choose products that they like the best and for the lowest cost.

5. **Critical Thinking:** *Cause and Effect* Possible answer: It led many people to work in factories rather than on farms. It led many people to live in cities rather than in rural areas. It attracted many immigrants to the United States.

Link to ⚬⚬ Mathematics
A total of 132,000 miles of track were built between 1865 and 1890. The average yearly total was 5,280 miles (132,000 divided by 25).

182 Unit 2 • An Expanding Nation

Help Wanted

The rise of big business in the late 1800s changed the United States. Before the Civil War, most Americans lived and worked on farms. By 1900 more Americans worked in industries than on farms. The United States had become the world's biggest producer of manufactured goods. By the early 1900s, businesses in the United States were producing about 35 percent of all the manufactured goods in the world. The United States economy was one of the strongest and fastest growing economies in the world.

Growing industries created millions of new jobs in American cities. Many people moved from rural areas to cities to take these jobs. The jobs also attracted people from other countries. Immigrants came from all over the world to find new opportunities in the United States. You will read about this "job rush," along with some of the immigrants' stories, in the next lesson.

REVIEW How did growing businesses lead to the growth of cities? **Draw Conclusions**

Summarize the Lesson

- **1859** Oil was found in Pennsylvania, leading to the rise of a huge new industry.

- **1893** The United States had five transcontinental railroad lines and more than 160,000 miles of railroad track.

- **1900** The rise of big business made the United States the world's leading producer of manufactured goods.

LESSON 2   **REVIEW**

Check Facts and Main Ideas

1. **Main Idea and Details** Complete the chart below by filling in three details about the rise of big business in the United States.

Entrepreneurs built big businesses in many industries during the late 1800s and early 1900s.

Carnegie's steel mills produced more steel than Great Britain.	By the early 1890s, Rockefeller's Standard Oil owned 90 percent of the oil business.	Westinghouse's electric company employed thousands of people.

2. How was Andrew Carnegie able to produce huge amounts of steel at low prices?

3. How did railroads help the United States economy grow?

4. What freedoms do business owners and **consumers** have in a **free enterprise** system?

5. **Critical Thinking:** *Cause and Effect* What are some ways that the rise of big business changed the United States?

Link to ⚬⚬ Mathematics

Measure the Railroad In 1865 the United States had 35,000 miles of railroad track. By 1890 the United States had 167,000 miles of track. How many miles of track were built in this 25-year period? What was the average number of miles of track built each year?

182

Practice and Extend

SOCIAL STUDIES STRAND
Geography

Urban vs. Rural Population

- Have students use Internet or library resources to determine when the United States urban population first exceeded its rural population. (1920)

- Have students find the distribution of urban and rural populations in the United States in 1790 (about 5 percent urban and about 95 percent rural) and in 2000 (about 79 percent urban and about 21 percent rural).

Workbook, p. 42

Lesson 2: The Rise of Big Business

Directions: Using information from this lesson, circle the term in parentheses that best completes each sentence.

1. A new process for making (steel, iron) helped spark a boom in industry in the late 1800s.
2. Carnegie built his fortune by (buying, selling) a number of businesses involved in the steel-making process.
3. (Railroad, Oil) companies became the nation's first large corporations.
4. Corporations are owned by (investors, employees).
5. By selling (stock, capital resources), corporations can raise money to help their businesses grow.
6. Standard Oil became a (free enterprise, monopoly) by gaining control of the nation's oil industry.
7. The oil industry boomed in the early 1900s along with the rise of the (automobile, electric) industry.
8. In a free enterprise system, (business owners, consumers) decide what to produce and what to charge for products and services.
9. A company's employees are its (human resources, capital resources).
10. The rise of big business in the late 1800s helped the United States become the world's leading producer of (manufactured goods, natural resources).

 **Also on Teacher Resources CD-ROM.**

Andrew Carnegie
1835–1919

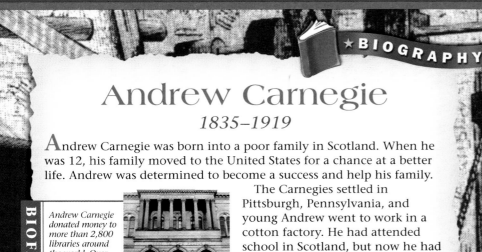

Andrew Carnegie was born into a poor family in Scotland. When he was 12, his family moved to the United States for a chance at a better life. Andrew was determined to become a success and help his family.

Andrew Carnegie donated money to more than 2,800 libraries around the world. Over the entrance to the Carnegie Library in Pittsburgh are his words, "Free to the People."

The Carnegies settled in Pittsburgh, Pennsylvania, and young Andrew went to work in a cotton factory. He had attended school in Scotland, but now he had no time for regular schooling. His family was so poor that he worked to help them. Even so, he believed education was the key to success, so he read on his own and took some classes at night school. As an adult, Carnegie worked for telegraph and railroad companies. He learned much about these businesses and became very successful. He also invested his money and made large profits. Carnegie was a rich man by the time he was 33. He wrote a letter to himself at the time, promising to take part "in public matters especially those connected with education and improvement of the poorer classes." ②

Carnegie went on to found a steel mill that became the Carnegie Steel Company. When Carnegie retired in 1901, he was one of the richest people in the world. Yet he never forgot the promise he had made to help others. Carnegie donated millions of dollars to universities, student financial aid, libraries, scientific research, and the promotion of world peace. He once said,

"Do not make riches, but usefulness, your first aim."

The charity organizations Carnegie established during his lifetime still give away money every year to help people.

Learn from Biographies

Carnegie did not finish school, but he gave much of his money to libraries and colleges. Why do you think this is so?

For more information, go to *Meet the People* at **www.sfsocialstudies.com.**

183

Andrew Carnegie

Objective

- Describe the accomplishments of significant figures in United States history, such as Andrew Carnegie.

1 Introduce and Motivate

Preview Remind students that Andrew Carnegie is remembered not only as a highly successful business leader, but also as a generous supporter of charitable causes. Tell students they will read about the early events that helped shape Carnegie's life.

2 Teach and Discuss

❶ **What did young Andrew Carnegie do to demonstrate his belief in the value of education?** Though he could not go to school, he read on his own and attended night classes. **Summarize**

❷ **Why do you think Carnegie was interested in "improvement of the poorer classes"?** He had come from the poorer classes himself, and he knew that poor people could achieve much if given the opportunity. **Draw Conclusions**

3 Close and Assess

Learn from Biographies Answer

Possible answer: Carnegie placed a high value on education.

CURRICULUM CONNECTION
Literature

Read About Andrew Carnegie

Andrew Carnegie: Builder of Libraries, by Charnan Simon (Children's Press, ISBN 0-516-26131-2, 1998) **Easy**

Andrew Carnegie: Steel King and Friend to Libraries, by Zachary Kent (Enslow Publishers, Inc., ISBN 0-766-01212-3, 1999) **On-Level** *NCSS Notable Book*

The Many Lives of Andrew Carnegie, by Milton Meltzer (Franklin Watts, Inc., ISBN 0-531-11427-9, 1997) **Challenge**

WEB SITE
Technology

Students can find out more about Andrew Carnegie by clicking on *Meet the People* at **www.sfsocialstudies.com.**

New Americans

Objectives

- Identify reasons why immigrants came to the United States in the late 1800s and early 1900s.

- Compare and contrast the immigration stations at Ellis Island and Angel Island.

- Evaluate the challenges that faced new immigrants.

Vocabulary

prejudice, p. 189; **diversity,** p. 190

Resources

- Workbook, p. 43
- Transparency 6
- Every Student Learns Guide, pp. 74–77
- Quick Study, pp. 38–39

Quick Teaching Plan

If time is short, have students prepare a web diagram and write the words *New Immigrants* in the center.

- As students read the lesson independently, have them add to the web details from the lesson about the experiences of new immigrants.

1 Introduce and Motivate

Preview To activate prior knowledge, ask students to think about other stories they have heard about newcomers to the United States—for example, the first settlers, enslaved Africans, or other immigrant groups. Tell students that they will learn in Lesson 3 about an era in which millions of people immigrated to the United States.

You Are There Explain that for many immigrants, the United States was unlike anything they had ever seen or experienced. Have students picture the thoughts that must have gone through Nathan's mind as he wandered the sidewalks of New York City in 1896.

184 Unit 2 • An Expanding Nation

LESSON 3

1890			1925
1894 Mary Antin arrives in the United States.	**Early 1900s** More than half of the people in most big Americans cities are immigrants or children of immigrants.		**1924** The United States government passes a law limiting immigration.

Angel Island ·   · Ellis Island

PREVIEW

Focus on the Main Idea
During the late 1800s and early 1900s, millions of immigrants arrived in the United States in search of freedom and opportunity.

PLACES
Ellis Island
Angel Island

PEOPLE
Mary Antin

VOCABULARY
prejudice
diversity

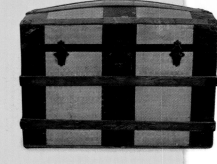

New Americans

You Are There Nathan Nussenbaum stands on a crowded New York City street. He stares at the tall buildings and rushing crowds of people.

The year is 1896. Nathan, a Jewish teenager from Austria, has just arrived in the United States. He has a total of nine dollars in his pocket. He speaks German and Yiddish—a language spoken by many Jews in Europe—but knows almost no English. He knows no one in this country.

He walks through the busy streets. Every time he hears the word *listen* he turns around. He thinks people are saying "Nisn," which is how you say the name Nathan in Yiddish. He soon realizes that people are not talking to him.

Nathan knows that it will be difficult to adjust to life in the United States. But he is not discouraged. "I was determined to try my luck in this country," he later said.

Summarize As you read, keep track of the different reasons that immigrants came to the United States.

184

Practice and Extend

READING SKILL
Summarize

In the Lesson Review, students complete a graphic organizer like the one below. You may want to provide students with a copy of Transparency 6 to complete as they read the lesson.

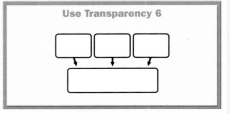

Use Transparency 6

VOCABULARY
Word Exercise

Related Word Study

Antonyms are words that mean the opposite of each other. Have students use thesauruses to find an antonym for *diversity. (uniformity)* Then describe a situation and have students tell you if the situation describes uniformity or diversity. Once they've identified which the situation is, have them describe for you a situation that illustrates the opposite. For example: a school attended by both boys and girls *(diversity),* and an all-girls school *(uniformity)*

New Immigrants

Nathan Nussenbaum was one of more than 23 million immigrants who arrived in the United States between 1880 and 1920. The entire population of the United States in 1880 was about 50 million, so this meant there was one new immigrant for every two people already in the country!

Before 1890 most immigrants came from the countries of northern Europe, including Ireland, Great Britain, Germany, and Sweden. After 1890 most came from southern and eastern European countries, such as Italy, Austria-Hungary, and Russia. However, not all immigrants who arrived at this time were European. People moved south from Canada and north from Mexico, Cuba, and Puerto Rico. Others came to the United States from China, Japan, and the Philippines.

Immigrants came for different reasons. Many were escaping poverty, hunger, or lack of jobs. For them, the farms and factories of the United States offered the hope of an income, food, and work. Others were escaping violence, war, or injustice.

Many Jewish immigrants left Europe to escape mistreatment because of their religion. A young immigrant named Mary Antin wrote that she had not been allowed to attend school in Russia because she was Jewish. In 1894 Antin and her family moved to Boston, Massachusetts, in search of a better life. You will read Antin's story in the Biography on page 191.

Most immigrants did not expect to find easy riches in the United States. They did expect to find jobs, political and religious freedom, and even some adventure. They came hoping for opportunities to make better lives for themselves and their families. Often that is just what they found.

REVIEW What opportunities did immigrants hope to find in the United States?
Main Idea and Details

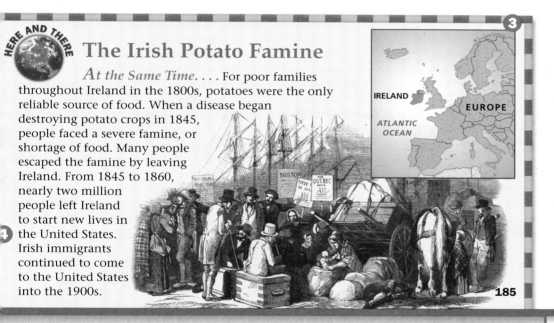

The Irish Potato Famine

At the Same Time. . . . For poor families throughout Ireland in the 1800s, potatoes were the only reliable source of food. When a disease began destroying potato crops in 1845, people faced a severe famine, or shortage of food. Many people escaped the famine by leaving Ireland. From 1845 to 1860, nearly two million people left Ireland to start new lives in the United States. Irish immigrants continued to come to the United States into the 1900s.

185

IRELAND
EUROPE
ATLANTIC OCEAN

---

2 Teach and Discuss

PAGE 185

New Immigrants

Quick Summary Millions of immigrants came to the United States between 1880 and 1920. Each had a different reason for leaving home, but they all hoped to create a better future in their new homeland.

1 **From which continent did most immigrants come in the late 1800s and early 1900s?** Europe
Main Idea and Details

Test Talk

Locate Key Words in the Question

2 **What were some of the reasons immigrants decided to leave their homes?** Students should ask themselves, "Who or what is this question about?" Possible answer: To escape bad economic conditions and to escape prejudice and discrimination
Cause and Effect

3 **What was the specific reason that Mary Antin's family left Russia?** To escape mistreatment because of their religion Main Idea and Details

✓ **REVIEW ANSWER** Possible answer: Immigrants hoped to find economic opportunity, freedom, and adventure.
Main Idea and Details

The Irish Potato Famine

4 **Why did many immigrants come from Ireland in the mid-1800s?** To escape the famine in Ireland caused by the destruction of the potato crops
Cause and Effect

Ellis Island

🕐 **Quick Summary** Many immigrants from Europe passed the Statue of Liberty in New York Harbor and were then taken to the immigration station at Ellis Island.

Primary Source

Cited in *Immigrant Kids*, by Russell Freedman

5 **Why do you think that the sight of the Statue of Liberty was so important to the new immigrants?** Possible answer: It offered immigrants hope and the promise of freedom and a better life in the United States.
Interpret National Symbols

✓ **Ongoing Assessment**

| **If...** students do not appreciate the significance of the Statue of Liberty, | **then...** have students reread p. 165 and the excerpt of the poem that appears on the statue. |

6 **Why do you think immigrants were checked for dangerous diseases upon their arrival in the United States?** Possible answer: Officials wanted to stop contagious illnesses from spreading in the United States.
Draw Conclusions

✓ **REVIEW ANSWER** Possible answer: They had to endure an often difficult voyage. They had to pass a medical exam and answer questions about their past, their occupations, and their future plans. 🔄 Sequence

Ellis Island

When he was 15 years old, Abraham Hyman (HEYE min) left his home in Russia and sailed to the United States. Like millions of immigrants from Europe in the late 1800s and early 1900s, Hyman and his family were poor. He could only afford a steerage class boat ticket. Steerage passengers were packed into crowded rooms beneath the deck of the ship. "The boat [ride] was about fifteen, sixteen days [long]," Hyman remembered. "It was bad. You wouldn't want to put pigs in it."

Most ships carrying immigrants from Europe landed in New York City. As the ships sailed into New York Harbor, passengers rushed to the deck to see the Statue of Liberty, a famous symbol of the United States. A young immigrant from Italy named Edward Corsi never forgot this moment:

> **5** *"Mothers and fathers lifted up babies so that they too could see, off to the left, the Statue of Liberty."*

When their ships landed in New York, most immigrants were taken by ferry boat to **Ellis Island.** This small island in New York Harbor was an immigration station—a place immigrants had to go before getting permission to enter the country. At Ellis Island, doctors checked immigrants for dangerous diseases. Government officials asked **6** immigrants questions about where they were from, what kind of work they did, and where they planned to live.

Immigrants often spent an entire day waiting in the long lines at Ellis Island. Once the examinations were over, they took a ferry back to New York City. Now they could begin their new lives in the United States.

REVIEW After leaving Europe, what steps did immigrants have to take before entering the United States? 🔄 Sequence

▶ Immigrants being checked at Ellis Island often ate at the huge dining hall (*above right*). Today visitors can tour the old immigration station, which is now a museum of immigration history on Ellis Island.

186

Practice and Extend

FYI **SOCIAL STUDIES Background**

About Ellis Island

- Ellis Island was the major—but not the only—immigration station on the East Coast. Immigrants also came through Boston, Savannah, and other ports.

- In general, only steerage passengers had to go to Ellis Island. Most healthy first- or second-class passengers were presumed to have enough money so that they would not become "public charges."

- Healthy immigrants who had no legal problems could expect to spend three to five hours on Ellis Island.

- About one out of every fifty immigrants was denied entry into the United States. Reasons for exclusion included contagious illness or the likelihood the person would become dependent on public assistance.

Angel Island

For immigrants from China in the early 1900s, the first stop was Angel Island in San Francisco Bay. At that time, a law limited the number of Chinese immigrants who could enter the United States. To get permission to enter, most Chinese immigrants had to prove that they had family members already living in the United States. Until they could prove this, they were held at Angel Island.

Inspectors questioned immigrants before they allowed them to leave the island. For example, if a young man said his father lived in San Francisco, inspectors would ask him many questions about his family life in China. Inspectors asked simple questions such as "How many people are in your family?" They also asked very detailed questions such as "How many windows did your house have?" or "Where do all your family members sleep?" Then the inspectors would ask the young man's father the same questions and compare the answers.

▶ Most immigrants at Angel Island were Chinese, but some came from other countries in Asia, as did these immigrants from Japan.

While waiting on Angel Island, some people expressed their frustration and anger by carving poems on the wooden walls. One person wrote,

> *"Counting on my fingers,*
> *several months have elapsed*
> *[passed].*
> *Still I am at the beginning*
> *of the road."*   ⑨

Many Chinese immigrants spent weeks or months on Angel Island. One immigrant, who was there for about a month, he summed up the feelings of many immigrants when he said, "All of us—all we wanted was to stay in this country."

REVIEW Why did it take a long time for some people to leave Angel Island?
Main Idea and Details

▶ This monument honors the immigrants who came through Angel Island. It says in Chinese, "Leaving their homes and villages, they crossed the ocean, only to endure confinement in these barracks [buildings]. Conquering frontiers and barriers, they pioneered a new life by the Golden Gate."

187

⏱ *Quick Summary* Many immigrants from Asia first entered the United States through Angel Island in San Francisco Bay.

🌐 **SOCIAL STUDIES STRAND**
Geography

Have students look at a map of the world. Have them locate China and other Asian countries and the United States.

❼ Why do you think Asian immigrants typically entered the United States through California? Possible answer: California was closer to Asia than other U.S. places of entry. Analyze Information

❽ What was the purpose of the difficult questions Asian immigrants had to answer at Angel Island? Possible answer: The questions were designed to ensure that people who said they were related were actually related.
Draw Conclusions

Primary Source

Cited in *Island: Poetry and History of Chinese Immigrants on Angel Island, 1910–1949,* by Him M. Lai, Genny Lim, and Judy Yung

❾ What can you infer about the meaning of the poet saying "Still I am at the beginning of the road"? Possible answer: He can't get beyond the beginning of his new life because he is still on Angel Island. Make Inferences

✓ **REVIEW ANSWER** It took some people a long time to prove that they had family members already living in the United States. Until they could prove it, they couldn't leave Angel Island.
Main Idea and Details

SOCIAL STUDIES
Background

About Angel Island
- Angel Island was thought of as the "Ellis Island of the West." However, unlike Ellis Island, Angel Island was designed for detaining immigrants rather than welcoming them.
- Chinese immigrants, who were excluded by the 1882 Chinese Exclusion Act, were the particular target on Angel Island.
- Most immigrants were detained on Angel Island for a few weeks to as long as a few months. Some were held for as long as two years.

A New World

⏱ **Quick Summary** Immigrants to the United States often faced a world very different from their original homelands. But they all faced the difficult task of finding new homes and jobs.

10 **Why did many immigrants feel like they were entering a "new world"?** Possible answer: Many who entered large, bustling U.S. cities were used to life in small villages. **Summarize**

11 **How did immigration change between the first and the last years of the twentieth century?** Possible answers: Fewer immigrants arrived at the end of the century, and most of them came from Latin America and Asia, not Europe. **Interpret Graphs**

12 **Why did immigrants often seek to live in communities with others from their homeland?** Possible answers: Such communities offered immigrants familiar languages and customs, which eased the transition to life in the U.S. **Summarize**

GRAPH SKILL **Answer** About eight million

A New World

What was it like for immigrants to arrive in a big American city in the late 1800s or early 1900s? For many, it was like stepping into a different world. Immigrants often came from small farming villages. Now they were suddenly surrounded by skyscrapers, electric streetcars, automobiles, and crowds of people rushing in all directions. An immigrant from Poland named Walter Mrozowski (mroh ZOW skee) felt very far from home when he first saw New York City. "I was in **10** a new world," he said.

Like most recent arrivals, Mrozowski needed to do two things right away—find a place to live and find a job. Some immigrants could go to friends or relatives for help. Those who did not know anyone usually headed to a neighborhood where there were other people from their homeland. Living in a community where the language and traditions were familiar made it a little easier to adjust to life in a new country.

After finding a place to live, most immigrants began looking for work. Many found jobs in the country's busy railroads, factories, and mines. Others started their own small businesses. If families did not have enough money to open a store, they could sell goods from pushcarts. Pushcarts were used to sell everything from food and clothing, to tools and eyeglasses. Streets in

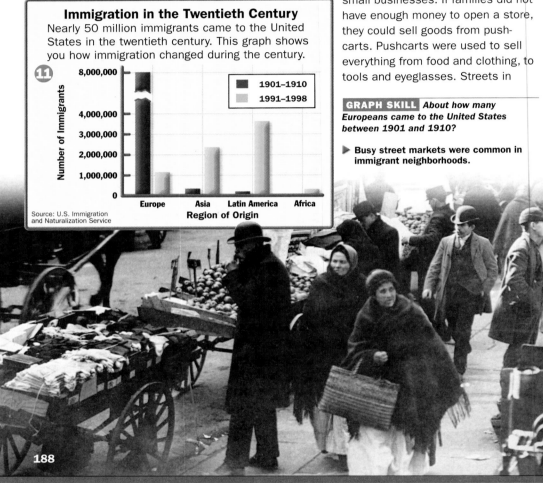

11 **Immigration in the Twentieth Century**
Nearly 50 million immigrants came to the United States in the twentieth century. This graph shows you how immigration changed during the century.

Legend: 1901–1910, 1991–1998

Number of Immigrants (y-axis): 0, 1,000,000, 2,000,000, 3,000,000, 4,000,000, 8,000,000

Region of Origin (x-axis): Europe, Asia, Latin America, Africa

Source: U.S. Immigration and Naturalization Service

GRAPH SKILL *About how many Europeans came to the United States between 1901 and 1910?*

▶ Busy street markets were common in immigrant neighborhoods.

188

Practice and Extend

MEETING INDIVIDUAL NEEDS
Leveled Practice

Make an Immigration "To Do" List Have students describe the challenges facing an immigrant to the United States.

Easy Tell students to create a flow chart showing the major steps an immigrant to the United States had to take to start building a new life. **Reteach**

On-Level Have students assume the point of view of an experienced immigrant and write a "to do" list explaining the key steps necessary for a new immigrant to take and the order he or she recommends they be taken. **Extend**

Challenge Have students assume the point of view of a new immigrant and write a one-page diary entry outlining the key steps he or she must take during the first week in the United States. **Enrich**

For a Lesson Summary, use Quick Study, p. 38.

▶ These immigrants ran a grocery store in San Francisco, California, in 1877.

immigrant neighborhoods were often lined with pushcarts and crowded with shoppers shouting to be heard in many different languages.

After finding a place to live and a job, immigrants could start thinking about how to improve their lives. Like so many people, 17-year-old Howard Ellis came to the United States with a dream. "I wanted to be a medical man," he said. Ellis came here from the West Indies in 1911. First he found a job as an elevator operator. Then he began studying. At the age of 26, he graduated from medical school. At first, Ellis had a hard time finding a job as a doctor. "They weren't hiring black doctors," he said. "I went back to work as an elevator operator. With a medical license!" Ellis never quit, though, and he finally got a job in a hospital.

Howard Ellis was not alone. Many immigrants faced the hardship of prejudice. **Prejudice** is an unfair negative opinion about a group of people. For example, job advertisements sometimes included phrases like "No Irish need apply." Immigrants from many different countries faced prejudice.

Like everyone else who was trying to get ahead in the growing cities, immigrants had to work long hours to make a living. Many worked 12 hours a day. Often, they would also go to school at night. It was hard to do well in school after such a long day of work, but these workers realized that an education was one key to a better life. Hard work was the other key. Though life remained hard for many, a large number of immigrants found great success in their new country.

REVIEW After arriving in New York, what two things did most recent arrivals need to do right away? ↺ Sequence

▶ This man sold potatoes from a pushcart in an immigrant neighborhood in New York City.

189

13 **Why were pushcarts common in many immigrant communities?** Possible answer: Pushcarts provided a relatively inexpensive way for an immigrant to go into business. **Draw Conclusions**

14 **Why do you think some immigrants faced prejudice in the United States?** Possible answer: Immigrants often spoke different languages and practiced different customs, which made certain people suspicious. Also, immigrants may have been viewed as competitors for jobs. **Hypothesize**

15 **What can you infer from the fact that immigrants often had to work long hours?** Possible answer: They were forced to take low-paying or generally undesirable jobs in order to make a living. **Make Inferences**

✓ **REVIEW ANSWER** Find a place to live and find a job ↺ Sequence

⬡ **CURRICULUM CONNECTION**
Literature

Read About Immigration

Use the following selections to extend students' knowledge of the immigrant experience.

When Jessie Came Across the Sea, by Amy Hest (Candlewick Press, ISBN 0-763-60094-6, 1997) **Easy**

Yang the Second and Her Secret Admirers, by Lensey Namioka (Yearling Books, ISBN 0-440-41641-8, 2000) **On-Level**

The Orphan of Ellis Island: A Time-Travel Adventure, by Elvira Woodruff (Scholastic, ISBN 0-590-48245-9, 1997) **Challenge**

Immigration and Diversity

Quick Summary The period from 1880 to 1924 saw more immigrants enter the United States than at any other period in history. The result was a richer, more diverse nation.

16 **Why do you think the United States decided to put a limit on immigration starting in 1924?** Possible answers: People in the United States may have developed prejudices against immigrants. Some may have thought that there were not enough jobs for everyone. **Predict**

✓ **REVIEW ANSWER** It increased their populations and made them more diverse. **Cause and Effect**

3 Close and Assess

Summarize the Lesson

Tell students to read the vertical time line. For each item, have students explain the significance of the event and relate it to the overall topic of immigration.

✓ **LESSON 3 REVIEW**

1. **Summarize** For possible answers, see the reduced pupil page.

2. Both Angel Island and Ellis Island were immigration stations. Most European immigrants had to go through Ellis Island, while most Asian immigrants went through Angel Island.

3. Sometimes immigrants were not allowed to apply for particular jobs because of their race and ethnicity.

4. The United States government passed a law limiting immigration.

5. **Critical Thinking:** *Express Ideas* Possible answer: Many people felt that the opportunities in the United States were greater than in their homelands.

Link to Writing

Letters should include details about what the immigrants have seen and their plans for the future.

190 Unit 2 • An Expanding Nation

Immigration and Diversity

From the 1880s through the 1920s, more immigrants arrived in the United States than at any other time in American history. Immigrants knew that life in a new country would be difficult. But they also knew that the United States offered freedoms and opportunities that they would not have found anywhere else in the world.

By the early 1900s, more than half of the people in most big American cities were immigrants or children of immigrants. More people of Irish background lived in New York City than in Dublin, Ireland's biggest city. Los Angeles, California, had the world's second-largest Mexican population—second only to Mexico City, Mexico. These examples show how immigrants contributed to the **diversity,** or variety, of the American population.

This period of largely unregulated immigration came to an end in 1924. The United States government passed new laws that put a limit on the number of immigrants who could enter the country each year.

16

REVIEW How did immigration affect the population of big American cities? **Cause and Effect**

Summarize the Lesson

- **1894** Mary Antin was one of 23 million immigrants to arrive in the United States in the late 1800s and early 1900s.

- **Early 1900s** More than half of the people in most big Americans cities were immigrants or children of immigrants.

- **1924** The period of largely unregulated immigration ended when the United States government passed a law limiting immigration.

LESSON 3 REVIEW

Check Facts and Main Ideas

1. **Summarize** Complete the chart below by filling in reasons that immigrants came to the United States.

| Many immigrants came to escape poverty and hunger. | Many Jewish immigrants came to escape mistreatment because of their religion. | Some immigrants came to find jobs. |

Immigrants had many reasons for coming to the United States.

2. How were Ellis Island and Angel Island similar? How were they different?

3. How did **prejudice** create problems for some immigrants in the late 1800s and early 1900s?

4. Why did the period of largely unregulated immigration come to an end in the 1920s?

5. **Critical Thinking:** *Express Ideas* Why do you think so many people were willing to face the challenge of starting new lives in the United States?

Link to Writing

Write a Letter Suppose the year is 1896 and you are a new immigrant in the United States. Write a letter home explaining why you decided to come to the United States. Describe what you have seen so far and how you feel about it. Explain what your plans are for the future.

190

Practice and Extend

SOCIAL STUDIES STRAND
Citizenship

Research Citizenship Requirements

- Have students use library and Internet resources to research the regulations and process by which an immigrant can obtain citizenship.

- They should discover how long it takes to become a citizen.

- They should learn what an immigrant must do to become a citizen.

Workbook, p. 43

Lesson 3: New Americans

Directions: Fill in the blanks with information from this lesson. You may use your textbook.

Between 1880 and 1920, more _____ immigrants arrived in the United States. Before 1890, most came from countries in _____. After that time, most came from _____. Many came to escape poverty, hunger and a lack of jobs. Some, such as Russian Jews, came in search of _____.

Millions of immigrants arriving on the East Coast passed through _____. Here they were checked for illnesses and asked questions about their plans. Chinese immigrants stopped at _____. The purpose of this stop was to ensure that they had _____ already living here. Many were forced to remain there for weeks or even longer. Once allowed into the United States, most immigrants had to find a _____ and a place to live. Many had to learn a new _____ and some faced the hardship of _____.

Directions: Suppose you are an immigrant arriving on Ellis Island in the late 1800s. Write a diary entry describing your experience. You may use a separate sheet of paper if you need more space.

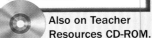

Also on Teacher Resources CD-ROM.

Mary Antin
1881–1949

Thirteen-year-old Mary Antin could not believe her eyes. After the Antins spent years waiting and hoping, her mother finally had ship tickets to take the whole family to the United States. Mary's father had sent the tickets. He had gone to Boston, Massachusetts, to find work three years  earlier. Mary's family was Jewish, and because of their religion they were denied many rights in their homeland of Russia. There was always the danger of pogroms, or organized attacks against Jews. Mary's father believed that they would all have better lives in the United States.

Mary Antin's autobiography, The Promised Land, *sold more than 80,000 copies.*

BIOFACT

Before Mary left for the United States, her uncle made her promise that she would write down everything about her journey. Just to reach the ship was difficult, and Mary was often scared. She and her family sometimes traveled in trains so crowded that there was no room to move.

Finally, the Antins boarded a ship to cross the Atlantic Ocean. Mary later described the end of their journey:

"And so suffering, fearing, brooding, rejoicing, we crept nearer and nearer to the coveted [desired] shore, until, on a glorious May morning, six weeks after our departure from [Russia], our eyes beheld the Promised Land, and my father received us in his arms."

Mary kept her promise to her uncle and wrote a long letter about the trip that brought her to a new land. Later she would use a copy of this letter as a basis for several successful books about her experiences.

Learn from Biographies
What did Mary mean when she said, "Our eyes beheld the Promised Land"?

For more information, go to *Meet the People* at **www.sfsocialstudies.com**.

191

Mary Antin

Objective
- Analyze the experiences of immigrants, such as Mary Antin.

1 Introduce and Motivate

Preview Ask students what they know about immigrants who came to the United States. Tell students that they will learn about Mary Antin, whose family left Russia in the late 1800s.

Ask why it is important to know about people who came to the United States. (Their stories can help us learn what it was like to come to the U.S.)

2 Teach and Discuss

1 Why do you think Mary's father sent for his family when he did? He found a job and a place to live. **Draw Conclusions**

2 Why do you think Mary's uncle asked her to write down her experiences? Possible answer: To share her experiences with family members who stayed in Russia; writing could also help her deal with the changes that she faced **Hypothesize**

3 Close and Assess

Learn from Biographies Answer
She believed that the United States held the promise of a better life for her family.

SOCIAL STUDIES Background

Religious Holidays
- Tell students that among the rights denied to Jews in Russia was the right to celebrate their religious holidays.
- Have students describe religious celebrations they may know about in the United States, such as Hanukkah, Christmas, or Ramadan.
- Have students discuss what is similar and different about these celebrations.

SOCIAL STUDIES Background

Mary Antin's Book
- Mary Antin's book, **The Promised Land** (Penguin USA, ISBN 0-140-18985-8, 1997), was published in 1912 and is still in print today.
- A picture book titled **Streets of Gold** (Dial Books for Young Readers, ISBN 0-803-72149-8, 1999), by Rosemary Wells, is based on Mary Antin's memoir.

The Labor Movement

Objectives

- Describe conditions that led to the rise of labor unions.

- Explain the main goals of labor unions such as the AFL.

- Identify ways in which conditions began to improve for workers in the early 1900s.

Vocabulary

sweatshop, p. 193, **labor union,** p. 195, **strike,** p. 195

Resources

- Workbook, p. 44
- Transparency 23
- Every Student Learns Guide, pp. 78–81
- Quick Study, pp. 40–41

Quick Teaching Plan

If time is short, have students create a two-column chart on a sheet of paper with the headings *Labor Problems* and *Solutions to Labor Problems.* Have students write down details from the lesson in the appropriate columns as they read the lesson independently.

1 Introduce and Motivate

Preview To activate prior knowledge, ask students if they can recall a time when they felt totally exhausted—after working at a job, playing outdoors, or hiking or walking somewhere. Tell students that they will learn about some of the difficulties faced by workers in the late 1800s and early 1900s.

You Are There Explain to students that many people in the early 1900s worked for long hours in uncomfortable and often dangerous conditions. Have students predict how workers would respond to these difficulties.

LESSON 4

New York City
• Homestead

1880			1890

1882
The first Labor Day celebration is held in New York City.

1886
Samuel Gompers forms the American Federation of Labor.

1892
Homestead Strike at Carnegie's Homestead Steel Works

PREVIEW

Focus on the Main Idea
Workers formed labor unions to fight for better wages and working conditions.

PLACES
Homestead, Pennsylvania
New York, New York

PEOPLE
Lewis Hine
Samuel Gompers
Mary Harris Jones

VOCABULARY
sweatshop
labor union
strike

The Labor Movement

You Are There The place is New York City. The time is the early 1900s. A teenager named Rose Cohen walks into a busy, noisy clothing factory. She sees a man standing at a table, folding coats. He looks up at her and demands, "Yes? What do you want?"

Rose explains that she is here for her first day of work. The man hands her pieces of a coat that need to be sewn together. "Let's see what you can do," he says.

Rose sits down at a crowded table and begins working. When she finishes sewing the coat, the man inspects her work. Then he gives her two more coats to sew. After twelve hours at the work table, Rose begins to wonder if the day will ever end. "My neck felt stiff and my back ached," she later said. "From this hour a hard life began for me."

Draw Conclusions As you read, think about the reasons why some people formed unions and went on strike.

192

Practice and Extend

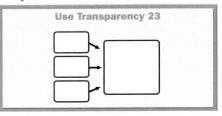

These women worked in a sweatshop in New York City. The front page headline *(right)* describes the fire at the Triangle Shirtwaist Company.

THE BROOKLYN DAILY EAGL

150 PERSONS, MOST OF THEM GIRLS, DIE AS FIRE TRAPS HAPLESS FACTORY WORKERS IN MANHATTAN SKYSCRAPER

Factories and Sweatshops

As you have read, big businesses created millions of new jobs in the late 1800s and early 1900s. Both immigrants and people born in the United States found work in factories and mines. However, it was a difficult time for many workers.

You know about the success of Andrew Carnegie's steel mills. Workers at Carnegie's mills, however, barely earned enough money to survive. At Carnegie's Homestead Steel Works in **Homestead, Pennsylvania,** steelworkers put in 12-hour days, seven days a week. The average salary was only about $10 a week.

Many women worked in clothing factories, where they earned even less. Women operated sewing machines in hot, cramped workshops known as **sweatshops.** A teenager named Sadie Frowne worked in a sweatshop in **New York, New York.** Frowne hoped to be able to sew fast enough to earn $7 a week. She described her experience,

"The machines go like mad all day because the faster you work the more money you can get. Sometimes in my haste I get a finger caught and the needle goes right through it. . . . I bind the finger up with a piece of cotton and go on working."

Sweatshops could be very dangerous places to work. At a sweatshop run by the Triangle Shirtwaist Company in New York City, workers were worried about the danger of fires. They asked the owners to build fire escapes and keep the workshop doors unlocked. The owners refused. On a Saturday afternoon in March 1911, a fire started. Workers were trapped inside. The fire killed almost 150 people, mostly young women.

REVIEW Why were the late 1800s and early 1900s a difficult time for workers? **Summarize**

193

CURRICULUM CONNECTION
Math

Calculate Hours and Pay Rates

- How many hours a week did workers at Homestead Steel Works work? ($12 \times 7 = 84$)
- How many hours per week did workers spend *outside* of work? ($12 \times 7 = 84$)
- On average, what did Homestead workers earn per hour? ($\$10.00 \div 84 = \$0.119$, or less than 12 cents an hour)
- How much did Homestead workers earn in a year? ($52 \times \$10 = \$520$)

---

2 Teach and Discuss

PAGE 193

Factories and Sweatshops

🕐 *Quick Summary* New factories and industries created millions of new jobs—but many of those jobs were low-paying, unpleasant, and even dangerous.

1 Why do you think so many people were willing to work in factories and mills like Carnegie's? Possible answer: They had no other better options available to them. **Draw Conclusions**

2 Why do you think women received lower pay than men? Possible answers: Employers thought that women could not do as much physical labor as men could. Women were the victims of prejudice and discrimination. **Draw Conclusions**

Primary Source
Cited in *Out of the Sweatshops: The Struggle for Industrial Democracy,* by Leon Stein

3 What can you infer from Frowne's statement about how workers were paid in the sweatshop? Possible answer: They were paid by how many pieces of work they produced. **Analyze Primary Sources**

4 Why do you think the factory owners refused to improve safety at the Triangle Shirtwaist Company? Possible answer: Making the changes would have cost the company money. **Draw Conclusions**

✔ **REVIEW ANSWER** Possible answer: Pay was low, hours were long, and working conditions were difficult and often unsafe. **Summarize**

Children at Work

🕐 *Quick Summary* Among the millions working in the nation's booming factories and mines were many children. Their situation caused some opposition in the United States.

Problem Solving

⑤ What was the problem that forced many children to seek work? Possible answer: Many parents were unable to make enough money to survive, so children's earnings were needed to support the family. Solve Problems

⑥ In what major way did the work experience of children differ from the work experience of adults? Possible answer: Children were paid much less than adults. Compare and Contrast

⑦ What did Lewis Hine believe was needed to put an end to child labor? Possible answer: More awareness of the problem Main Idea and Details

✓ **REVIEW ANSWER** Possible answer: He hoped to build greater public awareness of the issue of child labor and to eventually put an end to it. Draw Conclusions

---

Children at Work

⑤ Because wages were so low, children often had to work to help support their families. In 1900 about two million children under the age of 16 were working in the United States. Children were paid even less money than adults.

Children did all kinds of jobs. Many worked in textile mills, where machines were used to weave thread into cloth for clothing. Others worked canning fruits and vegetables, opening oyster shells, or picking crops on farms. In coal mining towns, young children worked as "breaker boys." After coal was brought up from the mines, it was broken up into small pieces. Breaker boys sat on benches and sorted through the coal. Their job was to pick out the rocks and keep only the clean coal.

⑥ At most of these jobs, children worked 12 or more hours a day for just 10 to 20 cents a day. There was no time for school. The working conditions were often unhealthy or dangerous. Breaker boys, for example, breathed in coal dust all day, often damaging their lungs. Children in textile mills could get their fingers caught in the spinning machines.

▶ Some people protested against child labor.

194

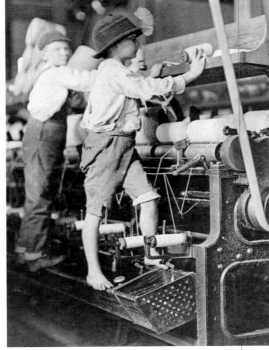

▶ Lewis Hine photographed these boys working in a cotton mill in Georgia.

⑦ Some people began speaking out against child labor. A New York City schoolteacher named **Lewis Hine** was a leader in this movement. Hine believed that more people would oppose child labor if they knew how terrible children's working conditions really were. "I wanted to show the things that had to be corrected," he said. Hine spent 12 years traveling around the United States, taking pictures of children at work. His powerful photographs helped convince many people to demand an end to child labor. You will read more about the struggle to end child labor in Issues and Viewpoints following this lesson.

REVIEW What did Lewis Hine hope to accomplish with his photographs? Draw Conclusions

---

Practice and Extend

More About Lewis Hine

- Hine was also deeply interested in photographing immigrants at Ellis Island. He sought to present immigrants as dignified people rather than helpless victims.
- His other well-known photographs document the construction of the Empire State Building in New York City. Again, his goal was to present a positive view of the worker.
- Hine's child-labor photographs were taken while he was working for the National Child Labor Committee.

Labor Unions

Low wages, long workdays, and disasters like the Triangle Shirtwaist Company fire encouraged many workers to join labor unions. *Labor* is another word for "work." In labor unions, people worked to gain improved working conditions and better wages. Labor unions also worked to end child labor.

One of the early union leaders in the United States was Samuel Gompers. As a teenager, Gompers worked in a cigar factory in New York City. He helped form a union of cigar factory workers. When owners lowered cigar makers' wages in 1877, Gompers led his union on a strike. In a strike, workers refuse to work to try to force business owners to meet their demands.

This strike was not successful. Factory owners ignored the union's demand for better wages. Gompers realized that unions would have more power if they joined together. In 1886 Gompers brought many workers' unions together to form the American

▶ Mary Harris Jones

Federation of Labor, or AFL. The AFL fought for better wages, an 8-hour work day, safer working conditions, and an end to child labor. ⑨

At the same time, a union called the United Mine Workers was struggling to improve working conditions for coal miners. A woman named Mary Harris Jones helped lead this effort. When she was in her 50s, Jones began traveling to coal mining towns in the Appalachian Mountains. "Join the union, boys," she urged the miners. Miners started calling her "Mother Jones."

Managers of coal mining companies did not usually welcome the sight of Mother Jones. They did not want their workers forming unions or going on strike. At one mining camp, Jones was warned that the manager did not want to see her around his mine. Jones refused to leave. "I am not coming to see him anyway," she replied. "I am coming to see the miners." Even when she was in her 90s, Jones continued organizing unions and speaking out in support of better treatment for workers. ⑩

REVIEW Why did Samuel Gompers want many labor unions to join together?
Main Idea and Details

▶ Samuel Gompers (*below*) and Mary Harris Jones (*above right*) helped workers join labor unions.

195

Labor Unions

🕐 *Quick Summary* The difficulties facing workers led many to join together in labor unions and use strikes in an effort to improve their situation.

❽ **What effect do you think Gompers hoped the cigar-factory strike would bring?** Possible answer: He hoped it would force the owners to raise workers' wages. Cause and Effect

❾ **What lesson did Gompers learn from his failed cigar-factory strike?** Possible answer: Unions that joined together would have more power to influence factory owners. Summarize

✓ **Ongoing Assessment**

| **If...** students do not recognize the value to labor organizations of building larger unions, | **then...** have students consider which is likely to be more effective: a strike in which workers force one fast-food restaurant to close, or a strike which forces every fast-food restaurant to close? |

❿ **What can you infer about Mother Jones and her success as a labor organizer?** Possible answer: She was very effective and popular with workers. Make Inferences

✓ **REVIEW ANSWER** Possible answer: He realized that a large labor organization would be more powerful. Main Idea and Details

Going on Strike

 Quick Summary Strikes were often tense events that sometimes erupted in violence. Most strikes, however, were settled peacefully.

Decision Making

11 What led Frick and Carnegie to decide to lower wages? Possible answer: Steel prices were dropping, so they were making less money.
Make Decisions

12 Why do you think that many years passed before the next attempt to form a union at Homestead? Possible answer: The strike had not been successful and in fact had led to some bad outcomes for workers. Unions were not considered effective. **Draw Conclusions**

Test Talk

Locate Key Words in the Text

13 How was the "newsies" strike settled? Ask students if the answer is *right there* or if they have to *think* and *search* for it. Possible answer: The newsies strike was settled peacefully when the newspaper owners offered to buy back unsold newspapers. The newsies returned to work.
Main Idea and Details

✓ **REVIEW ANSWER** Possible answer: The strikes were similar in that both involved complaints about pay for workers. They were different in that the former was violent and the latter was not; the former was not successful for workers and the latter was successful.
Compare and Contrast

Going on Strike

Tensions between striking workers and business owners sometimes led to violence. This happened at Andrew Carnegie's Homestead Steel Works in 1892. The Homestead Strike is remembered as one of the most famous strikes in American history.

The price of steel was falling in the early 1890s. Carnegie and his partner, Henry Frick, **11** decided to lower wages at Homestead. Union workers did not think this wage cut was fair. They voted to go on strike. Carnegie was out of the country, so Henry Frick handled the strike. He refused to talk with striking workers. Instead, he hired armed guards to break up the strike. When the guards arrived at night, thousands of striking workers were waiting for them. The guards and workers fought, and people on both sides were killed.

The Homestead Strike lasted several months. Finally, the workers decided to give up the strike. Many years passed before a new union was formed at the Homestead **12** plant.

Unlike the Homestead Strike, most strikes were settled peacefully. One example is the "newsies" strike of 1899. Newsies were children who sold newspapers on the street. In New York City, newsies could buy 100 newspapers for 50 cents. Then they sold as many as they could for one cent each.

Trouble started when the *New York World* and *New York Journal* decided to raise the price they charged to newsies. The newspaper owners said that 100 newspapers would now cost newsies 60 cents. Angry newsies gathered in a city park and voted to go on strike. They gained public support by handing out flyers that said, "Help us in our struggle to get fair play by not buying the *Journal* or the *World*."

After two weeks, sales of the two newspapers had fallen sharply. The newspaper owners decided to offer a deal. One hundred newspapers would still cost 60 cents, but the newspaper companies would now buy back any papers the newsies were not able to sell. Newsies thought this was fair, and they went back to work. **13**

REVIEW How were the Homestead Strike and newsies strike similar? How were they different? **Compare and Contrast**

▶ The diversity of workers is reflected in the signs they carried during this 1913 strike.

196

Practice and Extend

 ISSUES AND VIEWPOINTS
Critical Thinking

Analyze Different Viewpoints

• Many working people grew angry at business owners who seemed to get rich while the workers suffered. However, many others in the United States took a different view.

• Read the quote from Andrew Carnegie to the class. Then ask students to discuss Carnegie's viewpoint.

"It will be a great mistake for the community to shoot the millionaires, for they are the bees that make the honey, and contribute to the hive even after they have gorged themselves full."

Improving Conditions

Unions continued to gain members in the early 1900s. Many business owners, religious organizations, and political leaders also helped improve life for workers. New laws shortened hours and improved safety in the workplace.

Unions also created a new holiday—Labor Day. The first Labor Day celebration was held in New York City in September 1882. Thousands of workers paraded through the streets carrying signs saying "Shorter Hours, Fairer Pay" and "Stop Child Labor." Within a few years, workers were holding Labor Day celebrations in many cities. In 1894 Congress declared Labor Day to be an official national holiday. We still celebrate Labor Day on the first Monday in September.

REVIEW Explain how Labor Day became a national holiday. **Summarize**

▶ The first Labor Day celebration was held in New York City in 1882.

Summarize the Lesson

- **1882** The first Labor Day celebration was held in New York City.

- **1886** Under the leadership of Samuel Gompers, many unions joined together to form the American Federation of Labor.

- **1892** The Homestead Strike at Carnegie's Homestead Steel Works led to violence between workers and guards.

LESSON 4 REVIEW

Check Facts and Main Ideas

1. Draw Conclusions Complete the chart below on a separate sheet of paper. Fill in a conclusion that could be drawn from the information given.

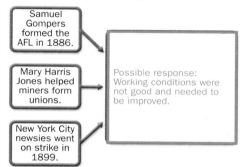

Samuel Gompers formed the AFL in 1886.

Mary Harris Jones helped miners form unions.

New York City newsies went on strike in 1899.

Possible response: Working conditions were not good and needed to be improved.

2. What conditions led to the rise of **labor unions**?

3. What were the main goals of labor unions such as the AFL?

4. In what ways did conditions begin to improve for workers in the early 1900s?

5. Critical Thinking: *Evaluate* Why do you think a disaster like the Triangle Shirtwaist Factory fire might have encouraged people to join unions?

Link to Citizenship

Research Changing Laws Citizens worked hard to change child labor laws in the early 1900s. Do research to find out about a national law called the Fair Labor Standards Act. What year was this law passed? What did it do?

197

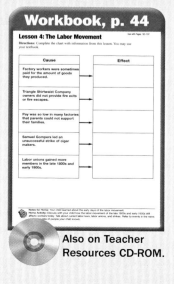

Workbook, p. 44

Lesson 4: The Labor Movement

Directions: Complete the chart with information from this lesson. You may use your textbook.

Cause	Effect
Factory workers were sometimes paid for the amount of goods they produced.	
Triangle Shirtwaist Company owners did not provide fire exits or fire escapes.	
Pay was so low in many factories that parents could not support their families.	
Samuel Gompers led an unsuccessful strike of cigar makers.	
Labor unions gained more members in the late 1800s and early 1900s.	

Also on Teacher Resources CD-ROM.

Improving Conditions

🕐 ***Quick Summary*** In the early 1900s, workers began to see some improvements in their lives. The Labor Day holiday, started in 1882, is still celebrated today.

14 **What facts support the idea that labor unions became increasingly successful in the early 1900s?** Possible answers: They steadily gained new members. New laws were passed to shorten working hours and to improve workplace safety. **Apply Information**

✓ **REVIEW ANSWER** Possible answer: Workers in New York City held a parade, which began a tradition of annual Labor Day celebrations. Then Congress established a national holiday. **Summarize**

3 Close and Assess

Summarize the Lesson

For each item on the time line, have students explain the significance and impact of the event on the labor movement.

✓ **LESSON 4 REVIEW**

1. **Draw Conclusions** For possible answers, see the reduced pupil page.

2. Poor and unsafe working conditions, long hours, and low pay led many workers to join together in unions.

3. They wanted higher pay, shorter hours, better working conditions, and the end of child labor.

4. Laws were passed leading to shorter workdays and safer workplaces.

5. **Critical Thinking: *Evaluate*** The disaster showed that the stakes were high for workers if employers were not watching out for their needs.

Link to Citizenship

Ensure that students' research is thorough and accurate. Assist them with an Internet search. The Act, passed in 1938, sets minimum standards for wages, overtime, child-labor regulations, and equal pay.

Working Against Child Labor

Objectives

- Explain how the Industrial Revolution caused changes in society that led to clashes between certain groups of Americans.

- Explain how industry changed many Americans' way of life.

- Explain how an individual is able to take part in civic affairs at the national level.

1 Introduce and Motivate

Preview To activate prior knowledge, ask students what they know about working conditions in the late 1800s and early 1900s. Ask how these conditions might affect a child. Tell students that they will learn about child labor and what people did about it.

2 Teach and Discuss

1 **At the age of twelve, what did Florence Kelley observe at a glassmaking factory?** Boys about her size were doing hard, dangerous work. Main Idea and Details

2 **Summarize what Kelley did about her observation and tell the results.** She wrote reports and encouraged people not to buy products made with child labor. The result was that laws were passed forbidding child labor. Summarize

3 **Why did Kelley use the word *robbed* when she said that not going to school was a result of child labor?** The word *robbed* has a strong meaning, which shows that Kelley believed children were being denied their rights when they were working in factories rather than attending school. Analyze Primary Sources

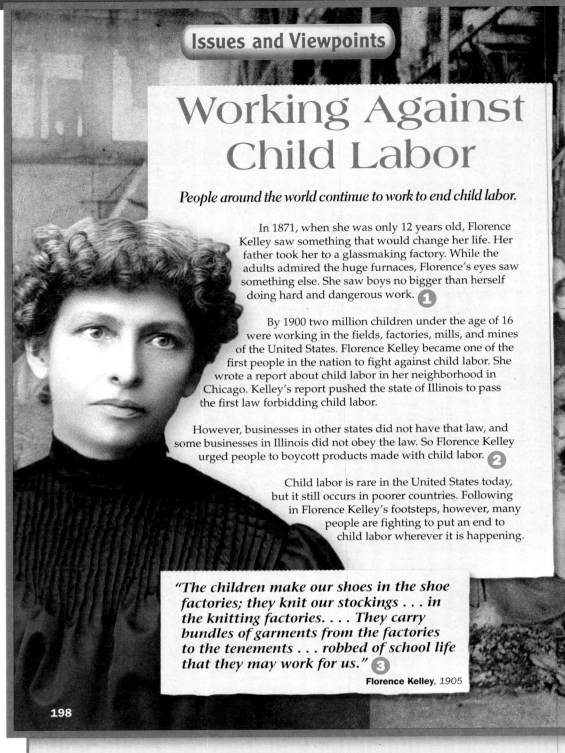

Issues and Viewpoints

Working Against Child Labor

People around the world continue to work to end child labor.

In 1871, when she was only 12 years old, Florence Kelley saw something that would change her life. Her father took her to a glassmaking factory. While the adults admired the huge furnaces, Florence's eyes saw something else. She saw boys no bigger than herself doing hard and dangerous work. **1**

By 1900 two million children under the age of 16 were working in the fields, factories, mills, and mines of the United States. Florence Kelley became one of the first people in the nation to fight against child labor. She wrote a report about child labor in her neighborhood in Chicago. Kelley's report pushed the state of Illinois to pass the first law forbidding child labor.

However, businesses in other states did not have that law, and some businesses in Illinois did not obey the law. So Florence Kelley urged people to boycott products made with child labor. **2**

Child labor is rare in the United States today, but it still occurs in poorer countries. Following in Florence Kelley's footsteps, however, many people are fighting to put an end to child labor wherever it is happening.

> *"The children make our shoes in the shoe factories; they knit our stockings . . . in the knitting factories. . . . They carry bundles of garments from the factories to the tenements . . . robbed of school life that they may work for us."* **3**
>
> **Florence Kelley**, *1905*

198

Practice and Extend

 SOCIAL STUDIES Background

Fighting Against Child Labor

- Librarian Helen Marot used her research and writing skills to speak out against child labor. She wrote a report that led to the New York legislature passing the Compulsory Education Act in 1903.
- Teacher Grace Abbott worked at Hull House and wrote articles and books to inspire people to address the issue of child labor. In 1917 she became the director of the United States Children's Bureau, which was formed to protect children.

Social Reform

- The creed of the Social Gospel movement of the late 1800s included abolition of child labor, better wages for workers, and better working conditions for women.
- Dwight L. Moody gave up a prosperous business to do missionary work in poor Chicago neighborhoods. An enthusiastic preacher, he founded the Moody Church and worked in urban areas across the country to provide recreation and education for youth.

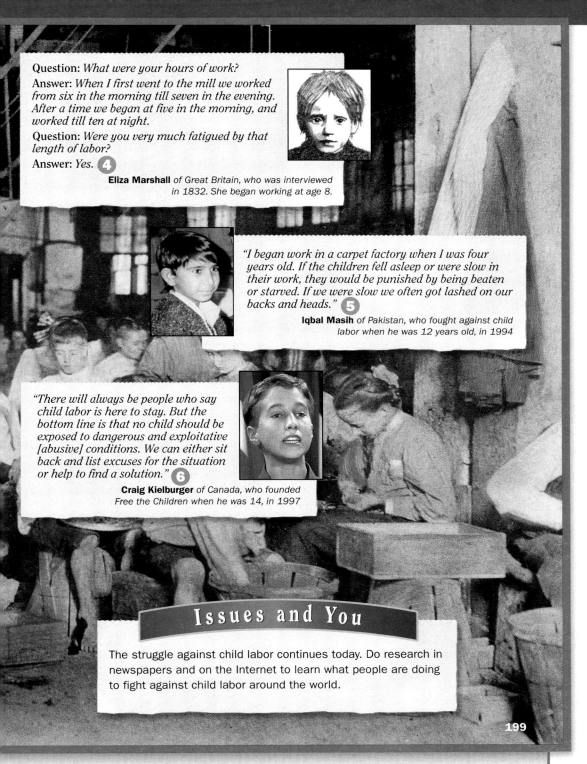

Question: *What were your hours of work?*

Answer: *When I first went to the mill we worked from six in the morning till seven in the evening. After a time we began at five in the morning, and worked till ten at night.*

Question: *Were you very much fatigued by that length of labor?*

Answer: *Yes.* ④

Eliza Marshall of Great Britain, who was interviewed in 1832. She began working at age 8.

"I began work in a carpet factory when I was four years old. If the children fell asleep or were slow in their work, they would be punished by being beaten or starved. If we were slow we often got lashed on our backs and heads." ⑤

Iqbal Masih of Pakistan, who fought against child labor when he was 12 years old, in 1994

"There will always be people who say child labor is here to stay. But the bottom line is that no child should be exposed to dangerous and exploitative [abusive] conditions. We can either sit back and list excuses for the situation or help to find a solution." ⑥

Craig Kielburger of Canada, who founded Free the Children when he was 14, in 1997

Issues and You

The struggle against child labor continues today. Do research in newspapers and on the Internet to learn what people are doing to fight against child labor around the world.

199

④ **Why do you think some parents permitted children to work the kinds of hours Eliza Marshall worked?** Possible answer: They may have felt their children had to work in order to make enough money for the family. Cause and Effect

⑤ **Compare Iqbal Masih's situation with that of children in the late 1800s and early 1900s.** In Masih's situation, as in the past, a young child was forced to work hard under difficult or dangerous conditions. Compare and Contrast

⑥ **What is Craig Kielburger's view about child labor?** He believes we should not tolerate it and should work to stop it. Main Idea and Details

③ Close and Assess

Issues and You

- After reviewing several reports about groups battling child labor, have each student focus on one group or activity.

- In conducting their research, have students search for answers to the following questions: What is the current situation involving child labor? Where is it taking place? Who is trying to help? What is the individual or group doing? What have been the results so far?

- Have students use a web with one of the questions on each branch for notes. Have students use these notes as the basis for oral reports.

SOCIAL STUDIES
Background

Craig Kielburger

- Craig Kielburger grew up in a suburb of Toronto, Ontario, Canada, with his parents and his older brother, Marc.

- Kielburger visits working children all over the world and speaks in defense of children's rights.

- Kielburger and his friends founded Free the Children, a worldwide network of children helping children. Their organization has more than 100,000 active members in more than 25 countries.

CURRICULUM CONNECTION
Writing

Write a Letter

- Have students discuss what questions they might ask Craig Kielburger and his friends about their organization and their efforts to improve children's lives.

- Direct students to write a letter to Craig Kielburger asking him about his life and his causes.

Resources

• Assessment Book, pp. 21–24
• Workbook, p. 45: Vocabulary Review

Chapter Summary

For possible answers, see the reduced pupil page.

Vocabulary

1. F; A monopoly is when one company controls an entire industry, **2.** T, **3.** F; Diversity is variety, **4.** T, **5.** F; When workers go on strike, they refuse to work until business owners meet their demands.

People and Places

Possible answers:

1. Alexander Graham Bell invented the telephone and changed the way people communicated.

2. Thomas Edison invented the light bulb in his laboratory in Menlo Park, New Jersey.

3. Orville Wright and his brother, Wilbur, flew the first successful airplane in 1903.

4. Andrew Carnegie used the Bessemer process to make steel at a low cost in Pittsburgh, Pennsylvania.

5. William Randolph Hearst built a successful newspaper business in the early 1900s by using big headlines and illustrations.

6. Many immigrants from Europe in the late 1800s and early 1900s first stopped at Ellis Island to answer questions and get checked by a doctor.

7. Most Chinese immigrants coming to the United States in the early 1900s first stopped at Angel Island to prove that they had family members already living in the country.

8. Lewis Hine took photographs of children at work that helped convince people to put an end to child labor.

1855	1865	1875

1856 Henry Bessemer develops a new way to make steel.

1876 Alexander Graham Bell invents the telephone.

1879 Thomas Edison invents a working light bulb.

Chapter Summary

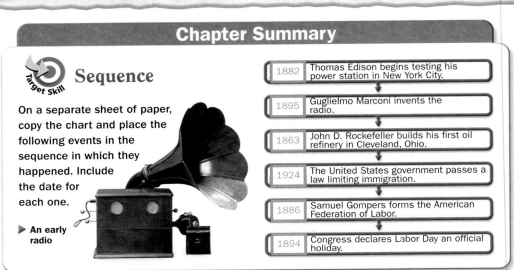

Sequence

Target Skill

On a separate sheet of paper, copy the chart and place the following events in the sequence in which they happened. Include the date for each one.

▶ An early radio

1882	Thomas Edison begins testing his power station in New York City.
1895	Guglielmo Marconi invents the radio.
1863	John D. Rockefeller builds his first oil refinery in Cleveland, Ohio.
1924	The United States government passes a law limiting immigration.
1886	Samuel Gompers forms the American Federation of Labor.
1894	Congress declares Labor Day an official holiday.

Vocabulary

On a separate sheet of paper, write **T** for each sentence that correctly defines the underlined word and **F** for each definition that is false. If false, rewrite the definition so it is correct.

1 A <u>monopoly</u> is when several companies have control of one industry.

2 A <u>consumer</u> is a person who buys or uses goods and services.

3 <u>Diversity</u> is an unfair negative opinion about a group of people.

4 <u>Sweatshops</u> are crowded and often unsafe workshops.

5 When workers go on <u>strike</u>, they work longer hours than usual.

People and Places

Write a sentence explaining the role of each of the following people or places in the changing United States of the late 1800s and early 1900s. You may use two or more in a single sentence.

1 Alexander Graham Bell (p. 167)

2 Menlo Park, New Jersey (p. 168)

3 Orville Wright (p. 172)

4 Pittsburgh, Pennsylvania (p. 177)

5 William Randolph Hearst (p. 180)

6 Ellis Island (p. 186)

7 Angel Island (p. 187)

8 Lewis Hine (p. 194)

Practice and Extend

Assessment Options

✓ Chapter 4 Assessment

• Chapter 4 Content Test: Use Assessment Book, pp. 21–22.

• Chapter 4 Skills Test: Use Assessment Book, pp. 23–24.

TEST PREP **Standardized Test Prep**

• Chapter 4 Tests contain standardized test format.

✓ Chapter 4 Performance Assessment

• Assign small groups the name of a person or organization discussed in this chapter. Have students act out an event or scene that tells something significant about the person or organization.

• Have the rest of the class watch the presentations to see if they can identify the individual or organization and its significance.

• Assess students' understanding of the significant people or organizations of the late 1800s and early 1900s.

1882
The first Labor Day celebration is held in New York City.

1892
The Homestead Strike occurs.

1900
About 2 million children under age 16 are working in the United States.

1903
The Wright Brothers build the world's first successful airplane.

1906
Madame C. J. Walker begins bottling shampoo and other products in her attic.

Facts and Main Ideas

1 What steps did Andrew Carnegie take to produce steel at the lowest possible cost?

2 How were the experiences of immigrants at Ellis Island and Angel Island alike and different?

3 **Time Line** How many years after the first Labor Day celebration did the Homestead Strike occur?

4 **Main Idea** What were some inventions that brought about major changes in the way people lived in the late 1800s and early 1900s?

5 **Main Idea** What industries did large business owners help build in the late 1800s?

6 **Main Idea** What challenges did many immigrants face when they arrived in the United States?

7 **Main Idea** Why did some workers form labor unions in the late 1800s?

8 **Critical Thinking:** *Draw Conclusions* Why do you think Lewis Hine's photographs of children at work helped convince people to put an end to child labor?

Internet Activity

To get help with vocabulary, people, and terms, select dictionary or encyclopedia from *Social Studies Library* at **www.sfsocialstudies.com.**

Apply Skills

Reread page 180 about free enterprise. Then answer the questions based on the outline.

I. George Westinghouse
  A. Westinghouse Electric Company
    1. Formed in 1886
    2. Developed alternating current to deliver electricity to homes
  B. "War of the Currents"
    1. _____
    2. Consumers chose Westinghouse's better product

II. Madame C. J. Walker
  A. _____
    1. Began bottling shampoo in her attic in 1906
    2. Sold her products door-to-door
  B. Success
    1. Ten years later she had thousands of employees
    2. First African American woman to become a millionaire

1 What detail would you write next to *1*?

2 What main idea belongs next to *A*?

3 How did Madame C. J. Walker start her business?

Write About History

1 **Write a short story** describing what it would have been like to see the first successful airplane flight.

2 **Write a letter to a friend** back home describing your experience as an immigrant at Ellis Island or Angel Island.

3 **Write an editorial** trying to convince workers either to join or not to join a labor union.

201

Hands-on Unit Project

✓ Unit 2 Performance Assessment

- See p. 206 for information about using the Unit Project as a means of performance assessment.
- A scoring guide is provided on p. 206.

WEB SITE
Technology

For more information, students can select the dictionary or encyclopedia from *Social Studies Library* at **www.sfsocialstudies.com.**

Workbook, p. 45

Vocabulary Review

Directions: Use the vocabulary terms from Chapter 4 to complete the crossword puzzle.

Across
1. unfair negative opinion about a group of people
8. a person
10. person who buys or uses goods and services
11. share of a company
12. business that is owned by investors
13. when workers refuse to work to try to force business owners to meet their demands

Down
2. tool or machine that a company can use to produce goods and services
3. variety
4. hot, cramped workshop
5. system in which people are free to start their own businesses and own their property
6. person who gives to a business or project hoping to gain a profit
7. company that has control of an entire industry
9. group of workers who join together to fight for improved working conditions and better wages

Also on Teacher Resources CD-ROM.

Facts and Main Ideas

Possible answers:

1. He bought iron and coal mines that supplied his mills with resources, and ships and railroads to deliver the resources.

2. Immigrants at both places had to answer questions, but Chinese immigrants at Angel Island had to prove that they had relatives living in the United States.

3. About 10 years

4. The telephone allowed people to communicate across distances, electric lights lit up businesses and homes at night, streetcars and automobiles moved people without horses, and the airplane was even faster.

5. Andrew Carnegie was a leader in the steel industry. John D. Rockefeller helped build the oil industry. George Westinghouse delivered electricity. William Randolph Hearst sold newspapers. J. P. Morgan helped build the banking industry.

6. Immigrants had to find a job and a place to live. Many had to learn English and faced discrimination.

7. To fight for safer working conditions and better pay

8. Possible answer: His photographs allowed many people to witness the poor and dangerous conditions for working children.

Apply Skills

1. Competed with Thomas Edison's direct current system

2. Started her own business

3. She bottled her own shampoo and sold her products door to door.

Write About History

1. Tell students that they would have never seen an airplane before.

2. Students' letters should reflect the conditions at Ellis or Angel Island.

3. Editorials should take a clear stand and provide a persuasive argument.

Red River Valley

Objectives

- Identify pieces of music from different periods in United States history.

- Explain how pieces of music reflect the times in which they were written.

1 Introduce and Motivate

Preview Ask students if they know the history of the song "Red River Valley." Tell students that they will learn more about this song and what it means.

Ask students how studying a song from a certain time can be useful. (It can provide another means to understand the people and the times.)

2 Teach and Discuss

1 **How is the singer of the song feeling? Why?** Sad, because a friend is leaving the Red River Valley
Cause and Effect

Red River Valley

If you had worked on the cattle drives of the 1800s, you would probably have known lots of cowboy songs. Cowboys sang these songs to keep their cattle calm. And they sang to pass the time during the long, lonely days and nights on the trail. What does the cowboy song "Red River Valley" tell you about what life was like for cowboys?

202

Practice and Extend

SOCIAL STUDIES
Background

"Red River Valley"

- The song was originally named "In the Bright Mohawk Valley" and was popular in New York.
- Later the song spread throughout the South and became a cowboy tune focused on the Red River Valley.

AUDIO CD
Technology

Play the CD, *Songs and Music,* to listen to "Red River Valley."

Cowboy Song from the United States

VERSE

1. From this val-ley they say you are go-ing, — We will
2. Won't you think of the val-ley you're leav-ing? — Oh, how

miss your bright eyes and sweet smile; For they say you are tak-ing the
lone-ly, how sad it will be. Oh, — think of the fond heart you're

 1

sun-shine, — That bright-ens our path-way a-while.
break-ing, — And the grief you are causing me to see.

2

REFRAIN

Come and sit by my side if you love me, — Do not

has-ten to bid me a-dieu; But re-mem-ber the Red Riv-er

3

Val-ley — And the girl that has loved you so true.

4

203

2 **What might the line "For they say you are taking the sunshine" mean?** Possible answer: It will seem like the sun will never shine again once the person leaves the valley. **Make Inferences**

3 **What is another way of saying, "Do not hasten to bid me adieu"?** Possible answer: Do not be in such a hurry to say goodbye. **Express Ideas**

4 **Why might the person be leaving the Red River Valley?** Possible answers: To begin a cattle drive, find a new job, or simply to go away. **Hypothesize**

3 Close and Assess

- Have students gather guitars and harmonicas to use in singing the song. Videotape the performance.

- Direct students to think of this song as a poem that tells a story. Have students discuss the events and characters in the "story." Point out the line "For they say you are taking the sunshine." Tell students to ask themselves if this is a logical action. They should ask themselves "Would this character really take the sunshine?" Then ask students to write a summary of the events and feelings described in the song.

CURRICULUM CONNECTION
Art

Paint a Setting

- Have students use watercolors or tempera paints to create an illustration of the setting of the song.
- Have students look at pictures of the area where the Red River flows to get ideas of how to depict the valley.

Resource
• Assessment Book, pp. 25–28

Main Ideas and Vocabulary TEST PREP

1. b, **2.** d, **3.** c, **4.** a

 Test Talk

Locate Key Words in the Text
Use Main Ideas and Vocabulary, Question 1, to model the Test Talk strategy.

Make sure that you understand the question.
Have students find the key words in the question. Students should finish the statement, "I need to find out…"

Find key words in the text that match the key words in the question.
Have students reread or skim the text to look for key words that will help them answer the question.

People and Places

1. d, **2.** c, **3.** f, **4.** b, **5.** a, **6.** e

 **Test Talk**

Find key words in the text.

Main Ideas and Vocabulary TEST PREP

Read the passage below and use it to answer the questions that follow.

From the middle to late 1800s, changes in technology helped people in the United States stay connected. The Pony Express began in 1860, but was replaced by the transcontinental telegraph only one year later. By 1869 the transcontinental railroad stretched from one coast of the country to the other.

As the West became easier to reach, more people decided to settle there. Pioneers moved to the Great Plains to farm, and miners rushed to the West to find gold. For Native Americans, these changes led to the loss of their traditional lands. When the government forced Native Americans to move to <u>reservations</u>, many fought to keep their homelands.

Inventors and business leaders also changed how people lived. In 1876 Alexander Graham Bell invented the telephone. Automobiles and electric streetcars moved people around faster than before. <u>Entrepreneurs</u> such as Andrew Carnegie and John D. Rockefeller made millions of dollars in the steel and oil businesses. Millions of people worked in new and growing industries.

Many of the workers in growing industries were immigrants. In the late 1800s and early 1900s, millions of immigrants came to the United States in search of opportunities. They often faced prejudice. In 1924 the United States passed a law limiting immigration.

Workers formed labor unions in the late 1800s to fight for better working conditions, shorter hours, and higher pay. Labor Day, made an official holiday in 1894, recognizes the contributions of workers across the country.

1 According to the passage, why did workers start labor unions?
 A to get new jobs
 B to fight for better working conditions
 C to protest against Labor Day
 D to work on new inventions

2 In the passage, the word <u>reservation</u> means—
 A land in the mountains
 B land on the Great Plains
 C farms
 D land set aside for Native Americans

3 In the passage, the word <u>entrepreneurs</u> means—
 A railroad workers
 B immigrants
 C people who start new businesses, hoping to make a profit
 D people who move to the Great Plains

4 According to the passage, technology
 A caused changes in the United States
 B helped the Native Americans keep their homelands
 C was not important in the late 1800s
 D caused people to leave the country

204

Practice and Extend

Assessment Options

✓ **Unit 2 Assessment**
• Unit 2 Content Test:
 Use Assessment Book, pp. 25–26.
• Unit 2 Skills Test:
 Use Assessment Book, pp. 27–28.

TEST PREP **Standardized Test Prep**
• Unit 2 Tests contain standardized test format.

✓ **Unit 2 Performance Assessment**
• See p. 206 for information about using the Unit Project as a means of Performance Assessment.
• A scoring guide for the Unit 2 Project is provided in the teacher's notes on p. 206.

 Test Talk
• Test Talk Practice Book

 **WEB SITE Technology**

For more information, students can select the dictionary or encyclopedia from *Social Studies Library* at **www.sfsocialstudies.com.**

People and Places

Match each person and place to its definition.

1 **Promontory Point, Utah Territory** (p. 133)

2 **Virginia City, Nevada** (p. 152)

3 **Crazy Horse** (p. 156)

4 **Lewis Latimer** (p. 168)

5 **Kitty Hawk, North Carolina** (p. 172)

6 **Mary Antin** (p. 185)

a. location of the first airplane flight

b. inventor of a long-lasting filament for light bulbs

c. large boom town

d. place where the transcontinental railroad was completed

e. immigrant from Russia

f. leader of the Lakota at the Battle of Little Bighorn

Apply Skills

Write an Outline Choose a page from a lesson in this unit. Reread the page and make note of the main ideas and the facts that support the main ideas. On a sheet of paper, use your notes to write an outline of the page you chose. Use Roman numerals to identify the main ideas, capital letters for subtopics, and numbers for important details.

Write and Share

Write a Class Newspaper Suppose you were a newspaper reporter in the late 1800s. Work with a group in your class to write an article about a business leader you read about in the unit. Conduct research to find out about how the leader's business affected the industry and its workers. When all the articles are finished, work together as a class to paste the articles into a newspaper. Remember to include headlines with your article, and decide together as a class what to call the newspaper. You can include pictures, drawings, and captions to help bring the stories to life.

Read on Your Own

Look for books like these in the library.

205

Revisit the Unit Question

✓ **Portfolio Assessment**

- Have students review their list of transportation methods used in the United States.
- Have students look at the list they created throughout Unit 2 of the types of transportation used in the 1800s and 1900s.

- Ask students to compare and contrast their lists.
- Have students write a paragraph discussing how these transportation methods affected where people lived.
- Have students add these lists and paragraphs to their Social Studies Portfolio.

Apply Skills

- Ensure that students correctly identify the main ideas and supporting details on the page they outline.
- Check to see that students follow the proper outline format.

Write and Share

- Help students identify some of the business leaders discussed in the unit. Students can use the Places, People, and Vocabulary sections at the start of each lesson for ideas.
- Guide students to find information on their subjects in the text and in outside resources.
- Use the following scoring guide.

✓ **Assessment Scoring Guide**

Write a Class Newspaper	
6	Article thoroughly discusses the leader and his or her impact. Includes clear headline, effective illustrations, and captions.
5	Article thoroughly discusses the leader and his or her impact. Includes headline, illustrations, and captions.
4	Article thoroughly discusses the leader and his or her impact. Includes most of the following: headline, illustrations, and captions.
3	Article provides some information on the leader and his or her impact. Includes most of the following: headline, illustrations, and captions.
2	Article provides some information on the leader and his or her impact. Includes some of the following: headline, pictures, and captions.
1	Article provides little information on the leader and his or her impact. Does not include headline, pictures, or captions.

If you prefer a 4-point rubric, adjust accordingly.

Read on Your Own

Have students prepare oral reports using the following books.

Vision of Beauty: The Story of Sarah Breedlove Walker, by Kathryn Lasky (Candlewick Press, ISBN 0-763-70253-1, 2000) **Easy**

Ten Mile Day: And the Building of the Transcontinental Railroad, by Mary Ann Fraser (Henry Holt & Company, ISBN 0-805-04703-4, 1996) **On-Level**

Alexander Graham Bell: An Inventive Life, by Elizabeth MacLeod (Kids Can Press, ISBN 1-550-74456-9, 1999) **Challenge**

Inventions Change the Country

Objective
- Research an invention from the late 1800s or early 1900s and create an advertisement.

Resource
- Workbook, p. 46

Materials
reference materials, paper, poster board, pencils, paints, markers

Follow This Procedure
- Tell students that they will advertise inventions from the late 1800s or early 1900s. Discuss how inventions have changed the world. For example, automobiles allowed people to travel farther.

- Divide students into groups. Have students choose an invention to research, including who the inventor was, and the features, benefits, and effects of the invention.

- Have students create posters to advertise their invention. Invite students to present their advertisements to the class.

- Use the following scoring guide.

✓Assessment Scoring Guide

Inventions Change the Country	
6	Extremely detailed with accurate content and precise word choices
5	Detailed with accurate content and precise word choices
4	Detailed with mostly accurate content and clear word choices
3	Provides some details with mostly accurate content and clear word choices
2	Provides some details with somewhat accurate content and vague word choices
1	Provides few details with inaccurate content and poor word choices

If you prefer a 4-point rubric, adjust accordingly.

UNIT 2 Project

Inventions Change the Country

Advertise a product from the past.

1 Form a group and choose an invention from the late 1800s or early 1900s that you read about in this unit.

2 Research the invention and describe what made the invention popular or revolutionary. Write who invented it and why, how it helped people, if it saved time or money, and if it changed the world.

3 Make a poster or large advertisement for this invention. Include a picture of the product.

4 Present your advertisement to the class. You may make the presentation as if you were the inventor.

The First Typewriter

Internet Activity
Explore immigration to the United States. Go to **www.sfsocialstudies.com/activities** and select your grade and unit.

Practice and Extend

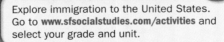
Hands-on Unit Project

✓Performance Assessment
- The Unit Project can also be used as a performance assessment activity.
- Use the scoring guide to assess each group's work.

WEB SITE
Technology

Students can launch the Internet Activity by clicking on *Grade 5, Unit 2* at **www.sfsocialstudies.com/activities.**

Workbook, p. 46

2 Project Inventions Change the Country

Directions: Make a poster or advertisement for an invention from the late 1800s or early 1900s.

1. The invention we chose is _____
2. The name of the inventor is _____
3. The purpose of the invention is _____
4. Special features of this invention include _____
5. The (or?) shows how this invention helped people.
    _____ saved money _____ saved time _____ other: _____
6. Reasons people should use this invention are _____
7. This invention changed the world because _____
8. This is what the invention looked like:

✓ Checklist for Students
_____ We chose an invention from the late 1800s.
_____ We identified the inventor, and we described the invention's purpose, features, and benefits.
_____ We made a poster or advertisement for the invention.
_____ We included a picture of the invention on the poster.
_____ We presented our poster or advertisement to the class.

Notes for Home: Your child researched an invention from the late 1800s and advertised its features to the class.
Home Activity: With your child, identify a modern invention you both agree has changed the world. Discuss how it has impacted your life.

Also on Teacher Resources CD-ROM.

Vocabulary Routines

The following examples of reading and vocabulary development strategies can be used to instruct students about unit vocabulary.

BEFORE READING

Related Word Study

Words with Prefixes Through the structural analysis of words with prefixes, students will learn that prefixes change the meaning of a base word. Introducing common prefixes and their meanings such as *re-* ("to do again"), *un-* ("the opposite of" or "not"), and *dis-* ("opposite of" or "lack of") will aid students in both their comprehension and writing skills.

Look at the word **unlike***. We know that the word means "not like or different from." But what if we didn't know that? How could we figure out the meaning of the word?*

First, we would think about the meaning of the base word: **like***. We know that one of its meanings is "the same as." If you put the prefix* **un-** *in front of* **like***, it changes the meaning of* **like***. So the word* **unlike** *means "the opposite of or not"* like.

Now think about the word **connected***. We know it means "fastened or joined together." Can you think of any prefixes that could be added to* **connected** *to create a word that was opposite in meaning? In this case there are two.* **Un-** *and* **dis-** *can be added to create words that are opposites:* **unconnected** *and* **disconnected***.*

DURING READING

Context Clues

Use Context Clues Teaching students to recognize and analyze context clues will help them to determine the meanings of difficult words when a dictionary or glossary is not available. By looking closely at the way in which a new word is used in a sentence, students will also learn how to use these words in their own writing.

Direct students to the following sentence on p. 219, then read it aloud.

"Sometimes when there were no local phone companies, farmers banded together and put up their own poles and lines."

Look at the word **banded***. What do you think the word means? Write the context clues that helped you to figure out the definition. Now try using the word* **banded** *to describe something that could happen to you.*

What are the context clues?	How can I use the word?
• no local phone companies • together • put up their own poles and lines	• My friends and I <u>banded</u> together to paint the animal shelter.

AFTER READING

Individual Word Study

Student-friendly Definitions At times, dictionary definitions can be as difficult to understand as the words they define. Students can benefit greatly if a definition is written in language that they use themselves. Sometimes descriptive sentences can serve the same function as a definition.

We read about residential areas in Lesson 2. The dictionary definition for **residential** *is "having something to do with residences." That definition doesn't really help you understand what* **residential** *means, does it? If we look up* **residence***, however, we find it means "places people live." We could then rewrite the definition of* **residential** *to read "having something to do with the places people live" or "related to the places people live." We could also use the word in a sentence to describe what it means:*

I live in a residential area where there are four large apartment buildings and two smaller ones. Most residential areas have streets and, sidewalks, and some have trees, and playgrounds.

Teaching with Leveled Readers

This series of readers focuses on the changes in the United States in the late 1800s and early 1900s.

Below Level

On Level

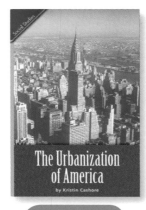

Above Level

LEVELED READER VOCABULARY ACTIVITY

- Have students preview the vocabulary words before they begin reading.

- Explain to students that the suffix *–ation* can mean "the condition or state of being."

- Have students predict the definitions of the two *-ation* vocabulary words.

Urbaniz | ation

Mechaniz | ation

CONNECTIONS TO THE LESSON

Chapter 5, Lesson 2: Life in the Growing Cities

CONNECTIONS TO TODAY

- Have students read the lesson. Then provide the leveled readers to enhance students' understanding of how cities have developed and changed since the 1800s, and how they continue to change even today.

- **Points for Discussion:**
  1. Have students discuss the greatest differences between cities in the 1800s and today?

  2. Students can also make predictions about how cities will continue to change in the future.

Expansion and Change

UNIT 3

Unit Planning Guide

Unit 3 • Expansion and Change

Begin with a Primary Source pp. 208–209

Meet the People pp. 210–211

 Reading Social Studies, Compare and Contrast pp. 212–213

Chapter Titles	Pacing	Main Ideas
Chapter 5 **Changing Ways of Life** pp. 214–245 ✓ **Chapter 5 Review** pp. 246–247	11 days	• During the Industrial Revolution of the 1800s, new machines and technologies affected the lives of people in the rural areas of the United States. • During the late 1800s and the early 1900s, people in American cities found that life was changing as populations grew larger. • In the late 1800s and well into the 1900s, African Americans, along with other racial and ethnic groups, faced lives that were affected by prejudice, segregation, and unequal opportunities. • Women hoped to benefit from the spirit of reform that began in the mid-1800s.
Chapter 6 **Becoming a World Power** pp. 248–281 ✓ **Chapter 6 Review** pp. 282–283	13 days	• By the end of the 1800s, the United States had gained new territory and became a world power. • Reformers worked to improve conditions in the United States in the early years of the industrial age. • When it appeared the United States might be in danger, the country became involved in World War I.

End with a Song pp. 284–285

✓ **Unit 3 Review** pp. 286–287

✓ **Unit 3 Project** p. 288

✓ = Assessment Options

▶ **Inventions such as the electric washing machine saved labor, although water still had to be wrung from the clothes.**

The passage of the Nineteenth Amendment meant that women could vote in all elections.

Resources	Meeting Individual Needs
• Workbook, pp. 48–53	• Learning Styles, TE p. 217
• Every Student Learns Guide, pp. 82–97	• ESL Support, TE pp. 218, 225, 235, 242
• Transparencies 1, 10, 14, 21	• Leveled Practice, TE pp. 219, 226, 230, 234, 241
• Quick Study, pp. 42–49	
• Workbook, p. 54	
✓ Chapter 5 Content Test, Assessment Book, pp. 29–30	✓ Chapter 5 Performance Assessment, TE p. 246
✓ Chapter 5 Skills Test, Assessment Book, pp. 31–32	
• Workbook, pp. 55–61	• ESL Support, TE pp. 253, 257, 264, 273
• Every Student Learns Guide, pp. 98–109	• Leveled Practice, TE pp. 254, 265, 276
• Transparencies 14, 21	
• Quick Study, pp. 50–55	
• Workbook, p. 62	
✓ Chapter 6 Content Test, Assessment Book, pp. 33–34	✓ Chapter 6 Performance Assessment, TE p. 282
✓ Chapter 6 Skills Test, Assessment Book, pp. 35–36	

Providing More Depth

Additional Resources

- Trade Books
- Family Activities
- Vocabulary Workbook and Cards
- Social Studies Plus! pp. 68–91
- Daily Activity Bank
- Read Alouds and Primary Sources
- Big Book Atlas   • Student Atlas
- Outline Maps   • Desk Maps

 Technology

- AudioText
- Video Field Trips
- Songs and Music
- Digital Learning CD-ROM Powered by KnowledgeBox (Video clips and activities)
- MindPoint® Quiz Show CD-ROM
- ExamView® Test Bank CD-ROM
- Colonial Williamsburg Primary Sources CD-ROM
- Teacher Resources CD-ROM
- Map Resources CD-ROM
- SF SuccessNet: iText (Pupil Edition online), iTE (Teacher's Edition online), Online Planner
- **www.sfsocialstudies.com** (Biographies, news, references, maps, and activities)

 To establish guidelines for your students' safe and responsible use of the Internet, use the Scott Foresman Internet Guide.

Additional Internet Links

To find out more about:

- the Brooklyn Bridge, search under that term at **www.pbs.org**
- the National Park System, visit **www.nps.gov**
- the Spanish-American War and World War I, go to "jump back in time" at **www.loc.gov**

Unit 3 Objectives

Beginning of Unit 3

- Use primary sources to acquire information. (p. 208)
- Identify the contributions of significant individuals in the United States in the late 1800s and early 1900s. (p. 210)
- Analyze information by identifying similarities and differences. (p. 212)

Chapter 5

Lesson 1 Rural Life Changes
pp. 216–221

- Explain how mechanization changed farm life.
- Relate how industrialization provided access to consumer goods.
- Explain the impact of the increased availability of telephones.
- Describe the changes brought about by advancements in electrification.

Lesson 2 Life in the Growing Cities
pp. 222–229

- Explain the reasons for the growth of cities, including immigration and urbanization.
- Relate how rapid industrialization and urbanization led to overcrowding.
- Identify the challenges faced by urban areas as a result of population and technological changes.
- Describe efforts to solve problems faced by urban areas.
- Compare and contrast the purposes of line and circle graphs. (p. 230)
- Describe the skill of reading line and circle graphs. (p. 230)

Lesson 3 Unequal Opportunities
pp. 232–238

- Explain how prejudice and segregation affected people's lives.
- Relate the effect of Jim Crow laws on African Americans.
- Explain the economic and social reasons for the migration of African Americans to the North.
- Examine issues facing African Americans in the North.
- Describe the African American response to discrimination.
- Identify contributions of significant individuals during the early 1900s, such as Booker T. Washington. (p. 239)

Lesson 4 Women's Rights
pp. 240–244

- Describe the effects of the women's suffrage movement.
- Relate the rights and educational opportunities gained for women.
- Explain the role of Susan B. Anthony in the suffrage movement.
- Describe the accomplishments of significant leaders in the women's rights movement, such as Susan B. Anthony. (p. 245)

Chapter 6

Lesson 1 Expanding Overseas
pp. 250–258

- Discuss the expansion of U.S. territories during the late 1800s.
- Analyze settlement patterns and movement of people after the Civil War.
- Explain the causes and events of the Spanish-American War.
- Explain the results of the Spanish-American War.
- Identify the achievements of people who have made contributions to society, such as Theodore Roosevelt. (p. 259)
- Identify credible sources of information. (p. 260)

Lesson 2 The Progressive Movement
pp. 262–267

- Analyze how social, political, moral, and economic reforms during the Roosevelt presidency affected Americans.
- Explain the role of media and the arts in the Progressive Movement.
- Explain the effects of the Progressive Movement reforms on the workplace.
- Discuss the accomplishments and limitations of the Progressive Movement.
- Interpret information in political cartoons. (p. 268)
- Identify the accomplishments of a leading reformer of the Progressive Era. (p. 270)

Lesson 3 World War I
pp. 272–280

- Relate the causes of World War I and identify the countries of the Allied Powers and Central Powers.
- Explain issues of isolationism and the reasons for U.S. involvement in the war.
- Discuss the technological advances in warfare as they affected society.
- Describe the impact at home and abroad of the U.S. involvement in World War I.
- Use primary sources, such as photographs, to acquire information about World War I. (p. 281)

End of Unit 3

- Identify significant examples of music from various periods in United States history. (p. 284)
- Explain how examples of music reflect the times during which they were written. (p. 284)
- Analyze an important invention through the creation of an infomercial. (p. 288)

◀ **Elisha Graves Otis invented the first safety elevator in 1852. By 1857, he had installed a passenger elevator in a New York City department store.**

Assessment Options

✓ Formal Assessment

- **Lesson Reviews,** PE/TE pp. 221, 229, 238, 244, 258, 267, 280
- **Chapter Reviews,** PE/TE pp. 246–247, 282–283
- **Chapter Tests,** Assessment Book, pp. 29–36
- **Unit Review,** PE/TE pp. 286–287
- **Unit Tests,** Assessment Book, pp. 37–40
- **ExamView® Test Bank CD-ROM** (test-generator software)

✓ Informal Assessment

- **Teacher's Edition Questions,** throughout Lessons and Features
- **Section Reviews,** PE/TE pp. 217–219, 221, 223–227, 229, 233–238, 241, 243–244, 251–255, 257–258, 263–265, 267, 274–280
- **Close and Assess,** TE pp. 213, 221, 229, 231, 238–239, 244–245, 258–259, 261, 267, 269, 271, 280–281, 285

Ongoing Assessment

Ongoing Assessment is found throughout the Teacher's Edition lessons using an **If...then** model.

If = students' observable behavior,   **then** = reteaching and enrichment suggestions

✓ Portfolio Assessment

- **Portfolio Assessment,** TE pp. 207, 208, 287
- **Leveled Practice,** TE pp. 219, 226, 230, 234, 241, 254, 265, 276
- **Workbook Pages,** pp. 47–63
- **Chapter Review: Write About History,** PE/TE pp. 247, 283
- **Unit Review: Apply Skills,** PE p. 287; TE p. 286
- **Curriculum Connection: Writing,** PE/TE pp. 221, 229; TE pp. 209, 236, 266, 281

✓ Performance Assessment

- **Hands-on Unit Project** (Unit 3 Performance Assessment), TE pp. 207, 247, 283, 286, 288
- **Internet Activity,** PE/TE p. 288
- **Chapter 5 Performance Assessment,** TE p. 246
- **Chapter 6 Performance Assessment,** TE p. 282
- **Unit Review: Write and Share,** PE/TE p. 287
- **Scoring Guides,** TE pp. 287–288

Test Talk

Test-Taking Strategies

Understand the Question
- **Locate Key Words in the Question,** TE pp. 254, 263
- **Locate Key Words in the Text,** TE p. 241

Understand the Answer
- **Choose the Right Answer,** PE p. 287; TE p. 286
- **Use Information from the Text,** TE pp. 218, 274
- **Use Information from Graphics,** TE p. 225
- **Write Your Answer to Score High,** TE p. 235

For additional practice, use the Test Talk Practice Book.

Featured Strategy

Choose the Right Answer
Students will:
- Narrow the answer choices and rule out choices they know are wrong.
- Choose the best answer.

PE p. 287; **TE** p. 286

Curriculum Connections

Integrating Your Day

The lessons, skills, and features of Unit 3 provide many opportunities to make connections between social studies and other areas of the elementary curriculum.

READING

Reading Skill—Compare and Contrast, PE/TE pp. 212–213, 216, 262, 272

Lesson Review—Compare and Contrast, PE/TE pp. 221, 267, 280

MATH

Figure Ratios, TE p. 220

Calculate Population Growth Rates, TE p. 223

Compute Percentages, TE p. 231

Calculate Square Mileage, TE p. 267

WRITING

Write a Speech, TE p. 209

Accessing Language, TE p. 236

Write a Poem, TE p. 266

Write About Modern Airplanes, TE p. 281

LITERATURE

Read Biographies, TE p. 210

Read About Rural Life Before Electricity, TE p. 221

Booker T. Washington, TE p. 239

Susan B. Anthony, TE p. 245

Ida Tarbell, TE p. 271

Social Studies

SCIENCE

Research Mosquito-Borne Illnesses, TE p. 256

Link to Science, PE/TE p. 280

MUSIC / DRAMA

Give a "Yellow Journalism" News Report, TE p. 253

Write a Tune, TE p. 279

Write a New Verse, TE p. 285

ART

Create an Urban Scene, TE p. 228

Design a Masthead, TE p. 238

Link to Art, PE/TE pp. 244, 267

Create a Political Cartoon, TE p. 268

Create a Poster, TE p. 278

 Look for this symbol throughout the Teacher's Edition to find **Curriculum Connections.**

Professional Development

Improving History Instruction

by Rita Geiger
Norman Public Schools

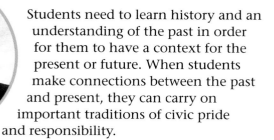

Students need to learn history and an understanding of the past in order for them to have a context for the present or future. When students make connections between the past and present, they can carry on important traditions of civic pride and responsibility.

There are two major concepts of social studies—*space* and *time*. Children develop these concepts over the course of the elementary school years. Effective teachers use these concepts as they incorporate history instruction into their social studies lessons. Think about the concepts of space and time as you teach *Scott Foresman Social Studies*.

Space

- Space includes the immediate environment—home, school, neighborhood, and city—which students learn about through direct experience. Space also includes the remote environment—state, nation, and world—which students learn about vicariously.

- *Create an Urban Scene on TE p. 228 has students use their knowledge of their immediate environment to picture a typical city in the United States. Students compare their pictures to find common elements.*

Time

- Time consists of the past, present, and future. Elementary children relate primarily to the present. The effective elementary social studies teacher should focus mainly on present experiences in the immediate environment. However, the children can begin to understand the past through a variety of activities. Developing a sense of history by placing events on a time line helps students begin to understand chronological relationships.

- *Have students study the time line showing the expansion of the United States and other events on PE/TE pp. 208–209. Help students to understand how the events relate to each other.*

ESL Support

by Jim Cummins, Ph.D.
University of Toronto

In Unit 3, you can use the following fundamental strategies to help ESL students access the concepts of social studies.

Access Content

One important strategy in making the language of social studies comprehensible to ESL students involves activating and building students' background knowledge. The more background knowledge students have, the more text they can understand and the more content they can access.

An additional way in which we can support or *scaffold* students' learning is by modifying the input itself. For example, language clarification is a way of modifying the presentation to students of academic content. It includes strategies and language-oriented activities that clarify the meanings of new words and concepts. Paraphrasing ideas, explaining new concepts, and providing synonyms, antonyms, or definitions are ways to clarify language. Grammatical structures, such as those that express comparison and contrast and sequence of events, provide ways for students to think about and describe specific events and relationships.

The following examples in the Teacher's Edition will help ESL students access content:

- *Practice Comparing and Contrasting on TE p. 212 helps ESL students to see relationships by asking them to compare and contrast.*

- *Describe a Process on TE p. 218 helps students to expand their understanding of mail-order shopping and its significance for people in the United States during the 1800s.*

Read Aloud

from Theodore Roosevelt's Inaugural Speech, March 4, 1905

Power invariably means both responsibility and danger. Our forefathers faced certain perils which we have outgrown. We now face other perils, the very existence of which it was impossible that they should foresee.

Modern life is both complex and intense, and the tremendous changes wrought by the extraordinary industrial development of the last half-century are felt in every fiber of our social and political being. Never before have men tried so vast and formidable an experiment as that of administering the affairs of a continent under the forms of a democratic republic.

Build Background

- Theodore Roosevelt was a forceful leader who was very willing to use the power of the government. His presidency was marked by the use of American power in foreign countries and against large corporations in the United States.
- When Roosevelt gave this speech, he had already served as President since 1901. Elected Vice-President in 1900, he took office when President McKinley was assassinated.
- Theodore Roosevelt's biography appears on PE/TE p. 259.

Definitions

- *invariably:* in all cases
- *wrought:* produced
- *formidable:* challenging

Read Alouds and Primary Sources

- *Read Alouds and Primary Sources* contains additional selections to be used with Unit 3.

Bibliography

Battles of the Spanish-American War, by Diane Smolinski (Heinemann Library, ISBN 1-403-43152-3, 2002) **Easy**

The New Land: A First Year on the Prairie, by Marilynn Reynolds (Orca Book Publishers, ISBN 1-551-43071-1, 1999) **Easy**

World War I (America at War), by Scott Marquette (Rourke Publishing, LLC, ISBN 1-589-52392-X, 2002) **Easy**

The Panama Canal (Great Building Feats), by Lesley A. DuTemple (Lerner Publishing Group, ISBN 0-822-50079-5, 2002) **On-Level**

The Rise and Fall of Jim Crow, by Richard Wormser (St. Martin's Press, ISBN 0-312-31326-8, 2004) **On-Level**

Woman's Suffrage, by JoAnne Weisman Deitch (Discovery Enterprises Ltd., ISBN 1-579-60066-2, 2000) **On-Level**

Andrew Carnegie: Steel King and Friend to Libraries, by Zachary Kent (Enslow Publishers, Inc., ISBN 0-766-01212-3, 1999) **Challenge** *NCSS Notable Book*

Theodore Roosevelt: Letters from a Young Coal Miner, by Jennifer Armstrong (Winslow Press, ISBN 1-890-81727-9, 2001) **Challenge** *NCSS Notable Book*

Ida B. Wells: Mother of the Civil Rights Movement, by Dennis Brindell Fradin and Judith Bloom Fradin (Houghton Mifflin Co., ISBN 0-395-89898-6, 2000) **Challenge** *NCSS Notable Book*

Great Bridge: The Epic Story of the Building of the Brooklyn Bridge, by David McCullough (Simon & Schuster, ISBN 0-671-45711-X, 1983) **Teacher reference**

How the Other Half Lives, by Jacob A. Riis (Viking Penguin, ISBN 0-140-43679-0, 1997) **Teacher reference**

The Souls of Black Folk, by W. E. B. Du Bois (Viking Penguin, ISBN 0-140-18998-X, 1996) **Teacher reference**

Booker T. Washington, Vol. 2: The Wizard of Tuskegee, 1901–1915, by Louis R. Harlan (Oxford University Press, ISBN 0-195-04229-8, 1986) **Teacher reference**

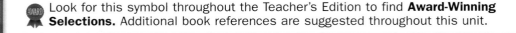 Look for this symbol throughout the Teacher's Edition to find **Award-Winning Selections.** Additional book references are suggested throughout this unit.

Expansion and Change

What kinds of changes do nations face?

207

Expansion and Change

Unit Overview

The territory, population, and world influence of the United States grew in the late 1800s and early 1900s. This created many challenges and opportunities for the people of the United States as the new century dawned.

Unit Outline

Chapter 5 *Changing Ways of Life*
pp. 214–247

Chapter 6 *Becoming a World Power*
pp. 248–283

Unit Question

- Have students read the question under the picture.

- To activate prior knowledge, ask students to think about what changes this nation had faced in its first 100 years of existence.

- Create a list of the changes students think they will read about occurring in the United States during the decades of the 1800s and early 1900s.

- ✓**Portfolio Assessment** Keep this list to review with students at the end of the unit on p. 287.

Practice and Extend

Hands-on Unit Project

✓**Unit 3 Performance Assessment**

- The Unit Project, *Arts and Letters,* found on p. 288, is an ongoing performance assessment project to enrich students' learning throughout the unit.

- This project, which has students create an infomercial about an important invention, may be started now or at any time during this unit of study.

- A performance assessment scoring guide is located on p. 288.

Begin with a Primary Source

Objective
- Use primary sources to acquire information.

Resources
- Poster 6

Interpret a Primary Source

- Tell students that this quotation comes from a speech delivered by Wilson just as the United States prepared to enter World War I.

- Wilson was trying to inspire the nation to rise to the challenge ahead. Ask students what kinds of things Wilson might have had in mind when he referred to those things "nearest our hearts." (Possible answers: Our democratic values; peace and prosperity; justice for all)

✓ **Portfolio Assessment** Remind students of the list of changes they thought they would read about (see TE p. 207). Have students keep a list of the changes the nation experienced in the 1800s and early 1900s as they read the unit. Review students' lists at the end of the unit on p. 287.

Interpret Fine Art

- Childe Hassam painted this city scene, called *Rainy Day in Boston,* in 1885.

- Hassam was interested in the way light acted. He painted many city scenes with people. He was one of the first American Impressionists.

- Have students discuss whether the painting looks realistic.

UNIT
3
Begin with a Primary Source

1835	1855	1875

1834
Cyrus McCormick invents mechanical reaper.

1867
United States buys Alaska from Russia.

1885
First skyscraper is built in Chicago.

208

Practice and Extend

FYI SOCIAL STUDIES
Background

About the Primary Source
- Woodrow Wilson was in his second term of office when he spoke these words.
- Wilson's campaign slogan in 1916 was "He kept us out of war"—a reference to Wilson's goal of maintaining the neutrality of the United States.
- By the time the United States entered the war, millions of Europeans had already died in the conflict.

> "...we shall fight for the things which we have always carried nearest our hearts...."
>
> —President Woodrow Wilson to Congress, April 2, 1917, before the U.S. entered World War I

Artist Childe Hassam's painting *Rainy Day in Boston* shows the growing city of Boston, Massachusetts, in 1885.

Use the Time Line

The time line at the bottom of the pages shows the dates for some major national and global events in which the United States was involved during the 1800s and early 1900s.

1 **How many years passed between the Spanish-American War and the entry of the United States into World War I?** About 19 years
Interpret Time Lines

2 **Which event reflects a major development in the nation's ability to transport goods and people around the world?** The opening of the Panama Canal meant that goods and people could travel more easily from the Atlantic to the Pacific Ocean. Analyze Information

3 **What two events occurred in the same year?** The passage of the Nineteenth Amendment and the Treaty of Versailles that ended World War I
Interpret Time Lines

1895	1915	1935

1898 Spanish-American War

1906 Upton Sinclair publishes *The Jungle.*

1914 The Panama Canal opens. **2**

1917 United States enters World War I. **1**

1919 Treaty of Versailles ends World War I.
Nineteenth Amendment passes. **3**   209

CURRICULUM CONNECTION
Writing

Write a Speech

Have students suppose that they have been asked to write a speech to soldiers as they prepare to ship off for Europe and combat in World War I. Provide the following information for students to think about as they prepare their speeches:

- The United States had sought to remain neutral in the conflict, yet Germany had been attacking American shipping.
- The fighting in Europe had seen the introduction of aircraft, poison gas, tanks, and machine guns that had caused unheard-of devastation.
- The allies of the United States had suffered terribly from the fighting over the past three years.

Have students present their speeches to the class.

Meet the People

Objective
- Identify the contributions of significant individuals in the United States in the late 1800s and early 1900s.

Resource
- Poster 8

Research the People

Each of the people pictured on these pages played an important role in the growth and development of the United States in the late 1800s and early 1900s. Have students do research to find out answers to the following questions.

- **Which two people worked closely together on the cause of women's suffrage?** Elizabeth Cady Stanton and Susan B. Anthony

- **Which two people worked closely together to help preserve what eventually became Yosemite National Park?** John Muir and Theodore Roosevelt

- **Of which university was Woodrow Wilson president before he became President of the United States?** Princeton University

- **Which of these people was born into slavery?** Booker T. Washington

Students may wish to write their own questions about other people on these pages for the rest of the class to answer.

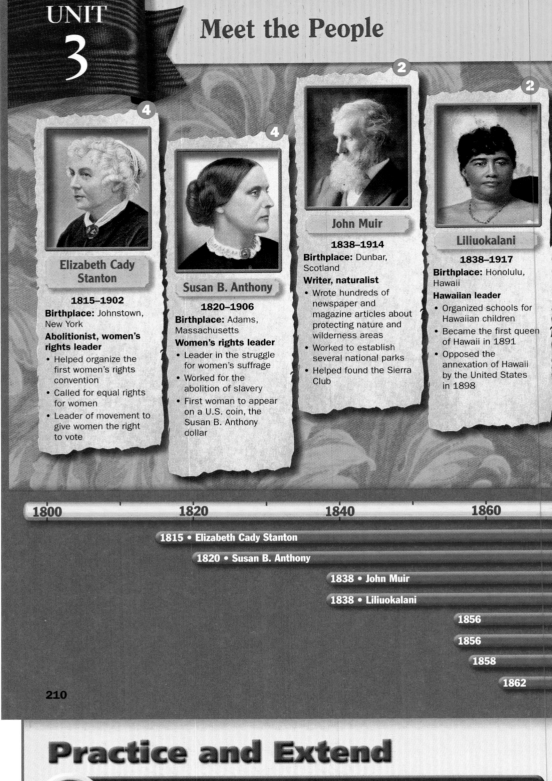

Meet the People

John Muir
1838–1914
Birthplace: Dunbar, Scotland
Writer, naturalist
- Wrote hundreds of newspaper and magazine articles about protecting nature and wilderness areas
- Worked to establish several national parks
- Helped found the Sierra Club

Liliuokalani
1838–1917
Birthplace: Honolulu, Hawaii
Hawaiian leader
- Organized schools for Hawaiian children
- Became the first queen of Hawaii in 1891
- Opposed the annexation of Hawaii by the United States in 1898

Elizabeth Cady Stanton
1815–1902
Birthplace: Johnstown, New York
Abolitionist, women's rights leader
- Helped organize the first women's rights convention
- Called for equal rights for women
- Leader of movement to give women the right to vote

Susan B. Anthony
1820–1906
Birthplace: Adams, Massachusetts
Women's rights leader
- Leader in the struggle for women's suffrage
- Worked for the abolition of slavery
- First woman to appear on a U.S. coin, the Susan B. Anthony dollar

1800	1820	1840	1860

1815 • Elizabeth Cady Stanton
1820 • Susan B. Anthony
1838 • John Muir
1838 • Liliuokalani
1856
1856
1858
1862

210

Practice and Extend

CURRICULUM CONNECTION
Literature

Read Biographies
Use the following biography selections to extend the content.

Woodrow Wilson, by Henry M. Holden (Enslow Publishers, ISBN 0-766-05123-4, 2003) **Easy**

John Muir: My Life with Nature, by John Muir and Joseph Bharat Cornell (Dawn Publications, ISBN 1-584-69009-7, 2000) **On-Level**

 Elizabeth Cady Stanton: The Right Is Ours, by Harriet Sigerman (Oxford University Press Children's Books, ISBN 0-195-11969-X, 2001) **Challenge**
NCSS Notable Book

For more information, go online to *Meet the People* at www.sfsocialstudies.com.

Woodrow Wilson

Theodore Roosevelt

Ida Wells-Barnett

Booker T. Washington

1856–1915
Birthplace: Hardy, Virginia
Educator, leader for African American rights
• Founded Tuskegee Institute in 1881
• Gave "Atlanta Compromise" speech, in which he stated that hard work and economic security would eventually bring equality to African Americans
• Wrote autobiography, *Up From Slavery*

1856–1924
Birthplace: Staunton, Virginia
Governor, President
• Passed federal act to stop unfair business practices in 1914
• Brought the United States into World War I in 1917
• Developed the League of Nations in an attempt to prevent future wars

1858–1919
Birthplace: New York, New York
Soldier, President
• Led troops in the Spanish-American War
• Became the youngest President of the United States in 1901 at age 42
• Won the Nobel Prize for Peace for his help in ending the Russo-Japanese War

1862–1931
Birthplace: Holly Springs, Mississippi
Journalist
• Wrote and spoke about unjust treatment of African Americans
• Worked to help women get the right to vote
• Wrote an autobiography called *Crusade for Justice*

1880	1900	1920	1940

1902
1906
1914
1917
Booker T. Washington 1915
Woodrow Wilson 1924
Theodore Roosevelt 1919
Ida Wells-Barnett 1931

211

WEB SITE
Technology

Students can research the lives of people on this page by clicking on *Meet the People* at **www.sfsocialstudies.com.**

Use the Time Line

Have students use the time line and biographies to answer the following questions.

1 Which two people were born in the same year? Booker T. Washington and Woodrow Wilson **Interpret Time Lines**

2 What do John Muir and Liliuokalani have in common? Both were born outside of the United States **Compare and Contrast**

3 Which person fought in a war, but also worked for peace? Theodore Roosevelt **Analyze Information**

4 What did Ida Wells-Barnett have in common with Booker T. Washington, Susan B. Anthony, and Elizabeth Cady Stanton? They all worked to improve life for African Americans **Compare and Contrast**

Biographies

Three of the people shown here are discussed more extensively on the Biography pages in Unit 3.

• Booker T. Washington, p. 239
• Susan B. Anthony, p. 245
• Theodore Roosevelt, p. 259

Read About the People

The people shown here are discussed in the text on the following pages in Unit 3.

• Elizabeth Cady Stanton, p. 242
• Susan B. Anthony, pp. 242, 245
• John Muir, p. 266
• Liliuokalani, p. 252
• Theodore Roosevelt, pp. 254–257, 259, 264–267
• Ida Wells-Barnett, p. 238
• Booker T. Washington, pp. 237, 239
• Woodrow Wilson, pp. 275, 280

Reading Social Studies

Compare and Contrast

Objective

Analyze information by identifying similarities and differences.

Resource

• Workbook, p. 47

About the Unit Target Skill

• The target reading skill for this unit is Compare and Contrast.
• Students are introduced to the unit target skill here and are given an opportunity to practice it.
• Further opportunities to use Compare and Contrast are found throughout Unit 3.

1 Introduce and Motivate

Preview To activate prior knowledge, ask students to compare two people or events and to contrast two people or events from previous units in the textbook. (For example, a comparison is: Robert E. Lee and Ulysses S. Grant were both skilled leaders. A contrast is: The South was heavily agricultural at the outset of the Civil War, but the North had a great deal of industry.)

2 Teach and Discuss

• Explain that comparing two items means telling how they are alike. Sometimes comparisons include clue words such as *both, as,* or *like.* Tell students that to contrast means to tell how two items are different. Writers might use clue words or phrases such as *unlike, in contrast,* or *different,* but often the reader has to read and look for the similarities and differences.

Expansion and Change

Compare and Contrast

Using graphic organizers can help you compare and contrast as you read. A Venn diagram, shown at far left, can help you show how two things or events are different and similar. The graphic organizer on the right shows differences only.

• To compare, writers may use clue words or phrases such as *both, like, as,* and *also.* To contrast, writers may use clue words such as *unlike, different,* and *in contrast.* Other clues can be *before* and *after.*

• When there are no clue words, ask yourself, *How are these events or things similar? How are they different?*

Read the following paragraph. Comparisons and contrasts have been highlighted.

In Unit 2 you learned how the United States grew as a nation. It gained land across the continent. Stagecoaches moved settlers and goods across the new land. However, stagecoaches were limited in the amount they could carry. In contrast, the new railroads could carry larger numbers of people and goods. Both forms of transportation were important to the growth of the West.

Word Exercise

Use Context Clues As you read a sentence, you may have to use clues from the text and what you already know to figure out the meaning of new words. How can you figure out the meaning of *appliances* in this passage?

Taking care of the home was once difficult and time-consuming. There were few, if any, machines to make the job go more quickly. But this would soon change. Inventors were hard at work. They created new electrical appliances to make housework easier.

212

Practice and Extend

ESL ACCESS CONTENT ESL Support

Practice Comparing and Contrasting Reinforce the meaning of the terms *compare* and *contrast.*

Beginning Have students examine a pencil and a pen and describe how they compare. Then have students describe how the objects contrast.

Intermediate Have students create a Venn diagram showing how a pen and a pencil compare and contrast. Make sure students write their observations in the correct segments of the diagram.

Advanced Have students create a Venn diagram to compare two objects or events of their choice.

Compare and Contrast Events in a Changing Nation

Following Reconstruction, the United States was again a united country. More settlers moved west. Unlike travelers of the early 1800s, who walked or rode in wagons, travelers of the late 1800s could cross the country more quickly by railroad.

Inventors produced useful new technologies that became more widely available by the late 1800s. New farming tools made it possible for a farmer to farm more land. Electric lines supplied electricity to homes, and new electrical appliances made housework easier. As telephone lines spread across the country, communication became easier.

Industry continued to grow. More and more factories were built in or near cities. People who needed jobs moved into the cities. Some workers came from farms, while others were immigrants who moved to the United States from other countries.

Cities across the country grew rapidly. The rapid growth of cities created many problems. Cities became overcrowded and dirty. There were more violence and more disease. Many men and women worked to improve the difficult city conditions and to make the lives of immigrants better.

Life changed for many in the United States, but some changes came slowly. Slavery was outlawed, but laws in many states made it legal to continue treating African Americans unfairly. African American leaders fought discrimination and worked hard for equality.

The United States had always had a policy of letting other countries handle their own problems. As the United States entered the 1900s, the government found it necessary to go to war to protect itself and its allies in Cuba and Europe.

Use the reading strategy of comparing and contrasting to answer questions 1 and 2. Then answer the vocabulary question.

1 How did inventions in the 1800s change farming?

2 Compare and contrast cities before the growth of industry and after.

3 What clues can help you figure out the meaning of the word *industry* in the third paragraph above? Read the paragraph carefully. What does it tell you about industry? When you think you know the meaning, check a dictionary to see if you are correct.

213

 Standardized Test Prep

- Use Workbook p. 47 to give students practice with standardized test format.
- Chapter and Unit Tests in the Assessment Book use standardized test format.
- Test-taking tips are contained in the front portion of the Assessment Book Teacher's Edition.

Also on Teacher Resources CD-ROM.

Workbook, p. 47

Compare and Contrast

Directions: Read the passage below. Then fill in the circle next to the correct answer.

Following the Civil War, both the North and the South faced adjustments. Soldiers in both regions returned from the battlefield to their homes and jobs. All across the now-reunited country, people faced the terrible reality that thousands would never be returning home. Thousands more, maimed in the fighting, looked forward to an uncertain future. The South's adjustments, however, were far more complicated than the North's. Unlike the North, which saw little actual fighting, much of the South was a smoking ruin. In addition, the system of slavery no longer existed. This had a dramatic effect on the social and economic systems in the South.

1. Which statement best compares the experiences of the North and the South after the Civil War?
Ⓐ The North faced a more difficult adjustment than the South.
Ⓑ The South faced a more difficult adjustment than the North.
Ⓒ Both the North and South faced an adjustment period.
Ⓓ The South had to deal with the end of slavery.

2. Which statement best contrasts the experiences of the North and the South after the Civil War?
Ⓐ Both the North and South faced adjustments.
Ⓑ The South faced a more complicated adjustment than the North.
Ⓒ Both sides lost many war dead.
Ⓓ The end of slavery dramatically affected both the North and the South.

3. In the passage, which clue word helps you identify a comparison being made between the North and the South?
Ⓐ had
Ⓑ following
Ⓒ unlike
Ⓓ addition

4. In the passage, which clue word helps you identify a contrast being made between the North and the South?
Ⓐ following
Ⓑ unlike
Ⓒ both
Ⓓ no

Notes for Home: Your child learned to identify comparisons and contrasts in a passage.
Home Activity: Work with your child to write a two-paragraph description of two buildings in your neighborhood that both compare and contrast the buildings.

- Have students read the sample paragraph on p. 212. Make sure they can explain why the highlighted sentences compare and contrast stagecoaches and railroads.

- Then have students read the longer practice sample on p. 213 and answer the questions that follow.

- Ask students why it is helpful to compare and contrast when reading about history. (If you can tell how specific people and events in history are similar or different, it can help you make generalizations and apply lessons about different times in history.)

Use Context Clues   **Word Exercise**

Direct students' attention to the paragraph in the passage on p. 213 that ends with the sentence "African American leaders fought **discrimination** and worked hard for equality." Ask students what context clues help them figure out what *discrimination* means. (African Americans were being treated unfairly at this time; African American leaders wanted equality, not *discrimination*.) Ask students what they know already about *discrimination*. (People today talk about *discrimination* when a person or group of people is treated differently than another person or group of people.) Ask students what they think discrimination means. ("the act of treating some people unfairly") Remind students to check their definitions in a dictionary.

Close and Assess

Apply it!

1. Possible answer: New tools made it possible for a farmer to farm more land.

2. Possible answer: After the growth of industry, there were more jobs near cities, so people moved to cities. Bigger cities were more crowded and dirtier, and they had more violence and disease.

3. Clue words include *factories, jobs,* and *workers*. Industry is any form of business, trade, or manufacture.

Chapter Planning Guide

Chapter 5 • Changing Ways of Life

Locating Time and Place pp. 214–215

Lesson Titles	Pacing	Main Ideas
Lesson 1 **Rural Life Changes** pp. 216–221	2 days	• During the Industrial Revolution of the 1800s, new machines and technologies affected the lives of people in the rural areas of the United States.
Lesson 2 **Life in the Growing Cities** pp. 222–229	3 days	• During the late 1800s and the early 1900s, people in American cities found that life was changing as populations grew larger.
Chart and Graph Skills: Read Line and Circle Graphs pp. 230–231		• Line graphs help show change over time, and circle graphs show how a whole is divided into parts.
Lesson 3 **Unequal Opportunities** pp. 232–238	3 days	• In the late 1800s and well into the 1900s, African Americans, along with other racial and ethnic groups, faced lives that were affected by prejudice, segregation, and unequal opportunities.
Biography: Booker T. Washington p. 239		• Booker T. Washington used his love of education to become a key African American leader.
Lesson 4 **Women's Rights** pp. 240–244	3 days	• Women hoped to benefit from the spirit of reform that began in the mid-1800s.
Biography: Susan B. Anthony p. 245		• Susan B. Anthony devoted her life to the fight for the abolition of slavery and equal rights for women.
✓ **Chapter 5 Review** pp. 246–247		

✓ = Assessment Options

In the 1800s, people began ordering a variety of things from mail-order catalogs.

Vocabulary	Resources	Meeting Individual Needs
manual labor mechanization reaper threshing machine	• Workbook, p. 49 • Transparency 14 • Every Student Learns Guide, pp. 82–85 • Quick Study, pp. 42–43	• Learning Styles, TE p. 217 • ESL Support, TE p. 218 • Leveled Practice, TE p. 219
urbanization tenement settlement house political machine suspension bridge line graph circle graph	• Workbook, p. 50 • Transparency 21 • Every Student Learns Guide, pp. 86–89 • Quick Study, pp. 44–45 • Workbook, p. 51	• ESL Support, TE p. 225 • Leveled Practice, TE pp. 226, 230
tenant enfranchise Great Migration	• Workbook, p. 52 • Transparency 1 • Every Student Learns Guide, pp. 90–93 • Quick Study, pp. 46–47	• Leveled Practice, TE p. 234 • ESL Support, TE p. 235
suffrage suffragist Nineteenth Amendment	• Workbook, p. 53 • Transparency 10 • Every Student Learns Guide, pp. 94–97 • Quick Study, pp. 48–49	• Leveled Practice, TE p. 241 • ESL Support, TE p. 242
	✓ Chapter 5 Content Test, Assessment Book, pp. 29–30 ✓ Chapter 5 Skills Test, Assessment Book, pp. 31–32	✓ Chapter 5 Performance Assessment, TE p. 246

Providing More Depth

Additional Resources

- Vocabulary Workbook and Cards
- Social Studies Plus! pp. 80–85
- Daily Activity Bank
- Big Book Atlas
- Student Atlas
- Outline Maps
- Desk Maps

 Technology

- AudioText
- MindPoint® Quiz Show CD-ROM
- ExamView® Test Bank CD-ROM
- Teacher Resources CD-ROM
- Map Resources CD-ROM
- SFSuccessNet: iText (Pupil Edition online), iTE (Teacher's Edition online), Online Planner
- **www.sfsocialstudies.com** (Biographies, news, references, maps, and activities)

 To establish guidelines for your students' safe and responsible use of the Internet, use the Scott Foresman Internet Guide.

Additional Internet Links

To find out more about:
- Jane Addams, visit **www.hullhouse.org**
- the Great Migration, visit the "African-American Mosaic" exhibition at **www.loc.gov**
- the 19th Amendment, search under this term at **www.archives.gov**

Key Internet Search Terms
- McCormick reaper
- tenements
- *Plessy* v. *Ferguson*
- women's rights

Workbook Support

Use the following Workbook pages to support content and skills development as you teach Chapter 5. You can also view and print Workbook pages from the Teacher Resources CD-ROM.

Workbook, p. 47

Compare and Contrast

Use with Pages 212–213.

Directions: Read the passage below. Then fill in the circle next to the correct answer.

> Following the Civil War, both the North and the South faced adjustments. Soldiers in both regions returned from the battlefield to their homes and jobs. All across the now-reunited country, people faced the terrible reality that thousands would never be returning home. Thousands more, maimed in the fighting, looked forward to an uncertain future.
>
> The South's adjustments, however, were far more complicated than the North's. Unlike the North, which saw little actual fighting, much of the South was a smoking ruin. In addition, the system of slavery no longer existed. This had a dramatic effect on the social and economic systems in the South.

1. Which statement best compares the experiences of the North and the South after the Civil War?
   - Ⓐ The North faced a more difficult adjustment than the South.
   - Ⓑ The South faced a more difficult adjustment than the North.
   - ● Both the North and South faced an adjustment period.
   - Ⓓ The South had to deal with the end of slavery.

2. Which statement best contrasts the experiences of the North and the South after the Civil War?
   - Ⓐ Both the North and South faced adjustments.
   - ● The South faced a more complicated adjustment than the North.
   - Ⓒ Both sides lost many war dead.
   - Ⓓ The end of slavery dramatically affected both the North and the South.

3. In the passage, which clue word helps you identify a comparison being made between the North and the South?
   - ● *both*
   - Ⓑ *following*
   - Ⓒ *unlike*
   - Ⓓ *addition*

4. In the passage, which clue word helps you identify a contrast being made between the North and the South?
   - Ⓐ *following*
   - ● *unlike*
   - Ⓒ *both*
   - Ⓓ *no*

Notes for Home: Your child learned to identify comparisons and contrasts in a passage.
Home Activity: Work with your child to write a two-paragraph description of two buildings in your neighborhood that both compares and contrasts the buildings.

Use with Pupil Edition, p. 213

Workbook, p. 48

Vocabulary Preview

Use with Chapter 5.

Directions: Look at the vocabulary words in Chapter 5 of your textbook. Choose the vocabulary word from the chapter that best completes each sentence. Write the word on the line provided.

1. The moving of people from rural areas to cities is ___**urbanization**___
2. A center that provides help for people with little money is a ___**settlement house**___
3. Someone who pays rent to use land or buildings that belong to someone else is a ___**tenant**___.
4. A ___**reaper**___ is a machine that cuts wheat.
5. A ___**suspension bridge**___ hangs from steel cables.
6. The right to vote is ___**suffrage**___
7. During the ___**Great Migration**___ about 5 million African Americans moved north.
8. Using machines to do work is called ___**mechanization**___
9. An organization of people that controls votes to gain political power is a ___**political machine**___
10. A building that is divided into small apartments is called a ___**tenement**___
11. A ___**threshing machine**___ separates grain from plant stalks.
12. The ___**Nineteenth Amendment**___ to the Constitution gave women the right to vote.
13. Before machines were invented, ___**manual labor**___ was the only way to get jobs done.
14. To ___**enfranchise**___ is to give someone the right to vote.
15. A ___**suffragist**___ was a person who worked for women's voting rights.

Notes for Home: Your child learned the vocabulary terms for Chapter 5.
Home Activity: Practice saying, spelling, and using these words correctly with your child.

Use with Pupil Edition, p. 214

Workbook, p. 49

Lesson 1: Rural Life Changes

Use with Pages 216–221.

Directions: Complete the outline with information from this lesson. You may use your textbook.

Changes in Rural Life in the Late 1800s

I. Mechanization on the Farm
  A. New machinery made farm work easier.
    1. Cyrus McCormick invented the ___**reaper**___ to cut wheat.
    2. The ___**threshing machine**___ helped separate grain from stalks.
    3. L. O. Colvin and Gustav de Laval's inventions helped farms that produced ___**milk**___
  B. Easier farm work meant bigger farms and the planting of ___**cash crops**___

II. Industry's Impact
  A. Industry provided a variety of goods that were ___**less expensive**___ to buy than in the past.
  B. Shoppers in rural areas could get these goods through ___**mail-order catalogs**___, such as the ones put out by Aaron Montgomery Ward and Sears and Roebuck.

III. Getting Connected
  A. The invention of the telephone helped connect people across the country.
    1. ___**Rural**___ areas were slower to get this technology.
    2. Farmers in ___**Ahwahnee Valley, California,**___ were the first to show how rural people could set up their own phone system.

IV. Electrifying the Countryside
  A. Electricity helped farmers do work more efficiently and safely.
    1. The building of ___**power stations**___, such as the first hydroelectric power plant in Appleton, Wisconsin, made electricity widely available.
    2. The federal government helped more rural areas get electricity in 1936 with the ___**Rural Electrification Act**___

Notes for Home: Your child learned how industrial, economic, and technological changes especially affected rural people in the United States in the late 1800s and early 1900s.
Home Activity: Discuss with your child how much you rely on technology (electricity, telephone, and cable) and machinery to do work in your home.

Use with Pupil Edition, p. 221

Workbook, p. 50

Lesson 2: Life in the Growing Cities

Use with Pages 222–229.

Directions: Answer the following questions on the lines provided. You may use your textbook.

1. How did changes on the farm help lead to the growth of cities in the late 1800s and early 1900s?
   The growing efficiency of farms meant that there was less need for farm labor, forcing many rural people to seek work in the cities.

2. Give two examples of challenges facing urban immigrants in the late 1800s and early 1900s.
   Possible answers include overcrowding, unsafe living conditions, and disease.

3. How did Jane Addams try to help urban residents in the late 1800s and early 1900s?
   Addams started a settlement house in Chicago. Immigrants could get help learning English in order to find jobs. Daycare was provided.

4. How were political machines able to achieve power in spite of complaints about their often corrupt practices?
   Political machines helped needy and powerless people get jobs and solve other problems in return for their votes.

5. How did the development of steel help change the look of cities in the late 1800s and early 1900s?
   Steel made it possible to build taller buildings and longer bridges.

Notes for Home: Your child has learned about the changes the United States experienced as its urban areas expanded in the late 1800s and early 1900s.
Home Activity: Work with your child to write a letter to an immigrant who is coming to the United States around the year 1900. The letter should discuss the positive and negative aspects of the urban experience awaiting the immigrant.

Use with Pupil Edition, p. 229

Workbook Support

Workbook, p. 51

Read Line and Circle Graphs

Use with Pages 230–231.

Directions: Look at the graphs below and answer the questions that follow.

Change in Foreign-Born Population 1850–1910

United States Population, 1910

1. Which of these graphs shows the change in population over time?
   The line graph

2. Which of these graphs tells you how the foreign-born and native populations compare?
   The circle graph

3. Between which years did the United States see the largest increase in its number of foreign-born residents?
   Between 1900 and 1910

 Notes for Home: Your child learned how to read line and circle graphs and how they are different.
Home Activity: Present your child with information—for example, how your family has grown in number over the last 15 years or how many males and females are in your family. Have your child create an appropriate graph of the information you provide.

Use with Pupil Edition, p. 231

Workbook, p. 52

Lesson 3: Unequal Opportunities

Use with Pages 232–238.

Directions: Write the number of each item in Column A in the blank next to its description in Column B.

Column A		Column B
1. sharecropping	**3**	The system by which African Americans and whites were separated in public places
2. George Washington Carver	**5**	Law passed in Congress in 1882 to limit immigration on the basis of race
3. racial segregation	**8**	An organization that sought the immediate end to racial discrimination in the early 1900s
4. Homer Plessy	**2**	A noted African American scientist who organized the agriculture department at the Tuskegee Institute
5. Chinese Exclusion Act	**1**	The system by which African Americans received the use of land in return for a share of their crop
6. Jack L. Cooper	**6**	The first African American disc jockey in the United States
7. W. E. B. Du Bois	**10**	An African American who fought segregation and established voting rights for African American women
8. NAACP	**9**	Helped found Tuskegee Institute and worked to improve the lives of African Americans
9. Booker T. Washington	**4**	Challenged a Jim Crow Law, which helped lead to a famous Supreme Court case of the late 1800s
10. Ida Wells-Barnett	**7**	A writer and editor who helped start the NAACP

 Notes for Home: Your child learned about the obstacles to equality for many ethnic groups in the late 1800s and early 1900s, and about the people who worked to overcome those obstacles.
Home Activity: Discuss racial prejudice with your child. Ask whether he or she thinks conditions today have improved or gotten worse since the early 1900s.

Use with Pupil Edition, p. 238

Workbook, p. 53

Lesson 4: Women's Rights

Use with Pages 240–244.

Directions: Using information from this lesson, circle the term in parentheses that best completes each sentence.

1. In the 1800s, women's opportunities and rights (did, **did not**) equal those of men.

2. In 1848, women's rights leaders Lucretia Mott and Elizabeth Cady Stanton invited people to gather in (**Seneca Falls, New York,** Argonia, Kansas) to discuss women's rights.

3. The most controversial idea of the convention was that women should be able to (**vote,** own property).

4. Suffragist (**Lucy Stone,** Carrie Chapman Catt) founded the American Woman Suffrage Association in 1870.

5. Women came closer to having equality in (urban, **rural**) areas.

6. The first woman mayor in the United States was (**Susannah Medora Salter,** Susan B. Anthony).

7. (**Susan B. Anthony,** Marguerite Harrison), who worked for women's rights until her death in 1906, said that "There will never be complete equality until women themselves help to make laws and elect lawmakers."

8. By 1912, (**many,** no) states had approved a woman's right to vote.

9. World War I helped (**strengthen,** weaken) the cause of women's suffrage.

10. In 1919, Congress passed the (**Nineteenth,** Fifteenth) Amendment, which gave women the right to vote.

 Notes for Home: Your child learned about the changes in women's roles and rights in the 1800s and early 1900s.
Home Activity: With your child, look at a newspaper or magazine and note every time you see a story that includes a woman holding a job, political office, or other position of authority.

Use with Pupil Edition, p. 244

Workbook, p. 54

Vocabulary Review

Use with Chapter 5.

Directions: Match each vocabulary term to its meaning. Write the letter of the word on the blank next to its meaning.

l	1. large-scale movement of African Americans from the South to the North in the early 1900s	a. manual labor
e	2. movement of people from rural areas to cities	b. mechanization
b	3. using machines to do work	c. reaper
m	4. the right to vote	d. threshing machine
c	5. machine that cuts wheat	e. urbanization
o	6. gave women right to vote	f. tenement
j	7. someone who pays rent for land or buildings	g. settlement house
f	8. building divided into small apartments	h. political machine
n	9. person who fought to win suffrage	i. suspension bridge
k	10. to give somone the right to vote	j. tenant
d	11. machine for separating grain from its stalk	k. enfranchise
g	12. a place where needy people receive assistance	l. Great Migration
a	13. work performed by hand	m. suffrage
i	14. bridge supported by steel cables	n. suffragist
h	15. organization of people who control votes to gain power	o. Nineteenth Amendment

Notes for Home: Your child learned the vocabulary terms for Chapter 5.
Home Activity: Discuss the vocabulary terms and how they relate to people and events in the news.

Use with Pupil Edition, p. 247

Assessment Support

Use these Assessment Book pages and the ExamView® Test Bank CD-ROM to assess content and skills in Chapter 5. You can also view and print Assessment Book pages from the Teacher Resources CD-ROM.

Assessment Book, p. 29

Chapter 5 Test
Part 1: Content Test

Directions: Fill in the circle next to the correct answer.

Lesson Objective (1:1)

1. How did the mechanization of farms change the lives of rural people in the 1800s and early 1900s?
   Ⓐ It led them to grow fewer crops.
   Ⓑ It increased the need for farm labor.
   Ⓒ It forced farmers into deeper and deeper debt.
   ● It led to larger farms that raised cash crops.

Lesson Objective (1:2)

2. Which is NOT an example of how industry in the late 1880s gave people greater access to all kinds of goods?
   Ⓐ More goods were being invented and produced.
   ● People on farms and ranches made almost everything they needed by hand.
   Ⓒ Goods were less expensive to buy than ever before.
   Ⓓ Stores increased in number, and mail-order businesses were established.

Lesson Objective (1:3)

3. In what way did telephones affect life in the 1800s?
   ● People were pleased to be able to communicate without having to travel.
   Ⓑ Most people no longer wanted or needed to use the mail system.
   Ⓒ Alexander Graham Bell's company filled rural areas with telephone poles.
   Ⓓ People protested against the sight of poles and lines.

Lesson Objective (1:4)

4. What was the main purpose of the Rural Electrification Act?
   Ⓐ to encourage the use of wind and water power
   Ⓑ to create streetcar systems in cities
   ● to create and improve electric service in rural areas
   Ⓓ to end people's need for electricity

Lesson Objective (2:1)

5. Which of the following was NOT a factor in the growth of cities in the late 1800s?
   ● agricultural depression
   Ⓑ mechanization of farms
   Ⓒ immigration
   Ⓓ urbanization

Lesson Objective (2:2)

6. What was one result of rapid industrialization and urbanization?
   Ⓐ Most people in cities started living in large homes.
   Ⓑ Factories moved away from residential areas.
   Ⓒ People quit their city jobs and moved to the country.
   ● Cities became overcrowded.

Lesson Objective (2:3)

7. Which is NOT one of the challenges faced by urban areas as a result of population and technological changes?
   Ⓐ There was more garbage and waste.
   Ⓑ The air became polluted.
   ● Fewer workers were available for factory jobs.
   Ⓓ Diseases spread quickly among people living close together.

Use with Pupil Edition, p. 246

Assessment Book, p. 30

Lesson Objective (2:4)

8. How did Jane Addams try to solve some of the problems faced by the city of Chicago?
   Ⓐ She started schools for under-privileged city children.
   ● She opened a settlement house to help immigrants and working families.
   Ⓒ She wrote articles for the *New York Tribune* about the hardships faced by immigrants.
   Ⓓ She was active in the YMCA.

Lesson Objective (3:1)

9. What is one thing that African Americans, Hispanic groups, Chinese immigrants, and Jews had in common in the late 1800s?
   ● Many faced prejudice and segregation in different areas of their lives.
   Ⓑ They ran for public office in great numbers and quickly gained political power.
   Ⓒ Most moved away from cities to work on farms.
   Ⓓ Many became leaders in the manufacturing industry and earned a great deal of money.

Lesson Objective (3:2)

10. What effect did the passage of Jim Crow laws in the 1880s have on the lives of African Americans?
   Ⓐ It made racial segregation illegal in the United States.
   ● It made racial segregation legal in the South.
   Ⓒ It made better jobs available to African Americans.
   Ⓓ It improved education for African American schoolchildren.

Lesson Objective (3:4)

11. Which of the following was NOT a factor in the Great Migration?
   Ⓐ World War I
   Ⓑ northern African American newspapers
   Ⓒ encouragement of northern African Americans
   ● total equality for African Americans in the North

Lesson Objective (3:5)

12. How did African American activist Booker T. Washington respond to discrimination and work toward equality?
   Ⓐ He started an African American newspaper.
   Ⓑ He became a scientist.
   ● He founded the Tuskegee Institute, a college for African Americans.
   Ⓓ He helped start the National Association for the Advancement of Colored People.

Lesson Objective (4:1)

13. What happened as a result of the women's suffrage movement?
   Ⓐ Women were no longer allowed to do certain jobs in factories or on farms.
   ● Congress passed the Nineteenth Amendment, which gave women the right to vote.
   Ⓒ Women were allowed to enter the armed services.
   Ⓓ New inventions made housework and farm work easier to do.

Use with Pupil Edition, p. 246

Assessment Support

Assessment Book, p. 31

Lesson Objective (4:2)

14. Which is NOT an example of the new rights and educational opportunities gained for women in the 1800s?
    - ● Women could work on farms.
    - Ⓑ Women earned the right to vote.
    - Ⓒ Some colleges opened their doors to women.
    - Ⓓ A woman was elected mayor of a town.

Lesson Objective (4:3)

15. For what is Susan B. Anthony most famous?
    - Ⓐ working as a spy during World War I
    - Ⓑ climbing mountains all over the world
    - Ⓒ becoming the first woman mayor in the United States
    - ● working for women's suffrage

Part 2: Skills Test

Directions: Use complete sentences to answer questions 1–5. Use a separate sheet of paper if you need more space.

1. Complete the chart below. Compare and contrast Booker T. Washington and W. E. B. Du Bois. **Compare and Contrast**

Alike	Different
Possible answers: Both worked for African American rights. Both were popular, educated leaders.	Du Bois demanded immediate change, while Washington accepted slower change.

2. Explain how sharecropping often led to a life of poverty and debt. **Cause and Effect**

   Sharecroppers had to buy goods from the landowner and pay for them out of their crop. Often, the crop was not sufficient to pay debts, and the sharecropper fell deeper into debt.

3. How did the roles of women in the 1800s differ depending on whether they lived in rural or urban areas? **Summarize**

   In general, the roles of women in rural areas were not much different than the roles of men. In urban areas, women's roles were limited and very different from men's.

Use with Pupil Edition, p. 246

Assessment Book, p. 32

4. What can you conclude from the fact that many African Americans in the South did not accept the idea of "separate but equal"? **Draw Conclusions**

   Possible answer: Separate facilities were not considered equal by African Americans.

5. Look at the graph below. In which year did the urban population first become greater than the rural population? **Read a Line Graph**

   Urban population surpassed rural population sometime between 1910 and 1940.

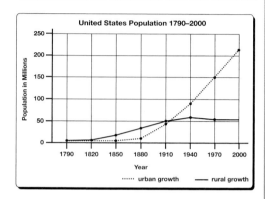

United States Population 1790–2000

····· urban growth —— rural growth

Use with Pupil Edition, p. 246

CHAPTER 5

Changing Ways of Life

Chapter 5 Outline
- **Lesson 1, *Rural Life Changes*,** pp. 216–221
- **Lesson 2, *Life in the Growing Cities*,** pp. 222–229
- **Chart and Graph Skills: *Read Line and Circle Graphs*,** pp. 230–231
- **Lesson 3, *Unequal Opportunities*,** pp. 232–238
- **Biography: *Booker T. Washington*,** p. 239
- **Lesson 4, *Women's Rights*,** pp. 240–244
- **Biography: *Susan B. Anthony*,** p. 245

Resources
- Workbook, p. 48: Vocabulary Preview
- Vocabulary Cards
- Social Studies Plus!

1834, Walnut Grove, Virginia: Lesson 1

This picture shows an early McCormick reaper that required two workers. Ask students what the illustration shows about farming in the 1830s. (Possible answer: In the 1830s, farmers were starting to use mechanical machines to help them harvest crops.)

1885, Chicago, Illinois: Lesson 2

This photo shows the first skyscraper. What does this photo suggest about how cities were developing in the late 1800s? (Possible answer: Larger buildings were being built in the cities.)

1881, Tuskegee, Alabama: Lesson 3

Ask students to describe what they see in this picture. What are the people doing in this picture? (Possible answer: The people in this picture are in a shop that appears to be putting together a newspaper or publication of some sort.)

1887, Argonia, Kansas: Lesson 4

What does the fact that Susannah Medora Salter became a mayor in 1887 show about the role of women? (Possible answer: Women were gaining new opportunities.)

214 Unit 3 • Expansion and Change

CHAPTER 5

Changing Ways of Life

1834

Walnut Grove, Virginia
Cyrus McCormick perfects the mechanical reaper.

Lesson 1

1

1885

Chicago, Illinois
The first skyscraper is built.

Lesson 2

2

1881

Tuskegee, Alabama
Booker T. Washington founds the Tuskegee Institute, a school for African Americans.

Lesson 3

3

1887

Argonia, Kansas
Susannah Medora Salter is the first woman elected mayor in the United States.

Lesson 4

4

214

Practice and Extend

Vocabulary Preview

- Use Workbook p. 48 to help students preview the vocabulary words in this chapter.
- Use Vocabulary Cards to preview key concept words in this chapter.

 Also on Teacher Resources CD-ROM.

Workbook, p. 48

Vocabulary Preview

Directions: Look at the vocabulary words in Chapter 5 of your textbook. Choose the vocabulary word from the chapter that completes each sentence. Write the word on the line provided.

1. The moving of people from rural areas to cities is _____
2. A center that provides help for people with little money is a _____
3. Someone who pays rent to use land or buildings that belong to someone else is a _____
4. A _____ is a machine that cuts wheat.
5. A _____ hangs from steel cables.
6. The right to vote or _____
7. During the _____ about 5 million African Americans moved north.
8. Using machines to do work is called _____
9. An organization of people that controls votes to gain political power is a _____
10. A building that is divided into small apartments is called a _____
11. A _____ separates grain from plant stalks.
12. The _____ to the Constitution gave women the right to vote.
13. Before machines were invented, _____ was the only way to get jobs done.
14. To _____ is to give someone the right to vote.
15. A _____ was a person who worked for women's voting rights.

Notes for Home: Your child learned the vocabulary terms for Chapter 5.
Home Activity: Practice saying, spelling, and using these words correctly with your child.

Locating Time and Place

Why We Remember

As the 1800s came to an end, the United States saw changes that solved some problems and created others. New tools and technologies made life easier for many people. Factories made goods more widely available. However, as people moved to the cities to work in factories, the cities grew too quickly. Also, people were not always treated equally. Many immigrants had trouble finding jobs. Women still could not vote in national elections. African American men could vote but were kept separate from whites. But for every problem, there were people who worked to find solutions. The United States continued its work of building a country that offered equality and hope to all of its citizens.

215

- Have students examine the pictures shown on p. 214 for Lessons 1, 2, 3, and 4.

- Remind students that each picture is coded with both a number and a color to link it to a place on the map on p. 215.

Why We Remember

Have students read the "Why We Remember" paragraph on p. 215, and ask them how the events in this chapter might compare or contrast to things that are happening in the United States today. Point out that today there are still many people who are working to build a country that offers equality and opportunity to all its citizens.

WEB SITE
Technology

You can learn more about Walnut Grove, Virginia; Chicago, Illinois; Tuskegee, Alabama; and Argonia, Kansas, by clicking on *Atlas* at **www.sfsocialstudies.com.**

SOCIAL STUDIES
Geography

Mental Mapping Have students picture in their minds what life was like in both rural and urban areas of the United States around the year 1900. Have them discuss how changes in technology and in the population might have affected the character of urban and rural places.

Rural Life Changes

Objectives

- Explain how mechanization changed farm life.
- Relate how industrialization provided access to consumer goods.
- Explain the impact of the increased availability of telephones.
- Describe the changes brought about by advancements in electrification.

Vocabulary

manual labor, p. 217;
mechanization, p. 217; **reaper,** p. 217;
threshing machine, p. 217

Resources

- Workbook, p. 49
- Transparency 14
- Every Student Learns Guide, pp. 82–85
- Quick Study, pp. 42–43

Quick Teaching Plan

If time is short, have students write *Before* and *After* at the top of a sheet of paper.

- As they read the lesson independently, have students write examples of what life was like before and after the technological developments discussed in the lesson.

1 Introduce and Motivate

Preview To activate prior knowledge, ask students to describe some type of machine or device they use regularly, such as a car or bus, computer, or electronic game. Encourage them to think about what life would be like without the machine or device. Tell students they will learn how the invention of new machinery changed life in the 1800s as they read Lesson 1.

You Are There: Have students predict how the development of new machinery will change life for rural people in the United States.

1830   1900

1834
Cyrus McCormick invents a mechanical reaper.

1879
First electric power station opens in San Francisco.

1893
New telephone companies form.

PREVIEW

Focus on the Main Idea
During the Industrial Revolution of the 1800s, new machines and technologies affected the lives of people in the rural areas of the United States.

PLACES
Walnut Grove, Virginia
Ahwahnee Valley, California
Appleton, Wisconsin

PEOPLE
Cyrus McCormick
L. O. Colvin
Gustav de Laval
Ellen Eglui
Aaron Montgomery Ward
Richard Sears
Alvah C. Roebuck

VOCABULARY
manual labor
mechanization
reaper
threshing machine

216

Rural Life Changes

You Are There

"Wake up," Father says. "Time for work."

You roll out of bed, dress quickly, and join him on the front porch of your farmhouse. It is still dark outside, and the Kansas air is cool. In the dim light of the moon, you can see the field of wheat waving in the wind. You follow your father to the barn.

"We have a lot to do today," Father says. "The wheat is ripe, and it is time to harvest."

You smile and your father smiles too. Harvesting has always been hard work, but this year it will be easier and faster! You have been reading for months about the new machine that cuts wheat. At last, your father was able to buy one. Your family used to pay laborers to help you cut the wheat by hand, but with this machine, you can do it all yourselves.

You get the horses, Molly and Millie, out of the barn and head for the wheat fields. The sun is coming up, and you are happy for this exciting, new day!

Compare and Contrast As you read, compare and contrast the life of a rural farmer before and after the invention of farm machines.

Practice and Extend

READING SKILL
Compare/Contrast

In the Lesson Review, students complete a graphic organizer like the one below. You may want to provide students with a copy of Transparency 14 to complete as they read the lesson.

Use Transparency 14

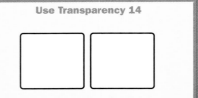

VOCABULARY
Word Exercise

Context Clues

To help build context for *reaper* and *threshing machine,* ask students what they can think of that are made from grains. (cereal, bread, noodles, and so on) If possible, show pictures of growing grain and grain processing. Have students look up *reap* and *thresh* in the dictionary. Ask students why they think people would want to make these processes easier. Point out that *reap* and *thresh* are the bases of the two vocabulary words.

Mechanization on the Farm

Farming in the early 1800s was difficult and tiring. Manual labor was the only way to get tasks done. Manual labor means the jobs done by hand, without the help of machines. The larger the farm, the more laborers it took to do the work.

Inventors in the 1800s, some of whom were farmers themselves, created new machines to help make farming easier. Using machines to do work is called mechanization. Mechanization dramatically changed farming in the United States.

A farmer was no longer limited to a "walking plow" but could buy a wheeled one that was pulled by horses. It had a seat, so the farmer could ride rather than walk. In 1834 Cyrus McCormick, a farmer and inventor from Walnut Grove, Virginia, perfected the mechanical reaper. A reaper is a machine that cuts grain. One reaper could cut as much wheat as 16 men with hand-held blades. Steam engines were put to use running threshing machines that separated the grain from the plant stalks. New binding machines made the farmer's chore of tying up hay into bundles or bales much easier.

Farmers who raised milk cows also benefited from mechanization. In 1862 L. O. Colvin developed the first milking machine. Farmers could now milk more than one cow at a time. The cream separator was another useful tool. Cream takes about 24 hours to rise to the top of the milk on its own. The cream separator invented by Gustav de Laval in 1879 spun the milk and separated the cream in minutes.

Machines worked faster than people could. Because of this, farmers with new machines were able to get more work done in less time. This meant they could farm more land, and farms increased in size. In the time it once took to plant or harvest a small plot of land, farmers could now plant and harvest many acres.

Once farmers provided food mainly for their families. As farms increased in size, farmers could sow fields with crops they grew only to sell. These were called "cash crops," because farmers grew them for cash. Cash crops brought in more money, so farmers could buy more land.

REVIEW Contrast how farmers worked before and after mechanization.
Compare and Contrast

▶ The first McCormick reaper required two workers, one to drive and one to move the cut wheat away from the machine. Later reapers needed only one worker.

217

Teach and Discuss

PAGE 217

Mechanization on the Farm

🕐 *Quick Summary* Inventions in the 1800s allowed farmers to do more work with less effort.

① Contrast farming before the 1800s with farming after the 1800s. Before: All tasks required manual labor. After: Machines helped with many tasks.
Compare and Contrast

② What was the effect of mechanization on the size of farms? Many farms increased in size because farmers could do more work in less time. Cause and Effect

💲 **SOCIAL STUDIES STRAND Economics**

Explain that without cash, people obtain goods and services by engaging in barter—the trade of one good or service for another.

③ How did farm machinery change the way people obtained goods and services? Machinery enabled farmers to earn cash and buy things rather than trading for them. Draw Conclusions

✓ **REVIEW ANSWER** Possible answers: Before machines, farmers did work by hand. The work was harder and took longer. After the introduction of machines, the farm work could be done faster with fewer people.
Compare and Contrast

❄️ **MEETING INDIVIDUAL NEEDS Learning Styles**

Create an Advertisement Have students create an ad about the benefits of farm machinery.

Verbal Learning Write and deliver a brief "sales pitch" for one of the farm machines described on p. 217.

Visual Learning Create a poster advertising the benefits of one of the farm machines described on p. 217.

Kinesthetic Learning Act out a demonstration of one of the farm machines described on p. 217, with the goal of encouraging a viewer to purchase the machinery.

Industry's Impact

Quick Summary Industry made many goods, and mail-order catalogs helped rural consumers obtain them.

SOCIAL STUDIES STRAND
Geography

Tell students that merchants prefer places where there is enough population density to ensure adequate customers.

Test Talk

Use Information from the Text

4 **How did shops in rural areas differ from shops in cities?** Students should look back at the text to make sure they have the right information. There were fewer shops in rural areas. City shops carried many goods. **Compare and Contrast**

Primary Source

Cited in 1897 Sears Roebuck Catalogue, ed. Fred L. Israel

Tell students that in the 1800s, many people in the United States had little education, and many came from foreign countries.

5 **Why do you think Sears and Roebuck stressed that people feel free to order "in their own way"?** Possible answer: They wanted people to order even if they did not write well or know English well. **Analyze Primary Sources**

✓ **REVIEW ANSWER** Possible answer: Unlike the farmer, the worker in Chicago could shop at stores. Both the worker and farmer could order from a mail-order catalog. **Compare and Contrast**

Mail-Order Catalogs

6 **Compare and contrast ordering from a mail-order catalog today and in the 1800s.** Similar: In the 1800s and today, people can send an order to a mail-order company. Different: Today, people can use the telephone or the Internet to order goods. **Compare and Contrast**

218 Unit 3 • Expansion and Change

Industry's Impact

Industry was growing in cities such as New York and Chicago. Factories produced all kinds of goods. There were dresses and buckets, tractors and birdcages. A shopper could buy a washing machine with the new clothes wringer invented by **Ellen Eglui.** More goods were being produced, and they were less expensive to buy. Stores increased in number and size to sell these affordable goods to people in the cities.

However, not everyone lived in or near cities. In the late 1800s, many Americans lived on farms and ranches. Almost everything they needed was made by hand, including clothes, soap, and furniture. People's homes were often far from the nearest town. Getting **4** supplies was a challenge.

How could farmers hope to buy new, factory-made items if they lived far from a city? **Aaron Montgomery Ward** had an answer: mail order. In 1872 in Chicago, Ward established the first mail-order business. A customer could just flip through the pages of a Montgomery Ward catalog, select an item, and then write an order. Whether a customer lived in the city of Boston or on a homestead in Texas, the goods were available. Ordered goods were carried across the country by train.

In 1893 **Richard Sears** and **Alvah C. Roebuck** formed a mail-order company that soon grew to be larger than Montgomery Ward's. Even houses could be bought from Sears and Roebuck. They promised that their prices were cheapest. They also said:

> *"Tell us what you want in your own way, written in any language, no matter whether good or poor writing, and the goods will be promptly sent to you."* **5**

REVIEW Compare and contrast the shopping experiences of a farmer far from the city and a worker in Chicago. **Compare and Contrast**

Mail-Order Catalogs

Mail-order catalogs became popular with people in big cities, small towns, and farms. Catalogs are still popular today. They arrive in mailboxes across the country on a regular basis.

Many catalogs are now online. Shoppers don't have to write their orders on paper like people did in the 1800s. They can choose what they want and press a key. **6**

▶ Early pages from Montgomery Ward and Sears, Roebuck catalogs reflect the styles and products of their day.

218

Practice and Extend

ACCESS CONTENT
ESL Support

Describe a Process Help students understand the significance of mail-order shopping for people in the United States in the 1800s.

Beginning Ask students to act out the process of finding an item in a catalog and writing out an order.

Intermediate Have students describe how they would find and order an item using a catalog.

Advanced Have students write out the steps involved in finding an item, placing an order, and receiving the item by mail.

For additional ESL support, use Every Student Learns Guide, pp. 82–85.

Getting Connected

In Unit 2, you read about the invention of the telephone by Alexander Graham Bell in 1876. Before this time, if people wanted to stay in touch, the only choices they had were to write letters, send telegrams, or go for a visit. With the telephone's invention, people had a new way to communicate.

Telephone poles and lines quickly spread west across the country. Phones were installed in homes and businesses. A Chicago factory owner could now talk about business with a supplier in St. Louis without having to travel. Families who lived far apart could hear each other's voices again. An emergency was less frightening when you could call a doctor or firefighter. Until the 1890s, however, telephone rates were very high. Some rural areas and small towns had no service at all.

Alexander Graham Bell owned the first telephone company, because he owned the patent on the equipment. Bell's company had to install all the telephone poles and lines his system needed. In cities, each mile of telephone line Bell put up could serve 40 customers. In rural areas, that same mile of line only served two customers. Because of this, Bell's company did not serve many people in rural areas. It was too expensive.

▶ Telephones were available in many rural areas by the early 1900s.

In 1893 Bell's patent expired. Small telephone companies began to form in rural areas. Sometimes when there were no local phone companies, farmers banded together and put up their own poles and lines. One of the first places where this happened was in **Ahwahnee Valley, California.** Farmers in this valley, which is now part of Yosemite National Park, each contributed money and labor to create their own phone system. The building materials could be ordered from mail-order catalogs, so could the telephones.

REVIEW Contrast the ways people could communicate before and after telephones were available. ↻ Compare and Contrast

▶ Before computers existed, all telephone connections had to be made by hand. Notice the plugs and cords these operators from 1900 used to make the connections.

219

PAGE 219

Getting Connected

🕐 *Quick Summary* Telephones helped link people across the nation, though rural areas faced big challenges in obtaining phone service.

7 **Summarize the impact of the invention of the telephone.** Possible answer: Telephones helped change the way people do business, maintain relationships, and deal with emergencies. **Summarize**

✓ Ongoing Assessment

If... students do not recognize the importance of the invention of the telephone,	then... have them write a list of all the phone calls or Web site visits they can remember making in the last 24 hours.

G SOCIAL STUDIES STRAND
Government

Tell students that the government of the United States issues patents to give inventors the sole opportunity to profit from their invention for a period of years.

8 **What happened when Bell's telephone patent expired?** Possible answer: Areas without phone service began to consider building their own systems. **Cause and Effect**

SOCIAL STUDIES STRAND
Decision Making

9 **Suppose you lived in a rural area in 1900. Would you be willing to spend your own money to help build a phone system for your area? Give reasons for your answer.** Accept all answers, but make sure students support their answers. **Make Decisions**

✓ REVIEW ANSWER Before the telephone was invented, people wrote letters, sent telegrams, or visited in person. After the telephone was invented, they could speak to each other with this new tool. ↻ **Compare and Contrast**

❄ MEETING INDIVIDUAL NEEDS
Leveled Practice

Write an Editorial Encourage students to write a newspaper editorial about a plan to build a telephone system in a rural area.

Easy Ask students to brainstorm a list of the benefits of having a telephone system in a rural area. **Reteach**

On-Level Have students write a brief paragraph arguing either for or against plans to build a telephone system in their rural area. **Extend**

Challenge Have students write two paragraphs, one for and one against plans to build a telephone system in their rural area. **Enrich**

For a Lesson Summary, use Quick Study, p. 42.

Electrifying the Countryside

Quick Summary In the late 1800s the growth of power stations helped harness the power of electricity and put it to work in homes, factories, and farms.

FACT FILE

Electric Appliances Change Work

10 **What do these examples suggest about how electricity changed life in many homes in the late 1800s and early 1900s?** Possible answer: Electricity was used to power appliances that made housework easier. Analyze Information

11 **What was necessary in order to make electricity useful on a large scale in the United States?** Power stations Apply Information

12 **Why did many rural areas not have electricity in the early 1900s?** It was costly to run lines over long distances to provide electricity for only a small number of homes. Analyze Information

FACT FILE

Electric Appliances Change Work

New electric appliances began to appear in the late 1800s. Rugs no longer had to be taken outside and beaten. Irons stayed hot without a nearby stove. Scrubbing clothes by hand was a thing of the past. Appliances run by electricity made work easier and faster.

ORION takes the leaning out of cleaning

▶ Electric washing machine, 1914

10

▶ Electric iron, 1893

▶ Electric upright vacuum cleaner, 1907

▶ Electric sewing machine, 1880s

Electrifying the Countryside

People had known about electricity for a long time. The first electric battery was made in 1800. The first electric motor was built in 1821. However, it took the building of electric power stations to make electricity widely

11 available.

The first power station in the United States opened in San Francisco, California, in 1879. But the first hydroelectric power plant, which opened in 1882, was built in the town of **Appleton, Wisconsin.** Hydroelectric power plants use running water to generate electricity.

Power stations made electricity available for more than just lighting homes. The power

plant in Appleton helped run paper mills. It also supplied power for an electric streetcar system that was opened in 1886.

Although some rural towns had electricity early, it was difficult to set up electrical lines over long distances. People who lived far from power plants had to wait to get electricity, sometimes for years. Farmers in these areas continued to rely on wind power, water-power, machine power, and their own power to get work done.

12

In 1936 the Rural Electrification Act was passed. This act gave the government the right to lend money to states to use for creating and improving electric service to rural areas. Slowly, electricity came to the country. Farmers' lives changed for the better.

Practice and Extend

SOCIAL STUDIES
Background

About Rural Electrification

- In 1930 only one in ten rural dwellers in the United States had electricity; some areas had a much lower ratio than that.
- By the end of the 1930s, the nation had more than 400 rural electric cooperatives, which provided electric power to nearly 300,000 homes.
- Government-sponsored programs also helped rural families, many of whom were poor, to buy electrical appliances.

CURRICULUM CONNECTION
Math

Figure Ratios

- Tell students that electric companies make money by selling electricity.
- Ask students to solve the following problem: A mile of electrical power line serves 2 customers in a rural area and 200 customers in an urban area. How much more would the electric company have to charge its rural customers to equal the amount earned from a mile of urban line? *Answer: 100 times more*

New electric appliances helped farmers and their families with daily chores. An electric iron made ironing faster, because an iron no longer had to be heated on a stove. The electric stove didn't need coal or wood to create heat. Electric vacuum cleaners helped keep floors clean. A family with enough money could buy an electric washing machine. This machine cleaned clothes faster and better, and was easier to use than doing laundry by hand.

Electricity also came in handy outside the farmhouse. Electric pumps brought water from the ground. Farmers didn't have to wait for the wind as they had when using windmills. Electric lights helped the farmer see inside the barn without a lantern, and they were safer than lanterns, which could

cause fires. Feed for animals could be prepared with an electric feed grinder.

Mechanical reapers and threshers had helped farmers and their families years earlier. Electricity brought additional changes to work and life in rural areas. **13**

REVIEW Compare and contrast housework before and after the invention of electric appliances. Compare and Contrast

Summarize the Lesson

- **1834** Cyrus McCormick invented a mechanical reaper.

- **1879** First electric power station opened in San Francisco.

- **1893** New telephone companies formed when Bell's patent expired.

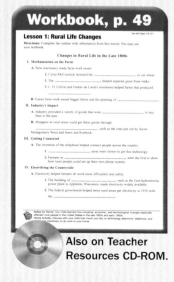

▶ Edison's "electric lamp"

LESSON 1 REVIEW

Check Facts and Main Ideas

1. **Compare and Contrast** On a separate sheet of paper, fill in the boxes to contrast rural people's lives before and after the arrival of electricity.

Before electricity	After electricity
Daily chores took much time and work. Wind was needed to run pumps for water. Lanterns could cause fires inside the barn.	Chores were done more quickly and easily. Electricity powered pumps for water and to grind grain for feed. Electric lights helped farmers see.

2. How did advances in **mechanization** affect farm life in the late 1800s? Use the highlighted word in your answer.

3. How did the growth of industry make it easier for farmers to get goods?

4. Why did big cities have new services such as telephone systems and electricity before rural areas did?

5. Critical Thinking: *Draw Conclusions* Why do you think people in the 1880s were so eager to have telephones?

Link to ━◯◯━ **Writing**

Create an Advertisement Suppose you are **Cyrus McCormick.** Write a newspaper advertisement about your **reaper,** to be placed in a rural 1800s newspaper. How can you excite farmers about this new invention? Use the term **manual labor** in your advertisement.

221

Workbook, p. 49

Lesson 1: Rural Life Changes
Directions: Complete the outline with information from this lesson. You may use your textbook.

Changes in Rural Life in the Late 1800s

I. Mechanization on the Farm
  A. New machinery made farm work easier.
    1. Cyrus McCormick invented the _____ to cut wheat.
    2. The _____ helped separate grain from stalks.
    3. L. O. Colvin and Gustav de Laval's inventions helped farms that produced _____
  B. Easier farm work meant bigger farms and the planting of _____
II. Industry's Impact
  A. Industry provided a variety of goods that were _____ to buy than in the past.
  B. Shoppers in rural areas could get these goods through _____
    _____ such as the ones put out by Aaron Montgomery Ward and Sears and Roebuck.
III. Getting Connected
  A. The invention of the telephone helped connect people across the country.
    1. _____ areas were slower to get this technology.
    2. Farmers in _____ were the first to show how rural people could set up their own phone system.
IV. Electrifying the Countryside
  A. Electricity helped farmers do work more efficiently and safely.
    1. The building of _____ such as the first hydroelectric power plant in Appleton, Wisconsin, made electricity widely available.
    2. The federal government helped more rural areas get electricity in 1936 with the _____

Notes for Home: Your child learned how industrial, economic, and technological changes especially affected rural people in the United States in the late 1800s and early 1900s.
Home Activity: Discuss with your child how much you rely on technology (electricity, telephone, and machinery) to work in your home.

▶ **Also on Teacher Resources CD-ROM.**

---

13 **What effect do you predict rural electrification would have on the productivity of farms?** Possible answer: Electricity would make farms more productive. **Predict**

✓ **REVIEW ANSWER** Before the invention of electric appliances, housework took many hours of heavy labor. After the invention of appliances, housework was often faster and easier. Compare and Contrast

3 Close and Assess

Summarize the Lesson

Have students add other items to the time line and use it to summarize the lesson.

✓ **LESSON 1** **REVIEW**

1. **Compare and Contrast** For possible answers, see the reduced pupil page.

2. Advances in mechanization gave farmers tools to make their work easier and faster.

3. Possible answer: Factories created more goods; mail-order catalogs made goods readily available.

4. It was more expensive to get phone lines or electric lines to homes that were far away and far apart.

5. **Critical Thinking:** *Draw Conclusions* Possible answer: The telephone made it easier to communicate over long distances for business or personal reasons. People could save time by using the telephone.

Link to ━◯◯━ **Writing**

Make sure advertisements use the term *manual labor* correctly.

Life in the Growing Cities

Objectives

- Explain the reasons for the growth of cities, including immigration and urbanization.

- Relate how rapid industrialization and urbanization led to overcrowding.

- Identify the challenges faced by urban areas as a result of population and technological changes.

- Describe efforts to solve problems faced by urban areas.

Vocabulary

urbanization, p. 224; **tenement,** p. 224; **settlement house,** p. 226; **political machine,** p. 227; **suspension bridge,** p. 229

Resources

- Workbook, p. 50
- Transparency 21
- Every Student Learns Guide, pp. 86–89
- Quick Study, pp. 44–45

Quick Teaching Plan

If time is short, have students create a web diagram with the words *Growth of Cities* in the center and several blank balloons surrounding it.

- Have students supply details from the lesson as they read it independently.

1 Introduce and Motivate

Preview To activate prior knowledge, ask students to generate a list of words they would use to describe cities today. Tell students that they will learn about the growth of cities in the United States as they read Lesson 2.

You Are There — Ask students to think about the opportunities and challenges cities might provide people in the United States in the late 1800s and early 1900s.

LESSON 2

1880			1900
1885 First skyscraper is built in Chicago.	**1889** Jane Addams opens Hull House for the poor.		**1900** New York City's population nears 3.5 million.

PREVIEW

Focus on the Main Idea
During the late 1800s and the early 1900s, people in American cities found that life was changing as populations grew larger.

PLACES
New York, New York
Chicago, Illinois
Philadelphia, Pennsylvania
St. Louis, Missouri
Boston, Massachusetts

PEOPLE
Jane Addams
Jacob Riis
"Boss" William M. Tweed
Elisha Graves Otis
James Buchanan Eads
John Roebling

VOCABULARY
urbanization
tenement
settlement house
political machine
suspension bridge

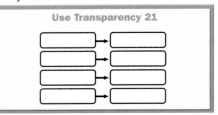

222

Life in the Growing Cities

You Are There — It is 1895, and you and your family have just moved to Philadelphia. You had thought you knew what to expect. You had been to the town near your farm at least once a month. You had gone to the fair, where you saw almost everyone in the county. But that didn't prepare you for this. Your whole town could fit in one street here. And the whole county could probably fit in one of the city's tall buildings.

The size of the city and the crowds are not the only differences. The air is not as fresh as it was back on the farm. And there is so much noise. Cars, horses, wagons, and people fill the streets. Horns are honking and people are shouting. You know how to read, but you can't read many of the signs. Your mother tells you that it is because they are in different languages. There is so much that is new. It is a little bit scary, but exciting too.

Cause and Effect As you read, pay attention to the changes that occurred in big cities as their populations grew.

Practice and Extend

READING SKILL
Cause and Effect

In the Lesson Review, students complete a graphic organizer like the one below. You may want to provide students with a copy of Transparency 21 to complete as they read the lesson.

Use Transparency 21

VOCABULARY
Word Exercise

Individual Word Study

Point out that *urbanization* has two suffixes, *-ize* and *-ation*. Explain that *urban* is used to talk about cities. The suffix *-ize* means "make" or "become," so *urbanize* means "becoming a city." Tell students that *-ation* means "act or process," then have them predict the meaning of *urbanization* using this information. Have them compare their predictions to the definition in the text. Discuss how the definition is related to the meaning created by the suffixes.

Growing Cities

In the late 1800s and early 1900s, the United States was changing. It was transforming from a largely rural, agricultural nation into a nation of city dwellers.

New York City, **Chicago**, and **Philadelphia**, the country's three largest cities at this time, grew rapidly. So did other cities. Cities near good transportation grew fastest. Access to both trains and water contributed to the growth of San Francisco, California; Buffalo, New York; Toledo, Ohio; and Chicago, Illinois. Other cities grew dramatically because they were on major railroad lines. The railroad cities included Atlanta, Georgia; Indianapolis, Indiana; Minneapolis, Minnesota; Fort Worth,

Texas; and Tacoma, Washington.

REVIEW What factor determined which cities grew fastest during the late 1800s? Cause and Effect

Growth of 3 Largest Cities, 1890-1910

▶ Some cities saw dramatic growth.

GRAPH SKILL Use a Bar Graph *How much did the population of New York increase between 1890 and 1900?*

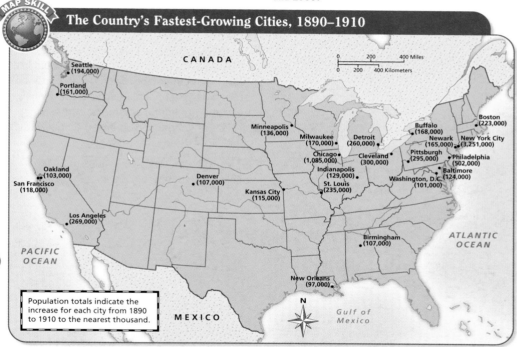

The Country's Fastest-Growing Cities, 1890–1910

Seattle (194,000)
Portland (161,000)
CANADA
0   200   400 Miles
0   200   400 Kilometers
Minneapolis (136,000)
Milwaukee (170,000)
Detroit (260,000)
Buffalo (168,000)
Boston (223,000)
Newark (165,000)
New York City (3,251,000)
Chicago (1,085,000)
Cleveland (300,000)
Pittsburgh (295,000)
Philadelphia (502,000)
Oakland (103,000)
Denver (107,000)
Indianapolis (129,000)
Baltimore (124,000)
San Francisco (118,000)
Kansas City (115,000)
St. Louis (235,000)
Washington, D.C. (101,000)
Los Angeles (269,000)
Birmingham (107,000)
ATLANTIC OCEAN
PACIFIC OCEAN
New Orleans (97,000)
N
MEXICO
Gulf of Mexico
Population totals indicate the increase for each city from 1890 to 1910 to the nearest thousand.

▶ During this time, existing cities grew and new cities were born.

MAP SKILL Using a Map Key *What do the numbers below each city's name tell you about the city?*

223

2 Teach and Discuss

PAGE 223

Growing Cities

Quick Summary In the late 1800s and early 1900s, the United States grew more urban, and many cities increased in size rapidly.

① **What major change was the population of the United States undergoing in the late 1800s and early 1900s?** It was becoming more urban and less rural. Summarize

✓ **REVIEW ANSWER** Access to good transportation determined which cities grew fastest. Cause and Effect

② **Which city in the chart grew at the fastest rate between 1890 and 1910?** New York Analyze Information

GRAPH SKILL Answer It grew from about 1.5 million to nearly 5 million.

The Country's Fastest-Growing Cities, 1890–1910

③ **Which city on the West Coast of the United States experienced the most growth in population between 1890 and 1910?** Los Angeles Interpret Maps

MAP SKILL Answer The increase in each city's population from 1890 to 1910, to the nearest thousand

---

CURRICULUM CONNECTION
Math

Calculate Population Growth Rates

Have students calculate the rate of growth for each of the three cities in the chart on p. 223. For each city:

- Write down the city's approximate population in 1910.
- Divide that number by the city's approximate population in 1890. (Answers: New York = 3.15; Chicago = 1.99; Philadelphia = 1.48)
- Explain to students that the answer represents the rate of growth of the city between 1890 and 1910. For example, the population of New York was 3.15 times greater in 1910 than it was in 1890. Chicago's population was 1.99 times greater.

Immigration and Urbanization

 Quick Summary Cities became crowded with immigrants and people from rural areas, creating difficult conditions—and the urge to ease them.

SOCIAL STUDIES STRAND
Geography

Tell students that immigration is often explained as the result of "push" factors that drive people from their home countries and "pull" factors that lead them to their new homes.

4 **What factor "pulled" many immigrants to cities of the United States in the late 1800s and early 1900s?** Possible answer: The growth of factories and the jobs they produced Cause and Effect

5 **What group besides immigrants contributed to urban growth in the late 1800s and early 1900s?** People from rural areas Main Idea and Details

6 **Explain how the development of farm machinery contributed to the growth of cities.** Farm machinery reduced the need for rural labor and encouraged many rural workers to seek jobs in the cities. Cause and Effect

✓ Ongoing Assessment

If... students do not understand how mechanization affected urban populations,

then... have students reread PE pp. 216–217 and the discussion of mechanization on the farm.

✓ **REVIEW ANSWER** Possible answer: People had to think about urban planning because uncontrolled industrial and population growth was creating problems in the growing cities. Cause and Effect

---

Immigration and Urbanization

Between 1890 and 1910, the population of the United States grew from about 63 million to more than 92 million people. Of this 29-million-person increase, nearly two-thirds were immigrants. This was the largest number of arrivals the United States had ever experienced in such a short time span.

Industrialization had created millions of new jobs. The flood of immigrants had come to the United States to fill these jobs, most of which were in cities.

4 But it was not just immigrants swelling the country's urban population. This was a time of rapid urbanization. **Urbanization** is the movement of people from rural areas to cities. With new machines making farm work easier, fewer farm workers were needed.
5
6 People who had always worked the land now moved to the city to find factory jobs.

With so many people moving to the cities, there was a shortage of housing. New arrivals crowded into **tenements,** or buildings that are divided into small apartments. Factories

▶ City children often had nowhere to play except the sidewalk.

began to move into residential areas. Tenements were built between houses. No one had ever thought about urban planning, so there were no rules about where it was appropriate to build.

The "city beautiful" movement started in the 1890s. This represented the earliest efforts to fight what was seen as the ugliness and disorder of uncontrolled industrial growth. People also built parks and playgrounds for city dwellers. But the cities grew so fast that these facilities were soon not enough.

Transportation both solved and created problems. As foot and horse traffic changed to streetcar, subway, and automobile traffic, city boundaries expanded. Workers could live farther from their jobs. Soon the streets were so crowded that people had to start thinking about how to improve traffic patterns.

More and more people began to realize that rapid growth had disadvantages.

REVIEW Why did people have to begin thinking about urban planning during this time? Cause and Effect

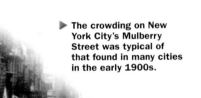
▶ The crowding on New York City's Mulberry Street was typical of that found in many cities in the early 1900s.

224

Practice and Extend

FYI **SOCIAL STUDIES**
Background

About the "City Beautiful" Movement

- The movement stressed improving the function of cities through better planning and management. It also sought to improve the appearance of cities through design and public art displays.

- The movement held that a "city beautiful" would uplift its residents and lead them to abandon socially unacceptable behaviors.

- A "city beautiful" was also thought to inspire loyalty, which would lead to civic virtue.

▶ Many immigrant families lived and worked in small tenement apartments like this one in New York City.

Urban Woes

In 1880 a report in the *Chicago Times* read: "The river stinks. The air stinks. People's clothing . . . stinks. No other word expresses it so well as stink."

This report reflected the conditions in many of the cities around the country. Urban growth had brought about some good changes. Record numbers of people had jobs, and many people were making more money than they had ever dreamed of making. However, the uncontrolled growth had also created many problems.

Overcrowding was one of the biggest problems. As people continued to arrive, housing became increasingly difficult to find. Families of eight or more often lived together in one tiny tenement apartment. Family members often shared beds, because there was so little space.

In addition to being crowded, many tenements were often unsafe or uncomfortable. Some apartments lacked heat. Others had no windows, making it hard to get fresh air.

With so many people living close together, diseases spread quickly. In southern states, thousands died from yellow fever. Across the country, epidemics of polio, tuberculosis, smallpox, and scarlet fever killed tens of

thousands of people. In 1918 an outbreak of influenza killed more than 500,000 Americans. Also, because milk was rarely refrigerated, it could spoil in hot weather. As a result, thousands of babies died every summer. Doctors, researchers, and concerned citizens realized that, with so many people living together, they had to think about caring for whole cities, not just individuals. This idea became known as public health.

The cities were becoming dirtier. Many factories spouted smoke and soot into the air. Traffic increased on the roads. There was more garbage and waste, some of it dumped in the streets, much of it dumped into rivers. Dirt and noise became the constants of city life.

As you read in Unit 2, immigrants sometimes faced prejudice when looking for work. Some people thought immigrants were taking jobs away from local people. Some feared people who were "different." Sometimes the prejudice was an old grudge that one group of immigrants still carried against another group. Prejudice contributed to making life in the city harder.

REVIEW What were some of the troubles that people faced in cities as the populations grew? **Main Idea and Details**

225

Urban Woes

Quick Summary The booming cities were plagued by a number of problems, including overcrowding, unhealthful conditions, and prejudice aimed at immigrants.

7 **What was the leading cause of overcrowding in immigrant neighborhoods?** Lack of available housing **Cause and Effect**

Test Talk

Use Information from Graphics

8 **How does this photograph help you understand overcrowding in cities during the late 1800s and early 1900s?** Remind students to use details from the photograph to support their answers. Possible answer: In this photograph, at least seven people are working and living in what appears to be a small tenement apartment. It is easier to understand how people lived when a photograph shows how small and crowded tenement apartments could be. **Draw Conclusions**

SOCIAL STUDIES STRAND
Economics

Explain that if the supply of workers exceeds the demand for them, the wage paid to those workers will drop. The available jobs may then go to those willing to work for the lower wage.

9 **Why did locals sometimes resent immigrant workers?** Possible answer: The locals believed the immigrants were taking the available jobs. **Apply Information**

✓ **REVIEW ANSWER** Possible answers: Overcrowding, noise, dirt and waste, smoke, and violence **Main Idea and Details**

Seeking Solutions

Quick Summary The challenges of urban life were met by reformers who sought to help urban residents and raise awareness of their plight.

10 **What kinds of help did Jane Addams provide to poor urban residents?**
Possible answer: She helped people adjust to life in the cities, find work, and deal with practical issues such as child care. **Summarize**

11 **How did Jacob Riis try to help immigrants and the urban poor?**
Possible answer: He tried to raise awareness of the problems of the poor. **Generalize**

⭐ **SOCIAL STUDIES STRAND**
Citizenship

Democratic Values and Institutions
Citizens have a responsibility to help others in their communities.

12 **Why do you think Theodore Roosevelt called Riis "the most useful citizen in New York"?** Possible answer: Riis identified a common problem and thought of a way to help resolve it. **Draw Conclusions**

✓ **REVIEW ANSWER** Possible answer: Riis remembered his own struggle as a poor immigrant. **Draw Conclusions**

Seeking Solutions

Many organizations were already hard at work trying to solve the problems created by the rapid growth of cities. Still active today are the YMCA, YMHA, and Salvation Army, all of which started during the 1800s. In fact, it was in 1891 at the YMCA in Springfield, Massachusetts, that Dr. James Naismith invented the game of basketball, in order to give city children a sport they could play indoors during the winter. Dwight L. Moody started schools in Chicago for underprivileged city children, and he mobilized people across the country to address the problems of the inner cities. There were groups of successful immigrants who aided struggling newcomers, as well as groups who banded together to help each other. But the cities grew too fast, and more help was needed.

In 1889 **Jane Addams** rented a house in a poor neighborhood in Chicago. She fixed it up and opened it as a settlement house called Hull House. A **settlement house** is a center that provides help for those who have little money. At Hull House, immigrants could take free English classes and get help in finding work. There was day care for the children **10** of families in which both parents worked.

▶ **Hull House was designed to make people feel comfortable and at home.**

▶ **Jane Addams, at right, opened Hull House, one of the country's first settlement houses.**

The idea of settlement houses spread across the country. Following the example of Hull House, hundreds opened in other cities.

Jacob Riis was an immigrant from Denmark. He settled in New York City in 1870. Like many other immigrants, he was poor when he arrived, and he struggled to get ahead. Then he got a job as a police reporter for the *New York Tribune*. He began writing articles about the hardships faced by immigrants at home and at work.

In 1890 Riis published a book called *How the Other Half Lives*. In words and photographs, he revealed the terrible conditions faced by poor urban immigrants. Some wealthy New Yorkers were saddened by what Riis wrote. They donated money to build parks and medical centers for the poor. City officials tore down several of the worst tenements. **11** Theodore Roosevelt, who became President of the United States in 1901, called Riis "the most useful citizen of New York." **12**

REVIEW Why do you think Riis was interested in helping poor immigrants? **Draw Conclusions**

Practice and Extend

✳ **MEETING INDIVIDUAL NEEDS**
Leveled Practice

Describe City Life Have students explore the challenges of urban life during this time period.

Easy Have students write a one-paragraph description of an urban scene in the late 1800s and early 1900s. The paragraph should strive to raise awareness of the problems and inspire support for reforms. **Reteach**

On-Level Have students write a descriptive paragraph and create an accompanying picture of an urban scene in the late 1800s and early 1900s, aimed at raising awareness and inspiring reform. **Extend**

Challenge Have students create a "book" that features two to three paragraphs and accompanying pictures of urban problems from the late 1800s and early 1900s. **Enrich**

For a Lesson Summary, use Quick Study, p. 44.

Rise of Political Machines

Growing cities needed better streets, more housing, and better sewage disposal. Plans were needed to control building and traffic. Immigrants needed help finding jobs and fighting prejudice.

Because city governments were having trouble handling the problems, people were unhappy. Political machines formed to take advantage of this unhappiness. A **political machine** is an organization of people who control votes to gain political power. Many of the votes controlled by political machines were those of immigrants.

Here is how a political machine would work. Members of the machine wanted to get certain candidates elected to city offices. They told immigrants that they would help them get homes and jobs if the immigrants voted for the candidates selected by the machine. Sometimes they did help, but most were more interested in power than kindness. The candidates that the machines put in city offices did what the political machines told them to do.

A powerful political machine in New York City was called Tammany Hall. Tammany Hall did improve sewer, water, police, and other services. However, it was best known for its dishonesty. A Tammany leader named **"Boss" William M. Tweed** was known for bribing leaders and cheating people out of money. He also stole millions of dollars from the city.

SHERIFF'S OFFICE

$10,000 Reward.

WM. M. TWEED.

▶ "Boss" Tweed was sent to jail for his crimes. This poster was published when he escaped.

George W. Plunkitt, another Tammany leader, grew wealthy from the "deals" he made but liked the power more than the money. He said, "If a family is burned out, I don't ask whether they are Republicans or Democrats. I just . . . fix them up till they are runnin' again. Who can tell how many votes these fires will bring me?"

Political machines also could be found in Boston, Philadelphia, Pittsburgh, Chicago, and other cities. Although most political machines were dishonest and influenced by bribes, many immigrants wanted their help. They were glad that someone seemed to be taking their side.

REVIEW What was a cause of the formation of political machines?
Cause and Effect

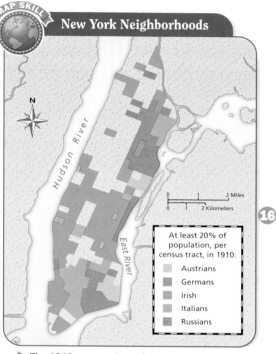

MAP SKILL — New York Neighborhoods

N

Hudson River

East River

At least 20% of population, per census tract, in 1910:
- Austrians
- Germans
- Irish
- Italians
- Russians

0 1 2 Miles
0 1 2 Kilometers

▶ The 1910 census showed that ethnic groups often settled together. This helped machine politicians gain power, because they could appeal to ethnic pride.

MAP SKILL Place *What can you determine about the speckled, tan areas of the map?*

227

Rise of Political Machines

⏱ *Quick Summary* The challenges of urban life helped lead to the growth of political machines, which used corrupt methods to build power and win support among urban residents.

13 How did political machines win the support of voters? They provided them with things they needed, such as jobs or housing. Main Idea and Details

G SOCIAL STUDIES STRAND
Government

Explain that once in power, political machines used the government to enrich themselves and their friends illegally.

14 Why did some people feel political machines were a bad influence on the cities? Possible answer: Though they helped people, the machines' goal was to use government power for their own benefit. Make Inferences

15 What do Plunkitt's words suggest about his motives in helping people? Possible answer: He helped people in order to win their votes.
Analyze Primary Sources

✓ **REVIEW ANSWER** Possible answer: Immigrants needed housing, jobs, and sanitation, but city governments were unable to fulfill all these needs.
Cause and Effect

MAP SKILL — New York Neighborhoods

16 Which ethnic group settled many of the neighborhoods near the Hudson River? Irish Interpret Maps

MAP SKILL Answer That less than 20% of the population in these areas was Austrian, German, Italian, Russian, or Irish

Up, Over, and Under

🕐 **Quick Summary** Key inventions in the 1800s made possible the creation of skyscrapers and enormous suspension bridges, and they helped change the face of the nation's cities.

17 Why did builders want to make taller buildings? Possible answer: To help the cities grow without expanding outward **Express Ideas**

18 What two factors made possible the building of tall skyscrapers? The development of affordable steel and elevators helped make skyscrapers possible. **Summarize**

S|T SOCIAL STUDIES STRAND
Science • Technology

Tell students that there were many challenges in using tall buildings, including the challenge of lifting water to higher and higher floors.

19 What challenges would you expect taller buildings to present? Possible answers: Providing fire protection, water, waste handling, and heating **Predict**

Up, Over, and Under

A city can expand by moving its limits outward, but that makes it harder to reach people with the services they need. So rather than build out, a city can build up. In the late 1800s, two things came together that made ⑰ taller buildings possible.

As you have read, the process for creating affordable steel was developed in England in the mid-1800s. With the rise of industrialization in the United States, steel was suddenly widely available. Steel is strong enough to support the weight of buildings with many floors.

▶ Otis demonstrated his safety elevator to New Yorkers in 1854.

In 1852 inventor **Elisha Graves Otis** created the first safety elevator. This elevator had brakes that would keep it from falling. He installed the first passenger elevator in a five-story department store in New York City in 1857. The stage was set. Steel and elevators would make very tall buildings, or ⑱ skyscrapers, possible.

The Great Chicago Fire had destroyed all of Chicago's downtown area in 1871, so Chicago was the perfect place to experiment with new types of buildings. The first skyscraper was built in 1885. This skyscraper, the Home Insurance Building in Chicago, was the

tallest building in the country. It was ten stories tall!

Some people doubted that tall buildings were a good idea, but people wanted and needed more space for apartments, offices, and stores. Skyscrapers soon appeared in St. Louis, New York, and Buffalo. ⑲

Steel also helped create stronger bridges. The first steel bridge was built in 1874 by **James Buchanan Eads**. It spanned the Mississippi River from Illinois to **St. Louis, Missouri**. To test the bridge for strength, fourteen trains weighing a total of 700 tons were sent across the center span. The bridge passed the test.

The world's first suspension bridge was built in Cincinnati, Ohio, in 1866. A **suspension bridge** is one that is suspended, or hung, from steel cables. The designer of this bridge, a German immigrant named **John Roebling**, was hired by leaders of New York City to create a larger version of this new type of bridge. John

▶ This building, shown being constructed in Chicago in 1894, is made strong by its steel frame.

Practice and Extend

CURRICULUM CONNECTION
Art

Create an Urban Scene

Discuss with students what images come to mind when they think of the word *city*.

- Have students create a picture of their idea of a typical city in the United States.
- Next, have students compare their pictures. What common features do the pictures have? (Examples might include tall buildings and busy streets.)

Roebling died before construction began, but his son, Washington Roebling, took over the project. When he was injured during construction, Washington's wife, Emily Roebling, completed the construction of the great bridge. The Brooklyn Bridge crossed the East River, connecting Brooklyn to the island of Manhattan. When the bridge opened in 1883, it was the longest bridge in the world.

If builders could go up, could they also go down? As the streets became more crowded, city planners and engineers began to consider underground transportation. Many cities were experimenting with ideas, but it was **Boston, Massachusetts** that built the country's first successful underground train system, or subway. Boston's electric subway system opened in 1897.

REVIEW Why was steel so important to the continued growth of cities?
Main Idea and Details

Summarize the Lesson

- **1885** The first skyscraper was built in Chicago.
- **1889** Jane Addams opened Hull House for the poor.
- **1900** New York City's population neared 3.5 million.

LESSON 2 REVIEW

Check Facts and Main Ideas

1. Cause and Effect Complete this chart by filling in one effect of each event listed below.

Cause	Effect
The population grew so fast that housing couldn't keep up with it.	People lived in crowded tenements.
Immigrants were offered help from political machines.	Immigrants voted for the candidates supported by the political machines.
Jane Addams wanted to help immigrants.	She opened Hull House.
Steel was strong enough to support great weight.	Buildings became taller, bridges became longer.

2. How did **urbanization** bring about the need for **settlement houses**? Write two or three sentences to answer the question. Be sure to use the highlighted words.

3. List three problems faced by some immigrants who moved to big cities in the late 1800s.

4. Why did political machines want to control the votes of immigrants?

5. Critical Thinking: *Draw Conclusions* You have read that immigrants faced many hardships in the big cities of the United States. Why do you think so many people continued to immigrate?

Link to —∞— **Writing**

Write a Profile As you read on page 226, many people in the 1800s wanted to make life better for people in the cities. Research a social reformer or organization that worked to improve the lives of others during this era. What problems did they try to solve? What actions did they take to make improvements? Write a profile of the reformer or organization you chose.

229

Workbook, p. 50

Lesson 2: Life in the Growing Cities

Also on Teacher Resources CD-ROM.

SOCIAL STUDIES STRAND Geography

20 **How would the ability to build longer bridges help cities to grow in size?** Possible answer: Longer bridges would help cities overcome certain natural barriers, such as rivers or bays. **Solve Problems**

21 **Why were cities interested in underground transportation?** Possible answer: To remove some of the crowding from city streets **Solve Problems**

REVIEW ANSWER Steel made it possible for cities to expand upward instead of outward. This meant that people still had access to the services provided by cities. **Main Idea and Details**

3 Close and Assess

Summarize the Lesson

Have students convert each heading in the lesson into a question and then use the answers to these questions to summarize the lesson.

LESSON 2 REVIEW

1. **Cause and Effect** For possible answers, see the reduced pupil page.

2. Possible answer: **Urbanization** brought many new people into the big cities. Many of these people were poor and had to live in tenements. People such as Jane Addams built **settlement houses** to help the poor.

3. Overcrowding, disease, prejudice

4. Controlling votes of immigrants put the political machines' candidates in office. The political machines then told the candidates what to do.

5. **Critical Thinking:** *Draw Conclusions* Possible answer: They came because there were many jobs, and because people who worked hard could become successful.

Link to —∞— **Writing**

Make sure students address the two questions in their profile of the reformer or organization.

Read Line and Circle Graphs

Objectives

- Compare and contrast the purposes of line and circle graphs.

- Describe the skill of reading line and circle graphs.

Vocabulary

line graph, p. 230; circle graph, p. 230

Resource

- Workbook, p. 51

1 Introduce and Motivate

What are line and circle graphs?
Remind students that graphs are ways of presenting types of information in a visual way. Different types of graphs are most appropriate for showing certain types of information. Have students read the **What?** section of text on p. 230.

Why use line and circle graphs?
Have students read the **Why?** section of text on pp. 230–231. Ask students which type of graph they would use if they wanted to show how the average height of students changed over time. (Answer: A line graph)

Read Line and Circle Graphs

What? Graphs show information in a visual way. A line graph can show change over time. The line graph below compares the growth of the urban population, or people living in the cities, in the United States with the country's rural population, or people living out in the country, in farming areas or small towns. The graph gives information for the years 1790 to 2000. A circle graph shows how a whole is divided into parts. It can show how different groups compare to each other in size. The circle graphs on page 231 show the percentage of people who worked in rural professions such as farming in 1900 and in 2000, as well as the percentage of those who performed jobs more likely to be found in urban areas.

Why? As you read in Lesson 2, cities in the United States grew because of immigration and urbanization. Of course people still moved to rural areas too, but by the early 1900s, urban growth was greater. A line graph like the one on this page makes it possible to see, at a glance, how the population grew in both the urban and rural areas. It lets you compare their growth rates.

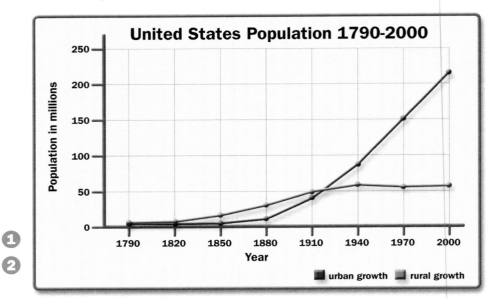

1
2

230

Practice and Extend

MEETING INDIVIDUAL NEEDS
Leveled Practice

Constructing Appropriate Graphs Have students distinguish between line and circle graphs and construct them accurately.

Easy Have students construct the appropriate graph for the numbers of girls and boys in the class. (Students should identify that a circle graph is appropriate here.) **Reteach**

On-Level Ask students to collect their own data in the class or at home and construct the proper type of graph to show those data. **Extend**

Challenge Have students collect their own data for the construction of both a circle graph and a line graph. **Enrich**

Unlike a line graph, a circle graph does not show change over time. Instead, it gives a certain view of the subject being studied at one moment in time. For example, when you look at the circle graph on the left on this page, you get a picture of how many workers in the United States in 1900 were employed in such rural occupations as farming compared with those who were employed in occupations more likely to be found in or near cities, such as manufacturing and service industries.

The circle graph on the right makes the same comparison of occupations for the year 2000.

How? When you use a line graph, look first at the title. Notice that the title of the line graph on page 230 tells you what it is about. It shows the growth in both rural and urban areas in the United States from 1790 to 2000. After you have read the title, look at the words along the axes, the lines at the edge of the graph, to see what the graph is showing. This line graph, for example, shows years along the bottom and population along the side. The dots in the middle of the graph show population in a certain year. When you connect those dots with a line, you have a line graph showing how the population has changed over time. This graph has a line showing growth of the urban population and another line showing growth of the rural population. Each is a different color to make the differences easier to identify. The graph shows that the country's urban population reached about 42 million in 1910. When did the rural population reach 55 million?

United States Labor Force

others 12%
manufacturing 19%
Farming 38%
Service Industries 31%

1900

Farming 2%
manufacturing 21%
Service Industries 77%

2000

③

To use a circle graph, first look at the title. Then read the words in the graph to learn what each section represents. In these circle graphs, each section represents a percentage of the workforce in the United States in 1900 and in 2000. You can see that the largest percentage of the labor force in 1900 worked in farming.

What occupation represented the smallest percentage of the workforce in the year 2000?

Think and Apply

① Which type of graph shows change over time? Which type shows information for only a single year?

② How many more people lived in rural areas than in urban areas in 1850?

③ How does each graph reflect the increase in improved farming technology and the rise of urbanization?

231

How is this skill used? Examine with students the graphs on pp. 230 and 231.

- Help students recognize that both of the graphs provide data in a graphic form.

- Make sure students recognize that each graph presents a different kind of data, with the circle graph showing how a whole is divided, and the line graph showing change over time.

- Have students read the **How?** section of text on p. 231.

① **What changing factors are measured in the line graph on p. 230?** Rural and urban population **Analyze Information**

② **Over what time period does the line graph provide data?** Between 1790 and 2000 **Interpret Graphs**

③ **What is the "whole" about which these circle graphs provide data?** The United States labor force
Analyze Information

3 **Close and Assess**

Think and Apply

1. Line graphs show change over time. Circle graphs show information for a certain time.

2. About 16 million

3. The line graph shows a drop in rural population. The circle graph shows a decrease in the percentage of people involved in rural occupations.

CURRICULUM CONNECTION
Math

Compute Percentages

- Tell students to look at the graph on p. 230 and write down the numbers *4 million* for urban and *1 million* for rural population in 1790. (These numbers have been rounded.)

- Have students use these numbers to calculate what percentage of the population was rural and what percentage was urban. (The total population was 5 million; 1 million divided by 5 million equals 0.20, or 20 percent. Four million divided by 5 million is 0.80, or 80 percent.)

- Have students use percentages to create circle graphs for different years.

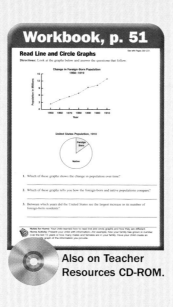

Workbook, p. 51

Read Line and Circle Graphs
Directions: Look at the graphs below and answer the questions that follow.

Change in Foreign-Born Population 1850–1910

United States Population, 1910

Foreign-Born
Native

1. Which of these graphs shows the change in population over time?

2. Which of these graphs tells you how the foreign-born and native populations compare?

3. Between which years did the United States see the largest increase in its number of foreign-born residents?

Notes for Home: Your child learned how to read line and circle graphs and how they are different.
Home Activity: Present your child with information—for example, how your family has grown in number over the last 15 years or how many males and females are in your family. Have your child create an appropriate graph of the information you provide.

Also on Teacher Resources CD-ROM.

Unequal Opportunities

Objectives

- Explain how prejudice and segregation affected people's lives.

- Relate the effect of Jim Crow laws on African Americans.

- Explain the economic and social reasons for the migration of African Americans to the North.

- Examine issues facing African Americans in the North.

- Describe the African American response to discrimination.

Vocabulary

tenant, p. 233; **enfranchise,** p. 233; **Great Migration,** p. 235

Resources

- Workbook, p. 52
- Transparency 1
- Every Student Learns Guide, pp. 90–93
- Quick Study, pp. 46–47

Quick Teaching Plan

If time is short, have students work in small groups to summarize the lesson.

- Have each group member read one to two sections of the lesson.

- Each student summarizes what he or she has read for the group.

1 Introduce and Motivate

Preview To activate prior knowledge, discuss what students know about some whites' attitudes toward African Americans in the late 1800s. Tell students they will learn more about the challenges facing minority groups as they read Lesson 3.

You Are There Ask students to predict what kinds of challenges might lie ahead for the newly freed African Americans in the late 1800s.

232 Unit 3 • Expansion and Change

LESSON 3

1875 — 1915

1877 Remaining federal troops leave the South after Reconstruction ends.

1909 NAACP is founded.

1915 Great Migration of African Americans begins.

Tuskegee

PREVIEW

Focus on the Main Idea
In the late 1800s and well into the 1900s, African Americans, along with other racial and ethnic groups, faced lives that were affected by prejudice, segregation, and unequal opportunities.

PLACES
Chicago, Illinois
Tuskegee, Alabama

PEOPLE
Jack L. Cooper
W. E. B. Du Bois
Booker T. Washington
George Washington Carver
Ida Wells-Barnett

VOCABULARY
tenant
enfranchise
Great Migration

▶ The people known as carpetbaggers often carried large traveling bags like these, which were made of carpet.

232

Unequal Opportunities

You Are There You stand with your uncle at the edge of town. The Union soldiers are leaving, and you watch the troops march by. "They're heading north," your uncle says. "They think their work is finished, but I'm not so sure."

"Well, at least those greedy carpetbaggers are leaving too," you note. "They did no one any good."

"Yes, everyone is glad to see them leave," your uncle agrees.

You watch the soldiers, wondering what will happen next. "Lots of our friends have moved away. If we stay, how will we get by?" you ask.

"Mr. Johnson has offered me a deal that sounds pretty good," your uncle tells you. "He will give us a piece of land to farm, and we just have to pay him with some of the crops."

Your family has farmed for generations, so you feel hopeful about this news. Still, you wonder how sharing crops with an owner will work.

Main Idea and Details As you read, keep in mind the main idea and supporting details that tell you more about life after Reconstruction.

Practice and Extend

READING SKILL
Main Idea and Details

In the Lesson Review, students complete a graphic organizer like the one below. You may want to provide students with a copy of Transparency 1 to complete as they read the lesson.

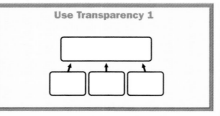

Use Transparency 1

VOCABULARY
Word Exercise

Related Word Study

Write the word *franchise* on the board. Tell students that one meaning of *franchise* is "right to vote." Then write the word *enfranchise*. Tell students the prefix *en-* means "cause to be." Therefore, *enfranchise* means or "to cause to have the right to vote." Then write *disenfranchise*. Explain that the prefix *dis-* means "opposite of" and ask students to figure out what *disenfranchise* means. (to take away someone's right to vote)

The South After Reconstruction

After Reconstruction, the South remained the poorest section of the country. It was to remain impoverished until the 1930s. Many blacks and poor whites became tenant farmers. A **tenant** is someone who pays rent to use land or buildings that belong to someone else. Most tenants make monthly payments with cash. But not everyone had cash in the 1870s. As you read in Unit 1, when a tenant pays rent with crops he or she has grown, the tenant is called a sharecropper. Sharecropping began during Reconstruction, and it lasted well into the 1940s.

At first, sharecropping had seemed to be a great bargain. It offered people a degree of independence and the ability to work for themselves, and they got to keep as much as half of the crop. But falling crop prices often meant too little income. Also, in order to buy seed and tools, sharecroppers often borrowed against future crops. People usually have to pay interest when they borrow money. Interest is a type of fee that gets paid to the lender. If interest rates were high and crops didn't get good prices, sharecroppers could be in debt after the harvest. Sharecroppers often felt trapped by debt.

The South's poverty was rooted largely in the destruction caused by the Civil War. It was worsened by the carpetbaggers of the Reconstruction era. Though many of the so-called carpetbaggers were truly concerned about the welfare of African Americans, the many dishonest ones gave a bad name to everyone who had come to help. They exploited the region and supported corrupt financial schemes.

Three institutions grew up in the South in reaction to the poverty and the involvement of the federal government. One was sharecropping. Growing cotton, tobacco, and rice required a lot of work, so there were millions of farm jobs available. In many southern states, nearly half of the population was sharecroppers.

Another institution was one-party politics. Southern Democrats soon controlled all the southern states, even states that did not have white majorities. Much as the big-city political machines had turned to immigrants for votes, Southern Democrats turned to the newly enfranchised African Americans. **Enfranchised** means having the right to vote. Once again, promises turned into election victories.

The third institution was racial segregation, which you will read about in the next section.

REVIEW What contributed to the poverty of the South after Reconstruction?
Main Idea and Details

Library of Congress

▶ The departure of Federal troops from the South marked the end of Reconstruction.

233

2 Teach and Discuss

PAGE 233

The South After Reconstruction

Quick Summary The system of sharecropping seemed to offer economic survival to many in the South in the late 1800s. Yet, poverty remained a serious problem throughout the region.

❶ Who was likely to become a tenant farmer in the post–Civil War South?
Poor whites and freed African Americans
Categorize

❷ What factor was necessary in order to make sharecropping pay off for sharecroppers? High prices for crops
Make Inferences

Problem Solving

❸ What two problems was sharecropping supposed to help solve?
The need for labor to raise crops, and the need for economic opportunity for the poor of the South Solve Problems

✓ **REVIEW ANSWER** The destruction of the war and the exploitation of the carpetbaggers contributed to the poverty of the South. Main Idea and Details

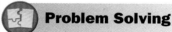

FYI SOCIAL STUDIES
Background

About Sharecropping

- Sharecropping was practiced widely in the South. In some areas, as much as 80 percent of the farmland was worked by sharecroppers.
- Sharecroppers generally had to plant what the landowner wanted them to plant—often cotton. This led to overproduction and low cotton prices.
- When sharecroppers fell into debt, as they often did, they were forced to keep working for the landowner. In this way, sharecroppers often became bound to their landowner in a system not unlike slavery.

Prejudice and Segregation

⏱ **Quick Summary** Jim Crow laws and the Supreme Court ruling in *Plessy* v. *Ferguson* helped segregate the South. Elsewhere in the nation, minority groups also faced harsh treatment.

④ Why did white southern leaders want to segregate the races? Possible answer: They meant to control African Americans and limit their political strength.
Make Inferences

✓ Ongoing Assessment

If... students do not recognize what southern whites hoped to accomplish by requiring segregation of African Americans,

then... ask them to discuss how African Americans may have felt when told that places were off-limits to them just because of their skin color.

Primary Source

Cited in "A Memorial from Representative Chinamen in America to His Excellency U. S. Grant, President of the United States of America" by Lee Ming How, et al

⑤ On what do the Chinese business leaders blame the prejudice against them? Misinformation
Analyze Primary Sources

⑥ What were two main reasons for segregationist laws and policies?
Possible answer: Fear and prejudice
Summarize

✓ **REVIEW ANSWER** Possible answer: He boarded a whites-only train car. When he was arrested, he sued the state over the legality of the segregation law.
Main Idea and Details

Prejudice and Segregation

As you read in Unit 1, Jim Crow laws passed in the 1880s made racial segregation legal in the South. Although the laws required that facilities be equal, they enforced the separation of races. Schools, train cars, ④ buses, and even cemeteries were segregated.

In 1892 Homer Plessy was chosen by a group of influential African American leaders to challenge the Jim Crow laws. He entered the whites-only section of a train car in Louisiana. Plessy was of mixed race, but he was considered black by southern law. Blacks could not be in the whites-only car, so he was arrested. Plessy sued the state. By 1896 his case had reached the United States Supreme Court. Plessy was found guilty of breaking the law. This court case made it clear that, as long as facilities for blacks and whites were equal, it was legal to keep the races separate.

African Americans were not the only group to face prejudice and segregation. In some areas, Hispanics experienced discrimination. This happened even in areas where Hispanic communities had been in place for several generations.

▶ **In the West, Chinese immigrants often faced prejudice and anger.**

234

▶ Segregation laws required that equal facilities be available for blacks and whites, but that they be separate.

Chinese immigrants in the West faced years of prejudice and violence. In the 1870s, a group of Chinese businessmen wrote to President Ulysses S. Grant, relating how badly they were being treated. They also wrote:

> *"Many charges are made against our people . . . [that are] calculated to mislead honest minds, and create unjust prejudice against us."* ⑤

In spite of this appeal, Congress passed the Chinese Exclusion Act in 1882. This law prevented immigration on the basis of race. In 1905 San Francisco established a segregated school for Chinese children, including those who were born in the United States.

Different racial or ethnic groups were segregated well into the 1900s. Often the segregation was limited to housing. For example, residential areas were sometimes closed to Jews, although these same people might be welcomed into the business community. While not everyone agreed with these policies, fear and prejudice caused many people to demand laws to protect their jobs or separate them from those who were "different." ⑥

REVIEW How did Homer Plessy challenge the Jim Crow laws? Main Idea and Details

---

Practice and Extend

❄ MEETING INDIVIDUAL NEEDS
Leveled Practice

Give a Speech Ask students to speak against the practice of segregation from the point of view of a person who is subject to it.

Easy Have students offer a brief speech explaining why they feel "separate" is not "equal." The "speech" may consist of short sentences giving the definitions of the words *separate* and *equal*. **Reteach**

On-Level Students' speeches should explain not only why "separate" is not "equal," but also how segregation makes them feel. **Extend**

Challenge Have students address why "separate" is not "equal," how segregation makes them feel, and what they think those favoring segregation are trying to accomplish. **Enrich**

For a Lesson Summary, use Quick Study, p. 46.

Great Migration

Some African Americans living in the South during the late 1800s and early 1900s began to wonder if there might be a better place to live. Was there a place with greater rights, better jobs, and good schools? Many believed this place was the North. Newspapers from northern cities told of homes and jobs for African Americans. Friends who had already moved north shared stories of greater freedom and new-found success.

 A **Chicago, Illinois,** newspaper, *The Chicago Defender,* encouraged African Americans to come to its city. This paper often listed black churches and other organizations that offered help to African Americans when they arrived. Thousands of African Americans wrote anxious letters to the churches, asking for assistance.

Between 1915 and the 1940s, more than a million African Americans moved north. This came to be called the **Great Migration.** There were many jobs available in factories in the North, especially when the United States entered World War I in 1917. You will read more about this war in the next chapter. The military needed tanks, ships, and weapons. Factories that made these items offered jobs with higher pay. African Americans hoped to fill these jobs. As northern workers left to fight the war, more and more jobs became available. Some of the open jobs went to women, but most of them went to the arriving African Americans.

REVIEW What issues led to the Great Migration? **Cause and Effect**

MAP SKILL — The Great Migration

▶ During the early 1900s, many African Americans moved to the North.

MAP SKILL *Movement In the South, African Americans lived mainly in rural areas. To what types of areas did they migrate?*

235

Great Migration

Quick Summary In the late 1800s and 1900s, millions of African Americans left the South and moved to the North.

7 **How did African Americans in the South learn about life in the North?** Possible answers: In newspapers or from friends and family members who moved there **Main Idea and Details**

Test Talk

Write Your Answer to Score High

8 **What can you infer about life in the North based on the activities of *The Chicago Defender?*** Written answers should be complete, focused, and correct. Possible answer: Life in the North did offer some opportunities for African Americans to improve their lives. **Make Inferences**

SOCIAL STUDIES STRAND
Geography

Remind students that migrations often result from "push" factors that cause people to leave and "pull" factors that draw them to their new homes.

9 **What event created the "pull" factor that drew millions of African Americans to the North during the Great Migration?** Jobs, especially after the start of World War I **Cause and Effect**

✓ **REVIEW ANSWER** Possible answer: African Americans wanted good schools, jobs, more pay, and less discrimination. **Cause and Effect**

MAP SKILL — The Great Migration

10 **Which cities were major destinations during the Great Migration?** St. Louis, Chicago, Detroit, New York City, Philadelphia, and Baltimore **Interpret Maps**

MAP SKILL Answer Urban

ESL — ACTIVATE PRIOR KNOWLEDGE
ESL Support

Describe the Challenges of Migration Help students recognize the hopes and challenges facing people who move to a new land.

Beginning Have students recall their first day of school. Then ask them to say any words they know that describe their feelings on that day. Alternatively, you could have them draw pictures that show their impressions of that first day.

Intermediate Ask students to write or say three sentences in English that describe how they felt on their first day at school.

Advanced Have students write three sentences in English about their hopes and three sentences about their fears on their first day at school.

For additional ESL support, use Every Student Learns Guide, pp. 90–93.

Life in the North

🕐 **Quick Summary** Many African Americans continued to experience discrimination in the North, yet many were able to rise above the challenges and achieve success.

⓫ What are two ways by which African Americans were segregated in the North? Possible answers: Jim Crow laws and the refusal of some white property owners to sell or rent property to African Americans **Analyze Information**

⓬ In what way was life for African Americans in the North similar to life in the South? Possible answer: African Americans were sometimes subject to discrimination and Jim Crow laws in the North, just as in the South. 🔄 **Compare and Contrast**

⓭ In what way was life for African Americans in the North different from life in the South? Possible answer: African Americans were able to find jobs in a variety of different settings, and some were able to achieve considerable success. 🔄 **Compare and Contrast**

✔ **REVIEW ANSWER** Possible answers: Many African Americans started their own businesses or found better-paying jobs. They also faced discrimination in housing, education, and job promotion. **Summarize**

This painting by Jacob Lawrence is titled *The Migrants Arrived in Great Numbers.* It shows families on the move during the Great Migration. You will read more about Lawrence in Unit 4.

The Museum of Modern Art, New York. Gift of Mrs. David M. Levy. Tempera on gesso on composition board, 12" x18".

Life in the North

Unfortunately, African Americans faced discrimination in the North as well. Some whites did not welcome their new black neighbors. Jim Crow laws were passed in many northern cities. These laws kept African Americans out of many restaurants, hotels, stores, and theaters.

⓫ Many white property owners would not rent or sell to blacks. Because of this, African American were often forced to live only in certain neighborhoods. These neighborhoods were often overcrowded. Many African American children were not allowed to attend school with white children. Although there were jobs in factories, black workers were ⓬ seldom promoted as often as white workers.

Some African Americans did find a better life in the North, however. Some started their own businesses. African Americans published newspapers such as *The Chicago Defender.* The "Perfect Eat Shop" was a restaurant in Chicago opened by Ernest Morris. **Jack L. Cooper** created his own radio show. He became the first African American disc jockey in the United States. And African Americans made a huge contribution to the development of music in the North. In addition, African Americans who worked in factories, packing-houses, steel mills, and railroad yards still earned more than most blacks living in the South. ⓭

REVIEW Summarize the experience of African Americans who moved north with the Great Migration. **Summarize**

236

Practice and Extend

CURRICULUM CONNECTION
Writing

Accessing Language
• Have students find out more about the meaning of the terms *explore* and *settle.*
• Explain that people who *explore* an area spend time looking around to discover what that place is like.
• When people *settle* in a place, they work, build homes, and stay in that area.
• Have students use what they learn and additional information from the dictionary to write meanings for *explorer* and *exploration* as well as *settler* and *settlement.*

New Leaders Arise

As had happened since before the Civil War, African American leaders spoke out against discrimination.

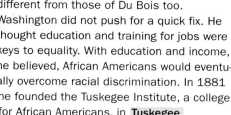

▶ W. E. B. Du Bois

W. E. B. Du Bois (doo BOYZ) was born in Massachusetts in 1868. His family had not been enslaved, and he attended school with white students. As a young man, he went to Fisk University, an African American college in Nashville. He saw how African Americans were affected by discrimination outside the college campus. He believed discrimination had to be challenged. He said, "We refuse to allow the impression to remain that African Americans assent to inferiority."

Du Bois became a successful writer and editor. In 1909 he helped to start the National Association for the Advancement of Colored People, or NAACP. The association's main goal was to bring an immediate end to racial discrimination.

Unlike Du Bois, **Booker T. Washington** had been enslaved. Washington's ideas and work for the rights of African Americans were different from those of Du Bois too. Washington did not push for a quick fix. He thought education and training for jobs were keys to equality. With education and income, he believed, African Americans would eventually overcome racial discrimination. In 1881 he founded the Tuskegee Institute, a college for African Americans, in **Tuskegee, Alabama**. In his autobiography *Up from Slavery,* Washington wrote:

> *"It is important and right that all privileges of the law be ours, but it is vastly more important that we be prepared for . . . these privileges."*

Noted African American scientist **George Washington Carver** joined him in 1896. Carver, who had also been enslaved, shared Washington's vision. He organized the school's agriculture department, and then taught and did research there for the rest of his life.

The institute changed many lives, and it soon rose to national prominence. Washington remained its president until his death in 1915. You will read more about Washington in the biography on p. 239.

REVIEW Compare and contrast the ideas of Du Bois and Washington concerning African Americans. ⟳ **Compare and Contrast**

▶ In the Tuskegee Institute printing shop, students could prepare for careers in publishing. This photograph of students at work is from 1902.

237

🕐 *Quick Summary* African American leaders offered new and sometimes competing visions of how to improve the lives of African Americans.

14 **What does Du Bois's quote imply about the basis of discrimination against African Americans?** Possible answer: Discrimination is based on the idea that African Americans are inferior to white Americans. **Make Inferences**

Primary Source
Cited in *Up From Slavery* by Booker T. Washington

15 **How would you summarize the message of Washington's quotation?** Possible answer: African Americans should be protected by the law, but they should be prepared for the privileges of the law. **Summarize**

✓ **REVIEW ANSWER** Both Du Bois and Washington sought to improve the lives of African Americans. Du Bois wanted immediate action, while Washington was willing to allow change to happen more slowly. ⟳ **Compare and Contrast**

 Decision Making

Use a Decision-Making Process

- Have students consider the following decision-making scenario: **Suppose you are weighing the views of Du Bois and Washington. You share their goal of improved rights for African Americans; however, you are unsure whose ideas are more likely to lead to success.**

- Students should use the decision-making process to decide whether to support Washington or Du Bois. For each step in the process, have students work in small groups to discuss and write about what must be considered as they make their decision. Write the steps above on the board or read them aloud.

1. **Identify a situation that requires a decision.**
2. **Gather information.**
3. **Identify options.**
4. **Predict consequences.**
5. **Take action to implement a decision.**

FYI SOCIAL STUDIES **Background**

More about Du Bois and Washington

- Washington favored training African Americans in useful job skills to help prepare them for the rights and freedoms they had gained.

- Du Bois stressed higher education for leading African Americans.

- Washington's views enjoyed more acceptance among white Americans.

- Du Bois was controversial because of his belief in Marxism.

Others Join the Fight

🕐 **Quick Summary** Du Bois and Washington were supported by a number of African American leaders.

16 Were Wells-Barnett's methods more similar to Booker T. Washington's or W. E. B. Du Bois's? Possible answer: Du Bois's, because Wells-Barnett fought for a quick end to discrimination against African Americans
↻ **Compare and Contrast**

✓ **REVIEW ANSWER** Possible answer: She started a newspaper, worked for voting rights for women, and fought a segregation law. **Main Idea and Details**

**Close and Assess**

Summarize the Lesson

Tell students to examine the vertical time line and to provide an "effect" for each of the "causes" that appear there.

✓ **LESSON 3** **REVIEW**

1. **Main Idea and Details** For possible answers, see the reduced pupil page.

2. Crop prices were often too low for them to earn enough money to pay off their debts.

3. Many faced discrimination and segregation in the North. They got jobs, but could not always get promoted as quickly as whites.

4. Possible answers: Du Bois wrote and helped start the NAACP. Washington founded a school to help African Americans. Wells-Barnett started a newspaper and fought segregation.

5. **Critical Thinking: Make Generalizations** Possible answers: When they moved North with the Great Migration, African Americans might have hoped to avoid discrimination and poverty, and to gain an education and work skills.

Link to ∞ Mathematics

47 days—752 divided by 16

238 Unit 3 • Expansion and Change

Others Join the Fight

Men and women of many races and backgrounds joined the fight for equality. There was much at stake for many groups. **Ida Wells-Barnett** was born in 1862 in Mississippi, the daughter of slaves. Wells-Barnett went to Chicago in 1893, where she helped start an African American newspaper. She also started one of the first organizations to seek voting

▶ Ida Wells-Barnett told her story in an autobiography called *Crusade for Justice.*

rights for African American women. She fought—and won—a battle against the passage of a state law that would have segregated blacks and whites on trains and buses in Illinois.

16

REVIEW What actions taken by Ida Wells-Barnett support the main idea that she was a fighter against discrimination? Main Idea and Details

Summarize the Lesson

— **1877** The remaining federal troops left the South after Reconstruction.

— **1909** The National Association for the Advancement of Colored People was founded.

— **1915** The Great Migration of African Americans began.

LESSON 3 **REVIEW**

Check Facts and Main Ideas

1. Main Idea and Details Complete the chart below by filling in three details that support the main idea that Jim Crow laws led to segregation.

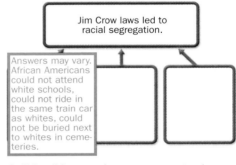

Jim Crow laws led to racial segregation.

Answers may vary. African Americans could not attend white schools, could not ride in the same train car as whites, could not be buried next to whites in cemeteries.

2. Why did most sharecroppers stay in debt?

3. What issues did African Americans face in the North?

4. What are some of the ways in which African American leaders responded to discrimination?

5. Critical Thinking: *Make Generalizations* Describe some of the hopes African Americans might have had when they moved North during the **Great Migration.** Use the highlighted term in your answer.

Link to ∞ Mathematics

Plan a Trip Suppose a family from Atlanta moves to Chicago during the Great Migration. The distance is 752 miles. They travel by wagon at 16 miles a day. How many days will it take?

238

Practice and Extend

 CURRICULUM CONNECTION Art

Design a Masthead

Show students examples of mastheads from modern newspapers. Have students design a masthead for an African American newspaper. Student designs should incorporate the name of their newspaper and images or slogans that would be meaningful to African Americans living in the early 1900s.

Workbook, p. 52

Also on Teacher Resources CD-ROM.

BIOGRAPHY

Booker T. Washington
1856–1915

Booker T. Washington was born into slavery on a Virginia plantation. Because he was enslaved, he did not go to school, but he remembered carrying the schoolbooks of the young white mistress of the plantation when she went. Going to school, he thought, must be like going to paradise. **1**

After emancipation, Washington's family moved to West Virginia to work in the coal mines. Washington never lost his desire for an education, and in 1872 he attended Hampton Institute, a school for former slaves. Going to school simply increased his love of education and his belief that education and character building were the keys to equality.

BIOFACT

Booker T. Washington was the first African-American to ever dine at the White House with the President.

Top Hat, TUIN 888
National Park Service, Museum Managent Program and Tuskegee Institute National Historic Site

In 1881 he moved to Tuskegee, Alabama, and founded the Tuskegee Institute. The institute started as a teacher's college. It offered the state's first nursing program. Soon it added instruction in other trades. Students not only studied, they also built their own buildings and grew their own food. They sold their products to the white community nearby.

Washington became a well-respected African American leader. He started educational institutions throughout the South, encouraged African American businesses, and advised American Presidents. He taught that equal rights could be gained through education, hard work, and understanding. He said: **2**

> *"Success is to be measured not so much by the position that one has reached in life as by the obstacles which he has overcome."*

Learn from Biographies
How did Booker T. Washington's early life affect his feelings about the way equal rights should be gained?

For more information, go to *Meet the People* at **www.sfsocialstudies.com.**

239

BIOGRAPHY

Booker T. Washington

Objective
- Identify contributions of significant individuals during the early 1900s, such as Booker T. Washington.

1 Introduce and Motivate

Preview Ask students to recall what they have read about Booker T. Washington on p. 237. Explain that they will now read about some of Washington's early experiences.

2 Teach and Discuss

1 When did Washington first discover his love of education? While still enslaved, he had the job of carrying a white girl's schoolbooks.
Main Idea and Details

2 What were some of the obstacles that Washington overcame in his career? Possible answers: Being enslaved, poverty, not having an early education **Summarize**

3 Close and Assess

Learn from Biographies Answer
Washington learned early to love education and to work hard for goals.

WEB SITE
Technology

Students can find out more about Booker T. Washington by clicking on *Meet the People* at **www.sfsocialstudies.com.**

CURRICULUM CONNECTION
Literature

Booker T. Washington

The Story of Booker T. Washington, by Patricia C. McKissack and Fredrick McKissack (Children's Press, ISBN 0-516-04758-2, 1991) **Easy**

Booker T. Washington, by Don Troy (Child's World, ISBN 1-567-66556-X, 1999) **On-Level**

Booker T. Washington: Educator, Alan Schroeder (Chelsea House Publishing, ISBN 0-791-00252-7, 1992) **Challenge**

Women's Rights

Objectives

- Describe the effects of the women's suffrage movement.

- Relate the rights and educational opportunities gained for women.

- Explain the role of Susan B. Anthony in the suffrage movement.

Vocabulary

suffrage, p. 242; **suffragist,** p. 242; **Nineteenth Amendment,** p. 243

Resources

- Workbook, p. 53
- Transparency 10
- Every Student Learns Guide, pp. 94–97
- Quick Study, pp. 48–49

Quick Teaching Plan

If time is short, have students create outlines of the lesson.

- As students read the lesson independently, have them list the main idea for each section.

- Under each main idea, ask students to list two to three supporting details.

1 Introduce and Motivate

Preview To activate prior knowledge, ask students to recall what opportunities men and women have in our society today. Tell students that the privileges and opportunities people have today are based in part on a debate over men's and women's roles that has been going on throughout history. Students will learn about one chapter in this debate as they read Lesson 4.

You Are There Ask students why the scene described might have been unusual or notable in the early 1900s. Tell students that in this section, they will read about how the attitude toward women in public life began to change in the United States.

240 Unit 3 • Expansion and Change

1840

1848 Seneca Falls Convention is held.

1869 The Territory of Wyoming leads the nation in giving women the vote.

1887 First woman mayor is elected in Argonia, Kansas.

1920

1919 Nineteenth Amendment is passed.

PREVIEW

Focus on the Main Idea
Women hoped to benefit from the spirit of reform that began in the mid-1800s.

PLACES
Seneca Falls, New York
Argonia, Kansas

PEOPLE
Lucretia Mott
Elizabeth Cady Stanton
Lucy Stone
Susannah Medora Salter
Susan B. Anthony
Carrie Chapman Catt

VOCABULARY
suffrage
suffragist
Nineteenth Amendment

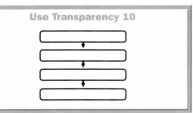

240

Women's Rights

You Are There

The city street is crowded with men and women. All eyes are focused on a speaker who is standing in the back of a wagon. You look up at your mother as she speaks to the crowd. It is spring 1912.

"We only demand what is rightfully ours!" your mother shouts. She wears a long white skirt, a white blouse, and a hat covered in bows. She also wears a banner reading "Votes for Women!"

Around the wagon are other women. Some wave American flags. Some have babies with them. The baby carriages are covered in red, white, and blue.

"Aren't you proud of your mother?" asks a woman near you. You nod. You are very proud. You have come with her to this rally to demand the right for women to vote. Many women out West already have this right. Surely, someday soon, all American women will be able to vote!

Sequence As you read, be aware of the sequence of events that led to increased rights for women.

Practice and Extend

READING SKILL
Sequence

In the Lesson Review, students complete a graphic organizer like the one below. You may want to provide students with a copy of Transparency 10 to complete as they read the lesson.

Use Transparency 10

VOCABULARY
Word Exercise

Context Clues

Explain that not all words that look similar are related. Students can use context to help them determine if a meaning they have predicted is a possibility. For example, *suffrage* looks a lot like *suffer*. However, in the lesson, people want suffrage, so *suffering* doesn't make sense. Tell students that they should always rely on context to let them know when predictions don't fit. Then they can turn to a dictionary or glossary.

Women's Roles in the 1800s

Why were women rallying for the right to vote in 1912? Though other rights for women were increasing, most women still could not vote.

Women's roles changed dramatically during the 1800s. Women were still expected to care for the house and children. Before the rise of industrialization, women spun yarn, wove cloth, hand made all clothes, and produced necessities such as butter and soap. As more goods became available, much of this work became unnecessary. In rural areas, life changed more slowly. But as you have read, mail-order catalogs soon made goods available there too.

Some women worked outside the home as teachers or factory workers, and many in the cities worked as maids or housekeepers. But few women were allowed to pursue the same careers as men.

This was less true in rural areas. Pioneer couples had to work together to survive.

Almost nothing was considered purely "men's work." Women helped work the crops, tended livestock, and chopped wood. Some hunted. Pioneer women had fewer comforts than city women, but they were more nearly equal to men in work and rights.

▶ In rural areas, women often had equal rights and equal work.

As new inventions for both housework and farm work became available, people's lives changed even more. Many city women had free time for visiting and shopping. As a result, the first department stores were opened, often with tea rooms. Some women who had been housekeepers now found jobs in these new stores.

REVIEW During the 1800s, why were rural women more nearly equal to men in work and rights? Draw Conclusions

▶ Because of new inventions, women gained time for leisure activities, often for the first time in their lives. In urban areas, women might use this time to shop or have tea with friends.

241

2 Teach and Discuss

PAGE 241

Women's Roles in the 1800s

🕐 *Quick Summary* The role of women began a dramatic change in the 1800s, as industrialization made consumer goods available and reduced the need for household labor.

Test Talk

Locate Key Words in the Text

1 **What event was largely responsible for the changes in women's roles in the 1800s?** Ask students whether the answer is right there or whether they have to think and search for it. Industrialization was a major cause of the change in women's roles. Main Idea and Details

C SOCIAL STUDIES STRAND
Culture

Prejudice Reduction Tell students that ways of living in the United States have always varied based on location, the type of work people do, and other factors.

2 **How did women's roles vary based on location in the 1800s?** Possible answer: In rural areas, women's roles were more similar to men's roles. In more urban areas, men and women had very different roles. Evaluate

✓ **REVIEW ANSWER** In rural areas, everyone had to work in order to ensure survival, and women often did the same work as men. Draw Conclusions

Women Work for More Rights

 Quick Summary The movement to reform women's roles gathered force in the 1800s and eventually began to focus on voting rights as a key goal.

⭐ **SOCIAL STUDIES STRAND**
Citizenship

Democratic Values and Institutions
Remind students that women had been fighting for equal rights for many years, but they still were not allowed to vote.

3 **What do Stanton's words imply about the equality of men and women at the time of her speech?** Possible answer: Women were not recognized as equal to men at that time.
Analyze Primary Sources

4 **What can you infer about public opinion toward women's rights based on the negative press coverage of the convention?** Possible answer: Many people did not support the idea of women's rights. *Make Inferences*

5 **What was it about the Fifteenth Amendment that amazed suffragists?** It ensured the vote for African American men but not for women.
Main Idea and Details

Primary Source
Cited in *The Quotable Woman*, by Elaine Partnow, ed.

6 **What does Anthony's quotation suggest about men and their ability to represent women's interests?** Possible answer: Anthony did not believe men would ever be able to fully represent women's interests.
Analyze Primary Sources

Women Work for More Rights

Women in the United States enjoyed the freedom and protection offered by citizenship. But in the 1800s their opportunities and rights did not equal those of men. Colleges were closed to women. Married women did not have the right to own property. The social and legal status of women was not equal to that of men. Many women wanted to participate in the reform movements of the day, including abolition and temperance. The temperance movement was trying to stop the widespread abuse of alcohol. But involvement in reforms was off limits for women.

In 1848 women's rights leaders **Lucretia Mott** and **Elizabeth Cady Stanton** invited interested women and men to gather in **Seneca Falls, New York,** to discuss women's rights. At the Seneca Falls Convention, Stanton stated, "Woman is man's equal, was intended to be so by the Creator, and . . . she should be recognized as such." **3**

Issues discussed at the convention included education and jobs. The most controversial issue was whether women should

▶ **Elizabeth Cady Stanton (left) and Lucretia Mott called a convention to discuss women's rights.**

be able to vote. Almost half of the people at the convention were against this idea. Stanton and abolitionist Frederick Douglass were determined that it be included as a goal. Much of the press criticized the convention. Stanton thought the reports would at least get people thinking about the issues. **4**

After the Civil War, the passage of the Fifteenth Amendment gave newly freed African American men the right to vote. Women were amazed that the new law had not included them. Women's rights leaders now felt that gaining the right to vote was their most important goal. Another term for the right to vote is **suffrage,** which is why people working for women's voting rights were called **suffragists.** Suffragist **Lucy Stone** founded the American Woman Suffrage Association at this time. This organization supported the Fifteenth Amendment and worked for women's suffrage as well. **5**

As you read, women came closer to having equality in rural areas, and it was in rural areas that they first got the vote. In 1869, the Territory of Wyoming led the nation in giving women the vote. Kansas allowed women to vote in local elections, and in 1887 the small town of **Argonia, Kansas,** elected **Susannah Medora Salter** mayor. She was the first woman mayor in the United States.

Susan B. Anthony's fight for women's rights began in the mid-1800s and continued until her death in 1906. As you will read in her biography on page 245, Anthony traveled and lectured on women's suffrage. Anthony said:

> *"There will never be complete equality until women themselves help to make laws and elect lawmakers."* **6**

Practice and Extend

ESL **BUILD BACKGROUND**
ESL Support

Discuss Women's Voting Rights

Beginning Have students state whether women are allowed to vote in their country of origin.

Intermediate Ask students to complete this sentence: "The right to vote is important because. . . ."

Advanced Tell students to write a sentence that explains why women's suffrage is necessary.

For additional ESL support, use Every Student Learns Guide, pp. 94–97.

FYI **SOCIAL STUDIES**
Background

About the Seneca Falls Convention

- Mott and Stanton called the convention after Mott was not allowed to take part fully in an antislavery convention in London, England.

- The convention issued a "Declaration of Sentiments" based on the Declaration of Independence and containing the words: "We hold these truths to be self-evident: that all men and women are created equal."

Another suffragist leader in the early 1900s was Carrie Chapman Catt. Catt was a teacher in Iowa when she became involved in the suffrage movement. At first she worked locally in her home state. She then began traveling, writing, and speaking to promote women's suffrage.

Catt's goal was to get Congress and the states to pass an amendment to the Constitution that would give women the right to vote. Catt felt certain of victory. She said:

> *"When a just cause reaches its flood tide . . . whatever stands in its way must fall before its overwhelming power."*

REVIEW When did women's suffrage become the most important goal for women's rights leaders? Sequence

▶ **Women lined up to vote after the passage of the Nineteenth Amendment.**

The Nineteenth Amendment

By 1912 many states had approved a woman's right to vote. These included Colorado, Idaho, Kansas, Utah, Oregon, and Arizona. However, it would take the Congress of the United States to make voting legal for women throughout the country. ⑧

World War I helped strengthen the cause of women's suffrage. As men went into the armed forces, women replaced them in the workforce. Women performed jobs they had never done before, such as repairing automobiles and driving buses. Women worked in factories producing weapons. About 11,000 women joined the women's branch of the United States Navy, which had never before allowed women to serve in its ranks. If women could do all this, they argued, they should be allowed to vote! ⑨

Even though Congress was made up entirely of men, women had successfully made their case. In 1919 Congress passed the Nineteenth Amendment to the Constitution. It stated:

> *"The right of citizens to vote shall be denied or abridged [limited] by the United States or by any state on account of [the] sex [of a person.]"* ⑩

In August 1920, the states ratified the amendment, and it became law.

REVIEW How did World War I help the suffragists' cause? Cause and Effect

243

Primary Source
Cited in a speech by Carrie Chapman, "Is Woman Suffrage Progressing?", Stockholm, 1911

⑦ **How would you summarize Catt's words?** Possible answer: The cause of women's suffrage will eventually become so popular that its opponents will be unable to resist it.
Analyze Primary Sources

✓ **REVIEW ANSWER** After the Civil War
Sequence

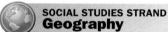

The Nineteenth Amendment

🕐 **Quick Summary** World War I strengthened the cause of women's suffrage. The Nineteenth Amendment to the Constitution, which gave women the right to vote, was ratified in 1920.

🌐 **SOCIAL STUDIES STRAND**
Geography

⑧ **What generalization can you make about the location of the earliest states to approve women's suffrage?** Possible answer: They were all located in the western part of the United States.
Generalize

⑨ **How did World War I affect the debate over women's suffrage?** Possible answer: It helped women demonstrate their ability to contribute in all levels of society. **Summarize**

Primary Source
Cited in the Nineteenth Amendment of the United States Constitution

⑩ **Why do you think the Nineteenth Amendment includes the words "denied or abridged," and not just "denied"?** Possible answer: To prevent states from allowing women to vote by limiting (abridging) their power in some other way
Analyze Primary Sources

✓ **REVIEW ANSWER** World War I provided opportunities for women to work and to serve in the Navy. This participation supported the argument that women should be allowed to vote.
Cause and Effect

Other Opportunities

Quick Summary While women were trying to win the vote, they were also winning new opportunities in a variety of fields—and accomplishing many great deeds.

11 **What resulted from the new availability of college education for women?** Women had new opportunities in careers. Cause and Effect

✓ **REVIEW ANSWER** Possible answer: Women had opportunities in education and careers, including politics. Main Idea and Details

3 Close and Assess

Summarize the Lesson

Tell students to examine the vertical time line. For each item, have students write one sentence to explain the significance of the event.

✓ **LESSON 4** **REVIEW**

1. **Sequence** For possible answers, see the reduced pupil page.

2. Suffragists wanted women to have the right to vote. Suffrage became more important because the Fifteenth Amendment only gave the vote to African American men and not to women.

3. She traveled for 30 years, lecturing on women's suffrage.

4. Women had more opportunities for education, jobs, and even exploration, and they gained the right to vote.

5. **Critical Thinking: *Evaluate*** Possible answers: Women had more time to think about such things. As life improved in some areas, they wanted it to improve in all areas.

Students' posters should show changes in the home and in the community.

Other Opportunities

In the late 1800s, many colleges opened to women students. Soon women worked as professors too. Women pursued new careers, including politics.

Some women wanted even greater adventures. Annie Smith Peck was a university professor before she became a mountain climber. She climbed mountains all over the world. In 1906 she reached the top of Peru's Mount Huascaran, the tallest peak in the Western Hemisphere. She was 60 years old!

▶ By the late 1800s, women were graduating from colleges.

Delia Akeley was an African explorer. Marguerite Harrison, a journalist, became a spy during World War I. Louise Arner Boyd was an Arctic explorer. The whole world was now open to women.

REVIEW What new opportunities opened for women in the late 1800s and early 1900s? Main Idea and Details

Summarize the Lesson

- **1848** The Seneca Falls Convention was held.
- **1869** The Territory of Wyoming led the nation in giving women the right to vote.
- **1887** The first woman mayor was elected in Argonia, Kansas.
- **1919** The Nineteenth Amendment was passed.

LESSON 4 REVIEW

Check Facts and Main Ideas

1. **Sequence** Redraw this chart on a separate sheet of paper, putting the events in their correct order.

Congress approves the right to vote for all American women.

↓

African American men get the right to vote.

↓

The Seneca Falls Convention proposes equality for women.

↓

Susannah Medora Salter is the first woman in the United States to be elected mayor.

Seneca Falls Convention, African American men get vote, Salter first woman mayor, Congress approves vote for all American women

2. What was the goal of the **suffragists**? Why did **suffrage** become more important to women's rights leaders after the passage of the Fifteenth Amendment?

3. How did **Susan B. Anthony** contribute to the cause of women's rights?

4. What rights and opportunities did women gain during the late 1800s and early 1900s?

5. **Critical Thinking: *Evaluate*** How do you think the work-saving tools mentioned at the beginning of this lesson, along with the way they changed people's lives, might have contributed to women having greater interest in equal rights?

Link to **Art**

Create a Poster Illustrate a poster to show how women's lives changed during the late 1800s and early 1900s.

244

Practice and Extend

FYI **SOCIAL STUDIES Background**

Firsts for Women The early 1900s was a time of many "firsts" for women.

- 1900—first time women compete in the Olympic Games
- 1916—Montana's Jeannette Rankin becomes the first woman to serve in the United States Congress.
- 1925—Nellie Tayloe Ross of Wyoming becomes the first woman governor in the United States.
- 1928—Aviator Amelia Earhart becomes the first woman to complete a transcontinental flight.

Workbook, p. 53

Lesson 4: Women's Rights

Directions: Using information from this lesson, circle the term in parentheses that best completes each sentence.

1. In the 1800s, women's opportunities and rights (did, did not) equal those of men.

2. In 1848, women's rights leaders Lucretia Mott and Elizabeth Cady Stanton invited people to gather in (Seneca Falls, New York, Argonia, Kansas) to discuss women's rights.

3. The most controversial idea of the convention was that women should be able to (vote, own property).

4. Suffragist (Lucy Stone, Carrie Chapman Catt) founded the American Woman Suffrage Association in 1890.

5. Women came closer to having equality in (urban, rural) areas.

6. The first woman mayor in the United States was (Susannah Medora Salter, Susan B. Anthony).

7. (Susan B. Anthony, Marguerite Harrison), who worked for women's rights until her death in 1906, said that "There will never be complete equality until women themselves help to make laws and elect lawmakers."

8. By 1912, (many, no) states had approved a woman's right to vote.

9. World War I helped (strengthen, weaken) the cause of women's suffrage.

10. In 1919, Congress passed the (Nineteenth, Fifteenth) Amendment, which gave women the right to vote.

Notes for Home: Your child learned about the changes in women's roles and rights in the 1800s and early 1900s.
Home Activity: With your child, look at a newspaper or magazine and note every time you see a story that shows women holding a job, political office, or other position of authority.

💿 **Also on Teacher Resources CD-ROM.**

Susan B. Anthony
1820–1906

As a teenager and young woman, Susan B. Anthony taught school. Yet she felt there was other work that needed her efforts. She saw injustice around her. African Americans were enslaved. Some laws prevented women from having the same rights as men.

In 1849 Anthony began to campaign for social reform. These reforms included the abolition of slavery and the promotion of women's rights. In 1850 she met Elizabeth Cady Stanton, who became her friend and partner in the fight for justice.

After slavery was abolished at the end of the Civil War, Anthony turned her energies toward working to gain the right to vote for women. It was to be a long, hard struggle. Newspaper articles attacked her. This did not deter Anthony. She believed the cause could not fail.

Anthony and Stanton traveled, gave speeches, and helped form suffrage groups across the country. They founded the National Woman Suffrage Association. In 1872 Anthony took a step few women dared to take. She voted illegally in her hometown of Rochester, New York. She was arrested and fined $100.

BIOFACT
Anthony was the first woman to appear on United States currency. The Susan B. Anthony dollar coin first appeared in 1979.

Anthony died in 1906, before women gained the right to vote. Her work, however, helped make the passage of the Nineteenth Amendment a reality. Of the future of women's rights, she said:

> *"The woman of the twentieth century will be the peer [equal] of man."*

Learn from Biographies

How do you think Susan B. Anthony's voting, arrest, and fine might have affected the cause of women's suffrage?

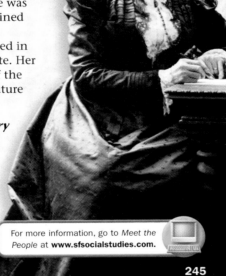

For more information, go to *Meet the People* at **www.sfsocialstudies.com.**

245

★ BIOGRAPHY ★

Susan B. Anthony

Objective

- Describe the accomplishments of significant leaders in the women's rights movement, such as Susan B. Anthony.

1 Introduce and Motivate

Preview To activate prior knowledge, ask students to recall what they have just read about the history of the women's rights movement in the United States. Tell students that they will read about Susan B. Anthony, a notable leader of this cause.

2 Teach and Discuss

1 What cause besides women's rights did Anthony work for? The abolition of slavery **Main Idea and Details**

2 Why do you think Anthony chose to break the law and get arrested? Possible answer: She felt the laws were wrong and wanted to call attention to them. **Hypothesize**

3 Close and Assess

Learn from Biographies Answer

Possible answer: It angered her opponents but it also inspired others to sacrifice as much as she had sacrificed.

CURRICULUM CONNECTION
Literature

Susan B. Anthony

America in the Time of Susan B. Anthony, by Sally Senzell Isaacs (Heinemann Library, ISBN 1-575-72941-5, 2002) **Easy**

Failure Is Impossible: The Story of Susan B. Anthony, by Lisa Frederiksen Bohannon (Morgan Reynolds, ISBN 1-883-84677-3, 2001) **On-Level**

Susan B. Anthony: And Justice for All, by Jeanne Gehret (Verbal Images Press, ISBN 0-962-51368-7, 2003) **Challenge**

WEB SITE
Technology

Students can find out more about Susan B. Anthony by clicking on *Meet the People* at **www.sfsocialstudies.com.**

Resources

- Assessment Book, pp. 29–32
- Workbook, p. 54: Vocabulary Review

Chapter Summary

For possible answers, see the reduced pupil page.

Vocabulary

1. c, **2.** d, **3.** e, **4.** b, **5.** a

People and Terms

Possible answers:

1. With a new threshing machine, a farmer could separate grain from stalks much faster than by hand.

2. Cyrus McCormick created a reaper to help farmers cut their crops faster and easier.

3. Richard Sears helped found a successful mail-order company.

4. Jane Addams felt she had a responsibility to help poor immigrants in Chicago.

5. With his writings and photographs, Jacob Riis showed the conditions faced by immigrants.

6. A political machine offered favors to immigrants in exchange for votes.

7. John Roebling designed the Brooklyn Bridge.

8. Booker T. Washington believed that job training would help African Americans obtain equality.

9. Susan B. Anthony traveled around the United States lecturing on women's suffrage.

10. The Nineteenth Amendment gave all women the right to vote.

Facts and Main Ideas

1. Their inventions made it possible to milk more than one cow at once and to separate cream more quickly.

2. The Great Migration was the movement of African Americans from the South to the North between 1915 and the 1940s.

3. Industrialization made many products available that women once had to make themselves. This allowed time for other activities, such as education.

1830   **1850**   **1870**

1834
Cyrus McCormick invents a mechanical reaper.

1848
Seneca Falls Convention is held.

1869
Territory of Wyoming leads the nation in giving women the vote.

Chapter Summary

Compare and Contrast

Target Skill

On a separate sheet of paper, copy the graphic organizer to compare and contrast the United States before and after the beginning of the Industrial Revolution of the 1800s.

Before Industrial Revolution began	After Industrial Revolution began

Possible answers might include:

Before– people lived in the country, manual labor, few goods available

After– people moved to cities, work done by machines, catalogs made more goods available

Vocabulary

Match each word with the correct definition or description.

1. **mechanization** (p.217)
2. **urbanization** (p. 224)
3. **settlement house** (p. 226)
4. **enfranchised** (p. 233)
5. **suffragist** (p. 242)

a. person working for women's voting rights

b. having the right to vote

c. use of machines to do work

d. movement of people from rural to urban areas

e. a center that provides help for the poor

People and Terms

Write a sentence explaining the importance of each of the following people or terms in the changing United States. You may use two or more in a single sentence.

1. **threshing machine** (p. 217)
2. **Cyrus McCormick** (p. 217)
3. **Richard Sears** (p. 218)
4. **Jane Addams** (p. 226)
5. **Jacob Riis** (p. 226)
6. **political machine** (p. 227)
7. **John Roebling** (p. 228)
8. **Booker T. Washington** (p. 237)
9. **Susan B. Anthony** (p. 242)
10. **Nineteenth Amendment** (p. 243)

Practice and Extend

Assessment Options

✓ Chapter 5 Assessment

- Chapter 5 Content Test: Use Assessment Book, pp. 29–30.
- Chapter 5 Skills Test: Use Assessment Book, pp. 31–32.

Standardized Test Prep

- Chapter 5 Tests contain standardized test format.

✓ Chapter 5 Performance Assessment

- Assign small groups one of the following topics: science and technology, politics and government, business, and education and social services.
- Have groups use information from the chapter to create a summary of developments in their topic. Groups should prepare a presentation of their findings for the class.
- Have one member of each group present the group's summary.
- Assess students' understanding of their topic area.

1879
First electric power station opens in San Francisco.

1885
First skyscraper is built in Chicago.

1889
Jane Addams opens Hull House for the poor.

1915
Great Migration of African Americans begins.

1919
Nineteenth Amendment is passed.

Facts and Main Ideas

❶ How did the inventions of L. O. Colvin and Gustav de Laval help farmers?

❷ What was the Great Migration?

❸ How did industrialization contribute to changes in women's roles?

❹ **Time Line** How many years were there between the time Wyoming gave women the vote and the passage of the Nineteenth Amendment?

❺ **Main Idea** Name two or three inventions from the late 1800s and describe how they changed the way people lived.

❻ **Main Idea** What were the main problems faced by big cities in the late 1800s?

❼ **Main Idea** Identify two or three of the difficulties African Americans faced in the late 1800s and into the 1900s?

❽ **Main Idea** What were some of the ways women worked to gain suffrage?

❾ **Critical Thinking:** *Draw Conclusions* In 1916, many African Americans moved from the South to the North. In what ways was their experience similar to that of immigrants from other countries? In what ways do you think their experience was different?

Internet Activity

To get help with vocabulary, people, and terms, select dictionary or encyclopedia from *Social Studies Library* at **www.sfsocialstudies.com**.

Apply Skills

Read Line and Circle Graphs

Look back at the graphs on pages 230 and 231. Use them to answer the following questions.

❶ How many more people lived in urban areas than in rural areas in 1970?

❷ Which careers did most workers hold in the year 1900? in the year 2000?

❸ If you were to make a graph comparing the kinds of jobs people in different areas of the United States held in the present year, which type of graph would you use and why?

Write About History

❶ **Write a letter** to a friend describing a new invention from the late 1800s. Explain how it will change the way people live.

❷ **Write an editorial** trying to convince people that women should have the right to vote.

❸ **Write a story** about an immigrant family who has just arrived in the United States. Describe their home, workplace, and other experiences.

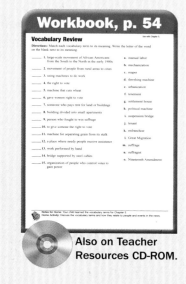

247

Hands-on Unit Project

✓ Unit 3 Performance Assessment

• See p. 288 for more information about using the Unit Project as a means of performance assessment.

• A scoring guide is provided on p. 288.

WEB SITE
Technology

For more information, students can select the dictionary or encyclopedia from *Social Studies Library* at **www.sfsocialstudies.com**.

Workbook, p. 54

Vocabulary Review

Directions: Match each vocabulary term to its meaning. Write the letter of the word on the blank next to its meaning.

_____ 1. large-scale movement of African Americans from the South to the North in the early 1900s

_____ 2. movement of people from rural areas to cities

_____ 3. using machines to do work

_____ 4. the right to vote

_____ 5. machine that cuts wheat

_____ 6. gave women right to vote

_____ 7. someone who pays rent for land or buildings

_____ 8. building divided into small apartments

_____ 9. person who fought to win suffrage

_____ 10. to give someone the right to vote

_____ 11. machine for separating grain from its stalk

_____ 12. a place where needy people receive assistance

_____ 13. work performed by hand

_____ 14. bridge supported by steel cables

_____ 15. organization of people who control votes to gain power

a. manual labor
b. mechanization
c. reaper
d. threshing machine
e. urbanization
f. tenement
g. settlement house
h. political machine
i. suspension bridge
j. tenant
k. enfranchise
l. Great Migration
m. suffrage
n. suffragist
n. Nineteenth Amendment

Notes for Home: Your child learned the vocabulary terms for Chapter 5.
Home Activity: Discuss the vocabulary terms and how they relate to people and events in the news.

Also on Teacher Resources CD-ROM.

---

4. About 50 years

5. Possible answers: Mechanical reapers and threshers changed farmers' lives. Now they could farm more land and grow cash crops. Telephones made it easier for people to communicate. Elevators made skyscrapers possible.

6. Cities were overcrowded, dirty, and noisy. Traffic was bad, and there was increasing violence.

7. In some cases they were not allowed to vote, they could not hold many of the jobs whites held, they were segregated in many places, and sometimes they were the target of racial violence.

8. Women held rallies, gave speeches, went door to door with fliers, formed suffrage organizations, and wrote letters, articles, and books.

9. Similar: African Americans and immigrants both faced distrust and discrimination in jobs and housing. Different: African Americans spoke English and many immigrants did not. African Americans may have understood the American culture better than many immigrants. Some immigrants may have had better educations than the average African American.

Apply Skills

1. About 96 million

2. Farming, 1900; service industries such as sales, education, trade, and others, 2000

3. A circle graph, because it shows how a whole is divided into parts

Write About History

1. Tell students that their letter should describe the invention and its effects on their lives.

2. Tell students that newspaper editorials take a clear position on a topic or issue and argue for that position.

3. Encourage students to include colorful details that help bring the story to life.

Chapter Planning Guide

Chapter 6 • Becoming a World Power

Locating Time and Place pp. 248–249

Lesson Titles	Pacing	Main Ideas
Lesson 1 **Expanding Overseas** pp. 250–258		• By the end of the 1800s, the United States had gained new territory and became a world power.
Biography: Theodore Roosevelt p. 259	5 days	• Theodore Roosevelt used his role as governor and later as President to preserve the environment and to help people who could not protect themselves.
Thinking Skills: Credibility of a Source pp. 260–261		• It is important to evaluate the credibility of information by considering the author's background and purpose.
Lesson 2 **The Progressive Movement** pp. 262–267		• Reformers worked to improve conditions in the United States during the early years of the industrial age.
Research and Writing Skills: Interpret Political Cartoons pp. 268–269	4 days	• A political cartoon is a drawing of people or news events, often designed to make people laugh but also to make them think about the topic.
⭐ **Citizen Heroes:** (Responsibility) **Investigating and Sharing the Truth** pp. 270–271		• In spite of obstacles, Ida Tarbell became a journalist and worked hard to live up to her responsibility to the public.
Lesson 3 **World War I** pp. 272–280		• When it appeared the United States might be in danger, the country became involved in World War I.
📖 **War in the Air** p. 281	4 days	• Although airplanes were a new invention when World War I began, people soon discovered many uses for them as the war progressed.
✓ **Chapter 6 Review** pp. 282–283		

✓ = Assessment Options

Vocabulary	Resources	Meeting Individual Needs
yellow journalism Spanish-American War Rough Riders Buffalo Soldiers isthmus source credible	• Workbook, p. 56 • Transparency 21 • Every Student Learns Guide, pp. 98–101 • Quick Study, pp. 50–51 • Workbook, p. 57	• ESL Support, TE pp. 253, 257 • Leveled Practice, TE p. 254
trust Progressives muckraker Blue Laws conservation political cartoon	• Workbook, p. 58 • Transparency 14 • Every Student Learns Guide, pp. 102–105 • Quick Study, pp. 52–53 • Workbook, p. 59	• ESL Support, TE p. 264 • Leveled Practice, TE p. 265
World War I nationalism alliance isolationism League of Nations Treaty of Versailles	• Workbook, p. 60 • Transparency 14 • Every Student Learns Guide, pp. 106–109 • Quick Study, pp. 54–55 • Workbook, p. 61	• ESL Support, TE p. 273 • Leveled Practice, TE p. 276

	✓ Chapter 6 Content Test,
	  Assessment Book,
	  pp. 33–34
	✓ Chapter 6 Skills Test,
	  Assessment Book,
	  pp. 35–36
		✓ Chapter 6 Performance
		  Assessment, TE p. 282

Providing More Depth

Additional Resources

- Vocabulary Workbook and Cards
- Social Studies Plus! pp. 86–91
- Daily Activity Bank
- Big Book Atlas
- Student Atlas
- Outline Maps
- Desk Maps

 Technology

- AudioText
- MindPoint® Quiz Show CD-ROM
- ExamView® Test Bank CD-ROM
- Teacher Resources CD-ROM
- Map Resources CD-ROM
- SFSuccessNet: iText (Pupil Edition online), iTE (Teacher's Edition online), Online Planner
- **www.sfsocialstudies.com** (Biographies, news, references, maps, and activities)

 To establish guidelines for your students' safe and responsible use of the Internet, use the Scott Foresman Internet Guide.

Additional Internet Links

To find out more about:
- the Spanish-American War, search this term at **www.loc.gov**
- the Progressive Era, click on "Jump Back in Time" at **www.americaslibrary.gov**
- World War I, search under "Great War" at **www.pbs.org**

Key Internet Search Terms
- imperialism
- Theodore Roosevelt
- World War I
- Woodrow Wilson

Workbook Support

Use the following Workbook pages to support content and skills development as you teach Chapter 6. You can also view and print Workbook pages from the Teacher Resources CD-ROM.

Workbook, p. 55

Vocabulary Preview

Use with Chapter 6.

Directions: Choose the vocabulary word from Chapter 6 that best completes each sentence. Write the word on the line provided. You may use your textbook.

1. Theodore Roosevelt organized the **Rough Riders** to fight in Cuba.
2. The **Treaty of Versailles** heavily punished the Germans for their role in World War I.
3. In an effort to control people's behavior, leaders passed **Blue Laws**
4. Because of its **alliance** with Belgium, Great Britain entered World War I.
5. **Yellow journalism**, or exaggerated reporting, whipped up public anger against Spain.
6. Upton Sinclair was a well-known **muckraker** who uncovered the truth about meat packing plants.
7. The United States never joined President Wilson's **League of Nations**
8. The United States emerged from the **Spanish-American War** as a world power.
9. The **Buffalo Soldiers** fought Native Americans before fighting in Cuba.
10. John Muir encouraged **conservation** of the nation's scenic places.
11. The United States planned to build the canal at the **Isthmus** of Panama.
12. The **Progressive** Era was dedicated to reform.
13. Standard Oil was a powerful **trust** of the late 1800s.
14. **Nationalism** was a contributing factor in World War I.
15. The great conflict that swept Europe starting in 1914 was called **World War I**
16. One reason the United States did not enter World War I at first was a strong feeling of **isolationism** in the country.

 Notes for Home: Your child learned the vocabulary terms for Chapter 6.
Home Activity: Make flip cards to quiz your child on the meaning of these terms.

Use with Pupil Edition, p. 248

Workbook, p. 56

Lesson 1: Expanding Overseas

Use with Pages 250–258.

Directions: Using information from this lesson, circle the term in parentheses that best completes each sentence.

1. William Seward sought to expand the territory of the United States through the purchase of (Alaska, Hawaii).
2. Alaska proved to be a valuable addition to the United States after the discovery of (salmon, gold).
3. American planters in Hawaii wanted the United States to (free, annex) the islands.
4. Many people in the United States were (pleased, angered) by Spain's reaction to the Cuban revolution of 1895.
5. The destruction of the *Maine* and yellow journalism reports about it helped tip public opinion (in favor of, against) war with Spain.
6. Commodore George Dewey led the attack on the Spanish Fleet in (the Philippines, Cuba).
7. Theodore Roosevelt helped organize a force known as the (Buffalo Soldiers, Rough Riders).
8. The Spanish-American War showed that the United States was a (powerful, weak) nation.
9. Theodore Roosevelt emerged from the war as a (villian, hero).
10. (Mosquitoes, The Panamanian people) were a major obstacle to building the Panama Canal.

 Notes for Home: Your child learned about the emergence of the United States as a major world power.
Home Activity: With your child, review a newspaper or Internet news site for stories about the United States and its role in international affairs today.

Use with Pupil Edition, p. 258

Workbook, p. 57

Credibility of a Source

Use with Pages 260–261.

Some sources of information are more believable than others. This is due, in part, to who is presenting the information.

Directions: Read the two passages about General George Armstrong Custer and answer the questions that follow.

Passage A comes from a historical novel. The story is presented as a part-fact, part-fiction presentation of Custer's journal. As you read the words, imagine them to be directly from Custer, himself.

Perhaps I have worshiped my superiors too well with not enough thought of myself. [My wife,] Libbie, says that I have always been too hasty in putting the needs of others ahead of my own.

Passage B comes from a biography. It is based on fact. At times the author includes a personal point of view or conclusion, as well as reports from others who were involved in the actual situation.

What [Custer] did was perfectly in keeping with his nature. He did what he had always done: push ahead, disregard orders, start a fight. . . .

So he marched his men most of the night and flung them into battle when—as a number of Native Americans noted—they were so tired their legs shook when they dismounted.

1. According to Passage A, how did Custer treat his superiors? According to Passage B?

    Passage A says Custer worshiped his superiors. Passage B states that he disregarded orders.

2. According to Passage A, how did Custer treat others, in general? According to Passage B?

    Passage A says Custer put the needs of others ahead of his own. Passage B states that he marched his men into battle when they were too tired to fight.

3. Which passage has more credibility? Why?

    Possible answer: Passage B is more credible because it is based on fact and contains information from actual participants in the events. Passage A is based only partially on fact.

 Notes for Home: Your child learned how to determine the credibility of a source.
Home Activity: With your child, brainstorm various sources of information and discuss the credibility of each.

Use with Pupil Edition, p. 261

Workbook, p. 58

Lesson 2: The Progressive Movement

Use with Pages 262–267.

Directions: Answer the following questions on the lines provided. You may use your textbook.

1. What kinds of problems did the growth of industry create in the United States?
    Many factories were unhealthy and unsafe places to work. Many employed children. Many caused pollution.

2. What were trusts?
    Trusts were combinations of different companies that joined together to control an entire industry. They were considered harmful because they limited competition.

3. Who were the Progressives and what were their goals?
    Progressives were reformers who wanted to change what they saw as unfair or corrupt practices in business and government.

4. Who were the muckrakers and how did they get their name?
    Muckrakers were writers who exposed problems in industry. They got their name because they exposed the "muck" in American business.

5. Who was John Muir, and what role did he play in the Progressive Movement?
    Muir was a writer who helped inspire government efforts to conserve and protect many of the nation's natural resources.

 Notes for Home: Your child learned about the key individuals and issues of the Progressive Movement in the United States.
Home Activity: Discuss the word *Progressive* and what it means. Talk with your child about whether there is a continuing need for Progressive-type activities in the United States.

Use with Pupil Edition, p. 267

Workbook, p. 59

Interpret Political Cartoons

Use with Pages 268–269.

A political cartoon is a drawing that shows people or events in the news in a way that makes you smile or laugh. The goal of political cartoons is to make you think about events.

Directions: Use this cartoon about women's rights to answer the questions below.

1. Where do the women appear in this cartoon? What are they doing? Why do you think the cartoonist portrayed these characters as she did?

    On top of the world; Fighting together; Possible answer: To show that women have gained power and now are in control of the world

2. What do you think the signs in the cartoon represent?
    Possible answer: The causes for which the women are fighting

3. In this cartoon, men are being pushed off the world. What do you think this means?
    Possible answer: Women have gained power and no longer need men.

4. A woman named Laura Foster drew this political cartoon. How do you think she felt about women's rights? Explain.

    Possible answer: I think she supported women's rights because her cartoon shows women on top of the world and in control.

 Notes for Home: Your child learned how to interpret political cartoons.
Home Activity: With your child, look through recent newspapers or magazines to find a political cartoon. Discuss the cartoon's message and the cartoonist's point of view.

Use with Pupil Edition, p. 269

Workbook, p. 60

Lesson 3: World War I

Use with Pages 272–280.

Directions: Complete the chart with information from this lesson. You may use your textbook.

Cause	Effect
Competition, rising nationalism in Europe	Increased tension in Europe, formation of alliances
Trench warfare and use of new weapons, such as poison gas	Casualty figures rise shockingly
United States pursues policy of isolationism	**United States stays out of the war at first**
United States enters the fighting	**Tide on the battlefield turns against Central Powers**
Some in United States fear the League of Nations would draw the United States into future conflicts	United States does not join League of Nations

Notes for Home: Your child learned about the causes and events of World War I.
Home Activity: Read a newspaper article about an armed conflict taking place in the world today. Discuss the terrible sacrifices that war requires of the people involved.

Use with Pupil Edition, p. 280

Workbook Support

Workbook, p. 61

Directions: Suppose that you are a pilot during World War I. Write a diary entry in which you describe your flying gear, your aircraft, and your experiences as you fly over enemy territory.

Use with Page 281.

Students' diary entries should accurately reflect information from the time period.

Use with Pupil Edition, p. 281

Workbook, p. 62

Vocabulary Review

Use with Chapter 6.

Directions: Use each of the vocabulary terms from Chapter 6 in a sentence. Write the sentences on the lines provided. You may use your glossary.

Rough Riders	yellow journalism	Spanish-American War	Progressive
Treaty of Versailles	muckrakers	Buffalo Soldiers	trust
Blue Laws	League of Nations	conservation	nationalism
alliance		isthmus	isolationism
			World War I

1. **Sentences will vary. Students should use each**
2. **vocabulary term correctly.**
3. _____
4. _____
5. _____
6. _____
7. _____
8. _____
9. _____
10. _____
11. _____
12. _____
13. _____
14. _____
15. _____
16. _____

Use with Pupil Edition, p. 283

Workbook, p. 63

UNIT 3 Project Arts and Letters

Create an infomercial about an important invention. Form a group, choose an invention studied in this unit, and research the invention.

1. The invention we chose is _____

2. Below is some information about the invention. The ✔ shows my role in the infomercial.

   ___ **Business or product representative:** Describe the invention and its history. Then describe the inventor and why he or she made the invention.

   ___ **Satisfied customer:** Tell about your experience with the invention and why you recommend it.

   ___ **Local resident or official:** Tell how the invention is different from other products and how it has helped people and made their lives easier.

Instruct students to write their scripts on a separate sheet or on index cards.

✔ Checklist for Students
___ We chose an invention from the unit.
___ We found information about our invention.
___ We wrote a script for our infomercial.
___ We made a poster or banner to use in our infomercial.
___ We presented our infomercial to the class.

Use with Pupil Edition, p. 288

Use these Assessment Book pages and the ExamView® Test Bank CD-ROM to assess content and skills in Chapter 6 and Unit 3. You can also view and print Assessment Book pages from the Teacher Resources CD–ROM.

Assessment Book, p. 33

Chapter 6 Test

Part 1: Content Test

Directions: Fill in the circle next to the correct answer.

Lesson Objective (1:1)

1. Which of the following did NOT come under United States control in the late 1800s?
   - Ⓐ Puerto Rico
   - Ⓑ Alaska
   - ● Cuba
   - Ⓓ Hawaii

Lesson Objective (1:2)

2. What eventually drew settlers to areas of Alaska?
   - Ⓐ large cities
   - Ⓑ war
   - ● gold
   - Ⓓ farmland

Lesson Objective (1:3)

3. Yellow journalism helped contribute to the start of the Spanish-American War by
   - ● inflaming public opinion in the United States against Spain.
   - Ⓑ providing an accurate and thorough record of events in Cuba.
   - Ⓒ uncovering the truth about what happened to the *Maine*.
   - Ⓓ forcing the Spanish to negotiate.

Lesson Objective (1:4)

4. Which of the following was NOT a result of the Spanish-American War?
   - ● The United States was no longer viewed as a powerful nation.
   - Ⓑ Theodore Roosevelt became a national hero.
   - Ⓒ The United States gained control of Puerto Rico, the Philippines, and Guam.
   - Ⓓ The United States proved that it was a powerful nation.

Lesson Objective (2:1)

5. Which of the following is NOT a reform that occurred during the Roosevelt presidency?
   - Ⓐ the Meat Inspection Act
   - ● the end of income tax
   - Ⓒ the Pure Food and Drug Act
   - Ⓓ improvement of education for children

Lesson Objective (2:1)

6. Why was Roosevelt convinced that he must break up trusts?
   - Ⓐ Trusts weren't making enough money.
   - Ⓑ He was afraid of Progressives.
   - Ⓒ He felt leaders of trusts would eventually drive him from office.
   - ● Trusts were driving out competition and charging unfair prices.

Lesson Objective (2:2)

7. Who is the muckraker who wrote a series of articles about the dangers of trusts?
   - Ⓐ John Muir
   - Ⓑ Upton Sinclair
   - ● Ida Tarbell
   - Ⓓ Theodore Roosevelt

Lesson Objective (2:2)

8. With what is Progressive Upton Sinclair credited?
   - ● writing a novel called *The Jungle* that told about conditions in the meatpacking plants of Chicago
   - Ⓑ signing various reform acts and speaking out against trusts
   - Ⓒ writing a series of articles about coal mining
   - Ⓓ creating Blue Laws

Use with Pupil Edition, p. 282

Assessment Book, p. 34

Lesson Objective (2:3)

9. Which of the following is NOT one of the ways in which the Progressive Movement changed workplaces?
   - Ⓐ Coal mines were inspected.
   - Ⓑ Building codes made factories safer.
   - Ⓒ Young children were kept from working in factories.
   - ● Children could work in factories as long as they attended school.

Lesson Objective (2:4)

10. Which of the following was NOT one of the accomplishments of Progressives?
    - Ⓐ income tax
    - Ⓑ larger companies
    - Ⓒ Blue Laws
    - Ⓓ building codes

Lesson Objective (3:1)

11. Which of the following was NOT one of the factors that helped set the stage for the outbreak of World War I?
    - Ⓐ growing nationalism in Europe
    - Ⓑ competition between the nations of Europe
    - Ⓒ alliances among different nations of Europe
    - ● isolationism among the nations of Europe

Lesson Objective (3:1)

12. During World War I, what did the countries of Great Britain, France, Russia, Serbia, and Belgium become known as?
    - Ⓐ the Central Alliance
    - ● the Allied Powers
    - Ⓒ the Central Powers
    - Ⓓ the European Alliance

Lesson Objective (3:2)

13. Which is NOT one of the reasons why the United States decided to break its policy of isolationism and enter World War I?
    - Ⓐ A German submarine sank the British steamship *Lusitania* and killed more than 100 U.S. citizens.
    - Ⓑ Germany promised to help Mexico get back lands it had lost to the United States.
    - ● Immigrants in the United States were born in some of the countries that were fighting the war.
    - Ⓓ German submarines sank three American-owned trade ships.

Lesson Objective (3:3)

14. What is one example of the way in which new technologies in World War I changed the way battles were fought?
    - Ⓐ Soldiers dug trenches.
    - Ⓑ Soldiers traveled by sea.
    - Ⓒ Guns were used regularly in battle.
    - ● Airplanes became a weapon of war.

Lesson Objective (3:4)

15. Which is NOT a true statement about the impact of World War I in the United States?
    - Ⓐ Some women went to work in factories to take over jobs men had done.
    - ● Most Americans argued against the war and refused to support the war effort in any way.
    - Ⓒ The government set up a Food Administration to encourage people to eat less and send food to soldiers.
    - Ⓓ People started growing food in "war gardens" to send to soldiers fighting overseas.

Use with Pupil Edition, p. 282

Assessment Book, p. 35

Part 2: Skills Test

Directions: Use complete sentences to answer questions 1–5. Use a separate sheet of paper if you need more space.

1. What was the effect of the Spanish-American War on the United States and its place in the world? **Cause and Effect**

   The United States emerged from the Spanish-American War as a major world power.

2. Summarize the actions of the United States throughout World War I. **Summarize**

   The United States originally chose to avoid involvement in World War I. German attacks on shipping and attempts to draw Mexico into the conflict finally led the United States to join the war. Once involved in the fighting, the United States helped turn the tide and bring victory to the Allies.

3. Complete the chart below. Compare and contrast the U.S. acquisition of Hawaii and Alaska. **Compare and Contrast**

Alike	Different
Possible answers: Alike: Both were lands far from the United States. Many people in the United States wanted to control them because both held promise of valuable resources.	Alaska's resources were largely unknown, while Hawaii was already being used by Americans. Hawaii somewhat resisted the United States takeover, whereas Alaska was acquired through agreement with its owner.

Use with Pupil Edition, p. 282

Assessment Book, p. 36

4. Suppose you are living in the United States during the Theodore Roosevelt era. You don't know much about the activities of the Progressives and want to gather background information about them. Which of the following sources is probably most credible for this purpose? For what might the other sources be useful? Explain your reasoning on the lines that follow. **Credibility of a Source**

   A piece by the owner of a large company that must now follow new rules.

   A news article by a reporter who is looking at only facts.

   A letter by a factory worker whose work conditions have improved as a result of the Progressives.

   The news article that presents only the facts would probably be the best source of general information about the Progressives. The other pieces would be useful in presenting different views on the activities of the Progressives, but they probably wouldn't present the facts as clearly. The personal experiences of each writer would affect the information in each piece.

5. What is a political cartoon? Write your answer on the lines provided. Then, in the space below, draw a political cartoon that tries to get people thinking about the problems of industrial society in the early 1900s. Think about what details you might include in your cartoon in order to make your point. **Interpret Political Cartoons**

   Students should understand that a political cartoon is a drawing that shows people or events in the news in a way that often makes people smile or laugh.

   Students' drawings will vary.

Use with Pupil Edition, p. 282

Assessment Support

Assessment Book, p. 37

Unit 3 Test
Part 1: Content Test

Directions: Fill in the circle next to the correct answer.

Lesson Objective (5–1:1)

1. In general, how did the spread of farm mechanization affect the size of farms in the United States?
   - ● It made them larger.
   - Ⓑ It made them smaller.
   - Ⓒ It had no effect.
   - Ⓓ It made some smaller and some larger.

Lesson Objective (5–1:2)

2. How did manufacturers help make it possible for rural residents to acquire manufactured goods?
   - Ⓐ They sent out salespeople.
   - Ⓑ They organized regular bus trips to urban shopping districts.
   - ● They developed mail-order catalogs.
   - Ⓓ They installed telephones.

Lesson Objective (5–2:1)

3. Which of the following was a major factor in causing urban populations to grow in the United States in the late 1800s and early 1900s?
   - Ⓐ war with Spain
   - Ⓑ Progressive reforms
   - Ⓒ rural depression
   - ● immigration

Lesson Objective (5–2:3)

4. Which was a result of population and technological changes in urban areas in the late 1800s?
   - Ⓐ There was less pollution.
   - ● There was more garbage, waste, and disease.
   - Ⓒ There were too few workers.
   - Ⓓ People moved away from cities.

Lesson Objective (5–3:1)

5. In the late 1800s and early 1900s, racial segregation
   - Ⓐ had largely been wiped out in the United States.
   - Ⓑ affected only African Americans.
   - ● affected a number of minority groups, including the Chinese and African Americans.
   - Ⓓ was declared unconstitutional by the Supreme Court.

Lesson Objective (5–3:4)

6. Which answer most closely represents what African Americans found in the North during the Great Migration?
   - Ⓐ many jobs and much fairer treatment
   - Ⓑ no jobs but social equality
   - Ⓒ much worse conditions than they had faced in the South
   - ● better job opportunities but continued discrimination and segregation

Lesson Objective (5–4:1)

7. What was the main purpose of the women's suffrage movement?
   - Ⓐ to get women elected to Congress
   - ● to get voting rights for women
   - Ⓒ to get people to take inventions by women seriously
   - Ⓓ to get women the right to work on farms

Use with Pupil Edition, p. 286

Assessment Book, p. 38

Lesson Objective (5–4:2)

8. In general, women had their earliest success in winning voting rights in rural areas of the West because
   - Ⓐ few men lived there.
   - Ⓑ more African Americans lived in these areas than urban areas.
   - Ⓒ few immigrants lived in rural areas.
   - ● women enjoyed more overall equality in these areas.

Lesson Objective (6–1:1)

9. This was considered to be a useless, frozen wasteland until gold was discovered there in the late 1800s.
   - ● Alaska
   - Ⓑ Hawaii
   - Ⓒ Guam
   - Ⓓ Cuba

Lesson Objective (6–1:4)

10. Theodore Roosevelt emerged from the Spanish-American War as
    - Ⓐ a wounded soldier.
    - ● a national hero.
    - Ⓒ President of the United States.
    - Ⓓ an honorary Buffalo Soldier.

Lesson Objective (6–2:1)

11. Which of the following is a reform that occurred during the Roosevelt presidency?
    - Ⓐ less powerful laws for companies that produce food
    - ● the breakup of trusts
    - Ⓒ the end of income tax
    - Ⓓ the strengthening of oil companies

Lesson Objective (6–2:2)

12. With what is Progressive Ida Tarbell credited?
    - ● writing a series of articles about the dangers of trusts
    - Ⓑ creating Blue Laws
    - Ⓒ changing child labor laws
    - Ⓓ writing a novel about dangerous practices in the meatpacking industry

Lesson Objective (6–2:3)

13. Which of the following was NOT considered an achievement of the Progressives?
    - Ⓐ Blue Laws
    - Ⓑ breaking up of trusts
    - Ⓒ laws to ensure pure food and medicine
    - ● building the Panama Canal

Lesson Objective (6–3:1)

14. Which of the following countries was NOT a member of the Allied Powers?
    - ● Germany
    - Ⓑ Great Britain
    - Ⓒ Serbia
    - Ⓓ Russia

Lesson Objective (6–3:3)

15. When United States troops entered World War I, what effect did they have on the war?
    - Ⓐ The Central Powers became energized.
    - Ⓑ There was more trench warfare.
    - ● The Allied Powers quickly gained a military advantage.
    - Ⓓ The Germans decided to use poison gas for the first time.

Use with Pupil Edition, p. 286

Assessment Book, p. 39

Part 2: Skills Test

Directions: Use complete sentences to answer questions 1–5. Use a separate sheet of paper if you need more space.

1. If you wanted to show how the entire United States population was divided into different racial groups, which would be better: a line graph or a circle graph? Explain your answer. **Compare Line and Circle Graphs**

   A circle graph would be the better choice. Circle graphs show how a whole is divided into different parts.

2. Complete the chart below. Compare and contrast the role of women of the 1800s before and after industrialization. What changed? What stayed the same? **Compare and Contrast**

   Before Industrialization   **After Industrialization**

   Women produced most household goods themselves. | **Women had no voting rights.** | **Many women could now purchase household goods.**

Use with Pupil Edition, p. 286

Assessment Book, p. 40

3. Write the following events in the order in which they took place. **Sequence**

   The Panama Canal is built.

   Spain is defeated.

   Hawaii is annexed.

   Theodore Roosevelt becomes President.

   Alaska is purchased.

   1. Alaska is purchased. 2. Hawaii is annexed. 3. Spain is defeated. 4. Theodore Roosevelt becomes President. 5. The Panama Canal is built.

4. Which of the following is most likely the more credible source: A newspaper story that is based on "unnamed sources" or one that provides several sources, all of whom tell the same story. Explain your answer. **Determine Credibility of a Source**

   Possible answer: The more credible source is the one that names its sources and gives more than one of them. Naming sources allows you and others to check into the story. And, having several sources, each with the same story, increases the likelihood that the story is true.

5. Explain the purpose of a political cartoon. In the space provided, draw a rough cartoon that shows how Progressives viewed large companies during the Roosevelt era.

   Students should understand that the goal of a political cartoon is to get people to think about a person, event, or idea in a new way.

   Students' drawings will vary.

Use with Pupil Edition, p. 286

Chapter 6 Outline

Resources

- Workbook, p. 55: Vocabulary Preview
- Vocabulary Cards
- Social Studies Plus!

1914, Panama Canal: Lesson 1

This picture shows a boat passing through the Panama Canal. Ask students what the photograph shows about transportation and engineering in the early 1900s. (Possible answer: In the early 1900s, transportation possibilities were expanding.)

1908, Grand Canyon National Monument: Lesson 2

Have students note what this photograph shows about the Grand Canyon. Ask students to suggest words that might describe the Grand Canyon. (Possible answers: majestic, deep, wild, interesting, a national treasure)

1919, Versailles, France: Lesson 3

Ask students to describe what they see in this photograph. What are the people doing? (Possible answer: The people in this photograph are signing a document.)

1914

Panama Canal
The Panama Canal connects the Atlantic and Pacific oceans.

Lesson 1

1

1908

Grand Canyon National Monument
President Theodore Roosevelt protects the Grand Canyon from developers.

Lesson 2

2

1919

Versailles, France
Allied leaders meet in Versailles, France, to draw up a peace treaty to end World War I.

Lesson 3

3

248

Practice and Extend

Vocabulary Preview

- Use Workbook p. 55 to help students preview the vocabulary words in this chapter.
- Use Vocabulary Cards to preview key concept words in this chapter.

Workbook, p. 55

Vocabulary Preview

Directions: Choose the vocabulary word from Chapter 6 that best completes each sentence. Write the word on the line provided. You may use your textbook.

1. Theodore Roosevelt organized the _____ to fight in Cuba.
2. The _____ heavily punished the Germans for their role in World War I.
3. In an effort to control people's behavior, leaders passed _____.
4. Because of its _____ with Belgium, Great Britain entered World War I.
5. _____, or exaggerated reporting, whipped up public anger against Spain.
6. Upton Sinclair was a well-known _____ who uncovered the truth about meat packing plants.
7. The United States never passed President Wilson's _____.
8. The United States emerged from the _____ as a world power.
9. The _____ fought Native Americans before fighting in Cuba.
10. John Muir encouraged _____ of the nation's scenic places.
11. The United States planned to build the canal at the _____ of Panama.
12. The _____ Era was dedicated to reform.
13. Standard Oil was a powerful _____ of the late 1800s.
14. _____ was a contributing factor in World War I.
15. The great conflict that swept Europe starting in 1914 was called _____.
16. One reason the United States did not enter World War I at first was a strong feeling of _____ in the country.

Notes for Home: Your child learned the vocabulary terms for Chapter 6.
Home Activity: Make flip cards to quiz your child on the meaning of these terms.

Also on Teacher Resources CD-ROM.

Locating Time and Place

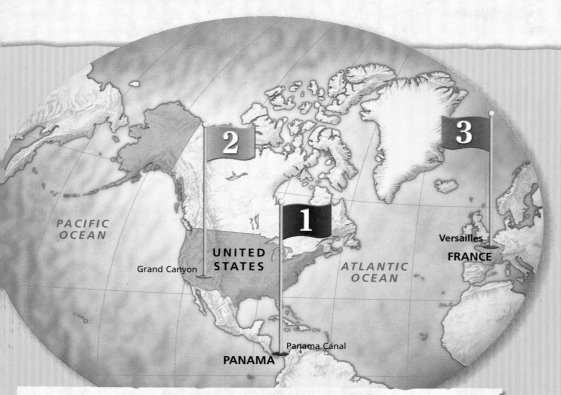

PACIFIC OCEAN

2

3

1

Grand Canyon

UNITED STATES

ATLANTIC OCEAN

Versailles

FRANCE

Panama Canal

PANAMA

Why We Remember

The United States continued to expand, gaining new lands and becoming involved outside its borders. As the country grew, so did its challenges. In the late 1800s, the rapid growth of industry created problems for people and cities. Some industries were dirty or unsafe, and sometimes both. A few businesses were not fair to other companies. Many people worked to stop these abuses. With problems to solve at home, most Americans felt that the United States did not need to get involved in the problems of other countries. Attacks on U.S. ships and citizens changed that, however. The United States found it could no longer remain isolated. In the early 1900s, the nation was drawn into war overseas.

249

Locating Time and Place

- Have students examine the pictures shown on p. 248 for Lessons 1, 2, and 3.

- Remind students that each picture is coded with both a number and a color to link it to a place on the map on p. 249.

Why We Remember

Have students read the "Why We Remember" paragraph on p. 249, and ask them why events in this chapter might be important to them. Have students identify possible reasons for the involvement of the United States in the problems and issues of other countries. Elicit that while reading this chapter, students may compare and contrast the reasons that the United States entered World War I with the reasons for entering more recent conflicts.

WEB SITE
Technology

You can learn more about the Panama Canal; the Grand Canyon National Monument; and Versailles, France, by clicking on *Atlas* at **www.sfsocialstudies.com.**

SOCIAL STUDIES
Background

Other Key Events of the Late 1800s–Early 1900s

- 1885—The Statue of Liberty, France's gift to the United States, arrives in New York.
- 1896—United States Supreme Court issues ruling in *Plessy* v. *Ferguson,* establishing constitutionality of "separate but equal."
- 1900—The first radio transmission of human speech is accomplished.
- 1906—San Francisco is heavily damaged by an earthquake.
- 1912—Arizona and New Mexico become states.

Expanding Overseas

Objectives

- Discuss the expansion of U.S. territories during the late 1800s.
- Analyze settlement patterns and movement of people after the Civil War.
- Explain the causes and events of the Spanish-American War.
- Explain the results of the Spanish-American War.

Vocabulary

yellow journalism, p. 253;
Spanish-American War, p. 253;
Rough Riders, p. 254;
Buffalo Soldiers, p. 254;
isthmus, p. 256

Resources

- Workbook, p. 56
- Transparency 21
- Every Student Learns Guide, pp. 98–101
- Quick Study, pp. 50–51

Quick Teaching Plan

If time is short, have students write the headings *Cause* and *Effect* at the top of a sheet of paper.

- Have students write down causes and effects from each section of the lesson as they read the lesson independently.

1 Introduce and Motivate

Preview To activate prior knowledge, ask students to think about the place of the United States in the world compared to such countries as Great Britain and France in the 1700s and early 1800s. Tell students that in this lesson, they will read about how the United States first emerged as a world power.

You Are There Have students predict whether the purchase of Alaska will prove to be a "good deal" for the United States.

LESSON 1

Panama Canal

1865			1915

1867 The United States buys Alaska from Russia.

July 1898 Hawaii is annexed by the United States.

August 1898 Spanish-American War ends with U.S. victory.

1914 Panama Canal opens.

PREVIEW

Focus on the Main Idea
By the end of the 1800s, the United States had gained new territory and became a world power.

PLACES
Hawaii
Puerto Rico
Cuba
Panama Canal

PEOPLE
William Seward
Liliuokalani
Theodore Roosevelt
Walter Reed
John Stevens

VOCABULARY
yellow journalism
Spanish-American War
Rough Riders
Buffalo Soldiers
isthmus

▶ Alaska is beautiful, rugged, and cold. It is also bigger than Texas, California, and Montana combined.

Expanding Overseas

You Are There   It is March 1867. Your father and mother have gone out to dinner. As they left, they were talking about a place called Alaska, but you don't know what they are discussing. You pick up your father's newspaper to learn more, and you read that:

- Russia has offered to sell Alaska to the United States for $7.2 million, which works out to about two cents an acre.
- Several thousand people live in Alaska—most are native Inuit people; some are Russian.
- There are reports that the land is rich in resources such as timber, coal, and fish.

You think it sounds like a good deal. But how will Congress vote on this sale?

Cause and Effect As you read, note the causes of the actions of individuals or countries.

250

Practice and Extend

READING SKILL
Cause and Effect

In the Lesson Review, students complete a graphic organizer like the one below. You may want to provide students with a copy of Transparency 21 to complete as they read the lesson.

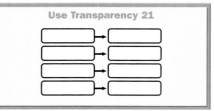

Use Transparency 21

VOCABULARY
Word Exercise

Individual Word Study

Students may not know what *yellow* in *yellow journalism* means. Tell them that two New York newspapers were competing for readers. One of them began printing a comic strip with a character named The Yellow Kid. Soon the other newspaper began printing a comic strip about a second Yellow Kid. Both papers were also printing many exaggerated stories. Because of the Yellow Kids, people began referring to exaggerated stories as *yellow journalism*.

Alaska

It seemed an incredible bargain—land for two cents an acre! Why was it for sale? Russia had claimed Alaska since 1741. As Canadian and American settlement closed in around Alaska, Russians worried that they might lose the land, so they offered to sell it. But many Americans opposed the deal. Hadn't the Civil War cost the country too much?

William Seward had been interested in Alaska since before the Civil War. He was the secretary of state for Abraham Lincoln and had continued in that job with President Andrew Johnson. Seward wanted to see the United States grow. Alaska was so large that it would increase the size of the United States by nearly 20 percent. Seward also believed that Alaska's fishing, fur trade, and mining were valuable.

The Civil War had interrupted Seward's plans. In 1866 the Russians began dis-

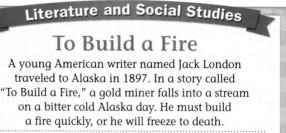
▶ **William Seward**

cussions again. The terms of the sale were approved by Russia on March 30, 1867. The United States would buy Alaska for $7.2 million in gold. The United States Senate approved the purchase in April 1867 and the House of Representatives approved it the next year.

At first, newspapers attacked Seward. They called the new territory "Seward's Icebox" and "Seward's Folly" (foolish act or silly idea). But Alaska's value would soon be recognized.

Gold had been discovered in Alaska as early as 1861, but new discoveries at Juneau (1880), Nome (1898), and Fairbanks (1903) brought fortune seekers north. Fishing became increasingly important to Alaska's economy. In 1878 Alaska's first salmon cannery was built. This was the beginning of what has become the largest salmon industry in the world.

In 1906 Alaska sent its first elected representative to Congress, though this delegate could not vote on laws. Alaska had an elected legislature by 1912. This was the beginning of the road to statehood.

REVIEW Contrast people's feelings about the purchase of Alaska before and after the discovery of gold.
↪ **Compare and Contrast**

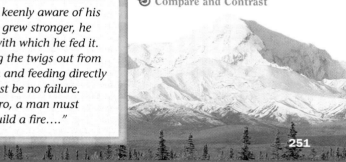

251

Decision Making

Use a Decision-Making Process

- Have students consider the following decision-making scenario: **You are a member of Congress considering the proposal to buy Alaska. You recognize the possible benefits of the purchase. But you also know the nation faces an expensive rebuilding task after the Civil War.**

- Students should use the decision-making process to decide whether or not to vote for the Alaska purchase. For each step in the process, have students work in small groups to discuss and write about what must be considered as they make their decision. Write the steps above on the board or read them aloud.

1. Identify a situation that requires a decision.
2. Gather information.
3. Identify options.
4. Predict consequences.
5. Take action to implement a decision.

---

2 Teach and Discuss

PAGE 251

Alaska

Quick Summary The decision to purchase Alaska after the Civil War drew some criticism, but it helped expand and enrich the United States.

1 Why did many people in the United States initially oppose the purchase of Alaska? Possible answer: It cost too much money, especially given that the United States had just fought a costly war. Cause and Effect

Literature and Social Studies

Read the passage aloud to students. Ask them to listen for words that help explain the situation in which the man finds himself.

2 What does this passage reveal about Alaska? Possible answer: Alaska can be a very dangerous place where failure to build a fire can lead to death. Apply Information

H SOCIAL STUDIES STRAND History

Tell students that the discovery of gold in California in 1848 led to the development of California and to its statehood just two years later.

3 What event helped spur interest in the development of Alaska? The discovery of gold Cause and Effect

---

✓ **REVIEW ANSWER** Possible answer: Before the discovery of gold, many viewed Alaska as a useless area. After the discovery of gold, many saw the land as valuable. ↪ Compare and Contrast

Hawaii

🕐 **Quick Summary** In spite of resistance by native Hawaiians, planters from the United States managed to gain control of Hawaii and bring about the annexation of the islands.

④ What factor first attracted Americans to the Hawaiian Islands? The suitability of the islands for the growth of valuable crops **Make Inferences**

⑤ Why did Queen Liliuokalani resist renewing her brother's earlier agreement with the American planters? She did not want foreigners to have so much control over things such as trade and ports. **Draw Conclusions**

Primary Source
Cited in "Official Protest to the Treaty of Annexation," Liliuokalani

⑥ What can you conclude about the intentions of the United States based on this quotation? The U.S. government was willing to fight to control Hawaii. **Analyze Primary Sources**

✓ **REVIEW ANSWER** Possible answer: American planters wanted control of Hawaii. **Sequence**

Hawaii

Thousands of miles southwest of Alaska lies **Hawaii,** a group of islands in the Pacific Ocean. Europeans discovered these islands in 1778. The Hawaiian people were impressed with the Europeans and their tools. In the early 1800s, one Hawaiian leader used European weapons to take control of the islands. He became Hawaii's first king.

People soon came to Hawaii from many countries. Houses, schools, and stores were built. Cows and horses were introduced. New ideas were also introduced. Even Hawaii's king took an interest in the idea of constitutional government.

④ American planters began moving to Hawaii in the mid-1800s. The islands' warm climate was perfect for growing sugarcane and pineapples. The planters established large plantations for these valuable cash crops. The Hawaiian king signed an agreement that gave Americans special trading rights and the port of Pearl Harbor for shipping.

Liliuokalani (li lee uh who kuh LAH nee) became Hawaii's queen in 1891—the first woman to rule Hawaii. She was well educated, had traveled in Europe, and was married to an American. However, she did not want foreigners having so much control. She thought that the previous king should not

⑤ have agreed to work with the Americans. She would not renew the agreement.

The many foreigners in Hawaii were not ready to be sent home. In 1893 they asked Liliuokalani to give up the throne, and then declared that she was no longer queen and took control of the government. President Grover Cleveland told the American planters that Liliuokalani must be queen. They ignored his order, because the islands were not under U.S. authority.

A group of Hawaiians gathered weapons and planned a revolt, but they were discovered. Queen Liliuokalani was arrested and forced to stay in her palace. The queen realized she could not win this battle. She said:

> *"I yielded [gave up] my authority to the forces of the United States in order to avoid bloodshed."* ⑥

The American planters, who had gained greater power than other groups living in the islands, wanted Hawaii to be annexed, or added to the United States. Hawaii was annexed in July 1898.

REVIEW What led up to the annexing of Hawaii to the United States? **Sequence**

▶ Queen Liliuokalani, pictured here, wrote many songs about Hawaii that are still sung today.

▶ Hawaii is famous for its warm climate and great beauty. The Hawaiian islands have many lovely beaches like this one.

252

Practice and Extend

C SOCIAL STUDIES STRAND
Culture

About Hawaiian Culture
- Hawaii has its own native language, which is currently spoken throughout the islands. Though it had fallen into disuse in the 1900s, it was reestablished as an official state language in 1978. Hawaii is the only state in which a native language is used for official purposes.
- Hawaii has a rich musical heritage, which includes the distinctive Hawaiian slack-key guitar music.
- Hula dancing is an ancient Hawaiian storytelling dance.

▶ The explosion of the *Maine* shocked Americans.

Causes of the Spanish-American War

Islands closer to the United States than Hawaii were also demanding attention at this time. By the late 1800s, Spain's empire in the Western Hemisphere had been reduced to just two Caribbean islands: **Puerto Rico** and **Cuba.** In 1895 the Cuban people revolted against Spanish rule. The Spanish army reacted harshly. To keep people from joining the revolution, Spanish soldiers imprisoned hundreds of thousands of Cubans.

 Many people in the United States were angered by Spain's treatment of the Cuban people. They were also upset because businesses in Cuba owned by American citizens were being destroyed. They worried that Americans living in Cuba might be in danger too. The United States government decided to act. In January 1898 President William McKinley sent the battleship USS *Maine* to Cuba's Havana harbor. The *Maine's* goal was to protect the lives and property of Americans in Cuba.

On the night of February 15, a huge explosion destroyed the *Maine,* killing 260 Americans. Several United States newspapers reported that Spain had caused the explosion. In the years since, studies have shown that an accident aboard the ship probably caused the explosion, although we may never know the true cause. However, newspaper reporters of the day were convinced that it must be Spain's fault. One even stated that a torpedo hole had been discovered. Such false or exaggerated reporting is called **yellow journalism.** The newspaper publishers **8** knew that these types of reports sold more papers. Yellow journalism also gave them greater political power, because they could control voters' opinions.

United States citizens already believed bad things about Spain. Newspapers had published many biased and exaggerated articles on how the Spaniards treated the Cubans. Also, Cuban refugees living in the United States were urging Americans to help free their country. People called for action, crying,

> *"Remember the* Maine*!"* **9**

Congress declared war on April 25, 1898, and the **Spanish-American War** began.

REVIEW Why were Americans willing to go to war against Spain? *Summarize*

253

Causes of the Spanish-American War

🕐 *Quick Summary* Unrest in Cuba led to U.S. involvement—and to war with the Spanish empire.

⭐ **SOCIAL STUDIES STRAND**
Citizenship

Democratic Values and Institutions Remind students that in the United States, the Constitution protects people's right to protest against the government.

7 **Why do you think many in the United States were angry at Spain's jailing of thousands of Cubans?** Possible answer: They felt Spain was going too far in trying to put down protests. **Draw Conclusions**

8 **Why do you think sensational yellow journalism sold more newspapers than accurate reporting?** Possible answer: Readers were interested in reading sensational stories. **Hypothesize**

9 **What do you think is the meaning of the cry "Remember the *Maine*"?** Possible answer: Use the memory of the *Maine* as motivation for punishing the Spanish. **Analyze Primary Sources**

✓ **REVIEW ANSWER** Possible answer: Americans did not like the way Spain treated the Cubans and how the unrest threatened American businesses and individuals. **Summarize**

CURRICULUM CONNECTION
Drama

Give a "Yellow Journalism" News Report

Have students assume the role of a reporter covering the destruction of the *Maine*. Students should give a 30-second news report in the style of yellow journalism—with exaggerated facts and with the goal of inflaming public opinion.

ESL **BUILD BACKGROUND**
ESL Support

Create Propaganda Help students understand the effect of yellow journalism by having them create their own propaganda statements.

Beginning Have students create and speak a newspaper headline about the destruction of the *Maine* in a yellow-journalism style.

Intermediate Have students write a lead sentence of a news story about the destruction of the *Maine* in a yellow-journalism style.

Advanced Encourage students to write two lead sentences for two news stories about the destruction of the *Maine,* one in a yellow-journalism style and one in a more straightforward, fact-based style.

For additional ESL support, use Every Student Learns Guide, pp. 98–101.

War with Spain

 **Quick Summary** The United States responded to the call for war with great energy and enthusiasm, resulting in a decisive defeat of Spain.

10 **Why did Commodore Dewey's fleet sail to the Philippines?** To meet and battle the Spanish fleet located there
Main Idea and Details

Test Talk

Locate Key Words in the Question

11 **How did Theodore Roosevelt demonstrate his dedication to the U.S. war effort?** Have students tell who or what in the question are key words. Possible answer: He quit his job in the government to organize a force of volunteers. Summarize

12 **What were the key events in the Spanish-American War, as described in this section?** Possible answer: The destruction of the Spanish fleet in the Philippines, the Battle of San Juan Hill, and the destruction of the Spanish fleet in Cuba Main Idea and Details

✓ **REVIEW ANSWER** The Buffalo Soldiers were experienced African American soldiers who had served in battle against Native Americans on the Great Plains. Main Idea and Details

War with Spain

In addition to Cuba and Puerto Rico, Spain had colonies in the Philippines and Guam, groups of islands in the Pacific Ocean. The United States Navy's first goal was to destroy the powerful Spanish fleet in the Philippines. The Navy's Pacific fleet had been stationed in Hong Kong since January 1898. When war was declared in April, battleships sailed to the Philippines under the command of **10** Commodore George Dewey. When Dewey spotted the Spanish ships in Manila Bay, he gave Captain Charles Gridley the order, "You may fire when you are ready, Gridley." The Spanish fleet was completely destroyed.

In the United States, people prepared for battle. Nearly one million Americans volunteered to fight in the Spanish-American War. **Theodore Roosevelt,** the assistant secretary of the navy, left his job to organize a group of **11** volunteer soldiers. He put together a fighting force of cowboys, Native Americans, college athletes, and wealthy New Yorkers. Newspapers began calling Roosevelt's soldiers the **Rough Riders.**

Also chosen to go to Cuba to fight were several units of experienced African American soldiers. These soldiers were known as **Buffalo Soldiers,** a nickname they got while serving in the wars against Native Americans on the Great Plains.

American soldiers fought their way across Cuba through dense, tropical forest. On July 1, 1898, they reached Spain's main force on Cuba's San Juan Hill. Rough Riders, Buffalo Soldiers, and other American soldiers charged the Spanish troops.

The Spanish were defeated at the Battle of San Juan Hill. Two days later, American ships destroyed the Spanish fleet in Cuba. In **12** August 1898 the United States and Spain agreed to a treaty ending the war.

REVIEW Who were the Buffalo Soldiers? Main Idea and Details

▶ This statue honors the Buffalo Soldiers, a group of African Americans who had fought out west. They also went into battle alongside the Rough Riders.

▶ Theodore Roosevelt led the Rough Riders up San Juan Hill.

Practice and Extend

MEETING INDIVIDUAL NEEDS
Leveled Practice

Make a Recruiting Poster Have students design and create a poster that could have been used to recruit volunteers for the war against Spain.

Easy Students can create a slogan and artwork that might encourage people to join in the fight against Spain. **Reteach**

On-Level Have students create a poster that incorporates ideas from the lesson about the events that led to the outbreak of war with Spain. **Extend**

Challenge Ask students to create a poster specifically designed to recruit volunteers for Theodore Roosevelt's Rough Riders. **Enrich**

For a Lesson Summary, use Quick Study, p. 50.

Results of War

On the map below, you can see some effects of the United States victory over Spain in the Spanish-American War. The United States gained control of several Spanish territories, including Puerto Rico, the Philippines, and Guam. Cuba gained independence from Spain, but remained under U.S. protection for a few years, while it set up a new government. The Philippines remained an American territory until 1946, when it became an independent nation. Puerto Rico and Guam are still part of the United States, and their people are United States citizens.

With its swift victory over Spain, the United States showed that it had become a powerful nation. The United States was now a world power, or one of the most powerful nations in the world.

Theodore Roosevelt became a national hero. As he stepped off the boat from Cuba, the crowds shouted, "Hurrah for Teddy and the Rough Riders!" Roosevelt was soon elected governor of New York and later became President of the United States. In the Biography on page 259, you will find out how childhood experiences helped prepare Roosevelt for leadership.

Victory in the Spanish-American War, however, was costly. More than 5,000 American soldiers died. Of these, fewer than 400 were killed in battle. The rest died from diseases such as malaria and yellow fever.

REVIEW How did the Spanish-American War change the role of the United States in the world? *Cause and Effect*

New United States Territories, 1898

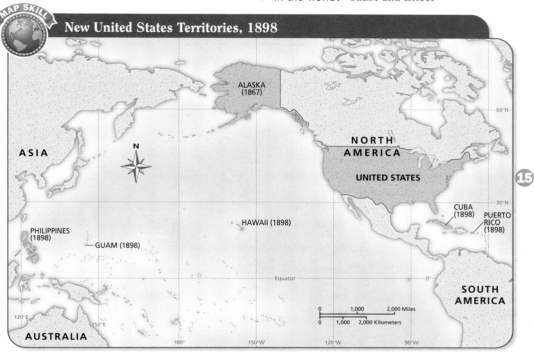

ALASKA (1867)

ASIA

NORTH AMERICA

UNITED STATES

HAWAII (1898)

PHILIPPINES (1898)

GUAM (1898)

CUBA (1898)

PUERTO RICO (1898)

SOUTH AMERICA

AUSTRALIA

Equator

0   1,000   2,000 Miles
0   1,000   2,000 Kilometers

▶ By 1898 the United States controlled territories throughout the Pacific Ocean.

MAP SKILL Use Latitude and Longitude *Estimate the location of Guam using latitude and longitude.*

255

Results of War

 Quick Summary With its quick victory over Spain in the Spanish-American War, the United States showed it was a powerful nation.

13 **What, besides an enhanced place in the world, did the United States gain from the war with Spain?** Possible answer: The United States gained control of Puerto Rico, Guam, and the Philippines. Cause and Effect

14 **How did the Spanish-American War affect Theodore Roosevelt?** It made him a national hero and helped propel him into political leadership. Cause and Effect

✓ **REVIEW ANSWER** The United States emerged from the war as a world power. Cause and Effect

New United States Territories, 1898

Point out that many of these territories were gained by the United States in 1898, but have students note the date of the purchase of the Alaskan territory.

15 **How many years after the purchase of Alaska did Hawaii become a territory of the United States?** About 31 years Sequence

MAP SKILL Answer About 13°N, 145°E

ISSUES AND VIEWPOINTS
Critical Thinking

Examine Points of View About Imperialism

- Though some Americans took pride in the nation's status as an imperial power, others did not.

- Read the following quote to students. It came from a group called the American Anti-Imperialist League, which disagreed with the domination of the Philippines and Puerto Rico by the United States. Then ask students to discuss the league's viewpoint.

"This policy which we oppose gives to the Filipinos and Puerto Ricans no constitutional rights, no American citizenship, no hope of statehood, no voice in the Congress which rules them; it leaves them without a country, the subjects of a republic. To believers in free government this policy is monstrous."

—*To the American People,* by the Anti-Imperialist League, July 4, 1901

Panama Canal

Quick Summary A canal across the Isthmus of Panama offered the hope of faster, safer shipping. Building it, however, required tremendous effort and ingenuity.

16 **What two major advantages would a canal across the Isthmus of Panama provide?** Speedier and safer travel
Main Idea and Details

✓ Ongoing Assessment

If... students do not recognize the tremendous advantages a Panama canal would provide,

then... have them examine a globe or map and measure the distance of a journey from New York to San Francisco by both the canal route and the route around South America.

17 **Why do you think the United States supported Panamanian independence?**
Possible answer: The United States wanted to build a canal through Panama, and Panamanian independence would further that goal. **Make Inferences**

Map Adventure Answers

1. Southeast
2. Colon; Panama City
3. Gatun, Pedro Miguel, Miraflores

Panama Canal

To sail from one coast of the United States to the other, ships had to sail around Cape Horn at the southern tip of South America. The trip took more than two months! The trip was not simply long; the cape's strong current and fierce storms could make it dangerous too. Like many other Americans, Theodore Roosevelt wanted U.S. ships to be able to travel between the Atlantic and Pacific Oceans quickly, for both trading and military purposes. After the Spanish-American War, this seemed even more important, because the navy had played such a big part in the war.

The trip could be shortened from months to days if a canal could be cut across the **16** Isthmus of Panama. An **isthmus** is a narrow strip of land that connects two larger areas. The Isthmus of Panama connects North and South America. Roosevelt set out to build such a canal. But first, he had to solve a number of problems.

First, the United States had to get control of the land. Panama at that time belonged to the South American nation of Colombia. Colombia refused to give it up. But backed by the United States, Panama declared independence in 1903. Panama then agreed to **17** let the United States build a canal through its land. (In 1921, the United States repaid Colombia for the loss of Panama.)

Second, deadly diseases such as yellow fever and malaria were common in hot, wet areas such as Panama. These diseases killed thousands every year. Army doctor **Walter Reed**, considered one of the world's great doctors and medical researchers, discovered that these diseases were carried by mosquitoes. He even tested his theory on himself.

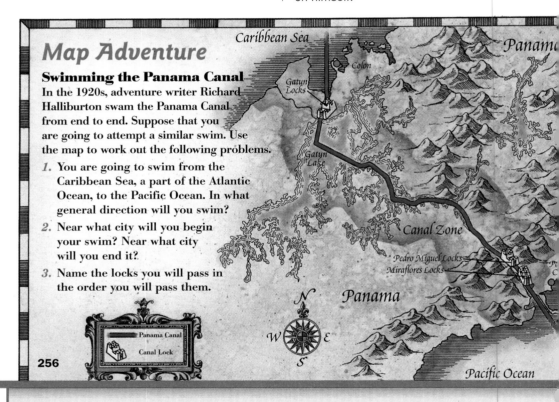

Map Adventure

Swimming the Panama Canal

In the 1920s, adventure writer Richard Halliburton swam the Panama Canal from end to end. Suppose that you are going to attempt a similar swim. Use the map to work out the following problems.

1. You are going to swim from the Caribbean Sea, a part of the Atlantic Ocean, to the Pacific Ocean. In what general direction will you swim?
2. Near what city will you begin your swim? Near what city will you end it?
3. Name the locks you will pass in the order you will pass them.

Panama Canal
Canal Lock

256

Practice and Extend

CURRICULUM CONNECTION
Science

Research Mosquito-Borne Illnesses

- Have students use library or online resources to gather information about mosquito-borne illnesses, such as malaria and yellow fever.
- Students should explore whether malaria and yellow fever are still threats to people in the United States and the rest of the world.
- Tell students to explore illnesses such as the West Nile virus that have recently appeared in the United States.

Disease-carrying mosquitoes swarmed in the dense rainforest through which the canal would be built. Another Army doctor, W. C. Gorgas, led the effort to drain the areas of standing water where mosquitoes laid their eggs. The mosquito population shrank, and so did the number of cases of yellow fever and malaria.

Third, the mountains, swamps, and mud of Panama would make the job of digging a canal very difficult. But in 1904, more than 40,000 people and lines of steam shovels set to work.

At first the digging was slow. Then in 1905 John Stevens was appointed chief engineer for the project. It was Stevens who approved and funded Gorgas's efforts to eliminate mosquitoes. He then dramatically increased the workforce, hiring Americans, Panamanians, and people from the Caribbean islands. He paved the streets of Panama's main cities and built new towns, with hospitals, hotels, and schools, to house the workers. He then created an efficient system of railroad tracks for moving equipment and carrying dirt away

► President Roosevelt, in the white suit, takes a turn at the controls of a steam shovel in Panama.

► A huge ship cruises through the Panama Canal.

from the digging sites.

Among the many important contributions Stevens made was convincing Theodore Roosevelt and Congress of the wisdom of building a system of locks. Others had wanted a sea-level canal, where the canal was dug so deep that ships could simply sail through. Several factors made the use of locks important. The tides in the Pacific are much greater than those in the Atlantic. This would make navigation difficult. The land was high above sea level, and the deeper digging would cost vastly more, in dollars and lives, and would take many years longer. It was likely that a sea-level canal would be a complete failure. Congress approved Stevens's plan, but only by a narrow margin. **20**

The creation of the canal was a huge task. Sometimes it seemed impossible. But on August 15, 1914, the 50-mile long Panama Canal was opened for shipping. Roosevelt called it "the greatest engineering feat of the ages." Now a steamship could move from one end of the canal to the other in just nine hours! **21**

REVIEW What problems did the United States have to solve in order to build the Panama Canal? Summarize

257

18 **What two major achievements helped reduce the threat of illness in the Panama Canal project?** The discovery that mosquitoes carried diseases and the effort to drain the areas where mosquitoes bred
Main Idea and Details

19 **How did John Stevens go about increasing the speed of the canal project?** Possible answer: He found a number of ways to increase the workforce, including removing mosquitoes, finding new sources of workers, and providing good facilities for workers to live in. Summarize

ST SOCIAL STUDIES STRAND
Science • Technology

Explain to students that a sea-level canal involves digging away all the earth down to sea level. A lock system allows a canal to actually travel "uphill" by creating isolated compartments, or locks, in which the water level can be raised or lowered.

20 **Why would a lock system reduce the amount of digging compared to a sea-level canal?** Each lock would only have to be deep enough to allow passage of ships to the next lock, while a sea-level canal would require very deep digging in higher elevations to get down to sea level. Compare and Contrast

21 **How many years did it take to build the Panama Canal?** About 10 years
Apply Information

✓ **REVIEW ANSWER** Possible answer: The United States had to gain control of the land, identify the cause of disease and remove the source of the disease, provide enough workers, and find a method for building a canal across mountains and through swamps. Summarize

ESL ACCESS CONTENT
ESL Support

Understand Terminology Students can enhance their understanding of key terms in the discussion above.

Beginning Have students work in pairs to look up the word *lock* in an English-language dictionary and identify the meaning that is appropriate to the discussion of canals. Student pairs should help each other read the definitions.

Intermediate Ask students to write a definition of the terms *lock* and *sea level* in their own words.

Advanced Have students write a brief description of how locks work and the advantage of a lock system over a sea-level canal.

For additional ESL support, use Every Student Learns Guide, pp. 98–101.

Panama Today

 Quick Summary The United States originally controlled the Panama Canal, but a 1977 treaty gave Panama control of the canal in the year 2000.

$ SOCIAL STUDIES STRAND
Economics

Tell students that ships are charged tolls to pass through the Panama Canal.

㉒ Why do you think Panama would want to control the Panama Canal?
Some of Panama's citizens wanted to control the canal because they wanted the collected tolls. **Draw Conclusions**

✓ **REVIEW ANSWER** Some of Panama's citizens wanted to control the canal. **Cause and Effect**

3 Close and Assess

Summarize the Lesson

Tell students to examine the vertical time line. For each item, have students write a sentence that explains its significance.

✓ **LESSON 1** **REVIEW**

1. **Cause and Effect** For possible answers, see the reduced pupil page.

2. He wanted the United States to expand. Alaska's fur, mines, and fish were valuable.

3. The climate was perfect for growing sugarcane and pineapples.

4. Newspapers used yellow journalism when they wrote exaggerated reports about Spanish actions in Cuba. The reports angered Americans, and soon the Spanish-American War started.

5. **Critical Thinking: *Draw Conclusions*** The United States emerged as a world power with its quick, decisive defeat of Spain, its territorial conquests, and control over transportation with the Panama Canal.

Link to ⚭ Geography

Students' reports should include facts about the landforms, resources, plant and animal life, and people.

258 Unit 3 • Expansion and Change

Panama Today

The treaty signed in 1903 gave the United States the right to control the Panama Canal "in perpetuity," or forever. In exchange, the United States would pay Panama millions of dollars and guarantee the country's independence. The United States managed the canal without challenge until 1964. Some of Panama's citizens felt that they should control the canal, because it ㉒ was in their country.

In 1977 a new treaty was signed between the two countries. In the year 2000 the

▶ **U.S. President Jimmy Carter turns over control of the canal to Panamanian President Mireya Moscoso.**

treaty went into effect. It gave Panama full control of the canal. Today, most of the ships passing through the canal are from the United States and Asia. Petroleum is the main product transported through the canal.

REVIEW What caused the United States to sign a new treaty with Panama? **Cause and Effect**

Summarize the Lesson

- **1867** The United States bought Alaska from Russia.
- **July 1898** Hawaii was annexed by the United States.
- **August 1898** Spanish-American War ended with a United States victory.
- **1914** Panama Canal opened.

LESSON 1 **REVIEW**

Check Facts and Main Ideas

1. **Cause and Effect** On a separate sheet of paper, fill in an effect of each major event from this lesson.

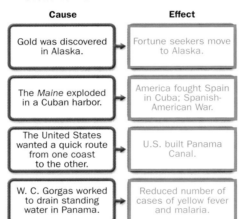

Cause	Effect
Gold was discovered in Alaska.	Fortune seekers move to Alaska.
The *Maine* exploded in a Cuban harbor.	America fought Spain in Cuba; Spanish-American War.
The United States wanted a quick route from one coast to the other.	U.S. built Panama Canal.
W. C. Gorgas worked to drain standing water in Panama.	Reduced number of cases of yellow fever and malaria.

2. Why did **William Seward** want to buy **Alaska**?

3. Why did American planters move to **Hawaii**?

4. How did **yellow journalism** help bring about the **Spanish-American War**? Answer in two or more sentences. Use the highlighted terms.

5. **Critical Thinking: *Draw Conclusions*** By 1900 the United States was seen as a world power. How do you think the events described in this lesson helped the United States become a world power?

Link to ⚭ Geography

Research United States Territories Look back at the map of the new United States territories on page 255. Choose one of these places and find out more about it. Write a short oral report describing the land and people of this place. Share your report.

258

Practice and Extend

FAST FACTS

- The Panama Canal handles as many as 14,000 vessels every year. This represents some 5% of world commercial trade.
- Today, the canal provides jobs for 9,000 people in Panama.
- All kinds of shipping vessels use the canal, from container ships to submarines to cruise ships.

Workbook, p. 56

Lesson 1: Expanding Overseas

Directions: Using information from this lesson, circle the term in parentheses that best completes each sentence.

1. William Seward sought to expand the territory of the United States through the purchase of (Alaska, Hawaii).

2. Alaska proved to be a valuable addition to the United States after the discovery of (salmon, gold).

3. American planters in Hawaii wanted the United States to (free, annex) the islands.

4. Many people in the United States were (pleased, angered) by Spain's reaction to the Cuban revolution of 1895.

5. The destruction of the *Maine* and yellow journalism reports about it helped tip public opinion (in favor of, against) war with Spain.

6. Commodore George Dewey led the attack on the Spanish Fleet in the (Philippines, Cuba).

7. Theodore Roosevelt helped organize a force known as the (Buffalo Soldiers, Rough Riders).

8. The Spanish-American War showed that the United States was a (powerful, weak) nation.

9. Theodore Roosevelt emerged from the war as a (villain, hero).

10. (Mosquitoes, The Panamanian people) were a major obstacle to building the Panama Canal.

Notes for Home: Your child learned about the emergence of the United States as a major world power. **Home Activity:** With your child, review a newspaper or internet news site for stories about the United States and its role in international affairs today.

Also on Teacher Resources CD-ROM.

★ BIOGRAPHY ★

Theodore Roosevelt
1858–1919

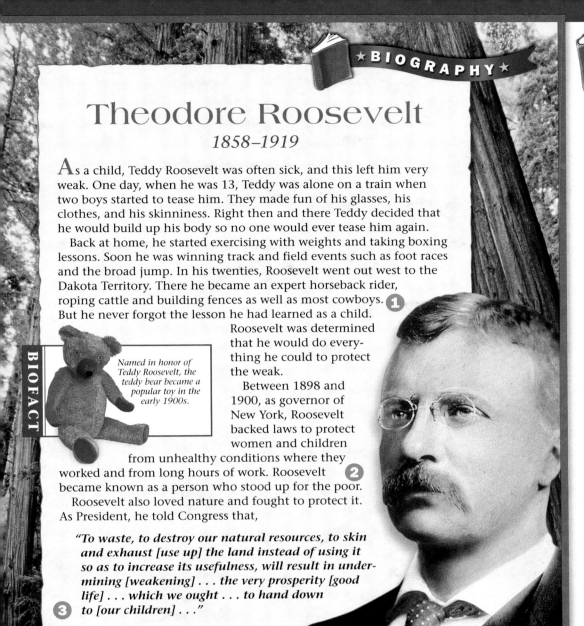

As a child, Teddy Roosevelt was often sick, and this left him very weak. One day, when he was 13, Teddy was alone on a train when two boys started to tease him. They made fun of his glasses, his clothes, and his skinniness. Right then and there Teddy decided that he would build up his body so no one would ever tease him again.

Back at home, he started exercising with weights and taking boxing lessons. Soon he was winning track and field events such as foot races and the broad jump. In his twenties, Roosevelt went out west to the Dakota Territory. There he became an expert horseback rider, roping cattle and building fences as well as most cowboys. ❶ But he never forgot the lesson he had learned as a child.

Roosevelt was determined that he would do everything he could to protect the weak.

Between 1898 and 1900, as governor of New York, Roosevelt backed laws to protect women and children from unhealthy conditions where they worked and from long hours of work. Roosevelt ❷ became known as a person who stood up for the poor.

Roosevelt also loved nature and fought to protect it. As President, he told Congress that,

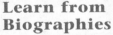

Named in honor of Teddy Roosevelt, the teddy bear became a popular toy in the early 1900s.

"To waste, to destroy our natural resources, to skin and exhaust [use up] the land instead of using it so as to increase its usefulness, will result in undermining [weakening] . . . the very prosperity [good life] . . . which we ought . . . to hand down ❸ *to [our children] . . ."*

Learn from Biographies

Describe how Roosevelt's experience with childhood illness affected his ideas as an adult.

For more information, go to *Meet the People* at **www.sfsocialstudies.com.**

259

WEB SITE
Technology

Students can find out more about Theodore Roosevelt by clicking on *Meet the People* at **www.sfsocialstudies.com.**

SOCIAL STUDIES
Background

Theodore Roosevelt

- Roosevelt had asthma and poor eyesight.
- Due to his poor health as a child, he was tutored at home. He went on to graduate from Harvard University.
- He used his time in the Dakota Territory to strengthen his body and to recover from the grief he felt when both his mother and wife died on the same day— February 14, 1884.

★ BIOGRAPHY ★

Theodore Roosevelt

Objective
- Identify the achievements of people who have made contributions to society, such as Theodore Roosevelt.

1 Introduce and Motivate

Preview To activate prior knowledge, ask students what they know about Theodore Roosevelt. Tell them that they will read more about his life.

2 Teach and Discuss

❶ **Summarize the actions Roosevelt took to build up his body.** Possible answer: He lifted weights, boxed, ran races, and rode horses. Summarize

❷ **What fact supports the opinion that Roosevelt built a strong character and a strong body?** He stood up for what he believed in and he became an experienced outdoorsman. Fact and Opinion

❸ **What did Roosevelt fear might happen to our natural resources?** People would destroy them without thought. Analyze Primary Sources

3 Close and Assess

Learn from Biographies Answer

As a child, he was teased about his weakness, so as an adult, he wanted to protect the weak.

BIOFACT

Credibility of a Source

Objective
- Identify credible sources of information.

Vocabulary
> **source,** p. 260
> **credible,** p. 260

Resource
- Workbook, p. 57

1 Introduce and Motivate

What is "credibility of a source"?
Ask students to share any prior knowledge about the meaning of *credibility* and its relationship to sources of information. Then have students read the **What?** section of text on p. 260.

Why determine the credibility of a source? Have students read the **Why?** section of text on pp. 260–261. Ask them to give examples of sources of information that they think are likely to be credible and ones they think are not.

2 Teach and Discuss

How is this skill used? Examine with students Source A and Source B on pp. 260–261.

- Discuss the term *motivation* with students. Have them discuss the probable motivations of the writers of Source A and Source B.

- Point out that word choice can be a clue to credibility. Have students identify examples of objective (giving facts without bias) and subjective (influenced by personal feelings) ways to describe an event.

- Have students read the **How?** section of text on p. 261.

Credibility of a Source

What? A source is any written or oral account that may provide information. Some sources are credible, or reliable. Other sources are not credible, or not reliable. When you decide whether a source is credible or not credible, you are determining whether or not to believe the information the source is giving you.

Why? Do you sometimes read or hear about things you find difficult to believe? Perhaps you should believe them.

▶ This painting shows one artist's view of the explosion of the *Maine.*

Source A

I was...so quiet that Lieutenant J. Hood came up and asked laughingly if I was asleep. I said "No, I am on watch." Scarcely had I spoken when there came a dull, sullen roar. Would to God that I could blot out the sound and the scenes that followed. Then came a sharp explosion—some say numerous detonations [blasts]. I remember only one....I have no theories as to the cause of the explosion. I cannot form any. I, with others, had heard the Havana harbor was full of torpedoes [mines], but the officers whose duty it was to examine into that reported that they found no signs of any. Personally, I do not believe that the Spanish had anything to do with the disaster. ❶ ❷

—Lieutenant John J. Blandin

260

Practice and Extend

SOCIAL STUDIES
FYI Background

Journalism
- Remind students that sensationalized news is often called *yellow journalism.* In this type of journalism, the writer will exaggerate information and use colorful adjectives to entertain the reader. However, an article written in this style might not contain accurate or factual information.

- The practice of using extreme sensationalism by city papers died out around 1900. Some techniques such as banner headlines, colored comics, and widespread use of illustrations continue today.

- Journalists today strive to write in an objective manner in order to maintain their credibility. Newspaper articles, television reports, and other examples of journalism also go through rigorous fact-checking to try to ensure that the reader is presented with an accurate and fair accounting of an event or topic.

Or perhaps you should not. You need to know how to determine the credibility of any source of information.

In 1898 the U.S. battleship *Maine* exploded in Havana Harbor. Americans and others wondered what caused the explosion. The ship's officers and sailors who survived wrote reports.

At the same time, some newspaper publishers decided that they could sell many newspapers if they printed sensational stories, or stories that would make people excited or interested. They also knew that they could affect public opinion.

Source A is from a report by Lieutenant John J. Blandin, who was on board the *Maine* when it exploded. Source B is from a front-page article published in the *New York Journal* on February 17, 1898.

How? To determine whether a source is credible, the first step is to consider the author of the source. Decide whether the author has first-hand or expert knowledge about the event. Decide whether the author has any reason to exaggerate, change the facts, or describe events in a particular way. It also helps to find out whether the author does or does not have a reputation for being truthful and accurate. You can also check another source.

Source B

Think and Apply

❶ What is Source A? What is Source B?

❷ What did Lieutenant Blandin say about the probable cause of the explosion? What did the newspaper say about the probable cause of the explosion?

❸ Which report do you think has more credibility? Why?

261

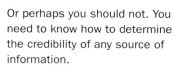

Workbook, p. 57

Credibility of a Source

Also on Teacher Resources CD-ROM.

❶ **What is one fact and one opinion in Lieutenant Blandin's report?** Possible answers: It is a fact that he heard an explosion. It is his opinion that the Spanish were not responsible. **Fact and Opinion**

❷ **What could have caused parts of the lieutenant's report to be incorrect even though he was there?** The terror of the situation might have caused him to remember incorrectly. **Analyze Information**

❸ **What are examples of strong words and phrases the *Journal* reporter used to try to convince people the explosion was Spain's fault?** Possible answers: "Naval officers think the *Maine* was destroyed by a Spanish mine"; "Spanish officials protest too much." **Recognize Bias**

③ Close and Assess

Think and Apply

1. Source A is a report by an officer who was on the *Maine* when it exploded. Source B is a newspaper.

2. Lieutenant Blandin says he does not know what caused the explosion, but he does not think the Spanish had anything to do with it. The *Journal* suggests that the explosion was not an accident and reports that officers on the *Maine* think it was caused by a Spanish mine.

3. Most students will say that the lieutenant's report is more credible because he was there, and he cites the reports of investigating officers. He does not appear to have a personal reason for holding one opinion or another, and he admits to uncertainty. In contrast, the *Journal* draws a conclusion without offering any firsthand evidence. The *Journal* may have decided that it could sell more newspapers by stirring up public anger and excitement.

The Progressive Movement

Objectives

- Analyze how social, political, moral, and economic reforms during the Roosevelt presidency affected Americans.

- Explain the role of media and the arts in the Progressive Movement.

- Explain the effects of the Progressive Movement reforms on the workplace.

- Discuss the accomplishments and limitations of the Progressive Movement.

Vocabulary

trust, p. 263; **Progressives,** p. 264; **muckraker,** p. 264; **Blue Laws,** p. 265; **conservation,** p. 266

Resources

- Workbook, p. 58
- Transparency 14
- Every Student Learns Guide, pp. 102–105
- Quick Study, pp. 52–53

 Quick *Teaching Plan*

If time is short, have students create a web diagram with the word *Progressives* in the center and a number of blank balloons surrounding it.

- Have students fill in the blank balloons with content from the lesson as they read the lesson independently.

1 Introduce and Motivate

Preview To activate prior knowledge, ask students to recall some of the challenges facing the nation's growing cities and their residents. Tell students that in this lesson, they will read about how the United States began to address some of these and other problems.

You Are There Have students predict how the people of the United States will respond to the question asked by the child in the *You Are There* segment.

LESSON 2

1900   1915

1901
Theodore
Roosevelt
becomes
President.

1906
Upton Sinclair
publishes *The
Jungle.*

1913
The Sixteenth
Amendment creates a
national income tax.

PREVIEW

Focus on the Main Idea
Reformers worked to improve conditions in the United States during the early years of the industrial age.

PLACES
Yosemite National Park
Grand Canyon National Monument

PEOPLE
Ida Tarbell
Upton Sinclair
John Muir

VOCABULARY
trust
Progressives
muckraker
Blue Laws
conservation

The Progressive Movement

You Are There You and your family have just settled into your new tenement apartment. The apartment is not really new, however. It is old.

Your family has moved to the city to work in a cotton mill. Both your mother and father work at the mill, and so do all of your neighbors. The mill seems to provide most of the jobs in this part of town.

When your parents think you have fallen asleep, your father reads aloud from the newspaper. You can hear him say, "Yesterday there was an accident at the cotton mill. A floor collapsed under the weight of the spinning machines. Several people were hurt." He stops reading and adds, "You know, it is not just the floors that have me worried. Those machines move so fast. I don't know if the bosses care about what happens, but I worry about it sometimes."

As you lie in the dark, you wonder, *Does anyone care about workers like my Mom and Dad?*

 Compare and Contrast As you read, think about how life changed because of the work of reformers.

262

Practice and Extend

READING SKILL
Compare/Contrast

In the Lesson Review, students complete a graphic organizer like the one below. You may want to provide students with a copy of Transparency 14 to complete as they read the lesson.

Use Transparency 14

VOCABULARY
Word Exercise

Individual Word Study

Remind students that if they are unfamiliar with a compound word, they can break it into its component words and see if they are familiar with those. Write *muckraker* on the board and draw a line between *muck* and *raker*. Have students define these two words. (filth; someone who rakes things) Discuss with students what the definition of *muckraker* is. (someone who rakes up filth, or shameful conditions in business or other areas of American life)

Problems of an Industrial Society

Cotton mills were not the only source of worry for Americans during the early 1900s. As industry grew in the United States, the problems created by industry grew too.

As you read in Unit 2, factories at this time could be dangerous places, both for adults and for the children that many industries hired. Workers operating dangerous machines were sometimes poorly trained. Many factories were not healthful places in which to work. Factories were often fire hazards too.

Children were small enough to climb in and out of the machinery to repair it, which could be dangerous. Also, children who worked often could not attend school.

Some industries filled the air with smoke. Some dumped waste into rivers or lakes. Forests were cut down for mines, ships, and buildings, but few companies planted new trees. There were frequent explosions and accidents in coal mines.

▶ In 1908 in this Indiana factory, young boys were still at work at midnight.

As industry became more important to everyone, some companies joined together to form groups that could control whole industries. These groups, often called trusts, had the power to drive out any competition. Companies usually compete with one another, which leads to better products and fairer prices. Without competition, trusts could act like monopolies. They could charge higher prices for their products. ③

REVIEW What problems arose because of the increase in industry during the early 1900s? Summarize

▶ Like many other cities in the early 1900s, Chicago suffered from problems caused by the rapid growth of industry.

263

2 Teach and Discuss

PAGE 263

Problems of an Industrial Society

🕐 **Quick Summary** As industry grew and expanded in the United States, a host of problems grew along with it.

❶ What made children a valuable source of labor for factory owners? Possible answer: Because of their size, children could fix machines. Summarize

❷ In what ways did industry threaten the health of the environment? Industry polluted the air and water; forests were cut down. Summarize

 **Test Talk**

Locate Key Words in the Question

❸ What harmful effect can the absence of competition have in an economy? Have students skim the text to look for key words that match key words in the question. Possible answer: Lack of competition can lead to higher prices. **Cause and Effect**

✓ **REVIEW ANSWER** Both people and the environment suffered with increased industry. Summarize

---

 SOCIAL STUDIES STRAND
Economics

Understanding Key Economic Principles

To help students understand the discussion about trusts, have them use a dictionary, encyclopedia, or online resources to look up the meaning of the following terms:

- free enterprise
- supply and demand
- monopoly
- trust

Have students discuss the meanings of these terms and why competition is important to the economic system in the United States.

 SOCIAL STUDIES
Background

About the Triangle Shirtwaist Fire

- One infamous example of the hazards of early 1900s industry occurred in March 1911, when fire broke out on the upper floors of the Triangle Shirtwaist factory in New York City.
- Some fire exits in the factory had been blocked to keep factory workers—mainly young women—at their work.
- Within a few minutes of the first report of fire, 146 workers had perished, many after jumping from ninth-floor windows to escape the flames.

Theodore Roosevelt and the Progressives

🕐 **Quick Summary** Reformers known as the Progressives sought to improve the behavior of industry and the effectiveness of government. Their cause was supported by President Theodore Roosevelt and by many writers.

4 **Why do you think the muckrakers chose to write about shameful conditions in business and other areas of American life?** Possible answer: They hoped that by exposing these problems, people would be motivated to correct them. **Draw Conclusions**

5 **What effect did Ida Tarbell's work have on Theodore Roosevelt?** Possible answer: It persuaded him of the need to attack trusts. **Summarize**

6 **What led to Progressive legislation that helped clean up the food and drug industries?** Possible answer: Upton Sinclair's book, *The Jungle* **Cause and Effect**

✓ **REVIEW ANSWER** They were writers who worked to uncover shameful conditions in business and other areas of American life. **Main Idea and Details**

Theodore Roosevelt and the Progressives

As problems related to industry increased, people came forward who wanted to solve the problems. Theodore Roosevelt helped lead the way to reform.

The Spanish-American War had made Roosevelt a national hero. In 1900 he was elected Vice-President under President McKinley. When McKinley was assassinated in 1901, Roosevelt became President. He was elected for a full term in 1904.

Roosevelt agreed with the goals of a group of reformers known as Progressives. **Progressives** were reformers who worked to stop unfair practices by businesses and to improve the way in which government worked.

One group of Progressives was made up of writers. They were called **muckrakers,** because they uncovered what some people saw as "muck"—shameful conditions in business and other areas of American life.

In 1902 muckraker **Ida Tarbell** wrote a series of magazine articles about Standard Oil, the company founded by John D. Rockefeller. She wrote about the dangers of trusts such as Standard Oil, which controlled the oil industry. Other trusts were formed in the railroad and steel industries. Trusts could hurt smaller businesses, she argued, and they could hurt the reputations of large companies that did not form trusts. Tarbell's work helped convince Roosevelt that he should be an active "trust-buster." He used the Sherman Antitrust Act, passed in 1890, to attack trusts. This law allowed the government to force trusts to break up into smaller companies.

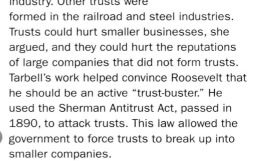

264

In 1906 muckraker **Upton Sinclair** wrote a novel called *The Jungle*. This book tells about conditions in the meat-packing plants of Chicago. Roosevelt had barely finished reading the book when he told his secretary of agriculture, James Wilson, to investigate the lack of cleanliness in food processing.

Soon Roosevelt supported and signed two reform acts—the Meat Inspection Act and the Pure Food and Drug Act. The Meat Inspection Act allowed government inspectors to check meat to make sure it was safe to eat. The Pure Food and Drug Act helped make food and medicine safer by requiring companies to tell the truth about their products.

Progressives did not limit their concern to business and government. Wherever they saw a problem, Progressives went to work, trying to improve education, health, and more. They also tried to solve social, moral, and family problems, although this was not always as welcome as other reforms.

REVIEW What were muckrakers? **Main Idea and Details**

▶ This famous political cartoon shows the cartoonist's impression of President Roosevelt's response to problems in the meat industry.

North Wind Picture Archives

Practice and Extend

ESL **EXTEND LANGUAGE**
ESL Support

Explore Word Meanings Have students explore the meaning of the word *progressive* and related words.

Beginning Work with students and model how to use a dictionary to find the meaning of the word *progressive* that most accurately reflects the spirit of the Progressive Movement. Write the definition on the board.

Intermediate Ask students to identify another word that is related to the word *progressive* (for example, *progress*).

Advanced Have students write a sentence that uses the words *progressive* and *progress* correctly.

For additional ESL support, use Every Student Learns Guide, pp. 102–105.

FACT FILE

Growing Concern for Worker Safety

The factories being built across the United States were filled with machinery and workers. Before industrialization, safety equipment was not very important. But now there were big machines and new problems. Everything happened faster, and many jobs were dangerous.

In the late 1800s, safety laws were passed to make the machines safer and to protect workers. Goggles and helmets are now required in many industries. Can you think of other safety equipment used in factories today to protect workers?

Impact of Reforms

Progressives believed that change could come through laws. They had been working for change for many years, but their efforts gained strength with Theodore Roosevelt in the White House. As you have read, Roosevelt broke up the big trusts and passed laws to make food and medicine safer.

Progressives were responsible for the passing of many new laws. Building codes made tenements and factories safer. Coal mines were inspected. Young children were kept from working in factories. Children were now required to attend school. And schools were required to hire nurses to protect children's health. In Chapter 5 you read about two other important concerns of the Progressives: civil rights and women's rights.

Progressives also helped pass Blue Laws in many towns. These were laws designed to solve some of the social problems of the day. A very serious problem was that many people abused alcohol. One Blue Law said that people could not buy alcohol on Sundays. In some areas, this law did help reduce abuses. However, some people did not want the government to force morals on them.

One long-lasting change introduced by the Progressives was the income tax. Before the late 1800s, the United States had few taxes. The country needed money to pay for reforms and other projects. In 1913 the Sixteenth Amendment gave Congress the legal right to tax income, or money earned from work or investing.

REVIEW What was the goal of the laws passed because of the Progressive Movement? **Summarize**

265

Impact of Reforms

Quick Summary The Progressives sought to bring change to the United States through the passage of laws, including those for the regulation of behavior, business, and government.

FACT FILE

Growing Concern for Worker Safety

7 **How did the growth of factories create new hazards for workers?** Possible answer: Machinery became bigger and it moved faster. **Summarize**

✓ Ongoing Assessment

If... students do not appreciate the hazards facing workers in the growing factories of the late 1800s,	**then...** have students review the Fact File on this page and observe the safety measures that are now in place to protect workers.

8 **What types of safety equipment might help keep the people in the two photographs safer?** Possible answer: The worker on the left could use safety equipment to prevent him from getting burned, while the worker on the right could use similar equipment to avoid getting something in her eyes. **Analyze Information**

9 **In what way did Blue Laws "try to force morals" on people?** Possible answer: They focused on problems such as alcohol abuse, which many people saw as personal decisions. **Make Inferences**

Problem Solving

10 **What problem was the income tax designed to solve?** Money was needed to pay for Progressive programs. **Solve Problems**

✓ **REVIEW ANSWER** Possible answer: The goal of the laws passed because of the Progressive Movement was to improve life and solve problems facing the people of the United States. **Summarize**

Caring for Nature

🕐 *Quick Summary* Progressives promoted the conservation of the nation's most valuable natural places and resources.

11 **Explain how a place or area would need to be protected against being destroyed or used up.** Possible answer: Places could be stripped of their beauty or their resources if industry or settlement moved into the area. Resources such as forests and water could be removed or polluted. **Express Ideas**

12 **How did John Muir promote conservation?** Possible answer: He wrote about beautiful places so that people who had never seen them would appreciate them. He helped establish a club that worked for conservation. He helped establish a park. **Summarize**

Primary Source

Cited in speech by Theodore Roosevelt, Sacramento, CA, May 19, 1903

13 **What did Theodore Roosevelt mean when he said "We are not building this country of ours for a day"?** Possible answer: We must not do things to our environment that will destroy its treasures for the future. **Analyze Primary Sources**

Caring for Nature

As interest in the West increased, some people became concerned that wilderness areas might be damaged. A movement to save western lands started shortly after the Civil War. Yellowstone National Park became the world's first national park in 1872. The Progressives continued this work.

John Muir, a naturalist and writer, had a great impact on the conservation of some of the country's most beautiful areas. **Conservation** is protecting something **11** from being destroyed or used up.

Muir traveled across the United States, visiting the great wilderness areas. He wrote magazine articles that described the beauty of these places. He helped establish **Yosemite National Park** (yoh SEM it ee) in California in 1890 and helped found the **12** Sierra Club in 1892. The club was named for the Sierra Nevada, the mountain range where Yosemite is located. Muir hoped that the club would contribute to the preservation of the environment.

Theodore Roosevelt had always loved being outdoors. He and Muir were good friends. They shared an appreciation of America's natural beauty. "I want to drop politics absolutely for four days and just be in the open with you," President Roosevelt wrote to Muir in 1903. Soon afterward, Roosevelt joined Muir on a camping trip in Yosemite.

For the next three days, the two men rode Yosemite's trails on horseback. They rested by rushing streams. They admired the magnificent mountains, trees, and waterfalls. The trip convinced Roosevelt that he must do more to conserve the nation's natural resources. Of the sights he had seen on the trip, he said,

> *"It would be a shame to our civilization to let them disappear . . . . We are not building this country of ours for a day. It is to last through the ages."*

13

▶ This postcard from 1912 shows visitors enjoying a view of the Grand Canyon, which Theodore Roosevelt had set aside as a National Monument in 1908.

266

Practice and Extend

CURRICULUM CONNECTION
Writing

Write a Poem

- Have students write a poem that expresses their appreciation for nature.
- Encourage students to begin by listing images from nature that appeal to them—for example, lofty mountains, shimmering lakes, and so on.
- Then, have students work these images into lines and verses.
- Tell students that their poems need not rhyme, though they may.
- Invite students to share their poems with the rest of the class.

Roosevelt wanted the country's many natural wonders protected—and he did something about it. He created the National Wildlife Refuge Program and organized the U.S. Forestry Service. He stopped the sale of 235 million acres of timberland and made them into national forests. In 1908 he set aside 800,000 acres in Arizona as the **Grand Canyon National Monument.** This protected the canyon from developers until Congress decided, eleven years later, to make it a national park. Roosevelt also

▶ John Muir and Teddy Roosevelt shared a love of the wilderness.

preserved Crater Lake in Oregon and the Anasazi ruins of Mesa Verde, Colorado. By the time he left office in 1909, Roosevelt had created 16 national monuments, 51 wildlife refuges, and 5 new national parks. **⑭**

REVIEW How did Muir's work promote conservation? *Main Idea and Details*

Summarize the Lesson

- **1901** Theodore Roosevelt became President.
- **1906** Upton Sinclair published *The Jungle,* a book that exposed unsafe conditions in Chicago's meatpacking plants.
- **1913** The Sixteenth Amendment created a national income tax.

LESSON 2   REVIEW

Check Facts and Main Ideas

1. **Compare and Contrast** Pick three or four problems the **Progressives** tried to solve. On a separate sheet of paper, complete this diagram by comparing life before Progressives tried to solve the problems to life after they acted.

Before	After
	Answers will vary. Possible response: Companies formed trusts to control industries. Progressives broke up trusts. People abused alcohol. Progressives passed laws against selling alcohol on Sundays. Factories were not safe. Progressives passed laws to require safer conditions.

2. What were the **Blue Laws**? Why did some people not like them?

3. Why did **Progressives** want to see **trusts** broken up?

4. Describe some of the work that **John Muir** did to promote **conservation.** Use the highlighted terms in your answer.

5. Critical Thinking: *Draw Conclusions* Why do you think writers such as **Ida Tarbell** and **Upton Sinclair** were so important to the Progressive Movement?

Link to **Art**

Create a Brochure Look for information about the United States National Parks. Combine information and pictures to create a brochure that could be used to interest people in visiting one or more of the national parks. Use the word **conservation** in your brochure.

267

---

⑭ What generalization can you make about the location of the land set aside by Theodore Roosevelt, mentioned in the text? Possible answer: Much of it was in the western portion of the United States. **Make Generalizations**

✓ **REVIEW ANSWER** Possible answer: Muir's writings showed people why the country might want to conserve the nation's natural resources. **Main Idea and Details**

③ Close and Assess

Summarize the Lesson

Have students read the events listed on the vertical time line. Ask them to add two or three events from the lesson to expand the time line.

✓ **LESSON 2   REVIEW**

1.  **Compare and Contrast** For possible answers, see the reduced pupil page.

2. Possible answer: The Blue Laws were laws designed to solve social problems. Some people did not like laws that forced morals on them.

3. Possible answers: The trusts controlled industries and forced out competition. Because of this, they could charge higher prices. This was not good for consumers.

4. Possible answers: John Muir traveled through the wilderness and wrote articles about his experiences. Because he believed in conservation, he helped found the Sierra Club.

5. **Critical Thinking:** *Draw Conclusions* Possible answer: These writers could change public opinion. Also, they got information to the people who could use it. Roosevelt changed laws after reading books by Sinclair and Tarbell.

Link to **Art**

Students' brochures should include information and illustrations that help inspire interest, and they should incorporate the word *conservation.*

CURRICULUM CONNECTION
Math

Calculate Square Mileage

Theodore Roosevelt established 235 million acres of timberland as national forests. Ask students the following math question:

If there are 640 acres per square mile, how many square miles of national forest did Roosevelt help create? (Answer: 367,187.5 square miles)

Workbook, p. 58

Lesson 2: The Progressive Movement

Directions: Answer the following questions on the lines provided. You may use your textbook.

1. What kinds of problems did the growth of industry create in the United States?

2. What were trusts?

3. Who were the Progressives and what were their goals?

4. Who were the muckrakers and how did they get their name?

5. Who was John Muir, and what role did he play in the Progressive Movement?

Notes for Home: Your child learned about the key individuals and issues of the Progressive Movement in the United States.
Home Activity: Discuss the word *Progressive* and what it means. Talk with your child about whether there is a need for Progressive-type activities in the United States.

Also on Teacher Resources CD-ROM.

Interpret Political Cartoons

Objective
- Interpret information in political cartoons.

Vocabulary
political cartoon, p. 268

Resource
- Workbook, p. 59

1 Introduce and Motivate

What is a political cartoon? Ask students how a political cartoon might be used by historians in the future to study our time. Then have students read the **What?** section of text on p. 268 to help set the purpose of the lesson.

Why use political cartoons? Have students read the **Why?** section of text on p. 268. Ask them what a cartoon for current people or events might look like.

2 Teach and Discuss

How is this skill used? Examine the political cartoons on p. 268 with students.

- Tell students that political cartoonists use symbols to represent different ideas in their messages.

- Explain that the symbols, along with other illustrations, take the place of written words. Some cartoons may have words as labels, but to understand the message a person has to examine the drawings and symbols.

- Have students read the **How?** section of text on pp. 268–269.

Interpret Political Cartoons

What? A political cartoon is a drawing that shows people or events in the news in a way that makes you smile or laugh. The goal of political cartoons is to make you think about events. Political cartoons often have a point of view.

Why? You can find political cartoons in newspapers and magazines. Often the cartoonist wants to express an opinion about people or events. You may or may not agree with the opinion, but a good political cartoon should make you think about the issue.

How? To understand a political cartoon, you need to understand the symbols that the cartoonist uses. For example, a drawing of a character called Uncle Sam is often a symbol for the United States. A drawing of a donkey is a symbol for the Democratic Party, and a drawing of an elephant is a symbol for the Republican Party. Political cartoonists first created these symbols.

Republican Party

Democratic Party

Uncle Sam

268

Practice and Extend

 SOCIAL STUDIES STRAND Government

Analyze Different Viewpoints
- Have students look at the political cartoon on p. 84.
- Ask students to identify the point of view expressed in this cartoon. (The Union will defeat the Confederacy.)
- Have students identify an opposing point of view. (The Confederacy will overwhelm the Union.)
- Lead a discussion of how the idea of the Confederacy winning might be shown in a political cartoon.

 CURRICULUM CONNECTION Art

Create a Political Cartoon
- Ask students to think about an issue or topic that is important at the local, state, or national level, and which relates to a person, place, or event.
- Have students decide what they think about the issue or topic and then design and draw a cartoon to show their feelings.
- Encourage students to look at others' cartoons and try to interpret the message.

In Lesson 2, you read about President Theodore Roosevelt's reforms. Look at the political cartoon on this page. Do you recognize the lion tamer? He is President Roosevelt. The cartoonist made the face look like Roosevelt's. Just in case you did not recognize the face, he wrote "San Juan" on the chest medal to show that the lion tamer is the hero of the Battle of San Juan Hill, during the Spanish-American War.

In the cartoon, Roosevelt is holding a whip to tame the lions. Each lion has a label to show what it stands for. For example, the lion closest to the reader is labeled "BEEF TRUST." The lions are walking out of a door labeled "WALL ST." The stocks of many large companies are traded in the New York Stock Exchange, located on Wall Street in New York City.

The cartoonist is saying something about Theodore Roosevelt and the trusts. If you have ever seen a lion tamer, you probably can figure out what the cartoonist intended.

Think and Apply

❶ What labels are shown on the other lions?

❷ What is the label on the door from which another lion appears? Why do you think the door has that label?

❸ What do you think the cartoonist intends to say about Theodore Roosevelt and the trusts?

269

❶ **Why did the cartoonist include the words "San Juan" on the lion tamer's chest?** People would know that the lion tamer is the hero of the Battle of San Juan Hill, Theodore Roosevelt.
Main Idea and Details

❷ **Why would the cartoonist use lions to represent the trusts?** Possible answer: Lions are strong and fierce.
Make Inferences

❸ **What do you notice about Roosevelt's arms in the cartoon? What does this tell you about the cartoonist's opinion of Roosevelt?** They are muscular. The cartoonist probably thinks Roosevelt is strong and tough.
Analyze Primary Sources

3 Close and Assess

Think and Apply

1. Oil trust, steel trust, coffee trust, sugar trust, railroad trust

2. The label is Wall Street, and it probably means that some of these trusts are part of Wall Street, where the New York Stock Exchange is located.

3. The cartoonist probably means to say that Roosevelt is taming the trusts with the antitrust laws.

Workbook, p. 59

Interpret Political Cartoons

A political cartoon is a drawing that shows people or events in the news in a way that makes you smile or laugh. The goal of political cartoons is to make you think about events.

Directions: Use this cartoon about women's rights to answer the questions below.

1. Where do the women appear in this cartoon? What are they doing? Why do you think the cartoonist portrayed these characters as she did?

2. What do you think the sign in the cartoon represent?

3. In this cartoon, men are being pushed off the world. What do you think this means?

4. A woman named Laura Foster drew this political cartoon. How do you think she felt about women's rights? Explain.

Notes for Home: Your child learned how to interpret political cartoons.
Home Activity: With your child, look through recent newspapers or magazines to find a political cartoon. Discuss the cartoon's message and the cartoonist's point of view.

Also on Teacher Resources CD-ROM.

Investigating and Sharing the Truth

Objective
- Identify the accomplishments of a leading reformer of the Progressive Era.

1 Introduce and Motivate

To activate prior knowledge, have students think about the importance of having fire alarms in buildings. Ask them why it is important for people to have systems for warning others about possible problems.

2 Teach and Discuss

❶ What can you infer about Ida Tarbell from the fact that she was the only woman in her class at Allegheny College? Possible answer: She was an unusual person who expected a lot of herself and who challenged herself to do different things than what women of her day usually did. Make Inferences

❷ What method did Tarbell use to make her stories responsible and effective? Possible answer: Careful research and hard work
Main Idea and Details

❸ What motivated Tarbell to write about Standard Oil? Possible answer: Her belief that Standard Oil was acting illegally and memories of her father's loss at the hands of Standard Oil Draw Conclusions

CITIZEN HEROES

Investigating and Sharing the Truth

Ida Tarbell investigated problems in United States businesses. She used her pen to share her findings in order to bring about change.

❶ Ida Tarbell did not follow the traditional role of women in the late 1800s. She attended Allegheny College in Pennsylvania and was the only woman in her class. She wanted to be a journalist, or news reporter and writer, which was unusual for women of the time.

As a girl, Tarbell had seen how some people who ran businesses, when not regulated, could cause harm to others. Her father owned an independent oil company. John D. Rockefeller's Standard Oil Company gained control over most of the country's oil companies, forming a powerful trust. Ida's father could not compete. He went bankrupt and lost his business. This event would later lead to Tarbell's most famous and important writings.

Tarbell went to Paris, France, to study. While there, she wrote articles for several American magazines, which she mailed back to the United States for publication. She came to know that a good reporter must do research and work ❷ hard to write well. While other magazines and newspapers exaggerated stories to make them more exciting, Tarbell wrote responsible stories that got the facts straight.

When back in the United States, Tarbell decided to write about the Standard Oil Company. She took her responsibility as a reporter seriously. She closely examined the trust that the Standard Oil Company had formed. She collected documents from government investigations. She interviewed a Standard Oil executive. She found that Standard Oil used illegal methods, such as ❸ bribes, to take control of the oil industry.

In 1904 she wrote a series of articles for *McClure's Magazine* about Standard Oil. John D. Rockefeller claimed that Tarbell did not tell the

270

Practice and Extend

SOCIAL STUDIES
Background

About John D. Rockefeller and the Standard Oil Company

- John D. Rockefeller first got into the oil refining business in Cleveland, Ohio, in the 1860s. In 1865, he bought out his partners for $72,500. Within a few years, Rockefeller's company was the world's largest refiner of oil.

- Rockefeller established Standard Oil in 1870 and set out to control the entire oil industry. He did this in part by good management. But he also used techniques such as forcing railroads to charge his competitors more for shipping—thus driving the competitors out of business.

- Standard Oil was finally dissolved in 1911, when the United States Supreme Court found the company was in violation of U.S. antitrust laws.

- John D. Rockefeller was a noted philanthropist who gave away hundreds of millions of dollars.

BUILDING CITIZENSHIP

Caring

Respect

★ Responsibility

Fairness

Honesty

Courage

truth. But she had done her work too well, and he could not prove her wrong. Tarbell's investigation and reporting helped lead to new government acts. President Theodore Roosevelt read her reports and worked to end the Standard Oil Company trust. The company was broken into several smaller companies.

Ida Tarbell realized that it was her education that had put her in a position to make a difference. She believed that a good education would help make better citizens. When speaking about the responsibility of college graduates, she said,

> "[College graduates] recognize that their education is not merely a personal matter, it is a community matter." **4**

Today, we are protected from trusts because responsible people such as Ida Tarbell worked to correct a problem. Others have learned from her example and continue to strive to change things that need changing.

Responsibility in Action

Discuss with your class ways that students can act responsibly. Have you ever stood up for something you felt was right? Have you ever stood up for another student even when others have not? Have you ever tried to change something that was wrong? How can you best share your views with others?

271

Primary Source

Cited in "The College Graduate in Her Community," Ida Tarbell

4 **What do you think Tarbell meant by saying ". . . education . . . is a community matter"?** Possible answer: People who have a good education can use it for the good of all people, not just themselves. **Analyze Primary Sources**

3 Close and Assess

Responsibility in Action

- Help students identify examples of standing up for something that is right.

- You may want to provide newspapers or other sources with examples of people in your community who have acted with notable responsibility.

CURRICULUM CONNECTION
Literature

Ida Tarbell and Responsibility

Ida Tarbell: Pioneer Investigative Reporter, by Barbara A. Somervill (Morgan Reynolds, ISBN 1-883-84687-0, 2002) **Easy**

You Decide!: Making Responsible Choices, by Jean Bunnell (McGraw-Hill Children's Publishing, ISBN 1-56822-427-3, 2003) **On-Level**

Ida Tarbell: Portrait of a Muckraker, by Kathleen Brady (University of Pittsburgh Press, ISBN 0-8229-5807-4, 1989) **Challenge**

World War I

Objectives

- Relate the causes of World War I and identify the countries of the Allied Powers and Central Powers.

- Explain issues of isolationism and the reasons for U.S. involvement in the war.

- Discuss the technological advances in warfare as they affected society.

- Describe the impact at home and abroad of the U.S. involvement in World War I.

Vocabulary

World War I, p. 273; **nationalism,** p. 273; **alliance,** p. 273; **isolationism,** p. 275; **League of Nations,** p. 280; **Treaty of Versailles,** p. 280

Resources

- Workbook, p. 60
- Transparency 14
- Every Student Learns Guide, pp. 106–109
- Quick Study, pp. 54–55

Quick Teaching Plan

If time is short, have students write each section heading at the top of a separate index card.

- Have students write down details from each section on the appropriate card as they read the lesson independently.

1 Introduce and Motivate

Preview To activate prior knowledge, have students recall what they have read about the terrible bloodshed and devastation wrought by the Civil War and other conflicts in United States history. Tell students that they will be reading about World War I, which raised the destructive power of warfare to a terrifying new level.

You Are There The United States was in 1916 one of the world's great military powers, but it had not yet entered World War I as a combatant. Have students predict how the U.S. entry into the war would affect the war and the people of this country.

272 Unit 3 • Expansion and Change

LESSON 3

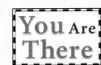

1910   1920

1914   1917   1919
World War I   United States   Treaty of
begins in Europe. enters World   Versailles ends
                   War I.   World War I.

Versailles
FRANCE   AUSTRIA-HUNGARY
               SERBIA

PREVIEW

Focus on the Main Idea
When it appeared the United States might be in danger, the country became involved in World War I.

PLACES
Austria-Hungary
Serbia
Versailles, France

PEOPLE
Woodrow Wilson
John J. Pershing
Eddie Rickenbacker
Alvin C. York

VOCABULARY
World War I
nationalism
alliance
isolationism
League of Nations
Treaty of Versailles

World War I

You Are There
It is 1916. One of the bloodiest battles in history has just ended at Verdun in France. A young American, Samuel Benson, is there to help wounded French soldiers. Benson is a volunteer in the American Ambulance Service. For months he has been transporting wounded soldiers to medical aid stations. Now he sits down to write himself a letter:

"My dear sir, self: . . . You may sometimes think you have it pretty hard staying out here in France away from home and loved ones . . . laboring without pay, and often getting little rest or sleep. But listen . . . you are at this hour in the midst of the biggest crisis of history. The world has never seen such a moment . . . and [you are] living for others."

That "moment" is World War I. It is being fought mainly in Europe, but also in Africa and Asia. Soon the United States will enter the war.

Compare and Contrast As you read, compare and contrast the United States before and during World War I.

272

Practice and Extend

READING SKILL
Compare/Contrast

In the Lesson Review, students complete a graphic organizer like the one below. You may want to provide students with a copy of Transparency 14 to complete as they read the lesson.

Use Transparency 14

VOCABULARY
Word Exercise

Context Clues

Homographs are words that have the same pronunciation and spelling, but different meanings and origins. Explain that *league* is a homograph. One meaning of *league* is "a union of persons, parties, or nations formed to help one another." Another meaning of *league* is "a unit for measuring distance." Tell students to use the lesson context to help them decide which meaning of *league* is used in the phrase *League of Nations.* (union)

A Gathering Storm

What brought on this war, which would one day be called **World War I**? Fierce rivalries had developed among European nations. Countries competed for military power and ownership of European lands. Strong feelings of nationalism existed. **Nationalism** is a love of one's country and the desire to have that country free from the control of others. Tensions grew because many lands were under the control of other nations. European nations also competed for new land in Africa, Asia, and the Middle East. New land meant new trading opportunities, greater wealth, and more power.

Fearing attack from their rivals, several European nations formed alliances. An **alliance** is an agreement among nations to defend one another. If one ally, or member of an alliance, is attacked, the other members promise to come to its aid. The two major alliances were the Allied Powers and the Central Powers. The Allied Powers included Great Britain, France, Russia, Serbia, and Belgium. The Central Powers included Germany, Austria-Hungary, Bulgaria, and Turkey.

In 1914 **Austria-Hungary,** a country in south central Europe, was in control of land that another country, **Serbia,** believed it owned. On June 28, 1914, a Serbian nationalist assassinated Archduke Franz Ferdinand, heir to the Austria-Hungarian throne. Austria-Hungary declared war on Serbia.

REVIEW How did nationalism help bring about war in 1914? **Draw Conclusions**

MAP SKILL

The Allied Powers and Central Powers in 1915

Allied Powers
Central Powers
Neutral nations

► The Allied and Central Powers fought during World War I. Some alliances changed after the war began.

MAP SKILL Use a Map Key *In 1914 Italy was a member of the Central Powers. What happened in 1915?*

ESL **ACCESS CONTENT**
ESL Support

Discuss Alliances Encourage students to explore the meaning of *alliances* as a way of understanding the events that brought about World War I.

Beginning Have students work in groups of three to act out the effects of an alliance (that is, parties cooperating either to protect or support each other).

Intermediate Ask students to summarize in their own words why the nations of Europe may have sought to make alliances in the early 1900s.

Advanced Have students describe in writing or orally one benefit and one drawback of being involved in an alliance.

For additional ESL support, use Every Student Learns Guide, pp. 106–109.

---

2 Teach and Discuss

PAGE 273

Gathering Storm

🕐 *Quick Summary* Throughout Europe, nationalism, rivalry, and alliances created tension. An assassination led to war.

H SOCIAL STUDIES STRAND
History

Tell students that nationalism in the 1900s caused nations to be very competitive and to protect their own interests.

1 **Why do you think nationalism helped create a "gathering storm" in Europe?** Possible answer: Nationalism made it difficult for countries to cooperate. **Express Ideas**

2 **Given the alliances that existed among European powers, what was the danger of Austria-Hungary's declaration of war against Serbia?** Possible answer: It would draw other nations into the conflict. **Draw Conclusions**

✓ **Ongoing Assessment**

If... students do not see the potential problem of Austria-Hungary's declaration of war on Serbia,

then... have them review the paragraph that begins "Fearing attack..." and the extent of the alliances that entangled Europe in 1914.

✓ **REVIEW ANSWER** Possible answer: Serbia wanted to gain control of land its people believed should have been part of its territory, and this led to the assassination of Archduke Ferdinand. **Draw Conclusions**

MAP SKILL
The Allied Powers and Central Powers in 1915

3 **Which countries shown on the map were neutral in 1915?** Norway, Sweden, Denmark, Netherlands, Switzerland, Spain, Portugal, Greece, Albania, and Romania **Use Map Key**

MAP SKILL **Answer** Italy changed its alliance to the Allied powers.

Fighting Begins in Europe

Quick Summary One by one, the nations of Europe were drawn into World War I. The fighting was fierce and was characterized by bloody "trench warfare."

Test Talk

Use Information from the Text

4 **What drew Russia and Germany into the war against each other?** Students should look back at the text to make sure they have the right information. Possible answer: Both entered in part to help defend another country. **Cause and Effect**

5 **What can you infer about Germany's motives for declaring war on France?** Possible answer: Germany feared an attack by France, so it decided to attack first. **Make Inferences**

6 **What would you predict happened to soldiers who crossed into no-man's land and charged the enemy's trenches?** Possible answer: Many of them were killed. **Predict**

✓ **REVIEW ANSWER** Possible answer: Belgium refused to let Germany march through its territory to attack France. **Main Idea and Details**

Fighting Begins in Europe

When Austria-Hungary declared war on Serbia, Russia worried that the fighting would threaten the trade route it had from the Black Sea to the Mediterranean Sea. On July 30, 1914, Russia prepared for war to protect its trade route and to help Serbia defeat Austria-Hungary.

Germany, allied with Austria-Hungary, demanded that Russia demobilize, or dismiss its army, and not fight. Russia did not listen to Germany's demands. On August 1, 1914, **4** Germany declared war on Russia.

Germany was afraid that it would have to fight in two different places. Russia was to Germany's east. France, Russia's ally, was to the west. Germany asked France if it planned to fight on the side of Russia. France did not give a clear answer, so Germany declared war **5** on France on August 3.

In order to reach France, German forces needed to march through Belgium. Germany asked the Belgian king for permission to cross his country. The king refused. There-fore, on August 4 the German army invaded

▶ Soldiers fought from trenches during World War I. Climbing out to attack was known as "going over the top."

Belgium. Great Britain, an ally of Belgium, declared war on Germany. Soon every major European country was involved in the war.

The fighting was fierce. Soldiers on each side dug a system of trenches that faced each other and could extend hundreds of miles. Barbed-wire fences protected the front of each trench. A "no-man's land"—the land between trenches that neither side con-trolled—spread out between the opposing armies. Soldiers ate and slept in the trenches, which were often flooded or filled with rats.

Each side shot at the other's trenches or sent poison gases into them. Occasionally, troops on one side would go "over the top." They climbed out, crawled through the barbed wire, and raced across no-man's land to attack the enemy. As casualties climbed month after month, it seemed that the killing **6** would never end.

REVIEW What caused Germany to invade Belgium? **Main Idea and Details**

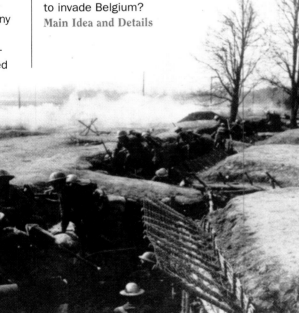

274

Practice and Extend

FYI **SOCIAL STUDIES** **Background**

About Poison Gases Used in World War I

- Poisonous gas as a weapon was first used on a significant scale in 1915, when the Germans used chlorine gas against entrenched French and Canadian troops.
- Poisonous gases were employed by both the Allies and the Central Powers at different points during the war.
- There were many different chemical agents used. Some, such as chlorine and phosgene gas, caused irritation of the lungs. Others, such as mustard gas, caused burns and blisters on contact.
- The development of gas masks limited the effectiveness of gas as a battlefield weapon. Gas killed fewer than 100,000 soldiers during the war but injured hundreds of thousands more.

The United States Enters the War

At first, the United States stayed out of World War I. The country had not become involved in European wars in the past. There was a policy of **isolationism.** This meant that the United States preferred to remain neutral and let other countries handle their own affairs. With an ocean between the United States and Europe, it was easy to stay isolated. Also, many European immigrants living in the United States did not want the country to take sides. They feared that they might have to fight the countries from which they had come.

On May 7, 1915, a German submarine torpedoed and sank the British steamship *Lusitania.* More than 100 U.S. citizens were killed. President Woodrow Wilson wrote a letter to the German government stating that the United States objected to attacks on non-military ships. Some Americans called for war.

Early in 1917 other events caused the United States to turn firmly against the Central Powers. In January the United States learned that a telegram had been sent from Germany to Mexico asking Mexico to enter the war on the side of the Central Powers. In return, Germany promised to help Mexico get back lands it had lost to the United States.

Then in February 1917, Germany ordered its submarines

► President Wilson asked Congress to declare war in 1917.

to attack any ships suspected of carrying weapons to the Allied Powers. German submarines sank three American-owned trade ships in March. The deaths of American sailors angered many in the United States.

On April 2 President Wilson asked Congress to declare war on the Central Powers. He stated,

> *"It is a fearful thing to lead this great peaceful people into war, into the most terrible and disastrous of all wars. . . . But the right is more precious than the peace."*

President Wilson hoped that by entering the war, the United States would make the world "safe for democracy." On April 6, 1917, Congress declared war on Germany.

REVIEW Why did the United States enter World War I? **Summarize**

► American officer's uniform from World War I

275

The United States Enters the War

🕐 *Quick Summary* The United States tried to stay out of the war, but German submarine warfare and dealings with neighboring Mexico finally drew the United States into the fight.

SOCIAL STUDIES STRAND
Geography

Help students understand that in the early 1900s, transportation and communication across the Atlantic Ocean was far slower than it is today. There was relatively less contact between Europe and the United States.

7 **Why do you think the distance between Europe and the United States affected American attitudes toward the war?** Possible answer: People in the United States may have felt that events in Europe did not have a direct effect on them. **Draw Conclusions**

8 **What was the sequence of events described in the text that led the United States into World War I?** The *Lusitania* was sunk in 1915. In January 1917, it was discovered that Germany had been seeking support from Mexico in return for helping Mexico regain land it had lost to the United States. In February 1917, Germans again began submarine warfare on American shipping. **Sequence**

Primary Source

Cited in "War Message," President Wilson's address to Congress, April 2, 1917

9 **What reason does Wilson give for bringing the United States into the war?** Possible answer: Entering the war is the right and just thing to do. **Analyze Primary Sources**

✓ **REVIEW ANSWER** Possible answer: German forces killed American civilians by sinking ships; Germany sought Mexican support in exchange for help in regaining territory Mexico had lost to the United States. **Summarize**

America at War

⏱ **Quick Summary** The entry of the United States into World War I proved decisive in defeating the Central Powers. Several American soldiers distinguished themselves on the battlefield.

⑩ What do you think Colonel Stanton meant when he spoke at Lafayette's tomb? Possible answer: He meant that the United States was there to repay the favor Lafayette had paid to the United States during the American Revolution. **Analyze Primary Sources**

⑪ What advantage did the United States military have over its enemies in World War I? Possible answer: It was not weary and wounded from three years of terrible fighting. ↩ **Compare and Contrast**

⑫ What made Sergeant Alvin York's performance so remarkable? Possible answer: He was outnumbered and had an inferior weapon compared to the German machine-gunners. **Summarize**

✓ **REVIEW ANSWER** He destroyed 35 machine guns and helped capture 132 German prisoners. **Main Idea and Details**

America at War

American forces began landing in France in June 1917, with General **John J. Pershing** in command. Pershing was an experienced soldier and had fought in many battles, including at San Juan Hill. On July 4, 1917, Pershing led a parade through Paris to the tomb of the Marquis de Lafayette, who had aided George Washington during the American Revolution. Standing in front of the tomb, Pershing's aide, Colonel Charles Stanton, said,

⑩ *"Lafayette, we are here!"*

These words gave hope to the allies. They showed that Americans were ready to help.

The arrival of American troops in Europe dramatically increased the fighting strength of the Allied Powers, who had already been ⑪ fighting for three years. More than four million American soldiers, sailors, and marines fought in World War I. Skilled leaders and fierce battles soon molded them into a powerful fighting force. The American presence began to turn the war around—it was one of the deciding factors in the Allied Powers' eventual victory.

The war produced many heroes. **Eddie Rickenbacker** was one of the first U.S. fighter pilots. He was considered an "ace"

because he shot down 22 German planes and 4 observation balloons. When World War I planes fought each other in the air, it was called a "dog fight."

One of the most famous heroes of the war was Sergeant **Alvin C. York.** Raised in the mountains of Tennessee, York had needed to learn to use a rifle to hunt food for his family. Even before the war, he was well known for his "sharp shooting." But he was also known as a man of peace. What happened when he went to war?

In October 1918, York was among a patrol of 17 men sent out to stop the German machine guns that were keeping American soldiers from moving forward. The patrol was behind enemy lines, and they came under heavy attack. Six men were killed and three were wounded. Alone, York traded fire with the Germans, a rifle against German machine guns. He shot quickly and accurately. He knocked out 35 machine guns. At last the ⑫ German major said in English, "Don't shoot anymore!" York and the ten other American soldiers returned to the American lines with 132 German prisoners. York was given the Medal of Honor and was promoted to rank of sergeant.

REVIEW Why was Alvin York promoted to the rank of sergeant? **Main Idea and Details**

▶ Soldiers were taught how to use gas masks to protect themselves during poison gas attacks.

Practice and Extend

❄ **MEETING INDIVIDUAL NEEDS**
Leveled Practice

Research World War I, 1914–1917 Encourage students to use the text and online library resources to learn about the events of World War I prior to the entry of the United States.

Easy Have students use information from the text to create a time line including at least one key event from each year of World War I prior to the U.S. entry. **Reteach**

On-Level Have students create a time line that identifies at least two key events from each year of the war prior to the entry of the United States. **Extend**

Challenge Ask students to create an illustrated time line that identifies at least four important events from each year of the war prior to the U.S. entry. **Enrich**

For a Lesson Summary, use Quick Study, p. 54.

New Technologies

When you read about the American Civil War, you learned that technology changed the way war was fought. By 1915, fifty years later, new technology had once again created weapons that were more powerful and deadly than older ones. For example, in April 1915 Germany began using poison gas as a weapon. The gas burned lungs and blinded eyes. Soon, both sides were using gas against each other. The Germans continued to develop deadlier gases.

Gas masks were developed to protect soldiers from the fumes.

Engineers turned the airplane, a new invention, into a weapon of war. Airplanes dropped bombs on enemy targets and fired machine guns, another new technology, at troops on the ground or enemy planes in the air.

Tanks were used for the first time by the British during World War I. Submarines, which had been in development for many years, were now put to use on a large scale to destroy enemy ships.

REVIEW How did new technologies affect the fighting in World War I? **Summarize**

▶ **Tanks were used for the first time in World War I.**

ANZACs at Gallipoli

Anyone fighting Britain faced all the countries of the British Commonwealth. In April 1915 the Australian and New Zealand Army Corps, or ANZACs, landed on the Gallipoli Peninsula in western Turkey. The ANZACs had been told they would land on flat beaches. What they found were steep cliffs. At the top of the cliffs were heavily armed Turkish forces. Gallipoli overlooks the Dardanelles, the narrow waterway connecting the Mediterranean and Black Seas. Controlling the Dardanelles could help the Allies win the war.

The ANZACs were the first soldiers to arrive at Gallipoli. They were attacked from the cliffs above by artillery and gunfire. Many were killed in the first hours and thousands more in the weeks to follow. The battle raged for eight months. The ANZACs did not get the supplies or medical care they needed, but they fought on. In January 1916 the ANZACs and other Allied soldiers were ordered to withdraw. The battle was a failure, but the ANZACs earned great respect for their valor and sacrifices.

▶ **ANZACs dug into the cliffs for shelter between battles.**

▶ **Gallipoli's steep cliffs made fighting difficult.**

277

PAGE 277

New Technologies

🕐 *Quick Summary* World War I saw the introduction of several deadly technological innovations in warfare, including poison gas, aircraft, and tanks.

S|T SOCIAL STUDIES STRAND
Science • Technology

Tell students that gas was capable of covering a wide area and reaching soldiers in trenches or otherwise out of sight or out of reach from conventional weapons.

13 **Why do you think poison gas was an effective weapon?** It could reach soldiers who were not vulnerable to bullets, bombs, or other conventional weapons. **Apply Information**

14 **What advantage did submarines have against surface ships?** Possible answer: Submarines could approach surface ships without being seen by human eyes. **Evaluate**

✓ **REVIEW ANSWER** Possible answer: Airplanes were used to drop bombs or fire at enemy troops. Poison gas was used to kill or injure the enemy. Tanks were used in battle. Submarines could destroy enemy ships. **Summarize**

ANZACs at Gallipoli

15 **Why do you think the cliffs made it harder for the ANZACs to fight at Gallipoli?** Possible answer: It is hard to fire on an enemy and defend oneself when climbing a hill. **Draw Conclusions**

FYI SOCIAL STUDIES
Background

About Zeppelins

• Zeppelins are gas-filled, balloon-like structures that float in the air.

• At the outset of World War I, the German military had zeppelins in its arsenal. Able to float above the range of existing aircraft and weapons, the zeppelins were used to bomb Great Britain and terrorize the public.

• The British quickly developed weapons and methods for combating the use of zeppelins. Dozens of the German airships were destroyed.

• By 1917, zeppelin warfare was obsolete.

War's Impact at Home

⏱ *Quick Summary* While the fighting took place in Europe, people in the United States rallied behind the war effort by raising money and saving food.

16 **What was the purpose of the recruitment posters?** Possible answer: The recruitment posters were intended to encourage young men to join the armed forces and fight for the United States in Europe. Make Inferences

17 **Why did people think raising food in their gardens would help win the war?** Possible answer: It would leave more food available for the soldiers in Europe. Draw Conclusions

18 **How did women contribute to the war effort?** Possible answer: They took over important jobs left vacant by men who went to war. Main Idea and Details

✓ **REVIEW ANSWER** Possible answer: The need for food supplies to be conserved and used wisely so that soldiers and Allied civilians would have enough to eat Cause and Effect

---

War's Impact at Home

While machine-gun fire and cannon shot blazed through Europe, people in the United States were busy doing what they could to help win the war. Americans sang the new patriotic song "Over There." They gave money to the Red Cross. Uncle Sam pointed out from posters, saying "I Want You" to young men who had not yet joined the army.

There were fewer hands to work the farms

▶ This poster used the symbol of Uncle Sam to encourage young men to volunteer for the army.

Poster by James Montgomery Flagg, 1918

I WANT YOU FOR U.S. ARMY
NEAREST RECRUITING STATION

16

with the men off at war. Because of this, less food was being produced. In spite of the shortages, a lot of food was needed for the soldiers fighting overseas. People started raising vegetables in "war gardens." Town squares and parks across the country were dug up and planted with food crops, to help feed people at home and overseas.

▶ These children are harvesting cabbage in a New York City "War Garden."

17

The government set up a Food Administration. It still looked like there might not be enough food. The administration encouraged people to eat less, using posters and slogans such as "Food Will Win the War!" Extra food was sent to soldiers and Allied civilians overseas.

Some women went to work in factories, taking over jobs men had done. Women helped produce weapons, tanks, and ammunition. African Americans who had moved North also took over many of the jobs now available.

18

REVIEW What caused the government to set up the Food Administration? Cause and Effect

278

▶ Children and adults across the United States worked in "war gardens" like this one. The food they grew helped the war effort, feeding workers and their families at home and soldiers overseas.

Practice and Extend

CURRICULUM CONNECTION
Art

Create a Poster

- Tell students that the government worked to win support from the public through the use of inspirational posters.
- Posters served many purposes—from encouraging enlistment in the military, to promoting food conservation, to stirring up resolve to fight the enemy.
- Have students create their own wartime poster. Students should be encouraged to create posters that support or oppose war.
- Posters should include art and an inspirational message.

The War Ends

The war raged into 1918. In September 1918 more than one million United States troops fought in a huge battle in the Meuse-Argonne (MUZ ahr GOHN), a region of northeastern France. More Americans fought in this battle than in any other single battle in United States history. The Allied Powers won the battle, which led to the final defeat of the Central Powers. The United States had helped turn the tide of the war.

On November 11, 1918, the Central Powers surrendered. Today, November 11 is celebrated as Veterans Day, to remember the Americans who fought in World War I and our nation's other wars.

In World War I, losses were huge for both sides. The Central Powers lost more than 3 million soldiers and nearly 3.5 million civilians. The Allied Powers lost nearly 5 million soldiers and more than 3 million civilians. The United States alone lost about 120,000 individuals. Many more were wounded. The war had been devastating and costly. Everyone hoped there would never be another war like that again. They called it "The War to End All Wars," because no one could imagine it happening again.

REVIEW Why did people hope there would never again be another war like World World I? **Draw Conclusions**

In Flanders Fields

Flanders in Belgium is the site of a cemetery and monument for Americans who died fighting to free Belgium. In 1919 Lieutenant Colonel John McCrae, a Canadian soldier and physician, wrote a poem about those who had lost their lives and the cause for which they died.

In Flanders fields the poppies blow
Between the crosses, row on row,
That mark our place; and in the sky
The larks, still bravely singing, fly
Scarce heard amid the guns below.

We are the Dead. Short days ago 21
We lived, felt dawn, saw sunset glow,
Loved, and were loved, and now we lie
In Flanders fields.

Take up our quarrel with the foe:
To you from failing hands we throw
22 *The torch; be yours to hold it high.*
If ye break faith with us who die
We shall not sleep, though poppies grow
In Flanders fields.

▶ Poppies grow where the dirt has been recently dug. The poem reflects the time when all the graves were new. Here you see the graves of Flanders fields as they appear today. Veterans groups still use paper poppies, like the one at left, to honor the war dead.

279

The War Ends

Quick Summary Aided by United States forces, the Allied Powers achieved victory in 1918. The joy of victory was restrained by the staggering numbers of war dead.

19 **What detail supports the idea that the Meuse-Argonne was a huge battle?** More than one million United States troops took part in the battle. **Main Idea and Details**

20 **Why was World War I known as "The War to End All Wars"?** Possible answer: Because people hoped that such a terrible conflict would never happen again **Express Ideas**

✓ **REVIEW ANSWER** Possible answer: Many died and were injured in the war. There was loss and sacrifice for civilians in both Europe and the United States. Terrible new weapons had been introduced, and these caused much death and destruction. **Draw Conclusions**

Literature and Social Studies

21 **From what point of view is this poem written?** From the point of view of soldiers killed in the war **Point of View**

22 **What do you think the torch mentioned in the last stanza represents?** Possible answer: The cause for which the soldiers were fighting **Analyze Primary Sources**

CURRICULUM CONNECTION
Music

Write a Tune

Have students come up with a tune (or use a melody they already know) to accompany the poem above. Encourage students to think about the tone of the poem and to create or use a melody that reflects that tone. Have student volunteers sing or play their song to the class.

The United States and the Peace Process

🕐 **Quick Summary** After the war, Woodrow Wilson failed to prevent a punishing peace treaty and to find support for a League of Nations.

㉓ **What did Woodrow Wilson think would result from a peace that punished the Central Powers?** It would set the stage for a future war. **Make Inferences**

✓ **REVIEW ANSWER** He wanted to prevent future wars. **Draw Conclusions**

3 Close and Assess

Summarize the Lesson

Have students write an explanation of each item in the vertical time line.

LESSON 3	**REVIEW**

1. 🔄 **Compare and Contrast** For possible answers, see the reduced pupil page.

2. The Allied Powers consisted of Great Britain, France, Russia, Serbia, and Belgium. The Central Powers consisted of Germany, Austria-Hungary, Bulgaria, and Turkey.

3. Possible answer: The United States believed that other countries should work out their own problems. When U.S. ships were attacked, the country joined the war.

4. Possible answer: Airplanes were used in air battles. Tanks were developed for land battles. Machine guns could fire more quickly than rifles. Poison gas was used to injure/kill the enemy.

5. **Critical Thinking: Draw Conclusions** Possible answers: People at home thought the war was just. Many people knew soldiers.

Link to ∞ Science
Ensure that students use several sources to support their reports.

The United States and the Peace Process

In January 1919, President Wilson and the other Allied leaders met in Versailles, France (vair SIGH), outside Paris, to draw up a peace treaty. Wilson hoped the treaty would not punish the Central Powers and would make sure ㉓ there would be a lasting peace. He suggested an international organization be formed to prevent wars—a **League of Nations.**

The **Treaty of Versailles** officially ended World War I. Against Wilson's wishes, the treaty did punish the Central Powers. It demanded that Germany pay heavy fines and not rebuild its army. However, the treaty also created the League of Nations, which Wilson had wanted.

The United States Senate did not approve the treaty. They disagreed with the harsh treatment of Germany. Also, many Americans feared that joining the League of Nations might force the United States into future wars. People wanted to return to a policy of isolationism. Peace and isolation would last only about 20 years.

REVIEW Why did President Wilson want a League of Nations? **Draw Conclusions**

Summarize the Lesson

- **1914** World War I began in Europe.
- **1917** United States entered World War I.
- **1919** Treaty of Versailles ended World War I.

LESSON 3	**REVIEW**

Check Facts and Main Ideas

1. 🔄 **Compare and Contrast** On a separate sheet of paper, fill in the boxes to describe what life was like in the United States before and during World War I.

Before World War I	During World War I
Answers may vary. The United States had a policy of isolationism. The United States had plenty of food from farms. The United States had not fought in wars overseas.	Answers may vary. The United States, for a while, lost its isolationist attitude. The United States faced some food shortages. The United States developed a strong army.

2. Identify the two alliances that fought each other in World War I and the nations that belonged to each. Answer in one or two sentences. Use the highlighted terms.

3. Why did the United States have a policy of isolationism, and what happened to change the policy?

4. Describe new technologies that were developed and used during World War I and how these technologies affected the way people fought.

5. **Critical Thinking: Draw Conclusions** Why did so many people at home get involved in the effort to help win the war?

Link to ∞ Science

Study Technology Look at the new technologies that were used in World War I. Choose one, such as tanks, airplanes, or submarines. Research the technology to find out how it has changed with time. Write a short report to share with the class.

Practice and Extend

FYI SOCIAL STUDIES
Background

About the League of Nations

- The idea for the league did have some support in the United States, but it could not win the two-thirds vote in the Senate required for ratification.
- Wilson campaigned tirelessly in support of the league. During this stressful campaign, he suffered a debilitating stroke.
- Even without the United States present, the League of Nations met throughout the 1920s and 1930s. By and large, it was a powerless and ineffectual body.
- The league was eventually replaced by the United Nations after World War II.

Workbook, p. 60

Lesson 3: World War I

Directions: Complete the chart with information from this lesson. You may use your textbook.

Cause	Effect
	Increased tensions in Europe, formation of alliances
	Casualty figures rose shockingly
United States pursues policy of isolationism	
United States enters the fighting	
	United States does not join League of Nations

Notes for Home: Your child learned about the causes and events of World War I.
Home Activity: Read a newspaper article about an armed conflict taking place in the world today. Discuss the terrible sacrifices that war requires of the people involved.

Also on Teacher Resources CD-ROM.

War in the Air

When World War I started in 1914, the history of powered flight was barely 10 years old. The first warplanes flew as observation craft. They scouted enemy lines from the air and helped direct artillery fire. Soon planes were carrying bombs to drop on enemy targets. By the end of the war, the role of military aircraft had changed from being a minor help to a major force in their own right. **1**

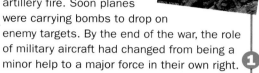

Leather hood and mask

Leather face mask and anti-splinter glass goggles

Raised collar to keep neck warm

Sheepskin lined leather gloves to protect against frostbite

Flying Gear
Pilots flew in open cockpits, so they wore special clothing to keep out the cold.

Sheepskin boots

Thick sole to give a good grip

Air "Aces"
To qualify as an air "ace", a pilot had to bring down at least 10 enemy aircraft. Captain Eddie Rickenbacker, an American "ace" and war hero, had 24 1/3 hits.

Wooden box-structure wings covered with canvas

wooden struts

26 ft. 11 in. wingspan

Symbol of British Royal Flying Corps, later the Royal Air Force

Sopwith Camel
The Sopwith F1 Camel first flew in battle in June 1917. It became the most successful Allied fighter in shooting down German aircraft. Pilots enjoyed flying the Camel because it was easy to steer and could make sharp turns at high speed.

CURRICULUM CONNECTION
Writing

Write About Modern Airplanes Tell students to use the library or Internet resources to learn more about the latest generation of airplanes. Have students research both civilian and military airplanes. Each student should then write about the features of one particular type of airplane and present a short report to the class.

War in the Air

Objective
- Use primary sources, such as photographs, to acquire information about World War I.

Resource
- Workbook, p. 61

1 Introduce and Motivate

- Tell students that new technologies, such as aircraft, changed the ways that wars were fought.

- Have students list ways airplanes were used in World War I. Tell students they will learn more as they read this page.

- Students will add to their lists later.

2 Teach and Discuss

1 For what sorts of actions were airplanes used in World War I? Combat, bombing, and scouting of enemy troops
Main Idea and Details

3 Close and Assess

Ask students to add to their lists of the uses of airplanes that they began earlier. Have students discuss what uses they learned about from the pictures and text on this page.

Workbook, p. 61

Directions: Suppose that you are a pilot during World War I. Write a diary entry in which you describe your flying gear, your aircraft, and your experiences as you fly over enemy territory.

Also on Teacher Resources CD-ROM.

Resources

- Assessment Book, pp. 33–36
- Workbook, p. 62: Vocabulary Review

Chapter Summary

For possible answers, see the reduced pupil page.

Vocabulary

1. d, **2.** c, **3.** e, **4.** b, **5.** a

People and Terms

Possible answers:

1. William Seward was responsible for the purchase of Alaska from Russia.

2. After the Spanish-American War, the United States gained control of several Spanish territories.

3. Army doctor Walter Reed discovered that yellow fever and malaria were carried by mosquitoes.

4. The Progressives were reformers who tried to solve many of the problems that the United States faced in the late 1800s and early 1900s.

5. Ida Tarbell was a muckraker who wrote about the dangers of trusts.

6. Progressives passed Blue Laws to try to solve some of the social problems of the day, such as alcohol abuse.

7. John Muir was a naturalist and writer who helped establish Yosemite National Park.

8. General John J. Pershing led American soldiers during World War I.

9. One of America's most famous World War I heroes was Sergeant Alvin C. York, who fought Germans single-handedly and helped capture 132 German prisoners.

10. The Treaty of Versailles, which officially ended World War I, severely punished the Central Powers.

CHAPTER 6
REVIEW

1890		1900

July 1898 Hawaii is annexed by the United States.

August 1898 Spanish-American War ends with United States victory.

1901 Theodore Roosevelt becomes President.

Chapter Summary

Compare and Contrast

On a separate sheet of paper, copy the graphic organizer. Use it to contrast the gaining of Alaska with the gaining of Hawaii. Write several points in each box.

Gaining Alaska	Gaining Hawaii
	• was valuable for growing sugarcane and pineapples

Answers will vary and may include—
Alaska: "valuable for fishing, furs, mines," "William Seward wanted it," "purchased from Russia"
Hawaii: "American growers wanted it," "taken over from Queen Liliuokalani and the Hawaiians"

Vocabulary

Match each word with the correct definition or description.

1. **yellow journalism** (p. 253)

2. **isthmus** (p. 256)

3. **muckraker** (p. 264)

4. **conservation** (p. 266)

5. **alliance** (p. 273)

a. an agreement among nations to defend one another

b. the protection of forests, rivers, and other natural resources

c. a narrow strip of land that connects two larger areas

d. false or exaggerated reporting

e. person who uncovered shameful conditions in businesses

People and Terms

Write a sentence explaining why each of the following people or terms was important to the United States becoming a world power. You may use two or more in a single sentence.

1. **William Seward** (p. 251)

2. **Spanish-American War** (p. 253)

3. **Walter Reed** (p. 256)

4. **Progressives** (p. 264)

5. **Ida Tarbell** (p. 264)

6. **Blue Laws** (p. 265)

7. **John Muir** (p. 266)

8. **General John J. Pershing** (p. 276)

9. **Sergeant Alvin C. York** (p. 276)

10. **Treaty of Versailles** (p. 280)

Practice and Extend

Assessment Options

✔**Chapter 6 Assessment**
- Chapter 6 Content Test: Use Assessment Book, pp. 33–34.
- Chapter 6 Skills Test: Use Assessment Book, pp. 35–36.

Standardized Test Prep
- Chapter 6 Tests contain standardized test format.

✔**Chapter 6 Performance Assessment**
- Have students present the concerns and challenges facing the people highlighted in this chapter.
- Each student can play the role of one of the persons mentioned in this chapter.
- Students should mention these individuals' roles in the events of the late 1800s and early 1900s discussed in this chapter.
- Assess students' understanding of the people and their effects on life in the late 1800s and early 1900s.

1906
Upton
Sinclair
publishes
The Jungle.

1910

1914
Panama
Canal
opens.

1917
United States
enters World
War I.

1920

1919
Treaty of
Versailles
ends World
War I.

Facts and Main Ideas

❶ Who were the Buffalo Soldiers? What did they accomplish?

❷ Why did John Stevens prove to be a good choice for chief engineer in building the Panama Canal?

❸ What did Woodrow Wilson suggest be formed to prevent war in the future?

❹ **Time Line** How many years were there between the end of the Spanish-American War and the United States, entering of World War I?

❺ **Main Idea** How did the Spanish-American War help expand the power of the United States abroad?

❻ **Main Idea** What major changes did the Progressives bring about in the United States?

❼ **Main Idea** Identify two reasons for tensions in Europe before World War I.

❽ **Critical Thinking:** *Make Inferences* Before World War I, the United States had a policy of isolationism. What might have happened if the United States had kept that policy and not fought in World War I?

Internet Activity

To get help with vocabulary, people, and terms, select dictionary or encyclopedia from *Social Studies Library* at www.sfsocialstudies.com.

Apply Skills

Interpret Political Cartoons
Answer the questions about this cartoon.

RECYCLING? BAH! TOO MUCH WORK

❶ What is this cartoon about?

❷ What is the man throwing? What does it stand for?

❸ What do you think is the cartoonist's point of view?

Write About History

❶ **Write a brief news story** describing the building of the Panama Canal.

❷ **Write an editorial** trying to convince Americans of the importance of conservation.

❸ **Draw a political cartoon** about one of the Progressives' issues of the time, such as unsafe work conditions, powerful trusts hurting competition, the need to conserve nature, or alcohol abuse.

283

Hands-on Unit Project

✓ Unit 3 Performance Assessment

- See p. 288 for more information about using the Unit Project as a means of performance assessment.
- A scoring guide is provided on p. 288.

💻 WEB SITE
Technology

For more information, students can select the dictionary or encyclopedia from *Social Studies Library* at **www.sfsocialstudies.com.**

Workbook, p. 62

Vocabulary Review

Directions: Use each of the vocabulary terms from Chapter 6 in a sentence. Write the sentences on the lines provided. You may use your glossary.

Rough Riders	yellow journalism	Spanish-	Progressive
Treaty of	muckrakers	American War	trust
Versailles	League of	Buffalo Soldiers	nationalism
Blue Laws	Nations	conservation	isolationism
alliance		reforms	World War I

Also on Teacher Resources CD-ROM.

Facts and Main Ideas

1. The Buffalo Soldiers were African American soldiers who helped win the Battle of San Juan Hill.

2. John Stevens increased the workforce, built towns for the workers, created an efficient system of railroad tracks to move equipment, and pushed for the use of a lock system for the canal.

3. The League of Nations

4. About 19 years

5. The United States gained control of several Spanish territories, including Guam, Puerto Rico, and the Philippines.

6. The Progressives helped bring about changes in working conditions, established new national parks, introduced a national income tax, helped make food and medicine safer, and reformed business practices.

7. Strong feelings of nationalism existed; also, many lands were under the control of other nations. People in these lands wanted independence.

8. Possible answer: If the United States had not fought in World War I, the Central Powers might have won the war. Germany might have taken over more land and become the most powerful nation in Europe. Germany might have aided Mexico in seeking to reconquer land from the United States.

Apply Skills

1. The importance of recycling and how people can be lazy about doing it

2. A globe; the environment

3. If we do not make recycling a way of life, the environment will be damaged.

Write About History

1. Remind students that a news story should focus on the main facts—who, what, where, why, and when.

2. Tell students that newspaper editorials take a clear position on a topic or issue and argue for that position.

3. Cartoons should use a combination of words and images to communicate their message.

Over There

Objectives

- Identify significant examples of music from various periods in United States history.

- Explain how examples of music reflect the times during which they were written.

1 Introduce and Motivate

Preview To activate prior knowledge, ask students if they are familiar with the song "Over There" and know its history. Tell students they will learn more about this song and its background.

Ask students how studying a popular song from a particular time might be useful in learning about that time. (It can help show how many people felt about events and issues.)

2 Teach and Discuss

1 **What kind of mood and attitude does this song project?** Possible answer: A positive, confident mood
Analyze Primary Sources

"Over There"

by George M. Cohan

By the time the United States decided to enter World War I, there was a feeling of patriotism and responsibility in joining the fight. Songwriters created thousands of new songs in support of American soldiers. George M. Cohan's "Over There" was optimistic and energetic. It was also one of the most popular songs during the war.

284

Practice and Extend

SOCIAL STUDIES Background

"Over There"

- George M. Cohan wrote the song just as the United States was entering the war—but before troops had seen combat.

- The song was perhaps the most popular song of the war era and helped the nation prepare for the struggle.

- The United States government recognized Cohan's contribution to the war effort with a Congressional Gold Medal awarded in 1936.

- Cohan also wrote "You're a Grand Old Flag" and other patriotic songs.

AUDIO CD Technology

Play the CD, *Songs and Music,* to listen to "Over There."

Words and Music by George M. Cohan

O - ver there, o - ver there,

Send the word, send the word o - ver there

That the Yanks are com-ing, the Yanks are com-ing, The

drums rum tum - ming ev - 'ry - where.

So pre - pare, say a pray'r,

Send the word, send the word to be - ware

We'll be o - ver, we're com - ing o - ver, And we

won't come back 'till it's o - ver o - ver there.

❶ ❷ ❸ ❹

285

❷ Why do you think the song tells people to "send the word over there"? Possible answer: Sending the word that the Yanks are coming will encourage our friends and frighten our enemies. **Analyze Primary Sources**

❸ Besides sending word that the Yanks are coming, what does the song tell people to do? Prepare and say a prayer. **Analyze Primary Sources**

❹ What is the meaning of "we won't be back till it's over over there"? Possible answer: The Yanks are determined to win the war. **Express Ideas**

❸ Close and Assess

Remind students that the song was meant to lift the nation's spirits during wartime. Have students discuss why they think it was important for the nation to feel positive and resolved as it headed into World War I. Ask them to consider what might have happened if people hadn't been as supportive of the troops and the war effort.

CURRICULUM CONNECTION
Music

Write a New Verse
- After students read or listen to the song, have them write a new verse for "Over There."
- Encourage students to try to match the tone and spirit of the original verses and chorus when writing their new verses.

Resource
- Assessment Book, pp. 37–40

Main Ideas and Vocabulary
TEST PREP

1. a, **2.** c, **3.** b, **4.** d

People and Places

1. b, **2.** f, **3.** a, **4.** e, **5.** c, **6.** d

Test Talk

Choose the Right Answer
Use People and Places, Question 4, to model the Test Talk strategy.

Narrow the answer choices.
Tell students to read each answer choice carefully. Students should rule out any choice that they know is wrong.

Choose the best answer.
After students mark their answer choice, tell them to check their answer by comparing it with the text.

Apply Skills

- Political cartoons from local newspapers may be easier for students to understand, since they may deal with familiar issues.

- Provide guided practice in deciphering the symbolism, irony, and exaggeration of political cartoons before starting.

UNIT 3 Review

Main Ideas and Vocabulary
TEST PREP

Read the passage below and use it to answer the questions that follow.

In the late 1800s and early 1900s, major changes occurred in the United States. New technologies improved the lives of many Americans. Telephones became widely available. Electric appliances saved time and energy. By the late 1800s, farmers no longer had to rely on <u>manual labor</u> alone. Mechanical reapers and threshing machines made harvesting faster and easier.

Goods of all kinds were produced in factories and mills. People moved from farms to the cities to fill the new jobs. Immigrants came to American cities to work in the factories. Cities became overcrowded and unsafe.

Women and African Americans worked to gain equal rights as citizens. Progressives pushed for laws to protect workers in the workplace. They wrote about the dangers of <u>trusts</u>. They also worked to conserve the wilderness.

Events outside the United States created changes too. To help Cubans gain independence from Spain, the United States fought the Spanish-American War. The United States became a world power.

The United States entered World War I in 1917. Americans helped the Allied Powers defeat the Central Powers.

Life for Americans was very different at the end of World War I from what it had been at the end of the Civil War.

1 According to the passage, what changed farm work in the late 1800s?
  A New machines made harvesting faster.
  B New laws made farmers hire more workers.
  C More people became farmers.
  D Americans bought less food.

2 In the passage, the term <u>manual labor</u> means—
  A work done with machines
  B work done slowly
  C work done by hand
  D work done quickly and easily

3 In the passage, the word <u>trusts</u> means—
  A relies or counts on
  B companies that have joined together to control an industry
  C industries that make farm machines
  D factories with unsafe working conditions

4 What is the main idea of the passage?
  A Progressives exposed shameful conditions.
  B African Americans and women worked for equal rights.
  C The United States fought in two wars.
  D Many events in the late 1800s and early 1900s changed life in the United States.

286

Practice and Extend

Assessment Options

✓ Unit 3 Assessment
- Unit 3 Content Test: Use Assessment Book, pp. 37–38.
- Unit 3 Skills Test: Use Assessment Book, pp. 39–40.

- Unit 3 Tests contain standardized test format.

✓ Unit 3 Performance Assessment
- See p. 288 for information about using the Unit Project as a means of Performance Assessment.
- A scoring guide for the Unit 3 Project is provided in the teacher's notes on p. 288.

Test Talk
- Test Talk Practice Book

WEB SITE Technology

For more information, you can select the dictionary or encyclopedia from *Social Studies Library* at **www.sfsocialstudies.com**.

Test Talk

Narrow the answer choices. Rule out answers you know are wrong.

People and Places

Match each person and event to its definition.

1 Walnut Grove, Virginia (p. 217)

2 James Buchanan Eads (p. 228)

3 Hawaii (p. 252)

4 Rough Riders (p. 254)

5 Upton Sinclair (p. 264)

6 Austria-Hungary (p. 273)

a. chain of islands annexed by the United States in 1898

b. home of inventor Cyrus McCormick

c. wrote the muckraking book *The Jungle*

d. country in south central Europe where World War I began

e. Roosevelt's soldiers during the Spanish-American War

f. built the first steel bridge in 1874

Apply Skills

Create a Political Cartoon Display Make a poster of political cartoons you have found in newspapers or magazines. You can add cartoons that you draw yourself. Under each cartoon, write a sentence or two explaining what the cartoon is about and what point of view it shows about the subject.

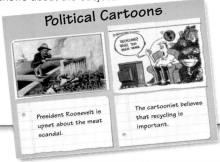

Write and Share

Create a Brochure Work in a group to create a brochure to advertise one of the important technologies developed or improved during the 1800s or early 1900s. Possible technologies include the milking machine, mechanical reaper, elevator, subway, and electric stove. Use the textbook or other resources to fill in details about the chosen technology. Create pictures, graphs, or diagrams to help illustrate the technology. Share the brochure with the class, explaining the technology's uses and benefits.

Read on Your Own

Look for books like these in the library.

287

Revisit the Unit Question

Portfolio Assessment

- Have students look at the list they created at the beginning of Unit 3 of the changes they think the United States faced in the 1800s and early 1900s.
- Have students look at the list they created throughout Unit 3 of the challenges the United States faced at home and abroad.

- Ask students to compare and contrast their lists.
- Have students write a paragraph comparing the United States at the beginning of the unit with the United States that emerged from World War I.
- Have students add these lists and paragraphs to their Social Studies Portfolio.

Write and Share

- Provide students with magazines and newspapers in order for them to get some ideas for their brochures.

- Help students locate resources for learning about their selected technologies.

- Encourage students to discuss and plan their illustrations before drawing them.

- Use the following scoring guide.

✓ Assessment Scoring Guide

Create a Brochure	
6	Elaborate details about uses, improvements, and benefits; clear, accurate information and graphics.
5	Includes details about uses, improvements, and benefits; clear, accurate information and graphics.
4	Some details about uses, improvements, and benefits; accurate information and graphics.
3	Mostly accurate information; some graphics; unclear details about uses, improvements, and benefits.
2	Few details or graphics; unclear information; does not cover one of the following: uses, improvements, or benefits.
1	Inaccurate information; does not cover uses, benefits, or improvements; graphics are missing or irrelevant.

If you prefer a 4-point rubric, adjust accordingly.

Read on Your Own

Have students prepare oral reports using the following books.

Where Poppies Grow: A World War I Companion, by Linda Granfield (Stoddart Publishing Co., Limited, ISBN 0-773-73319-1, 2001) **Easy**

The Panama Canal, by Elizabeth Mann (Mikaya Press, ISBN 0-965-04934-5, 1998) **On-Level**

Up from Slavery, by Booker T. Washington (Oxford University Press, ISBN 0-192-83562-9, 2000) **Challenge**

Arts and Letters

Objective

- Analyze an important invention through the creation of an infomercial.

Resource

- Workbook, p. 63

Materials

paper, pencils, paints, markers, reference materials

Follow This Procedure

- Tell students that they will present an infomercial about an invention created in the time period studied in this unit. They will advertise the invention and present the infomercial to the class.

- Explain to students that an infomercial is like a long commercial. It provides information about a particular product to encourage viewers to purchase the product.

- Divide students into groups. Have students choose an invention and research who the inventor was, why the invention was created, and how it helped people.

- Have students create posters or backdrops to advertise their invention. Encourage them to wear clothing of the time period. Invite students to present their infomercials to the class.

- Use the following scoring guide.

✓ Assessment Scoring Guide

Arts and Letters	
6	Elaborate details, very accurate content, precise word choices.
5	Good details, very accurate content, precise word choices.
4	Good details, accurate content, clear word choices.
3	Uses several details, accurate content, clear word choices.
2	Uses some details, some inaccurate content, vague word choices.
1	Uses few details, mostly inaccurate content, incorrect word choices.

If you prefer a 4-point rubric, adjust accordingly.

UNIT 3 Project

Arts and Letters

Create an infomercial about an important invention.

1 **Form** a group and choose an invention studied in this unit.

2 **Research** the invention. Write about the inventor and the time during which he or she lived. Explain why he or she made the invention. Describe how the invention has helped people.

3 **Make** a poster or backdrop to advertise your invention.

4 **Present** your infomercial to your class. You may want to dress in the clothing of the time and add sound effects.

Internet Activity

Find more about women's rights. Go to **www.sfsocialstudies.com/activities** and select your grade and unit.

288

Practice and Extend

 **Hands-on Unit Project**

✓ Performance Assessment

- The Unit Project can also be used as a performance assessment activity.
- Use the scoring guide to assess each group's work.

WEB SITE Technology

Students can launch the Internet Activity by clicking on *Grade 5, Unit 3* at **www.sfsocialstudies.com/activities**.

Workbook, p. 63

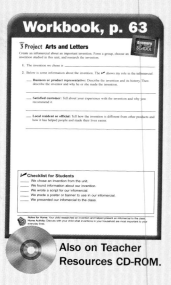

 **Also on Teacher Resources CD-ROM.**

Reference Guide

Table of Contents

Atlas
Photograph of the Continents

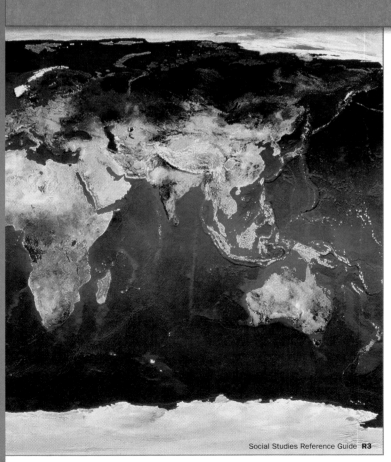

Atlas
Map of the World: Political

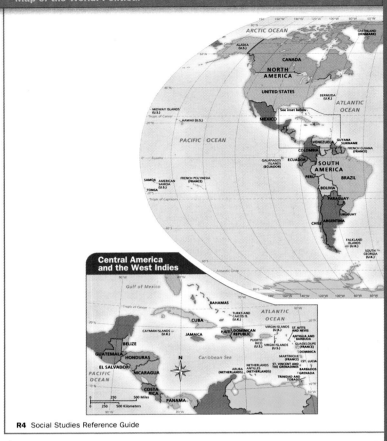

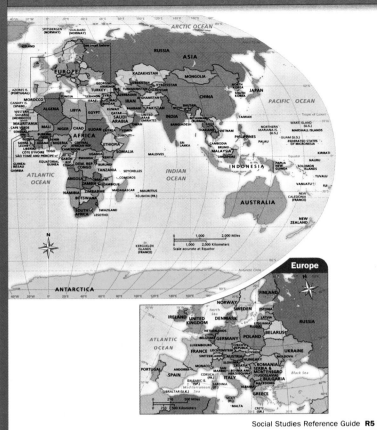

Atlas
Map of the Western Hemisphere: Political

Map of the Western Hemisphere: Physical

Atlas
Map of North America: Political

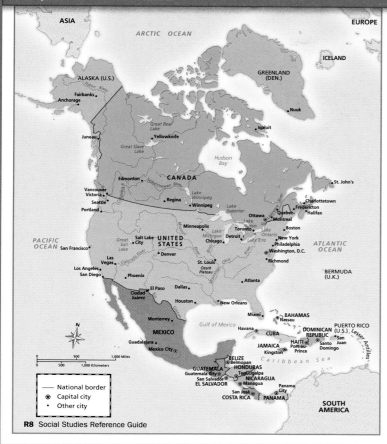

ASIA   EUROPE

ARCTIC OCEAN

ICELAND

ALASKA (U.S.)
Fairbanks
Anchorage

GREENLAND (DEN.)

Nuuk

Juneau

Yellowknife
Iqaluit

Great Bear Lake

Great Slave Lake

Hudson Bay

CANADA

Edmonton

Vancouver
Victoria
Seattle
Portland

Regina
Winnipeg

Lake Winnipeg

Lake Superior

St. John's

Charlottetown
Fredericton
Halifax
Ottawa Québec
Montreal

PACIFIC OCEAN

San Francisco

Las Vegas
Los Angeles
San Diego

Minneapolis

Salt Lake City

UNITED STATES

Denver

Phoenix

El Paso

Ciudad Juárez

Dallas

Houston

Monterrey

MEXICO

Guadalajara
Mexico City

Lake Michigan
Chicago
Detroit

St. Louis

Ozark Plateau

Atlanta

Chicago Toronto
Lake Erie
New York
Philadelphia
Washington, D.C.
Richmond

Boston

ATLANTIC OCEAN

BERMUDA (U.K.)

New Orleans
Miami

Gulf of Mexico

Havana

CUBA

BAHAMAS
Nassau

JAMAICA
Kingston

HAITI
Port-au-Prince

DOMINICAN REPUBLIC
Santo Domingo

San Juan

PUERTO RICO (U.S.)

Lesser Antilles

Caribbean Sea

BELIZE
Belmopan

GUATEMALA
Guatemala City
San Salvador
EL SALVADOR

HONDURAS
Tegucigalpa
NICARAGUA
Managua
San José
COSTA RICA

Panama City
PANAMA

SOUTH AMERICA

500   1,000 Miles
500   1,000 Kilometers

— National border
⊛ Capital city
• Other city

R8 Social Studies Reference Guide

Map of North America: Physical

ASIA   EUROPE

ARCTIC OCEAN

Chukchi Sea

Bering Sea

Queen Elizabeth Islands
Ellesmere Island

Greenland

Iceland

Beaufort Sea

Banks Island

Victoria Island

Baffin Bay

Baffin Island

Cape Farewell

Aleutian Islands
Bristol Bay
Kodiak Island

Mt. McKinley 20,320 ft. (6,194 m)

Gulf of Alaska

Alaska Peninsula

Brooks Range

Yukon River

Mackenzie Mts.

Great Bear Lake

Great Slave Lake

Lake Athabasca

CANADIAN SHIELD

Hudson Bay

Foxe Basin

Hudson Strait

Labrador Sea

Newfoundland

Gulf of St. Lawrence

PACIFIC OCEAN

Queen Charlotte Islands

Vancouver Island

Coast Mountains

ROCKY MOUNTAINS

GREAT PLAINS

Columbia Plateau

Black Hills

NORTH AMERICA

Lake Manitoba
Lake Winnipeg

Lake Superior
Lake Huron
Lake Michigan
Lake Erie
Lake Ontario

St. Lawrence River

Bay of Fundy
Cape Cod

Long Island

ATLANTIC OCEAN

Cape Hatteras

Chesapeake Bay

APPALACHIAN

GREAT BASIN

Great Salt Lake

Colorado Plateau

Mt. Whitney 14,495 ft. (4,418 m)
Death Valley (lowest point in N.A.) -282 ft. (-86 m)

Mojave Desert

Platte R.
Arkansas R.

INTERIOR PLAINS

Red River

Ohio R.
Tennessee R.

Bermuda

Sierra Nevada

Sierra Madre Occidental

Gila R.
Rio Grande

Sierra Madre Oriental

Gulf of California

Bay of Campeche

Yucatán Peninsula

Citlaltépetl 18,701 ft. (5,700 m)

COASTAL PLAIN

Gulf of Mexico

Straits of Florida

Cuba

Bahamas

Hispaniola

Puerto Rico

Lesser Antilles

Greater Antilles

WEST INDIES

Jamaica

Caribbean Sea

Lake Nicaragua

Isthmus of Panama

Gulf of Panama

SOUTH AMERICA

500   1,000 Miles
500   1,000 Kilometers

▲ Mountain peak
— National border

Social Studies Reference Guide R9

Atlas
Map of the United States of America

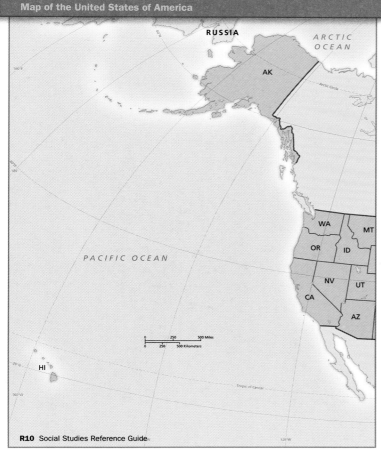

RUSSIA

ARCTIC OCEAN

AK

Arctic Circle

PACIFIC OCEAN

WA   MT
OR   ID
NV   UT
CA   AZ

WY
CO

HI

Tropic of Cancer

250   500 Miles
250   500 Kilometers

R10 Social Studies Reference Guide

Greenland (DENMARK)

CANADA

WA MT ND MN WI MI NY ME VT NH MA CT RI
OR ID SD IA IL IN OH PA NJ DE MD DC
NV UT WY NE KS MO KY WV VA
CA AZ CO OK AR TN NC SC
NM TX LA MS AL GA
FL

ATLANTIC OCEAN

Gulf of Mexico

MEXICO

BAHAMAS

CUBA

HAITI
DOM. REP.

JAMAICA

State or area	Abbreviation
Alabama	AL
Alaska	AK
Arizona	AZ
Arkansas	AR
California	CA
Colorado	CO
Connecticut	CT
Delaware	DE
District of Columbia	DC
Florida	FL
Georgia	GA
Hawaii	HI
Idaho	ID
Illinois	IL
Indiana	IN
Iowa	IA
Kansas	KS
Kentucky	KY
Louisiana	LA
Maine	ME
Maryland	MD
Massachusetts	MA
Michigan	MI
Minnesota	MN
Mississippi	MS
Missouri	MO
Montana	MT
Nebraska	NE
Nevada	NV
New Hampshire	NH
New Jersey	NJ
New Mexico	NM
New York	NY
North Carolina	NC
North Dakota	ND
Ohio	OH
Oklahoma	OK
Oregon	OR
Pennsylvania	PA
Rhode Island	RI
South Carolina	SC
South Dakota	SD
Tennessee	TN
Texas	TX
Utah	UT
Vermont	VT
Virginia	VA
Washington	WA
West Virginia	WV
Wisconsin	WI
Wyoming	WY

Social Studies Reference Guide R11

Atlas
Map of Our Fifty States: Political

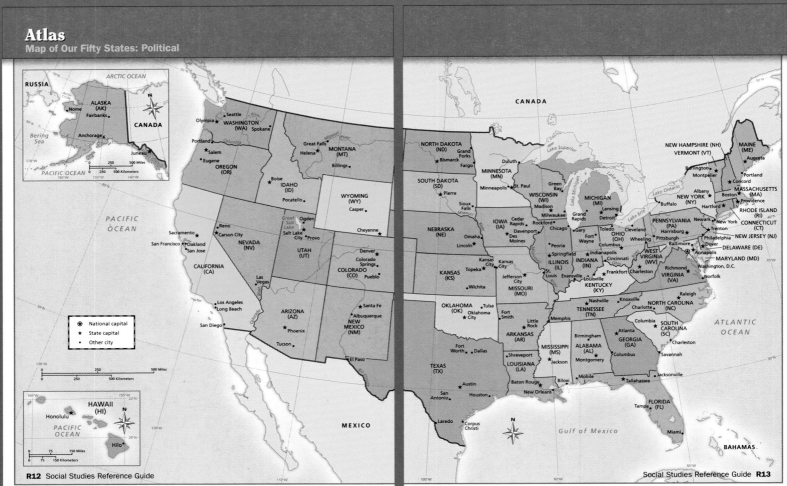

Atlas
Map of Our Fifty States: Physical

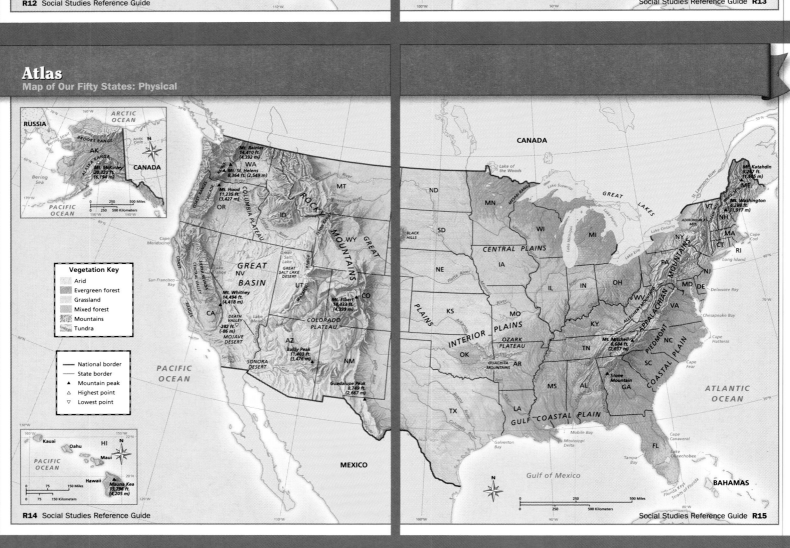

Geography Terms

basin bowl-shaped area of land surrounded by higher land

bay narrower part of an ocean or lake that cuts into land

canal narrow waterway dug across land mainly for ship travel

canyon steep, narrow valley with high sides

cliff steep wall of rock or earth, sometimes called a bluff

coast land at the edge of a large body of water such as an ocean

coastal plain area of flat land along an ocean or sea

delta triangle-shaped area of land at the mouth of a river

desert very dry land

fall line area along which rivers form waterfalls or rapids as the rivers drop to lower land

floodplain flat land, near a river, that is formed by dirt left by floods

foothills hilly land at the bottom of a mountain

glacier giant sheet of ice that moves very slowly across land

gulf body of water, larger than most bays, with land around part of it

harbor sheltered body of water where ships safely tie up to land

hill rounded land higher than the land around it

inlet narrow strip of water running from a large body of water either into land or between islands

island land with water all around it

lake large body of water with land all or nearly all around it

mesa flat-topped hill with steep sides

mountain a very tall hill; highest land on Earth

mountain pass narrow channel or path through a mountain range

mountain range long row of mountains

mouth place where a river empties into another body of water

ocean any of the four largest bodies of water on Earth

peak pointed top of a mountain

peninsula land with water on three sides

plain very large area of flat land

plateau high, wide area of flat land, with steep sides

prairie large area of flat land, with few or no trees, similar to a plain

river large stream of water leading to a lake, another river, or an ocean

riverbank land at a river's edge

sea large body of water somewhat smaller than an ocean

sea level an ocean's surface, compared to which land can be measured either above or below

source place where a river begins

swamp low, water-covered land filled with trees and other plants

tributary stream or river that runs into a larger river

valley low land between mountains or hills

volcano mountain with an opening at the top, formed by violent bursts of steam and hot rock

waterfall steep falling of water from a higher to a lower place

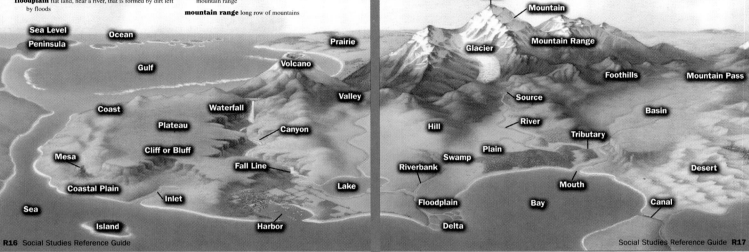

Facts About Our Fifty States

	AL Alabama	AK Alaska	AZ Arizona	AR Arkansas	CA California	CO Colorado
Capital	Montgomery	Juneau	Phoenix	Little Rock	Sacramento	Denver
Date and order of statehood	1819 (22)	1959 (49)	1912 (48)	1836 (25)	1850 (31)	1876 (38)
Nickname	Heart of Dixie	The Last Frontier	Grand Canyon State	Land of Opportunity	Golden State	Centennial State
Population	4,447,100	626,932	5,130,632	2,673,400	33,871,648	4,301,261
Square miles and rank in area	50,750 (28)	570,374 (1)	113,642 (6)	52,075 (27)	155,973 (3)	103,730 (8)
Region	Southeast	West	Southwest	Southeast	West	West

	CT Connecticut	DE Delaware	FL Florida	GA Georgia	HI Hawaii	ID Idaho	IL Illinois
Capital	Hartford	Dover	Tallahassee	Atlanta	Honolulu	Boise	Springfield
Date and order of statehood	1788 (5)	1787 (1)	1845 (27)	1788 (4)	1959 (50)	1890 (43)	1818 (21)
Nickname	Constitution State	Diamond State; First State	Sunshine State	Peach State	Aloha State	Gem State	Land of Lincoln
Population	3,405,565	783,600	15,982,378	8,186,453	1,211,537	1,293,953	12,419,293
Square miles and rank in area	4,845 (48)	1,955 (49)	53,997 (26)	57,919 (21)	6,423 (47)	82,751 (11)	55,593 (24)
Region	Northeast	Northeast	Southeast	Southeast	West	West	Midwest

	IN Indiana	IA Iowa	KS Kansas	KY Kentucky	LA Louisiana	ME Maine
Capital	Indianapolis	Des Moines	Topeka	Frankfort	Baton Rouge	Augusta
Date and order of statehood	1816 (19)	1846 (29)	1861 (34)	1792 (15)	1812 (18)	1820 (23)
Nickname	Hoosier State	Hawkeye State	Sunflower State	Bluegrass State	Pelican State	Pine Tree State
Population	6,080,485	2,926,324	2,688,418	4,041,769	4,468,976	1,274,923
Square miles and rank in area	35,870 (38)	55,875 (23)	81,823 (13)	39,732 (36)	43,566 (33)	30,865 (39)
Region	Midwest	Midwest	Midwest	Southeast	Southeast	Northeast

	MD Maryland	MA Massachusetts	MI Michigan	MN Minnesota	MS Mississippi	MO Missouri	MT Montana
Capital	Annapolis	Boston	Lansing	St. Paul	Jackson	Jefferson City	Helena
Date and order of statehood	1788 (7)	1788 (6)	1837 (26)	1858 (32)	1817 (20)	1821 (24)	1889 (41)
Nickname	Free State	Bay State	Wolverine State	North Star State	Magnolia State	Show Me State	Treasure State
Population	5,296,486	6,349,097	9,938,444	4,919,479	2,844,658	5,595,211	902,195
Square miles and rank in area	9,775 (42)	7,838 (45)	56,809 (22)	79,617 (14)	46,914 (31)	68,898 (18)	145,556 (4)
Region	Northeast	Northeast	Midwest	Midwest	Southeast	Midwest	West

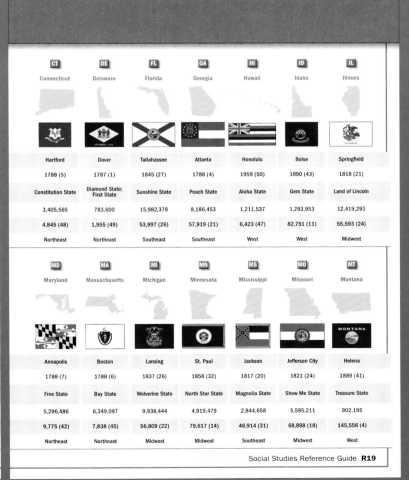

Facts About Our Fifty States

	NE Nebraska	NV Nevada	NH New Hampshire	NJ New Jersey	NM New Mexico	NY New York
Capital	Lincoln	Carson City	Concord	Trenton	Santa Fe	Albany
Date and order of statehood	1867 (37)	1864 (36)	1788 (9)	1787 (3)	1912 (47)	1788 (11)
Nickname	Cornhusker State	Silver State	Granite State	Garden State	Land of Enchantment	Empire State
Population	1,711,263	1,998,257	1,235,786	8,414,350	1,819,046	18,976,457
Square miles and rank in area	76,644 (15)	109,806 (7)	8,969 (44)	7,419 (46)	121,365 (5)	47,224 (30)
Region	Midwest	West	Northeast	Northeast	Southwest	Northeast

	SC South Carolina	SD South Dakota	TN Tennessee	TX Texas	UT Utah	VT Vermont
Capital	Columbia	Pierre	Nashville	Austin	Salt Lake City	Montpelier
Date and order of statehood	1788 (8)	1889 (40)	1796 (16)	1845 (28)	1896 (45)	1791 (14)
Nickname	Palmetto State	Mount Rushmore State	Volunteer State	Lone Star State	Beehive State	Green Mountain State
Population	4,012,012	754,844	5,689,283	20,851,820	2,233,169	608,827
Square miles and rank in area	30,111 (40)	75,898 (16)	41,220 (34)	261,914 (2)	82,168 (12)	9,249 (43)
Region	Southeast	Midwest	Southeast	Southwest	West	Northeast

	NC North Carolina	ND North Dakota	OH Ohio	OK Oklahoma	OR Oregon	PA Pennsylvania	RI Rhode Island
Capital	Raleigh	Bismarck	Columbus	Oklahoma City	Salem	Harrisburg	Providence
Date and order of statehood	1789 (12)	1889 (39)	1803 (17)	1907 (46)	1859 (33)	1787 (2)	1790 (13)
Nickname	Tar Heel State	Sioux State	Buckeye State	Sooner State	Beaver State	Keystone State	Ocean State
Population	8,049,313	642,200	11,353,140	3,450,654	3,421,399	12,281,054	1,048,319
Square miles and rank in area	48,718 (29)	68,994 (17)	40,953 (35)	68,679 (19)	96,003 (10)	44,820 (32)	1,045 (50)
Region	Southeast	Midwest	Midwest	Southwest	West	Northeast	Northeast

	VA Virginia	WA Washington	WV West Virginia	WI Wisconsin	WY Wyoming
Capital	Richmond	Olympia	Charleston	Madison	Cheyenne
Date and order of statehood	1788 (10)	1889 (42)	1863 (35)	1848 (30)	1890 (44)
Nickname	Old Dominion	Evergreen State	Mountain State	Badger State	Equality State
Population	7,078,515	5,894,121	1,808,344	5,363,675	493,782
Square miles and rank in area	39,598 (37)	66,582 (20)	24,087 (41)	54,314 (25)	97,105 (9)
Region	Southeast	West	Southeast	Midwest	West

Facts About Our Presidents

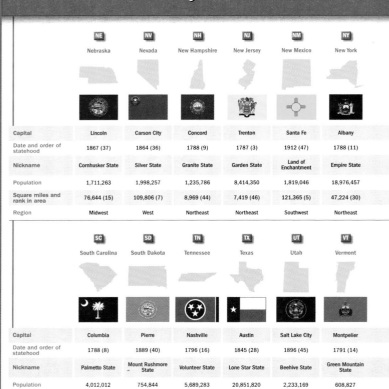

	1 George Washington	2 John Adams	3 Thomas Jefferson	4 James Madison	5 James Monroe
Years in Office	1789–1797	1797–1801	1801–1809	1809–1817	1817–1825
Life Span	1732–1799	1735–1826	1743–1826	1751–1836	1758–1831
Birthplace	Westmoreland County, Virginia	Braintree County, Massachusetts	Albemarle County, Virginia	Port Conway, Virginia	Westmoreland County, Virginia
Home State	Virginia	Massachusetts	Virginia	Virginia	Virginia
Political Party	Federalist	Federalist	Democratic-Republican	Democratic-Republican	Democratic-Republican
First Lady	Martha Dandridge Washington	Abigail Smith Adams	None	Dolley Payne Madison	Elizabeth Kortright Monroe
Religion	Episcopalian	Unitarian	Deist	Episcopalian	Episcopalian

	6 John Quincy Adams	7 Andrew Jackson	8 Martin Van Buren	9 William H. Harrison	10 John Tyler	11 James K. Polk
Years in Office	1825–1829	1829–1837	1837–1841	1841	1841–1845	1845–1849
Life Span	1767–1848	1767–1845	1782–1862	1773–1841	1790–1862	1795–1849
Birthplace	Braintree, Massachusetts	Waxhaw, South Carolina	Kinderhook, New York	Charles City County, Virginia	Charles City County, Virginia	Mecklenburg County, North Carolina
Home State	Massachusetts	Tennessee	New York	Ohio	Virginia	Tennessee
Political Party	Democratic-Republican	Democratic	Democratic	Whig	Whig	Democratic
First Lady	Louisa Johnson Adams	None	None	Anna Symmes Harrison	Letitia Christian Tyler; Julia Gardiner Tyler	Sarah Childress Polk
Religion	Unitarian	Presbyterian	Dutch Reformed	Episcopalian	Episcopalian	Presbyterian

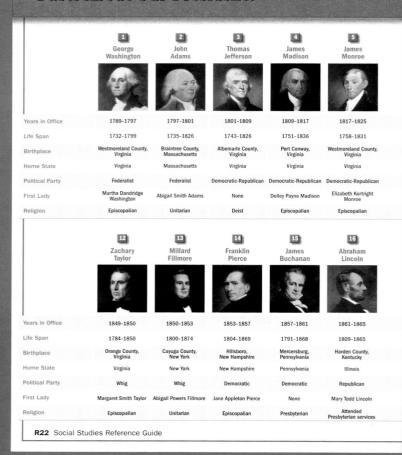

	12 Zachary Taylor	13 Millard Fillmore	14 Franklin Pierce	15 James Buchanan	16 Abraham Lincoln
Years in Office	1849–1850	1850–1853	1853–1857	1857–1861	1861–1865
Life Span	1784–1850	1800–1874	1804–1869	1791–1868	1809–1865
Birthplace	Orange County, Virginia	Cayuga County, New York	Hillsboro, New Hampshire	Mercersburg, Pennsylvania	Harden County, Kentucky
Home State	Virginia	New York	New Hampshire	Pennsylvania	Illinois
Political Party	Whig	Whig	Democratic	Democratic	Republican
First Lady	Margaret Smith Taylor	Abigail Powers Fillmore	Jane Appleton Pierce	None	Mary Todd Lincoln
Religion	Episcopalian	Unitarian	Episcopalian	Presbyterian	Attended Presbyterian services

	17 Andrew Johnson	18 Ulysses S. Grant	19 Rutherford B. Hayes	20 James A. Garfield	21 Chester A. Arthur	22 24 Grover Cleveland
Years in Office	1865–1869	1869–1877	1877–1881	1881	1881–1885	1885–1889; 1893–1897
Life Span	1808–1875	1822–1885	1822–1893	1831–1881	1829–1886	1837–1908
Birthplace	Raleigh, North Carolina	Point Pleasant, Ohio	Delaware, Ohio	Orange, Ohio	Fairfield, Vermont	Caldwell, New Jersey
Home State	Tennessee	Illinois	Ohio	Ohio	New York	New York
Political Party	Democratic	Republican	Republican	Republican	Republican	Democratic
First Lady	Eliza McCardle Johnson	Julia Dent Grant	Lucy Webb Hayes	Lucretia Rudolph Garfield	None	Frances Folsom Cleveland
Religion	No specific affiliation	Methodist	Methodist	Disciples of Christ	Episcopalian	Presbyterian

Facts About Our Presidents

	23 Benjamin Harrison	25 William McKinley	26 Theodore Roosevelt	27 William H. Taft	28 Woodrow Wilson
Years in Office	1889–1893	1897–1901	1901–1909	1909–1913	1913–1921
Life Span	1833–1901	1843–1901	1858–1919	1857–1930	1856–1924
Birthplace	North Bend, Ohio	Niles, Ohio	New York, New York	Cincinnati, Ohio	Staunton, Virginia
Home State	Indiana	Ohio	New York	Ohio	New Jersey
Political Party	Republican	Republican	Republican	Republican	Democratic
First Lady	Caroline Scott Harrison	Ida Saxton McKinley	Edith Carow Roosevelt	Helen Herron Taft	Ellen Axson Wilson; Edith Galt Wilson
Religion	Presbyterian	Methodist	Dutch Reformed	Unitarian	Presbyterian

	29 Warren G. Harding	30 Calvin Coolidge	31 Herbert Hoover	32 Franklin D. Roosevelt	33 Harry S. Truman	34 Dwight D. Eisenhower
Years in Office	1921–1923	1923–1929	1929–1933	1933–1945	1945–1953	1953–1961
Life Span	1865–1923	1872–1933	1874–1964	1882–1945	1884–1972	1890–1969
Birthplace	Morrow County, Ohio	Plymouth, Vermont	West Branch, Iowa	Hyde Park, New York	Lamar, Missouri	Denison, Texas
Home State	Ohio	Massachusetts	California	New York	Missouri	Kansas
Political Party	Republican	Republican	Republican	Democratic	Democratic	Republican
First Lady	Florence DeWolfe Harding	Grace Goodhue Coolidge	Lou Henry Hoover	Anna Eleanor Roosevelt	Bess Wallace Truman	Marie "Mamie" Doud Eisenhower
Religion	Baptist	Congregational	Quaker	Episcopalian	Baptist	Presbyterian

	35 John F. Kennedy	36 Lyndon B. Johnson	37 Richard M. Nixon	38 Gerald R. Ford	39 James E. Carter
Years in Office	1961–1963	1963–1969	1969–1974	1974–1977	1977–1981
Life Span	1917–1963	1908–1973	1913–1994	1913–2006	1924–
Birthplace	Brookline, Massachusetts	Stonewall, Texas	Yorba Linda, California	Omaha, Nebraska	Plains, Georgia
Home State	Massachusetts	Texas	California	Michigan	Georgia
Political Party	Democratic	Democratic	Republican	Republican	Democratic
First Lady	Jacqueline Bouvier Kennedy	Claudia "Lady Bird" Taylor Johnson	Thelma "Pat" Ryan Nixon	Elizabeth (Betty) Warren Ford	Rosalynn Smith Carter
Religion	Roman Catholic	Disciples of Christ	Quaker	Episcopalian	Southern Baptist

	40 Ronald Reagan	41 George H. W. Bush	42 William J. Clinton	43 George W. Bush
Years in Office	1981–1989	1989–1993	1993–2001	2001–
Life Span	1911–2004	1924–	1946–	1946–
Birthplace	Tampico, Illinois	Milton, Massachusetts	Hope, Arkansas	New Haven, Connecticut
Home State	California	Texas	Arkansas	Texas
Political Party	Republican	Republican	Democratic	Republican
First Lady	Anne "Nancy" Davis Reagan	Barbara Pierce Bush	Hillary Rodham Clinton	Laura Welch Bush
Religion	Disciples of Christ	Episcopalian	Baptist	Methodist

United States Documents
The Declaration of Independence

Sometimes in history it becomes necessary for a group of people to break political ties with the country that rules it. When this happens, it is proper to explain the reasons for the need to separate.

We believe that all men are created equal and given by their Creator certain rights that cannot be taken away. People have the right to live, be free, and seek happiness.

Governments are established to protect these rights. The government gets its power from the support of the people it governs. If any form of government tries to take away the basic rights, it is the right of the people to change or end the government and to establish a new government that seems most likely to result in their safety and happiness.

Wise judgment will require that long-existing governments should not be changed for unimportant or temporary reasons. History has shown that people are more willing to suffer under a bad government than to get rid of the government they are used to. But when there are so many abuses and misuses of power by the government, it is the right and duty of the people to throw off such government and form a new government to protect their basic rights.

The colonies have suffered patiently, and now it is necessary for them to change the government. The king of Great Britain has repeatedly abused his power over these states. To prove this, the following facts are given.

In Congress, July 4, 1776
The unanimous Declaration of the thirteen United States of America

When, in the course of human events, it becomes necessary for one people to dissolve the political bands which have connected them with another, and to assume, among the powers of the earth, the separate and equal station to which the laws of nature and nature's God entitle them, a decent respect to the opinions of mankind requires that they should declare the causes which impel them to the separation.

We hold these truths to be self-evident, that all men are created equal, that they are endowed by their Creator with certain unalienable rights, that among these are life, liberty, and the pursuit of happiness.

That to secure these rights, governments are instituted among men, deriving their just powers from the consent of the governed; that whenever any form of government becomes destructive of these ends, it is the right of the people to alter or to abolish it, and to institute new government, laying its foundation on such principles, and organizing its powers in such form, as to them shall seem most likely to effect their safety and happiness.

Prudence, indeed, will dictate that governments long established should not be changed for light and transient causes; and accordingly all experience hath shown that mankind are more disposed to suffer, while evils are sufferable, than to right themselves by abolishing the forms to which they are accustomed. But when a long train of abuses and usurpations, pursuing invariably the same object, evinces a design to reduce them under absolute despotism, it is their right, it is their duty, to throw off such government, and to provide new guards for their future security.

Such has been the patient sufferance of these colonies; and such is now the necessity which constrains them to alter their former systems of government. The history of the present king of Great Britain is a history of repeated injuries and usurpations, all having in direct object the establishment of an absolute tyranny over these states. To prove this, let facts be submitted to a candid world.

He has refused his assent to laws the most wholesome and necessary for the public good. He has forbidden his governors to pass laws of immediate and pressing importance, unless suspended in their operation till his assent should be obtained; and when so suspended, he has utterly neglected to attend to them.

He has refused to pass other laws for the accommodation of large districts of people, unless those people would relinquish the right of representation in the legislature, a right inestimable to them, and formidable to tyrants only.

He has called together legislative bodies at places unusual, uncomfortable, and distant from the depository of their public records, for the sole purpose of fatiguing them into compliance with his measures.

He has dissolved representative houses repeatedly, for opposing, with manly firmness, his invasions on the rights of the people.

He has refused, for a long time after such dissolutions, to cause others to be elected; whereby the legislative powers, incapable of annihilation, have returned to the people at large for their exercise; the state remaining, in the meantime, exposed to all the dangers of invasion from without and convulsions within.

He has endeavored to prevent the population of these states; for that purpose obstructing the laws for the naturalization of foreigners, refusing to pass others to encourage their migrations hither, and raising the conditions of new appropriations of lands.

He has obstructed the administration of justice, by refusing his assent to laws for establishing judiciary powers.

He has made judges dependent on his will alone for the tenure of their offices, and the amount and payment of their salaries.

He has erected a multitude of new offices, and sent hither swarms of officers to harass our people and eat out their substance.

He has kept among us, in times of peace, standing armies, without the consent of our legislatures.

He has affected to render the military independent of, and superior to, the civil power.

He has combined with others to subject us to a jurisdiction foreign to our constitution and unacknowledged by our laws, giving his assent to their acts of pretended legislation:

The king has not given his approval to needed laws. He has not allowed his governors to pass laws needed immediately. The king has made the governors delay laws until they can get his permission and then he has ignored the laws.

He has refused to pass other laws for the help of large districts of people, unless those people would give up the right of representation in the legislature, a right priceless to them, and threatening only to tyrants.

He has called together legislative bodies at unusual and uncomfortable places, distant from where they store their public records, and only for the purpose of tiring them into obeying his measures.

He has repeatedly done away with legislative groups that firmly opposed him for taking away the rights of the people.

After he has dissolved these representative meetings, he has refused to allow new elections. Because of this lack of legislative power, the people are exposed to the dangers of invasion from without and violence within.

He has tried to prevent people from immigrating to these states by blocking the process for foreigners to become citizens, refusing to pass laws to encourage people to travel to America, and making it harder to move to and own new lands.

He has interfered with the administration of justice, by refusing to approve laws for establishing courts.

He has made judges do what he wants by controlling how long they serve and how much they are paid.

He has created many new government offices, and sent many officials to torment our people and live off of our hard work.

In times of peace, he has kept soldiers among us, without the consent of our legislatures.

He has tried to make the military separate from, and superior to, the civil government.

He and others have made us live under laws that are different from our laws. He has given his approval to these unfair laws that parliament has adopted:

United States Documents
The Declaration of Independence

For forcing us to feed and house many British soldiers;

For using pretend trials to protect British soldiers from punishment for murdering people in America;

For cutting off our trade with the world;

For taxing us without our consent;

For taking away, in many cases, the benefits of trial by jury;

For taking us to Great Britain to be tried for made-up offenses;

For doing away with the free system of English laws in a neighboring province, and establishing a harsh government there, and enlarging its boundaries, as a way to introduce the same absolute rule into these colonies;

For taking away our governing documents, doing away with our most valuable laws, and changing our governments completely;

For setting aside our own legislatures, and declaring that Great Britain has power to make laws for us in all cases whatsoever.

He has deserted government here, by not protecting us and waging war against us.

He has robbed our ships on the seas, destroyed our coasts, burned our towns, and destroyed the lives of our people.

He is at this time sending large armies of foreign hired soldiers to complete the works of death, destruction, and injustice he has already begun. These deeds are among the cruelest ever seen in history, and are totally unworthy of the head of a civilized nation.

He has forced our fellow citizens, who were captured on the high seas, to fight against America, to kill their friends and family, or to be killed themselves.

He has stirred up civil disorder among us, and has tried to cause the merciless killing of the people living on the frontiers by the Indians, whose rule of warfare includes the deliberate killing of people regardless of age, sex, or conditions.

In every stage of these mistreatments we have asked for a solution in the most humble terms; our repeated requests have been answered only by repeated injury. A leader who is so unfair and acts like a dictator is unfit to be the ruler of a free people.

For quartering large bodies of armed troops among us;

For protecting them, by a mock trial, from punishment for any murders which they should commit on the inhabitants of these states;

For cutting off our trade with all parts of the world;

For imposing taxes on us without our consent;

For depriving us, in many cases, of the benefits of trial by jury;

For transporting us beyond seas, to be tried for pretended offenses;

For abolishing the free system of English laws in a neighboring province, establishing therein an arbitrary government, and enlarging its boundaries, so as to render it at once an example and fit instrument for introducing the same absolute rule into these colonies;

For taking away our charters, abolishing our most valuable laws, and altering fundamentally the forms of our governments;

For suspending our own legislatures, and declaring themselves invested with power to legislate for us in all cases whatsoever.

He has abdicated government here, by declaring us out of his protection and waging war against us.

He has plundered our seas, ravaged our coasts, burned our towns, and destroyed the lives of our people.

He is at this time transporting large armies of foreign mercenaries to complete the works of death, desolation, and tyranny already begun with circumstances of cruelty and perfidy scarcely paralleled in the most barbarous ages, and totally unworthy the head of a civilized nation.

He has constrained our fellow citizens, taken captive on the high seas, to bear arms against their country, to become the executioners of their friends and brethren, or to fall themselves by their hands.

He has excited domestic insurrection among us, and has endeavored to bring on the inhabitants of our frontiers, the merciless Indian savages, whose known rule of warfare is an undistinguished destruction of all ages, sexes, and conditions.

In every stage of these oppressions we have petitioned for redress in the most humble terms; our repeated petitions have been answered only by repeated injury. A prince, whose character is thus marked by every act which may define a tyrant, is unfit to be the ruler of a free people.

Nor have we been wanting in attentions to our British brethren. We have warned them, from time to time, of attempts by their legislature to extend an unwarrantable jurisdiction over us. We have reminded them of the circumstances of our emigration and settlement here. We have appealed to their native justice and magnanimity; and we have conjured them, by the ties of our common kindred, to disavow these usurpations, which would inevitably interrupt our connections and correspondence. They, too, have been deaf to the voice of justice and consanguinity. We must, therefore, acquiesce in the necessity which denounces our separation, and hold them, as we hold the rest of mankind, enemies in war; in peace, friends.

We, therefore, the representatives of the United States of America, in General Congress assembled, appealing to the Supreme Judge of the world for the rectitude of our intentions, do, in the name and by the authority of the good people of these colonies, solemnly publish and declare that these United Colonies are, and of right ought to be, free and independent states; that they are absolved from all allegiance to the British crown, and that all political connection between them and the state of Great Britain is, and ought to be, totally dissolved; and that, as free and independent states, they have full power to levy war, conclude peace, contract alliances, establish commerce, and do all other acts and things which independent states may of right do. And, for the support of this declaration, with a firm reliance on the protection of Divine Providence, we mutually pledge to each other our lives, our fortunes, and our sacred honor.

Button Gwinnett (GA)	Benjamin Harrison (VA)	Lewis Morris (NY)
Lyman Hall (GA)	Thomas Nelson, Jr. (VA)	Richard Stockton (NJ)
George Walton (GA)	Francis Lightfoot Lee (VA)	John Witherspoon (NJ)
William Hooper (NC)	Carter Braxton (VA)	Francis Hopkinson (NJ)
Joseph Hewes (NC)	Robert Morris (PA)	John Hart (NJ)
John Penn (NC)	Benjamin Rush (PA)	Abraham Clark (NJ)
Edward Rutledge (SC)	Benjamin Franklin (PA)	Josiah Bartlett (NH)
Thomas Heyward, Jr. (SC)	John Morton (PA)	William Whipple (NH)
Thomas Lynch, Jr. (SC)	George Clymer (PA)	Samuel Adams (MA)
Arthur Middleton (SC)	James Smith (PA)	John Adams (MA)
John Hancock (MA)	George Taylor (PA)	Robert Treat Paine (MA)
Samuel Chase (MD)	James Wilson (PA)	Elbridge Gerry (MA)
William Paca (MD)	George Ross (PA)	Stephen Hopkins (RI)
Thomas Stone (MD)	Caesar Rodney (DE)	William Ellery (RI)
Charles Carroll of Carrollton (MD)	George Read (DE)	Roger Sherman (CT)
George Wythe (VA)	Thomas McKean (DE)	Samuel Huntington (CT)
Richard Henry Lee (VA)	William Floyd (NY)	William Williams (CT)
Thomas Jefferson (VA)	Philip Livingston (NY)	Oliver Wolcott (CT)
	Francis Lewis (NY)	Matthew Thornton (NH)

We have also asked for help from the British people. We have warned them, from time to time, of attempts by their government to extend illegal power over us. We have reminded them of why we came to America. We have appealed to their sense of justice and generosity; and we have begged them, because of all we have in common, to give up these abuses of power. They, like the king, have not listened to the voice of justice and brotherhood. We must, therefore, declare our separation. In war the British are our enemies. In peace, they are our friends.

We, therefore, as the representatives of the people of the United States of America, in this General Congress assembled, appealing to God for the honesty of our purpose, do solemnly publish and declare that these United Colonies are, and rightly should be, free and independent states. The people of the United States are no longer subjects of the British crown. All political connections between the colonies and Great Britain are totally ended. These free and independent states have full power to declare war, make peace, make treaties with other countries, establish trade, and do all other acts and things that independent states have the right to do. To support this declaration, with a firm trust on the protection of Divine Providence, we pledge to each other our lives, our fortunes, and our sacred honor.

"Among the natural rights of the Colonists are these: First, a right to life; Secondly, to liberty; Thirdly, to property; together with the right to support and defend them in the best manner they can."

Samuel Adams, The Report of the Committee of Correspondence to the Boston Town Meeting

"All, too, will bear in mind this sacred principle, that though the will of the majority is in all cases to prevail, that will to be rightful must be reasonable; that the minority possess their equal rights, which equal law must protect, and to violate would be oppression."

Thomas Jefferson, First Inaugural Address

United States Documents
The Constitution of the United States of America

We the people of the United States, in order to form a more perfect union, establish justice, insure peace in our nation, provide for our defense, promote the general welfare, and secure the blessings of liberty to ourselves and our descendants, do authorize and establish this Constitution for the United States of America.

ARTICLE 1
Legislative Branch

SECTION 1. Congress
Only the Congress of the United States has the power to make national laws. Congress is made up of a Senate and House of Representatives.

SECTION 2. House of Representatives
Members of the House of Representatives will be chosen every two years. People who are eligible to vote for state legislators are also eligible to vote for members of the House of Representatives.

To be a member of the House of Representatives, a person must be at least twenty-five years of age, must have been a citizen of the United States for at least seven years, and must live in the state the person is chosen to represent.

The number of representatives a state has is determined by the state's population. A census, or count, of the population must be taken every ten years. Each state shall have at least one representative.

We the people of the United States, in order to form a more perfect union, establish justice, insure domestic tranquility, provide for the common defense, promote the general welfare, and secure the blessings of liberty to ourselves and our posterity, do ordain and establish this Constitution for the United States of America.

ARTICLE 1
Legislative Branch

SECTION 1. Congress
All legislative powers herein granted shall be vested in a Congress of the United States, which shall consist of a Senate and House of Representatives.

SECTION 2. House of Representatives
The House of Representatives shall be composed of members chosen every second year by the people of the several states, and the electors in each state shall have the qualifications requisite for electors of the most numerous branch of the State legislature.

No person shall be a representative who shall not have attained to the age of twenty-five years, and been seven years a citizen of the United States, and who shall not, when elected, be an inhabitant of that state in which he shall be chosen.

Representatives ~~and direct taxes~~ shall be apportioned among the several states which may be included within this Union, according to their respective numbers~~, which shall be determined by adding to the whole numbers of free persons, including those bound to service for a term of years, and excluding Indians not taxed, three fifths of all other persons.~~* The actual enumeration shall be made within three years after the first meeting of the Congress of the United States, and within every subsequent term of ten years, in such manner as they shall by law direct. The number of representatives shall not exceed one for every thirty thousand, but each State shall have at least one representative~~; and until such enumeration shall be made, the State of New Hampshire shall be entitled to choose three, Massachusetts eight, Rhode Island and Providence Plantations one, Connecticut five, New York six, New Jersey four, Pennsylvania eight, Delaware one, Maryland six, Virginia ten, North Carolina five, South Carolina five, and Georgia three.~~* *(*Changed by the Fourteenth Amendment)*

When vacancies happen in the representation from any state, the executive authority thereof shall issue writs of election to fill such vacancies.

The House of Representatives shall choose their speaker and other officers, and shall have the sole power of impeachment.

SECTION 3. Senate
The Senate of the United States shall be composed of two senators from each state, ~~chosen by the legislature thereof,~~* for six years; and each senator shall have one vote. *(*Changed by the Seventeenth Amendment)*

Immediately after they shall be assembled in consequence of the first election, they shall be divided as equally as may be into three classes. The seats of the senators of the first class shall be vacated at the expiration of the second year, of the second class at the expiration of the fourth year, and of the third class at the expiration of the sixth year, so that one third may be chosen every second year; ~~and if vacancies happen by resignation, or otherwise, during the recess of the legislature of any State, the executive thereof may make temporary appointments until the next meeting of the legislature, which shall then fill such vacancies.~~* *(*Changed by the Seventeenth Amendment)*

No person shall be a senator who shall not have attained to the age of thirty years, and been nine years a citizen of the United States, and who shall not, when elected, be an inhabitant of that State for which he shall be chosen.

The Vice President of the United States shall be president of the Senate, but shall have no vote, unless they be equally divided.

The Senate shall choose their other officers, and also a president pro tempore, in the absence of the Vice President, or when he shall exercise the office of President of the United States.

The Senate shall have the sole power to try all impeachments. When sitting for that purpose, they shall be on oath or affirmation. When the President of the United States is tried, the Chief Justice shall preside: and no person shall be convicted without the concurrence of two thirds of the members present.

Judgment in cases of impeachment shall not extend further than to removal from office, and disqualification to hold any office of honor, trust or profit under the United States: but the party convicted shall nevertheless be liable and subject to indictment, trial, judgment and punishment, according to law.

When open positions occur happen in the representation from any state, the governor of the state will call a special election to fill the empty seat.

The House of Representatives shall choose their speaker and other officers, and only the House of Representatives may impeach, or accuse, government officials of crimes in office.

SECTION 3. Senate
The Senate of the United States shall be made up of two senators from each state. Each senator serves for six years; and each senator shall have one vote.

(Until the Seventeenth Amendment, the senators were chosen by the legislature of the state they represented).

Only one-third of the senators are up for election at one time.

(The remaining section was changed by the Seventeenth Amendment).

A senator must be at least thirty years old, a citizen of the United States for at least nine years, and live in the state the senator is chosen to represent.

The Vice-President of the United States is also the president of the Senate, but has no vote unless there is a tie.

The Senate chooses its own officers. The Senate also chooses a senator to be the president pro tempore who serves as the temporary president of the Senate in the absence of the Vice-President, or when the Vice-President acts as President of the United States.

Only the Senate has the power to bring all impeachments to trial. When meeting on an impeachment, the senators shall take an oath or affirmation. When the President of the United States is tried on impeachment charges, the Chief Justice shall be in charge, and no person shall be found guilty without the agreement of two-thirds of the members present.

Impeached officials who are convicted can be removed from office, and disqualified from holding any other government office. Other courts in the country may still try, judge, and punish the impeached official.

SECTION 4. Elections and Meetings of Congress
The times, places, and manner of holding elections for senators and representatives shall be prescribed in each State by the legislature thereof; but the Congress may at any time by law make or alter such regulations, except as to the places of choosing senators.

The Congress shall assemble at least once in every year, ~~and such meeting shall be on the first Monday in December,~~* unless they shall by law appoint a different day. *(*Changed by the Twentieth Amendment)*

SECTION 5. Rules for Congress
Each house shall be the judge of the elections, returns and qualifications of its own members, and a majority of each shall constitute a quorum to do business; but a smaller number may adjourn from day to day, and may be authorized to compel the attendance of absent members, in such manner, and under such penalties as each house may provide.

Each house may determine the rules of its proceedings, punish its members for disorderly behavior, and, with the concurrence of two thirds, expel a member.

Each house shall keep a journal of its proceedings, and from time to time publish the same, excepting such parts as may in their judgment require secrecy; and the yeas and nays of the members of either house on any question shall, at the desire of one fifth of those present, be entered on the journal.

Neither house, during the session of Congress, shall, without the consent of the other, adjourn for more than three days, nor to any other place than that in which the two houses shall be sitting.

SECTION 6. Rights and Restrictions of Members of Congress
The senators and representatives shall receive a compensation for their services, to be ascertained by law, and paid out of the Treasury of the United States. They shall in all cases, except treason, felony and breach of the peace, be privileged from arrest during their attendance at the session of their respective houses, and in going to and returning from the same; and for any speech or debate in either house, they shall not be questioned in any other place.

No senator or representative shall, during the time for which he was elected, be appointed to any civil office under the authority of the United States, which shall have been created, or the emoluments whereof shall have been increased during such time; and no person holding any office under the United States shall be a member of either house during his continuance in office.

SECTION 4. Elections and Meetings of Congress
The state legislature determines the times, places, and method of holding elections for senators and representatives. Congress may make laws that change some of the regulations.

The Congress shall meet at least once in every year.

(Until the passing of the Twentieth Amendment, Congress met on the first Monday in December.)

SECTION 5. Rules for Congress
The Senate and House of Representatives judge the fairness of the elections and the qualifications of their own members. At least half of the members must be present to do business; but a smaller number may end the meeting from day to day, and may force absent members to attend and may penalize a member for not attending.

Each house may determine the rules of its proceedings and punish its members for disorderly behavior. Each house may, with the agreement of two-thirds of its members, force a member out of office.

Each house of Congress shall keep a record of its proceedings, and from time to time publish the record, except those parts that may need to be kept secret. If one-fifth of the members want it, the votes on any matter shall be published.

During the session of Congress, neither house shall adjourn for more than three days without the permission of the other, nor can either house decide to meet at any other place than where both houses agree.

SECTION 6. Rights and Restrictions of Members of Congress
The senators and representatives shall receive a payment for their services, to be decided by law, and paid out of the Treasury of the United States. Except for very serious crimes, senators and representatives are protected from arrest during their attendance at the session of Congress, and in going to and returning from Congress. Members of Congress shall not be arrested for anything they say in Congress.

No senator or representative shall be appointed to any government job while serving in Congress. No senator or representative is allowed to take a government job that is created or has its salary increased during the senator's or representative's term of office. While holding a government office, no person shall also be a member of Congress.

SECTION 7. How Laws Are Made
All bills for raising revenue shall originate in the House of Representatives; but the Senate may propose or concur with amendments as on other bills.

Every bill which shall have passed the House of Representatives and the Senate shall, before it become a law, be presented to the President of the United States; if he approve he shall sign it, but if not he shall return it, with his objections to that house in which it shall have originated, who shall enter the objections at large on their journal, and proceed to reconsider it. If after such reconsideration two thirds of that house shall agree to pass the bill, it shall be sent, together with the objections, to the other house, by which it shall likewise be reconsidered, and if approved by two thirds of that house, it shall become a law. But in all such cases the votes of both houses shall be determined by yeas and nays, and the names of persons voting for and against the bill shall be entered on the journal of each house respectively. If any bill shall not be returned by the President within ten days (Sundays excepted) after it shall have been presented to him, the same shall be a law, in like manner as if he had signed it, unless the Congress by their adjournment prevent its return, in which case it shall not be a law.

Every order, resolution, or vote to which the concurrence of the Senate and House of Representatives may be necessary (except on a question of adjournment) shall be presented to the President of the United States; and before the same shall take effect, shall be approved by him, or being disapproved by him, shall be repassed by two thirds of the Senate and House of Representatives, according to the rules and limitations prescribed in the case of a bill.

SECTION 8. Powers of Congress
The Congress shall have power:

To lay and collect taxes, duties, imposts and excises, to pay the debts and provide for the common defense and general welfare of the United States; but all duties, imposts and excises shall be uniform throughout the United States;

To borrow money on the credit of the United States;

To regulate commerce with foreign nations, and among the several States, and with the Indian tribes;

To establish a uniform rule of naturalization, and uniform laws on the subject of bankruptcies throughout the United States;

To coin money, regulate the value thereof, and of foreign coin, and fix the standard of weights and measures;

To provide for the punishment of counterfeiting the securities and current coin of the United States;

To establish post offices and post roads;

SECTION 7. How Laws Are Made
All bills for raising money shall begin in the House of Representatives. The Senate may suggest or agree with amendments to these tax bills, as with other bills.

Every bill that has passed the House of Representatives and the Senate must be presented to the President of the United States before it becomes a law. If the President approves of the bill, the President shall sign it. If the President does not approve, then the bill may be vetoed. The President then sends it back to the house in which it began, with an explanation of the objections. That house writes the objections on its record and begins to reconsider it. If two-thirds of each house agree to pass the bill, it shall become a law. But in all such cases the votes of both houses shall be determined by "yes" and "no" votes, and the names of persons voting for and against the bill shall be entered on the record of each house. If any bill is neither signed nor vetoed by the President within ten days (except for Sundays) after it has been sent to the President, the bill shall be a law. If Congress adjourns before ten days have passed, the bill does not become a law.

Every order, resolution, or vote that passes in the Senate and House of Representatives shall be presented to the President of the United States to be signed or vetoed. A bill that is vetoed by the President can become a law only if it is passed again by two-thirds of the Senate and House of Representatives.

SECTION 8. Powers of Congress
The Congress shall have power to:
- establish and collect taxes on imported and exported goods and on goods sold within the country. Congress also shall pay the debts and provide for the defense and general welfare of the United States. All federal taxes shall be the same throughout the United States;
- borrow money on the credit of the United States;
- make laws about trade with other countries, among the states, and with the American Indian tribes;
- establish one procedure by which a person from another country can become a legal citizen of the United States, and establish bankruptcy laws to deal with people and businesses who cannot pay what they owe;
- print or coin money and regulate its value. Congress has the power to determine how much foreign money is worth in American money. Congress sets the standard of weights and measures;

United States Documents
The Constitution of the United States of America

To promote the progress of science and useful arts by securing for limited times to authors and inventors the exclusive right to their respective writings and discoveries;

To constitute tribunals inferior to the Supreme Court;

To define and punish piracies and felonies committed on the high seas, and offenses against the law of nations;

To declare war~~, grant letters of marque and reprisal, and make rules concerning captures on land and water;~~* *(*These powers are no longer exercised by Congress.)*

To raise and support armies, but no appropriation of money to that use shall be for a longer term than two years;

To provide and maintain a navy;

To make rules for the government and regulation of the land and naval forces;

To provide for calling forth the militia to execute the laws of the Union, suppress insurrections and repel invasions;

To provide for organizing, arming, and disciplining the militia, and for governing such part of them as may be employed in the service of the United States, reserving to the States respectively the appointment of the officers, and the authority of training the militia according to the discipline prescribed by Congress;

To exercise exclusive legislation in all cases whatsoever, over such district (not exceeding ten miles square) as may, by cession of particular States and the acceptance of Congress, become the seat of the government of the United States, and to exercise like authority over all places purchased by the consent of the legislature of the State in which the same shall be, for the erection of forts, magazines, arsenals, dockyards, and other needful buildings; and

To make all laws which shall be necessary and proper for carrying into execution the foregoing powers, and all other powers vested by this Constitution in the government of the United States, or in any department or officer thereof.

SECTION 9. Powers Denied to Congress
~~The migration or importation of such persons as any of the States now existing shall think proper to admit shall not be prohibited by the Congress prior to the year one thousand eight hundred and eight, but a tax or duty may be imposed on such importation, not exceeding ten dollars for each person.~~

The privilege of the writ of habeas corpus shall not be suspended, unless when in cases of rebellion or invasion the public safety may require it.

No bill of attainder or ex post facto law shall be passed.

- establish punishments for counterfeiting, or making fake money, stocks, and bonds;
- establish post offices and roads for mail delivery;
- promote the progress of science and useful arts by protecting, for limited times, the writings and discoveries of authors and inventors by issuing copyrights and patents;
- create courts lower than the Supreme Court;
- define and punish crimes committed on the high seas, and crimes that break international laws;
- declare war and make rules about taking enemy property on land or sea;
- set up and supply armies. Congress cannot provide funding for the armies for more than two years at a time;
- set up and supply a navy;
- make rules for the armed forces;
- provide for calling the militia to action to carry out the laws of the country, put down revolts and riots and fight off invasions;
- provide for organizing, arming, and disciplining the militia, and for governing those employed in the armed service of the United States. The states have the right to appoint the officers, and the authority of training the militia according to the rules made by Congress;
- govern the nation's capital [Washington, D.C.] and military bases in the United States; and
- make all laws needed to carry out the powers mentioned earlier in the Constitution, and all other powers placed by this Constitution in the government of the United States, or in any department or officer of the government.

SECTION 9. Powers Denied to Congress
Congress does not have the power to prevent enslaved people from being brought into the country until 1808, but a tax may be placed on each imported person.

(Congress passed a law in 1808 forbidding the slave trade.)

Congress may not do away with laws that protect an individual from being jailed unless the person goes to trial or unless specific criminal charges are filed, unless the public safety requires it during a rebellion or invasion.

No law shall be passed that penalizes a person or group without the benefit of a trial or makes an action illegal after the action was taken.

No capitation, or other direct,* tax shall be laid~~, unless in proportion to the census or enumeration herein before directed to be taken.~~* *(*Changed by the Sixteenth Amendment)*

No tax or duty shall be laid on articles exported from any State.

No preference shall be given by any regulation of commerce or revenue to the ports of one State over those of another; nor shall vessels bound to, or from, one State be obliged to enter, clear, or pay duties in another.

No money shall be drawn from the Treasury, but in consequence of appropriations made by law; and a regular statement and account of the receipts and expenditures of all public money shall be published from time to time.

No title of nobility shall be granted by the United States; and no person holding any office of profit or trust under them, shall, without the consent of the Congress, accept of any present, emolument, office, or title of any kind whatever, from any king, prince, or foreign State.

SECTION 10. Powers Denied to the States
No State shall enter into any treaty, alliance, or confederation; grant letters of marque and reprisal; coin money; emit bills of credit; make anything but gold and silver coin a tender in payment of debts; pass any bill of attainder, ex post facto law, or law impairing the obligation of contracts, or grant any title of nobility.

No State shall, without the consent of the Congress, lay any imposts, or duties on imports or exports, except what may be absolutely necessary for executing its inspection laws; and the net produce of all duties and imposts, laid by any State on imports or exports, shall be for the use of the Treasury of the United States; and all such laws shall be subject to the revision and control of the Congress.

No State shall, without the consent of Congress, lay any duty of tonnage, keep troops, or ships of war in time of peace, enter into any agreement or compact with another State, or with a foreign power, or engage in war, unless actually invaded, or in such imminent danger as will not admit of delay.

ARTICLE 2
The Executive Branch

SECTION 1. The President and Vice President
The executive power shall be vested in a President of the United States of America. He shall hold his office during the term of four years, and, together with the Vice President, chosen for the same term, be elected as follows:

No person in the United States may be taxed unless everyone is taxed the same.

(The Sixteenth Amendment allowed an income tax.)

No tax shall be put on articles exported from any state.

No laws shall be passed that give special treatment to one state over those of another in trade. Ships shall not be required to pay a tax to enter another state.

No money shall be taken from the Treasury, without a law passed by Congress. A public record must be kept of money raised and money spent.

The United States shall not give any titles of nobility, such as king or queen. No person holding any government office shall accept any present, payment, office, or title of any kind from another country, without the consent of the Congress.

SECTION 10. Powers Denied to the States
No state can make treaties or alliances with other nations or issue official documents permitting private citizens to capture merchant ships or engage warships of another nation. No state can issue its own money or make anything, other than gold or silver, legal as currency. No state can pass laws that apply to actions done before the law was passed. No state may allow a person to be punished without a fair trial. No state can pass laws that excuse anyone from a contract. No state can give anyone a title of nobility.

Without approval from Congress, no state can collect taxes on goods coming in or going out of the state, except those small fees needed for customs inspections. Any taxes from trade become the property of the United States government.

Without approval from Congress, states are forbidden to tax ships or keep troops or warships in peacetime, unless endangered by actual invasion. States may not enter into an agreement with another state or foreign nation.

ARTICLE 2
The Executive Branch

SECTION 1. The President and Vice-President
The President has the power to carry out the laws of Congress, and the President and Vice-President serve a four-year term.

Each State shall appoint, in such manner as the legislature thereof may direct, a number of electors, equal to the whole number of senators and representatives to which the State may be entitled in the Congress, but no senator or representative, or person holding an office of trust or profit under the United States, shall be appointed an elector.

~~The electors shall meet in their respective States, and vote by ballot for two persons, of whom one at least shall not be an inhabitant of the same State with themselves. And they shall make a list of all the persons voted for, and of the number of votes for each; which list they shall sign and certify, and transmit sealed to the seat of the government of the United States, directed to the president of the Senate. The president of the Senate shall, in the presence of the Senate and House of Representatives, open all the certificates, and the votes shall then be counted. The person having the greatest number of votes shall be the President, if such number be a majority of the whole number of electors appointed; and if there be more than one who have such majority, and have an equal number of votes, then the House of Representatives shall immediately choose by ballot one of them for President; and if no person have a majority, then from the five highest on the list the said House shall in like manner choose the President. But in choosing the President, the votes shall be taken by States, the representation from each State having one vote; a quorum for this purpose shall consist of a member or members from two thirds of the States, and a majority of all the States shall be necessary to a choice. In every case, after the choice of the President, the person having the greatest number of votes of the electors shall be the Vice President. But if there should remain two or more who have equal votes, the Senate shall choose from them by ballot the Vice President.~~* (*Changed by the Twelfth Amendment)*

The Congress may determine the time of choosing the electors, and the day on which they shall give their votes; which day shall be the same throughout the United States.

No person except a natural-born citizen, or a citizen of the United States, at the time of the adoption of this Constitution, shall be eligible to the office of President; neither shall any person be eligible to that office who shall not have attained to the age of thirty-five years, and been fourteen years a resident within the United States.

In case of the removal of the President from office, or of his death, resignation, or inability to discharge the powers and duties of the said office, the same shall devolve on the Vice President~~, and the Congress may by law provide for the case of removal, death, resignation, or inability, both of the President and Vice President, declaring what officer shall then act as President, and such officer shall act accordingly, until the disability be removed, or a President shall be elected.~~* (*Changed by the Twenty-Fifth Amendment)*

The legislature of each state determines the process for electing its representatives in the Electoral College, which officially elects the President and the Vice-President. Each state's total number of electors is determined by the state's total number of members in Congress. No person holding any office in the federal government can become an elector.

(Until this was changed by the Twelfth Amendment, the person who received the most electoral votes became the President and the person with the next highest number became the Vice-President. The Twelfth Amendment overruled this clause and changed the way the election process worked.)

Congress determines the date and time when each state's electors are to cast their votes for President and Vice-President.

To become President a person must be born a citizen of the United States, be at least thirty-five years old, and have lived in the United States for at least fourteen years.

If a President dies, is disabled, or is removed from office, the Vice-President becomes President.

(The Twenty-Fifth Amendment changed the method for filling these offices if they become vacant.)

The President shall, at stated times, receive for his services a compensation, which shall neither be increased nor diminished during the period for which he shall have been elected, and he shall not receive within that period any other emolument from the United States, or any of them.

Before he enter on the execution of his office, he shall take the following oath or affirmation: — "I do solemnly swear (or affirm) that I will faithfully execute the office of President of the United States, and will to the best of my ability, preserve, protect and defend the Constitution of the United States."

SECTION 2. Powers of the President

The President shall be Commander in Chief of the Army and Navy of the United States, and of the militia of the several States, when called into the actual service of the United States; he may require the opinion, in writing, of the principal officer in each of the executive departments, upon any subject relating to the duties of their respective offices, and he shall have power to grant reprieves and pardons for offenses against the United States, except in cases of impeachment.

He shall have power, by and with the advice and consent of the Senate, to make treaties, provided two-thirds of the senators present concur; and he shall nominate, and by and with the advice and consent of the Senate, shall appoint ambassadors, other public ministers and consuls, judges of the Supreme Court, and all other officers of the United States, whose appointments are not herein otherwise provided for, and which shall be established by law; but the Congress may by law vest the appointment of such inferior officers, as they think proper, in the President alone, in the courts of law, or in the heads of departments.

The President shall have power to fill up all vacancies that may happen during the recess of the Senate, by granting commissions which shall expire at the end of their next session.

SECTION 3. Duties of the President

He shall from time to time give to the Congress information of the state of the Union, and recommend to their consideration such measures as he shall judge necessary and expedient; he may, on extraordinary occasions, convene both houses, or either of them, and in case of disagreement between them, with respect to the time of adjournment, he may adjourn them to such time as he shall think proper; he shall receive ambassadors and other public ministers; he shall take care that the laws be faithfully executed, and shall commission all the officers of the United States.

The President will receive a salary, but it cannot be increased or decreased during the term(s) of office. The President cannot have another occupation or receive outside compensation while in office.

Before assuming the duties of the office, the President must take the following oath or affirmation: "I do solemnly swear (or affirm) that I will faithfully execute the office of President of the United States, and will to the best of my ability, preserve, protect and defend the Constitution of the United States."

SECTION 2. Powers of the President

The President is the leader of the armed forces of the United States and of the state militias during times of war. The President may require the principal officer in each of the executive departments to write a report about any subject relating to their duties, and can grant delays of punishment or pardons for criminals, except in cases of impeachment.

With the advice and consent of two-thirds of the members of the Senate, the President can make treaties with foreign nations and can appoint ambassadors and other officials as necessary to handle the countries diplomatic affairs with other countries. The President can appoint federal judges and other key officers in the executive branch of government, with the consent of two-thirds of the Senate. Congress may give power to the President to appoint minor government officials and heads of departments.

When the Senate is not in session, the President can make temporary appointments to offices that require Senate approval. These appointments expire when the next session ends.

SECTION 3. Duties of the President

The President must make a report to Congress on a regular basis, providing information concerning important national developments and goals. Lawmaking requests for Congress should be given as well. The President can call for special sessions of one or both houses of Congress for special reasons. If the houses of Congress cannot agree on a common date for adjournment, the President has the power to make that decision. The President is to officially receive foreign ambassadors and other public ministers. The President is to fully and faithfully carry out the laws of Congress and sign the documents required to give officers the rights to perform their duties.

SECTION 4. Removal from Office

The President, Vice President, and all civil officers of the United States, shall be removed from office on impeachment for, and conviction of, treason, bribery, or other high crimes and misdemeanors.

ARTICLE 3
The Judicial Branch

SECTION 1. Federal Courts

The judicial power of the United States shall be vested in one Supreme Court, and in such inferior courts as the Congress may from time to time ordain and establish. The judges, both of the Supreme and inferior courts, shall hold their offices during good behavior, and shall, at stated times, receive for their services a compensation, which shall not be diminished during their continuance in office.

SECTION 2. Powers of Federal Courts

The judicial power shall extend to all cases, in law and equity, arising under this Constitution, the laws of the United States, and treaties made, or which shall be made, under their authority; — to all cases affecting ambassadors, other public ministers and consuls; — to all cases of admiralty and maritime jurisdiction; — to controversies to which the United States shall be a party; — to controversies between two or more States; — between a State and citizens of another State; —between citizens of different states — between citizens of the same State claiming lands under grants of different States, and between a State, or the citizens thereof, and foreign States, citizens or subjects.

In all cases affecting ambassadors, other public ministers and consuls, and those in which a State shall be party, the Supreme Court shall have original jurisdiction. In all the other cases before mentioned, the Supreme Court shall have appellate jurisdiction, both as to law and fact, with such exceptions, and under such regulations as the Congress shall make.

The trial of all crimes, except in cases of impeachment, shall be by jury; and such trial shall be held in the State where the said crimes shall have been committed; but when not committed within any State, the trial shall be at such place or places as the Congress may by law have directed.

SECTION 3. Treason

Treason against the United States shall consist only in levying war against them, or in adhering to their enemies, giving them aid and comfort. No person shall be convicted of treason unless on the testimony of two witnesses to the same overt act, or on confession in open court.

SECTION 4. Removal from Office

The President, Vice-President, and all civil officers can be removed from office if convicted on impeachment charges for treason, bribery, or other high crimes and misdemeanors.

ARTICLE 3

The Judicial Branch

SECTION 1. Federal Courts

The Supreme Court is the highest court in the land. Congress has the power to create all other federal courts. Federal judges may hold office for life as long as they act properly, and they shall receive a salary that cannot be lowered during the judge's time of service.

SECTION 2. Powers of Federal Courts

The power of the federal courts covers two types of cases: (1) those involving the interpretation of the Constitution, federal laws, treaties, and laws relating to ships on the high seas; and (2) those involving the United States government itself, foreign diplomats, two or more state governments, citizens of different states, and a state or its citizens versus foreign countries or their citizens.

Cases involving foreign diplomats and any state in the United States will be tried by the Supreme Court. Other cases tried by the Supreme Court are those appealed or brought forward from lower federal courts or from state courts. Congress can decide to make exceptions to these regulations.

Except for those trials involving impeachment, all persons accused of crimes are guaranteed a jury trial in the same state where the crime was committed. When a crime is committed outside of any state, such as on a ship at sea, Congress will decide where the trial will take place.

SECTION 3. Treason

Anyone who makes war against the United States or gives help to the nation's enemies, can be charged with treason. No one can be convicted of treason unless two witnesses support the charge or unless the person confesses to the charge in open court.

The Congress shall have power to declare the punishment of treason, but no attainder of treason shall work corruption of blood, or forfeiture except during the life of the person attainted.

ARTICLE 4
Relations Among the States

SECTION 1. Recognition by Each State

Full faith and credit shall be given in each State to the public acts, records, and judicial proceedings of every other State. And the Congress may by general laws prescribe the manner in which such acts, records, and proceedings shall be proved, and the effect thereof.

SECTION 2. Rights of Citizens in States

The citizens of each State shall be entitled to all privileges and immunities of citizens in the several States.

A person charged in any State with treason, felony, or other crime, who shall flee from justice, and be found in another State, shall on demand of the executive authority of the State from which he fled, be delivered up to be removed to the State having jurisdiction of the crime.

~~No person held to service or labor in one State, under the laws thereof, escaping into another, shall, in consequence of any law or regulation therein, be discharged from such service or labor, but shall be delivered up on claim of the party to whom such service or labor may be due.~~ *
*(*Changed by the Thirteenth Amendment)*

SECTION 3. New States

New States may be admitted by the Congress into this Union; but no new State shall be formed or erected within the jurisdiction of any other State; nor any State be formed by the junction of two or more States, or parts of States, without the consent of the legislatures of the States concerned as well as of the Congress.

The Congress shall have power to dispose of and make all needful rules and regulations respecting the territory or other property belonging to the United States; and nothing in this Constitution shall be so construed as to prejudice any claims of the United States, or of any particular State.

SECTION 4. Guarantees to the States

The United States shall guarantee to every State in this Union a republican form of government, and shall protect each of them against invasion; and on application of the legislature, or of the executive (when the legislature cannot be convened), against domestic violence.

Congress has the power to decide punishments for acts of treason. The family of the traitor does not share in the guilt.

ARTICLE 4

Relations Among the States

SECTION 1. Recognition by Each State

Each state must recognize the laws, records, and legal decisions made by all the other states. Congress has the power to make laws to determine how these laws, records, and legal decisions can be proved.

SECTION 2. Rights of Citizens in States

States must give the same rights to citizens from other states that they give their own citizens.

If a person charged with a crime runs away to another state, the person must be returned to the original state for a trial.

No person who was a slave in one state may become free by escaping to a different state.

(This was changed by the Thirteenth Amendment, which made slavery illegal in all states.)

SECTION 3. New States

New states may become part of the United States with the permission of Congress. New states cannot be formed from land in an existing state, nor can two or more states or their parts join to create a new state without the consent of the states involved and of Congress.

Congress may sell or give away land or property belonging to the United States. Congress has the power to make all laws related to territories or other property owned by the United States and to make laws to govern federal territories and possessions.

SECTION 4. Guarantees to the States

The United States government is required to guarantee that each state has a republican form of government, a government that is responsible to the will of its people through their elected representatives. The federal government also must protect the states if they are invaded by foreign nations, and to do the same in case of riots, if requested by the governor or legislature of the state.

ARTICLE 5
Amending the Constitution

Amendments may be proposed by a two-thirds vote of each house of Congress or by a national convention called by Congress at the request of two-thirds of the states. To add an amendment to the Constitution, the legislatures or special conventions of three-fourths of the states must give approval or ratify it. However, no amendment can be added that keeps a state from having an equal vote in the United States Senate. No amendment may be added before 1808 that affects the slave trade or certain taxes. *(Congress passed a law in 1808 forbidding the slave trade protected under Article 1.)*

ARTICLE 6
Debts, Federal Supremacy, Oaths of Office

The federal government must pay all debts owed by the United States, including those debts which were taken on under the Articles of Confederation.

The Constitution and the laws of the United States are the supreme, or highest, laws of the land. All public officials in the federal government or within the states, regardless of other laws to the contrary, are bound by the Constitution and the national laws.

All officials in both federal and state governments must promise to obey and support the Constitution. No religious qualifications can be required as a condition for holding public office.

ARTICLE 7
Ratifying the Constitution

The Constitution will take effect when it is approved by at least nine of the thirteen states.

On September 17, 1787, all twelve state delegations present have given approval for adopting the Constitution. As proof, the delegates have each placed their signatures on the document.

ARTICLE 5
Amending the Constitution

The Congress, whenever two thirds of both houses shall deem it necessary, shall propose amendments to this Constitution, or, on the application of the legislatures of two thirds of the several States, shall call a convention for proposing amendments, which, in either case, shall be valid to all intents and purposes, as part of this Constitution, when ratified by the legislatures of three fourths of the several States, or by conventions in three fourths thereof, as the one or the other mode of ratification may be proposed by the Congress; provided ~~that no amendment which may be made prior to the year one thousand eight hundred and eight shall in any manner affect the first and fourth clauses in the ninth section of the first article~~ and that no State, without its consent, shall be deprived of its equal suffrage in the Senate.

ARTICLE 6
Debts, Federal Supremacy, Oaths of Office

All debts contracted and engagements entered into, before the adoption of this Constitution, shall be as valid against the United States under this Constitution, as under the Confederation.

This Constitution, and the laws of the United States which shall be made in pursuance thereof, and all treaties made, or which shall be made, under the authority of the United States, shall be the supreme law of the land; and the judges in every State shall be bound thereby, anything in the Constitution or laws of any State to the contrary notwithstanding.

The senators and representatives before mentioned, and the members of the several State legislatures, and all executive and judicial officers, both of the United States, and of the several States, shall be bound by oath or affirmation to support this Constitution; but no religious test shall ever be required as a qualification to any office or public trust under the United States.

ARTICLE 7
Ratifying the Constitution

The ratification of the conventions of nine States shall be sufficient for the establishment of this Constitution between the States so ratifying the same.

Done in Convention by the unanimous consent of the States present the seventeenth day of September in the year of our Lord one thousand seven hundred and eighty-seven and of the independence of the United States of America the twelfth. In witness whereof we have hereunto subscribed our names.

George Washington, *President* (Virginia)

Massachusetts
Nathaniel Gorham
Rufus King

New York
Alexander Hamilton

Georgia
William Few
Abraham Baldwin

Delaware
George Read
Gunning Bedford, Jr.
John Dickinson
Richard Bassett
Jacob Broom

Virginia
John Blair
James Madison, Jr.

Pennsylvania
Benjamin Franklin
Thomas Mifflin
Robert Morris
George Clymer
Thomas FitzSimons
Jared Ingersoll
James Wilson
Gouverneur Morris

New Hampshire
John Langdon
Nicholas Gilman

New Jersey
William Livingston
David Brearley
William Paterson
Jonathan Dayton

Connecticut
William Samuel Johnson
Roger Sherman

North Carolina
William Blount
Richard Dobbs Spaight
Hugh Williamson

South Carolina
John Rutledge
Charles Cotesworth Pinckney
Charles Pinckney
Pierce Butler

Maryland
James McHenry
Daniel of St. Thomas Jenifer
Daniel Carroll

"Let virtue, honor, and love of liberty and of science be and remain the soul of this constitution, and it will become the source of great and extensive happiness to this and future generations."

From Jay's charge to the Grand Jury of Ulster County. The Correspondence and Public Papers of John Jay, Henry P. Johnston, editor (New York: Burt Franklin, 1970), Vol. I, pp. 158–165, September 9, 1777.

"The power under the Constitution will always be in the people."

George Washington, The Writings of George Washington, Jared Sparks, editor (Boston: Russell, Odiorne and Metcalf, 1835), Vol. IX, p. 279, to Bushrod Washington on November 10, 1787.

FIRST AMENDMENT—1791
Freedom of Religion, Speech, Press, Assembly, and Petition

Congress shall not make any laws that set up an official national religion or that keeps people from worshiping according to their conscience. Congress may not limit the freedom of speech or the press, or the freedom to meet peaceably. People must have the right to ask the government to correct a problem.

SECOND AMENDMENT—1791
Right to Have Firearms

Because an organized militia is needed to protect the states, the right of people to keep and bear firearms shall not be violated.

THIRD AMENDMENT—1791
Right Not to House Soldiers

Soldiers may not be housed in private homes, without the consent of the owner, unless a law for that purpose is passed during a time of war.

FOURTH AMENDMENT—1791
Freedom from Unreasonable Search and Seizure

People and their property are to be protected from unreasonable search and seizure. Government authorities must have good cause and have a written order from a judge describing the place to be searched and the person or things to be seized.

FIFTH AMENDMENT—1791
Rights of People Accused of Crimes

A person may not be put on trial for a crime that is punishable by death or imprisonment without first being accused by a grand jury. [A grand jury is a group of citizens selected to decide whether there is enough evidence against a person to hold a trial.] However, during wartime or a time of public danger, people in military service may not have that right.

A person may not be put on trial twice for the same crime.

FIRST AMENDMENT—1791
Freedom of Religion, Speech, Press, Assembly, and Petition

Congress shall make no law respecting an establishment of religion, or prohibiting the free exercise thereof; or abridging the freedom of speech, or of the press; or the right of the people peaceably to assemble, and to petition the government for a redress of grievances.

SECOND AMENDMENT—1791
Right to Have Firearms

A well-regulated militia, being necessary to the security of a free state, the right of the people to keep and bear arms shall not be infringed.

THIRD AMENDMENT—1791
Right Not to House Soldiers

No soldier shall, in time of peace, be quartered in any house, without the consent of the owner, nor in time of war, but in a manner to be prescribed by law.

FOURTH AMENDMENT—1791
Freedom from Unreasonable Search and Seizure

The right of the people to be secure in their persons, houses, papers, and effects, against unreasonable searches and seizures, shall not be violated, and no warrants shall issue, but upon probable cause, supported by oath or affirmation, and particularly describing the place to be searched, and the persons or things to be seized.

FIFTH AMENDMENT—1791
Rights of People Accused of Crimes

No person shall be held to answer for a capital or otherwise infamous crime, unless on a presentment or indictment of a grand jury, except in cases arising in the land or naval forces, or in the militia, when in actual service in time of war or public danger; nor shall any person be subject for the same offense to be twice put in jeopardy of life or limb; nor shall be compelled in any criminal case to be a witness against himself, nor be deprived of life, liberty, or property, without due process of law; nor shall private property be taken for public use without just compensation.

SIXTH AMENDMENT—1791
Right to a Jury Trial in a Criminal Case

In all criminal prosecutions, the accused shall enjoy the right to a speedy and public trial, by an impartial jury of the state and district wherein the crime shall have been committed, which district shall have been previously ascertained by law, and to be informed of the nature and cause of the accusation; to be confronted with the witnesses against him; to have compulsory process for obtaining witnesses in his favor, and to have the assistance of counsel for his defense.

SEVENTH AMENDMENT—1791
Right to a Jury Trial in a Civil Case

In suits at common law, where the value in controversy shall exceed twenty dollars, the right of trial by jury shall be preserved, and no fact tried by a jury shall be otherwise reexamined in any court of the United States, than according to the rules of the common law.

EIGHTH AMENDMENT—1791
Protection from Unfair Bail and Punishment

Excessive bail shall not be required, nor excessive fines imposed, nor cruel and unusual punishments inflicted.

NINTH AMENDMENT—1791
Other Rights

The enumeration in the Constitution of certain rights shall not be construed to deny or disparage others retained by the people.

TENTH AMENDMENT—1791
Powers of the States and People

The powers not delegated to the United States by the Constitution, nor prohibited by it to the States, are reserved to the states respectively, or to the people.

People cannot be required to give evidence against themselves.

People may not have their lives, liberty, or property taken away without fair and equal treatment under the laws of the land.

People may not have their property taken for public use without receiving reasonable payment.

SIXTH AMENDMENT—1791
Right to a Jury Trial in a Criminal Case

A person accused of a crime must have a speedy, public trial held before an open-minded jury made up of citizens living in the community where the crime occurred. The accused person must also be told about the nature of the charge of wrongdoing. Accused people are allowed to meet and question witnesses against them, to have witnesses testify in their favor, and to have the services of a lawyer.

SEVENTH AMENDMENT—1791
Right to a Jury Trial in a Civil Case

In civil cases, where the value of the property in question is over $20, the right to a jury trial is guaranteed. The decision of the jury is final and cannot be changed by a judge but only by a new trial.

EIGHTH AMENDMENT—1791
Protection from Unfair Bail and Punishment

Bails and fines must not be too large, and punishments may not be cruel and unusual.

NINTH AMENDMENT—1791
Other Rights

Fundamental rights not listed in the Constitution remain guaranteed to all citizens.

TENTH AMENDMENT—1791
Powers of the States and People

The states or the people keep all powers not granted to the federal government and not denied to the states by the Constitution.

ELEVENTH AMENDMENT—1795
Limits on Right to Sue States

The judicial power of the United States shall not be construed to extend to any suit in law or equity, commenced or prosecuted against one of the United States by citizens of another State, or by citizens or subjects of any foreign State.

TWELFTH AMENDMENT—1804
Election of President and Vice President

The electors shall meet in their respective States, and vote by ballot for President and Vice President, one of whom, at least, shall not be an inhabitant of the same State with themselves; they shall name in their ballots the person voted for as President, and in distinct ballots the person voted for as Vice President, and they shall make distinct lists of all persons voted for as President, and of all persons voted for as Vice President, and of the number of votes for each, which lists they shall sign and certify, and transmit sealed to the seat of the government of the United States, directed to the president of the Senate;—The president of the Senate shall, in the presence of the Senate and House of Representatives, open all the certificates and the votes shall then be counted;—The person having the greatest number of votes for President shall be the President, if such number be a majority of the whole number of electors appointed; and if no person have such majority, then from the persons having the highest numbers not exceeding three on the list of those voted for as President, the House of Representatives shall choose immediately, by ballot, the President. But in choosing the President, the votes shall be taken by States, the representation from each State having one vote; a quorum for this purpose shall consist of a member or members from two thirds of the States, and a majority of all the States shall be necessary to a choice. ~~*And if the House of Representatives shall not choose a President whenever the right of choice shall devolve upon them, before the fourth day of March next following,*~~* *then the Vice President shall act as President,* as in the case of the death or other constitutional disability of the President. The person having the greatest number of votes as Vice President shall be the Vice President, if such number be a majority of the whole number of electors appointed, and if no person have a majority, then from the two highest numbers on the list, the Senate shall choose the Vice President; a quorum for the purpose shall consist of two thirds of the whole number of senators, and a majority of the whole number shall be necessary to a choice. But no person constitutionally ineligible to the office of President shall be eligible to that of Vice President of the United States. *(*Changed by the Twentieth Amendment)*

ELEVENTH AMENDMENT—1795
Limits on Right to Sue States

A state government cannot be sued in a federal court by people from a different state or from a foreign country.

TWELFTH AMENDMENT—1804
Election of President and Vice-President

In each state, members of the Electoral College vote on separate ballots for one person as President and another person as Vice-President. At least one of these choices may not live in the same state as the electors. Each person on the ballot receiving votes in a given state must be listed by the total numbers of votes. Final counts of votes from each state must be signed and officially recognized as accurate and complete. These results must be delivered to the national capital to be opened and read aloud by the president of the Senate at a joint session of Congress.

If a person receives a majority of votes for President, that person shall be the President. If no person has a majority, then from the three who received the most votes, the House of Representatives will immediately choose the President by ballot. But in choosing the President, the votes shall be taken by states, with each state having one vote. Two-thirds of the states must participate in this choice. *(Until changed by the Twentieth Amendment, if the House of Representatives failed to elect a President by March 4, the Vice-President served as President.)*

If a person receives a majority of votes as Vice-President, that person shall be the Vice-President. If no person has a majority, then from the two highest numbers on the list, the Senate will choose the Vice-President, provided that two-thirds of the senators are present to vote. A simple majority, with each senator voting individually, is necessary to make a final choice. A person who is not eligible to be President cannot be eligible for the office of Vice-President.

THIRTEENTH AMENDMENT—1865
Abolition of Slavery

SECTION 1. Slavery Outlawed
Neither slavery nor involuntary servitude, except as a punishment for crime whereof the party shall have been duly convicted, shall exist within the United States, or any place subject to their jurisdiction.

SECTION 2. Enforcement
Congress shall have power to enforce this article by appropriate legislation.

FOURTEENTH AMENDMENT—1868
Rights of Citizens

SECTION 1. Citizenship
All persons born or naturalized in the United States, and subject to the jurisdiction thereof, are citizens of the United States and of the State wherein they reside. No State shall make or enforce any law which shall abridge the privileges or immunities of citizens of the United States; nor shall any State deprive any person of life, liberty, or property, without due process of law; nor deny to any person within its jurisdiction the equal protection of the laws.

SECTION 2. Representation in Congress
Representatives shall be apportioned among the several States according to their respective numbers, counting the whole number of persons in each State, ~~excluding Indians not taxed~~. But when the right to vote at any election for the choice of electors for President and Vice President of the United States, representatives in Congress, the executive and judicial officers of a State, or the members of the legislature thereof is denied to any of the ~~male~~ inhabitants of such State, being ~~twenty-one years of age, and~~ citizens of the United States, or in any way abridged, except for participation in rebellion, or other crime, the basis of representation therein shall be reduced in the proportion which the number of such ~~male~~ citizens shall bear to the whole number of ~~male~~ citizens ~~twenty-one years of age~~ in such State.* *(*Restriction on race and ethnicity changed by the Fifteenth Amendment; restriction on gender changed by the Nineteenth Amendment; restriction regarding taxation changed by the Twenty-Fourth Amendment; restriction on age changed by the Twenty-Sixth Amendment)*

THIRTEENTH AMENDMENT—1865
Abolition of Slavery

Slavery shall not exist anywhere in the United States or anyplace governed by the United States. Forced labor may only be required after a person has been fairly convicted of a crime.

Congress may make laws to enforce this article.

FOURTEENTH AMENDMENT—1868
Rights of Citizens

All persons born in the United States or granted citizenship are citizens of both the United States and of the states in which they live.

No state may pass laws that take away or limit the freedoms or privileges of any of its citizens. Citizens may not have their lives, liberties, or property taken away without access to a regular judicial process conducted according to the laws. All people must be protected equally by the laws.

A state's representation in Congress is determined by the state's population. A state which does not allow qualified voters to vote may have its representation in Congress reduced. *(Other provisions of this section were changed by the Fifteenth, Nineteenth, Twenty-Fourth, and Twenty-Sixth Amendments.)*

SECTION 3. Penalties for Leaders of the Confederacy
No person shall be a senator or representative in Congress, or elector of President and Vice President, or hold any office, civil or military, under the United States, or under any State, who, having previously taken an oath, as a member of Congress, or as an officer of the United States, or as a member of any State legislature, or as an executive or judicial officer of any State, to support the Constitution of the United States, shall have engaged in insurrection or rebellion against the same, or given aid or comfort to the enemies thereof. But Congress may by a vote of two thirds of each house, remove such disability.

SECTION 4. Responsibility for the Public Debt
The validity of the public debt of the United States, authorized by law, including debts incurred for payment of pensions and bounties for services in suppressing insurrection or rebellion, shall not be questioned. But neither the United States nor any State shall assume or pay any debt or obligation incurred in aid of insurrection or rebellion against the United States, or any claim for the loss or emancipation of any slave; but all such debts, obligations and claims shall be held illegal and void.

SECTION 5. Enforcement
The Congress shall have power to enforce, by appropriate legislation, the provisions of this article.

FIFTEENTH AMENDMENT—1870
Voting Rights

SECTION 1. Suffrage for African Americans
The right of citizens of the United States to vote shall not be denied or abridged by the United States or by any State on account of race, color, or previous condition of servitude.

SECTION 2. Enforcement
The Congress shall have power to enforce this article by appropriate legislation.

SIXTEENTH AMENDMENT—1913
Income Tax

The Congress shall have power to lay and collect taxes on incomes, from whatever source derived, without apportionment among the several States, and without regard to any census or enumeration.

No person may hold a civil or military office in the federal or a state government who had previously taken an oath to uphold the Constitution and then aided or helped the Confederacy during the Civil War or other rebellions against the United States. Congress may remove this provision by a two-thirds vote of both houses.

Any federal debts resulting from fighting to end a civil war or put down a rebellion must be paid in full. However, the federal or state government shall not pay debts made by those who participate in a rebellion against the United States.
Former owners of slaves shall not be paid for the financial losses caused by the freeing of slaves.

Congress has the power to pass laws to enforce the provisions of this article.

FIFTEENTH AMENDMENT—1870
Voting Rights

A citizen's right to vote in any election cannot be denied based on the person's race or color, or because they were once enslaved.

Congress has the power to pass laws to enforce the provisions of this article.

SIXTEENTH AMENDMENT—1913
Income Tax

Congress has the power to tax all individuals directly based on their personal incomes, without collecting taxes based on a division among the states or in consideration of a state's population.

SEVENTEENTH AMENDMENT—1913
Direct Election of Senators

The Senate of the United States shall be composed of two senators from each State, elected by the people thereof, for six years; and each senator shall have one vote. The electors in each State shall have the qualifications requisite for electors of the most numerous branch of the State legislatures.

When vacancies happen in the representation of any State in the Senate, the executive authority of such State shall issue writs of election to fill such vacancies: Provided, that the legislature of any State may empower the executive thereof to make temporary appointments until the people fill the vacancies by election as the legislature may direct.

This amendment shall not be so construed as to affect the election or term of any Senator chosen before it becomes valid as part of the Constitution.

EIGHTEENTH AMENDMENT*—1919
Prohibition

SECTION 1. Liquor Banned
~~After one year from the ratification of this article, the manufacture, sale, or transportation of intoxicating liquors within, the importation thereof into, or the exportation thereof from the United States and all territory subject to the jurisdiction thereof for beverage purposes is hereby prohibited.~~*

SECTION 2. Enforcement
~~The Congress and the several States shall have concurrent power to enforce this article by appropriate legislation.~~*

SECTION 3. Time Limit for Ratification
~~This article shall be inoperative unless it shall have been ratified as an amendment to the Constitution by the legislatures of the several States, as provided in the Constitution, within seven years from the date of the submission hereof to the States by the Congress.~~* *(*Repealed by the Twenty-First Amendment)*

SEVENTEENTH AMENDMENT—1913
Direct Election of Senators

Two senators will represent each state in Congress, each elected for six-year terms and having one vote in the Senate. They will be elected directly by the qualified voters in the states *(not by state legislatures, which was originally provided for in Article I, Section 3, Clause 1).*

When vacancies occur in the Senate, the governor of the state will call for an election to fill the vacancy. In the meantime the state legislature will permit the governor to make a temporary appointment until the election occurs. The legislature organizes the election.

This amendment shall not affect the election or term of any Senator chosen before it becomes part of the Constitution.

EIGHTEENTH AMENDMENT*—1919
Prohibition

The making, selling, and transporting of alcoholic beverages anywhere in the United States and its territories is outlawed. This amendment takes effect one year after the amendment is passed.

Congress and the states will share lawmaking powers to enforce this article.

This amendment will become part of the Constitution only if it is ratified within seven years after Congress has sent it to the States.
(This amendment was repealed by the Twenty-First Amendment.)

NINETEENTH AMENDMENT—1920
Women's Right to Vote

SECTION 1. Suffrage for Women
The right of citizens of the United States to vote shall not be denied or abridged by the United States or by any State on account of sex.

SECTION 2. Enforcement
Congress shall have power to enforce this article by appropriate legislation.

TWENTIETH AMENDMENT—1933
Terms of Office

SECTION 1. Start and End of Terms
The terms of the President and Vice President shall end at noon on the 20th day of January, and the terms of senators and representatives at noon on the third day of January, of the year in which such terms would have ended if this article had not been ratified; and the terms of their successors shall then begin.

SECTION 2. Congressional Meeting
The Congress shall assemble at least once in every year, and such meeting shall begin at noon on the third day of January, unless they shall by law appoint a different day.

SECTION 3. Successor for the President-Elect
If, at the time fixed for the beginning of the term of the President, the President-elect shall have died, the Vice President-elect shall become President. If a President shall not have been chosen before the time fixed for the beginning of his term, or if the President-elect shall have failed to qualify, then the Vice President-elect shall act as President until a President shall have qualified; and the Congress may by law provide for the case wherein neither a President-elect nor a Vice President-elect shall have qualified, declaring who shall then act as President, or the manner in which one who is to act shall be selected, and such persons shall act accordingly until a President or Vice President shall have qualified.

SECTION 4. Elections Decided by Congress
The Congress may by law provide for the case of the death of any of the persons from whom the House of Representatives may choose a President

NINETEENTH AMENDMENT—1920
Women's Right to Vote
A citizen's right to vote in any election cannot be denied based on the person's sex.

Congress shall have power to pass laws to enforce the provisions of this article.

TWENTIETH AMENDMENT—1933
Terms of Office
The terms of the President and Vice-President end at noon on January 20th, and the terms of senators and representatives end at noon on January 3rd, following the federal elections held the previous November. The terms of their successors begin at that time.

Congress must meet at least once a year, and the session will begin at noon on January 3rd unless a law is passed to change the day.

If the President-elect dies before taking office, the Vice-President-elect becomes President. If a President has not been chosen before January 20, or if the President-elect has not qualified, then the Vice-President-elect acts as President until a President becomes qualified. If neither the President-elect or Vice-President-elect is able to take office on the designated date, then Congress will decide who will act as President until a President or Vice-President has been qualified.

If a candidate fails to win a majority in the Electoral College, and then dies while the election is being decided in the House of Representatives, Congress will have the power to pass laws to resolve the problem. Congress has similar power in the event that a candidate for Vice-President dies while the election is in the Senate.

whenever the right of choice shall have devolved upon them, and for the case of the death of any of the persons from whom the Senate may choose a Vice President whenever the right of choice shall have devolved upon them.

SECTION 5. Effective Date
Sections 1 and 2 shall take effect on the 15th day of October following the ratification of this article.

SECTION 6. Time Limit for Ratification
This article shall be inoperative unless it shall have been ratified as an amendment to the Constitution by the legislatures of three fourths of the several States within seven years from the date of its submission.

TWENTY-FIRST AMENDMENT—1933
Repeal of Prohibition Amendment

SECTION 1. End of Prohibition
The eighteenth article of amendment to the Constitution of the United States is hereby repealed.

SECTION 2. Protection of State Prohibition Laws
The transportation or importation into any State, territory, or possession of the United States for delivery or use therein of intoxicating liquors, in violation of the laws thereof, is hereby prohibited.

SECTION 3. Time Limit for Ratification
This article shall be inoperative unless it shall have been ratified as an amendment to the Constitution by conventions in the several States, as provided in the Constitution, within seven years from the date of submission hereof to the States by the Congress.

TWENTY-SECOND AMENDMENT—1951
Limit on Terms of the President

SECTION 1. Two-Term Limit
No person shall be elected to the office of the President more than twice, and no person who has held the office of President, or acted as President, for more than two years of a term to which some other person was elected President shall be elected to the office of the President more than once.

Sections 1 and 2 of this amendment shall take effect on October 15, after this amendment is ratified.

This amendment will become part of the Constitution only if it is ratified by three-fourths of the states within seven years after Congress has sent it to the States.

TWENTY-FIRST AMENDMENT—1933
Repeal of Prohibition Amendment
The Eighteenth Amendment, prohibiting the making, sale, and transportation of alcoholic beverages in the United States and its possessions, is repealed.

Individual states may prohibit the transporting or importing of alcoholic beverages.

This amendment will become part of the Constitution only if it is ratified in seven years.

TWENTY-SECOND AMENDMENT—1951
Limit on Terms of the President
No person can be elected to the office of the President more than twice. If a President has served two or more years of a previous President's term, then the President may be reelected for one additional term.

But this Article shall not apply to any person holding the office of President when this Article was proposed by the Congress, and shall not prevent any person who may be holding the office of President, or acting as President, during the term within which this Article becomes operative from holding the office of President or acting as President during the remainder of such term.

SECTION 2. Time Limit on Ratification
This article shall be inoperative unless it shall have been ratified as an amendment to the Constitution by the legislatures of three-fourths of the several States within seven years from the date of its submission to the States by the Congress.

TWENTY-THIRD AMENDMENT—1961
Presidential Elections for District of Columbia

SECTION 1. Presidential Electors
The District constituting the seat of government of the United States shall appoint in such manner as the Congress may direct:

A number of electors of President and Vice President equal to the whole number of senators and representatives in Congress to which the District would be entitled if it were a State, but in no event more than the least populous state; they shall be in addition to those appointed by the States, but they shall be considered, for the purposes of the election of President and Vice President, to be electors appointed by a State; and they shall meet in the District and perform such duties as provided by the twelfth article of amendment.

SECTION 2. Enforcement
The Congress shall have power to enforce this article by appropriate legislation.

TWENTY-FOURTH AMENDMENT—1964
Outlawing of Poll Tax

SECTION 1. Ban on Poll Tax in Federal Elections
The right of citizens of the United States to vote in any primary or other election for President or Vice President, for electors for President or Vice President, or for senator or representative in Congress, shall not be denied or abridged by the United States or any State by reason of failure to pay any poll tax or other tax.

The current President in office at the time of this amendment's ratification process is not limited to term restrictions.

This amendment will become part of the Constitution only if it is ratified by three-fourths of the States within seven years after Congress has sent it to the States.

TWENTY-THIRD AMENDMENT—1961
Presidential Elections for District of Columbia
Citizens living in the District of Columbia may elect members to the Electoral College to vote in federal elections for President and Vice-President. The number of electors is limited to the number of votes of the least populated state. The voters must live in the district and follow all duties and procedures outlined in the Twelfth Amendment.

Congress has the power to make laws necessary to enforce this amendment.

TWENTY-FOURTH AMENDMENT—1964
Outlawing of Poll Tax
United States citizens may not have their voting rights restricted in federal elections by the establishment of a poll tax or other tax.

SECTION 2. Enforcement
The Congress shall have power to enforce this article by appropriate legislation.

TWENTY-FIFTH AMENDMENT—1967
Presidential Succession

SECTION 1. Filling Vacant Office of President
In case of the removal of the President from office or his death or resignation, the Vice President shall become President.

SECTION 2. Filling Vacant Office of Vice President
Whenever there is a vacancy in the office of the Vice President, the President shall nominate a Vice President who shall take the office upon confirmation by a majority vote of both houses of Congress.

SECTION 3. Disability of the President
Whenever the President transmits to the president pro tempore of the Senate and the Speaker of the House of Representatives his written declaration that he is unable to discharge the powers and duties of his office, and until he transmits to them a written declaration to the contrary, such powers and duties shall be discharged by the Vice President as Acting President.

SECTION 4. When Congress Names an Acting President
Whenever the Vice President and a majority of either the principal officers of the executive departments or of such other body as Congress may by law provide, transmit to the president pro tempore of the Senate and the Speaker of the House of Representatives their written declaration that the President is unable to discharge the powers and duties of his office, the Vice President shall immediately assume the powers and duties of the office as Acting President.

Thereafter, when the President transmits to the president pro tempore of the Senate and the Speaker of the House of Representatives his written declaration that no inability exists, he shall resume the powers and duties of his office unless the Vice President and a majority of either the principal officers of the executive department or of such other body as Congress may by law provide, transmit within four days to the president pro tempore of the Senate and the Speaker of the House of Representatives their written declaration that the President is unable to discharge the powers and duties of his office. Thereupon Congress shall decide the issue, assembling within forty-eight hours for that purpose if not in session. If

Congress has the power to make laws necessary to enforce this amendment.

TWENTY-FIFTH AMENDMENT—1967
Presidential Succession
If a President dies or is removed from office, then the Vice-President will become President.

If the office of Vice-President becomes vacant, the President may nominate a new Vice-President. The person nominated must be approved by a majority vote in both houses of Congress.

If the President sends a written notice to officers of both houses of Congress that the President is unable to perform the duties of the office, then the Vice-President will become Acting President. The Vice-President will act as the President until the President informs Congress that the President is again ready to take over the presidential responsibilities.

If the President is unconscious or has a disabling illness, the Vice-President and a majority of the Cabinet have the right to inform Congress in writing that the President is unable to carry out the duties of being President. The Vice-President then becomes Acting President until the President can return to work.

When the President informs the leaders of Congress in writing that the disability no longer exists, the President shall resume the office. But if there is a disagreement between the President and the Vice-President and a majority of the Cabinet about the President's ability to carry out the duties of being President, the Vice-President, or other appropriate authority, has four days to notify Congress, and Congress has the power to decide the issue. If not in session, both houses of Congress must meet within 48 hours for that purpose and will have 21 days to make a decision. A two-thirds vote in both houses of Congress is required to find the President unfit to perform the duties of the office.

United States Documents

The Constitution of the United States of America

the Congress, within twenty-one days after receipt of the latter written declaration, or, if Congress is not in session, within twenty-one days after Congress is required to assemble, determines by two-thirds vote of both houses that the President is unable to discharge the powers and duties of his office, the Vice President shall continue to discharge the same as Acting President; otherwise, the President shall resume the powers and duties of his office.

TWENTY-SIXTH AMENDMENT—1971
Voting Rights for Eighteen-Year-Olds
Citizens who are eighteen years of age or older have the right to vote in all elections.

TWENTY-SIXTH AMENDMENT—1971

Voting Rights for Eighteen-Year-Olds

SECTION 1. New Voting Age
The right of citizens in the United States, who are eighteen years of age or older, to vote shall not be denied or abridged by the United States or by any State on account of age.

Congress has the power to make laws necessary to enforce this amendment.

SECTION 2. Enforcement
The Congress shall have power to enforce this article by appropriate legislation.

TWENTY-SEVENTH AMENDMENT—1992
Limits on Congressional Salary Changes
Salary changes for Congress cannot take effect until after the next federal election.

TWENTY-SEVENTH AMENDMENT—1992

Limits on Congressional Salary Changes

No law varying the compensation for the services of the Senators and Representatives shall take effect, until an election of Representatives shall have intervened.

Gazetteer

This Gazetteer is a geographic dictionary that will help you locate and pronounce the names of places in this book. Latitude and longitude are given for cities. The page numbers tell you where each place appears on a map (m.) or in the text (t.).

A

Afghanistan (af gan′ ə stan) Country in Southwest Asia where United States soldiers defeated Taliban troops in 2001. (m. 449, 506; t. 448, 506)

Africa (af′ rə kə) Second largest of Earth's seven continents. (m. 9, t. 9)

Ahwahnee Valley (ä wä′ nē) Valley in California that was one of the first rural places with phone access; part of Yosemite National Park. (m. 216, t. 219)

Anaheim (an′ ə hīm) City in southwestern California where the first theme park in the world, Disneyland, opened in 1955; 34°N, 118°W. (m. 394, t. 401)

Angel Island (ān′ jəl ī′ lənd) Island in San Francisco Bay, California, that was the entry point for immigrants from Asia from 1910 to 1940. (m. 184, t. 187)

Antarctica (ant′ ärk′ tə kə) One of Earth's seven continents, around the South Pole. (m. R4–5)

Appleton (ap′ əl tən) Town in eastern Wisconsin where the first hydroelectric power plant in the United States was built in 1882; 44°N, 88°W. (m. 216, t. 220)

Appomattox Court House (ap′ ə mat′ əks kôrt′ hous) Town in central Virginia, site of Confederate General Lee's surrender to Union General Grant on April 9, 1865, ending the Civil War; 37°N, 79°W. (m. 99, t. 101)

Arctic Ocean (ärk′ tic ō′ shən) Smallest of Earth's four oceans. (m. R4–5)

Argonia (är gō′ nē ə) Town in southern Kansas where the first woman mayor in the United States was elected in 1887; 37°N, 98°W. (m. 240, t. 242)

Asia (ā′ zhə) Largest of Earth's seven continents. (m. 6, t. 7)

Atlanta (at lan′ tə) Capital and largest city in Georgia; 33°N, 84°W. (m. 99, 113; t.100)

Atlantic Ocean (at lan′ tik ō′ shən) One of Earth's four oceans. (m. R4–5)

Australia (ȯ strā′ lyə) Smallest of Earth's seven continents. (m. R5)

Austria-Hungary (ȯ′ strē ə hung′ gar ē) Country in south central Europe that declared war on Serbia, starting World War I. (m. 273, t. 273)

B

Bering Strait (bir′ ing strāt′) Narrow body of water that separates Asia from North America. During the Ice Age, it was a land bridge connecting the two continents. (m. 7, t. 7)

Black Hills (blak hilz) Mountain range in South Dakota and Wyoming, where gold was discovered in 1874. (m. 154, t. 155)

Boston (bȯ′ stən) Capital and largest city of Massachusetts; 42°N, 71°W. (m. 16; t. 23, 229, 494)

C

Chicago (shə kä′ gō) Largest city in Illinois, located on Lake Michigan; 41°N, 87°W. (m. 134, t. 150, 223, 235)

Cleveland (klēv′ lənd) Port city in Ohio, on Lake Erie; 41°N, 81°W. (m. 176, t. 179)

Coast Ranges (kōst rān′ jəz) Mountains extending along the Pacific coast of North America. (m. R14)

Cuba (kyü′ bə) Largest country in the West Indies. (m. 255, t. 253)

Pronunciation Key

a	in hat	ō	in open	sh	in she
ā	in age	ȯ	in all	th	in thin
â	in care	ô	in order	ᴛʜ	in then
ä	in far	oi	in oil	zh	in measure
e	in let	ou	in out	ə	= a in about
ē	in equal	u	in cup	ə	= e in taken
ėr	in term	ů	in put	ə	= i in pencil
i	in it	ü	in rule	ə	= o in lemon
ī	in ice	ch	in child	ə	= u in circus
o	in hot	ng	in long		

Gazetteer

D

Dallas (dal′ əs) City in northeastern Texas; 33°N, 97°W. (m. R13)

Death Valley (deth val′ ē) Lowest point in North America, located in the Mojave Desert in California. (m. R14)

Denver (den′ vər) Capital and largest city in Colorado; 40°N, 105°W. (m. 134, t. 151)

Detroit (di troit′) Largest city in Michigan, site of Henry Ford's automobile factory; 42°N, 83°W. (m. 298, t. 299, 402)

Dodge City (doj sit′ ē) City in southern Kansas, located on the Arkansas River; formerly a stop along a cattle trail in the late 1800s; 38°N, 100°W (m. 148, 328; t. 149, 332)

E

East Berlin (ēst bər lin′) Eastern section of the city of Berlin, Germany, divided from the western section by the Berlin Wall from 1961 to 1989. (m. 384, t. 389)

Eastern Hemisphere (ē′ stərn hem′ ə sfir) Half of Earth east of the prime meridian, including the continents of Africa, Asia, Europe, and Australia. (m. H10, t. H10)

Ellis Island (el′is ī′lənd) Island in New York Harbor, which was the entry point for immigrants from Europe from 1892 to 1954. (m. 184, t.186)

Europe (yůr′ əp) One of Earth's seven continents. (m. 17, t. 10)

F

Fort Sumter (fôrt sum′ tər) Fort in Charleston Harbor, South Carolina, site of the first battle of the Civil War in 1861. (m. 99, t. 75)

Fort Wagner (fôrt wag′ nər) Fort that protected the harbor of Charleston, South Carolina, attacked by the African American 54th Regiment in the Civil War in July 1863. (m. 88, t. 91)

France (frans) Country in Western Europe. (m. 273, t. 32)

G

Gettysburg (get′ ēz bėrg′) Town in southern Pennsylvania, site of a major Union victory during the Civil War in 1863; 40°N, 77°W. (m. 99, t. 97)

Grand Canyon National Monument (grand kan′ yən nash′ ə nəl mon′ yə mənt) Large wildlife area in Arizona set aside by President Theodore Roosevelt in 1908; the area later become a national park. (m. 262, t. 267)

Great Plains (grāt plānz) Region in central North America, east of the Rocky Mountains and extending from Canada to Texas. (m. 138, t. 139)

Great Salt Lake (grāt sȯlt lāk) Lake in northwestern Utah, largest salt lake in North America. (m. R14)

Greensboro (grēnz′ bėr ō) City in north central North Carolina where four African American students staged a sit-in for equal rights in 1960; 36°N, 80°W. (m. 418, t. 423)

H

Harlem (här′ ləm) Neighborhood in New York City where many African American artists lived and worked in the 1920s. (m. 310, t. 314)

Harpers Ferry (här′ pərz fer′ ē) Town in northeastern West Virginia, site of federal arsenal raided by abolitionist John Brown in 1859; 39°N, 78°W. (m. 66, t. 70)

Hawaii (hə wī′ ē) Group of volcanic islands in the central Pacific Ocean that became a state in 1959. (m. 255, t. 252)

Hiroshima (hir′ ō shē′ mə) City in southwestern Japan; the first city where an atomic bomb was dropped, on August 6, 1945; 35°N, 132°E. (m. 367, t. 361)

Homestead (hōm′ sted) Town in southwest Pennsylvania; site of a major labor strike at Andrew Carnegie's Homestead Steel Works in 1892; 40°N, 80°W. (m. 192, t. 193)

I

Iraq (i rak′) Country in Asia, site of the 1991 Persian Gulf War; invaded by the United States and other nations as part of the war on terrorism in 2003. (m. 506, t. 507)

Iwo Jima (ē′ wō jē′ mə) Small Pacific island off of Japan, site of major battle during World War II; 25°N, 141°E. (m. 359, t. 361)

J

Jamestown (jāmz′ toun) First permanent English colony in North America, founded in 1607 in eastern Virginia; 37°N, 77°W. (m. 13, t. 14)

K

Kansas Territory (kan′ zəs ter′ ə tôr′ ē) Territory created in 1854 by the Kansas-Nebraska Act; part of it became the state of Kansas. (m. 69, t. 69)

Kitty Hawk (kit′ ē hȯk) Town in North Carolina where the Wright Brothers flew the first powered airplane in 1903; 36°N, 76°W. (m. 166, t. 172)

Kuwait (kü wāt′) Country in Asia that was invaded by Iraq in 1990, leading to the Persian Gulf War. (m. 446, t. 450)

L

Los Alamos (lōs al′ ə mōs) City in northern New Mexico that was the site of a major atomic bomb research laboratory; 36°N, 106°W. (m. 348, t. 354)

Los Angeles (los an′ jə ləs) Largest city in California, located in southern part of the state; 34°N, 118°W. (m. 130, t. 304)

M

Manassas Junction (mə nas′ əs jungk′ shən) Town in Virginia near the site of the First Battle of Bull Run in 1861; 39°N, 78°W. (m. 82, t. 85)

Menlo Park (men′ lō pärk) Community in central New Jersey, site of inventor Thomas Edison's laboratory. (m. 166, t. 168)

Middle East (mid′ l ēst) A group of countries in Southwest Asia, including Iraq, Afghanistan, Egypt, and Israel. (m. 446, t. 448)

Midwest (mid′ west′) Region of the north central United States. (m. 473, t. 473)

Montgomery (mont gum′ ər ē) Capital of Alabama, site of African American bus boycott for equal rights from 1955 to 1956; 32°N, 86°W. (m. 418, t. 422)

Moscow (mos′ cō) Capital of Russia, located in the western part of the country; 56°N, 37°E. (m. 389, t. 388)

Mount Whitney (mount wit′ nē) Highest mountain in the contiguous states, located in southeastern California. (m. R14)

Pronunciation Key

a	in hat	ō	in open	sh	in she
ā	in age	ȯ	in all	th	in thin
â	in care	ô	in order	ᴛʜ	in then
ä	in far	oi	in oil	zh	in measure
e	in let	ou	in out	ə	= a in about
ē	in equal	u	in cup	ə	= e in taken
ėr	in term	ů	in put	ə	= i in pencil
i	in it	ü	in rule	ə	= o in lemon
ī	in ice	ch	in child	ə	= u in circus
o	in hot	ng	in long		

★ N ★

Nebraska Territory (nə brasʹ kə terʹ ə tôrʹ ē) Territory created in 1854 as a result of the Kansas-Nebraska Act; part of it became the state of Nebraska. (m. 69, t. 69)

New Amsterdam (nü amʹ stər dam) Settlement founded by the Dutch on Manhattan Island; became present-day New York City. (m. 13, t. 13)

New Haven (nü hāʹ vən) City in southern Connecticut, site of the trial of Africans who in 1839 took control of the Spanish slave ship *Amistad*; 41°N, 72°W. (m. 60, t. 62)

New Orleans (nü ôrʹ lē ənz) Port city in Louisiana, largest city in the state; 30°N, 90°W. (m. 310, t. 312)

New York City (nü yôrk sitʹ ē) Largest city in the United States, located in southeastern New York; 40°N, 73°W. (m. 223, t. 193, 223, 322, 443)

Nicodemus (nik ə dēʹ məs) Town in Kansas that was founded by African American pioneers; 39°N, 100°W. (m. 138, t. 141)

Normandy (nôrʹ mən dē) Region in northern France along the English Channel, where the Allies invaded Axis-occupied France in World War II; 49°N, 2°E. (m. 360, t. 363)

North America (nôrth ə merʹ ə kə) One of Earth's seven continents. (m. 7, t. 7)

Northeast (nôrthʹ ēstʹ) Region in the northeastern United States. (m. 473, t. 473)

Northern Hemisphere (nôrʹ Frarn hemʹ ə sfir) Half of Earth north of the equator. (m. H13, t. H13)

North Korea (nôrth kō rēʹ ə) Country occupying the northern part of the Korean peninsula. (m. 407, t. 407)

North Pole (nôrth pōl) Northernmost point on Earth; 90°N. (m. H13–15, t. H13–14)

North Vietnam (nôrth vē etʹ nämʹ) Northern part of Vietnam that was a separate nation from 1954 to 1975. (m. 431, t. 431)

★ O ★

Omaha (ōʹ mə hä) Largest city in Nebraska, located in the eastern part of the state; 41°N, 96°W. (m. 130, t. 130)

★ P ★

Pacific Ocean (pə sifʹ ik ōʹ shən) Largest of Earth's four oceans. (m. R4–5)

Panama Canal (panʹ ə mä kə nalʹ) Canal through the Isthmus of Panama, connecting the Atlantic and Pacific Oceans. (m. 250, t. 257)

Pearl Harbor (pėrl härʹ bər) Harbor in Hawaii, where Japanese planes bombed the United States naval base in a surprise attack on December 7, 1941. (m. 344, 346; t. 344)

Philadelphia (filʹ ə delʹ fē ə) City in southeastern Pennsylvania, which was the capital of the United States from 1790 to 1800; 40°N, 75°W. (m. 16, t. 23, 223)

Pittsburgh (pitsʹ bėrg) City in southwestern Pennsylvania, site of Andrew Carnegie's steel mill; 40°N, 79°W. (m. 176, t. 177)

Plymouth (plimʹ əth) Town in southeastern Massachusetts, founded by the Pilgrims in 1620; 42°N, 71°W. (m. 13, t. 15)

Promontory Point (promʹ ən tôrʹ ē point) Place in northwestern Utah where tracks of the Union Pacific and Central Pacific railroads met in 1869 to complete the transcontinental railroad; 41°N, 112°W. (m. 128, t. 133)

Puerto Rico (pwârʹ tō rēʹ kō) Island in the West Indies, a commonwealth of the United States. (m. 255, t. 253)

★ Q ★

Quebec (kwi bek) Capital of the Canadian province of Quebec, the first French colony in the Americas; 46°N, 71°W. (m. 13, t. 13)

Queens (kwēnz) Borough of New York City, site of the 1939 World's Fair. (m. 328, t. 334)

★ R ★

Richmond (richʹ mənd) Capital of Virginia, was capital of the Confederacy during the Civil War; 37°N, 77°W. (m. 99, t. 85, 170)

★ S ★

Sacramento (sakʹ rə menʹ tō) Capital of California; 38°N, 121°W. (m. 128, t. 130)

San Diego (san dē āʹ gō) Port city in southern California; 32°N, 117°W. (m. R12)

Savannah (sə vanʹ ə) Port city on the coast of Georgia; 32°N, 81°W. (m. 99, t. 100)

Seneca Falls (senʹ ə kə fölz) Town in west central New York, site of the first women's rights convention in the United States, in 1848; 43°N, 77°W. (m. 240, t. 242)

Serbia (sėrʹ bē ə) Country in southern Europe where Archduke Franz Ferdinand of Austria-Hungary was assassinated, leading to World War I. (m. 273, t. 273)

Southampton County (south ampʹ tən kounʹ tē) County in southeastern Virginia, location of Nat Turner's slave rebellion in 1831. (m. 60, t. 62)

Southeast (southʹ ēstʹ) Region in the southeastern United States. (m. 473, t. 473)

Southern Hemisphere (suᴛʜʹ ərn hemʹ ə sfir) Half of Earth south of the equator. (m. H13, t. H13)

South Korea (south kō rēʹ ə) Country occupying the southern part of the Korean peninsula. (m. 407, t. 407)

South Pole (south pōl) Southernmost point on Earth; 90°S. (m. H13–15, t. H13–14)

South Vietnam (south vē etʹ nämʹ) Southern part of Vietnam that was a separate nation from 1954 to 1975. (m. 431, t. 431)

Southwest (southʹ westʹ) Region in the southwestern United States. (m. 473, t. 473)

St. Louis (sānt lüʹ is) City in eastern Missouri; 39°N, 90°W. (m. 222, t. 228)

★ T ★

Tuskegee (təs kēʹ gē) City in central Alabama, site of Booker T. Washington's college for African Americans, Tuskegee Institute; 32°N, 86°W. (m. 232, t. 237, 239, 352)

★ V ★

Versailles (ver sīʹ) City in north central France, where treaty was signed ending World War I; 49°N, 2°E. (m. 272, t. 280)

Vicksburg (viksʹ bərg) City in western Mississippi on the Mississippi River, site of major Union victory during the Civil War in 1863; 32°N, 91°W. (m. 99, t. 99)

Virginia City (vər jinʹ yə sitʹ ē) Town in western Nevada on the eastern slope of the Sierra Nevada mountain range; 39°N, 120°W. (m. 148, t. 152)

Pronunciation Key		
a in hat	ò in open	sh in she
ā in age	ò in all	th in thin
â in care	ô in order	ᴛʜ in then
ä in far	oi in oil	zh in measure
e in let	ou in out	ə = a in about
ē in equal	u in cup	ə = e in taken
ėr in term	ù in put	ə = i in pencil
i in it	ü in rule	ə = o in lemon
ī in ice	ch in child	ə = u in circus
o in hot	ng in long	

★ W ★

Walnut Grove (wälʹ nət grōv) Estate in southwestern Virginia, where the mechanical reaper was perfected. (m. 216, t. 217)

Washington, D.C. (wäshʹ ing tən dē cē) Capital of the United States of America; 38°N, 77°W. (m. 30, 99; t. 31, 107, 443)

West (west) Region in the western United States. (m. 473, t. 473)

West Berlin (west bėr linʹ) Western section of the city of Berlin, Germany, divided from the eastern section by the Berlin Wall from 1961 to 1989. (m. 384, t. 389)

Western Hemisphere (westʹ ərn hemʹ ə sfir) Half of Earth west of the prime meridian; includes South America and North America. (m. H14, t. H14)

★ Y ★

Yorktown (yôrkʹ toun) Town in southeastern Virginia near Chesapeake Bay, which was the site of the last major battle of the American Revolution; 37°N, 76°W. (m. 22, t. 25)

Yosemite National Park (yō semʹ i tē nashʹ ə nəl pärk) National Park in California, established in 1890. (m. 262, t. 266)

Biographical Dictionary

This Biographical Dictionary tells you about the people in this book and how to pronounce their names. The page numbers tell you where the person first appears in the text.

★ A ★

Adams, Abigail (adʹ əmz) 1744–1818 Wife of second President John Adams, she was the first First Lady to live in what later became known as the White House. (p. 25)

Adams, John (adʹ əmz) 1735–1826 Second President of the United States, from 1797 to 1801. Member of committee that drafted the Declaration of Independence and Patriot leader during the American Revolution. (p. 24)

Adams, Samuel (adʹ əmz) 1722–1803 Political leader in the American Revolution who organized the Sons of Liberty in Boston; helped plan the Boston Tea Party. (p. 23)

Addams, Jane (adʹ əmz) 1860–1935 Social worker and reformer who founded Hull House in Chicago in 1889. (p. 226)

Albright, Madeleine (älʹ brīt) 1937– Former United States ambassador to the United Nations and the first woman to serve as secretary of state, appointed 1997. (p. 451)

Aldrin, Edwin "Buzz" (älʹ drin) 1930– Astronaut on the *Apollo 11* who became the second person to walk on the moon, in 1969. (p. 430)

Anthony, Susan B. (anʹ thə nē) 1820–1906 Women's suffrage leader who fought for voting rights for women and the abolition of slavery. (p. 242)

Antin, Mary (anʹ tin) 1881–1949 Russian-born writer who published *The Promised Land*, an autobiography about her experiences as an immigrant in the United States. (pp. 185, 191)

Armstrong, Louis (ärmʹ strông) 1901–1971 Trumpeter and singer who was the first major jazz soloist. (p. 312)

Armstrong, Neil (ärmʹ strông) 1930– Astronaut who was the first person to walk on the moon, in 1969. (p. 430)

★ B ★

Barton, Clara (bärtʹ n) 1821–1912 Nurse during the Civil War who founded the American Red Cross. (p. 92)

Bell, Alexander Graham (bel) 1847–1922 Inventor and educator of the deaf who built the first telephone in 1876. (p. 167)

bin Laden, Osama (bin läʹ dan) 1957– Leader of the terrorist organization al Qaeda, which planned and carried out the September 11, 2001, attacks on New York City and the Pentagon. (p. 506)

Boyd, Belle (boid) 1844–1900 Confederate spy during the Civil War. (p. 92)

Brady, Mathew (brāʹ dē) 1823–1896 Civil War photographer. (p. 89)

Brown, John (broun) 1800–1859 Abolitionist who led attacks on supporters of slavery in Kansas and led a raid on Harpers Ferry, Virginia, in 1859. (p. 70)

Bruce, Blanche K. (brüs) 1841–1898 Former slave who was elected to the United States Senate in 1874. (p. 108)

Bush, George H. W. (bùsh) 1924– 41st President of the United States, from 1989 to 1993. (p. 449)

Bush, George W. (bùsh) 1946– Became 43rd President of the United States in 2001, governor of Texas from 1995 to 2000 and son of 41st President George H. W. Bush. (pp. 452, 505)

Pronunciation Key		
a in hat	ò in open	sh in she
ā in age	ò in all	th in thin
â in care	ô in order	ᴛʜ in then
ä in far	oi in oil	zh in measure
e in let	ou in out	ə = a in about
ē in equal	u in cup	ə = e in taken
ėr in term	ù in put	ə = i in pencil
i in it	ü in rule	ə = o in lemon
ī in ice	ch in child	ə = u in circus
o in hot	ng in long	

Biographical Dictionary

C

Calhoun, John C. (kal hün′) 1782–1850 United States senator from South Carolina who believed in states' rights. (p. 67)

Carnegie, Andrew (kär′ nə gē) 1835–1919 Industrialist who made steel a major industry in the United States. (p. 177)

Carney, William (kär′ nē) 1840–1908 Civil War hero who was one of 16 African Americans to win the Congressional Media of Honor for heroism in the Civil War. (p. 91)

Carson, Rachel (kär′ sən) 1907–1964 Biologist who wrote *The Silent Spring* in 1962, a book that helped make more people aware of growing environmental problems. (p. 443)

Carter, Jimmy (kär′ tər) 1924– 39th President of the United States, from 1977 to 1981. Awarded the Nobel Peace Prize in 2002 for his work promoting peace around the world. (pp. 448, 514)

Carver, George Washington (kär′ vər) 1861–1943 Agricultural scientist and educator who taught at Tuskegee Institute, an African American college. He discovered hundreds of new uses for peanuts, sweet potatoes, and other crops. (p. 237)

Cather, Willa (kath′ ər) 1873–1947 Novelist who moved to the Great Plains as a child in the 1800s. Her writing was strongly influenced by Nebraska's immigrant settlers. (p. 140)

Catt, Carrie Chapman (kat) 1859–1947 Women's rights leader who helped win the passage of the Nineteenth Amendment. (p. 243)

Chávez, César (shä′ vez) 1927–1993 Mexican American leader who formed the National Farm Workers Association to gain rights for migrant workers. (p. 441)

Churchill, Winston (chərch′ hil) 1874–1965 British leader during World War II. (p. 343)

Cinque, Joseph (sin′ kā) 1813(?)–1879(?) West African captive who led the 1839 slave revolt on the Spanish slave ship *Amistad* and was allowed by the Supreme Court to return home to Africa. (p. 62)

Clark, William (klärk) 1770–1838 Shared command of the expedition to explore the Louisiana Territory with Meriwether Lewis. (p. 32)

Clay, Henry (klā) 1777–1852 United States senator who was nicknamed "The Great Compromiser" for organizing important agreements such as the Missouri Compromise in 1820 and the Compromise of 1850. (p. 67)

Clinton, Bill (klin′ tən) 1946– 42nd President of the United States, from 1993 to 2001. (p. 450)

Coffin, Catherine (ko′ fin) 1803–1881 Conductor on the Underground Railroad who, with her husband Levi Coffin, helped more than 2,000 people escape from slavery to freedom. (p. 63)

Coffin, Levi (ko′ fin) 1798–1877 Conductor on the Underground Railroad; married to Catherine Coffin. (p. 63)

Collins, Michael (ko′ lənz) 1930– One of the first astronauts to travel to the moon, with Neil Armstrong and Buzz Aldrin, in 1969. (p. 430)

Columbus, Christopher (kə lum′ bəs) 1451(?)–1506 Italian-born explorer who sailed across the Atlantic Ocean to the Americas in 1492. He was the first European to establish lasting contact between Europe and the Americas. (p. 10)

Colvin, L. O. (kōl′ vən) 1800s Farmer who developed the first cow-milking machine in 1862. (p. 217)

Conrad, Frank (kän′ rad) 1874–1941 Engineer for Westinghouse Electric whose work with radios led to the development of the first commercial radio station, KDKA in Pittsburgh, Pennsylvania, in 1920. (p. 302)

Cooper, Jack L. (kü′ pər) 1900s First African American radio disc jockey. (p. 236)

Crazy Horse (krā′ zē hôrs) 1842(?)–1877 Lakota leader who helped defeat Colonel George Custer at the Battle of Little Bighorn. (p. 156)

Cronkite, Walter (kron′ kīt) 1916– Journalist and television newscaster who was a war correspondent during World War II. (p. 402)

Custer, George (kus′ tər) 1839–1876 United States military leader who was defeated by the Lakota at the Battle of Little Bighorn in 1876. (p. 156)

D

Davis, Benjamin O., Jr., (dā′ vis) 1912–2002 Pilot who was the first African American general in the United States Air Force. He organized and commanded the Tuskegee Airmen in 1943. (p. 352)

Davis, Jefferson (dā′ vis) 1808–1889 President of the Confederacy during the Civil War and former United States senator from Mississippi. (p. 75)

Douglas, Stephen (dug′ ləs) 1813–1861 United States senator from Illinois who helped create the Kansas-Nebraska Act. (p. 69)

Douglass, Frederick (dug′ ləs) 1817–1895 Leading abolitionist who spoke and wrote about his life as a former slave. (p. 36)

Du Bois, W. E. B. (dü boiz′) 1868–1963 African American writer who helped start the National Association for the Advancement of Colored People (NAACP) in 1909. (p. 237)

Duryea, Charles (dər′ yā) 1861–1938 Inventor who, with his brother Frank, built the first working car in the United States in 1893. (p. 170)

Duryea, Frank (dər′ yā) 1869–1967 Inventor who, with his brother Charles, built the first working car in the United States in 1893. He produced an improved version in 1895 and won several races. (p. 170)

E

Eads, James Buchanan (ēdz) 1820–1887 Engineer who built the first bridge made entirely of steel, over the Mississippi River, in 1874. (p. 228)

Earhart, Amelia (âr′ härt) 1897–1937(?) Pilot who was the first woman to fly alone over the Atlantic Ocean in 1932. In 1937 she attempted to fly around the world and her plane mysteriously disappeared. (p. 315)

Edison, Thomas (ed′ ə sən) 1847–1931 Inventor whose many creations included the light bulb, the phonograph, and the microphone. (p. 168)

Eglui, Ellen (eg′ lü ē) 1800s Inventor who created a clothes wringer for washing machines in the late 1800s. (p. 218)

Einstein, Albert (īn′ stīn) 1879–1955 German-born physicist who told President Franklin D. Roosevelt about the possibility of atomic bombs. He made some of the most important contributions to science in the twentieth century. (p. 354)

Eisenhower, Dwight D. (ī′ zn hou′ ər) 1890–1969 34th President of the United States, from 1953 to 1961. Commander of Allied forces in western Europe during World War II. In 1957 he sent troops to a high school in Little Rock, Arkansas, to enforce desegregation. (p. 360)

Ellington, Duke (el′ ing tən) 1899–1974 Jazz composer, bandleader, and pianist who wrote over 2,000 pieces of music. (p. 312)

F

Fitzgerald, F. Scott (fits jer′ əld) 1896–1940 Writer famous for his novels and short stories about the 1920s. (p. 313)

Ford, Gerald (fôrd) 1913–2006 38th President of the United States, from 1974 to 1977. Took office when Richard Nixon resigned, becoming the nation's only President not elected. (p. 447)

Ford, Henry (fôrd) 1863–1947 Entrepreneur and inventor who built the Model T, the first car to become widely available in the United States. His method of assembly-line production was faster and cheaper than previous methods, forever changing factories in the United States. (p. 299)

Pronunciation Key

a	in hat	ō	in open	sh	in she
ā	in age	ȯ	in all	th	in thin
â	in care	ô	in order	ᴛʜ	in then
ä	in far	oi	in oil	zh	in measure
e	in let	ou	in out	ə	= a in about
ē	in equal	u	in cup	ə	= e in taken
ėr	in term	u̇	in put	ə	= i in pencil
i	in it	ü	in rule	ə	= o in lemon
ī	in ice	ch	in child	ə	= u in circus
o	in hot	ng	in long		

Biographical Dictionary

Frank, Anne (frank) 1929–1945 Jewish girl whose diary was published in 1947 and became a literary classic of the Holocaust. She hid with her family from the Nazis in Amsterdam during World War II before being captured and killed by the Nazis. (p. 362)

Franklin, Benjamin (frang′ klən) 1706–1790 Writer, printer, and inventor in Pennsylvania, and member of the committee that drafted the Declaration of Independence; a leading Patriot during the American Revolution. (p. 24)

G

Geronimo (jə rän′ ə mō) 1829–1909 Apache leader who fought United States soldiers to keep his land. He led a revolt of 4,000 of his people after they were forced to move to a reservation in Arizona. (p. 158)

Glenn, John (glen) 1921– First American astronaut to orbit Earth, in 1962. (p. 429)

Giuliani, Rudolph (jü lē ä′ nē) 1944– Mayor of New York City, from 1993 to 2002. He was praised for his handling of the city after the September 11, 2001 terrorist attacks. (p. 504)

Gompers, Samuel (gôm′ pərz) 1850–1924 Labor leader who, in 1886, founded the American Federation of Labor, which fought for better working conditions. (p. 195)

Goodnight, Charles (gu̇d′ nīt) 1836–1929 Rancher who established the Goodnight-Loving Trail, a cattle trail from Texas to Colorado, in 1866. (p. 149)

Gorbachev, Mikhail (gôr′ bə chof) 1931– Last leader of the Soviet Union, from 1985 to 1991. (p. 448)

Grant, Ulysses S. Grant (grant) 1822–1885 18th President of the United States, from 1869 to 1877. Commander of Union forces during the Civil War. (p. 99)

H

Hamilton, Alexander (ham′ əl tən) 1755(?)–1804 Delegate to the Constitutional Convention and leader of the Federalists; first secretary of the treasury. (p. 31)

Hearst, William Randolph (hėrst) 1863–1951 Newspaper publisher who built the leading newspaper chain in the United States in the early twentieth century. (p. 180)

Hine, Lewis (hīn) 1874–1940 Photographer who used his pictures to draw attention to social problems such as child labor and the poor living conditions of immigrants in New York City. (p. 194)

Hitler, Adolf (hit′ lər) 1889–1945 Nazi dictator of Germany during World War II. (p. 341)

Hoover, Herbert (hü′ vər) 1874–1964 31st President of the United States, from 1929 to 1933. (p. 321)

Huerta, Dolores (wer′ tä) 1930– Mexican American leader who helped establish the United Farm Workers of America, a group that fought for rights for migrant farm workers. (p. 441)

Hughes, Langston (hyüz) 1902–1967 Writer who was an important figure in the Harlem Renaissance. His poems often addressed race and discrimination. (p. 314)

Hurston, Zora Neale (hėr′ stən) 1903–1960 Writer who was an important figure in the Harlem Renaissance. (p. 314)

Hussein, Saddam (hü sān′) 1937– Dictator of Iraq who was removed from power by the United States in 2003. (p. 507)

J

Jackson, Andrew (jak′sən) 1767–1845 7th President of the United States, from 1829 to 1837, and war hero from the War of 1812. (p. 33)

Jackson, Thomas "Stonewall" (jak′ sən) 1824–1863 Confederate general who led the Confederate army to victory in several battles early in the Civil War. (p. 85)

Jefferson, Thomas (jef′ ər sən) 1743–1826 3rd President of the United States, from 1801 to 1809. He wrote the first draft of the Declaration of Independence. (p. 24)

Johnson, Andrew (jon′ sən) 1808–1875 17th President of the United States, from 1865 to 1869; became President after Abraham Lincoln's assassination. (p. 107)

Jones, Mary Harris (jōnz) 1830–1930 Labor organizer, known as "Mother Jones." She fought for coal workers' rights by speaking in Appalachian mining towns, encouraging them to join unions. (p. 195)

Joseph,Chief (jō′ səf) 1840–1904 Nez Percé leader who led his people in their unsuccessful effort to escape to Canada to avoid being forced onto a reservation. (p. 157)

K

Kennedy, John F. (ken′ ə dē) 1917–1963 35th President of the United States, from 1961 to 1963. He was the youngest person ever to be elected President, and was assassinated in 1963. (p. 410)

King, Martin Luther, Jr., (king) 1929–1968 Minister who led the Civil Rights movement during the 1950s and 1960s and believed in peaceful protests. He was assassinated in 1968. (p. 422)

L

Lange, Dorothea (lang) 1895–1965 Photographer whose pictures helped draw attention to the living conditions of the poor during the Great Depression. (p. 333)

Latimer, Lewis (lat′ ə mər) 1848–1928 Inventor who improved Thomas Edison's light bulb, making electric lighting more practical. (p. 168)

Laval, Gustav de (di läv äl′) 1845–1913 Farmer who invented the cream separator in 1879. (p. 217)

Lawrence, Jacob (lôr′ əns) 1917–2000 Painter whose work shows African American life and history. His best known works are *Life in Harlem* and his *Great Migration* series. (p. 314)

Lee, Robert E. (lē) 1807–1870 Commander of the Confederate forces in the Civil War. (p. 85)

Lewis, Meriwether (lü′ is) 1774–1809 Army captain appointed by Thomas Jefferson to lead the Lewis and Clark expedition to explore the lands gained in the Louisiana Purchase. (p. 32)

Libeskind, Daniel (lēbz′ kind) 1946– Architect whose plan was chosen as part of the design for the rebuilding of the World Trade Center site in New York City. (p. 508)

Liliuokalani (lē lē ü ō kä lä′ nē) 1838–1917 Last queen of the Hawaiian Islands, she protested the American takeover of Hawaii in the 1890s. (p. 252)

Lin, Maya Ying (lin) 1959– Architect and sculptor who designed the Vietnam Veterans Memorial in Washington, D.C. (p. 434)

Lincoln, Abraham (ling′ kən) 1809–1865 16th President of the United States, from 1861 to 1865, who led the United States during the Civil War and was assassinated in 1865. (p. 71)

Lindbergh, Charles (lind′ bėrg) 1902–1974 Pilot who was the first to fly solo across the Atlantic Ocean in 1927. (p. 315)

Love, Nat (luv) 1854–1921 Former slave who became a cowboy at fifteen and wrote a popular autobiography. (p. 149)

M

MacArthur, Douglas (mə kär′ thėr) 1880–1964 General who commanded American forces in the Southwest Pacific during World War II. (p. 302)

Malcom X (mal′ kəm eks) 1925–1965 Civil rights activist in the 1960s who urged African Americans to rely on themselves. (p. 425)

Marconi, Guglielmo (mär cō′ nē) 1874–1937 Italian physicist and inventor who sent the first radio message across the Atlantic Ocean. (p. 302)

Marshall, George C. (mär′ shəl) 1880–1959 World War II general and United States secretary of state from 1947 to 1949 who created the Marshall Plan, which aided Europe after World War II. (p. 386)

Marshall, Thurgood (mär′ shəl) 1908–1993 Lawyer and civil rights activist who was the first African American justice appointed to the Supreme Court, serving from 1967 to 1991. (p. 421)

Pronunciation Key

a	in hat	ō	in open	sh	in she
ā	in age	ȯ	in all	th	in thin
â	in care	ô	in order	ᴛʜ	in then
ä	in far	oi	in oil	zh	in measure
e	in let	ou	in out	ə	= a in about
ē	in equal	u	in cup	ə	= e in taken
ėr	in term	u̇	in put	ə	= i in pencil
i	in it	ü	in rule	ə	= o in lemon
ī	in ice	ch	in child	ə	= u in circus
o	in hot	ng	in long		

Biographical Dictionary

McCarthy, Joseph (mə kär′ thē) 1908–1957 United States senator who, in the 1950s, claimed that communists were working inside the United States government. (p. 409)

McCormick, Cyrus (mə kôr′ mik) 1809–1884 Farmer and inventor who perfected the mechanical reaper, a machine that cuts wheat. (p. 217)

Monroe, James (mən rō′) 1758–1831 fifth president of the United States, from 1817 to 1825. Issued the Monroe Doctrine in 1823, warning European nations against interfering in the Western Hemisphere. (p. 33)

Morgan, J. P. (môr′ gən) 1837–1913 Banker who invested millions in railroads, steel mills, and other companies, helping American industries to grow. (p. 181)

Morse, Samuel (môrs) 1791–1872 Inventor who helped develop the Morse code, which was used to send messages by telegraph. (p. 129)

Mott, Lucretia (mot) 1793–1880 Social reformer who fought to abolish slavery and to give women the right to vote. (p. 242)

Muir, John (myür) 1838–1914 Naturalist and conservationist who helped establish Sequoia and Yosemite national parks. (p. 266)

Murrow, Edward R. (mėr′ ō) 1908–1965 Radio and television broadcaster who became famous for his World War II coverage. (p. 402)

Mussolini, Benito (mü sə lē′ nē) 1883–1945 Italian dictator who led his country during World War II. (p. 341)

N

Nimitz, Chester (nim′ its) 1885–1966 Military commander of the United States Pacific Fleet during World War II; helped the United States win the Battle of Midway. (p. 358)

Nixon, Richard (nik′ sən) 1913–1994 37th President of the United States, from 1969 to 1974; first President to resign from office. (p. 430)

O

O'Connor, Sandra Day (ō kon′ ər) 1930– Judge who was the first woman appointed to the United States Supreme Court. (pp. 439, 484)

O'Keeffe, Georgia (ō kēf′) 1887–1986 Painter famous for her colorful flowers and natural scenes. (p. 316)

Otis, Elisha Graves (ō′ tis) 1811–1861 Inventor who developed the first safety elevator in 1852. (p. 228)

P

Parks, Rosa (pärks) 1913–2005 Civil rights leader arrested for protesting bus segregation in Montgomery, Alabama, in 1955. Her actions helped end the segregation of public buses. (p. 422)

Patton, George S. (pat′ n) 1885–1945 General in the United States Army who helped lead the Allies to victory in the Battle of the Bulge. (p. 360)

Pershing, John J. (pėr′ shing) 1860–1948 Army general who led American forces in Europe during World War I. (p. 276)

Pocahontas (pō′ kə hon′ təs) 1595(?)–1616 Native American woman who married John Rolfe and helped create peace between the Powhatan and the English. (p. 14)

Powell, Colin (pou′ əl) 1937– Highest-ranking American military leader during the Persian Gulf War; became the first African American secretary of state in 2001. (p. 450)

R

Reagan, Ronald (rā′ gən) 1911–2004 40th President of the United States, from 1981 to 1989. (p. 448)

Red Cloud (red kloud) 1822–1909 Lakota chief who objected to the United States forts and railroads being built on Lakota lands. (p. 131)

Reed, Walter (rēd) 1851–1902 United States Army doctor and medical researcher who proved diseases such as yellow fever and malaria are spread by mosquitoes. (p. 256)

Revels, Hiram R. (rev′ əlz) 1822–1901 First African American elected to the United States Senate in 1870. (p. 108)

Rice, Condoleezza (rīs) 1954– First woman appointed as national security advisor, by President George W. Bush, in 2001. (pp. 449, 507)

R64 Social Studies Reference Guide

Rickenbacker, Eddie (rik′ ən bä kər) 1890–1973 Pilot for the United States Army who shot down several German planes during World War I. (p. 276)

Riis, Jacob (rēs) 1849–1914 Newspaper reporter who wrote *How the Other Half Lives,* a book that revealed the living conditions of the poor in New York City. (p. 226)

Robinson, Jackie (rob′ ən sən) 1919–1972 Baseball player who became the first African American player in the United States Major Leagues in 1947, playing for the Brooklyn Dodgers; elected to the Baseball Hall of Fame in 1962. (p. 420)

Rockefeller, John D. (rok′ ə fel ər) 1839–1937 Industrialist who founded the Standard Oil Company, which had a near monopoly on the petroleum industry in the United States by 1881. (p. 179)

Roebling, John (rō′ bling) 1806–1869 German-born engineer who designed the world's first suspension bridge in Cincinnati and went on to design the Brooklyn Bridge in New York City. (p. 228)

Roebuck, Alvah C. (rō′ buk) 1864–1948 Businessman who, along with Richard Sears, founded the national mail-order company Sears, Roebuck, and Company. (p. 218)

Rolfe, John (rälf) 1585–1622 Colonist in Jamestown, Virginia, who grew tobacco, which became a valuable cash crop for Jamestown. In 1614 he married Pocahontas, a Native American woman, and their union led to a period of peace between the settlers and Native Americans. (p. 14)

Roosevelt, Eleanor (rō′ zə velt) 1884–1962 First Lady who traveled around the country during the Great Depression to report Americans' living conditions to her husband, President Franklin D. Roosevelt. In 1948 she helped draft the Universal Declaration of Human Rights. (p. 333)

Roosevelt, Franklin D. (rō′ zə velt) 1882–1945 32nd President of the United States, from 1933 to 1945. Created a group of programs called the New Deal to try to help the United States recover from the Great Depression; led the United States during World War II. (pp. 329, 341)

Roosevelt, Theodore (rō′ zə velt) 1858–1919 26th President of the United States, from 1901 to 1909. Led a group of soldiers called the Rough Riders during the Spanish-American War. As President, he established national forest reserves and parks. (p. 254)

S

Sacagawea (sa kä′ gä wā ə) 1786(?) –1812 Shoshone woman who was an interpreter and guide on the Lewis and Clark Expedition. (p. 32)

Salem, Peter (sā′ ləm) 1750(?)–1816 Soldier in the Continental Army. One of about 5,000 African Americans to serve in the American Revolution, he gained recognition for his heroism in battle. (p. 25)

Salter, Susannah Medora (sôlt′ ər) 1800s Politician who was elected mayor of Argonia, Kansas, in 1887, becoming the first female mayor in the United States. (p. 242)

Santiago, Esmeralda (sän tē ä′ gō) 1948– Writer who published books about her experience moving from Puerto Rico to New York City. (p. 477)

Sarnoff, David (sär′ nôf) 1891–1971 Russian-born radio pioneer who proposed selling radios for entertainment in 1916. By 1924 millions of radios had been sold. (p. 302)

Schlafly, Phyllis (shla′ flē) 1924– Lawyer and activist who opposed the proposed Equal Rights Amendment and wrote books supporting women who chose the traditional role of working in the home. (p. 440)

Scott, Blanche Stuart (skot) 1889–1970 Pilot who was the first American woman to fly an airplane. She was the first woman to drive across the United States. (p. 173)

Scott, Dred (skot) 1795(?)–1858 Enslaved African American who claimed he was free because he had lived in a free state. His case reached the Supreme Court, which decided against him. (p. 70)

Pronunciation Key

a in hat	ō in open	sh in she
ā in age	ȯ in all	th in thin
â in care	ô in order	ᴛʜ in then
ä in far	oi in oil	zh in measure
e in let	ou in out	ə = a in about
ē in equal	u in cup	ə = e in taken
ėr in term	u̇ in put	ə = i in pencil
i in it	ü in rule	ə = o in lemon
ī in ice	ch in child	ə = u in circus
o in hot	ng in long	

Social Studies Reference Guide R65

Biographical Dictionary

Scott, Winfield (skot) 1786–1866 General who fought in the Mexican War, and Union general in the Civil War; creator of the Anaconda Plan. (p. 84)

Sears, Richard (sērz) 1863–1914 Merchant who turned his small jewelry business into the national mail order company Sears, Roebuck and Company. (p. 218)

Sequoyah (si kwoi′ ə) 1770(?)–1843 Cherokee chief and scholar who developed a written alphabet for the Cherokee language. (p. 33)

Seward, William (sü′ wərd) 1801–1872 Secretary of state from 1861 to 1869. He negotiated the United States' purchase of Alaska from Russia in 1867. (p. 251)

Sherman, William Tecumseh (shėr′ mən) 1820–1891 Union general in the Civil War who helped defeat the Confederacy. (p. 100)

Shima, George (shē′ mə) 1863(?)–1926 Immigrant farmer from Japan who produced 80 percent of California's potato crop, becoming known as the "Potato King." (p. 144)

Sinclair, Upton (sin klâr′) 1878–1968 Writer of *The Jungle,* a book about poor conditions in the meatpacking plants in Chicago. (p. 264)

Singleton, Benjamin (sing′ gəl tən) 1809–1892 Leader of African American pioneers known as exodusters, who moved to the Great Plains after the Civil War. (p. 141)

Sitting Bull (sit′ ing bu̇l) 1831–1890 Lakota leader who defeated American soldiers at the Battle of Little Bighorn in 1876. (p. 155)

Slater, Samuel (slā′ tər) 1768–1835 British mechanic who built the country's first cotton-spinning factory in Rhode Island in 1790, bringing the Industrial Revolution to the United States. (p. 34)

Smith, Bessie (smith) 1894(?)–1937 Blues singer who often recorded with jazz legend Louis Armstrong. (p. 312)

Smith, John (smith) 1580–1631 Leader of the Jamestown colony. (p. 14)

Sprague, Frank (sprāg) 1857–1934 Inventor who designed the world's first system of electric streetcars in Richmond, Virginia, in 1888. (p. 170)

Squanto (skwon′ tō) 1590(?)–1622 Native American who helped the Pilgrims by teaching them key survival skills, such as how to grow corn. (p. 15)

Stalin, Joseph (stä′ lin) 1879–1953 Communist dictator of the Soviet Union, from 1923 to 1953. (p. 346)

Stanton, Elizabeth Cady (stan′ tən) 1815–1902 Women's suffrage leader and abolitionist who helped begin the women's rights movement in the United States. (p. 242)

Steinbeck, John (stīn′ bek) 1902–1968 Writer who described the hardships faced by migrant workers during the Great Depression in his novels. (p. 333)

Stevens, John (stē′ vənz) 1853–1943 Chief engineer of the Panama Canal, from 1905 to 1907. His improvements of the working conditions there helped the project to be completed successfully. (p. 257)

Stone, Lucy (stōn) 1818–1893 American suffragist who founded the American Woman Suffrage Association. (p. 242)

Stowe, Harriet Beecher (stō) 1811–1896 Author of *Uncle Tom's Cabin,* a novel that described the cruelties of slavery and which sold over 300,000 copies. (p. 70)

Strauss, Levi (strous) 1829–1902 Immigrant from Germany who produced the first denim pants in San Francisco during the California gold rush. (p. 152)

T

Tarbell, Ida (tär′ bəl) 1857–1944 Writer and journalist who exposed the unfair practices of large companies. (p. 264)

Tojo, Hideki (tō′ jō) 1884–1948 Military leader of Japan during World War II. (p. 344)

Truman, Harry S. (trü′ mən) 1884–1972 33rd President of the United States, from 1945 to 1953. In 1945 he decided to use atomic bombs against Japan, leading to the end of World War II. (pp. 361)

Tubman, Harriet (tub′ mən) 1820(?)–1913 Abolitionist who escaped from slavery in 1849 and became a conductor on the Underground Railroad; she led more than 300 slaves to freedom. (p. 63)

Turner, Nat (tėr′ nər) 1800–1831 Leader of an 1831 slave rebellion in Southampton County, Virginia. (p. 62)

R66 Social Studies Reference Guide

Twain, Mark (twān) 1835–1910 Pen name of American writer Samuel L. Clemens, who wrote *The Adventures of Huckleberry Finn* and *The Adventures of Tom Sawyer.* (p. 152)

Tweed, "Boss" William M. (twēd) 1823–1878 One of the leaders of the New York political group called Tammany Hall. He stole million of dollars from the city of New York and was eventually sent to prison. (p. 227)

W

Walker, David (wä′ kər) 1785–1830 Abolitionist who wrote a pamphlet in 1829 urging slaves to rebel. (p. 57)

Walker, Madame C. J. (wä′ kər) 1867–1919 Entrepreneur who was the first African American woman to become a millionaire. (p. 180)

Wang, An (wang) 1920–1990 Engineer and inventor who invented technology that improved computer memory. (p. 494)

Ward, Aaron Montgomery (wôrd) 1843–1913 Merchant who developed the first mail-order business in 1872. (p. 218)

Washington, Booker T. (wäsh′ ing tən) 1856–1915 Educator who founded the Tuskegee Institute, a college for African Americans, in Tuskegee, Alabama. (p. 237)

Washington, George (wäsh′ ing tən) 1732–1799 First President of the United States, from 1789 to 1797. Commander-in-chief of the Continental Army during the American Revolution. (p. 24)

Webster, Daniel (web′ stər) 1782–1852 Senator from Massachusetts and opponent of slavery who supported the Compromise of 1850. (p. 68)

Wells-Barnett, Ida (welz bär net′) 1862–1931 Journalist who helped to start an African American newspaper and fought against discrimination. (p. 238)

Westinghouse, George (wes′ ting hous) 1846–1914 Inventor and entrepreneur who developed a new technology called alternating current to deliver electricity to customers. (p. 180)

Westmoreland, William (west môr′ lənd) 1914– United States Army general who led American troops in Vietnam from 1964 to 1968. (p. 432)

Wilson, Luzena Stanley (wil′ sen) 1800s Settler whose family went to California during the 1849 gold rush. (p. 151)

Wilson, Woodrow (wil′ sən) 1856–1924 28th President of the United States, from 1913 to 1921; led the United States during World War I. (p. 275)

Wright, Orville (rīt) 1871–1948 Inventor who, with his brother Wilbur, built the first successful airplane in 1903. (p. 172)

Wright, Wilbur (rīt) 1867–1912 Inventor who, with his brother Orville, built the first successful airplane in 1903. (p. 172)

Y

York, Alvin C. (yôrk) 1887–1964 War hero from World War I, known for his bravery and expert shooting. (p. 276)

Pronunciation Key

a in hat	ō in open	sh in she
ā in age	ȯ in all	th in thin
â in care	ô in order	ᴛʜ in then
ä in far	oi in oil	zh in measure
e in let	ou in out	ə = a in about
ē in equal	u in cup	ə = e in taken
ėr in term	u̇ in put	ə = i in pencil
i in it	ü in rule	ə = o in lemon
ī in ice	ch in child	ə = u in circus
o in hot	ng in long	

Social Studies Reference Guide R67

Growth of a Nation • Social Studies Reference Guide R64–R67

Glossary

This Glossary will help you understand the meanings and pronounce the vocabulary words in this book. The page number tells you where the word first appears.

A

abolitionist (ab′ ə lish′ ə nist) Person who wants to abolish, or end, slavery. (p. 36)

AFL-CIO Largest labor organization in the nation, formed in 1955 by the merging of the American Federation of Labor and the Congress of Industrial Organizations. (p. 396)

aggressor (ə gres′ ər) Nation that starts war. (p. 385)

agriculture (ag′ rə kul′ chər) Science of farming, including growing crops and raising animals. (p. 7)

alliance (ə lī′ əns) Agreement among nations to defend one another. (p. 273)

Allies (al′ īz) Alliance among Great Britain, France, the United States, Canada, the Soviet Union, and other nations during World War II. (p. 342)

almanac (ôl′ mə nak) Reference book with helpful facts and figures. (p. H6)

Americans with Disabilities Act (ə mer′ ə kəns with dis′ ə bil′ ə tēz akt) Law passed in 1990 that protects people with disabilities from discrimination in employment and requires public services to be accessible. (p. 441)

Anaconda Plan (an′ ə kon′ də plan) Union strategy for defeating the Confederacy during the Civil War. (p. 84)

arms control (ärmz kən trōl′) Agreement to limit the production of weapons. (p. 447)

arms race (ärmz rās) Race to build more and better weapons than the enemy has. (p. 410)

artificial intelligence (är′ tə fish′ əl in tel′ ə jəns) The ability of a machine to learn and imitate human thought. (p. 516)

assassination (ə sas ə nā′ shən) Killing of a government or political leader. (p. 107)

assembly line (ə sem′ blē līn) Method of mass production in which a product is put together as it moves past a line of workers. (p. 299)

atlas (at′ ləs) Book of maps. (p. H6)

atmosphere (at′mə sfir) Gasses that surround a planet. (p. 513)

atomic bomb (ə tom′ ik bom) Type of bomb built during World War II that was more powerful than any built before it. (p. 354)

Axis (ak′ sis) Alliance of Germany, Italy, and Japan during World War II. (p. 342)

B

Battle of Antietam (bat′ l uv an tē′ təm) Civil War battle fought in 1862 near Sharpsburg, Maryland, that was an important victory for the Union. (p. 85)

Battle of Bull Run, First (fėrst bat′ l uv bůl run) First major battle of the Civil War, fought near Manassas Junction, Virginia, on July 21, 1861. (p. 85)

Battle of Gettysburg (bat′ l uv get′ ēz bėrg′) Union victory over Confederate forces in 1863 in Gettysburg, Pennsylvania, that was a turning point in the Civil War. (p. 97)

Battle of Little Big Horn (bat′ l uv lit′ l big′ hôrn′) Lakota victory over United States soldiers on June 25, 1876. (p. 156)

Battle of Midway (bat′ l uv mid′ wā′) World War II naval battle between the United States and Japan in 1942, which weakened the Japanese threat in the Pacific. (p. 358)

Battle of Stalingrad (bat′ l uv stä′ lin grad) Unsuccessful German attack on the city of Stalingrad during World War II, from 1942 to 1943, that was the furthest extent of German advance into the Soviet Union. (p. 359)

Battle of the Bulge (bat′ l uv ᴛʜə bulj) World War II battle in December 1944 between Germany and Allied troops that was the last German offensive in the West. General George S. Patton led the Allies to victory. (p. 360)

Battle of Vicksburg (bat′ l uv viks′ bərg) Union victory over Confederate forces in 1863 at Vicksburg, Mississippi, that gave the Union control of the Mississippi River. (p. 99)

Berlin Airlift (bər lin′ âr′ lift′) Program under which the United States aided West Berlin by flying in food and fuel when Soviet troops cut off the city from Western trade. (p. 389)

Berlin Wall (bər lin′ wól) Barrier that divided communist East Berlin from non-communist West Berlin from 1961 to 1989. (p. 412)

Bill of Rights (bil uv rīts) First ten amendments to the Constitution, ratified in 1790. (p. 28)

black codes (blak kōdz) Laws that denied African Americans many civil rights. (p. 107)

blockade (blo kād′) Shutting off of an area by troops or ships to keep people and supplies from moving in or out. (p. 84)

Blue Laws (blü lȯs) Laws introduced by Progressives in the early 1900s designed to solve social problems, such as alcohol abuse. (p. 265)

border state (bôr′ dər stāt) During the Civil War, a state located between the Union and the Confederacy that allowed slavery but remained in the Union. (p. 76)

Buffalo Soldiers (buf′ ə lō sōl′ jərz) Nickname for African American soldiers who fought in the wars against Native Americans living on the Great Plains during the 1870s. (p. 254)

C

Cabinet (kab′ ə nit) Officials appointed by the President as advisors and to head the departments in the Executive Branch. (p. 31)

capital resource (kap′ ə təl ri′ sôrs) Money, tools, and machines a company uses to produce goods and services. (p. 181)

cardinal direction (kärd′ n əl də rek′ shən) One of the four main directions on Earth: north, south, east, and west. (p. H17)

caring (kâr′ ing) Being interested in the needs of others. (p. H2)

cash crop (kash krop) Crop grown to be sold for a profit. (p. 14)

cattle drive (kat′ l drīv) Method cowboys used to move large herds of cattle north from ranches in Texas to towns along the railroads in the late 1800s. (p. 149)

century (sen′ chər ē) Period of 100 years. (p. 38)

checks and balances (cheks and bal′ ən səz) System set up by the writers of the Constitution that gives each of the three branches of government the power to check, or limit, the power of the other two. (p. 26)

circle graph (sėr′ kəl graf) Graph that shows how a whole is divided into parts. (p. 230)

citizen (sit′ ə zən) Member of a country. (p. 482)

Pronunciation Key

a	in hat	ō	in open	sh	in she
ā	in age	ȯ	in all	th	in thin
â	in care	ô	in order	ᴛʜ	in then
ä	in far	oi	in oil	zh	in measure
e	in let	ou	in out	ə	= a in about
ē	in equal	u	in cup	ə	= e in taken
ėr	in term	ů	in put	ə	= i in pencil
i	in it	ü	in rule	ə	= o in lemon
ī	in ice	ch	in child	ə	= u in circus
o	in hot	ng	in long		

Glossary

civil rights (siv′ əl rīts) Rights guaranteed to all United States citizens by the Constitution. (p. 420)

civil war (siv′ əl wôr) War between people of the same country. (p. 77)

climograph (klī′ mə graph) Graph that shows the average temperature and average precipitation for a place over time. (p. 146)

Cold War (kōld wôr) Struggle between the United States and the Soviet Union from the late 1940s to the early 1990s that was fought with ideas, words, and money, with no direct conflict between the two countries. (p. 390)

colony (kol′ ə nē) Settlement far from the country that rules it. (p. 10)

Columbian Exchange (kə lum′ bē ən eks chānj′) Movement of people, animals, plants, diseases, and ways of life between the Eastern and Western Hemispheres following the voyages of Christopher Columbus. (p. 10)

communism (kom′ yə niz′ əm) Political and economic system in which the government owns all businesses and land. (p. 388)

commute (kə myüt′) Trip to work, such as from the suburbs to a nearby city. (p. 401)

compass rose (kum′ pəs rōz) Pointer that shows directions on a map. (p. H17)

Compromise of 1850 (kom′ prə mīz uv) Law under which California was admitted to the Union as a free state and the Fugitive Slave Law was passed. (p. 68)

concentration camp (kon′ sən trā′ shən kamp) Prison in which the Nazis enslaved and murdered millions of Jews and other groups during World War II. (p. 362)

Confederacy (kən fed′ ər ə sē) Confederate States of America formed by the 11 Southern states that seceded from the Union after Abraham Lincoln was elected President. (p. 75)

conservation (kon′ sər vā′ shən) Protection and careful use of natural resources. (p. 266)

constitution (kon′ stə tü′ shən) Written plan of government. The United States Constitution, adopted in 1789, is the foundation of the national government. (p. 26)

consumer (kən sü′ mər) Person who buys or uses goods and services. (p. 180)

consumer credit (kən sü′ mər kre′d it) Credit used to buy goods that are consumed, such as clothing, rather than for investments, such as business equipment. (p. 398)

corporation (kôr′ pə rā′ shən) Business owned by investors. (p. 178)

courage (kėr′ ij) Doing what is right even when it is frightening or dangerous. (p. H2)

credible (kred′ ə bəl) Reliable. (p. 260)

credit (kred′ it) Borrowed money. (p. 323)

credit card (kred′ it kärd) Card that allows the cardholder to charge goods and services and then pay off the charge, along with an extra fee, over a period of time. (p. 398)

Cuban Missile Crisis (kyü′ bən mis′ əl krī′ sis) Tension between the United States and the Soviet Union in 1962 over nuclear missiles in Cuba. (p. 411)

culture (kul′ chər) Way of life of a group of people, including their religion, customs, and language. (p. 8)

D

decade (dek′ ād) Period of ten years. (p. 38)

Declaration of Independence (dek′ lə rā′ shən uv in′ di pen′ dəns) Document that declared the 13 Colonies independent from Great Britain, written mainly by Thomas Jefferson and approved on July 4, 1776. (p. 24)

degree (di grē′) Unit of measuring, used in latitude and longitude. (p. H15)

demand (di mand′) Amount of a product that people are willing to buy. (p. 489)

democracy (di mok′ rə sē) Government run by the people. (p. 481)

dictator (dik′ tā tər) Leader with complete control of a country's government. (p. 341)

dictionary (dik′ shə ner′ ē) Alphabetical collection of words that includes the meaning and pronunciation of each word. (p. H6)

discrimination (dis krim′ ə nā′ shən) Unfair treatment of a group or individual. (p. 108)

distribution map (dis′ trə byü′ shən map) Map that shows patterns of how things such as population or natural resources are spread out over an area. (p. 478)

diversity (də vėr′ sə tē) Variety. (p. 190)

draft (draft) Law that requires men of a certain age to serve in the military, if called. (p. 89)

drought (drout) Long period without rain. (p. 332)

Dust Bowl (dust bōl) Name given to much of the Great Plains during the long drought of the 1930s. (p. 332)

E

Earth Day (ėrth dā) Annual day of awareness to encourage respect for the environment. The first Earth Day celebration was held on April 22, 1970. (p. 443)

economist (i kon′ ə mist) Person who studies the economy. (p. 181)

economy (i kon′ ə mē) System for producing and distributing goods and services. (p. 16)

Eighteenth Amendment (ā′ tēnth ə mend′ mənt) Amendment to the Constitution, also called the Prohibition Amendment, passed in 1919, that outlawed the making, sale, and transporting of alcoholic beverages. (p. 311)

electoral college (i lek′ tər əl kol′ ij) Group of people chosen by the voters of each state who elect the President and Vice-President of the United States. (p. 483)

elevation (el′ ə vā′ shən) Height of the land above sea level. (p. H22)

elevation map (el′ ə vā′ shən map) Physical map that uses color to show elevation. (p. H22)

Emancipation Proclamation (i man′ sə pā′ shən prok′ lə mā′ shən) Statement issued by President Abraham Lincoln on January 1, 1863, freeing all slaves in Confederate states still at war with the Union. (p. 90)

encyclopedia (en sī′ klə pē′ dē ə) Book or set of books with articles, alphabetically listed, on various topics. (p. H6)

enfranchise (ən fran′ chīz) To give the right to vote. (p. 233)

entrepreneur (än′ trə prə nėr′) Person who starts a new business, hoping to make a profit. (p. 152)

Environmental Protection Agency (EPA) (en vī′ rən men′ təl prə tek′ shən ā′ jen sē) Federal agency formed in 1970 to enforce environmental laws. (p. 443)

Equal Employment Opportunity Commission (ē′ kwəl em ploi′ mənt op′ ər tü′ ni tē kə mish′ ən) Federal agency formed in 1965 that enforces civil rights laws that have to do with the workplace. (p. 442)

Pronunciation Key

a	in hat	ō	in open	sh	in she
ā	in age	ȯ	in all	th	in thin
â	in care	ô	in order	ᴛʜ	in then
ä	in far	oi	in oil	zh	in measure
e	in let	ou	in out	ə	= a in about
ē	in equal	u	in cup	ə	= e in taken
ėr	in term	ů	in put	ə	= i in pencil
i	in it	ü	in rule	ə	= o in lemon
ī	in ice	ch	in child	ə	= u in circus
o	in hot	ng	in long		

Glossary

equator (i kwā′ tər) Imaginary line around the middle of Earth, halfway between the North Pole and the South Pole; 0° latitude. (p. H12)

ethnic group (eth′ nik grüp) Group of people who share the same customs and language. (p. 476)

Executive Branch (eg zek′ yə tiv branch) Part of the federal government, led by the President, that makes sure the laws are carried out. (p. 484)

exoduster (ek′ sə dus tər) Name for African American pioneers who moved to the Great Plains after the Civil War. (p. 141)

export (ek′ spôrt) Good that one country sells to another country. (p. 492)

F

fact (fakt) Statement that can be proved to be true. (p. 306)

fairness (fâr′ nes) Not favoring one more than others. (p. H2)

fascism (fash′ iz′ əm) Form of government in which individual freedoms are denied and the government has complete power. (p. 341)

Fifteenth Amendment (fif′ tēnth ə mend′ mənt) Amendment to the United States Constitution, ratified in 1870, that gave male citizens of all races the right to vote. (p. 109)

Fourteenth Amendment (fôr′ tēnth ə mend′ mənt) Amendment to the United States Constitution, ratified in 1868, that gave African Americans citizenship and equal protection under the law. (p. 109)

Freedmen's Bureau (frēd′ mənz byůr′ ō) Federal agency set up in 1865 to provide food, schools, and medical care to freed slaves in the South. (p. 108)

free enterprise (frē en′ tər prīz) Economic system in which people are free to start their own businesses and own their own property. (p. 180)

free state (frē stāt) State in which slavery was not allowed. (p. 67)

French and Indian War (french and in′ dē ən wôr) War fought by the British against the French and their Native American allies in North America, from 1754 to 1763. (p. 18)

Fugitive Slave Law (fyü′ jə tiv slāv lò) Law passed in 1850 that said escaped slaves had to be returned to their owners even if they reached free states. (p. 68)

G

generalization (jen′ ər ə lə zā′ shən) Broad statement or idea about a subject. (p. 518)

Gettysburg Address (get′ ēz bėrg ə dres′) Civil War speech given by President Abraham Lincoln in 1863 at the site of the Battle of Gettysburg. (p. 98)

G.I. Bill of Rights (jē ī bil uv rīts) Law passed during World War II that provided benefits to help veterans return to civilian life. (p. 397)

glacier (glā′ shər) Thick sheet of ice. (p. 7)

globalization (glō′ bə li zā′ shən) Development of a world economic system in which people and goods move freely from one country to another. (p. 493)

global warming (glō′ bəl wôr′ ming) Idea that the increase in carbon dioxide in the atmosphere is leading to a slow warming of the global climate, which would cause environmental problems around the world. (p. 513)

globe (glōb) Round model of Earth. (p. H12)

gold rush (gōld rush) Sudden movement of many people to an area where gold has been found. (p. 151)

Great Depression (grāt di presh′ ən) Period of severe economic hardship that began in the United States in 1929. (p. 323)

Great Migration (grāt mī grā′ shən) Movement of millions of African Americans to the northern United States between 1915 and the 1940s in search of work and fair treatment. (p. 235)

grid (grid) Pattern of criss-crossing lines that can help find locations on a map. (p. 366)

guerrilla warfare (gə ril′ ə wôr′ fâr) Form of warfare that includes surprise, random attacks, often by fighters not in uniform. (p. 432)

H

Harlem Renaissance (här′ ləm ren′ ə säns) Artistic movement centered in Harlem, an African American neighborhood in New York City. (p. 314)

hemisphere (hem′ ə sfir) Half of a sphere or globe. Earth can be divided into hemispheres. (p. H13)

Holocaust (hol′ ə kòst) Murder of about 12 million people, including 6 million Jews, by the Nazis during World War II. (p. 362)

Homestead Act (hōm′ sted′ akt) Law signed in 1862 offering free land to people willing to start new farms on the Great Plains. (p. 139)

homesteaders (hōm′ sted ərz) Settlers who claimed land on the Great Plains under the Homestead Act. (p. 139)

honesty (on′ ə stē) Truthfulness. (p. H2)

House of Burgesses (hous uv bėr′ jis ez) Law-making assembly in colonial Virginia, the first in an English colony. (p. 14)

human resource (hyü′ mən ri sôrs′) People. (p. 181)

I

Ice Age (īs āj) Long period of time when Earth's climate was much colder than it is today. (p. 7)

ideals (ī dē′ əlz) Important beliefs. (p. 475)

ideology (ī′ dē ol′ ə jē) Set of beliefs. (p. 388)

impeachment (im pēch′ mənt) Bringing of charges of wrongdoing against an elected official by the House of Representatives. (p. 109)

import (im′ pôrt) Good that one country buys from another country. (p. 492)

Industrial Revolution (in dus′ trē əl rev′ ə lü′ shən) Period of change from making goods by hand to producing them with machines. (p. 34)

inflation (in flā′ shən) Rapid rise in prices. (p. 335)

inset map (in′ set′ map) Small map within a larger map. Shows areas outside of or in greater detail than the larger map. (p. H19)

interdependence (in′ tər di pen′ dəns) Result of globalization in which changes to the economy of one country can affect the economies of other countries. (p. 493)

intermediate direction (in′ tər mē′ dē it də rek′ shən) Pointer halfway between the main directions: northeast, northwest, southeast, southwest. (p. H17)

International Date Line (in′ tər nash′ ə nəl dāt līn) An imaginary line running along latitude 180°, in the middle of the Pacific Ocean, marking the time boundary between one day and the next. (p. 367)

Internet (in′ tər net′) Worldwide network of computers. (p. H7)

Pronunciation Key

a	in hat	ō	in open	sh	in she
ā	in age	ȯ	in all	th	in thin
â	in care	ô	in order	ᴛʜ	in then
ä	in far	oi	in oil	zh	in measure
e	in let	ou	in out	ə	= a in about
ē	in equal	u	in cup	ə	= e in taken
ėr	in term	ů	in put	ə	= i in pencil
i	in it	ü	in rule	ə	= o in lemon
ī	in ice	ch	in child	ə	= u in circus
o	in hot	ng	in long		

interstate highway (in′ tər stāt hī′ wā′) Road that connects cities in different states. (p. 102)

investor (in vest′ ər) Person who gives money to a business or project, hoping to make a profit. (p. 168)

isolationism (ī′ sə lā′ shə niz′ əm) Policy in which a nation prefers to remain neutral and let other countries handle their own affairs. (p. 275)

isthmus (is′ məs) A narrow strip of land that connects two larger areas. (p. 256)

J

jazz (jaz) Musical form that began in New Orleans, Louisiana, and was influenced by African American musical traditions. (p. 312)

Jim Crow laws (jim krō lòz) Laws passed in the South after Reconstruction enforcing the segregation of blacks and whites. (p. 110)

Judicial Branch (jü dish′ əl branch) Part of the federal government, made up of the court system, that decides the meaning of the laws. (p. 484)

K

Kansas-Nebraska Act (kan′ zəs nə bras′ kə akt) Law passed in 1854 allowing the people of these two territories to decide for themselves whether to allow slavery. (p. 69)

key (kē) Box explaining the symbols on a map. It is also known as a legend. (p. H16)

Korean War (kô rē′ ən wôr) War between South Korea, supported by the United States and the United Nations, and North Korea, supported by China, from 1950 to 1953. (p. 407)

L

labor union (lā′ bər yü′ nyən) Group of workers joined together to fight for improved working conditions and better wages. (p. 195)

large-scale map (lärj skāl map) Map showing a small area in detail. (p. 20)

latitude (lat′ ə tüd) Distance north or south of the equator, measured in degrees. (p. H15)

League of Nations (lēg uv nā′ shənz) International organization formed after World War I to prevent wars. (p. 280)

Legislative Branch (lej′ ə slā′ tiv branch) Part of the federal government, led by Congress, that makes the laws. (p. 484)

Lend-Lease (lend′ lēs) Policy that allowed Great Britain to borrow military supplies from the United States during World War II. (p. 343)

line graph (līn graf) Graph that shows change over time. (p. 230)

locator map (lō′ kā tər map) Small map that appears with a larger map; shows where the subject area of the larger map is located on Earth. (p. H16)

longitude (lon′ jə tüd) Distance east or west of the prime meridian, measured in degrees. (p. H15)

M

Manhattan Project (man hat′ n proj′ ekt) Code name given to the effort to build an atomic bomb in the United States. (p. 354)

manifest destiny (man′ ə fest des′ tə nē) Belief that the United States should expand west to the Pacific Ocean. (p. 35)

manual labor (man′ yü əl lā′ bər) Work done by hand without machines. (p. 217)

map projection (map prə jek′ shen) Way of showing Earth as a flat surface. (p. 454)

Marshall Plan (mär′ shəl plan) Program under which the United States provided funds to help European countries rebuild after World War II. (p. 386)

mass media (mas mē′ dē ə) Public forms of communication that reach large audiences. (p. 303)

mass production (mas prə duk′ shən) Making of a large number of goods that are exactly alike. (p. 302)

mechanization (mek′ ə ni zā′ shən) Using machines to do work. (p. 217)

meridian (mə rid′ ē ən) Imaginary line extending from the North Pole to the South Pole, also called longitude line. (p. H15)

migrant worker (mī′ grənt wėr′ kər) Person who moves from place to place harvesting crops. (p. 332)

migrate (mī′ grāt) To move from one area to another. (p. 7)

Missouri Compromise (mə zůr′ ē kom′ prə mīz) Law passed in 1820 that divided the Louisiana Territory into a southern area that allowed slavery and a northern area that did not. (p. 67)

monopoly (mə nop′ ə lē) A company that has control of an entire industry. (p. 179)

muckraker (muk′ rā′ kər) Writer or journalist of the early 1900s who uncovered shameful conditions in business and other areas of American life. (p. 264)

N

nationalism (nash′ ə nə liz′ əm) Love of country and the desire to have one's country free from the control of another. (p. 273)

National Organization for Women (nash′ ə nəl ôr′ gə nə zā′ shən fôr wim′ ən) Group founded in 1966 to work for equal rights and opportunities for women. (p. 440)

NATO (nā′ tō) North Atlantic Treaty Organization, a military alliance among the nations of Western Europe, United States, and Canada in which they agreed to help each other if attacked by the Soviet Union. (p. 389)

natural resource (nach′ ər əl ri sôrs′) Materials found in nature that people can use such as trees and water. (p. 16)

New Deal (nü dēl) Series of programs started by President Franklin D. Roosevelt in 1933 to try to help the nation recover from the Great Depression. (p. 329)

Nineteenth Amendment (nīn′ tēnth ə mend′ mənt) Amendment to the Constitution, ratified in 1920, that gave women the right to vote. (p. 243)

nonfiction book (non fik′ shən bůk) Book that is based on fact. (p. H6)

North American Free Trade Agreement (NAFTA) (nôrth ə mer′ ə kən frē trād ə grē′ mənt) Agreement among the United States, Canada, and Mexico that allows them to import and export goods with each other without having to pay taxes or fees. (p. 492)

Pronunciation Key

a	in hat	ō	in open	sh	in she
ā	in age	ȯ	in all	th	in thin
â	in care	ô	in order	ᴛʜ	in then
ä	in far	oi	in oil	zh	in measure
e	in let	ou	in out	ə	= a in about
ē	in equal	u	in cup	ə	= e in taken
ėr	in term	ů	in put	ə	= i in pencil
i	in it	ü	in rule	ə	= o in lemon
ī	in ice	ch	in child	ə	= u in circus
o	in hot	ng	in long		

O

opinion (ə pin′ yən) Personal view about an issue. (p. 306)

opportunity cost (op′ ər tü′ nə tē kôst) Value of what must be given up in order to produce a certain good. (p. 489)

outline (out′ līn′) Written plan for organizing information about a subject. (p. 174)

P

parallel (pâr′ ə lel) Imaginary circle around the Earth, also called latitude lines. (p. H15)

parallel time lines (pâr′ ə lel tīm līnz) Two or more time lines grouped together. (p. 38)

passive resistance (pas′ iv ri zis′ təns) Form of protest that does not use violence. (p. 423)

periodical (pir′ ē od′ ə kəl) Newspaper or magazine that is published on a regular basis. (p. H6)

Persian Gulf War (pėr′ zhən gulf wôr) War involving the United States and its allies against Iraq, triggered by Iraq's invasion of Kuwait in 1990. (p. 450)

physical map (fiz′ ə kəl map) Map showing geographic features, such as mountains and rivers. (p. H17)

pioneer (pī ′ ə nir′) Early settler of a region. (p. 139)

plantation (plan tā′ shən) Large farm with many workers who live on the land they work. (p. 16)

point of view (point uv vyü) A person's own opinion on an issue or event. (p. 58)

political cartoon (pə lit′ ə kəl kär tün′) Drawing that shows people or events in the news in a funny way. (p. 268)

political machine (pə lit′ ə kəl mə shēn′) Organization of people that controls votes to gain political power. (p. 227)

political map (pə lit′ ə kəl map) Map that shows borders between states or countries. (p. H16)

political party (pə lit′ ə kəl pär′ tē) Organized group of people who share a similar view of what government should do. (p. 31)

Pony Express (pō′ nē ek spres′) Service begun in 1860 that used a relay of riders on horses to deliver mail from Missouri to California in ten days. (p. 129)

popular sovereignty (pop′ yə lər sov′ rən tē) Idea that all people have a say in how the government is run. (p. 481)

population density map (pop′ yə lā′ shən den′ sə tē map) Map that shows the distribution of population over an area. (p. 478)

prejudice (prej′ ə dis) Unfair negative opinion about a group of people. (p. 189)

primary source (prī′ mer ē sôrs) Eyewitness account of a historical event. (p. H6)

prime meridian (prīm mə rid′ ē ən) Line of longitude marked 0 degrees. Other lines of longitude are measured in degrees east or west of the prime meridian. (p. H12)

producer (prə dü′ sər) Person who makes goods. (p. 489)

Progressives (prə gres′ ivz) Reformers who worked to stop unfair practices by businesses and improve the way government works. (p. 264)

Prohibition (prō′ ə bish′ ən) Complete ban on the making, transporting, and sale of alcoholic beverages in the United States from 1920 to 1933. (p. 311)

propaganda (prop′ ə gan′ də) Systematic effort to spread opinions or beliefs. (p. 390)

R

rationing (rash′ ən ing) Government limiting of the amount of food each person in the United States could buy during World War II. (p. 351)

reaper (rē′ pər) Machine that cuts wheat. (p. 217)

Reconstruction (rē′ kən struk′ shən) Period of rebuilding after the Civil War, during which the Southern states rejoined the Union. (p. 107)

Red Scare (red skâr) Period of panic and fear that communism was spreading in the United States in the early twentieth century. (p. 409)

region (rē′ jən) Large area that has common features that set it apart from other areas. (p. 473)

republic (ri pub′ lik) Form of government in which people elect representatives to make laws and run the government. (p. 26)

research (rē′ sėrch′) Way of gathering information to learn more about a subject. (p. 496)

reservation (rez′ ər vā′ shən) Land set aside by the government for Native Americans. (p. 155)

respect (ri spekt′) Consideration for others. (p. H2)

responsibility (ri spon′ sə bil′ ə tē) Doing what you are supposed to do. (p. H2)

road map (rōd map) Map showing roads, cities, and places of interest. (p. H24)

Rough Riders (ruf rī′ dərz) Volunteer soldiers led by Theodore Roosevelt during the Spanish-American War. (p. 254)

S

scale (skāl) Tool that helps you measure distances on a map. (p. H18)

search engine (sėrch en′ jən) Computer site that searches for information from numerous Internet Web sites. (p. H7)

secede (si sēd′) To break away from a group, as the Southern states broke away from the United States in 1861. (p. 75)

secondary source (sek′ ən der′ ē sôrs) Description of events written by a person who did not witness the events. (p. H6)

sectionalism (sek′ shə nə liz′ əm) Loyalty to a part of a country rather than to the country itself. (p. 55)

segregation (seg′ rə gā′ shən) Separation of people of different races. (p. 110)

settlement house (set′ l mənt hous) Center that provides help for immigrants and the poor. (p. 226)

sharecropping (shâr′ krop′ ing) System of farming in which farmers rent land and pay the landowner with a share of the crops they raise. (p. 110)

slave codes (slāv kōdz) Laws designed to control the behavior of enslaved people. (p. 61)

slave state (slāv stāt) State in which slavery was allowed before the Civil War. (p. 67)

small-scale map (smôl′ skāl map) Map showing a large area of land but not much detail. (p. 20)

Social Security (sō′ shəl si kyůr′ ə tē) New Deal program that provides monthly payments to people who are elderly, disabled, or unemployed. (p. 329)

sodbuster (sod′ bus tər) Great Plains farmer of the late 1800s who had to cut through sod, or thick grass, before planting crops. (p. 140)

source (sôrs) Written or oral account that may provide information. (p. 260)

Pronunciation Key

a	in hat	ō	in open	sh	in she
ā	in age	ȯ	in all	th	in thin
â	in care	ô	in order	ᴛʜ	in then
ä	in far	oi	in oil	zh	in measure
e	in let	ou	in out	ə	= a in about
ē	in equal	u	in cup	ə	= e in taken
ėr	in term	ů	in put	ə	= i in pencil
i	in it	ü	in rule	ə	= o in lemon
ī	in ice	ch	in child	ə	= u in circus
o	in hot	ng	in long		

Glossary

space race (spās rās) Race between the United States and the Soviet Union to explore outer space during the Cold War. (p. 429)

Spanish-American War (span′ ish ə mer′ ə kən wôr) War between the United States and Spain in 1898 in which the United States gained Spanish territory. (p. 253)

Stamp Act (stamp akt) British law approved in 1765 that taxed printed materials in the 13 Colonies. (p. 23)

standard time (stan′ dərd tīm) Time set by law for all places in a time zone. (p. 134)

states' rights (stāts rīts) Idea that states have the right to make decisions about issues that concern them. (p. 67)

stock (stok) A share of a company that is sold to an investor. (p. 178)

stock market (stok mär′ kit) Place where stocks are bought and sold. (p. 322)

strike (strīk) Refusal of workers to work until business owners meet their demands. (p. 195)

suburb (sub′ ėrb′) Community just outside or near a city. (p. 395)

suffrage (suf′ rij) Right to vote. (p. 242)

suffragist (suf′ rə jist) Person working for women's voting rights. (p. 242)

Sunbelt (sun′ belt′) An area of the United States made up of the Southeast and Southwest regions. (p. 474)

supply (sə plī′) Amount of a product that is available. (p. 489)

suspension bridge (sə spen′ shən brij) Bridge that hangs from steel cables. (p. 228)

sweatshop (swet′ shop′) Factory or workshop where people work under poor conditions. (p. 193)

symbol (sim′ bəl) Something that stands for something else. (p. H16)

T

technology (tek nol′ ə jē) Use of new ideas to make tools that improve people's lives. (p. 142)

telegraph (tel′ ə graf) Device that sends messages through wires using electricity. (p. 129)

tenant (ten′ ənt) Person who pays rent to use land or buildings that belong to someone else. (p. 233)

tenement (ten′ ə mənt) Building, especially in a poor section of a city, divided into small apartments. (p. 224)

terrorist (ter′ ər ist) Person who uses violence and fear to try to achieve goals. (p. 503)

Thirteenth Amendment (thėr′ tēnth ə mend′ mənt) Amendment to the United States Constitution that abolished slavery in 1865. (p. 107)

threshing machine (thresh′ ing mə shēn′) Machine that separates the grain from plant stalks. (p. 217)

time zone (tīm zōn) Region in which one standard of time is used. There are 24 time zones around the world. (p. 134)

time zone map (tīm zōn map) Map showing the world's or any country's time zones. (p. H21)

title (tī′ tl) Name of something, such as a book or map. (p. H16)

total war (tō′ təl wôr) Method of warfare that involves civilians as targets and is designed to destroy the opposing army and the people's will to fight. (p. 100)

transcontinental railroad (tran′ skon tə nen′ tl rāl′ rōd′) Railroad that crosses a continent. The first transcontinental railroad in the United States was completed in 1869. (p. 130)

Treaty of Versailles (trē′ tē uv ver sī′) Treaty signed in 1919 that officially ended World War I. (p. 280)

triangular trade route (trī ang′ gyə lər trād rout) Three-sided trade route among England, Africa, and the North American colonies; included the slave trade. (p. 17)

trust (trust) Large companies with the power to drive out competition in an industry. (p. 263)

Tuskegee Airmen (təs kē′ gē âr′ men) First African American fighter pilots. (p. 352)

Twenty-first Amendment (twen′ tē fėrst ə mend′ mənt) Amendment to the United States Constitution, adopted in 1933, that ended Prohibition. (p. 311)

U

Underground Railroad (un′ dər ground′ rāl′ rōd′) Organized system of secret routes used by people escaping slavery that led from the South to the North or Canada. (p. 63)

unemployment (un′ em ploi′ mənt) Number or percentage of workers without jobs. (p. 321)

Union (yü′ nyən) States that remained loyal to the United States government during the Civil War. (p. 75)

United Farm Workers of America (yü nī′ tid färm wėr′ kərs uv ə mer′ ə kə) Labor union founded by César Chávez and Dolores Huerta that works for the rights of migrant farm workers. (p. 441)

United Nations (yü nī′ tid nā′ shəns) International organization formed in 1945 to promote peace and end conflicts between countries. (p. 387)

urbanization (ėr bə niz ā′ shən) Movement of people from rural areas to cities. (p. 224)

V

Vietnam Conflict (vē et′ näm′ kon′ flikt) Conflict in the 1960s and 1970s during which the United States sent soldiers to South Vietnam to try to prevent communists from taking over the nation. (p. 432)

W

weapons of mass destruction (wep′ ənz uv mas di struk′ shən) Nuclear weapons and weapons that spread poison chemicals or deadly diseases. (p. 507)

World War I (wėrld wôr wun) War fought from 1914 to 1918 between the Central and Allied Powers. The United States joined the Allied Powers in 1917, helping them to victory. (p. 273)

World War II (wėrld wôr tü) War fought from 1939 to 1945 between the Allies and the Axis, involving most of the countries in the world. The United States joined the Allies in 1941, helping them to victory. (p. 342)

Y

yellow journalism (yel′ ō jėr′ nl iz′ əm) False or exaggerated reporting. (p. 253)

Pronunciation Key

a	in hat	ō	in open	sh	in she
ā	in age	ȯ	in all	th	in thin
â	in care	ô	in order	ᴛʜ	in then
ä	in far	oi	in oil	zh	in measure
e	in let	ou	in out	ə	= a in about
ē	in equal	u	in cup	ə	= e in taken
ėr	in term	ů	in put	ə	= i in pencil
i	in it	ü	in rule	ə	= o in lemon
ī	in ice	ch	in child	ə	= u in circus
o	in hot	ng	in long		

Index

Index

Index

Fort Sumter, 74–77, 84, *m99, p75*
Fort Wagner, 91, *m88, p91*
Fourteenth Amendment, 109–111, *c109*
France, 13, 18, 25, 32, 40, 273–274, 276, 279, 342, 350, 360, 408, 431, *mR5*
Frank, Anne, 362–363, *p363*
Franklin, Benjamin, 24, *p26–27*
Freedmen's Bureau, 51, 108
freedom, political, 341, 391, 469, 482. *See also* specific freedoms
freedom rides, 423, *p423*
free enterprise, 180, 388, 390, 449, 471, 489–490, 493
free states, 67, *m67, 69*
French and Indian War, 18, 22
Fugitive Slave Law, 68, *p68*
Fulton, Robert, 34

G

Gallipoli, Turkey, 277, *p277, m277*
Garfield, James A., R23, *pR23*
generalizations, making, 518–519
geography, H10–H11, H15–H24. *See also* specific themes
Georgia, R19, *m473*
Germany, 273–275, 280, 335, 341–342, 345–346, 349, 354, 359–360, 365, 385, *mR5*
Geronimo, 158, *p159*
Gershwin, George, 313, *p313*
Gershwin, Ira, 313, *p313*
Gettysburg, Battle of, 97, 99, *m97, 99*
Gettysburg, Pennsylvania, 81, 96–97,*m96, 99, p102*
Gettysburg Address, 47, 81, 98
G.I. Bill of Rights, 397
Giuliani, Rudolph, 466, 504, 511, *p466, 504*
glacier, 7
Glenn, John, 429, *p429*
Glidden, Joseph, *c143*
globalization, 493
Global Positioning System (GPS), 491, *p491*
global warming, 513
globe, H8
gold rush, 151–153
Gompers, Samuel, 195, *p195*
Goodnight, Charles, 149
Goodnight-Loving Trail, 149, *m150*
Gorbachev, Mikhail, 448–449
Gorgas, W. C., 257
Gore, Al, 452–453, 483
government, United States, 480–484
Grand Canyon National Monument, 267, *m262, p266*
Grant, Ulysses S., 49, 99–101, R23, *p49, 100, R23*
Grapes of Wrath, The, 333, 370–371
graphs, reading
  circle, 230–231, *c231*
  line, 230–231, *c230*
Graveley, Samuel Lee, Jr., 426
Great Britain, 18, 34–35, 40, 55, 84–85, 273–274, 342–345, 351, 388, 408, 505, 507, *m351. See also* England
Great Depression, 323–329, 333–335, 343, 349, 395, 400, *p323, 324, 325*
Great Migration, 235, 314, 318, *m235*
Great Plains, 138–144, 150–151, 155–156, 178, *m138, p139, 140, 142,*
Great Salt Lake, *mR14*
Great Seal of the United States, 475
Greensboro, North Carolina, 423, *m418*
grid, 366
Guam, 254–255, *m367*
guerrilla warfare, 432

H

Hamilton, Alexander, 31, *p31*
Harding, Warren G., R25, *pR25*
Harlem, 295, 314, 318, *p314, m310*
Harlem Renaissance, 295, 314
Harper's Ferry, Virginia, 70, *m66*
Harrison, Benjamin, R24, *pR24*
Harrison, William Henry, R23, *pR23*
Hawaii, 252, R19, *p252, m473*
Hayes, Rutherford B., R23, *pR23*
Hearst, William Randolph, 180
hemisphere, H9
hijack, 503
Hine, Lewis, 194
Hiroshima, Japan, 361, *m367*
Hispanics. *See* Latinos
Hitler, Adolf, 341–342, 346, 354, 359–360, 391, *p341*
Ho Chi Minh, 431–432, *p431*
Holocaust, 362–363
Homestead, Pennsylvania, 193, *m192*
Homestead Act, 139, 141
homesteader, 139–142, 150
Homestead Strike, 196
Hoover, Herbert, 321, 324–326, R25, *p321, R25*
House of Burgesses, 14
Huerta, Dolores, 379, 441, 445, *p379, 445*
Hughes, Langston, 295, 314, 325, *p314*
Hull House, 226, *p226*

human-environment interaction (as geographical theme), H10
human resource, 181
human rights, 387
Hurston, Zora Neale, 293, 314, *p293*
Hussein, Saddam, 450, 507

I

Ice Age, 7
Idaho, 160, R19, *m473*
ideals, 475, 505
ideology, 388, 390–391
Illinois, R19, *m473*
immigrants
  Africans, 16–17, 476
  Asian, 7, 185, 187, 476
  becoming a citizen, 486–487
  Chinese, 132, 187, 234, *p187*
  European, 184–186, 188–190
  Irish, 131, 185, 190, *p185*
  Japanese, 144, 145, *p187*
  Jewish, 184–185, 191
  life of, 184–190, 215, 476
  Mexican, 185, 190
  Russian, 141, 185, 191
  twentieth century, *c188*
  urbanization and, 224–227
impeachment, 109, 451
import, 492–493, *p492–493, c492*
inauguration, 328
income tax, 265
Indiana, R18, *m473*
Indians. *See* Native Americans
Indian Territory, *m8, c33*
Industrial Revolution, 34, 55
"In Flanders Fields," 279, *p279*
inflation, 335
inset map, H19
interdependence, 493
intermediate directions, H17
International Date Line, 367, *m367*
International Space Station, 430, 521, *p521*
Internet, H17, 452, 491, 496–497, 516
internment, 353, *p353*
interstate highway, 102
interview, H8
Intolerable Acts, *c23*
inventions, 10, 34, 166–173, 181, 213, 241, 297, 299, 302, 304, 308–309, 490, 495, *p308–309, c171. See also* technology
investor, 168, 322
Iowa, R18, *m473*
Iraq, 450, 507, *m506*
Ireland, 185, *m185*
Irish potato famine, 185
Iron Curtain, 388, 390, *m389*
Iroquois, 8–9, *m8, p9*
isolationism, 275, 280, 343–344, *p343*
isthmus, 256, *m256*
Italy, 341–342, 345, 356, 360, *mR5*
"I, too," 295, 314
Iwo Jima, 361, *p361, m359*

J

Jackson, Andrew, 33, R23, *p33, R23*
Jackson, Mahalia, 419
Jackson, Thomas "Stonewall," 85
Jamestown, Virginia, 14, 19, *m13, p14*
Japan, 341–342, 344–345, 349, 358–359, 361, 385–386, *mR5*
Japanese Americans, 353, *p353*
jazz, 310, 312
Jazz Age, 312–313
Jefferson, Thomas, 24, 29, 31–32, R22, *p31, R22*
Jews, 184–185, 191, 341, 362–363
Jim Crow laws, 51, 110, 234, 236
jobs, 490, *c490*
Johnson, Andrew, 107, 109, 251, R23, *pR23*
Johnson, Lyndon B., 413, 424, 431–432, 434, R24, *pR24*
Jones, Mary Harris, 195, *p195*
Joseph, Chief, 122, 157, 160–161, *p122, 157, 160*
Judicial Branch, 26–27, 484, *c27*
Jungle, The, 264, *p264*
jury, trial by, 469, 482

K

Kansas, 66, 69, 141, R18, *m473*
Kansas-Nebraska Act, 69, *m69*
Kansas Territory, 69, *m69*
Kelley, Florence, 198, *p198*
Kemble, Fanny, 58–59, *p58*
Kennedy, John F., 378, 410–413, 424, 431, R24, *p378, 413, R24*
Kentucky, 76, R18, *m473*
Key, Francis Scott, 40–41, *p40*
key, map, H16
Kielburger, Craig, 199, *p199*
King, Martin Luther, Jr., 379, 422–425, 427, 441, *p379, 424, 427*
Kitty Hawk, North Carolina, 172, *m166*
Korea, 381, 385, 407, *m407*
Korean War, 407–409
Ku Klux Klan, 108
Kuwait, 450, *m446*

Index

L

Labor Day, 197, *p197*
labor union, 195–197, 396, *p396*
Lakota, 9, 131, 154–156, *m8*
landmine, 94–95
Lange, Dorothea, 293, 333, *p293, 333*
Lantos, Tom, 487, *p487*
large-scale map, 20–21, *m21*
Latimer, Lewis, 123, 168, *p123, 168*
Latinos, 185, 190, 441, 445, 476–477, *p441, 445, 467, c188*
latitude, H15, 366–367, *m366, 367*
Laval, Gustav de, 217
Lawrence, Jacob, 293, 314, 318–319, *p293, 318*
Lazarus, Emma, 165
League of Nations, 280
Lee, Robert E., 48, 85, 87, 97, 99–101, *p48, 87, 100*
Legislative Branch, 26–27, 484, *c27. See also* Congress, United States
Lend-Lease, 343, 346
Lewis, Meriwether, 32, 160
Libeskind, Daniel, 467, 508–509, *p467, 509*
light bulb, electric, 168, 171, *p168, 171*
Liliuokalani, 210, 252, *p210, 252*
Lin, Maya Ying, 379, 434, 437, *p379*
Lincoln, Abraham, 47–48, 51, 71–73, 75–76, 83–85, 96, 98, 100–101, 106–107, 130, 251, 481, R22, *p48, 71, 73, R22*
Lindbergh, Charles, 315, *p315*
line graphs, reading, 230–231, *c230*
literature
  Declaration of Independence, 24, R26–R29
  Grapes of Wrath, The, 333, 370–371
  "I, too," 295, 314
  "In Flanders Fields," 279, *p279*
  Roughing It, 152
  Silent Spring, 443
  To Build a Fire, 251
  Uncle Tom's Cabin, 70, *p70*
  When I Was Puerto Rican, 476
Little Big Horn, Battle of, 156
location (as geographical theme), H10
locator map, H16
locks, 257
London, Jack, 251
longhouse, 9, *p9*
longitude, H15, 366–367, *m366–367*
Los Alamos, New Mexico, 354, *m348*
Los Angeles, California, 144, 190, 304, *m130*
Louisiana, R18, *m473*
Louisiana Purchase, 32, 67, *m32*
Love, Nat, 148–149, *p149*

M

MacArthur, Douglas, 361
Macedonia, 451, *mR5*
Madison, James, R22, *pR22*
mail-order catalog, 218, 241
main idea and details, 50–51, 57, 64, 72, 86, 93, 101, 111, 182, 238, 335, 355, 517
Maine, 67, R18, *m473*
Maine, 253, 260–261, *p253, 260*
malaria, 256–257
Malcolm X, 425, *p425*
Manassas Junction, Virginia, 85, *m82*
Mandela, Nelson, 451, *p451*
Manhattan Island, 13, *m227*
Manhattan Project, 354
manifest destiny, 35
manual labor, 217
map projection, 454–455, *m454, 455*
maps
  elevation, H22
  latitude on, H15, 366–367, *m366, 367*
  longitude on, H15, 366–367, *m366, 367*
  physical, H17
  political, H16
  population density, H23, 478–479, *m478, 479*
  projections of, 454–455, *m454, 455*
  road, H24, 102–103, *m103*
  scales of, comparing, H18, 20–21, *m20, 21*
  time zone, H21, 134–135, *m134*
Marconi, Guglielmo, 302, *p302*
Marshall, Eliza, 199, *p199*
Marshall, George C., 386
Marshall Plan, 386, 389, *p386*
Marshall, Thurgood, 378, 418, 421, 426, *p378, 418*
Maryland, 76, R19, *m473*
Masih, Iqbal, 199, *p199*
mass media, 303, 315
mass production, 302
Massachusetts, 15, 24, R19, *m473*
Mayflower, 15, *p15*
McCarthy, Joseph, 409, *p409*
McCormick, Cyrus, 217
McKinley, William, R24, *p180, R24*
mechanization, 217
Menlo Park, New Jersey, 168, *m166*
meridian, H12, H14–H15, 366–367, *m366*
Merrimack, 86
Mexican War, 35, 68, 84, 99

Mexico, 7, 35, 68, 275, *mR4*
Michigan, R19, *m473*
Middle Colonies, 16, 38, *m16, c38–39*
Middle East, 448, 450, *m446*
Midway, Battle of, 358–359, *m359, 367*
Midwest, 473, *m473*
migrant worker, 332–333, 441, 445
migrate, 7, *m7*
migration, 7, 235, 314, 318, 474, *m7, 235*
Miles, Nelson, 157
Minnesota, R19, *m473*
Mississippi, R19, *m473*
Mississippi River, 84, 99, 129, 228, *m32*
Missouri, 67, 76, R19, *m473*
Missouri Compromise, 67–68, *m67*
Model T, 298–299, *p298*
Monitor, 86
monopoly, 179
Monroe, James, 33, R22, *pR22*
Monroe Doctrine, 33
Montana, R19, *m473*
Montgomery, Alabama, 422, *m418*
Moody, Dwight L., 226
Morgan, J. P., 181, *p181*
Morse, Samuel, 122, 129, *p122*
Moscow, Soviet Union (now Russia), 388, *m389*
Mott, Lucretia, 242, *p242*
Mount Whitney *mR14*
Movement (as a geographical theme), H11
movies, 304–305, 307, 334, *p304, 334, c305*
muckraker, 264
Muir, John, 210, 266, *p210, 267*
Murrow, Edward R., 402
Mussolini, Benito, 341–342

N

Naismith, James, 226
National Aeronautics and Space Administration (NASA), 429, 439, 452, 516
National Association for the Advancement of Colored People (NAACP), 237, 423
nationalism, 273
National Organization for Women (NOW), 440
national park, 266
National Road, 125
Native Americans. *See also* specific groups
  colonists and, 14–15, 18–19
  conflicts and, 131, 154–158
  cultures of, 8–9, *m8*
  enslavement of, 11
  opportunities for, 441
  population, 158–159
  removal of, 33, *p33*
  reservation, 155–161, *m158*
  transcontinental railroad and, 131
  in World War II, 357, 442, *p357*
NATO, 389, 408
natural resource, 16, 181, 251, 259, 301, 513, *c513*
Navajo, 357, 442, *m8, p357*
Nazis, 341, 362–363
Nebraska, R20, *m473*
Nebraska Territory, 69, *m69*
Netherlands, The, 13, *mR5*
Nevada, R20, *m473*
New Amsterdam, 12–13, *m13*
New Deal, 329–333
New England Colonies, 16, 38, *m16, c38–39*
New Hampshire, R20, *m473*
New Haven, Connecticut, 62, *m60*
New Jersey, R20, *m473*
New Mexico, R20, *m473*
New Orleans, Louisiana, 64, 312, *m310*
New York, 25, R20, *m473*
New York, New York, 17, 31, 169, 186, 193, 223, 226, 227, 322, 387, 443, 503–504, 509, 510–511, *m192, 227, p169, 224, 503*
newsies, 196
Nez Percé, 157–158, 160–161, *p161*
Nicodemus, Kansas, 141, *m138, p141*
Nimitz, Chester, 358
Nineteenth Amendment, 243, 245
Nixon, Richard, 430, 433–434, 447, R24, *p447, R24*
Nobel Peace Prize, 426, 514
nonfiction book, H6
Normandy, France, 360, *m360*
North America, 7, *m7*
North American Free Trade Agreement (NAFTA), 492
North Atlantic Treaty Organization (NATO), 389, 408
North Carolina, R21, *m473*
North Dakota, R21, *m473*
Northeast, 473, *m473*
Northern Hemisphere, H9
North Korea, 390, 407–408, *m407*
North Pole, H13–H14, *mH13–H15*
North Vietnam, 431–434, *m431*
nuclear power, 513, *c513*

O

O'Connor, Sandra Day, 439–440, 466, 484, 485, *p442, 466, 485*
Ohio, R21, *m473*

Index

R88 Social Studies Reference Guide

Social Studies Reference Guide **R89**

Index

R90 Social Studies Reference Guide

Social Studies Reference Guide **R91**

Facing Fear: Helping Students Cope with Tragic Events

American Red Cross

Together, we can save a life

As much as we would like to protect our children, we cannot shield them from personal or community tragedies. We can, however, help them to be prepared for unforeseen dangerous events and to learn about facing and moving beyond their fears and related concerns.

Common Responses to Trauma and Disaster

Young people experience many common reactions after a trauma. These include reexperiencing the event (for example, flashbacks), avoidance and numbing of feelings, increased agitation, and changes in functioning. These reactions may be manifested in clingy behaviors, mood changes, increased anxieties, increased startle responses (for example, more jumpy with noises), physical complaints, and regressive behavior. Increased aggressive behaviors may also be seen. When the trauma or disaster is human-made, such as a terrorist event, young people may react with hurtful talk, behaviors, or play. All of these reactions are normal responses and will, in general, dissipate with time. However, should these persist or increase over time, a referral to a mental health professional might be considered. Similarly, should these reactions result in a danger to self or others, immediate action is warranted.

Issues of Safety, Security, and Trust

In the aftermath of terrorism or other tragic events, students can feel overwhelmed with concerns of safety, security, and trust. Worries about their own safety as well as the safety of those important in their lives are likely heightened. Although they have developed a sense of empathy and are concerned about others, their immediate needs for personal reassurance will take priority. They will need repeated reassurances about their safety and the safety of those around them. They may have concerns about the event reoccurring; this concern may be exacerbated by repeated exposure to media images. At times students may feel as if they are reexperiencing the event. They may have triggers for memories, such as noises, sights, or smells. These "flashbacks" may also occur without an obvious reminder. Reexperiencing can be very frightening for students this age. They may try (without success) to NOT think about the event. Their inability to block the thoughts may produce increased levels of stress. Although students will continue to process recent events, a return to a classroom routine is one of the best ways to reinforce a sense of security and safety.

Expressing Thoughts and Feelings

Young people seven to twelve years old have the ability to understand the permanence of loss from trauma. They may become preoccupied with details of it and want to talk about it continually. The questions and the details discussed are often disturbing to adults (for example, talk of gore and dismemberment). Such discussions are not meant to be uncaring or insensitive but rather are the way that many students attempt to make sense of a tragedy. Since their thinking is generally more mature than that of students under seven, their understanding of the disaster is more complete. They understand the irreversibility of death but may continue to ask questions about death and dying as they try to understand the repercussions of the event.

Students this age will attempt to create the "story" of the terrorist action or tragic event. Unfortunately, their attempts will contain misinformation as well as misperceptions. Unless addressed directly, the misunderstanding may be perpetuated and lead to increased levels of stress. Students are trying to make the story "fit" into their concept of the world around them. Questions related to the trauma may be equally repetitive. Teachers may answer students' questions only to have the same questions repeated within a few minutes. Having the same answer will increase the students' sense of security and help them process the trauma.

One result of a human-made tragedy may be intense feelings of anger and a sense of revenge. With an inaccurate understanding of events, these feelings may develop into hateful/hurtful talk or play. It may be directed toward classmates or groups of people. This behavior should be immediately addressed. Open discussions with these young students may improve their understanding of the event as well as reduce inappropriate direction of anger toward others.

Identifying Factors to Predict Students at Greatest Risk

Feelings accompanying the event may overwhelm elementary-aged students. In addition to the anger, they may also have feelings of guilt and intense sadness; nervousness is also seen. As they attempt to process these feelings, a change in school performance may be seen. Some students will have a drop in school performance as attention to and concentration on their work are diminished. They may not be able to grasp new concepts as easily as before the event, and grades may show a decline. Students may become more active in their behaviors as well as more impulsive and reckless. These behaviors often appear similar to attention deficit hyperactivity disorder and/or learning disabilities. Although either may be present, the impact of the event as a reason for the behavior changes should be considered. Students may develop problems in sleep and appetite after a traumatic event or disaster. These changes may contribute to a decrease in school performance.

It is important to note that some students may try to handle feelings of guilt and worry by an intense attention to schoolwork. These students may be worried about disappointing teachers and parents. Through their intense focus on school, they may be attempting to avoid activities and thoughts that are disturbing.

Students' anxiety and fear may be seen in an increased number of physical complaints. These may include headaches, stomachaches, feelings of nausea, or vague aches and pains. Expression of these emotions may also be seen in mood changes. *(continued on the following page)*

(continued from p. TR1)

Students may become more irritable and quarrelsome. They may become more aggressive at recess. Although some students may act out more, others may become more withdrawn and detached from activities and friends around them. They may be having an equally hard time processing the events, but because of their quietness, they are often overlooked as having any difficulties.

In the face of tragic events, students of this age will be seeking ways to help others. By finding positive avenues for expressing their concerns and need for involvement, initial negative reactions to the event may begin to diminish. Working to guide students in positive directions can be an important aspect of the healing process.

It is important to remember that all of these reactions are normal and, generally, will begin to diminish with time.

Moving Forward in Spite of Life-Affecting Events

Frightening events, such as the terrorist attacks in the United States on September 11, 2001, the Oklahoma City bombing in 1995, earthquakes, tornadoes, and hurricanes here and in other countries, massive transportation accidents, and war or armed conflict or other military action, impact us all. Events that are caused by human beings can be particularly frightening and raise unique concerns.

Terrorist actions and other violent acts are designed to instill fear in individuals and communities, if not countries. Because they happen without warning, there is no time to prepare. This unpredictability leaves us with a heightened sense of vulnerability and anxiety that the event could be repeated again, anywhere. With increased media coverage, even those not directly impacted can be significantly affected by an event. Images make us feel closer to the victims, and we may perceive ourselves as victims of the actions as well. The questions that arise from disasters of human design are difficult, if not impossible, to answer. We want answers to "Why?" and "How could they?" and are often left frustrated by the lack of satisfying responses. This frustration also gives rise to intense feelings of anger. The anger toward the perpetrators may be uncomfortable and difficult to express in productive ways. As adults struggle with reactions and feelings in the aftermath of a terrorist action or tragic event, young people are similarly searching for how to best handle their feelings. At all ages, they take cues from adults around them (parents, teachers, and community and national leaders).

Students need to know that their reactions to and feelings about such events are normal. They need to recognize that others feel very similarly. Most important, young people need to know that they will begin to feel better with time and that it is acceptable to enjoy friends, family, and activities. They need to know that there are things they can do to help themselves move forward in a positive way.

Activities to Help Students Address Fears

The following activities are designed to help you help your students address their fears and move beyond them.

- **What Happened**—Have students tell what they remember about the trauma/disaster. Validate their experiences, but be sure to correct any misperceptions and misunderstandings.

- **Searching for a Sense of Safety**—Review with students school and family emergency procedures for natural or human-made disasters. Have students list people to contact in an emergency as well as identifying a "buddy family" that will be available to check on their safety.

- **Dealing with Feelings**—Make a chart with *Uncomfortable Feelings* and *What We Can Do About Them* as heads. List feelings students may have following a traumatic event. Then work together to come up with things to do to feel better (examples may include talking to adults, writing letters, helping in the relief effort, relaxation exercises, activities with friends, and watching a funny movie together).

- **Redirecting Thoughts**—Have students make an activity wheel by writing or drawing an activity that they enjoy doing (playing with a pet, singing a song, reading a book, riding a bike, shooting baskets, kicking soccer balls, stringing beads, watching a favorite show or video). Show them how to put a paper arrow and a paper fastener through the middle of the wheel loosely enough to spin the arrow. Suggest that when an unwanted thought or picture pops into their mind, they can spin to choose an activity to help get rid of the thought or picture.

- **Looking Ahead and Setting Goals**—Help students identify and write short-range goals as well as long-range ones. Discuss setting realistic goals and how they can be achieved. Also discuss ways of keeping track of the goals and the progress toward meeting them, reminding students of the importance of sharing thoughts and feelings while working toward the goals.

Books for Young Readers

Molly's Pilgrim Cohen, Barbara. Illus. by Daniel M. Duffy. Beech Tree Books, 1998. A recent Jewish Russian immigrant teaches her third-grade class about all kinds of pilgrims.

Number the Stars Lowry, Lois. Laureleaf, 1998. In 1943, Jews in Denmark are hidden and smuggled to safety in Sweden.

Heroes Mochizuki, Ken. Illus. by Dom Lee. Lee and Low Books, 1997. A Japanese American child, treated as an outsider by classmates during the Vietnam War, begs his father and uncle to tell how they fought in the U.S. Army during World War II.

The Tenth Good Thing About Barney Viorst, Judith. Illus. by Eric Blegvad. Aladdin, 1976. After the death of a pet cat, a young child tries to think of ten good things about him.

Jumping into Nothing Willner-Pardo, Gina. Illus. by Heidi Chang. Houghton Mifflin, 1999. Sophie devises a plan to overcome her fear of jumping off the high dive.

 American Red Cross **Information on American Red Cross *Facing Fear: Helping Young People Deal with Terrorism and Tragic Events***

The American Red Cross *Facing Fear* curriculum contains lesson plans for teachers and includes hands-on or interactive activities for the classroom that will help students and their families prepare for disastrous situations and equip them with tools to sort out their feelings and fears.

For further information or to obtain copies of the *Facing Fear* curriculum materials, or the curriculum materials that focus on natural disaster preparedness, called *Masters of Disaster*™, contact your local American Red Cross chapter. Visit

http://www.redcross.org to find your nearest Red Cross chapter, and visit **www.redcross.org/disaster/masters** for specific information on the curriculum. American Red Cross products are available exclusively from local Red Cross chapters in the United States.

With permission, parts above were adapted from Healing After Trauma Skills, *Robin H. Gurwitch and Anne K. Messenbaugh, University of Oklahoma Health Sciences Center.*

School to Home

Overview

Newsletter

Here are the main ideas that we are learning:

★ A wide variety of Native American groups lived in North America when European explorers began arriving in the late 1400s.

★ By the early 1600s, many European countries had established colonies in North America.

★ The United States won independence from Britain and formed a new government under the Constitution.

★ During the first half of the 1800s, the United States expanded west to the Pacific Ocean, and the Industrial Revolution changed the way Americans lived and worked.

Fast Facts

• Around 1491 a mudslide buried an entire Native American village in what is now the state of Washington. The village was rediscovered in 1991 after some tourists found artifacts on the beach.

• Horses are not originally from the Americas. The Spanish introduced them in 1493.

• In 1790 the United States population was almost 4 million people. The 1990 census taken exactly 200 years later counted about 250 million people.

Family Activities

Talk Together

Ask your child to tell you about what life was like in the colonies. Have your child explain how the Native Americans helped the colonists survive. Discuss how life in the colonies was different from life today.

Learn Together

Help your child learn about differing viewpoints in a conflict.

✔ With your child look through magazines and newspapers for articles about countries that are involved in conflicts with other countries.

✔ Make a list of these conflicts. Help your child identify the views of people on each side of the conflict.

✔ Discuss with your child different ways conflicts between countries are resolved.

Read Together

James Towne: Struggle for Survival, by Marcia Sewall (Atheneum, ISBN 0-689-81814-9, 2001) NCSS Notable Book

Journeys In Time: A New Atlas of American History, by Susan Buckley and Elspeth Leacock (Houghton Mifflin Co., ISBN 0-618-31114-9, 2003) NCSS Notable Book

The Signers: The 56 Stories Behind the Declaration of Independence, by Dennis Brindell Fradin and Michael McCurdy (Walker & Co., ISBN 0-802-78849-1, 2002) NCSS Notable Book

 Go online to find more activities at **www.sfsocialstudies.com**

Thank you for supporting your child's Social Studies education!

De la escuela al hogar

Panorama general **Boletín**

Estas son las ideas principales que estamos estudiando:

★ Una gran variedad de grupos indígenas vivían ya en América del Norte cuando llegaron los primeros exploradores europeos, a finales del siglo XV.

★ Hacia principios del siglo XVII, muchos países europeos habían establecido colonias en América del Norte.

★ Los Estados Unidos obtuvieron su independencia de Inglaterra y formaron un nuevo gobierno bajo la Constitución.

★ Durante la primera mitad del siglo XIX, los Estados Unidos se expandieron hacia el oeste hasta el océano Pacífico, y la Revolución Industrial cambió la forma en que los estadounidenses vivían y trabajaban.

Datos curiosos

- Alrededor de 1491 un derrumbe de barro enterró todo un poblado de indígenas norteamericanos en lo que hoy es el estado de Washington. El poblado fue redescubierto en 1991 luego de que algunos turistas encontraran artefactos en la playa.

- Los caballos no son originarios de las Américas. Los introdujeron los españoles en 1493.

- En 1790 la población de los Estados Unidos era de casi 4 millones de personas. El censo de 1990, realizado exactamente 200 años después, registró 250 millones de personas.

Actividades en familia

Para conversar

Pregúntele a su hijo o hija cómo era la vida en las colonias. Pídale que explique de qué forma ayudaron los indígenas norteamericanos a la supervivencia de los colonos. Conversen sobre las diferencias entre la vida en las colonias y la vida hoy.

Para aprender juntos

Ayude a su hijo o hija a aprender sobre diferentes puntos de vista en un conflicto.

✔ Busquen en revistas y periódicos artículos sobre países que estén en conflicto con otros países.

✔ Hagan una lista de esos conflictos. Ayude a su hijo o hija a identificar los puntos de vista de las personas en cada lado del conflicto.

✔ Conversen sobre las diferentes maneras en que se resuelven los conflictos entre países.

Para leer juntos

Molly y los peregrinos, por Barbara Cohen y Michael J. Deraney (ilustrador), (Lectorum, ISBN 1-880507-34-X, 1995)

Una Unión más perfecta: La historia de nuestra constitución, por Betsy y Giulio Maestro (Lectorum, ISBN 0-962516-28-7, 1993) ALA Notable Book

El coraje de Sarah Noble, por Alice Dalgliesh y Leonard Weisgard (ilustrador), (Noguer y Caralt, ISBN 84-279-3462-9, 1992) Newbery Award

 Para encontrar más actividades, visite **www.estudiosocialessf.com**

¡Gracias por apoyar la educación de sus hijos en Estudios sociales!

School to Home

Unit 1   Newsletter

Here are the main ideas that we are learning:

★ Differences between North and South led to growing tensions between the two regions.

★ Enslaved African Americans resisted slavery in many different ways.

★ Despite attempts to compromise, the struggle over slavery threatened to tear the United States apart.

★ Eventually 11 Southern states seceded from the United States, leading to the outbreak of the Civil War.

★ In the early years of the Civil War, the North and South formed strategies in hopes of gaining a quick victory.

★ As the Civil War continued, people in the North and the South suffered many hardships including the growing loss of life.

★ A series of Northern victories led to the end of the Civil War by 1865.

★ The country faced many difficult challenges after the Civil War ended, including rebuilding the South and protecting the rights of newly freed African Americans.

Fast Facts

• Georgia's state flag changed three times between 1956 and 2003. From 1956 to 2001, the flag featured a large confederate battle flag in its design. In January 2001, that flag was replaced by one featuring a large state seal over a row of much smaller flags—including the old confederate flag. In April 2003, Georgia picked a brand-new flag, with no confederate flag in its design.

Family Activities

Talk Together

Ask your child to tell you how the life of a slave was different than the life of a free person. Discuss what life was like for freed slaves in the North, and what life was like for slaves in the South during the same time.

Learn Together

Help your child learn about the Underground Railroad.

✔ Discuss the purpose of the Underground Railroad with your child. Talk about the risks involved with being part of the "Railroad."

✔ Ask your child to describe character traits of "conductors" on the Underground Railroad, such as bravery, caring, and selflessness.

Read Together

A Freedom River, by Doreen Rappaport (Jump at the Sun Books, ISBN 0-786-80350-9, 2000) Coretta Scott King Honor Book

Lincoln: A Photobiography, by Russell Freedman (Houghton Mifflin Co., ISBN 0-899-19380-3, 1987) Newbery Medal

Anthony Burns: The Defeat and Triumph of a Fugitive Slave, by Virginia Hamilton (Laureleaf, ISBN 0-679-83997-6, 1993) ALA Notable Book, Boston Globe Horn Book Award, Jane Addams Book Award

 Go online to find more activities at **www.sfsocialstudies.com**

Thank you for supporting your child's Social Studies education!

De la escuela al hogar

Unidad 1

Boletín

Estas son las ideas principales que estamos estudiando:

★ Las diferencias entre el Norte y el Sur produjeron creciente tensión entre ambas regiones.

★ Los afroamericanos esclavizados se resistieron a la esclavitud de muchas maneras.

★ A pesar de los esfuerzos por llegar a un acuerdo, la disputa sobre la esclavitud amenazaba con partir en dos a los Estados Unidos.

★ Al final, 11 estados sureños se separaron de los Estados Unidos, motivando el inicio de la Guerra Civil.

★ En los primeros años de la guerra, el Norte y el Sur desarrollaron estrategias con la esperanza de lograr una victoria rápida.

★ Durante la Guerra Civil, los habitantes del Norte y del Sur sufrieron grandes penurias, incluyendo la pérdida de muchas vidas.

★ Una serie de victorias del Norte condujo al fin de la Guerra Civil en 1865.

★ El país se enfrentó a muchos desafíos después de la Guerra Civil, incluyendo la reconstrucción del Sur y la protección de los derechos de los afroamericanos liberados.

Datos curiosos

La bandera del estado de Georgia cambió tres veces entre 1956 y 2003. De 1856 a 2001, incluía en su diseño una gran bandera de batalla de la Confederación. En enero de 2001, este diseño fue reemplazado por otro que incluía el sello del estado y una hilera de banderas más pequeñas, incluyendo la antigua bandera confederada. En abril de 2003, Georgia escogió un nuevo diseño, esta vez sin la bandera confederada.

Actividades en familia

Para conversar

Pídale a su hijo o hija que le cuente en qué se diferenciaba la vida de un esclavo de la de una persona libre. Conversen sobre cómo era la vida para los esclavos en el Norte y cómo era en el Sur.

Para aprender juntos

Ayude a su hijo o hija a aprender sobre el Tren Clandestino

✔ Conversen sobre el propósito del Tren Clandestino. Hablen de los riesgos que corrían sus participantes.

✔ Pídale a su hijo o hija que describa las características de personalidad de los "conductores" del Tren Clandestino, por ejemplo el coraje, la bonad y el desprendimiento.

Para leer juntos

La Osa Menor: Una historia del ferrocarril subterráneo, por F. N. Monjo y Fred Brenner (ilustrador), (HarperCollins, ISBN 0-06-444217-9, 1997)

Azules contra grises, por William Camus (Ediciones SM, ISBN 84-3481-455-2, 1985)

Abraham Lincoln (Hombres famosos), por A. Guerrero (Ediciones Toray, ISBN 84-3101-740-6, 1990)

 Para encontrar más actividades, visite **www.estudiosocialessf.com**

¡Gracias por apoyar la educación de sus hijos en Estudios sociales!

School to Home

Unit 2 **Newsletter**

Here are the main ideas that we are learning:

★ In the 1860s new railroad lines made it possible to travel and move goods across the United States much more quickly than ever before.

★ Farmers began settling in the Great Plains in the 1860s, and they soon turned the plains into a productive farming region.

★ Cattle drives and the search for gold offered new opportunities and led to lasting changes in the western United States.

★ As more and more settlers came to the western United States, Native American groups fought to maintain control of their lands.

★ In the late 1800s and early 1900s, new inventions changed the way people lived and led to the rise of new industries.

★ In the late 1800s and early 1900s, big businesses helped the United States economy grow quickly.

★ During the late 1800s and early 1900s, millions of immigrants arrived in the United States in search of freedom and opportunity.

★ Workers formed labor unions to fight for better wages and working conditions.

Fast Facts

• Today you can fly from Europe to New York City in a few hours. In the 1860s the fastest way to travel was by the newly invented steamship, which took 10 days.

• The Native Americans of the Great Plains held powwows to celebrate. Today, Native American groups throughout the United States hold powwows, full of music and dancing, to celebrate their culture.

Family Activities

Talk Together

Ask your child to describe to you how the railroads were built. Have your child explain how the railroad companies built track across the mountains. Discuss who worked on the railroads, and what the work was like.

Learn Together

Help your child learn about time zones.

✔ Look at a time zone map of the United States with your child. Note how the country is divided into time zones. Then write down different cities in the United States on different pieces of paper.

✔ Put the pieces of paper in a hat or cap. Have your child pick a piece of paper. Then look at the clock in your own home. What time is it? Look at the map together, and figure out what time it is in that city.

Read Together

The New Land: A First Year on the Prairie, by Marilynn Reynolds (Orca Books, ISBN 1-551-43071-1, 1999)

Immigrant Kids, by Russell Freedman (Penguin Putnam Books for Young Readers, ISBN 0-140-37594-5, 1995)

 Sitting Bull and His World, by Albert Marrin (Dutton Books, ISBN 0-525-45944-8, 2000), NCSS Notable Book

 Go online to find more activities at **www.sfsocialstudies.com**

Thank you for supporting your child's Social Studies education!

De la escuela al hogar

Unidad 2
Boletín

Estas son las ideas principales que estamos estudiando:

★ En la década de 1860, nuevas líneas ferroviarias hicieron los viajes y el transporte de bienes a través de los Estados Unidos mucho más fáciles y rápidos.

★ Grupos de granjeros empezaron a llegar a las Grandes Llanuras en la década de 1860, y las llanuras se convirtieron en una región agrícola productiva.

★ Los arreos de ganado y la búsqueda de oro ofrecieron nuevas oportunidades y generaron cambios duraderos en el oeste de los Estados Unidos.

★ Cuando más y más colonos se establecieron en la parte oeste de los Estados Unidos, los grupos de indígenas norteamericanos lucharon por mantener el control de sus territorios.

★ A finales del siglo XIX y principios del XX, nuevos inventos cambiaron la vida de las personas y ayudaron al surgimiento de nuevas industrias.

★ A finales del siglo XIX y a principios del XX, las grandes empresas contribuyeron a que la economía de los Estados Unidos creciera rápidamente.

★ A finales del siglo XIX y a principios del XX, millones de inmigrantes llegaron a los Estados Unidos en busca de libertad y oportunidades.

★ Los trabajadores formaron sindicatos para luchar por mejores salarios y condiciones de trabajo.

Datos curiosos

- Hoy es posible volar de Europa a Nueva York en unas horas. En la década de 1860, la forma más rápida de hacer ese viaje era en un barco de vapor, que demoraba 10 días.

- Los indígenas norteamericanos de las Grandes Llanuras hacían *powwows*. Hoy, las tribus indígenas de los Estados Unidos hacen *powwows* llenos de música y bailes para celebrar su cultura.

Actividades en familia

Para conversar

Pídale a su hijo o hija que describa cómo se construyeron los ferrocarriles. Pídale que le explique cómo las compañías ferroviarias tendieron rieles a través de las montañas. Conversen sobre quiénes trabajaban en los ferrocarriles y cómo era el trabajo.

Para aprender juntos

Ayude a su hijo o hija a aprender sobre husos horarios.

✔ Busquen los husos horarios en un mapa de los Estados Unidos. Fíjense en que el país está dividido en zonas de acuerdo a los husos horarios. Luego escriban los nombres de varias ciudades en los Estados Unidos en pedazos de papel aparte.

✔ Coloquen los pedazos de papel en un sombrero o gorra. Pídale a su hijo o hija que escoja uno. Luego miren qué hora es en el reloj de su casa. Busquen la ciudad en el mapa, y trabajen juntos para determinar qué hora es ahí.

Para leer juntos

Cuando Jessie cruzó el océano, por Amy Hest y P. J. Lynch (ilustrador), (Lectorum, ISBN 1-8880507-46-3, 1998) Kate Greenaway Medal, Gran Bretaña, 1997

La Estatua de la Libertad, por Lynda Sorensen (Rourke, ISBN 1-55916-067-5, 1994)

Trenes, por John Coiley (Santillana, ISBN 84-3723772-6, 1993)

 Para encontrar más actividades, visite **www.estudiosocialessf.com**

¡Gracias por apoyar la educación de sus hijos en Estudios sociales!

School to Home

Unit 3

Newsletter

Here are the main ideas that we are learning:

★ During the Industrial Revolution of the 1800s, new machines and technologies affected the lives of people in the rural areas of the United States.

★ During the late 1800s and early 1900s, people in American cities found that life was changing as populations grew larger.

★ In the late 1800s and well into the 1900s, African Americans, along with other racial and ethnic groups, faced lives that were affected by prejudice, segregation, and unequal opportunities.

★ Women worked to benefit from the spirit of reform that began in the mid-1800s.

★ By the end of the 1800s, the United States had gained new territory and had become a world power.

★ Reformers worked to improve conditions in the United States during the early years of the Industrial Age.

★ When it appeared the United States might be in danger, the country became involved in World War I.

Fast Facts

• In 1910, almost two million children under the age of 15 worked in industrial jobs. Today, child labor is illegal under federal law.

• A Grand Canyon stamp issued by the U.S. Postal Service in 2000 was a mistake: the image on the stamp was printed in reverse. Since it was too expensive to reprint the stamps, they were released with the error.

Family Activities

Talk Together

Ask your child to describe to you what opportunities women had in the 1800s. Were they equal to the opportunities that men had in the 1800s? Have your child explain how women began to fight for their rights. Discuss the women who helped pave the way for equality.

Learn Together

Help your child learn about America's national parks.

✔ Look at photographs of Yosemite National Park and Yellowstone National Park. Have your child point out different elements in each photograph, such as animals or natural formations.

✔ Discuss why Theodore Roosevelt might have wanted to preserve these wild places. Discuss the idea of preserving wild places. What might those places be if they had not been designated as national parks?

Read Together

World War I (American at War), by Scott Marquette (The Rourke Book Company, ISBN 1-589-52392-X, 2002)

Woman's Suffrage, by JoAnne Weisman Deitch (Discovery Enterprises, Ltd., ISBN 1-579-60066-2, 2000)

 Theodore Roosevelt: Letters from a Young Coal Miner (Dear Mr. President), by Jennifer Armstrong (Winslow Press, ISBN 1-890-81727-9, 2001), NCSS Notable Book

 Go online to find more activities at **www.sfsocialstudies.com**

Thank you for supporting your child's Social Studies education!

De la escuela al hogar

Unidad 3 Boletín

Estas son las ideas principales que estamos estudiando:

★ Durante la Revolución Industrial del siglo XIX, nuevas máquinas y tecnologías influenciaron la vida de los pobladores de áreas rurales de los Estados Unidos

★ A finales del siglo XIX y a principios del siglo XX, la vida en las ciudades de los Estados Unidos cambió con el crecimiento de la población.

★ A finales del siglo XIX y a principios del siglo XX, los afroamericanos, junto con otros grupos raciales y étnicos, fueron afectados por los prejuicios, la segregación y la falta de oportunidades iguales.

★ Las mujeres trabajaron para beneficiarse con el espíritu de reforma que empezó a mediados del siglo XIX.

★ Hacia finales del siglo XIX, los Estados Unidos habían adquirido nuevos territorios y se habían convertido en una potencia mundial.

★ Los reformistas trabajaron para mejorar las condiciones en los Estados Unidos durante los primeros años de la Revolución Industrial.

★ Al verse en peligro, los Estados Unidos decidieron participar en la Primera Guerra Mundial.

Datos curiosos

- En 1910, casi dos millones de niños menores de 15 años trabajaban en empleos industriales. En la actualidad, el trabajo infantil es ilegal bajo las leyes federales.

- Un sello de correos del Gran Cañón fue emitido por error por el Servicio Postal de los Estados Unidos en el año 2000: la imagen estaba impresa al revés. Como resultaba muy caro volver a imprimir los sellos, fueron emitidos con el error.

Actividades en familia

Para conversar

Pídale a su hijo o hija que le explique qué oportunidades tenían las mujeres en el siglo XIX. ¿Eran iguales a las oportunidades que tenían los hombres? Pídale que explique cómo comenzaron las mujeres a luchar por sus derechos. Conversen sobre las mujeres que contribuyeron a allanar el camino a la igualdad.

Para aprender juntos

Ayude a su hijo o hija a aprender sobre los parques nacionales de los Estados Unidos

✔ Miren fotografías de parques nacionales como Yosemite o Yellowstone. Pídale a su hijo o hija que señale diferentes elementos en cada fotografía, como animales o formaciones naturales.

✔ Conversen sobre qué razones llevaron a Theodore Roosevelt a querer preservar estas áreas silvestres. ¿Cómo serían estas áreas si no se les hubiera designado parques nacionales?

Para leer juntos

Thomas Edison y la electricidad, por S. Parker (Celeste Ediciones, ISBN 84-87553-22-2, 1997)

El mundo de las máquinas maravillosas, por Brian Williams y Sebastian Quigley (ilustrador) (Susaeta, ISBN 84-305-7129-9, 1991)

 Para encontrar más actividades, visite **www.estudiosocialessf.com**

¡Gracias por apoyar la educación de sus hijos en Estudios sociales!

School to Home

Unit 4

Newsletter

Here are the main ideas that we are learning:

★ The automobile, radio, and movies changed American culture in the early 1900s.

★ Changes in culture and the roles of women in the 1920s had a major effect on life in the United States.

★ The Great Depression began with the stock market crash of 1929 and became the worst period of economic hardship in United States history.

★ The New Deal helped ease some problems of the Great Depression, but hard times continued throughout the 1930s.

★ The United States entered World War II when Japan attacked Pearl Harbor in 1941.

★ After the United States entered World War II, the Great Depression came to an end and many Americans found new opportunities.

★ The United States helped lead Allies to victory in World War II, the deadliest war in human history.

Fast Facts

• The United States Holocaust Memorial Museum in Washington, D.C., had 19.2 million visitors during the first decade that it was open.

• The Navajo code talkers of World War II were finally honored for their contributions to defense on Sept. 17, 1992, at the Pentagon in Washington, D.C. They were honored again in 2001 by President George W. Bush in a special ceremony at the White House.

Family Activities

Talk Together

Ask your child to explain to you how the war effort lifted the country out of the Great Depression. Have your child talk about rationing, and explain why it was needed. Discuss what the materials and items that were rationed were used for to help the war effort.

Learn Together

Help your child learn about what life was like during wartime.

✔ Make a list together of your favorite foods and household items. Discuss which foods and household items would have been rationed.

✔ Discuss the purpose of a "Victory Garden."

✔ Talk about how the war effort would change the roles in the family, as dads went to war and moms went to work.

Read Together

Remember Pearl Harbor: American and Japanese Survivors Tell Their Stories, by Thomas B. Allen (National Geographic, ISBN 0-792-26690-0, 2001) NCSS Notable Book

Jazz and Its History, by Giuseppe Vigna (Barrons Juveniles, ISBN 0-764-15132-0, 1999)

Rosie the Riveter: Women Working on the Home Front in World War II, by Penny Colman (Crown Publishers, Inc., ISBN 0-517-88567-0, 1998) ALA Notable Book

 Go online to find more activities at **www.sfsocialstudies.com**

Thank you for supporting your child's Social Studies education!

De la escuela al hogar

Unidad 4

Boletín

Estas son las ideas principales que estamos estudiando:

★ El automóvil, la radio y el cine cambiaron la cultura estadounidense a principios del siglo XX.

★ Los cambios en la cultura y en el papel de las mujeres durante la década de 1920 tuvieron un efecto importante en la vida en los Estados Unidos.

★ La Gran Depresión empezó con la caída de la bolsa de valores de 1929 y fue el período más difícil para la economía de los Estados Unidos en toda su historia.

★ El Nuevo Trato ayudó a superar algunos de los problemas causados por la Gran Depresión, pero los tiempos difíciles continuaron durante la década de 1930.

★ Los Estados Unidos entraron a la Segunda Guerra Mundial cuando Japón atacó Pearl Harbor, en 1941.

★ Después de que los Estados Unidos entraron a la Segunda Guerra Mundial, la Gran Depresión terminó y muchos estadounidenses encontraron nuevas oportunidades.

★ Los Estados Unidos contribuyeron a la victoria de los Aliados en la Segunda Guerra Mundial, la guerra más mortífera en la historia de la humanidad.

Datos curiosos

• El Museo del Holocausto en Washington, D.C. recibió a más de 19.2 millones de visitantes en la primera década desde su inauguración.

• Los "hablantes en código" navajos finalmente recibieron reconocimiento por sus contribuciones a la defensa de la nación durante la Segunda Guerra Mundial el 17 de septiembre de 1992, en el Pentágono de Washington, D.C. Fueron honrados nuevamente en 2001 por el presidente George W. Bush en una ceremonia especial en la Casa Blanca.

Actividades en familia

Para conversar

Pídale a su hijo o hija que le explique cómo contribuyó el esfuerzo de la guerra a rescatar al país de la Gran Depresión. Pídale que hable sobre el racionamiento, y que explique por qué fue necesario. Conversen sobre qué materiales y objetos racionados fueron usados para ayudar en la guerra.

Para aprender juntos

Ayude a su hijo o hija a aprender sobre cómo era la vida en tiempos de guerra.

✔ Hagan una lista de sus alimentos y objetos domésticos favoritos. Conversen sobre qué alimentos y objetos domésticos habrían sido racionados.

✔ Conversen sobre el propósito de los "jardines para la victoria".

✔ Hablen sobre la forma en que el esfuerzo de la guerra cambiaría los papeles en la familia, cuando los papás fueron a combatir y las mamás a trabajar.

Para leer juntos

El béisbol nos salvó, por Ken Mochizuki y Dom Lee (ilustrador) (Lee & Low Books, ISBN 1-880000-22-9, 1995) 1993 Parents Choice

Pasaje a la libertad: La historia de Shiune Sugihara, por Ken Mochizuki y Dom Lee (ilustrador) (Lee & Low Books, ISBN 1-880000-82-2, 1999) ALA Notable Book

Lejos del polvo, por Karen Hesse (Everest, ISBN 84-241-5928-4, 1997)

 Para encontrar más actividades, visite **www.estudiosocialessf.com**

¡Gracias por apoyar la educación de sus hijos en Estudios sociales!

School to Home

Unit 5

Newsletter

Here are the main ideas that we are learning:

★ The Cold War was a worldwide struggle between free Western nations, including the United States, and the communist countries of the Soviet Union.

★ Following World War II, the United States entered a time of economic growth and technological advancement.

★ As the United States and the Soviet Union moved into the second half of the 1900s, Cold War conflicts intensified.

★ In the 1950s and 1960s, the continued efforts of African Americans to gain civil rights began to be successful.

★ The United States continued to oppose the spread of communism and Soviet power in the 1960s and 1970s.

★ From the 1950s through the 1990s, Americans worked toward equal rights for women, minorities, and the disabled and gained new interest in protecting the environment.

★ In the late 1900s, events occurred that brought the Cold War to an end and put the United States on new courses for the future.

Fast Facts

According to the U.S. Census of 2000:

• There were 34,658,190 African Americans or Blacks in the United States, or 12.3% of the total population.

• There were 35,305,818 Hispanics or Latinos in the United States, or 12.5% of the total population.

Family Activities

Talk Together

Ask your child to explain to you what it means to have equal rights. Have your child talk about some of the rights that he or she thinks should be the same for everyone. Discuss ways in which, in daily life, one person may have fewer rights than another.

Learn Together

Help your child learn about heroes of the Civil Rights movement.

✔ Make a list of people who had a role in the Civil Rights movement.

✔ Discuss their lives and what they did.

✔ Find a picture of one of these people and find information about that person's life.

Read Together

 Martin's Big Words: The Life of Dr. Martin Luther King, Jr., by Doreen Rappaport (Hyperion Books for Children, ISBN 0-786-80714-8, 2001) NCSS Notable Book

Failure Is Impossible!: The History of American Women's Rights, by Martha E. Kendall (Lerner Publications Company, ISBN 0-822-51744-2, 2001) NCSS Notable Book

There Comes a Time: The Struggle for Civil Rights, by Milton Meltzer (Random House, ISBN 0-375-80414-5, 2002) NCSS Notable Book

 Go online to find more activities at **www.sfsocialstudies.com**

Thank you for supporting your child's Social Studies education!

De la escuela al hogar

Unidad 5

Boletín

Estas son las ideas principales que estamos estudiando:

★ La Guerra Fría fue una lucha a nivel mundial entre las naciones libres de Occidente, incluyendo los Estados Unidos, y los países comunistas aliados con la Unión Soviética.

★ Después de la Segunda Guerra Mundial, los Estados Unidos entraron en una etapa de crecimiento económico y avance tecnológico.

★ En la segunda mitad de la década de 1990, los conflictos de la Guerra Fría entre los Estados Unidos y la Unión Soviética se intensificaron.

★ En las décadas de 1950 y 1960, los esfuerzos de los afroamericanos por obtener derechos civiles empezaron a dar resultado.

★ En las décadas de 1960 y 1970, los Estados Unidos continuaron oponiéndose a la expansión del comunismo y del poder soviético.

★ Desde la década de 1950 a la de 1990, los estadounidenses trabajaron para lograr igualdad de derechos para las mujeres, las minorías, y las personas con limitaciones físicas, y desarrollaron un interés por la protección del ambiente.

★ A finales del siglo XX la Guerra Fría llegó a un final abrupto, y los Estados Unidos se embarcaron en un nuevo rumbo hacia el futuro.

Datos curiosos

De acuerdo con el censo del 2000, ese año:

• Había 24'658,190 afroamericanos o negros en los Estados Unidos, o 12.3% de la población total.

• Había 35'305,818 hispanos o latinos en los Estados Unidos, o 12.5% de la población.

Actividades en familia

Para conversar

Pídale a su hijo o hija que le explique qué significa tener igualdad de derechos. Pídale que hable acerca de algunos derechos que él o ella cree deben ser iguales para todos. Conversen sobre cómo una persona, en la vida diaria, puede tener menos derechos que otra.

Para aprender juntos

Ayude a su hijo o hija a aprender sobre los héroes del Movimiento por los Derechos Civiles.

✔ Hagan una lista de personas que tuvieron un papel en el movimiento por los derechos civiles.

✔ Conversen sobre sus vidas y sobre lo que hicieron.

✔ Busquen fotografías de estas personas e información sobre sus vidas.

Para leer juntos

John F. Kennedy: Una biografía ilustrada con fotografías, por Steve Potts Davis (Bridgestone Books, ISBN 1-56065-807-X, 1999)

César Chávez, por Consuelo Rodríguez (Chelsea House, ISBN 0-79103-102-0, 1994)

Para encontrar más actividades, visite **www.estudiosocialessf.com**

¡Gracias por apoyar la educación de sus hijos en Estudios sociales!

School to Home

Unit 6

Here are the main ideas that we are learning:

★ The United States is a land of varied geography and has a diverse population that is united by common ideals.

★ The United States is a republic in which the people elect representatives to run the government.

★ Technology has changed the way people work, study, and play.

★ Americans united in response to the terrorist attacks of September 11, 2001.

★ In the United States and around the world, people are working to develop new technologies and find new solutions to the challenges facing our world.

Fast Facts

The tiny silicon chip in a computer consists of thousands of transistors and it can store millions of bits of information.

Family Activities

Talk Together

Talk with your child about the changes you have witnessed as a result of new technology. Ask your child what changes he or she has noticed. Help your child recognize that new technologies, such as the computer, change societies.

Learn Together

Help your child learn how technology causes changes in society.

✔ With your child, walk through your home and make a list of any technology, such as a television or electric light, you see.

✔ Talk about how things changed as a result of the use of each item.

✔ Choose several items and have your child tell how his or her life might change if the items were no longer available.

Read Together

A Basket of Bangles; How a Business Begins, by Ginger Howard (Millbrook Press, ISBN 0-761-31902-6, 2002) NCSS Notable Book

Understanding September 11th: Answering Questions About the Attacks on America, by Mitch Frank (Viking Children's Books, ISBN 0-670-03587-4, 2002) NCSS Notable Book

Of Beetles and Angels: A Boy's Remarkable Journey from a Refugee Camp to Harvard, by Mawi Asgedom (Little Brown Children's Books, ISBN 0-316-82620-0, 2002) NCSS Notable Book

 Go online to find more activities at **www.sfsocialstudies.com**

Thank you for supporting your child's Social Studies education!

De la escuela al hogar

Unidad 6

Boletín

Estas son las ideas principales que estamos estudiando:

★ Los Estados Unidos son un país de geografía muy variada y tienen una población diversa, unida por ideales comunes.

★ Los Estados Unidos son una república en la que las personas eligen a representantes para que administren el gobierno.

★ La tecnología ha cambiado la forma en que la gente trabaja, estudia y juega.

★ Los estadounidenses se unieron en respuesta a los ataques terroristas del 11 de septiembre de 2001.

★ En los Estados Unidos y alrededor del mundo, muchas personas están trabajando para desarrollar nuevas tecnologías y encontrar soluciones a los desafíos que el mundo enfrenta.

Datos curiosos

Los minúsculos chips de computadora contienen miles de transistores que pueden almacenar millones de bits de información.

Actividades en familia

Para conversar

Converse con su hijo o hija sobre los cambios que usted ha visto como resultado de nuevas tecnologías. Pregúntele qué cambios él o ella ha notado. Ayúdelo/a a comprender que las nuevas tecnologías, como las computadoras, cambian la sociedad.

Para aprender juntos

Ayude a su hijo o hija a comprender cómo las nuevas tecnologías cambian la sociedad.

✔ Caminen por la casa haciendo una lista de los objetos tecnológicos que encuentren, como el televisor, la tostadora o la luz eléctrica.

✔ Conversen sobre cómo cambiaron las cosas como resultado de cada objeto. Por ejemplo, ¿qué hacían las personas antes de que la televisión se convirtiera en una fuente de entretenimiento en la casa?

✔ Escojan varios objetos, y pídale a su hijo o hija que explique cómo cambiaría su vida si ya no tuviera cada uno de ellos.

Para leer juntos

El libro de los inventos divertidos para niños, por John E. Thomas y Danita Pagel (Kid Concoctions, ISBN 0-966-10886-8, 2000)

Me pregunto por qué suena el teléfono y otras preguntas sobre las comunicaciones, por Richard Mead (Everest, ISBN 84-241-1964-9, 1997)

50 cosas que los niños pueden hacer para salvar la tierra, por John Javna y The Earth Works Group (Emecé, ISBN 950-04-1083-4, 1991)

 Para encontrar más actividades, visite **www.estudiosocialessf.com**

¡Gracias por apoyar la educación de sus hijos en Estudios sociales!

Calendar Pages

Each month of the year provides new opportunities for students to learn about history, geography, government, good citizenship, economics, culture, and technology through holidays, "firsts," and important birthdays and anniversaries. The 12-month format is ideal for year-round schools and summer schools but also provides a wealth of information for students who attend a standard 9-month school.

The following pages offer an entire year of calendar activities, including:

- A list of facts about the month: birthdays, holidays, and other red-letter days
- Detailed instructions for constructing a bulletin board for each month
- At least one additional activity per month
- A selection of books for students to read about a monthly subject
- A Web link for *This Day in History,* part of the Scott Foresman Social Studies Web site

An extra page is given for you to note state or community celebrations.

Class election, page TR20

Valentine cards, page TR25

Historical "movie," page TR19

Thanksgiving, page TR22

Ellis Island, page TR24

Notes

August _____

_____

September _____

_____

October _____

_____

November _____

_____

December _____

_____

January _____

_____

February _____

_____

March _____

_____

April _____

_____

May _____

_____

June _____

_____

July _____

_____

August

MARCH ON WASHINGTON, D.C., THE MOVIE

August Facts

- On August 10, 1864, the **Smithsonian Institution** was founded in Washington, D.C.
- August 12 is **United Nations International Youth Day.**
- The **Appalachian Trail** opened as a continuous footpath from Maine to Georgia on August 14, 1937.
- On August 15, 1914, the **Panama Canal opened.**
- The **March on Washington** took place on August 28, 1963.

Activities

The March on Washington, D.C.

After talking about the March on Washington and Dr. Martin Luther King, Jr.'s famous "I Have a Dream" speech, ask students to become movie directors and create a storyboard about that important day. Explain that a story-board lays out the most important scenes of a story in chronological order. As a class, decide what scenes to include in the "movie." Working with partners, have students illustrate one scene for the storyboard. Display the finished storyboard on a bulletin board labeled, "March on Washington, D.C., the Movie."

Read About the Smithsonian Institution

For more information on the Smithsonian Institution, look for books such as these:

The Smithsonian Institution, by Mary Collins (Children's Book Press, ISBN 0-516-26518-0, 2000)

Smithsonian Presidents and First Ladies, by James Barber and Amy Pastan (Dorling Kindersley, ISBN 0-789-48454-4, 2002)

The Appalachian Trail

The Appalachian Trail was not always one continuous trail. Many shorter trails were joined to create it. On August 14, 1937, the 2,168-mile footpath was finally connected from Maine to Georgia. Provide maps of the trail for students to study. Have students research the history of the Appalachian Trail. Discuss what challenges they might encounter along the different sections of the footpath. Ask students make their own trail around the school or community area. Have students prepare some trail mix to take along on the hike. Ask them what ingredients would be best for a long hike and what would be easiest to carry. Ingredients could include raisins, peanuts, small pretzels, and dried fruit.

This Day in History

For additional August events go to *This Day in History* at **www.sfsocialstudies.com**. Select a birthday or historic event for any day in August and then base an activity or assign a report on it.

September

NAME THAT COUNTRY

Activities

The United States of America

On September 9, 1776, the name "United States of America" was adopted for our country. Discuss why this name might have been chosen. Was it a good choice? If students had been part of the Continental Congress in 1776, what name would they have proposed? Have small groups propose and vote on a new name for our country. Groups have to agree by majority vote. Groups can make posters to show their name choice and to try to persuade others to vote their way. Display the posters on the bulletin board and then allow each group to "plead their case" before a final vote is taken to determine the overall winner.

Read About Labor Day

For more information on Labor Day, look for books such as these:

Labor Day, by Mari C. Schuh (Pebble Books, ISBN 0-736-81653-4, 2003)

Labor Day, by Mir Tamim Ansary (Heineman Library, ISBN 1-58810-431-1, 2002)

Our First Subway

The first subway in the United States opened in Boston on September 1, 1897. Part of it still operates today. Find out what students already know about subways. Explain that a subway is an underground railroad system that operates in tunnels or passageways.

Provide maps of subway systems from several major cities. Point out that there are stations where people get on and off subway trains and either go back up to the street level or switch to other trains. Have students design a new subway system for their own community.

This Day in History

For additional September events go to *This Day in History* at **www.sfsocialstudies.com**. Select a birthday or historic event for any day in September and then base an activity or assign a report on it.

October

TECHNOLOGIES: THEN AND NOW

October Facts

- In October, we set our clocks to **standard time** by turning them back an hour.
- The comic strip **"Peanuts"** debuted on October 2, 1950.
- October 24 is **United Nations Day.**
- **Columbus Day** is celebrated on the second Monday in October.
- **Fire Prevention Week** is the second week in October.
- October is **Family Health Month.**
- **National Popcorn Popping Month** is in October.

Activities

Celebrate Technology

In honor of the beginning of the Internet in October 1969, have students create a "Technologies: Then and Now" bulletin board to show how technologies, including the computer, have changed over time. The computer will be the given technology in this activity. A picture of a 1969 computer should be on hand to show students how it looked. Have students brainstorm other technologies that were available in 1969 and still exist in some form today.

Have students collect pictures from books or the Internet of the items they came up with, such as a television, car, record player, or home movie projector. They should then collect pictures of the present-day counterparts. Post the pictures on the bulletin board, with the 1969 items on the left and the present-day items on the right. Label items. Have students connect each 1969 technology with its present-day counterpart with colorful yarn. Students might add technologies to the board throughout the month. Discuss how technologies might change in another few decades.

"Peanuts" Debuted October 2, 1950

To learn more about Charles Shultz's comic strip "Peanuts," tell students to read the comics page in the newspaper or "Peanuts" trade books from the library. Ask students to choose characters from "Peanuts" and write character profiles. Are these characters like anyone the student know?

Read About the United Nations

For more information on the United Nations, look for books such as these:

If You Could Wear My Sneakers!, by Sheree Fitch (Firefly Books, ISBN 1-552-09259-3, 1998)

United Nations, by Linda Melvern (Scholastic Library Publishing, ISBN 0-531-14814-9, 2001)

This Day in History

For additional October events go to *This Day in History* at **www.sfsocialstudies.com**. Select a birthday or historic event for any day in October and then base an activity or assign a report on it.

November

THANK YOU, VETERANS!

November Facts
- **Election Day** is the Tuesday after the first Monday in November. Every four years there is a presidential election.
- **Sandwich Day** is November 3.
- November 11 is **Veterans Day.**
- **Thanksgiving** is the fourth Thursday in November.
- On November 19, 1863, President Lincoln delivered the **Gettysburg Address.**
- November is **National American Indian Heritage Month.**

Activities

Veterans Day

Veterans Day is a day to remember and honor men and women who have served in the armed forces. Have students research military uniforms from the Revolutionary War, Civil War, World War I, World War II, the Korean War, the Vietnam War, and the Gulf Wars. Ask them to choose one uniform to draw and label for a bulletin board display. Place all the drawings in time line order. Include photos and other information on the armed forces alongside the uniform pictures. Students can also bring in pictures of family members who have served in the military.

Read About Election Day

For more information on Election Day, look for books such as these:

Election Day, by Patricia J. Murphy (Children's Book Press, ISBN 0-516-27488-0, 2002)

Voting and Elections, by Patricia J. Murphy (Compass Point Books, ISBN 0-756-50144-X, 2001)

Thanksgiving

After studying about the first Thanksgiving, ask students to compare and contrast the original Thanksgiving celebration with their own celebrations of today. Distribute large sheets of construction paper and ask students to fold the paper in half. On the left half of the paper, students can illustrate the first Thanksgiving. On the right half, they can draw a modern Thanksgiving celebration. Ask students to think about what inventions and technologies help us celebrate differently today. Challenge students to draw what they think Thanksgiving Day will be like 300 years from now.

This Day in History

For additional November events go to *This Day in History* at **www.sfsocialstudies.com**. Select a birthday or historic event for any day in November and then base an activity or assign a report on it.

December

DECEMBER IS FLYING BY!

Happy Birthday, Bill of Rights

Happy Birthday, Basketball

Hooray for the Wright Brothers

December Facts
- **Winter** begins in December.
- **Basketball** was created on December 1, 1891.
- December 1 is **National Pie Day.**
- On December 15, 1791, the **Bill of Rights** was adopted.
- On December 17, 1903, the **Wright brothers** made the first motor-powered, controlled airplane flight.
- **Hanukkah, Christmas,** and **Kwanza** are celebrated in December.
- **Boxing Day** (Canada) is December 26.

Activities

The Wright Brothers

More than 100 years ago, Orville Wright made the first motor-powered, controlled airplane flight. Ask students how airplanes and flight have changed over the years. Have students predict what airplanes will look like in another 100 years.

Ask how many students have seen airplanes flying through the air pulling message signs behind them. Discuss where they have seen these planes and what types of messages were on the signs. If possible, provide pictures of airplanes pulling message signs for students who may have never seen one.

Read About the Bill of Rights

For more information on the Bill of Rights, look for books such as these:

The Bill of Rights, by Michael Burgan (Compass Point Books, ISBN 0-756-50151-2, 2001)

The Bill of Rights, by Patricia Ryon Quiri (Children's Book Press, ISBN 0-516-26427-3, 1999)

Basketball History

Basketball was created on December 1, 1891, by a man named James Naismith. He wanted to develop an indoor sport for his students to play during the cold Massachusetts winters. He used ordinary peach baskets and a soccer ball, and basketball was born.

Ask students to find out more about the beginning of basketball, then have them create their own new indoor sport. Tell them that ordinary objects from the classroom can be used in a different way to create something new. Each student should make up a name and rules for his or her new game. Give students a chance to try out these new games in the classroom.

This Day in History

For additional December events go to *This Day in History* at **www.sfsocialstudies.com**. Select a birthday or historic event for any day in December and then base an activity or assign a report on it.

January

NEW YEAR, NEW LIFE

Activities

Ellis Island Opened on January 1, 1892

Ask students to research Ellis Island and record information about some of the immigrants who came to the United States seeking a new life in the late 1800s.

Ask students to write down what they think their new year would have been like in this new country near the turn of the 20th century. These pages can be displayed on a January bulletin board along with pictures or drawings of Ellis Island and immigrants of the late 1800s and early 1900s.

Read About Benjamin Franklin

For more information on Benjamin Franklin, look for books such as these:

The Amazing Life of Benjamin Franklin, by James Giblin (Scholastic Press, ISBN 0-590-48534-2, 2000)

B. Franklin, Printer, by David A. Adler (Holiday House, ISBN 0-823-41675-5, 2001)

Martin Luther King, Jr. Day

Discuss the life and accomplishments of Dr. Martin Luther King, Jr. Ask students to share this information with younger children in the school by creating a big picture book about Dr. King. Explain that the text of the book should be simple, so that younger children can read and understand it. Allow students to share this big book with other classrooms throughout the school.

This Day in History

For additional January events go to *This Day in History* at **www.sfsocialstudies.com**. Select a birthday or historic event for any day in January and then base an activity or assign a report on it.

February

BLACK HISTORY MONTH

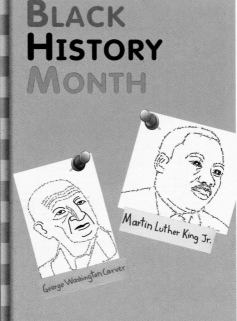

George Washington Carver

Martin Luther King Jr.

Shirley Chisolm

February Facts

- February is the second month of the year and has 28 days. It is the **shortest month of the year.**
- Every four years February has 29 days. This is called a **Leap Year.**
- **Presidents' Day** is celebrated on the third Monday in February because both George Washington and Abraham Lincoln were born in February.
- **Valentine's Day** is February 14.
- February is **American Heart Month** and **National Dental Health Month.**

Activities

Black History Month

Have students create a bulletin board for February illustrating the lives and achievements of some famous African American citizens. Search books or the Internet for some copyright-free blackline drawings of the men and women you have selected to highlight. Enlarge these pictures using an opaque projector or copy machine onto large construction paper or poster board.

Have students research these famous people and record facts about their lives and accomplishments. Now, ask students to write this information along the lines of the drawings, following the curves and features on the face of each person. The completed pictures look like the drawings are made from words instead of plain lines.

Read About Presidents' Day

For more information on Presidents' Day, look for books such as these:

George Washington, by Cheryl Harness (National Geographic Society, ISBN 0-792-27096-7, 2000)

So You Want to Be President?, by Judith St. George (Penguin Putnam, ISBN 0-399-23407-1, 2000)

Valentine's Day

Have students research the different types of valentine cards that have been sent through the years. Explain that valentines are usually sent to special people in your life to let them know you care about them. Tell students that they are going to create valentines for people that they don't know. Explain that they will make cards for people in hospitals, nursing homes, or community centers in their area. Students can look up LOVE, KINDNESS, and CARING in a thesaurus to help add cheerful messages to their colorful paper valentines.

This Day in History

For additional February events go to *This Day in History* at **www.sfsocialstudies.com**. Select a birthday or historic event for any day in February and then base an activity or assign a report on it.

March

WOMEN'S HISTORY MONTH

Activities

National Women's History Month

Ask students to name notable women who have made contributions to society. Have your own list of names, and have students research these women individually or with a partner and find pictures of each woman.

Now have students find photos or draw pictures that represent each woman's life and accomplishments. For example, for Sally Ride students could draw a space shuttle, and for Sandra Day O'Conner they could draw a judge's gavel. Students can then play a game to match each woman with the symbol that represents her. After the matches have been made, put up the pictures and the drawings on the bulletin board.

Music in Our Schools Month

Highlight the holiday and special events of the month, including Music in Our Schools Month, by asking students to write original songs. Have students choose one event in March to compose a tune and write some lyrics about. Ask students to perform their special "numbers" on their corresponding dates.

Read About the Peace Corps

For more information on the Peace Corps, look for books such as these:

The Peace Corps, by Anastasia Suen (Rosen Publishing Group, ISBN 0-823-96001-3, 2001)

Peace Corps, by Celeste A. Peters (Weigl Publishers, ISBN 1-590-36023-0, 2002)

This Day in History

For additional March events go to *This Day in History* at **www.sfsocialstudies.com**. Select a birthday or historic event for any day in March and then base an activity or assign a report on it.

April

PAUL REVERE RIDES AGAIN!

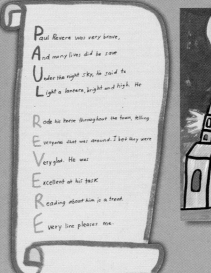

Paul Revere was very brave,
And many lives did he save
Under the night sky, he said to
Light a lantern, bright and high. He

Rode his horse throughout the town, telling
Everyone that was around. I bet they were
Very glad. He was
Excellent at his task
Reading about him is a treat.
Every line pleases me.

April Facts

- **Spring** begins in April.
- **Thomas Jefferson** was born on April 13, 1743.
- In April, we file income tax returns and set our clocks ahead for **daylight savings time.**
- April is **Math Education Month** and **National Poetry Month.**
- **National Library Week** is the second week in April.
- **Earth Day** is on April 22.
- The **midnight ride of Paul Revere** started on April 18, 1776.

Activities

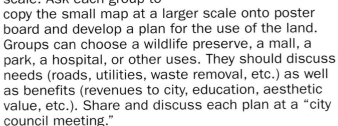

National Poetry Month

In honor of National Poetry Month, discuss different styles of poetry with your class. Read and interpret poems by some famous poets through the centuries. Ask students to memorize and recite some of their favorite poems.

Read Henry Wadsworth Longfellow's poem "Paul Revere's Ride" to the class. Explain that the famous event about which the poem was written took place in April 1776. Have students create their own versions of this famous story using a variety of poetic styles. Ask students to present their poems to the class. Display copies of the poems, along with student illustrations, on a bulletin board titled, "Paul Revere Rides Again!"

Read About Thomas Jefferson

For more information on Thomas Jefferson, look for books such as these:

The Declaration of Independence and Thomas Jefferson of Virginia, by Kathy Furgang (Rosen Publishing Group, ISBN 0-823-95589-3, 2002)

Thomas Jefferson, by Anne Welsbacher (ABDO Publishing, ISBN 1-562-39809-1, 1999)

Earth Day Land Use

Working in small groups, give students a photocopy of the same simple map showing an area of unused city land. This map should show a river, forest, or other natural features as well as a map scale. Ask each group to copy the small map at a larger scale onto poster board and develop a plan for the use of the land. Groups can choose a wildlife preserve, a mall, a park, a hospital, or other uses. They should discuss needs (roads, utilities, waste removal, etc.) as well as benefits (revenues to city, education, aesthetic value, etc.). Share and discuss each plan at a "city council meeting."

This Day in History

For additional April events go to *This Day in History* at **www.sfsocialstudies.com**. Select a birthday or historic event for any day in April and then base an activity or assign a report on it.

May

WE REMEMBER ON MEMORIAL DAY

I remember on Memorial Day. Many soldiers defend our country. Some soldiers have fought defending the United States and have died in battle. I am thankful. I am grateful that they are so brave, because it makes me feel safe.

Memorial Day is about remembering those men and women in the military who have passed away. Some people from our community are gone. But they will never be forgotten.

May Facts
- **Memorial Day** is the last Monday in Ma
- The second Sunday in May is **Mother's Day**.
- The Mexican holiday, **Cinco de Mayo**, i celebrated on May 5.
- **National Nurses Day** is May 6.
- The **transcontinental railroad** was completed on May 10, 1869.
- The **Lewis and Clark Expedition** began on May 14, 1804.

Activities

Memorial Day

Memorial Day is a national holiday when Americans remember and honor soldiers who died during wartime. Flowers are placed on soldiers' graves in honor of their sacrifice for our country. Have students research the history of Memorial Day and find out how it is celebrated in different parts of the country.

Students can make paper flowers and patriotic decorations for the bulletin board. Have students interview parents, teachers, and other members of the community, asking them to share stories, pictures, and photos of loved ones who died during time of war. Add these stories and pictures to the patriotic bulletin board.

Read About Lewis and Clark

For more information on Lewis and Clark, look for books such as these:

As Far as the Eye Can Reach: Lewis and Clark's Westward Quest, by Elizabeth Cody Kimmel (Random House, ISBN 0-375-82728-5, 2004)

Lewis and Clark's Voyage of Discovery, by James P. Burger (Rosen Publishing Group, ISBN 0-823-95848-5, 2003)

Transcontinental Railroad

Ask students to research information about the transcontinental railroad and the driving of the "Golden Spike" to complete it. Have students share their findings about the two companies who built the railroad across the country.

Divide students into two railroad "companies." Challenge the teams to build a "transclassroom bookway" that meets at the same place in the middle of the classroom. Each company will be given a stack of books and asked to start on an opposite side of the classroom. Using the books, each team will build a "track" across the room, heading toward the other team's track.

This Day in History

For additional May events go to *This Day in History* at **www.sfsocialstudies.com**. Select a birthday or historic event for any day in May and then base an activity or assign a report on it.

June

SIGNS OF SUMMER QUILT

June Facts
- **Summer** begins in June.
- The third Sunday in June is **Father's Day.**
- **Thurgood Marshall** became the first African American Supreme Court justice on June 13, 1967.
- **Flag Day** is June 14.
- **World Juggling Day** is on June 14.
- **Helen Keller** was born on June 27, 1880.
- June is **National Dairy Month.**

Activities

Signs of Summer Quilt

To recognize the first day of summer, June 21, students will help create a "summer quilt." Give each student a 10" × 10" square of construction paper. Students will use rulers and pencils to divide/mark the squares into sixteen 2 1/2" squares. They will then look through magazines to find and cut out colorful pictures of flowers, summer games or sports, etc. Students may also draw and color their own summer pictures. Then, have students cut eight 2 1/2" × 2 1/2" pieces out of the pictures. They will glue these squares onto every other square of the construction paper to make a basic, patterned quilt piece. Students may also use their own ideas to make symmetrically designed quilt pieces. Put the students' quilt pieces together as a whole "Summer Quilt" bulletin board.

Read About Flag Day

For more information on Flag Day, look for books such as these:

The American Flag, by Tamara L. Britton (ABDO Publishing Co., ISBN 1-577-65852-3, 2003)

Red, White, Blue, and Uncle Who?: The Stories Behind Some of America's Patriotic Symbols, by Teresa Bateman (Holiday House, ISBN 0-823-41285-7, 2001)

Helen Keller's Birthday: June 27, 1880

Provide a variety of books about Helen Keller and sign language. Ask students what they know about the life of Helen Keller or sign language. Discuss how Helen Keller had to have words spelled out into the palm of her hand because she was also blind. Challenge students to learn the manual alphabet, then practice spelling their own names and other words. See if students can understand a message spelled out into the palms of their hands.

This Day in History

For additional June events go to *This Day in History* at **www.sfsocialstudies.com**. Select a birthday or historic event for any day in June and then base an activity or assign a report on it.

July

NATIONAL PARK FACT HUNT

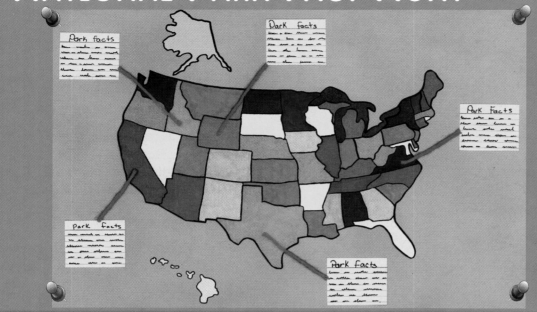

July Facts

- **Canada Day** is July 1.
- **Independence Day** is on July 4.
- **Disneyland** opened in California on July 18, 1955.
- The **first Moon landing** was on July 20, 1969.
- July is **National Hot Dog** and **National Ice Cream Month**.
- July is **Youth Art Month**.
- July is **Recreation and Parks Month**.

Activities

Recreation and Parks Month

In honor of Recreation and Parks Month, have students create a "National Park Fact Hunt" bulletin board. On a bulletin board, place a large, simple Unites States map, showing outlines of states and major cities. Have students research and choose six to eight national parks to highlight. Students should put a push pin on the map where the park is located and attach a piece of yarn to extend to the outside area of the bulletin board where a labeled picture of the park can be placed. Beneath the name and picture, place a sheet of paper with the title "Park Facts." Students can find out facts such as the tallest or lowest point in the park, the average temperature in January and July, when the park became a national park, and the average number of tourists who visit the park each year.

Read About Independence Day

For more information on Independence Day, look for books such as these:

The Declaration of Independence, by Michael Burgan (Compass Point Books, ISBN 0-756-50042-7, 2000)

Give Me Liberty!: The Story of the Declaration of Independence, by Russell Freedman (Holiday House, ISBN 0-823-41448-5, 2000)

Design a Theme Park

In honor of the opening of Disneyland in Anaheim, California, on July 18, 1955, have students create their own theme parks. Disneyland, created by Walt Disney, was a new concept in family recreation. Have each student draw a colorful, detailed map showing rides, shows, attractions, food stations, and other details of his or her own theme park.

This Day in History

For additional July events go to *This Day in History* at **www.sfsocialstudies.com**. Select a birthday or historic event for any day in July and then base an activity or assign a report on it.

Writing Rubrics

Rubric for Narrative Writing

	6	**5**	**4**
Content Quality and Idea Development	• well-focused on topic and purposeful • ideas thoroughly developed • reflects insight into writing situation • conveys sense of completeness	• focused on topic • ideas developed • reflects firm grasp of writing situation • conveys sense of completeness	• fairly focused on topic • moderately developed ideas • may include extraneous or loosely related material • conveys some sense of completeness
Voice	• clear and fitting for topic • expressive and engaging • well-suited for audience and purpose	• clear and fitting for topic • engaging • suited for audience and purpose	• fairly clear and seems to fit topic • fairly engaging style • suited for audience and purpose
Organization	• logical progression of ideas • sequence very clear	• logical progression of ideas • sequence clear	• organizational pattern apparent • some lapses may occur in organization • sequence fairly clear
Word Precision	• demonstrates mature command of language • precise and interesting word choice • wide variety of word choice	• demonstrates command of language • interesting word choice • variety of word choice	• adequate word choice • some variety of word choice
Sentence Fluency	• uses complete sentences • varied sentence structures and lengths	• uses complete sentences • varied sentence structures	• uses complete sentences • varied sentence structure attempted • some simple sentence structures
Mechanics	• correct spelling, punctuation, and capitalization • proper grammar and usage • errors do not prevent understanding	• few errors in spelling, punctuation, and capitalization • proper grammar and usage • errors do not prevent understanding	• mostly correct spelling, punctuation, and capitalization • few errors in grammar and usage • errors do not prevent understanding
If using a four-point rubric	**4**	**4**	**3**

③	②	①	Cannot be scored
• generally focused on topic • ideas may be vague • erratic development of ideas • some loosely related material • conveys some sense of completeness	• somewhat related to topic • insufficient development of ideas • includes extraneous or loosely related material • may lack sense of completeness	• minimally focused on topic • little, if any, development of ideas • lacks sense of completeness	• no focus on topic • no development of ideas • incomplete
• generally clear and seems to fit topic • engaging at times • generally suited for audience and purpose	• rarely comes through • basic attempt to engage reader • ill-suited for audience and purpose	• weak • basic attempt to engage reader • not suited for audience or purpose	• no attempt to engage reader • unaware of audience or purpose
• organizational pattern attempted • sequence generally clear	• little evidence of organizational pattern • sequence may be unclear	• no organizational pattern evident • sequence unclear	• no attempt at organization present • no sequence • cannot follow
• adequate word choice • limited, predictable, or occasionally vague word choice • some variety of word choice	• word choice limited, inappropriate, or vague • little variety of word choice	• limited or inappropriate word choice may obscure meaning • words/phrases repetitive and show minimal variety	• incorrect word choice • word choice shows no variety
• uses complete sentences • varied sentence structure attempted • generally simple sentence structures	• occasional sentence fragment or run-on sentence • limited to simple sentence structure	• excessive use of sentence fragments or run-on sentences • limited to simple sentence structure • sentences difficult to understand	• no complete sentences • sentence structure basic/below grade level
• generally correct spelling, punctuation, and capitalization • some errors in grammar and usage • errors do not prevent understanding	• some errors in spelling, punctuation, and capitalization • errors in grammar and usage • errors may prevent understanding	• errors in spelling, punctuation, and capitalization • frequent errors in grammar and usage • errors prevent understanding	• critical errors in spelling, punctuation, and capitalization/below grade level • critical errors in grammar and usage/below grade level • errors prevent understanding
3	**2**	**1**	

Rubric for Persuasive Writing

	6	**5**	**4**
Content Quality and Idea Development	• well-focused on topic • clear position stated • many facts and opinions to support position • convincing argument • conveys sense of completeness	• focused on topic • clear position stated • ample support • presents convincing argument • conveys sense of completeness	• fairly focused on topic • position apparent • adequate support, though perhaps uneven • may include extraneous or loosely related material • presents reasonable argument • conveys some sense of completeness
Voice	• clear and fitting for topic • confident, engaging, and credible • well-suited for audience and purpose	• clear and fitting for topic • engaging and credible • suited for audience and purpose	• fairly clear and seems to fit topic • fairly engaging • suited for audience and purpose
Organization	• logical organization with reasons presented in clear order • clearly contains beginning, middle, and end • easy to follow argument	• logical organization with reasons presented in order • contains beginning, middle, and end • easy to follow argument	• organizational pattern apparent • some lapses may occur in organization • vaguely contains beginning, middle, and end • fairly easy to follow argument
Word Precision	• demonstrates mature command of language • precise, persuasive, and interesting word choice • wide variety of word choice	• demonstrates command of language • interesting word choice • variety of word choice	• adequate word choice • some variety of word choice
Sentence Fluency	• uses complete sentences • varied sentence structures and lengths	• uses complete sentences • varied sentence structures	• uses complete sentences • varied sentence structure attempted • some simple sentence structures
Mechanics	• correct spelling, punctuation, and capitalization • proper grammar and usage • errors do not prevent understanding	• few errors in spelling, punctuation, and capitalization • proper grammar and usage • errors do not prevent understanding	• mostly correct spelling, punctuation, and capitalization • few errors in grammar and usage • errors do not prevent understanding
If using a four-point rubric	**4**	**4**	**3**

③	②	①	Cannot be scored
• generally focused on topic • position may be present • some support included, but erratic development • includes loosely related material • presents mediocre argument • conveys some sense of completeness	• somewhat related to topic • position may be unclear • inadequate support • includes extraneous or unrelated material • may lack sense of completeness	• minimally focused on topic • position unclear • little, if any, development of support • lacks sense of completeness	• no focus on topic • no position • no development of support • incomplete
• generally clear and seems to fit topic • engaging at times • generally suited for audience and purpose	• rarely comes through • basic attempt to engage reader • ill-suited for audience and purpose	• weak • basic attempt to engage reader • not suited for audience or purpose	• no attempt to engage reader • unaware of audience or purpose
• organizational pattern attempted • attempts to contain beginning, middle, and end • generally easy to follow argument	• little evidence of organizational pattern • somewhat difficult to follow argument	• no organizational pattern evident • difficult to follow argument	• no attempt at organization present • cannot follow argument
• adequate word choice • limited, predictable, or occasionally vague word choice • some variety of word choice	• word choice limited, inappropriate, or vague • little variety of word choice	• limited or inappropriate word choice may obscure meaning • words/phrases repetitive and show minimal variety	• incorrect word choice • word choice shows no variety
• uses complete sentences • varied sentence structure attempted • generally simple sentence structures	• occasional sentence fragment or run-on sentence • limited to simple sentence structure	• excessive use of sentence fragments or run-on sentences • limited to simple sentence structure • sentences difficult to understand	• no complete sentences • sentence structure basic/below grade level
• generally correct spelling, punctuation, and capitalization • some errors in grammar and usage • errors do not prevent understanding	• some errors in spelling, punctuation, and capitalization • errors in grammar and usage • errors may prevent understanding	• errors in spelling, punctuation, and capitalization • frequent errors in grammar and usage • errors prevent understanding	• critical errors in spelling, punctuation, and capitalization/below grade level • critical errors in grammar and usage/below grade level • errors prevent understanding
3	**2**	**1**	

Rubric for Expressive/Descriptive Writing

	6	5	4
Content Quality and Idea Development	• well-focused on topic • ideas supported with interesting and vivid details • "paints a picture" for reader • conveys sense of completeness	• focused on topic • ideas supported with details • sustains interest of reader • conveys sense of completeness	• fairly focused on topic • ideas supported with adequate detail, but development may be uneven • may include extraneous or loosely related material • conveys some sense of completeness
Voice	• clear and fitting for topic • thoughtful, expressive, and engaging • well-suited for audience and purpose	• clear and fitting for topic • expressive and engaging • suited for audience and purpose	• fairly clear and seems to fit topic • fairly engaging with some expression • suited for audience and purpose
Organization	• logical progression of ideas • easy to follow	• logical progression of ideas • easy to follow	• organizational pattern apparent • some lapses may occur in organization • fairly easy to follow
Word Precision	• demonstrates mature command of language • precise, vivid, and interesting word choice • wide variety of word choice	• demonstrates command of language • interesting word choice • variety of word choice	• adequate word choice • some variety of word choice
Sentence Fluency	• uses complete sentences • varied sentence structures and lengths	• uses complete sentences • varied sentence structures	• uses complete sentences • varied sentence structure attempted • some simple sentence structures
Mechanics	• correct spelling, punctuation, and capitalization • proper grammar and usage • errors do not prevent understanding	• few errors in spelling, punctuation, and capitalization • proper grammar and usage • errors do not prevent understanding	• mostly correct spelling, punctuation, and capitalization • few errors in grammar and usage • errors do not prevent understanding
If using a four-point rubric	4	4	3

3	2	1	Cannot be scored
• generally focused on topic • ideas may be vague • some details included, but erratic development • some loosely related material • conveys some sense of completeness	• somewhat related to topic • inadequate details • includes extraneous or unrelated material • may lack sense of completeness	• minimally focused on topic • little, if any, development of ideas • lacks sense of completeness	• no focus on topic • no development of ideas • incomplete
• generally clear and seems to fit topic • engaging at times • generally suited for audience and purpose	• rarely comes through • basic attempt to engage reader • ill-suited for audience and purpose	• weak • basic attempt to engage reader • not suited for audience or purpose	• no attempt to engage reader • unaware of audience or purpose
• organizational pattern attempted • generally easy to follow	• little evidence of organizational pattern • somewhat difficult to follow	• no organizational pattern evident • difficult to follow	• no attempt at organization present • cannot follow
• adequate word choice • limited, predictable, or occasionally vague word choice • some variety of word choice	• word choice limited, inappropriate, or vague • little variety of word choice	• limited or inappropriate word choice may obscure meaning • words/phrases repetitive and show minimal variety	• incorrect word choice • word choice shows no variety
• uses complete sentences • varied sentence structure attempted • generally simple sentence structures	• occasional sentence fragment or run-on sentence • limited to simple sentence structure	• excessive use of sentence fragments or run-on sentences • limited to simple sentence structure • sentences difficult to understand	• no complete sentences • sentence structure basic/below grade level
• generally correct spelling, punctuation, and capitalization • some errors in grammar and usage • errors do not prevent understanding	• some errors in spelling, punctuation, and capitalization • errors in grammar and usage • errors may prevent understanding	• errors in spelling, punctuation, and capitalization • frequent errors in grammar and usage • errors prevent understanding	• critical errors in spelling, punctuation, and capitalization/below grade level • critical errors in grammar and usage/below grade level • errors prevent understanding
3	2	1	

Rubric for Expository Writing

	6	**5**	**4**
Content Quality and Idea Development	• well-focused on topic • ideas supported with interesting details • conveys sense of completeness	• focused on topic • ideas supported with details • conveys sense of completeness	• fairly focused on topic • ideas supported with adequate detail, but development may be uneven • may include extraneous or loosely related material • conveys some sense of completeness
Voice	• clear and fitting for topic • engaging • well-suited for audience and purpose	• clear and fitting for topic • engaging • suited for audience and purpose	• fairly clear and seems to fit topic • fairly engaging • suited for audience and purpose
Organization	• logical progression of ideas • excellent transitions • easy to follow	• logical progression of ideas • good transitions • easy to follow	• organizational pattern apparent • some lapses may occur in organization • some transitions • fairly easy to follow
Word Precision	• demonstrates mature command of language • precise, interesting word choice • wide variety of word choice	• demonstrates command of language • precision in word choice • variety of word choice	• adequate word choice • some variety of word choice
Sentence Fluency	• strong topic sentence • uses complete sentences • varied sentence structures and lengths	• good topic sentence • uses complete sentences • varied sentence structures	• adequate topic sentence • uses complete sentences • varied sentence structure attempted • some simple sentence structures
Mechanics	• correct spelling, punctuation, and capitalization • proper grammar and usage • errors do not prevent understanding	• few errors in spelling, punctuation, and capitalization • proper grammar and usage • errors do not prevent understanding	• mostly correct spelling, punctuation, and capitalization • few errors in grammar and usage • errors do not prevent understanding
If using a four-point rubric	**4**	**4**	**3**

③	②	①	Cannot be scored
• generally focused on topic • some loosely related material • some details included, but erratic development	• somewhat related to topic • inadequate details • includes extraneous or unrelated material • may lack sense of completeness	• minimally focused on topic • little, if any, development of ideas • lacks sense of completeness	• no focus on topic • no development of ideas • incomplete
• generally clear and seems to fit topic • engaging at times • generally suited for audience and purpose	• rarely comes through • basic attempt to engage reader • ill-suited for audience and purpose	• weak • basic attempt to engage reader • not suited for audience or purpose	• no attempt to engage reader • unaware of audience or purpose
• organizational pattern attempted • few transitions • generally easy to follow	• little evidence of organizational pattern • no transitions • somewhat difficult to follow	• no organizational pattern evident • difficult to follow	• no attempt at organization present • cannot follow
• adequate word choice • limited, predictable, or occasionally vague word choice • some variety of word choice	• word choice limited, inappropriate, or vague • little variety of word choice	• limited or inappropriate word choice may obscure meaning • words/phrases repetitive and show minimal variety	• incorrect word choice • word choice shows no variety
• adequate topic sentence • uses complete sentences • varied sentence structure attempted • generally simple sentence structures	• weak topic sentence • occasional sentence fragment or run-on sentence • limited to simple sentence structure	• topic sentence not evident • excessive use of sentence fragments or run-on sentences • limited to simple sentence structure • sentences difficult to understand	• no topic sentence • no complete sentences • sentence structure basic/below grade level
• generally correct spelling, punctuation, and capitalization • some errors in grammar and usage • errors do not prevent understanding	• some errors in spelling, punctuation, and capitalization • errors in grammar and usage • errors may prevent understanding	• errors in spelling, punctuation, and capitalization • frequent errors in grammar and usage • errors prevent understanding	• critical errors in spelling, punctuation, and capitalization/below grade level • critical errors in grammar and usage/below grade level • errors prevent understanding
3	**2**	**1**	

Notes

Overview Bibliography

Columbus Day: Celebrating a Famous Explorer, by Elaine Landau (Enslow Publishers, Inc., ISBN 0-766-01573-4, 2001) **Easy** *NCSS Notable Book*

Jamestown: New World Adventure, by James E. Knight (Troll Associates, ISBN 0-816-74554-4, 1998) **Easy**

James Towne: Struggle for Survival, by Marcia Sewall (Atheneum, ISBN 0-689-81814-9, 2001) **Easy** *NCSS Notable Book*

Our Strange New Land: Elizabeth's Diary, Jamestown, Virginia, 1609, by Patricia Hermes (Scholastic Press, ISBN 0-439-36898-7, 2002) **Easy**

The Spinner's Daughter, by Amy Littlesugar (Pippin Press, ISBN 0-945-91222-6, 1994) **Easy**

Sybil Ludington's Midnight Ride, Marsha Amstel (Lerner Publishing Group, ISBN 1-575-05456-6, 2000) **Easy** *Horn Book Award*

Yonder Mountain: A Cherokee Legend, by Kay Thorpe Bannon, et al. (Marshall Cavendish Corp., ISBN 0-761-45113-7, 2002) **Easy** *NCSS Notable Book*

American Indian Cooking Before 1500, by Mary Gunderson (Capstone Press, ISBN 0-736-80605-9, 2000) **On-Level** *NCSS Notable Book*

How We Crossed the West: The Adventures of Lewis & Clark, by Rosalyn Schanzer (National Geographic, ISBN 0-792-26726-5, 2002) **On-Level**

Increase Mather: Clergyman and Scholar, by Norma Jean Lutz (Chelsea House Publishers, ISBN 0-7910-6119-1, 2001) **On-Level**

Journeys in Time: A New Atlas of American History, by Susan Buckley and Elspeth Leacock (Houghton Mifflin Co., ISBN 0-618-31114-9, 2003) **On-Level** *NCSS Notable Book*

Pocahontas: The True Story of the Powhatan Princess, by Catherine Iannone (Chelsea House Publishers, ISBN 0-791-02496-2, 1995) **On-Level**

The Secret Soldier: The Story of Deborah Sampson, by Ann McGovern (Scholastic, ISBN 0-590-43052-1, 1990) **On-Level**

The Captain's Dog: My Journey with the Lewis and Clark Tribe, by Roland Smith (Harcourt Brace, ISBN 0-152-02696-7, 2000) **Challenge**

The Declaration of Independence: The Words That Made America, by Sam Fink (text by Thomas Jefferson) (Scholastic Reference, ISBN 0-439-40700-1, 2002) **Challenge**

If You Were There in 1776, by Barbara Brenner (Simon and Schuster, ISBN 0-027-12322-7, 1994) **Challenge**

John and Abigail Adams: An American Love Story, by Judith St. George (Holiday House, ISBN 0-823-41571-6, 2001) **Challenge** *NCSS Notable Book*

The Paradox of Jamestown: 1585–1700, by Christopher Collier and James Lincoln Collier (Benchmark Books, ISBN 0-761-40437-6, 1998) **Challenge**

Pilgrims and Puritans: 1620–1676, by Christopher Collier and James Lincoln Collier (Benchmark Books, ISBN 0-761-40438-4, 1998) **Challenge**

The Signers: The 56 Stories Behind the Declaration of Independence, by Dennis Brindell Fradin and Michael McCurdy (Walker & Co., ISBN 0-802-78849-1, 2002) **Challenge** *NCSS Notable Book*

Slavery: Bondage Throughout History, by Richard Ross Watkins (Houghton Mifflin Co., ISBN 0-395-92289-5, 2001) **Challenge** *NCSS Notable Book*

This Vast Land: A Young Man's Journal of the Lewis and Clark Expedition, by Stephen E. Ambrose (Simon & Schuster, ISBN 0-689-86448-5, 2003) **Challenge**

In the Hands of the Great Spirit: The 20,000-Year History of American Indians, by Jake Page (Free Press, ISBN 0-684-85577-1, 2004) **Teacher reference**

A People's History of the United States: 1492–Present, by Howard Zinn (Harperperennial Library, ISBN 0-060-52837-0, 2003) **Teacher reference**

The U.S. Constitution: And Fascinating Facts About It, by Terry L. Jordan (Oak Hill Publishers, ISBN 1-891-74300-7, 1999) **Teacher reference**

Discovery Channel School Videos

George Washington: The Unknown Years Learn about George Washington's colonial life and what prepared him to become one of the country's Founding Fathers. (Item #716530, 26 minutes)

The Real Thomas Jefferson Discover the complexities and contradictions of a great American. (Item #716720, 26 minutes)

Look for this symbol throughout the Teacher's Edition to find **Award-Winning Selections.**

Unit 1 Bibliography

Abe Lincoln Remembers, by Ann Turner (HarperCollins Juvenile Books, ISBN 0-060-51107-4, 2003) **Easy**

 **Freedom River,** by Doreen Rappaport (Hyperion Books for Children, ISBN 0-786-80350-9, 2000) **Easy** *Coretta Scott King Honor Book*

 **Harriet and the Promised Land,** by Jacob Lawrence (Aladdin Paperbacks, ISBN 0-689-80965-4, 1997) **Easy New York** *Times Best Illustrated Book*

I Thought My Soul Would Rise and Fly: The Diary of Patsy, a Freed Girl, by Joyce Hansen (Scholastic, Inc., ISBN 0-590-84913-1, 1997) **Easy**

Robert E. Lee, Brave Leader, by Rae Bains (Troll Associates, ISBN 0-816-70546-1, 1989) **Easy**

Sweet Clara and the Freedom Quilt, by Deborah Hopkinson (Random House, ISBN 0-679-87472-0, 1995) **Easy**

Voice of Freedom: A Story About Frederick Douglass, by Maryann N. Weidt (Lerner Publishing Group, ISBN 1-575-05553-8, 2001) **Easy**

Abraham Lincoln the Writer: A Treasury of His Greatest Speeches and Letters, by Harold Holzer, ed. (Boyds Mills Press, ISBN 1-563-97772-9, 2000) **On-Level**

The Africans, by Jen Green (Crabtree Publishing, ISBN 0-778-70198-0, 2000) **On-Level**

Harriet Tubman: Conductor on the Underground Railroad, by Ann Petry (Harper Trophy, ISBN 0-064-46181-5, 1996) **On-Level**

 **Lincoln: A Photobiography,** by Russell Freedman (Houghton Mifflin Company, ISBN 0395-51848-2, 1989) **On-Level** *Newbery Medal*

My Brother's Keeper: Virginia's Civil War Diary, by Mary Pope Osborne (Scholastic, ISBN 0-439-15307-7, 2000) **On-Level**

 **Steal Away,** by Jennifer Armstrong (Scholastic Paperbacks, ISBN 0-590-46921-5, 1993) **On-Level** *ALA Notable Book*

The World in the Time of Abraham Lincoln, by Fiona MacDonald (Chelsea House Publishing, ISBN 0-791-06028-4, 2000) **On-Level**

Amistad Rising: A Story of Freedom, by Veronica Chambers (Raintree Publishers, ISBN 0-8172-5510-9, 1998) **Challenge**

 **Anthony Burns: The Defeat and Triumph of a Fugitive Slave,** by Virginia Hamilton (Random House Children's Books, ISBN 0-679-83997-6, 1993) **Challenge** *ALA Notable Book, Boston Globe Horn Book Award, Jane Addams Book Award*

Clara Barton: Civil War Nurse, by Nancy Whitelaw (Enslow Publishers, ISBN 0-894-90778-6, 1997) **Challenge**

Dear Ellen Bee: A Civil War Scrapbook of Two Union Spies, by Mary E. Lyons and Muriel M. Branch (Atheneum, ISBN 0-689-82379-7, 2000) **Challenge**

 **House of Dies Drear,** by Virginia Hamilton (Simon & Schuster, ISBN 0-020-43520-7, 1984) **Challenge** *Edgar Allan Poe Juvenile Book*

Lincoln: In His Own Words, by Milton Melzer, ed. (Harcourt, ISBN 0-152-45437-3, 1993) **Challenge**

Nightjohn, by Gary Paulsen (Random House, ISBN 0-440-91014-5, 1994) **Challenge**

Battle Cry of Freedom: The Civil War Era, by James M. McPherson (Oxford University Press, ISBN 0-19-516895-X, 2003) **Teacher reference**

With Malice Toward None: The Life of Abraham Lincoln, by Stephen B. Oates (Harperperennial Library, ISBN 0-060-92471-3, 1994) **Teacher reference**

Discovery Channel School Video Slave Ship Uncover the shocking facts about the transatlantic slave trade as African slaves take over the slave ship *Amistad.* (Item #716787, 26 minutes)

Look for this symbol throughout the Teacher's Edition to find **Award-Winning Selections.**

Unit 2 Bibliography

Andrew Carnegie: Builder of Libraries, by Charnan Simon (Children's Book Press, ISBN 0-516-26131-2, 1998) **Easy**

Chief Joseph: Chief of the Nez Percé, by Cynthia Fitterer Klingel and Robert B. Noyed (Child's World, ISBN 1-567-66165-3, 2002) **Easy**

Eyewitness: Cowboy, by David Hamilton Murdoch (DK Publishing, ISBN 0-789-45854-3, 2000) **Easy**

The New Land: A First Year on the Prairie, by Marilynn Reynolds (Orca Books, ISBN 1-551-43071-1, 1999) **Easy**

Pony Express!, by Steven Kroll (Scholastic, ISBN 0-590-20240-5, 1996) **Easy**

The Real McCoy: The Life of an African-American Inventor, by Wendy Towle (Scholastic, ISBN 0-590-48102-9, 1995) **Easy**

School Success: The Inside Story, by Peter Kline (Great Ocean Publishing, ISBN 0-915-55625-1, 1994) **Easy**

Streets of Gold, by Rosemary Wells (Dial Books for Young Readers, ISBN 0-803-72149-8, 1999) **Easy**

Vision of Beauty: The Story of Sarah Breedlove Walker, by Kathryn Lasky (Candlewick Press, ISBN 0-763-6-1834-9, 2003) **Easy**

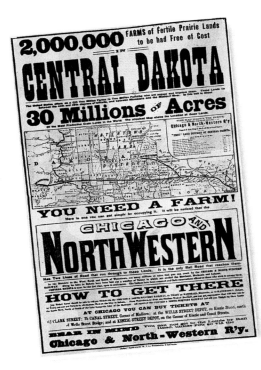

When Jessie Came Across the Sea, by Amy Hest (Candlewick Press, ISBN 0-763-61274-X, 1997) **Easy**

Always Inventing: A Photobiography of Alexander Graham Bell, by Tom Matthews (National Geographic, ISBN 0-792-27391-5, 1999) **On-Level**

 Andrew Carnegie: Steel King and Friend to Libraries, by Zachary Kent (Enslow Publishers, Inc., ISBN 0-766-01212-3, 1999) **On-Level** **NCSS Notable Book**

Chief Joseph: Nez Percé Leader, by Marian Taylor (Chelsea House, ISBN 0-791-01972-1, 1993) **On-Level**

Ellis Island, by Patricia Ryon Quiri (Scholastic, ISBN 0-516-26374-9, 1998) **On-Level**

How to Study, by David H. Griswold (Longman Publishing, ISBN 1-88334-157-3, 1993) **On-Level**

Immigrant Kids, by Russell Freedman (Penguin Putnam, ISBN 0-140-37594-5, 1995), **On-Level**

Industry and Business (Life in America 100 Years Ago), by Linda Leuzzi (Chelsea House, ISBN 0-791-02846-1, 1996) **On-Level**

The Story of Alexander Graham Bell: Inventor of the Telephone, by Margaret Davidson (Gareth Stevens Publishing, ISBN 0-836-81483-5, 1997) **On-Level**

Ten Mile Day: The Building of the Transcontinental Railroad, by Mary Ann Fraser (Henry Holt & Company, ISBN 0-805-04703-4, 1996) **On-Level**

Yang the Second and Her Secret Admirers, by Lensey Namioka (Yearling Books, ISBN 0-440-41641-8, 2000) **On-Level**

Alexander Graham Bell: An Inventive Life, by Elizabeth MacLeod (Kids Can Press, ISBN 1-550-74458-5, 1999) **Challenge**

Chief Joseph and the Nez Percés, by Robert A. Scott (Facts on File, Inc., ISBN 0-816-02475-8, 1993) **Challenge**

Hurry Freedom: African Americans in Gold Rush California, by Jerry Stanley (Crown Publishers, ISBN 0-517-80094-2, 2000) **Challenge**

Legendary Labor Leaders, by Thomas Streissguth (Oliver Press, ISBN 1-881-50844-7, 1998) **Challenge**

Lewis Latimer: Scientist, by Winifred Latimer Norman (Chelsea House, ISBN 0-791-01977-2, 1994) **Challenge**

The Many Lives of Andrew Carnegie, by Milton Meltzer (Franklin Watts, Inc., ISBN 0-531-11427-9, 1997) **Challenge**

The Orphan of Ellis Island: A Time-Travel Adventure, by Elvira Woodruff (Scholastic, ISBN 0-590-48246-7, 2000) **Challenge**

The Promised Land, by Mary Antin (Penguin USA, ISBN 0-140-18985-8, 1997) **Challenge**

 Sitting Bull and His World, by Albert Marrin (Dutton Books, 0-525-45944-8, 2000) **Challenge** **NCSS Notable Book**

Student Success Secrets, by Eric Jensen (Barron's Educational Series, ISBN 0-764-12007-7, 2003) **Challenge**

Thomas A. Edison: Young Inventor, by Sue Guthridge (Aladdin Library, ISBN 0-020-41850-7, 1986) **Challenge**

Encyclopedia of Indian Wars: Western Battles and Skirmishes, 1850–1890, by Gregory F. Michno (Mountain Press Publishing Co., ISBN 0-878-42468-7, 2003) **Teacher reference**

History of the Labor Movemens in the United States: From Colonial Times to the Founding of the American Federation of Labor, by Philip S. Foner (International Publishers Co., ISBN 0-717-80376-7, 1979) **Teacher reference**

Nothing Like It in the World: The Men Who Built the Transcontinental Railroad 1863–1869, by Stephen E. Ambrose (Touchstone Books, ISBN 0-743-20317-8, 2001) **Teacher reference**

Discovery Channel School Video *The Real American Cowboy* Learn about the real life of the American cowboy: It was tough and lonely. (Item #716688, 26 minutes)

Look for this symbol throughout the Teacher's Edition to find **Award-Winning Selections**.

Growth of a Nation • Unit 2 Bibliography **TR43**

Unit 3 Bibliography

America in the Time of Susan B. Anthony: (1845–1928), by Sally Senzell Isaacs (Heinemann Library, ISBN 1-575-72941-5, 2002) **Easy**

Battles of the Spanish-American War (Americans at War), by Diane Smolinski (Heinemann Library, ISBN 1-403-43152-3, 2002) **Easy**

Ida Tarbell: Pioneer Investigative Reporter, by Barbara A. Somervill (Morgan Reynolds, ISBN 1-883-84687-0, 2002) **Easy**

The New Land: A First Year on the Prairie, by Marilynn Reynolds (Orca Books, ISBN 1-551-43071-1, 1999) **Easy**

The Story of Booker T. Washington, by Patricia C. McKissack and Frederick L. McKissack (Children's Book Press, ISBN 0-516-04758-2, 1991) **Easy**

Welcome to Kirsten's World, 1854: Growing Up in Pioneer America, by Susan Sinnott (Pleasant Company Publications, ISBN 1-562-47770-6, 1999) **Easy**

Where Poppies Grow: A World War I Companion, by Linda Granfield (Stoddart Publishing Co., Limited, ISBN 0-773-73319-1, 2002) **Easy**

Woodrow Wilson, by Henry M. Holden (Enslow Publishers, ISBN 0-766-05123-4, 2003) **Easy**

World War I (America at War), by Scott Marquette (The Rourke Book Company, ISBN 1-589-52392-X, 2002) **Easy**

Booker T. Washington (Journey to Freedom), by Don Troy (Child's World, ISBN 1-567-66556-X, 1999) **On-Level**

Caleb's Story, by Patricia MacLachlan (HarperTrophy, ISBN 0-064-40590-7, 2002) **On-Level**

Failure Is Impossible: The Story of Susan B. Anthony, by Lisa Frederiksen Bohannon (Morgan Reynolds, ISBN 1-883-84677-3, 2001) **On-Level**

Ida M. Tarbell: Pioneer Woman Journalist and Biographer, by Adrian A. Paradis (Children's Book Press, ISBN 0-516-03217-8, 1985) **On-Level**

John Muir: My Life with Nature, by John Muir and Joseph Bharat Cornell (Dawn Publications, ISBN 1-584-69009-7, 2000) **On-Level**

The Panama Canal, by Elizabeth Mann (Mikaya Press, ISBN 0-965-04934-5, 1998) **On-Level**

The Panama Canal (Great Building Feats), by Lesley A. DuTemple (Lerner Publications Company, ISBN 0-822-50079-5, 2003) **On-Level**

The Rise and Fall of Jim Crow: The African-American Struggle Against Discrimination: 1865–1954, by Richard Wormser (St. Martin's Press, ISBN 0-312-31326-8, 2004) **On-Level**

Woman's Suffrage: Researching American History, by JoAnne Weisman Deitch (Discovery Enterprises Ltd., ISBN 1-579-60066-2, 2000) **On-Level**

 Andrew Carnegie: Steel King and Friend to Libraries, by Zachary Kent (Enslow Publishers, Inc., ISBN 0-766-01212-3, 1999) **Challenge** *NCSS Notable Book*

Booker T. Washington: Educator (Black Americans of Achievement), Alan Schroeder (Chelsea House Publishing, ISBN 0-791-00252-7, 1992) **Challenge**

Farmer Boy, by Laura Ingalls Wilder (HarperTrophy, ISBN 0-06-052238-0, 2003) **Challenge**

Ida B. Wells: Mother of the Civil Rights Movement, by Dennis Brindell Fradin and Judith Bloom Fradin (Houghton Mifflin Co., ISBN 0-395-89898-6, 2000) **Challenge** *NCSS Notable Book*

Ida Tarbell: First of the Muckrakers, by Alice Fleming (Ty Crowell Co., ISBN 0-690-42881-2, 1971) **Challenge**

Susan B. Anthony: And Justice for All, by Jeanne Gehret (Verbal Images Press, ISBN 0-962-51368-7, 2003) **Challenge**

Theodore Roosevelt: Letters from a Young Coal Miner, by Jennifer Armstrong (Winslow Press, ISBN 1-890-81727-9, 2001) **Challenge** *NCSS Notable Book*

Up from Slavery, by Booker T. Washington (Oxford University Press, ISBN 0-192-83562-9, 2000) **Challenge**

Great Bridge: The Epic Story of the Building of the Brooklyn Bridge, by David McCullough (Simon & Schuster, ISBN 0-671-45711-X, 1983) **Teacher reference**

How the Other Half Lives, by Jacob A. Riis (Penguin USA, ISBN 0-140-43679-0, 1997) **Teacher reference**

The Souls of Black Folk, by W. E. B. Du Bois (Penguin USA, ISBN 0-140-18998-X, 1996) **Teacher reference**

Booker T. Washington, Vol. 2: The Wizard of Tuskegee, 1901–1915, by Louis R. Harlan (Oxford University Press, ISBN 0-195-04229-8, 1986) **Teacher reference**

Look for this symbol throughout the Teacher's Edition to find **Award-Winning Selections**.

Unit 4 Bibliography

Franklin D. Roosevelt: A Photo-Illustrated Biography, by Steve Potts (Bridgestone Books, ISBN 1-560-65453-8, 1996) **Easy**

Georgia O'Keeffe (On My Own Biographies), by Linda Lowery (Carolrhoda Books, ISBN 0-876-14860-7, 2003) **Easy**

Harlem: A Poem, by Walter Dean Myers (Scholastic, ISBN 0-590-54340-7, 1997) **Easy Caldecott Honor Book**

Leah's Pony, by Elizabeth Friedrich (Boyds Mills Press, ISBN 1-563-97828-8, 2003) **Easy**

Model T: How Henry Ford Built a Legend, by David L. Weitzman (Crown Publishers, ISBN 0-375-81107-9, 2002) **Easy**

The Orphans of Normandy, by Nancy Amis (Atheneum, ISBN 0-689-84143-4, 2003) **Easy**

Remember Pearl Harbor: American and Japanese Survivors Tell Their Stories, by Thomas Allen (National Geographic, ISBN 0-792-26690-0, 2001) **Easy NCSS Notable Book**

Rent Party Jazz, by William Miller (Lee & Low Books, ISBN 1-584-30025-6, 2001) **Easy NCSS Notable Book**

Rose's Journal: The Story of a Girl in the Great Depression, by Marissa Moss (Harcourt, ISBN 0-15-204605-4, 2001) **Easy**

The Story of D-Day, by R. Conrad Stein (Children's Book Press, ISBN 0-516-44609-6, 1977) **Easy**

Story Painter: The Life of Jacob Lawrence, by John Duggleby (Chronicle Books, ISBN 0-811-82082-3, 1998) **Easy**

Airplanes of World War II, by Nancy Robinson-Masters (Capstone Press, ISBN 1-560-65531-3, 1998) **On-Level**

Angels of Mercy: The Army Nurses of World War II, by Betsy Kuhn (Atheneum, ISBN 0-689-82044-5, 1999) **On-Level**

Attack on Pearl Harbor: The True Story of the Day America Entered World War II, by Shelley Tanaka (Hyperion Press, ISBN 0-786-80736-9, 2001) **On-Level**

Black Stars of the Harlem Renaissance, by Jim Haskins (John Wiley & Sons, ISBN 0-471-21152-4, 2002) **On-Level**

D-Day, June 6, 1944 (Days that Shook the World), by Sean Sheehan (Raintree/Steck Vaughn, ISBN 0-739-85232-9, 2003) **On-Level**

Franklin D. Roosevelt (United States Presidents), by Paul Joseph (Checkerboard Library, ISBN 1-562-39813-X, 2000) **On-Level**

Georgia O'Keeffe (Artists in Their Time), by Ruth Thomson (Franklin Watts, ISBN 0-531-16620-1, 2003) **On-Level**

The Home Front During World War II in American History, by R. Conrad Stein (Enslow Publishers, Inc., ISBN 0-766-01984-5, 2003) **On-Level**

Jazz and Its History, by Giuseppe Vigna (Barrons Juveniles, ISBN 0-764-15132-0 1999) **On-Level**

Jump at de Sun: The Story of Zora Neale Hurston, by A. P. Porter and Lucy Ann Hurston (First Avenue Editions, ISBN 0-876-14546-2, 1993) **On-Level**

Welcome to Kit's World, 1934: Growing Up During America's Great Depression, by Harriet Brown (Pleasant Company Publications, ISBN 1-584-85359-X, 2002) **On-Level**

Anne Frank in the World: 1929–1945, by the Anne Frank House Staff (Knopf, ISBN 0-375-81177-X, 2001) **Challenge NCSS Notable Book**

Extraordinary People of the Harlem Renaissance, by P. Stephen Hardy and Sheila Jackson Hardy (Children's Book Press, ISBN 0-516-27170-9, 2001) **Challenge**

Fighting for Honor: Japanese Americans and World War II, by Michael L. Cooper (Houghton Mifflin, ISBN 0-395-91375-6, 2000) **Challenge**

Franklin D. Roosevelt: The Four-Term President, by Michael A. Schuman (Enslow Publishers, ISBN 0-894-90696-8, 1996) **Challenge**

Georgia O'Keeffe: Painter, by Michael L. Berry (Chelsea House, ISBN 0-7910-0420-1, 1989) **Challenge**

The Good Fight: How World War II Was Won, by Stephen Ambrose (Atheneum, ISBN 0-689-84361-5, 2001) **Challenge**

The Great Depression in American History, by David K. Fremon (Enslow Publishers, ISBN 0-894-90881-2, 1997) **Challenge**

Headin' for Better Times: The Arts of the Great Depression, by Duane Damon (Lerner Publishing Group, ISBN 0-822-51741-8, 2002) **Challenge**

My Secret War: The World War II Diary of Madeline Beck, by Mary Pope Osborne (Scholastic, Inc., ISBN 0-590-68715-8, 2000) **Challenge**

Restless Spirit: The Life and Work of Dorothea Lange, by Elizabeth Partridge (Penguin Putnam, ISBN 0-14-230024-1, 2001) **Challenge**

Rosie the Riveter: Women Working on the Home Front in World War II, by Penny Colman (Crown Publishers, Inc., ISBN 0-517-88567-0, 1998) **Challenge ALA Notable Book**

The Story of D-Day: June 6, 1944, by Bruce Bliven, Jr. (Random House, ISBN 0-394-84886-1, 1991) **Challenge**

The Greatest Generation, by Tom Brokaw (Dell Publishing, ISBN 0-385-33462-1, 1998) **Teacher reference**

Hard Times: An Oral History of the Great Depression in America, by Studs Terkel (New Press, ISBN 1-565-84656-7, 2000) **Teacher reference**

The Portable Harlem Renaissance Reader, by David L. Lewis, ed. (Penguin USA, ISBN 0-140-17036-7, 1995) **Teacher reference**

 Look for this symbol throughout the Teacher's Edition to find **Award-Winning Selections**.

Growth of a Nation • Unit 4 Bibliography   **TR45**

Unit 5 Bibliography

Dolores Huerta (Latinos in American History), by Rebecca Thatcher Murcia (Mitchell Lane Publishers, Inc., ISBN 1-584-15155-2, 2002) **Easy**

Footprints on the Moon, by Alexandra Siy (Charlesbridge Publishing, ISBN 1-57091-409-5, 2001) **Easy**

Freedom Summer, by Deborah Wiles (Atheneum, ISBN 0-689-83016-5, 2001) **Easy** *NCSS Notable Book*

Harvesting Hope: The Story of César Chávez, by Kathleen Krull (Harcourt Children's Books, ISBN 0-152-01437-3, 2003) **Easy**

High Hopes: A Photobiography of John F. Kennedy, by Deborah Heiligman (National Geographic, ISBN 0-792-26141-0, 2003) **Easy**

I Am Rosa Parks, by Rosa Parks and James Haskins (Puffin, ISBN 0-141-30710-2, 1999) **Easy** *Horn Book Award, NCSS Notable Book*

Leagues Apart: The Men and Times of the Negro Baseball Leagues, by Lawrence S. Ritter (Mulberry Books, ISBN 0-688-16693-8, 1999) **Easy**

Martin's Big Words: The Life of Dr. Martin Luther King, Jr., by Doreen Rappaport (Hyperion Books for Children, ISBN 0-786-80714-8, 2001) **Easy** *NCSS Notable Book*

Mikhail Gorbachev (Leading Lives), by Andrew Langley (Heinemann Library, ISBN 1-403-40831-9, 2003) **Easy**

One Giant Leap: The First Moon Landing, by Dana Meachen Rau (Soundprints Corp Audio, ISBN 1-568-99344-7, 1996) **Easy**

Stateswoman to the World: A Story About Eleanor Roosevelt, by Maryann N. Weidt (First Avenue Editions, ISBN 0-876-14562-4, 1992) **Easy**

César Chávez: A Hero for Everyone, by Gary Soto (Aladdin Library, ISBN 0-689-85922-8, 2003) **On-Level**

Eleanor Roosevelt: First Lady of the World, by Doris Faber (Puffin, ISBN 0-140-32103-9, 1996) **On-Level**

Failure Is Impossible!: The History of American Women's Rights, by Martha E. Kendall (Lerner Publications Company, ISBN 0-822-51744-2, 2001) **On-Level** *NCSS Notable Book*

A History of U.S. Involvement, by John M. Dunn (Gale Group, ISBN 1-560-06645-8, 2001) **On-Level**

John F. Kennedy (United States Presidents), by Paul Joseph (Checkerboard Library, ISBN 1-562-39745-1, 2000) **On-Level**

Martin Luther King, by Rosemary Bray (Harper Collins Children's Book, ISBN 0-688-15219-8, 1997) **On-Level**

Mikhail Gorbachev, by Tom Head (Gale Group, ISBN 0-7377-1297-X, 2003) **On-Level**

Satchel Paige, by Lesa Cline-Ransome (Simon and Schuster, ISBN 0-689-85681-4, 2003) **On-Level** *NCSS Notable Book*

Shadow Ball: The History of the Negro Leagues, by Geoffrey C. Ward (Knopf, ISBN 0-679-86749-X, 1994) **On-Level**

Their Names to Live: What the Vietnam Veterans Memorial Means to America, by Brent Ashabranner (The Millbrook Press, ISBN 0-761-33235-9, 1998) **On-Level**

Thurgood Marshall: Civil Rights Attorney and Supreme Court Justice, by Mark Rowh (Enslow Publishers, Inc., ISBN 0-766-01547-5, 2002) **On-Level**

Black Diamond: The Story of the Negro Baseball Leagues, by Patricia C. McKissack (Scholastic, Inc., ISBN 0-590-45810-8, 1996) **Challenge**

César Chávez (The Great Hispanic Heritage), by Hal Marcovitz (Chelsea House, ISBN 0-7910-7515-X, 2002) **Challenge**

The Cold War, by Ted Gottfried (21st Century Books, ISBN 0-761-32560-3, 2003) **Challenge**

Dare to Dream: Coretta Scott King and the Civil Rights Movement, by Angela Shelf Medearis (Puffin, ISBN 0-141-30202-X, 1999) **Challenge**

Eleanor Roosevelt: A Life of Discovery, by Russell Freedman (Houghton Mifflin, ISBN 0-395-84520-3, 1997) **Challenge** *Newbery Honor Book*

Eleanor Roosevelt: Fighter for Social Justice, by Ann Weil (Aladdin Library, ISBN 0-689-71348-7, 1989) **Challenge**

John Fitzgerald Kennedy: America's Youngest President, by Lucy Frisbee (Aladdin Library, ISBN 0-020-41990-2, 1986) **Challenge**

Malcolm X: By Any Means Necessary, by Walter Dean Myers (Scholastic, ISBN 0-590-48109-6, 1994) **Challenge**

Maya Lin: Architect and Artist, by Mary Malone (Enslow Publishers, Inc., ISBN 0-894-90499-X, 1995) **Challenge**

Mikhail Gorbachev: The Soviet Innovator, by Steven Otfinoski (Columbine Trade, ISBN 0-449-90400-8, 1989) **Challenge**

There Comes a Time: The Struggle for Civil Rights, by Milton Meltzer (Random House, ISBN 0-375-80414-5, 2002) **Challenge** *NCSS Notable Book*

Fire in the Lake: The Vietnamese and the Americans in Vietnam, by Frances FitzGerald (Little Brown & Co., ISBN 0-316-15919-0, 1973) **Teacher reference** *Pulitzer Prize, National Book Award*

Lenin's Tomb: The Last Days of the Soviet Empire, by David Remnick (Vintage Books, ISBN 0-679-75125-4, 1994) **Teacher reference** *Pulitzer Prize*

Parting the Waters: America in the King Years, 1954–1963, by Taylor Branch (Touchstone Books, ISBN 0-671-68742-5, 1989) **Teacher reference** *Pulitzer Prize*

Discovery Channel School Video *Free At Last* Meet the heroic men and women who were killed in the fight against racism. (Item #740001, 52 minutes)

 Look for this symbol throughout the Teacher's Edition to find **Award-Winning Selections.**

Unit 6 Bibliography

 A Basket of Bangles: How a Business Begins, by Ginger Howard (Millbrook Press, ISBN 0-761-31902-6, 2002) **Easy** *NCSS Notable Book*

Fire!, by Joy Masoff (Scholastic, ISBN 0-439-47217-2, 2002) **Easy**

How the U.S. Government Works, by Syl Sobel (Barrons Juveniles, ISBN 0-764-11111-6, 1999) **Easy**

Jimmy Carter: A MyReportLinks.Com Book, by Tim O'Shei (Enslow Publishers, ISBN 0-766-05051-3, 2002) **Easy**

Growing up in Ancient Greece, by Chris Chelepi (Troll Associates, ISBN 0-816-72720-1, 1997) **Easy**

Sandra Day O'Connor, by Mary Hill (Scholastic Library Publishing, ISBN 0-516-27890-8, 2003) **Easy**

Sandra Day O'Connor (First Biographies), by Gini Holland (Raintree/Steck Vaughn, ISBN 0-817-24455-7, 1997) **Easy**

The Story of Money, by Betsy Maestro (HarperTrophy, ISBN 0-688-13304-5, 1995) **Easy**

The U.S. Constitution and You, by Syl Sobel (Barrons Juveniles, ISBN 0-764-11707-6, 2001) **Easy**

Eyewitness: Ancient Greece, by Anne Pearson (DK Publishing, ISBN 0-789-45750-4, 2000) **On-Level**

Firefighting: Behind the Scenes, by Maria Mudd Ruth (Houghton Mifflin, ISBN 0-395-70129-5, 1998) **On-Level**

Heroes of the Day, by Nancy Louis (Abdo & Daughters, ISBN 1-577-65658-X, 2002) **On-Level**

Hydrogen Power: New Ways of Turning Fuel Cells into Energy, by Chris Hayhurst (Rosen Publishing Group, ISBN 0-823-93666-X, 2003) **On-Level**

The Kid's Guide to Money: Earning It, Saving It, Spending It, Growing It, Sharing It, by Steven Otfinoski (Scholastic, ISBN 0-590-53853-5, 1996) **On-Level**

Osama bin Laden: A War Against the West, by Elaine Landau (21st Century Books, ISBN 0-761-31709-0, 2002) **On-Level** *NCSS Notable Book*

President George W. Bush: Our Forty-Third President, by Beatrice Gormley (Aladdin Library, ISBN 0-689-84123-X, 2001) **On-Level**

Sandra Day O'Connor: Lawyer and Supreme Court Justice, by Jean Kinney Williams (Facts on File, ISBN 0-894-34355-6, 2001) **On-Level**

Understanding September 11th: Answering Questions About the Attacks on America, by Mitch Frank (Viking Children's Books, ISBN 0-670-03587-4, 2002) **On-Level** *NCSS Notable Book*

911: The Book of Help, by Michael Cart, Marianne Carus, and Marc Aronson (Cricket Books, ISBN 0-812-62676-1, 2002) **Challenge** *NCSS Notable Book*

Ancient Greece, by Peter Connolly (Oxford University Press Inc., ISBN 0-19-910810-2, 2001) **Challenge**

Ecology, by Steve Pollock (DK Publishing, ISBN 0-7894-5581-1, 2000) **Challenge**

Fire in Their Eyes: Wildfires and the People Who Fight Them, by Karen Magnuson Beil (Harcourt, ISBN 0-152-01042-4, 1999) **Challenge**

Global Warming: Opposing Viewpoints, by James Haley, ed. (Greenhaven Press, ISBN 0-737-70908-1, 2001) **Challenge**

Jimmy Carter (Major World Leaders), by Kerry Acker (Chelsea House Publishing, ISBN 0-791-07523-0, 2003) **Challenge**

Money Sense for Kids!, by Hollis Page Harman (Barrons Juveniles, ISBN 0-764-10681-3, 1999) **Challenge**

Of Beetles and Angels: A Boy's Remarkable Journey from a Refugee Camp to Harvard, by Mawi Asgedom (Little Brown & Co., ISBN 0-316-82620-0, 2002) **Challenge** *NCSS Notable Book*

Sandra Day O'Connor: Independent Thinker, by D. J. Herda (Enslow Publishers, Inc., ISBN 0-894-90558-9, 1995) **Challenge**

Global Political Economy: Understanding the International Economic Order, by Robert Gilpin and Jean M. Gilpin (Princeton University Press, ISBN 0-691-08677-X, 2001) **Teacher reference** *Pulitzer Prize*

Global Warming: A Guide to the Science, by Willie Soon, ed. (Fraser Institute, ISBN 0-889-75187-0, 2001) **Teacher reference**

Holy War, Inc.: Inside the Secret World of Osama bin Laden, by Peter L. Bergen (Touchstone Books, ISBN 0-743-23495-2, 2002) **Teacher reference**

Look for this symbol throughout the Teacher's Edition to find **Award-Winning Selections**.

Notes

Main Idea and Details

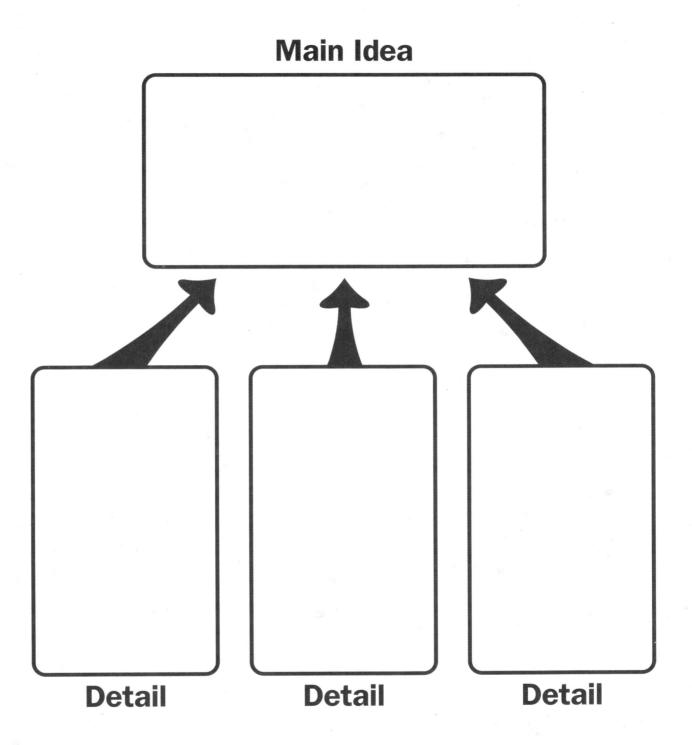

Main Idea

Detail   **Detail**   **Detail**

Sequence

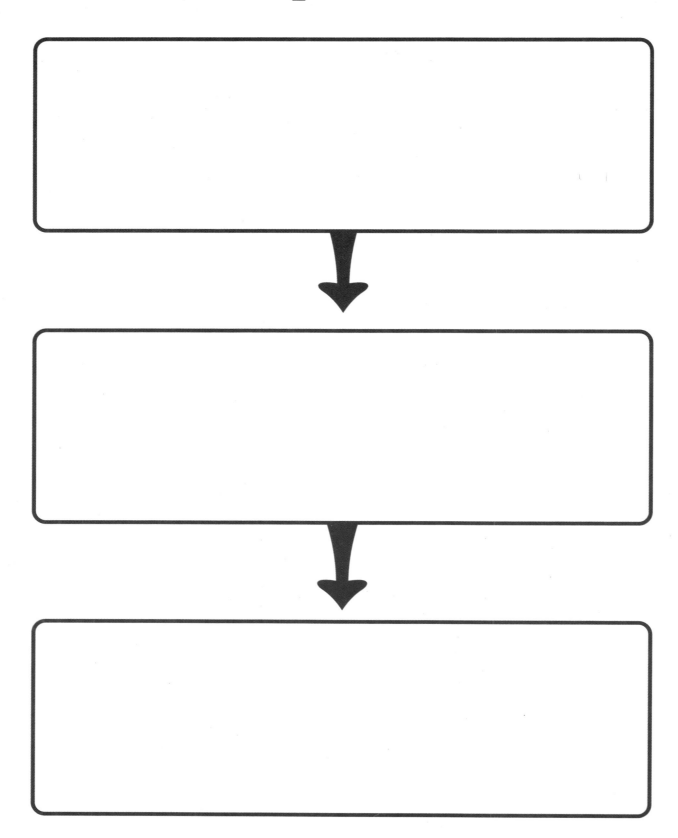

Cause and Effect

Cause

Effect

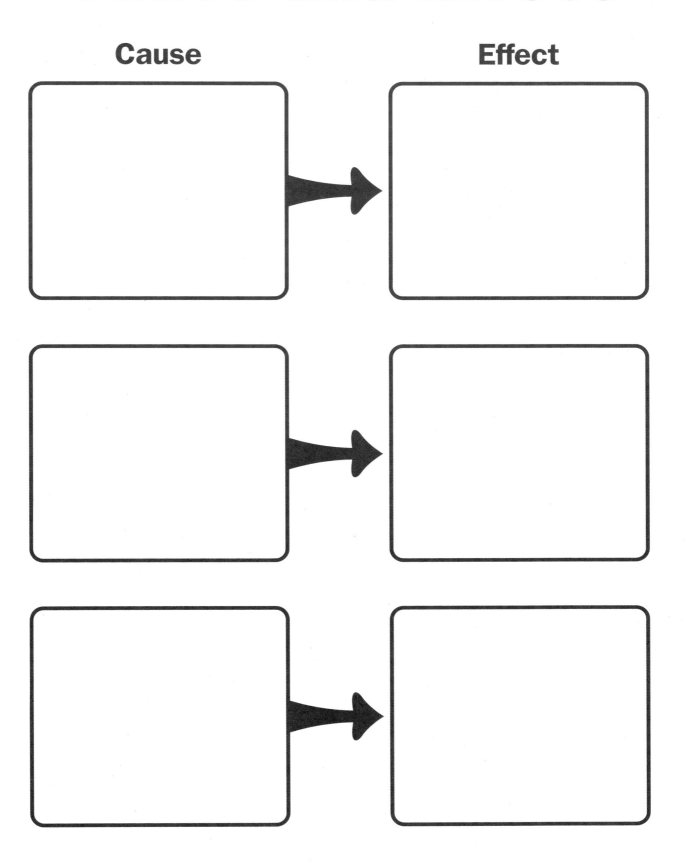

Compare and Contrast

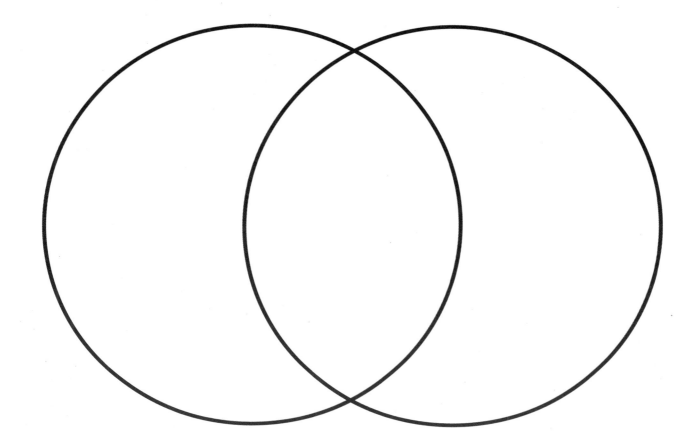

Compare and Contrast

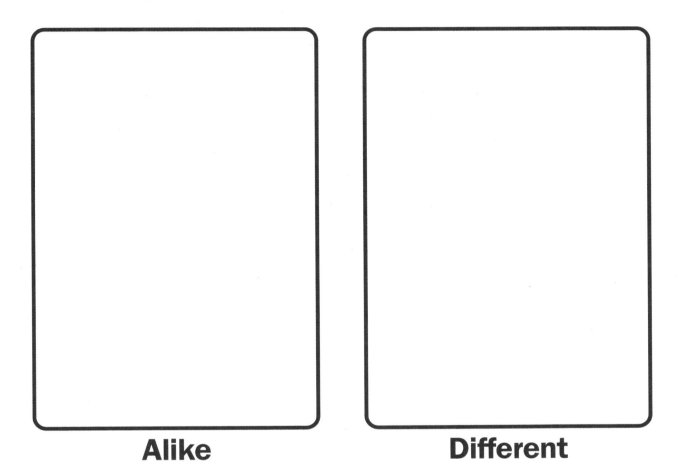

Alike   **Different**

Summarize

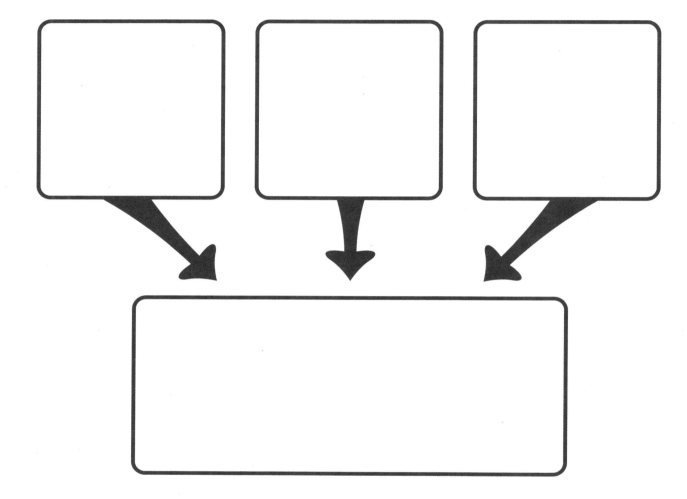

kidspiration Find a 30-day Kidspiration trial at www.inspiration.com/sf.

Draw Conclusions

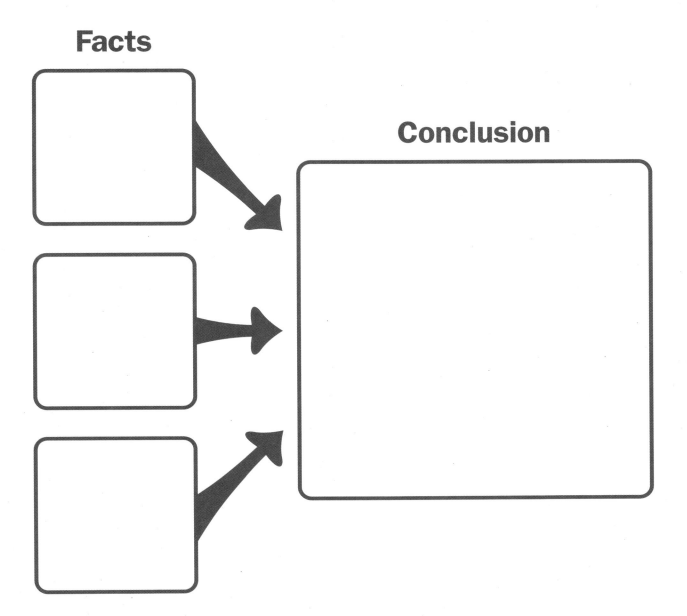

Facts

Conclusion

Make Generalizations

Fact

Fact

Generalization

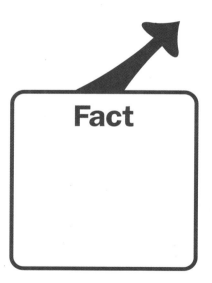

Fact

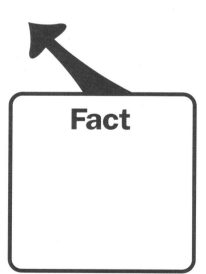

Fact

© Scott Foresman

K-W-L Chart

Topic _____

What We **K**now	What We **W**ant to Know	What We **L**earned

K-W-L Interactive Reading Strategy was developed and is reprinted by permission of Donna Ogle, National-Louis University, Evanston, Illinois.

Event Summary

Name of event _____

WHO? | Who was part of this event?

WHAT? | What happened?

WHEN? | When did this happen?

WHERE? | Where did this happen?

WHY? | Why did this happen?

Lesson Summary

Chapter _____ Lesson _____ Title _____

Section Title	Notes
Summary	

Section Title	Notes
Summary	

Section Title	Notes
Summary	

Section Title	Notes
Summary	

© Scott Foresman

Categorize

Topic	Category 1	Category 2	Category 3	Category 4

kidspiration **Find a 30-day Kidspiration trial at www.inspiration.com/sf.**

Social Studies Daily Journal

Today I learned...

Some new words I learned...

One way this relates to me...

I would like to learn more about...

Current Event Organizer

Article Title _____

Article Source _____ Article Date _____
(magazine/newspaper title)

TOPIC?
What is the article about?

WHAT?
What is the issue or event?

WHY?
Why is the event taking place? Why is it important?

WHERE?
Where is the event taking place?

WHEN?
When did the event take place? Is it still going on?

WHO?
Who are the people involved?

My reaction to this issue/event:

Solve a Problem

STEP 1: Name the problem.

STEP 2: Find out more about the problem.

STEP 3: List ways to solve the problem.   **STEP 4:** Consider advantages and disadvantages.

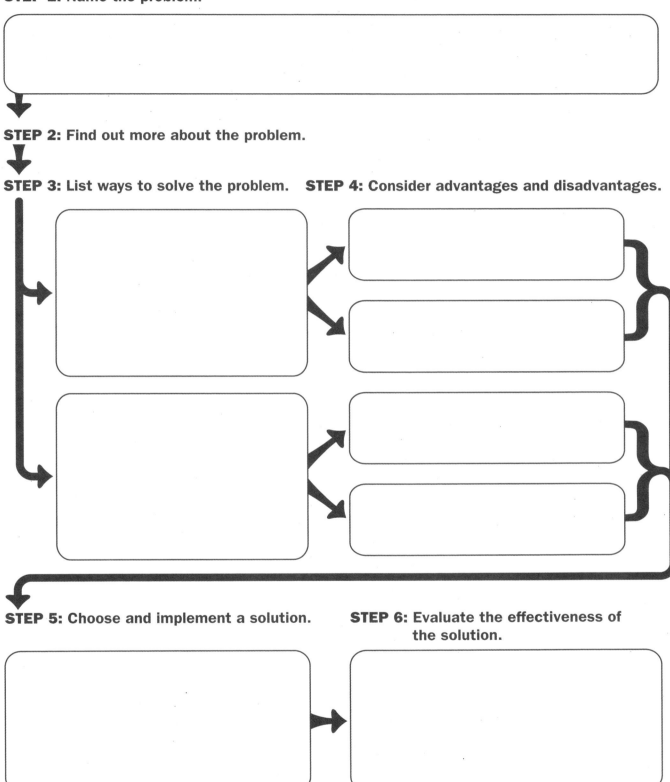

STEP 5: Choose and implement a solution.   **STEP 6:** Evaluate the effectiveness of the solution.

© Scott Foresman

Vocabulary Organizer

Word	Definition

One thing I learned about this word...

Word	Definition

One thing I learned about this word...

Word	Definition

One thing I learned about this word...

Word	Definition

One thing I learned about this word...

Writing Organizer

Topic of Writing Piece	Audience	Purpose

Main Idea	Supporting Details

Transition Sentence

Main Idea	Supporting Details

Transition Sentence

Main Idea	Supporting Details

© Scott Foresman

Artifact Analysis

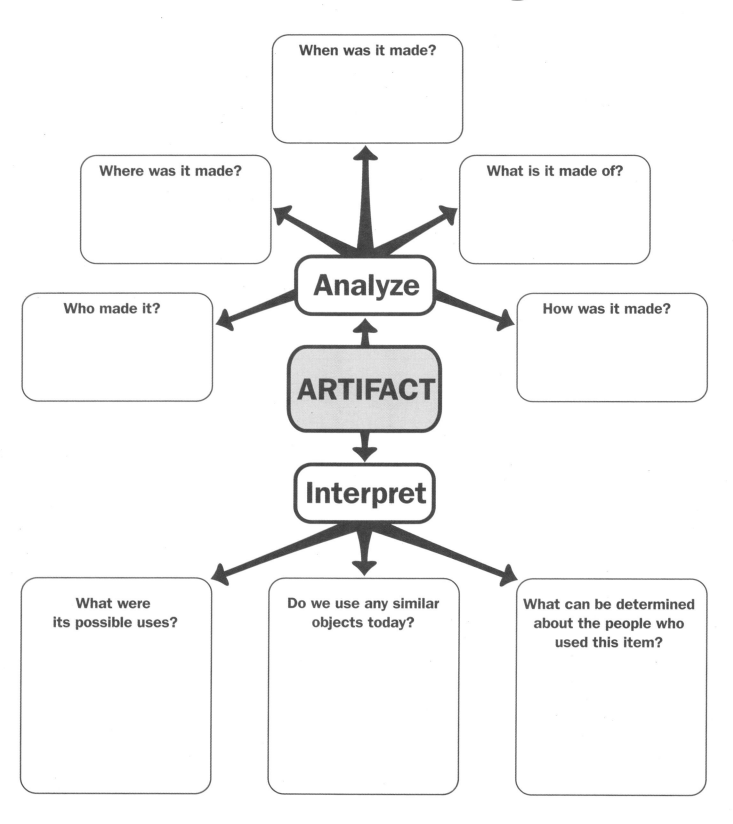

When was it made?

Where was it made?

What is it made of?

Analyze

Who made it?

How was it made?

ARTIFACT

Interpret

What were its possible uses?

Do we use any similar objects today?

What can be determined about the people who used this item?

© Scott Foresman

Document Analysis

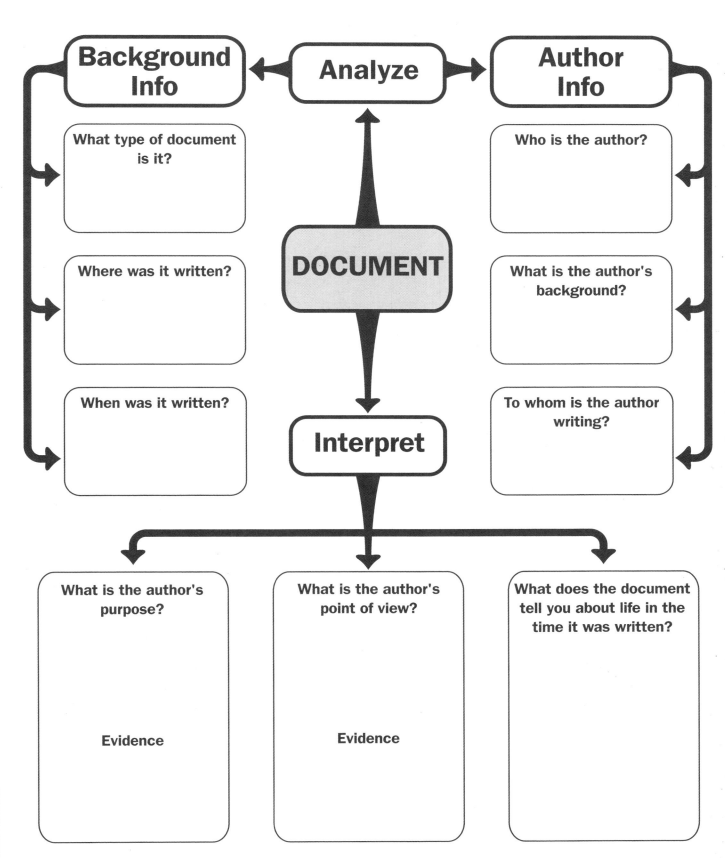

Analyze

Background Info
- What type of document is it?
- Where was it written?
- When was it written?

Author Info
- Who is the author?
- What is the author's background?
- To whom is the author writing?

DOCUMENT

Interpret
- What is the author's purpose?

  Evidence
- What is the author's point of view?

  Evidence
- What does the document tell you about life in the time it was written?

© Scott Foresman

Graph Paper

kidspiration Find a 30-day Kidspiration trial at www.inspiration.com/sf.

Time Line

Grid

kidspiration Find a 30-day Kidspiration trial at www.Inspiration.com/sf.

Name _____ Date _____

The World

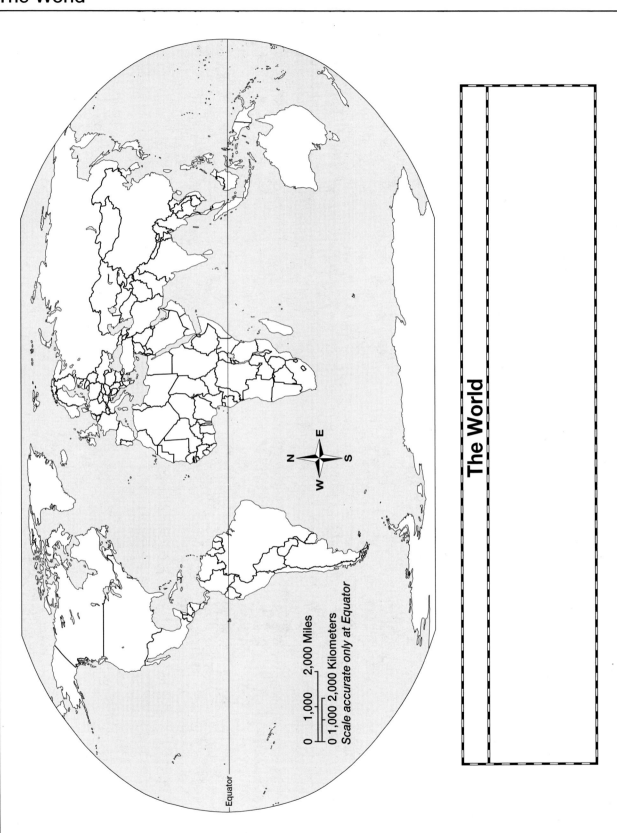

The World

Equator

N
E
W
S

0   1,000   2,000 Miles
0 1,000 2,000 Kilometers
Scale accurate only at Equator

© Scott Foresman

Name _____ Date _____

North America

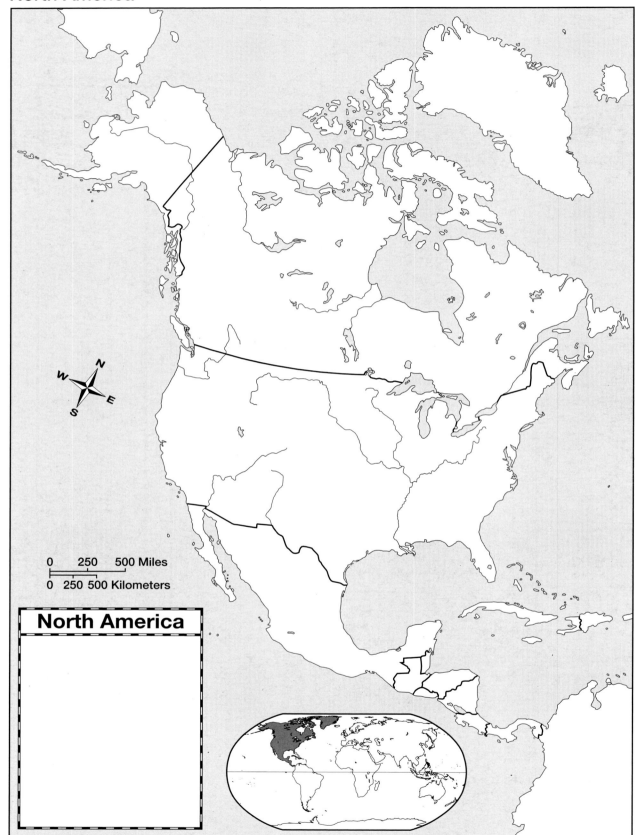

0   250   500 Miles

0 250 500 Kilometers

North America

Name _____ Date _____

The United States

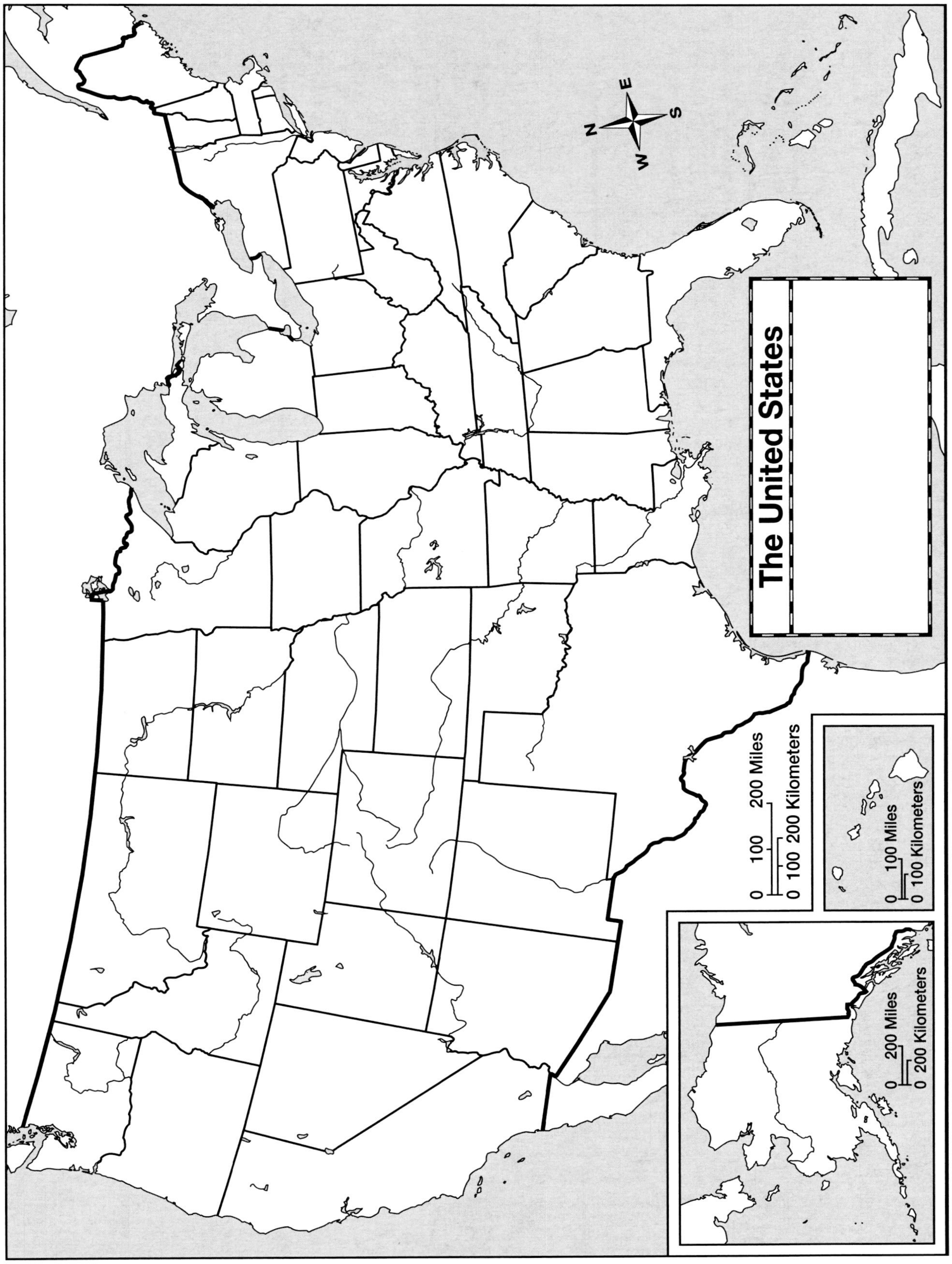

The United States

200 Miles
0 100 200 Kilometers

100 Miles
0 100 Kilometers

200 Miles
0 200 Kilometers

© Scott Foresman

Calendar

Sunday	Monday	Tuesday	Wednesday	Thursday	Friday	Saturday

Index

Index

Index

Index

Recognize Bias (see Reading Skills)

Research and Writing Skills
  Community Resources, H8
  Compare Primary and Secondary Sources, 392–393
  Gather and Report Information, H6–H9
  Internet Research, 496–497
  Interpret Political Cartoons, 268–269
  Print Resources, H6
  Technology Resources, H7
  Write an Outline, 174–175
  Writing a Research Report, H9

Reteach Activities (see Meeting Individual Needs, Leveled Practice—Easy, On-Level, Challenge Activities)
Rubrics (see also Assessment Scoring Guides [Rubrics])
  Expository, TR38–TR39
  Expressive/Descriptive, TR36–TR37
  Narrative, TR32–TR33
  Persuasive, TR34–TR35

Science
  Curriculum Connection, 1f, 10, 45f, 119f, 121, 147, 207f, 256, 289f, 332, 375f, 429, 445, 452, 463f, 495, 509, 530
  Link to Science, 11, 64, 173, 280, 435
Science and Technology
  Social Studies Strand, 20, 86, 228, 257, 277, 299, 304, 332, 354, 355, 366, 403, 429, 447, 519

Sequence (see Reading Skills)
Skills (see Chart and Graph Skills; Map and Globe Skills; Reading Skills; Research and Writing Skills; Thinking Skills)
Social Learning (see Meeting Individual Needs, Learning Styles)
Social Studies Strand (see Citizenship; Culture; Economics; Geography; Government; History; Science and Technology; Writing)
Sociology (see Culture)
Solve Problems (see Reading Skills)
Songs (see Music; Technology)
Songs and Music (see Music; Technology)
Standardized Test Prep, 5, 42, 51, 78, 112, 116, 125, 162, 200, 204, 213, 246, 282, 286, 295, 336, 368, 372, 381, 414, 456, 460, 469, 498, 522, 526
Summarize (see Reading Skills)

Technology
  Additional Internet Links, 1c, 45c, 52b, 80b, 119c, 126b, 164b, 207c, 214b, 248b, 289c, 296b, 338b, 375c, 382b, 416b, 463c, 470b, 500b
  Audio CD, 40, 114, 202, 284, 458, 524
  AudioText, 1c, 45c, 52b, 80b, 119c, 126b, 164b, 207c, 214b, 248b, 289c, 296b, 338b, 375c, 382b, 416b, 463c, 470b, 500b
  Colonial Williamsburg Primary Sources CD-ROM, H4–H5, 1c, 45c, 119c, 136–137, 207c, 289c, 375c, 463c
  Digital Learning CD-ROM, 1c, 45c, 119c, 207c, 289c, 375c, 463c
  ExamView® Test Bank CD-ROM, 1c, 1e, 6c, 45c, 45e, 52b, 52e, 80b, 80e, 119c, 119e, 126b, 126e, 164b, 164e, 207c, 207e, 214b, 214e, 248b, 248e, 289c, 289e, 296b, 296e, 338b, 338e, 375c, 375e, 382b, 382e, 416b, 416e, 463c, 470b, 470e, 500b, 500e
  Key Internet Search Terms, 52b, 80b, 126b, 164b, 214b, 248b, 296b, 338b, 382b, 416b, 470b, 500b
  Mindpoint® Quiz Show CD-ROM, 1c, 45c, 52b, 80b, 119c, 126b, 164b, 207c, 214b, 248b, 289c, 296b, 338b, 375c, 382b, 416b, 463c, 470b, 500b
  SF SuccessNet, 1c, 45c, 52b, 80b, 119c, 126b, 164b, 207c, 214b, 248b, 289c, 296b, 338b, 375c, 382b, 416b, 463c, 470b, 500b
  Songs and Music, 1c, 40, 45c, 114, 119c, 202, 207c, 284, 289c, 375c, 458, 463c, 524
  Teacher Resources CD-ROM, 1c, 3, 5, 6a, 6c, 11, 18, 21, 28, 36, 39, 43, 44, 45c, 51, 52b, 52c, 52e, 52, 57, 59, 64, 72, 77, 79, 80b, 80c, 80e, 80, 86, 93, 101, 103, 111, 113, 118, 119c, 125, 126b, 126c, 126e, 126, 133, 135, 137, 144, 147, 153, 159, 163, 164b, 164c, 164e, 164, 173, 175, 182, 190, 197, 201, 206, 207c, 213, 214b, 214c, 214e, 214, 221, 229, 231, 238, 244, 247, 248b, 248c, 248e, 248, 258, 261, 267, 269, 280, 281, 283, 288, 289c, 295, 296b, 296c, 296e, 296, 305, 307, 316, 326, 335, 337, 338b, 338c, 338e, 338, 347, 355, 364, 367, 369, 374, 375c, 381, 382b, 382c, 382e, 382, 391, 393, 403, 412, 415, 416b, 416c, 416e, 416, 426, 435, 444, 453, 455, 457, 462, 463c, 469, 470b, 470c,

470e, 470, 477, 479, 484, 494, 497, 499, 500b, 500c, 500e, 500, 508, 517, 519, 523, 528
  Video Field Trips, 1c, 45c, 119c, 207c, 289c, 375c, 463c
  Web Site (www.sfsocialstudies.com), 1c, 29, 35, 37, 42, 44, 45c, 49, 52b, 53, 65, 79, 80b, 81, 113, 116, 118, 119c, 123, 126b, 127, 145, 163, 164b, 165, 183, 201, 204, 206, 207c, 211, 214b, 215, 239, 245, 247, 248b, 249, 259, 283, 286, 288, 289c, 293, 296b, 297, 317, 327, 337, 338b, 339, 365, 366, 369, 372, 374, 375c, 379, 382b, 383, 413, 415, 416b, 417, 427, 445, 454, 457, 460, 462, 463c, 467, 470b, 471, 479, 485, 495, 499, 500b, 501, 509, 523, 526, 528

Technology Resources (see Research and Writing Skills)
Test Prep (see Standardized Test Prep)
Test Talk
  Choose the Right Answer, 1e, 45e, 119e, 207e, 286, 289e, 375e, 463e
  Locate Key Words in the Question, 1e, 26, 35, 42, 45e, 85, 116, 119e, 141, 180, 185, 207e, 254, 263, 289e, 312, 362, 375e, 390, 463e, 490
  Locate Key Words in the Text, 1e, 15, 34, 45e, 90, 119e, 151, 196, 204, 207e, 241, 289e, 324, 375e, 448, 463e, 505
  Use Information from Graphics, 1e, 27, 39, 45e, 103, 119e, 135, 169, 207e, 225, 289e, 301, 346, 375e, 400, 460, 463e, 479
  Use Information from the Text, 1e, 9, 45e, 70, 119e, 129, 207e, 218, 274, 289e, 343, 372, 375e, 396, 430, 463e, 475, 511
  Write Your Answer to Score High, 1e, 36, 45e, 79, 119e, 157, 207e, 235, 289e, 331, 350, 375e, 424, 463e, 526

Then and Now, 14, 62, 141, 218, 344, 408, 516
Thinking Skills
  Credibility of a Source, 260–261
  Fact and Opinion, 306–307
  Issues and Viewpoints, 198–199, 486–487
  Make Generalizations, 518–519
  Recognize Point of View, 58–59

Tolerance, 198–199, 486–487

Index

Credits

Cover: ©Craig Aurness/Corbis, (Bkgd) Getty Images

Front Matter
SF1 Everett Johnson/Stone
SF5 Photo from the collection of the Lexington, Massachusetts, Historical Society
SF12 Getty Images

Overview
1A ©Bettmann/Corbis
1C (B) Pitt Rivers Museum/© Dorling Kindersley, (T) Getty Images
1D Bettmann/Corbis

Unit 1
45A The Granger Collection, New York
45B The Granger Collection, New York
45C The Granger Collection, New York
45D North Wind Picture Archives
45H Stock Montage Inc.
52A The Granger Collection, New York
52B Richard Hamilton Smith/Corbis
80A Harper's Weekly, November 16, 1867
80B Corbis

Unit 2
119A ©Hulton Archive/Getty Images
119C The Granger Collection, New York
119D Brand X Pictures
119H Max Alexander/© Dorling Kindersley
126B The Granger Collection, New York

Unit 3
207A The Granger Collection
207B ©Schenectady Museum; Hall of Electrical History Foundation/Corbis
207C SuperStock
207D ©Bettmann/Corbis
214 (TL) The Granger Collection, New York, (TC) Brown Brothers, (TR) The Granger Collection, New York

Unit 4
289B SuperStock
289C Mary Evans Picture Library
289D Underwood & Underwood/Corbis
289H Dorothea Lange/Corbis
296A The Granger Collection, New York
296B Lake County Museum/Corbis
338A The Mariners' Museum/Corbis
338B AP/Wide World

Unit 5
375A Frank Whitney/Brand X Pictures
375B Hulton/Archive/Getty Images
375C The Military Picture Library/Corbis
375D ©AFP/William Philpott/Corbis
382A Corbis
382B H. Armstrong Roberts/Retrofile.com
416B Jack Moebes/Corbis

Unit 6
463A ©Diaphor Agency/Index Stock Imagery
463C Andy Sacks/Stone
463D (B, BL) Getty Images, (CL,BC,C) Corbis, (CR) ©Bill Aron/PhotoEdit
470A Corbis
470B ©Ed Lallo/Index Stock Imagery
500A NASA/Getty Images
500B The Image Works, Inc.

Back Matter
TR3, TR15 Hallogram Publishing
TR19 ©Flip Schulke/Corbis
TR21 (TC, TCR) Hemera Technologies, (TL) Getty Images
TR23 ©Bettmann/Corbis
TR24 Library of Congress
TR26 (BL) NASA, (TC) ©Hulton Archive/Getty Images, (TR) The Supreme Court Historical Society, (TL) Library of Congress
TR28 AP/Wide World Photos
TR29 Library of Congress

Notes

Notes